Troubles on the East Bank

DATE			

THE WASHINGTON PAPERS

... intended to meet the need for an authoritative, yet prompt, public appraisal of the major developments in world affairs.

Series Editors: Walter Laqueur; Amos A. Jordan

Associate Editors: William J. Taylor, Jr.; M. Jon Vondracek

Executive Editor: Jean C. Newsom

Managing Editor: Nancy B. Eddy

Editorial Assistant: Ann E. Ellsworth

President, CSIS: Amos A. Jordan

MANUSCRIPT SUBMISSION

The Washington Papers and Praeger Publishers welcome inquiries concerning manuscript submissions. Please include with your inquiry a curriculum vita, synopsis, table of contents, and estimated manuscript length. Manuscripts must be between 120–200 double-spaced typed pages. All submissions will be peer reviewed. Submissions to *The Washington Papers* should be sent to *The Washington Papers*; The Center for Strategic and International Studies; Georgetown University; 1800 K Street NW; Suite 400; Washington, DC 20006. Book proposals should be sent to Praeger Publishers; 521 Fifth Avenue; New York NY 10175.

The Washington Papers/123

Troubles on the East Bank

Challenges to the Domestic Stability of Jordan

Robert B. Satloff

Foreword by Robert G. Neumann

Published with The Center for
Strategic and International Studies
Georgetown University, Washington, D.C.

 PRAEGER

New York
Westport, Connecticut
London

Library of Congress Cataloging-in-Publication Data

Satloff, Robert B. (Robert Barry)
  Troubles on the East Bank.

  (The Washington papers, ISSN 0278-937X; vol. XIV,
123)
  "Published with the Center for Strategic and
International Studies, Georgetown University,
Washington, D.C."
  Bibliography: p.
  1. Jordan – Politics and government. I. Georgetown
University. Center for Strategic and International
Studies. II. Title. III. Series: Washington papers ;
123.
DS154.55.S27 1986   956.95   86-18675
ISBN 0-275-92617-6 (alk. paper)
ISBN 0-275-92618-4 (pbk. : alk. paper)

DS 154.55 .S27 1986

R00582 48539

The *Washington Papers* are written under the auspices of The Center
for Strategic and International Studies (CSIS), Georgetown University,
and published with CSIS by Praeger Publishers. The views expressed in these
papers are those of the authors and not necessarily those of The Center.

Library of Congress Catalog Card Number: 86-18675
ISBN: 0-275-92617-6 (cloth)
ISBN: 0-275-92618-4 (paper)

First published in 1986

Praeger Publishers, 521 Fifth Avenue, New York, NY 10175
A division of Greenwood Press, Inc.

Printed in the United States of America

The paper used in this book complies with the Permanent
Paper Standard issued by the National Information Standards
Organization (Z39.48-1984).

10 9 8 7 6 5 4 3 2 1

Contents

Foreword

One thing is certain: if there is ever to be peace in the Arab-Israeli conflict, Jordan, by its geographic position, its large Palestinian population, its previous occupation of the West Bank and East Jerusalem, is and must be at the center of any serious peace negotiations.

This fact automatically focuses attention on the internal stability of Jordan and the survival of King Hussein and the Hashemite dynasty, which has ruled the country ably and courageously for 40 turbulent and dangerous years. The author of this study, Robert B. Satloff, deserves great credit for concentrating on this important and frequently neglected subject.

As the author makes clear, Jordan faces a multiplicity of troubles. The plunge in oil prices has diminished the kingdom's income and subsidies as well as remittances from Jordanians working abroad, especially in the Gulf States. For a country with a diverse population, the threat of large-scale unemployment poses not only an economic but also a political problem.

Jordan is the only Arab state that has generously opened its borders to Palestinian refugees and has granted them citizenship. This and King Hussein's deep sense of responsibility for the occupied territories has plunged Jordan into the Palestinian problem in several ways. King Hussein can hardly afford to neglect this problem even if he wanted to — which he does not. But this means that he must work with representative Palestinians, which — thus far at least — means the PLO. This has proven very difficult.

Satloff argues that Jordan is engaged with Israel in a de facto accommodation of the status quo and that open peace negotiations would exacerbate instability in Jordan. I differ with this view. If progress is not achieved toward a viable peace with Israel, which would have to include the return to Arab control of substantial parts of the West Bank, grave danger for Jordan and the entire Middle East is bound to arise. Desperate Palestinians, especially those of the younger generation, are bound to resort to ever-increasing violent challenge to the Israeli occupation authorities. These, in turn, could and probably would push large numbers of West Bank Palestinians into Jordan. There they would probably destabilize the kingdom, thereby creating that very radical, Palestinian state that Israel has so long professed to fear. And in that case, Israeli intervention in Jordan would be only a matter of time.

Fundamentalist agitation, already present on both the West Bank and in Jordan, would then join in the fight, perhaps even taking leadership in the struggle. And this, in turn, could easily lead to the destabilization of the entire Middle East.

Satloff's paper deals largely with internal threats to Jordan's stability, which leads him to rather pessimistic conclusions, which I respect, but do not entirely share. King Hussein is a survivor of many plots and dangers. He is an extremely intelligent and resourceful man, who knows how to be tough when the occasion requires it.

Nor can the surrounding countries and the United States remain indifferent to Jordan's disintegration. But all this underscores how important peace is to the United States, the Middle East, and the entire West, which has a big stake in that area's stability.

This study merits well-deserved attention.

Robert G. Neumann
Senior Adviser and Director, Middle East Programs
Former Ambassador to Afghanistan,
Morocco, and Saudi Arabia

About the Author

Robert B. Satloff is a research fellow of The Washington Institute for Near East Policy, specializing in contemporary Arab and Islamic politics. He received an M.A. in Middle Eastern studies from Harvard University in 1985 and his articles on various Middle Eastern issues have appeared in the *New York Times,* the *Chicago Tribune,* the *Miami Herald, Defense News,* and *Middle Eastern Studies. Troubles on the East Bank* is his first book.

Acknowledgments

Although a short work, this monograph owes much to many. The original idea for studying the domestic affairs of the Hashemite Kingdom of Jordan sprang from a fall 1984 graduate seminar on comparative politics in the Arab world at Harvard University's Center for Middle Eastern Studies. I pursued my research in Jordan while enrolled in an Arabic language program sponsored jointly by Yarmouk University and the University of Virginia during the summer of 1985. The monograph itself was written while serving as a research fellow of The Washington Institute for Near East Policy. I am indebted to all those institutions for their generosity and support. I am particularly appreciative of the confidence and trust placed in me by Barbi Weinberg, president of The Washington Institute.

Institutional aid was necessary but not sufficient. I owe thanks to all those Jordanians – in both private and public life – who provided insight, information, and access to statistical data. Although they demand mention, it is best they not be named.

Many people answered questions, offered criticisms, suggested advice, and extended the sort of friendship, assistance, and encouragement without which this monograph could not have been written. They number far too many to enumerate, yet I owe them all my deepest gratitude. I am especially grateful to Paul Jureidini, Eliyahu Kanovsky, Elie Kedourie, Bruce Lawrence, Aaron David Miller, Daniel Pipes, David Pollock, Harold Rhode and the late M. H. Blinken. Stephen Glick artfully and graciously assisted in creating the charts and graphs.

My greatest debt is owed to my friends and colleagues of The Washington Institute. Each one offered valuable editorial and intellectual contributions. But it is the spirit of collegiality and camaraderie fostered by Brooke Joseph, Michael Lewis, Joshua Muravchik, Leonard Schoen, Harvey Sicherman, and especially Martin Indyk that was truly invaluable.

Of course I alone take responsibility for the contents of this work.

Washington, D.C.
June 1986

Introduction:
Fissures in the System

All is not well in the Hashemite Kingdom of Jordan. Among other problems, Jordan is beset by a growing economic crisis, rising unemployment, and the danger of a confrontationist Islamic political movement. And because of the special role envisaged for Jordan in America's Middle East policy, the United States is ill-prepared to deal with the portentous changes going on inside the kingdom.

Throughout the past decade, Jordanian society has witnessed a period of fast and fundamental change. In the mid-1970s, the oil revolution swept through Jordan just as it swept through the Persian Gulf. Because of Jordan's role within the Arab system — being a weak state that both imports and exports huge numbers of laborers — the shocks of that revolution were at least as ferocious as those felt in the Gulf. Indeed, Jordan has proved to be a caricature of the wealthier Gulf states, booming when they expand and busting when they contract.

Like its long-time monarch, Hussein bin Talal, Jordan has always been able to recover from national traumas and political upheavals. But the oil revolution of the 1970s has fueled a crisis unlike any other in Jordan's rocky history.

Billions of dollars of oil-derived revenue flowed in from sympathetic Arab capitals and expatriate workers in the

1

Persian Gulf. In turn, that money built hospitals, universities, airports, factories, and skyscrapers; paid for the importation of luxury cars, appliances, televisions, stereos, and VCRs; subsidized bread, water, fuel, meat, and clothing; and hired more than 125,000 foreign workers to do the menial jobs Jordanians refused to do themselves.

Processes of social change that had been proceeding at a slow and manageable rate before the expansion proceeded more rapidly. Urbanization, consumerism, the spread of bureaucracy, and the empowerment of the technocrats – all these phenomena were speeded up by the influx of foreign capital. But as long as oil revenues kept climbing, Jordanian society was cushioned against tensions arising from the rapid social change.

When the oil market began to buckle under the glut of the early 1980s, causing tremors of retrenchment in the Gulf, Jordan was trapped without the massive currency reserves of the nouveau riche oil exporters. By 1983, Arab aid had dropped precipitously and workers' remittances had leveled off. Moreover, thousands of expatriates were returning home because jobs in the Gulf had disappeared. In 1986, Jordan's resources are dwindling, yet it must pay off creditors not only for the spending spree of yesterday but also for today's debilitating dependence upon imports to feed, clothe, and sustain a fast-growing population. Having committed itself to wide-ranging capital expenditures and development projects, Jordan now finds itself dangerously overextended.

To cope with the sudden shortfall, the government has cut subsidies, suspended construction, postponed projects, and borrowed heavily. Prices of several basic commodities were permitted to rise and unemployment shot upwards, both among recent university graduates and repatriated workers. Temporary relief, such as the windfall from the diversion of some Arab banking services and tourism from Beirut to Amman, did little to offset the very real dangers to an economy that had been well regarded by international financiers for its fiscal responsibility. The "roaring" years have come to a close, and Jordan is now in the throes of economic recession.

But Jordan's problems are not just economic. Rather, the kingdom is witnessing a gradual but unmistakable challenge to the traditional order coming from within. The monarchy's ability to siphon off social tensions through labor exportation, commodity subsidies, and unlimited education and employment opportunities is vanishing. As a result, the processes of change that had been slowly gnawing away at the traditional Hashemite system now gnaw much more rapidly.

Jordan today is facing a challenge to a governing coalition that has provided the foundation for the Hashemite monarchy. The threat, however, does not emanate from hostile and belligerent forces such as a Damascus regime inspired by visions of a Greater Syria or a Palestinian nationalist fifth column. On the contrary, the threat is a product of the gradual weakening of the forces that have sustained the stability of the regime for so long, a weakening brought about by the economic aftershocks of boom and bust.

Since the late 1950s, Hussein has ruled by maintaining the image of moderation while brooking no serious internal opposition. Coup and assassination attempts aside, he built a coalition that buttressed his personal authority. The 1970–1971 civil war against Palestinian insurgents galvanized a spectrum of forces that have since formed the principal elements of that system. Included in that coalition are the military hierarchy (including armed forces and internal security), tribal shaykhs, religious leaders (including the Muslim Brotherhood), and elements of the wealthy Palestinian elite. Today, that coalition is in trouble because several of its basic elements are in flux:

• Islamic activism has spread throughout the kingdom in the past decade, spurred on both by the regional tide and by Hussein's policies in reaction to it, ultimately pitting Hussein and the activists in a confrontation over who legitimately speaks in the name of Islam.

• Faced with unalterable demographic facts, Jordan has been forced to alter the composition of its fiercely loyal, largely bedouin armed forces. Thousands of untested but better-educated Palestinians have been incorporated into the armed forces so that the country can field a modern, high-tech army. At the same time, the once-unquestioned role of tribalism in the kingdom's political culture has come under attack, leaving both traditional bedouin leaders and their forward-looking offspring unsure of their future role in society.

• Moreover, prominent establishment figures, whose lack of political power has long been assuaged by economic good fortune are beginning to flex their political muscles cautiously. Many are disenchanted with the maintenance of martial law and their disenfranchisement from the decision-making processes.

• In response, Hussein has yet to forge a national policy that addresses the conflicting demands of the traditionalists and the modernists, key groups whose support is essential to Hashemite rule. Although he has had some success at imposing a sense of Jordanian nationality (one hesitates to use the term Jordanian "nationalism"), it has been a success born out of times of plenty. Whatever compact exists among the elite groups that compete for power and authority inside the kingdom is just now being tested by the lean years of austerity and retrenchment.

• And as for the monarchy itself, the paradox of Hussein's spectacular record of personal survival is that – after more than 30 years on the throne – few Jordanians can conceive of the kingdom after the king. As Prime Minister Zaid al-Rifa'i said in a 1984 interview, "Everyone knows that King Hussein is Jordan and Jordan is King Hussein. It is difficult to imagine the Kingdom without him." After 20 years as heir apparent, Crown Prince Hassan will most likely accede to the throne upon the death of his older brother. But given Hassan's history as palace intellectual, political gadfly, and poor cultivator of key constituencies, a tranquil transfer of title from brother to brother may not also entail a similar transfer of power.

Indeed, much is happening in Jordan that is overlooked because it is not directly related to Arab-Israeli peacemaking, the focus of U.S. Middle East policy. But what is happening has profound ramifications for the existence of a regime upon which the United States has pinned its hopes for a successful outcome of that peace process. This paper, therefore, is an effort to examine important events and fundamental trends in Jordanian society that could affect the domestic stability of the Hashemite regime in the long run and will surely affect the peace process in the short run.

Chapter 1 chronicles the rise and fall of Jordan's "piggyback economy," with an analysis of the currently bleak prospects for economic recovery. Chapter 2 explains the growth of Islamic politics and the emerging confrontation between a self-proclaimed descendant of Muhammad and the self-appointed keepers of the faith. Chapter 3 discusses the more evolutionary dangers facing a monarchy caught between modernists pushing the country forward and traditionalists hesitant to depart from the status quo. Chapter 4 deals with the thorny issue of royal succession and broaches the larger — and more difficult — question of the fate of monarchical rule itself. Chapter 5 explores Jordan's current state of tacit peace with Israel and weighs the domestic political constraints that prohibit Hussein from making a de facto condition de jure. Chapter 6 offers a brief assessment of the current domestic challenges to the Hashemite regime and some observations on how dealing with those challenges may influence its future stability. Finally, a concluding section presents a critique of U.S. policy toward Jordan, arguing that the United States must look beyond the confines of the peace process if it is to assist Hussein and his heirs through economic crises and political challenges.

Taken alone, each chapter presents just one piece of a Jordanian puzzle that has received far too little attention for far too many years. But taken as a whole, it is hoped that this paper will direct the policymaker's attention and the scholar's interest away from the "headline politics" of Jordan — the peace process, inter-Arab conflicts, personal quarrels between Hussein and Yasir Arafat – and toward closer scrutiny of domestic issues whose potential impact on regime stability is of at least equal importance.

1

Oil and the Economy

In January 1985, Prime Minister Ahmad Obeidat stood on the floor of the Jordanian Senate and announced that a team of geologists had been trying for three days to plug the runaway flow of oil gushing from a new well near Azraq.[1] Obeidat reported optimistically that the resource-poor kingdom would soon produce 10,000 barrels of crude oil per day.[2]

Jordan does not have to wait for that day to arrive for it to boast an oil-based economy. Today, with but a trickle of its own petroleum production, Jordan's economy is already inexorably tied to oil. Indeed, Jordan can claim what has been termed the world's only non-oil exporting oil economy.[3] In 1981, for example, direct petro-revenue – that is, transfers from Arab governmental donors and remittances from expatriates working in the Gulf – amounted to nearly half the kingdom's gross national product (GNP).[4] In other words, grants and remittances from Arab countries contributed more to Jordan's economy than nearly all other sources – industrial, financial, agricultural, and commercial – combined. In short, the health of the Jordanian economy rides the crest of the volatile oil market.

Jordan has long relied on external sources of revenue to underwrite the kingdom's economy. In the early 1950s, for example, following King Abdallah's formal annexation of the

7

West Bank of the Jordan River to the East Bank, foreign aid exceeded domestic revenue by more than a third.[5] But what separates previous cycles of dependence on foreign revenue from the current situation is the magnitude of the infusion of outside capital and the fundamental changes in economy and society it has wrought.

Effects of the Oil Boom (1973–1981)

Between 1973 and 1981, Jordan enjoyed a remarkable economic boom. In that period, the kingdom consistently registered real annual growth rates (GNP) of around 9–10 percent; gross domestic product (GDP) increases averaged 8 percent per year.[6] Gold and foreign exchange reserves increased 6-fold; capital formation increased 11-fold — all in a country with little more than a drop of oil to its name.[7]

Statistics, however, do not quite capture the sense of growth, affluence, and easy money that characterized Amman in the late 1970s and early 1980s. One observer, writing in the *Atlantic Monthly*, offered this description of the boomtown mentality that transfixed the capital city in 1981.

> Even the minarets on today's skyline are new, and steel scaffolds continue to intrude unattractively upon the landscape. The shops bulge with food, fashions and imported gadgets. Peugeots and Mercedes race for space in the traffic circles. Amman has no unemployment. In fact, short of labor, it has become the host to Egyptians who tend the gardens, to Koreans who raise the skyscrapers, to Filipinos and Pakistanis who wait on the tables and clean the rooms in the Intercontinental and the Holiday Inn.[8]

The boom was entirely a function of Jordan's place in the Arab system. Between 1973 and 1981, direct Arab budget support rose more than 16-fold, from $71.8 million to $1.179 billion.[9] In the same period, the value of Jordanian exports jumped 12-fold, from $57.6 million to $734.9 million.[10] Most of that increase comprised exports to other Arab states, principally Gulf oil exporters. By 1982, exports to Iraq alone were 20 times their 1978 level.[11]

Jordanian trade statistics do not even include figures for the most precious national export – the 350,000 doctors, engineers, teachers, and construction workers remitting home salaries from their jobs in the Gulf.[12] By 1981, gross worker remittances were estimated at more than $1 billion, or about 30 percent of the kingdom's GDP.*[13] Even after deducting the outward flow of dinars from the 125,000 foreign workers inside Jordan holding agricultural and unskilled jobs, net workers' remittances (current prices) rose from $15 million in 1970 to $900 million in 1981 – a factor of 60.[14] In comparative terms, remittances nearly tripled their value in relation to total export earnings during this decade.[15]

In short, these three sources of revenue – Arab aid, merchandise exports, and gross workers remittances – were more than 17 times larger in 1981 than in 1973. Whereas these three sources of revenue equaled 37 percent of GDP in 1973, by 1981 they amounted to 84 percent of GDP.[16] (See table 1 and figure 1.)

The Price of Newfound Wealth

Jordan found itself suffering from many of the same ailments plaguing oil exporters suddenly awash in foreign exchange. Imports shot upward to supply the government with the goods and materials to build the dams, roads, schools, and hospitals outlined in boldly devised development plans and to satisfy the populace's newfound desires for Western clothes, foods, and appliances. By 1981, the total value of imported goods had grown to 10 times its 1973 level; interestingly,

---

*Most estimates only account for remittances funneled home via the Jordanian banking system. According to Eliyahu Kanovsky, an additional 50–100 percent is remitted through unofficial channels. *Middle East Contemporary Survey* 7, p. 401.

TABLE 1
Selected Components of Jordan's Economy, 1973–1984
(Millions of current $)

Year	GDP	Arab Grants	Gross Remittance Income	Exports (Goods)	Imports (Goods)	Government Debt
1973	665.5	71.8	44.8	57.9	333.0	360.1
1974	770.3	145.5	75.4	155.0	487.9	423.0
1975	1000.9	330.7	166.6	152.5	729.0	539.5
1976	1296.0	233.7	411.3	209.2	1022.5	651.2
1977	1596.1	402.0	470.0	249.5	1381.3	913.5
1978	2099.6	215.6	522.0	296.1	1494.9	1263.5
1979	2507.4	995.9	601.0	402.6	1950.2	1520.8
1980	3285.5	1243.4	794.4	575.5	2401.6	1945.2
1981	3531.2	1192.8	1032.5	735.0	3173.2	2303.2
1982	3755.8	952.1	1084.0	750.8	3242.8	2498.6
1983	3949.3	700.6	1109.6	580.1	3039.6	3098.7
1984	3965.3	593.8	1235.1	756.8	2718.9	3374.3

Source: Data on gross domestic product and government debt taken from International Monetary Fund, *International Financial Statistics*, various editions; Data on Arab grants and gross remittance income taken from International Monetary Fund, *Balance of Payments Yearbook*, various editions; Data on exports and imports taken from Jordan's Department of Statistics, *External Trade Statistics*, 1984, p. 4.

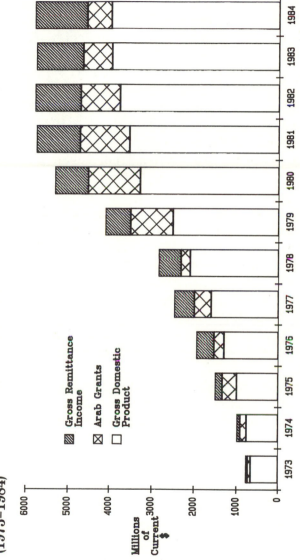

FIGURE 1
Selected Components of Jordan's Economy (1973–1984)

Source: International Monetary Fund, *International Financial Statistics,* and *Balance of Payments Yearbook,* various editions.

11

imports of Western goods (U.S. and European Community) grew 24 percent faster than imports of Arab goods.[17] In typical (though not uniform) fashion, inflation rose, agricultural production declined, and there was a mass migration from the hinterland to the lone urban center, Amman.

According to the Central Bank, the national cost of living index rose 168 percent from 1973 to 1981.[18] (See figure 2.) Prices of many basic items jumped even higher; vegetables were up 186 percent; meat, 188 percent; clothes, 232 percent; and fruit, 426 percent.[19] Concurrently, domestic agricultural output declined sharply — largely the result of poor climatic conditions. For example, Jordan produced no more wheat in 1981 than it did in 1975, although it had more than 25 percent more people to feed.[20] (See figure 3.)

To cover domestic shortfalls, the government turned to importing basic foodstuffs. Net annual wheat imports grew by a factor of seven in the decade following 1972, doubling in 1981 alone.[21] By that year, the kingdom was spending more than $3 billion on imports, a staggering sum that itself rivaled the GDP.[22] Even the impressive growth of exports in the late 1970s could not make a dent in the meteoric rise in imports. In 1981, the trade gap in goods stood at nearly $2.5 billion, or more than three times the total value of exports.[23] (See figure 4.)

A changing demography exacerbated Jordan's economic difficulties. According to the government's own estimates, Jordan's population grows at a phenomenal 4 percent per annum.[24] In 1984, the total East Bank population was 2.6 million, not including the hundreds of thousands of Jordanians working abroad.[25] And it is a young population. At the time of the last national census in 1979, more than half the population was under 15 years of age.[26] Moreover, tens of thousands of Jordanians are moving from the hinterland to Amman. Today, Greater Amman claims more than 1.4 million residents — 55 percent of the kingdom's total population.[27] Urban sprawl, internal migration, rising prices, and consumer price gouging have worsened the economic crunch in the capital.[28]

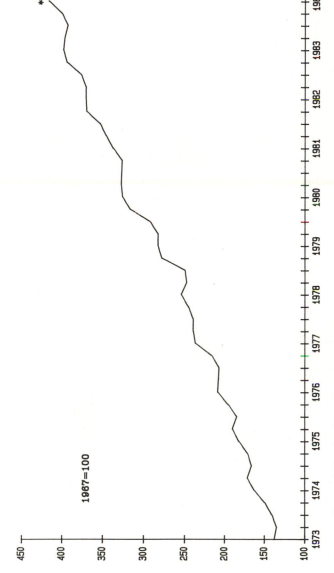

FIGURE 2
Cost of Living Index

Source: Central Bank of Jordan, *Quarterly Statistical Series,* 1984, and *Monthly Statistical Bulletin,* April 1985.

*1984 figure is year average.

13

FIGURE 3
Estimated Population and Wheat Supply (1979–1984)

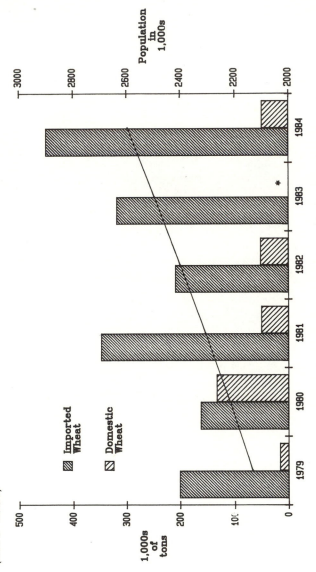

Source: Jordan's Department of Statistics, *Statistical Yearbook*, 1984, pp. 1, 104.

*1983 domestic wheat data not available.

Note: Population estimates (1980–1984) based on Housing and Population Census, November 1979. Includes East Bank residents only.

14

FIGURE 4
Imports and Exports of Goods
(1973–1984)

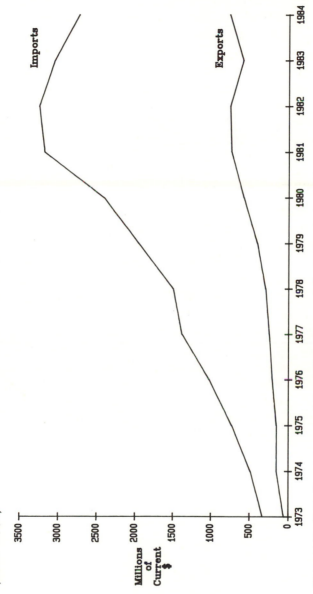

Source: Jordan's Department of Statistics, *External Trade Statistics*, 1984, p. 3.

15

Robust growth rates only obscured the fragility of the country's true economic condition. Economic vitality was an illusion; Jordan remained solvent largely through the magnanimity of fellow Arab states. As was presciently noted by economists J. S. Birks and C. A. Sinclair in 1978, "a rapid change in the perspective of aid donors or in the propensity of Jordanian workers to remit would cripple the economy."[29]

Spending the Windfall

In the midst of the kingdom's artificial boom, the government spent heavily to expand social services and finance large development projects. State agencies approved a hike in minimum wage laws and passage of a rudimentary social security and health insurance program.[30] Health facilities were dramatically improved; for example, the ratio of doctors per capita more than doubled.[31] Communications were modernized, so that by 1981 there were three times as many telephones in service as in 1973.[32] Millions of dinars were spent upgrading and reforming the country's educational system. By 1979, about 80 percent of the potentially volatile 15–30 age group were literate.[33] The jewel of the educational program was the groundbreaking of the billion-dollar campus of Yarmouk University, billed as the finest center of science and technology in the Arab world. Moreover, Jordan invested heavily in large industrial projects, like the massive fertilizer factory in Aqaba and the potash works on the Dead Sea. In total, the Five Year Plan inaugurated in 1976 authorized investment of $2.3 billion (JD 765 million) – $500 million more than that year's entire GNP.[34] (See figure 5 and table 2.)

At the same time, extensive commodity price supports, consumer subsidies, and market distribution schemes were implemented. Between 1973 and 1981, private consumption rose faster than the GDP and more than 70 percent faster than the rate of public consumption.[35] In response, by 1976, the government had imposed controls and subsidies on several basic commodities, including sugar, meat, bread, and fuel.[36] Within a year, subsidies were extended to all grain production,

FIGURE 5
Government Expenditures
(FY 1978–1984)

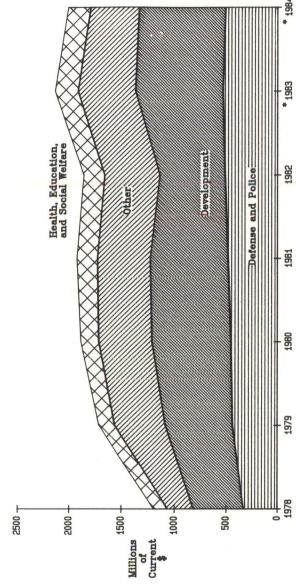

Millions of Current $

Health, Education, and Social Welfare

Other

Development

Defense and Police

2500

2000

1500

1000

500

0

1978   1979   1980   1981   1982   *1983   *1984

*planned estimates

Source: Jordan's Department of Statistics, *Statistical Yearbook*, 1984, pp. 162–163.

Notes: "Development" includes development budget and other capital expenditures under the regular budget. "Other" includes current costs of general administration, justice, posts, and telegraphs. Fiscal year ends on March 31.

17

TABLE 2
Government Expenditure, FY 1978–1984
(Millions of current $)

Year	Health, Social Welfare, and Education	Defense and Police	Development	Other	Total
1978	138.2	333.4	484.1	247.6	1203.3
1979	153.6	440.6	647.1	475.8	1717.1
1980	174.5	455.5	761.2	497.9	1889.1
1981	199.0	483.2	751.5	493.3	1927.0
1982	200.5	512.3	626.5	518.3	1857.6
1983	222.7*	533.9*	837.2*	541.9*	2137.7*
1984	217.9*	506.4*	827.1*	453.9*	2005.3*

Source: Jordan's Department of Statistics, *Statistical Yearbook,* 1984, pp. 163–164.
*planned estimate

Note: "Development" includes development budget and other capital expenditure under regular budget. "Other" includes cost of general administration, justice, posts, and telegraphs. Fiscal year ends on March 31.

and the government expanded its existing storage facilities for meat, rice, sugar, tea, and flour to ameliorate distribution bottlenecks.[37] A bonus system for agricultural products was instituted in 1980, in the hope of encouraging greater domestic productivity.[38] Total government spending on price supports was, in relative terms, quite large. In 1981, for example, the fuel subsidy alone cost more than $177 million — nearly equaling Iraq's entire $180-million development grant for the year.[39]

Meanwhile, despite the subsidy program, hoarding and price gouging persisted. In response, the government cracked down. Dozens of merchants were brought before military tribunals in 1979 for violating price regulations; in 1980, the cabinet approved the establishment of a Civilian Complaints Bureau and a special anticorruption court.[40] According to the *Middle East Contemporary Survey*, "scores" of merchants were fined or imprisoned for improprieties in 1979 and 1980; "hundreds" were arrested and punished the next year.[41]

At the same time, the government embarked on a series of spending programs to cushion several key constituencies against the inflationary spiral plaguing the country. Civil servants and military personnel were the prime beneficiaries of these programs. Army salaries were raised several times between 1975 and 1981, with two pay hikes in 1980 alone.[42] Special supermarkets and consumer cooperatives were established for the exclusive use of government employees, offering discounts on all manner of consumer goods of up to 50 percent.[43] In 1980, a royal decree mandated that children of these special groups receive preferential treatment in university admission, and in 1981, the government drew up plans for housing projects earmarked for, among others, internal security officers, key elements underpinning the foundation of the king's regime.[44]

The Market Busts (1982–1986)

Throughout the oil boom years, Jordan's economy floated uneasily on the munificence of wealthy Arab states. But the government spent dinars as though it were the motivator, not the beneficiary, of regional growth. During the past five years, however, oil prices dropped and the Organization of Petroleum Exporting Countries (OPEC) fractured. Revenue from each of the primary income sources has diminished sharply. Without the liquid investments and cash reserves of major oil exporters, Jordan feels the brunt of economic constriction far more keenly than its wealthy patrons. As a result, Jordan now suffers the ills of serious economic recession.

Arab aid was particularly hard hit by the economic turnaround. According to testimony offered by Secretary of State George P. Shultz before the Senate Foreign Relations Committee in June 1985, Arab grant aid to Jordan had fallen 54 percent, from $1.2 billion in 1982 to $550 million in 1984.[45] Of the seven Arab states that promised Jordan a huge annual subsidy at the 1978 Baghdad summit, only Saudi Arabia has faithfully continued to fulfill its commitment. But even Riyadh reneged on promises to pay the unfilled shares owed by Libya and Algeria, which failed to meet their own commitments almost immediately after they made them. In July 1985, Kuwait sharply curtailed its subsidy, ensuring that Jordan's foreign aid revenue will drop even further.[46] Moreover, development loans from several Arab states were slashed as well. Forced to draw on dwindling reserves to finance its war effort, Iraq, for example, completely cancelled its development assistance package in 1982.[47]

In an unusually blunt appraisal of the foreign aid situation, King Hussein complained in 1983 that the failure of Arab states to meet their financial obligations had compelled Jordan to rearrange payment for arms deals via normal commercial loans. "Indeed, this matter has caused us economic confusion," he stated.[48] Speaking before the Jordanian Senate in January 1985, Prime Minister Obeidat said that the drop in Arab aid had had "great adverse consequences" on both the economy and the military supply program.[49] All told, outstanding Arab debt on commitments to Jordan exceeds $3.6 billion in 1986.[50]

Worker remittances have shrunk as well. Vanishing oil revenues have curtailed the Gulf construction boom, threatening the jobs of the close to 40 percent of Jordanian migrants employed in that industry.[51] As early as 1980, even before the downturn in oil prices, Saudi Arabia cut the number of Jordanian worker permits in half.[52] Since then, Jordan's traditional outward flow of labor has reversed itself. In his optimistic presentation of the 1984 budget, Finance Minister Salim Masa'idah could not avoid reference to the "drop in the level of worker emigration."[53]

Today, immigration far surpasses emigration. More workers are entering or returning to Jordan than are leaving for work outside the kingdom.[54] Because of the sensitivity of the issue and the inherent difficulty in regulating remittance income, no one knows how great the drop in remittance revenue has been. The government hinted at the problem when it announced that "invisible earnings" had fallen 8 percent in 1984, but it placed the blame on the outflow from foreign labor and the high rate of Jordanian tourist spending overseas.[55] A *Washington Post* report, citing Jordanian government officials, stated that in 1985 remittance income fell by 10 percent.[56] Other reports, also citing official figures, claim that 1985 remittances were 17 percent below their 1984 level.[57] (For the effect of immigration on domestic employment, see below.)

Since 1981, the export sector has also proved itself to be an unreliable source of foreign exchange. The total value of Jordanian exports in 1983 dropped 22 percent from the previous year's $750 million, only to rise the next year by more than 30 percent.[58] Although the government has tried to target export toward non-Arab markets, Arab countries are still Jordan's prime trading area. And the economic side effects of regional politics and the Gulf war have rendered trade with key Arab neighbors especially volatile.

Between 1980 and 1984, for example, exports to Syria fell 81 percent.[59] Whereas those exports had accounted for more than one-fifth of all Jordan's exports to Arab countries in 1979 (the year before Syrian-Jordanian relations fell into a deep freeze), by 1984 the Syrian share had shrunk to just 2 percent of the total Arab market.[60] In 1986, bilateral trade was given a boost by the warming of relations between Amman and Damascus. The two countries promised to increase the level of exports for each to about $60 million.[61] Given Syria's poor economic condition, however, Jordan cannot expect to earn much foreign exchange from its economic relationship with cash-poor Syria.

There has been similar volatility in the trade relationship with Iraq. Exports to Iraq dropped 60 percent in just one year (1982–1983), only to be revived when Amman bankers extended a $125 million line of credit to Baghdad importers a year later.[62] In effect, Jordanian dinars paid for Jordanian exports.

It was hoped that with closer Jordanian-Egyptian relations and the reestablishment of diplomatic ties between the two countries, bilateral trade would ease Jordan's trade deficit burden. Indeed, between 1982 and 1984, exports to Egypt did rise an impressive 800 percent.[63] But there is still a long way to go before the Amman-Cairo route saves Jordanian trade. In 1984, exports to Egypt still constituted only one-tenth of one percent of Jordan's total export earnings.[64]

Much of Jordan's hope for invigorating the export sector rests on the untapped potential of its mineral resources, namely potash and its derivative chemicals and fertilizers. But prospects for windfall revenues from these resource deposits remain gloomy. In 1984, both the Arab Potash Company and the Jordan Fertilizer Industries Company (JFIC) experienced heavy losses. In 1985, JFIC suffered another multimillion dollar loss and was projected to continue to lose money through the rest of the decade. The company has since been merged with the national phosphate corporation in an effort to cut losses.[65]

Austerity and Retrenchment

A comparison of the goals of the 1983 and 1984 budgets highlights the severe macroeconomic problems facing the Hashemite regime. Decreases in government revenue forced state planners to deal with painful policy trade-offs. In late 1982, the finance minister outlined the five main bases of the 1983 budget: increasing security, providing support for Palestinians, honoring financial obligations, completing current development projects, and limiting government spending.[66] In contrast, the goals of the 1984 budget reordered national objectives and called for greater austerity measures. Defense funding was couched in terms of "retention" and "preservation" of its current levels; meeting debt requirements replaced assistance to the Palestinians as the second-ranking priority. Also, a new goal appeared on the list – "continued but rationalized subsidies" – foreshadowing the retrenchment demanded by shrinking revenues.[67]

Stripped of much of its foreign aid and remittance income, Jordan reacted by cutting development projects and consumer subsidies. Development expenditure in 1982 was cut roughly in half, and many projects outlined in the Five Year Plan were suspended or canceled.[68] Construction of the $128 million Yarmouk Hospital, for example, the showpiece of the billion-dollar university complex, was suspended in May 1985.[69]

The government canceled subsidies for all goods except grain and fuel in January 1983.[70] Support for even those staple items was substantially reduced; spending on the fuel subsidy was cut nearly 70 percent, from $177 million to $55 million.[71] The government "rationalized" the allocation of electricity and water throughout the country and placed a virtual hiring freeze on civilian employment.[72] Late in 1984, the government unveiled an ambitious scheme to reduce Jordan's high rate of growth in energy consumption from 14 percent to zero in two years.[73] In the 1985 budget, subsidy outlays continued their downward slide, with total subsidies (food, agriculture, and energy) amounting to only about $54 million.[74] In the proposed 1986 budget, subsidies were cut even more, with the fuel subsidy decreased by 80 percent.[75] Total expenditure on subsidies was limited to just $40 million.[76]

Given the extent of Jordan's financial squeeze, the government's official budget is becoming increasingly unrealistic. In April 1986, price gouging impelled the government to increase the bread subsidy by more than $5 million and to ban the use of all flour not purchased through government agencies.[77] According to government budget figures, Amman plans on paying for these and other subsidies by counting on a 30 percent increase in aid from Arab states in 1986.[78] The rationale for that optimistic forecast is not known.

Efforts to stimulate the private sector, improve productivity, and encourage exports have also been implemented. Prime Minister Zaid al-Rifa'i believes that freeing the private sector will stimulate needed export revenue. In April 1985, the new Rifa'i government canceled its predecessor's plans for the "Jordanization" of the kingdom's banks, a proposal that would have required all banks operating in the country to maintain 51 percent Jordanian ownership.[79] That same month, the cabinet approved the importation of food by private sector firms, leaving the Supply Ministry responsible only for the purchase of four commodities—flour, sugar, rice, and meat.[80] Four months later the government endorsed a wide range of proposals to boost domestic exports and curtail unnecessary consumption, including raising the customs duty on luxury goods and banning the import of goods similar to ones produced locally.[81] Moreover, the Rifa'i cabinet approved a series of measures to attract Arab capital to Jordan, the most significant of which was the removal from commercial regulations of most legal distinctions between Jordanians and non-Jordanian Arabs.[82]

But the failure of a government experiment to promote private initiative in agriculture underscores the difficulties of Rifa'i's plan to rely on the private sector as a means to reduce consumer imports, the main culprit behind the massive trade deficit. In January 1986, the government canceled its mandated pricing system for agricultural produce, hoping that farmers would take advantage of the free market to increase production and reap higher profits. After just one week, the produce market was out of control. Wholesale prices fell while retail prices skyrocketed. According to the minister of industry, trade, and supply, some prices soared more than 200 percent in less than one month, indicating "that the retail greengrocers were the only beneficiaries of the scrapping of the price system."[83] Under considerable pressure from consumers in Amman, the government reinstated the old system in March 1986 — less than three months after the start of the experiment. *Jordan Times* economic analyst Fahd Fanik soundly criticized the government's timid approach to solving structural economic problems: "Let's face it — intervention in the vegetable and fruit market is designed to serve the urban consumers and the new class of bureaucrat, at the expense of the rural producers and the long-term interest of the economy."[84]

Although the government should be applauded for reducing imports by 6 percent in 1984, it is clear that the kingdom is hooked on the high level of imports it grew to enjoy in the oil boom years.[85] As Rami Khouri, former editor of the *Jordan Times*, stated ominously, "Jordan cannot realistically cut its imports in the near future."[86] The kingdom continues to import half its food and virtually all its oil — together valued at more than $1 billion per year. In 1984, Jordan imported three times as much wheat as it did just seven years earlier, and the fuel bill ate up four-fifths of the country's export earnings.[87] Even with the precipitous drop in world oil prices, Jordan's $700-million annual oil import bill has not diminished substantially.[88] As Rifa'i admitted in March 1986, Jordan locked itself into long-term petroleum contracts at pre-glut prices.[89]

Continued high rates of imports mirror the downward spiral of the agricultural sector. Between 1977 and 1984, the ratio of imported wheat to domestically produced wheat was 5 : 1; in 1984 alone, that ratio was 9 : 1.[90] With "alarm," the *Jordan Times* noted that agriculture's share of the GDP was getting worse, not better. "Agriculture is almost dying or fading away despite all the lip service and financial public expenditure it is attracting," wrote Fahd Fanik in March 1985.[91]

Facing an Economic Crisis

In short, the kingdom's economic health is not good. Both the external public debt and the trade deficit hover at the $2.5 billion mark.[92] Domestic revenue provides little more than half the government's expenditure; direct taxes account for less than one-tenth.[93] Capital formation is down and the central government has resorted to hefty commercial borrowing from foreign banks to maintain solvency.[94] In 1983, the kingdom narrowly averted default on $200 million in foreign military sales loans to the United States, but in recent years, Amman has still been able to raise more than twice that through loans in the European market.[95] According to Khouri, Jordan "must be nearing the limit of what it can safely borrow abroad on reasonable terms."[96] (See figure 6.)

In 1984, stock market activity was down 58 percent and seven out of the eight banks operating in the kingdom lost money.[97] In January 1986, Chase Manhattan Bank opted to close its Amman branch rather than increase its cash reserves by $5.3 million to the government-mandated level of $13.5 million.[98] Jordan faces record budget deficits, and foreign exchange reserves have dropped 54 percent between 1980 and 1985.[99] The kingdom's economic problems are dangerously acute, with little hope for immediate improvement.

The Threat of Mass Unemployment

Despite that litany of economic ills, the worst and most threatening problem of all may be the prospect of thousands of migrant workers returning to Jordan in search of new jobs. Jordan produces far too many workers—both skilled and unskilled—for its domestic economy to absorb. Secretary Shultz presented this bleak assessment of Jordan's labor prospects in his Senate Foreign Relations Committee presentation:

The labor force is now growing at 6 percent a year.

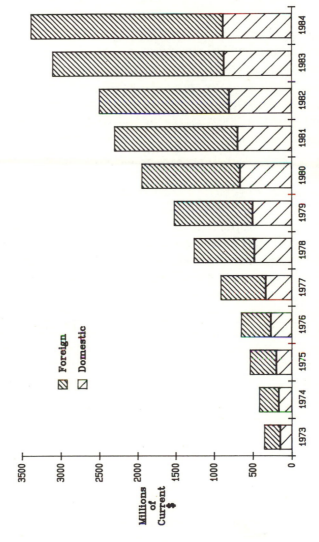

FIGURE 6
Government Debt
(1973–1984)

Source: International Monetary Fund, *International Financial Statistics*, various editions.

27

> Considering present trends, jobs can be found for only
> half of the new job seekers, which could lead to struc-
> tural unemployment of 30 percent by 1990.[100]

Job opportunities in the Gulf siphoned off much of the ex-
cess human capital throughout the 1970s. In fact, attractive
wage rates in the wealthy Arab states drained the Jordanian
labor force, overcompensating for the former labor surplus
and resulting in shortages of unskilled labor within the kingdom. Jordan became one of the world's few states both to
export and import large numbers of workers. Approximately
125,000 foreign workers—25 percent of the domestic work
force—are employed in Jordan in 1986, working for wages
uniformly lower than Gulf wage rates.[101]

   Upon returning home, Jordanian workers are not only
finding job opportunities scarce, but they are forced to compete with the cheaper foreign labor for the available openings.
Some steps have already been taken to ease expatriates back
into the domestic work force. In June 1984, the Labor Ministry began to implement "measures to tackle the employment
balance in the country," requiring all foreign workers to apply
for government work permits.[102] Until then, almost all migrants were undocumented. According to the director of the
ministry's employment office, "if Jordanians are found to
need such jobs, the Ministry will immediately refuse to issue
a work permit and contact the employer and inform him that
his non-Jordanian employee can be replaced."[103] Replacing
foreign workers with unemployed Jordanians will be given
high priority in the new Five Year Development Plan, highlighted by increased spending on labor-intensive projects.
Indeed, the proposed 1986 budget calls for increased spending on such projects as land reclamation and public works.[104]
And in early 1986, the government announced plans to crack
down on illegal foreign workers by posting checks at airports
and border crossings and by levying hefty fines on employers
hiring undocumented aliens.[105]

   So far, however, there has been little evidence of large-
scale dismissals of foreign workers to accommodate the re-

patriated Jordanians. At least 22,000 people have applied for employment to the Civil Service Commission, and Rifa'i admitted that the government is in no position to create jobs for all of them.[106] According to a *Jordan Times* editorial, "under the present circumstances, job opportunities are very limited and there is not much hope to reverse the picture in the immediate future."[107] And given Jordan's poor census procedures, no one knows exactly how many Jordanians are out of work. In January 1986, Labor and Social Development Minister Khalid al-Haj Hassan, pegged the unemployment rate at 6 percent.[108] Two months earlier, Fahd Fanik had already estimated the unemployment rate at 9 percent.[109] Manpower and employment statistics are uniformly poor in Jordan, but given the growth of immigration and the lack of job openings, there can be little doubt that the actual unemployment rate is probably much higher and climbing steadily.

Joblessness looms as an issue of massive proportion even among highly skilled and technical workers, for whom there are far too few available positions to accommodate the fantastic growth in supply. More than 65,000 Jordanians are now studying in foreign universities; an additional 24,000 are enrolled in Jordanian universities, with thousands more at local community colleges and vocational schools.[110] Each year Jordanian colleges and universities boast their largest graduating classes in history. Many of these graduates, however, already are — or are about to be — unemployed. As the *Middle East* magazine reported in March 1986, "entire classes of community college graduates are sometimes unable to find suitable employment."[111]

Especially hard hit are the prestigious professions like engineering. According to the Engineers Association, "practically none" of Jordan's young engineers had been recruited for employment in the Gulf since 1982, and, in 1983, unemployment among engineers began "to take shape."[112] In 1984, the *Jerusalem Star* chronicled the dismal employment prospects for Jordan's then 18,085 engineering students, a number expected to rise 56 percent in just five years:

> Warning. If you or any of your friends are thinking of
> studying engineering, stop now or suffer later. A recent
> barrage of shocking official statistics and forewarnings
> from official observers demonstrate that the employ-
> ment line holds the only vacancy for many of the once
> proud engineers.[113]

According to many indications, the same fate will befall large
numbers of well-educated Jordanians in all professions. The
director of the kingdom's Civil Service Commission stated
in 1984 that the "government is unable to absorb the great
number of people who are committed to serve in government
departments in accordance with previously arranged commitments and arrangements."[114] Mass unemployment could
cause greater strains in the fragile Jordanian economy than
any other of its myriad financial woes.

Economic Prospects and Potential Remedies

In his November 1983 speech discussing the "economic confusion" precipitated by diminished Arab aid, King Hussein
said, "If we manage through the rest of this year and next
year, Jordan will be able to depend on itself from then on."[115]
Since then the country has not collapsed. But with the passage of that critical period, there are no claims from Amman
of resolving financial shortfalls, no signs of substantially
decreased dependence on imports, no indication of movement
toward self-reliance, and, most important, no relief in sight.
In early 1985, Governor of the Central Bank Muhammad
Sa'id al-Nabulsi described Jordan's current economic hard-
ships as the worst the kingdom had faced since the June 1967
war.[116]

Jordan's treasury is so strapped for funds that in October
1985 the government ordered all ministries to cut by 15
percent all spending for the final 10 weeks of 1985.[117] Furthermore, the cabinet announced that in order to save money,
delegations to foreign countries would be pared down, enter-

tainment expenses would be trimmed back, and all government ministries would have to economize on the use of water, electricity, heating, and cooling equipment.[118]

The kingdom does not have many available options in its search for a cure to economic recession. Since his return to the prime ministry in 1985, Rifa'i has reopened ties with Damascus, resulting in the activation of a Syrian-Jordanian Free Trade Area, the resumption of rail and air traffic, and the enhancement of economic cooperation.[119] After Jordan began supplying three Syrian towns with electricity in December 1985, Amman television boasted that nearly 500,000 Syrians were tied into Jordan's national power grid. Moreover, the two countries have vowed to increase bilateral trade to unprecedented levels. But given Syria's own battered economy — in many ways more seriously impaired than Jordan's — it is foolhardy to look for economic recovery as a direct byproduct of an Amman-Damascus rapprochement. Although there may be powerful reasons for Hussein to seek reconciliation with his long-time adversary Hafiz al-Asad, direct economic windfall is not one of them.

Recent moves toward the north, however, may have been the result of enticement from Jordan's south. Hussein's erstwhile Kuwaiti benefactors and cautious Saudi patrons are far more hesitant to commit billions in direct aid than they were a few years ago. At that time, oil shaykhs volunteered billions of dollars for development projects, weapon purchases, and budget assistance throughout the Arab and Muslim worlds. But today, Saudi and Kuwaiti leaders have grown increasingly frugal as they are forced to draw upon reserves to finance their own budget deficits. Kuwait curtailed its aid to Jordan in July 1985, ostensibly to protest Hussein's February 11 accord with Yasir Arafat. The operational death of that agreement will reveal whether Kuwait was just masking its financial constraints behind a political rationalization. Subsidizing Jordan remains within the means of the Saudis and Kuwaitis, despite their shortage of cash. The unanswered questions, however, are whether the health of Jordan's economy ranks high enough on their priority list for them to accept

shortfalls elsewhere and whether Hussein is willing to pay
the political price that Gulf rulers are sure to extract in
return. Topping their list of quids pro quo is a demand for
Hussein to pursue rapprochement with Syria aggressively
and to abandon independent decision making in favor of the
wishes of the Arab consensus.*

For Jordan, the costs of supplicating to the Gulf states
by currying Asad's favor in return for massive infusions of
aid may seem to be a bargain compared to what the kingdom's superpower ally — the United States — is likely to demand. Although Washington is nearly always an accommo-
dating patron when Amman comes in need of financial help,
the magnitude of assistance required to bail Jordan out of
its current economic woes will dwarf all previous aid requests.
Just to make up for the shortfalls in Arab budget support,
Hussein will need approximately half-a-billion dollars per
year within the framework of a multiyear aid package; much
more will be required if Jordan wants to avoid shelving its
current development plan indefinitely and if it wants to create jobs for some of its unemployed. Jordan would then zoom
near the top of the list of U.S. economic aid recipients.[120]

When the Reagan administration sought special dispen-
sation for a 15-month, $250 million emergency grant to assist
Jordan through economic rough times in June 1985, Congress
and Israel's U.S. friends raised few voices in opposition, and
Congress eventually approved a $250 million supplemental
aid package spread over 36 months. But in exchange for a
long-term, multibillion dollar U.S. commitment, Hussein will
surely have to pay a price in the form of recognizing and
signing a peace treaty with Israel. And even though U.S.

----

*Jordan has continually — and vainly — sought ways to circum-
vent the Arab world's principle of unanimity on key policy issues.
Syria's carefully waged campaign to undermine the legitimacy of
the August 1985 Arab League summit in Casablanca put to rest
Jordan's hopes of replacing the unanimity or consensus system
with a majority-vote system.

financial patronage is more reliable than Gulf benefaction or precarious inter-Arab alliances, peace with Israel is a price Hussein is neither willing nor able to pay. As we shall see, viewed in light of other domestic Jordanian issues, the attendant burdens of peace make economic recession seem bearable and the inter-Arab remedies comparatively attractive.

2

The Politics of Islam

By themselves, high prices, unemployment, and economic frustration are not a surefire recipe for political instability. History remembers countless examples of nations in sorrier economic straits than Jordan that resigned themselves to their lot without resort to demonstrations, riots, and insurrection. Indeed, the kingdom itself has experienced periods of painful economic sacrifice and privation with barely a tremor of domestic turmoil.

But two factors render the current Jordanian case especially volatile. First, Jordan's recession is particularly acute in relative terms. For decades, Jordan was satisfied with a small, unpretentious – but growing – economy. Because it neither promised nor delivered much, there was little reason for disappointment. The boom of the late 1970s and early 1980s changed all that. In virtually one swift stroke, massive infusions of foreign capital opened up vistas of opportunity to all sectors of the population. Through education, travel, and foreign employment, the promise of houses, cars, and televisions was open to everyone. Today, that promise is slipping away, and in its place is the frustration, anger, and despair of relative deprivation.

Second, Jordan's political culture has evolved to the point when it may be ready to translate that frustration, anger, and despair into political action. There are trends and movements in the kingdom that can be catalyzed into more overt political activity by the effects of economic depression. The boundaries of political debate – constricted as they are – are straining under demands of a social change as varied as the call for Islamization and the desire for liberalization.

Neutralizing the Palestinian Threat

Paradoxically, King Hussein stands on the threshold of domestic instability today only because he has so artfully resolved the most menacing threat of yesterday – militant Palestinian nationalism in the form of an armed and insurrectionary Palestine Liberation Organization (PLO). Today, Palestinian nationalism poses little direct danger to the Hashemite regime. In 1970-1971, the king destroyed the Palestinian military threat, and since then he has worked diligently to prevent its return. Jordan's internal security apparatus controls Palestinian political activity on the East Bank zealously and efficiently. Jordan has shown little hesitance in suppressing what it considers subversive PLO activity on the East Bank, even during periods of political coordination with the Arafat leadership. During the February 1985–February 1986 Jordan-PLO dialogue, Jordan's intelligence service was not dissuaded from arresting and incarcerating two members of the Palestine National Council (PNC) and the director of the Amman office of the PLO's Department of Education in the Occupied Territories.[1] Even the Israelis have lauded Hussein's policy of severely limiting fedayeen terrorist activity from his country. Explaining why Israeli planes bombed Tunis in October 1985 instead of PLO offices in Amman, Prime Minister Shimon Peres said,

> Jordan is a country that actively fights against terrorism. Jordan, as a country, does not allow the terrorists to come across the Jordan River. Jordan, as a country, does not allow them to establish terrorist bases against Israel from her territory.[2]

Covert Palestinian nationalist organizations in Jordan are tiny, scattered, disorganized, poorly funded, and essentially powerless.[3]

Even more important in recent years has been Hussein's program of incorporating large segments of the Palestinian population into his governing system. Many Palestinians today have a hefty stake in the maintenance of Hashemite rule. Palestinians, or Jordanians of Palestinian parentage, hold powerful positions in government, academe, trade, finance, and industry. The king could convene a joint Jordanian-Palestinian negotiating team by calling a meeting of the Rifa'i cabinet. Of course, splits do exist within the Palestinian community—especially along the chronological lines separating the waves of refugees, those who came in 1948 versus those who came in 1967. On the whole, though, few Palestinians are willing to gamble the personal success and material wealth they have acquired under the king by demanding "national rights." As Professor Clinton Bailey has argued, "Owing to Jordan's development and prosperity, many Palestinians acquired an admiration for the monarchy and a stake in the stability it provided."[4] Under the current political climate, Palestinians would only openly oppose the regime within some other identity, such as unemployed engineers.

For the moment, at least, the domestic Palestinian threat has abated. New threats to the regime, however, have grown to take its place. And these areas of instability are potentially even more dangerous, because they have grown from inside the machinery of Hussein's governing system.

The Specter of Islamic Activism

The most dangerous and least studied area of instability in Jordan is the threat of Islamic activism.* In just the past decade, Islamic activism has—in various forms—toppled one

---

*Lexicographers have expended far too much time and energy jockeying over the precise labeling of this religious, social, and

regime, humbled rulers, and challenged traditional concep-
tions of Middle Eastern society. Yet it has received scant
attention in analyses of Jordan's internal security.[5] In fact,
a discernible, dynamic, and nationwide Islamic activist movement exists in Jordan, a movement waiting to feed off the
frustration of economic deprivation and the perceived igno-
miny of accommodation with Israel.

Politicizing Islam is not new in Jordan. For decades,
invoking Islam — through public manifestations of piety, support of religious institutions, and continual reference to the
Hashemite claim of direct lineage to the Prophet Muhammad — has been an integral part of Hussein's domestic policy.
Islamic activists in general, and members of the Muslim
Brotherhood (*Ikhwan*) in particular, have maintained cordial
relations with the monarchy and enjoyed rights of political
expression refused to other groups. Since the 1950s, the
Muslim Brotherhood has been Jordan's only legal political
organization.[6]

In response, Islamic activists have traditionally been
fiercely loyal to the king. They have appreciated their relative
political freedom and have been fully cognizant of the un-
written political limits beyond which they dare not pass.
Generally, Hussein's Islamic policy has met with remarkable
success. Except for a lone plot against the regime by the tiny
Islamic Liberation (*Tahrir*) Party uncovered by intelligence
agents in 1969, Hussein has had little worry about security
threats emanating from religious circles.[7]

After 1977, however, the Islamic factor in Jordanian
politics began to follow a more independent and defiant path.
Hussein's half-hearted denunciation of Egyptian President
Anwar Sadat's journey to Jerusalem, which failed to con-

---

political phenomenon that is easy to perceive but difficult to classify. Difference of nuance among "fundamentalism," "neofunda-
mentalism," "traditionalism," "revivalism," "militancy," etc., are
secondary to the essential thrust of these movements — a desire to
define personal behavior and political expression under the rubric
of Islam. In order to focus on this central issue, I prefer to employ
the more general term "Islamic activism" throughout this paper.

demn the initiative within an Islamic perspective, kindled a rethinking of one of the basic pillars upon which Hashemite legitimacy rests. Soon thereafter, the king publicly supported the shah against the Ayatollah Khomeini's Islamic revolution and volunteered to assist Iraqi President Saddam Hussein in his battle against Iran. In the early years of the Iranian revolution, public opinion did not focus on the Shi'ite character of Khomeinism. Rather, most Jordanians admired the revolutionaries simply for asserting themselves within an Islamic framework. Incongruities in Hussein's balance of Islam, Arabism, and Jordanian nationalism grew manifestly apparent. Throughout the past eight years, Hussein and Islamic activists in Jordan have competed in a minuet of political and religious one-upmanship, elevating the Islamic issue to the forefront of domestic politics.

Iran, Egypt, and the Amplification of State Islam

Hussein's backing of the shah was the first target of Islamic-based dissatisfaction with government policy. Throughout 1978, Jordan was one of the shah's staunchest defenders; the king himself visited Tehran three times that year to bolster the crumbling Pahlavi regime.[8] At home, many took exception to what was viewed as support for an illegitimate, anti-Islamic ruler against a legitimate Islamic revolution. In February 1979, even the state-supervised Jordanian press reprinted a message from *Ikhwan* leader Muhammad Abd-al-Rahman al-Khalifa to Iranian Prime Minister Shapur Bakhtiar asking him not to obstruct the establishment of an Islamic government.[9] Later that month, the city of Salt was the site of several small but significant demonstrations in support of Khomeini.

The signing of the Egyptian-Israeli peace treaty less than a month later sparked the second round of Islamic-based opposition to government policy. Amman's continuing relations with Cairo between November 1977 and March 1979 were cited as evidence of the shallowness of Hussein's commitment to what were perceived to be pan-Arab and pan-Islamic ideals. Economic ties between the two nations continued after the Jerusalem journey and even after the Camp David accords; Egypt and Jordan signed trade agreements in February and September 1978.[10] Despite the rhetoric of rebuke and denunciation, few saw any substantive change in the nature of bilateral relations. In response, at the end of March 1979 throngs of students throughout the country held protest demonstrations against the treaty – and implicitly against Hussein's flirtation with negotiations. In Amman, the government was compelled to deploy police and internal security forces to quell the demonstrations. One of the most significant events of that week was a mass sit-in by women at a mosque in Amman on March 30.[11]

In retrospect, the events of February–March 1979 had little direct impact on Jordanian society. There were no hordes of students and veiled women marching through the streets chanting "Death to the King," no vicious accounts of police brutality, no charismatic leaders to energize the opposition. Against the backdrop of the revolution in Iran, Islamic activism in Jordan was waged on a very low level.

But given Jordan's particular historical tradition and the relative intensity of the country's embryonic Islamic surge, those two months constituted a watershed period in the development of domestic Jordanian politics. In contrast to both Iran and Egypt, Jordan in the late 1970s was just beginning to experience the movement toward Islam. Only in 1978 did press reports begin to discuss the "new concern . . . about the recent Islamic revival movement."[12] Various sources started hinting at what have come to be the telltale signs of "Islamicness" – men growing beards, women wearing conservative dress, and stricter adherence to Ramadan prohibitions.[13]

There are several explanations for the tilt toward Islam. Many observers point to the role played by popular sympathy with the Islamic revolutionaries in Iran; others cite the general trend in the Arab world to seek Islamic solutions to problems that nationalist and pan-Arab formulas could not solve. But what is clear is that the Hashemite regime perceived this tilt and sought to place itself at its helm.

Newspapers and magazines increased their reportage of religious issues; radio and television boosted their level of religious programming.[14] Coverage accented the personal piety of both Hussein and his brother, Crown Prince Hassan, focusing on their regimen of prayer and their patronage of religious institutions. In 1979, the government introduced a plan to encourage payment of the *zakat* (alms) tax, exempting all those who paid this tax during the month of Ramadan from 25 percent of their regular income tax.[15] Moreover, the palace ordered a crackdown on some of the more flagrant violations of the Ramadan laws, directing provincial governors to close bars and night clubs and to make at least token arrests for eating, drinking, and smoking during proscribed periods.[16] In short, the state was quick to sense the growing Islamic sentiment and escalate the level of Islamic activity.

Islamic politics assumes greater significance, therefore, when viewed in light of the peculiar Jordanian experience. Within just two years, the level of Islamic activity expanded from the relative irrelevance of beard-growing to public protests evoking state intervention. In February 1979, Hussein traveled to Salt and personally dedicated a new mosque following pro-Khomeini demonstrations there.[17] Viewed in a vacuum, the events of February–March 1979 were minor. But in a larger context, they signaled a swift transition in the level of Islamic activity from the predominantly personal to the overtly political spheres.

The Muslim Brotherhood and the Confrontation with Syria

Since 1979, Islamic activism has assumed a position of pivotal importance in Jordan. Fueled by the mutual expansion in state and popular Islam, religion has emerged as a powerful factor in the kingdom's political life.[18]

An Amman meeting of the General Islamic Conference of Jerusalem, convened one week after the March 1979 demonstrations, pointed to the growing complexity of relations between state-supported and popular Islam. Chaired by Kamil al-Sharif, minister of Islamic affairs and Muslim Brotherhood supporter, the Congress approved two resolutions. First, it denounced the Egyptian-Israel peace treaty as a "stab to the Arab and Islamic nations" and endorsed Jordan's stance as a leader of the Arab rejection of the accord. Its second resolution, however, "praised the stand of the Islamic Iranian revolution and its support for the Arab cause" — its strident anti-Israeli position.[19] By criticizing Sadat and praising Khomeini, one of Jordan's most influential religious bodies met the king only halfway on issues of prime relevance to Islamic activists.

Tension grew following Iraq's invasion of Iran in September 1980. Two weeks after the attack, Hussein appeared on television to explain his support for Iraq's Saddam Hussein. Not only did he argue for Iraq as providing a "strategic depth" for the kingdom, but he termed Iraq's victory over Iran the "beginning of victory in Palestine."[20]

In the eyes of many Jordanians, the inconsistency in Hussein's Islamic policy was glaring. Popular opposition to Jordan's support for Iraq in the Gulf war was widespread. In a November 1980 interview with the Arabic magazine *al-Hawadith*, even the king conceded that "there exists in Jordan . . . an emotional gap, meaning that the Jordanian people are not in sympathy with the war because Iran is an Islamic state."[21] As the *Manchester Guardian* reported a few weeks earlier,

> [Hussein] has never been so out of tune with his people as he is today. The great majority see the Gulf War as Saddam's personal adventure and Hussein's intervention on his side as an adventure hardly less perplexing and disturbing.[22]

Less than a week after the king's televised address, several mosque preachers were arrested for championing Iran's Islamic republic in their Friday sermons. Within months, popular opposition to Jordan's alliance with Iraq grew considerably.[23]

Much of the popular support for Iran was channeled through the Muslim Brotherhood, the largest Islamic activist organization in the kingdom. At the same time though, the Brotherhood and the government maintained their peculiar client-patron relationship. The development of that connection highlights the complexity of Islamic politics in Jordan.

For more than 20 years, the *Ikhwan* has operated as the only legally recognized political organization in the kingdom. Its leader, Muhammad Abd-al-Rahman al-Khalifa, is an elderly disciple of Egyptian *Ikhwan* founder Hasan al-Banna. Kamil al-Sharif, who has known ties to the *Ikhwan*, served until 1984 as minister of Islamic affairs, and his brother manages the influential daily newspaper *al-Dustur*. Although the Jordanian branch originated as an offshoot of the mass opposition movement in Egypt, its political fortune has always been tied closely to the crown. Throughout Hussein's most desperate crises – in 1957, 1967, and 1970 – the Brotherhood has consistently defended the king.[24]

In recent years, the price of the *Ikhwan's* relative freedom has been to act as Hussein's agent in his feud with Syrian President Hafiz al-Asad. Although the *Ikhwan* may on its own seek to disrupt the Damascus regime through assisting its fellow brethren in Syria, Hussein clearly dictates what it can and cannot do.[25] For example, following the murder of cadets at the Aleppo Military Academy in June 1979 – for which Asad blamed the Brotherhood – Khalifa launched a propaganda campaign against Syria's Alawite regime and boosted the level of support to Jordanian-based camps training Syrian *Ikhwan* members for missions against Damascus.[26] Three months later, these efforts were halted, most likely on orders from Hussein.[27] In a February 1980 interview with *Le Monde*, Khalifa expressed satisfaction with the Brotherhood's tethered connection with the throne: "We understand our government. . . . We have accepted these constraints with a good face in order not to create internal dissension."[28] (Khalifa's statements came just weeks after the Brotherhood vigorously pursued allegations of sexual misconduct brought against high-ranking Jordanian officials. According to various published reports, three government ministers – including Interior Minister Sulayman Arar – were forced to resign after *Ikhwan* leaders presented Hussein with evidence of their guilt.)[29]

A second instance of the use of the Brotherhood as a pawn in the festering Syrian-Jordanian conflict came to light in the summer of 1980. According to a report in the *Quarterly Economic Review of Syria and Jordan*, Hussein warned Iraq's Saddam Hussein of a Syrian assassination plot in August, leading to a raid on the Syrian embassy in Baghdad and a series of retributive executions.[30] Asad retaliated against the king by threatening direct military intervention unless Jordanian-backed *Ikhwan* activities against his regime were checked. To avoid open conflict with Damascus, the king reportedly curtailed these activities and ordered the reappointment of two ministers known for their anti-*Ikhwan* attitudes, one of whom was Arar.[31] Two months later, Hussein made the next move in his clash with Asad, executing two Syrians dispatched to Jordan to assassinate an exiled *Ikhwan* leader.[32]

The two countries also moved closer to war over the issue of military training camps that the Jordanian *Ikhwan* was providing for Syrian allies operating against the Alawite regime:

> Jordanian Prime Minister Mudar Badran:
> We sincerely hope that nothing will happen, but if any soldier from whatever force steps on Jordanian soil, all Jordanian territory will turn into hell, burning everyone who tries to attack it.[33]

> Syrian President Asad:
> The dens from which plotting against Syria sprang and from which the sabotage acts were carried out in Syria remained in Jordan, in Amman and other cities. . . . I want to say that the Jordanian role has led to the treacherous murder of hundreds of people from all sectors of the Syrian population . . .[34]

Rhetoric was backed up by the deployment of forces along the Jordan-Syria border.

After several tense days in December 1980, Saudi and U.S. mediators persuaded Damascus and Amman to withdraw their troops.[35] One of the conditions for defusing the crisis was understood to be Hussein's promise to limit anti-Syrian Brotherhood activity inside the kingdom.[36] But other than stepping up surveillance of Brotherhood operations, Hussein did not restrict their freedom of action.[37]

A Larger and Bolder Brotherhood

During the 18-month Syrian-Jordanian jousting match, Jordan's *Ikhwan* underwent a profound change. Showcased by the government as its unofficial vanguard against a Syrian regime universally decried for its "un-Islamic" qualities, the Brotherhood gained new vitality. Although it was used as a tool of bilateral affairs, the *Ikhwan's* central role in shaping relations between the two countries appears to have emboldened it.

An aura of cautious but deliberate rebelliousness is evident in the statements of even the Brotherhood's top leadership, those most closely tied to the government. In February 1980, Khalifa had minimized the significance of Jordan's nascent Islamic activist movement and praised the broad-mindedness of Hashemite rule:

> In Jordan, nobody worries about the Islamic movement.
> . . . The Jordanian leaders are more wise than others.[38]

Just 10 months later, though, his remarks bordered on an open challenge to the king:

> This is an Islamic government, but it is not wholly Islamic. We would like to see the teachings of the Qur'an followed much more closely. The government can stop

us publishing, but they cannot stop our tongues. If they try to close our offices, we would go to the mosques. They cannot shut those.[39]

In a 1985 interview with the author, Khalifa repeated his resounding condemnation of Syria's Asad – calling him, among other things, an "American spy" – and not-too-implicitly criticized the king for passively submitting to U.S. will.[40]

Expressions of greater independence were coupled with a growth in popular support. Sources report that *Ikhwan* membership in early 1981 stood at "several thousands," with growing numbers of students at schools, community colleges, and universities joining Brotherhood circles.[41] In 1986, Islamic groups are the most powerful student organizations on the campuses of Jordan's two main universities, Jordan University in Amman and Yarmouk University in Irbid.[42] They control student electoral politics and oversee campus social activities, making sure they comply with traditional codes of behavior. At Yarmouk, for example, there exists a cell-based organization of educational, activist, and support groups for both male and female students. Campus *Ikhwan* leaders lobby hard to convince female students to forgo makeup and designer clothes for long skirts and head-coverings. Nationalist and Palestinian-oriented organizations, which have traditionally been the dominant student groups, are losing support to the Islamic activists. Indeed, few students are able to find any middle ground between the two movements – one is either with the *Ikhwanis* or against them. Networks of Islamic activists – supportive of the *Ikhwan's* goals but not themselves official members – have spread out to the neighboring communities, while a loosely organized oversight committee coordinates activities between the two universities on a national level.

Membership in these Islamic groups includes all elements of the social spectrum – urban and rural, rich and poor. Of prime significance is the appeal of Islamic groups to Palestinian youths. Palestinians do not believe they are forsaking their national aspirations by vowing allegiance to Islamic organizations; on the contrary, many feel these groups offer a more effective way to reach their goals than do radical nationalist groups. Also, Palestinian *Ikhwanis* dismiss much of the nationalist and socialist rhetoric of the old-line Palestinian groups, preferring to view the Palestinian issue within a more comprehensive, Islamic framework.

No single factor explains the change in Brotherhood attitude toward the government or its growth in popularity. As the country's largest and best organized Islamic organization, the Brotherhood was in the best position to accommodate – and benefit from – the surge in popular Islam. As Professor Nazih Ayubi stated in reference to the Egyptian case, "revolt takes an Islamic expression quite often because there are no other outlets for channeling political expression."[43] But the mere existence of such an Islamic outlet does not a priori ensure its appeal or expansion.

More important, the *Ikhwan* attracted wide-ranging support as a result of the prestige garnered through the Syrian connection. To Hussein, the *Ikhwan* was a tool in his contest with Asad. To the Brotherhood and to the growing activist segment of the populace, the *Ikhwan* was a legitimate instrument of Islamic advocacy.

The gulf between those two interpretations of the Brotherhood's role has far-reaching ramifications. Although Hussein and the *Ikhwan* shared some tactical goals against Syria such as disrupting the Alawite regime, they differ fundamentally on such basic strategic issues as Islamic politics inside the kingdom. The *Sunday Times* of London pointed out the paradox of royal Jordanian patronage of the Brotherhood following the execution of Syrian agents in October 1980:

> One Jordanian official pointed out the danger of "turning a blind eye" to the Brotherhood in Jordan in the absence of any other outlet for political expression. "While Brotherhood activity is undoubtedly strictly controlled here, it is tolerated and could easily become a vehicle for the expression of political frustration," he said.[44]

Middle East scholar Adeed Dawisha stated succinctly the catch-22 of Hussein's Syrian policy:

> The destabilizing influence of Iran's government on secularist and modernist regimes like those in Jordan can hardly fill the Hashemite monarch with confidence at the thought of the fundamentalist Muslim Brotherhood gaining power in neighboring Syria.[45]

Hussein, it is argued, can only suffer if he fuels Islamic opposition in Syria by exploiting domestic groups like the *Ikhwan*. That is precisely what occurred.

Many Islamic activists declared their independence from the regime, so to speak, over the issue of Jordanian support for Iraq in the Gulf war. Khalifa, who never ceased to express his admiration for the Islamic revolution in Iran, hailed the Khomeini government as a "regime of liberty."[46] University students in Amman began to circulate a clandestine journal called *Sawt al-Islam (Voice of Islam)*, professing their solidarity with the Iranian cause.[47] Because of government controls on unauthorized publications, *Sawt al-Islam* most likely lacked official sanction from the Brotherhood leadership. But its principal themes—support for Iran and condemnation of moral decline—meshed closely with long-standing *Ikhwan* doctrine.

A corollary to the growth of the Brotherhood was the spawning of several small, underground Islamic activist groups. Many of these organizations endorsed more radical positions than the Brotherhood's client-patron relationship with the state could allow. In 1981, *Le Monde* reported that Islamic activist students were split among "four or five organizations," including an extremist, predominantly Palestinian wing of the Brotherhood, the reincarnated, anti-regime Islamic Liberation Party, and a tiny group calling itself *Takfir wa-Hijra*, modeled after the Egyptian organization of that name.[48] Because of the paucity of reliable information, it is impossible to gauge precisely the size and influence of any of these groups. But if the mainstream Brotherhood

should cease to serve as a useful outlet for Islamic activists –
as a result of regime co-optation or government crackdown
– then radical Islamic groups will most likely assume greater
significance.

Islamization of the Iran–Iraq War

Hussein tried to fashion a response to the growth of an Islamic activist movement for whose creation he shares at least
partial responsibility. Handcuffed by the legitimacy he in-
advertently conferred upon the *Ikhwan* via his Syrian policy,
the king could not challenge the traditional leadership directly. Instead, he pursued a two-tiered policy aimed first at
minimizing the scope of popular Islamic activity and, second,
at claiming for himself once again the religious high ground.
Although his first effort was an appropriate, if not necessarily successful response, Hussein's move toward redefining
his own Islamic policy led to an escalation of Islamic activism
in the kingdom.

First, Hussein tried to restrict the expansion and influence of the activists by placing structural barriers to their
growth. In 1980, for example, the Jordanian cabinet established a new higher education authority headed by the rector
of Yarmouk University. Some observers noted that the authority may be "a way of checking the Muslim Brotherhood
does not get too much of a hold on the campuses – as it has
been threatening to do in Amman."[49] Moreover, Islamic activists won approval from Jordan University to hold prayers
in specially designated "prayer halls" away from the central
university mosque.[50] In practice, the new set-up should fa-
cilitate surveillance of group activities.

Meanwhile, Hussein launched the second element of his
plan in January 1982. In a speech broadcast on the prophet's
birthday, the king heightened the Islamic stakes in the Gulf
war. Throughout the previous 18 months, Jordan's alliance
with Iraq was primarily portrayed as a military necessity,
with Iraq's security described as the kingdom's strategic

depth.[51] By 1982, however, the king began to argue for the Islamization of the war. In the January speech, Hussein challenged the Khomeini regime directly by distinguishing between enlightened and fanatical Islam.[52] Two months later, he "expressed his anxiety over what he believed was a sinister drive by Iran to create a rift between Sunni and Shi'ite Islam."[53]

Hussein was quick to translate his polemical assault into military terms. In late January 1982, he announced the formation of the volunteer Yarmouk Brigade to join Iraqi soldiers in their battle against Iran, purposefully choosing the name "Yarmouk" to evoke images of the seventh-century battle between Arabian Muslims and the Byzantine empire. At the same time, the king called for "an Arabization of the war against the idolatrous Persians."[54] In fact, though, it was Islamization — not just Arabization — that underlies Hussein's charge, for the king went beyond framing the Gulf was solely in ethnic terms. He claimed for himself and his Iraqi allies the mantle of Muhammad and the early righteous companions; to Iran he relegated the mark of infidel. By challenging Khomeini on religious as well as ethnic grounds, Hussein escalated the level of Islamic politics inside the kingdom once again.

Electoral Success and Parliamentary Opposition

Hussein also attempted to assert control of Islamic activists through government appointments, an issue that assumed prime importance in light of two cabinet shake-ups within a 15-month period. In January 1984, Ahmad Obeidat replaced Mudar Badran as prime minister. At that time, long-time *Ikhwan* supporter Sharif was relieved from his post as minister of Islamic affairs in favor of a career civil servant and former provincial governor, Abd-al-Khalaf al-Dawudiyah.[55] After little more than year, Zaid al-Rifa'i took over Obeidat's post as prime minister, and a new Islamic affairs minister, Dr. Abd-al-Aziz al-Khayyat was named.[56] Khayyat is a traditionalist, and he represents the old-line religious hierarchy that has always viewed itself as an ally of the Hashemites. Moreover, he has occasionally adopted positions that earn him the wrath of Islamic activists. For example, he has argued publicly that there is nothing inherently Islamic about traditional women's dress.

These changes in government appointments should be viewed in light of Hussein's moves to reconvene Parliament and order public elections. Within days of the appointment of the Obeidat government in January 1984, Hussein moved toward the long-promised reestablishment of parliamentary life by calling for an election to fill eight vacant seats in the House of Representatives. Although no organized campaigning was permitted and political parties remained banned, more than 100 individuals competed in the eight winner-take-all elections. When the votes were counted, Islamic activists, including at least two *Ikhwan* members, were winners of three of the six seats reserved for Muslims; two other seats were reserved for Christians.[57]

Jordanian officials quickly dismissed the significance of the Islamic activists' electoral support, preferring to attribute their victories "more to structural than ideological factors."[58] One election official said that because of the high number of candidates,

> the middle class moderates took votes away from another. Those who had a strong religious commitment tended to vote in a block, which, because of the diffuse vote, appeared stronger than it actually was.[59]

Others cited the absence of runoff elections, pointing toward the unconvincing victory of one *Ikhwan* affiliate in Amman who received only 18,000 out of 108,000 votes in his district.[60]

Nevertheless, three issues cannot be overlooked. First, the seats won by the Islamic activists spanned the length of the country, from Irbid in the north, to Amman in the center, to Tafileh in the south.[61] Popular support for Islamic activism cannot be considered a phenomenon limited to the densely populated Amman metropolitan area. Second, the haste with which election officials tried to dismiss the final tally indicates their displeasure and probable surprise. The election results were obviously not welcome news. Third, regardless of all structural arguments, it was Islamic activists and not middle class liberals who worked well enough under the stringent electoral laws to gain victories. Elections enhancing the position of the Islamic activists—just weeks after Sharif's removal—were clearly not what government had bargained for.

In Parliament, the Islamic activists have formed the most vocal opposition to the king's government. They have criticized the prime minister's handling of basic national issues and have moved for no-confidence votes on several occasions.[62] Although they are only beginning to find support from other lawmakers for these and other parliamentary gambits, they persist in an effort to rally public opinion to their cause. Parliamentary debate receives wide and relatively uncensored press coverage in Jordan, which the activists have sought to use to their best advantage. By early 1986, 33 of Parliament's 60 members were persuaded to call on the government to introduce the Qur'anic *zakat* tax, and 22 backed the Islamic activists' demand for the total ban on the manufacture, sale, and distribution of alcohol by Muslims.[63]

After 15 months in office, Obeidat, former chief of internal security, was replaced by two-time prime minister and long-time friend of Hussein's, Zaid al-Rifa'i. Although most observers ascribe this April 1985 change to the king's desire to pursue a more aggressive foreign policy, there are indications that Islamic issues played an important role. *Middle East International* cited the king's displeasure with Obeidat's "lack of confrontationalist policies [toward] the Islamic fundamentalist groups," noting that some government ministers gave "public sermons in mosques indicating their preference for the establishment of Islamic rule in the country."[64]

Since taking office, the secular, Harvard-educated Rifa'i has not shied away from confronting the Islamic activists in parliament. For example, during a debate on the proposed

"Popular Army" civilian militia, the prime minister clashed with the activists on the highly charged issue of the proper role of women in society. Islamic activists had criticized a government proposal stipulating compulsory noncombat service for females and warned against any mixing of the sexes during training periods. In response, the prime minister labeled the opposition's position "incorrect," citing women's participation in the Prophet Muhammad's conquests as justification for his stand.[65]

Rifa'i has aggressively continued to heighten the rhetorical stakes in the campaign against the Islamic activists. In one parliamentary debate on the government budget proposal, he dedicated a hearty chunk of his speech to an attack on the maverick leader of the religious bloc, member of Parliament Laith Shubeilat.

> The government greatly regrets the words and methods used by the Honorable Representative Laith Shubeilat. . . . His reservations are a violation of truth and reality, and his indiscriminate accusations against the government not only prejudice the government but your noble chamber as a whole.[66]

In addition to confronting the Islamic activists inside Parliament, the Rifa'i government has tried to circumvent the activists' popular support by rewriting Jordan's election law. In March 1986, a parliamentary majority approved detailed legislation overhauling the kingdom's outdated election law.[67] Although the intent of the new law was largely to satisfy some of the demands of Jordanian liberals by expanding parliament's size and enfranchising residents of Palestinian refugee camps, the legislation was designed to limit the chances for Islamic activist success at the polls. First, increasing registration fees for parliamentary candidates to JD 500 — more than $1,200 — should dissuade the activists from fielding challengers in each district. Second, the government voted itself a potential safety valve against antigovernment activists by banning candidacies of persons belonging to "any illegal or other party which has aims, objectives and principles that clash with the Jordanian Constitution" (Article 17). Third, and most important, the new law redrew election districts, effectively diluting the activists' electoral strength. In short, the new electoral system has constructed a series of structural barriers to prevent an overwhelming *Ikhwani* success at the polls.

Rifa'i's Crackdown on the Brotherhood

A more direct approach to the problem of the Islamic activists was inaugurated in the fall of 1985, when Rifa'i implemented a clampdown on the *Ikhwan* as the price for better relations with Syria. Well known for his close ties to Damascus, Rifa'i's appointment to the prime ministry came as no surprise at a time when Hussein needed to shore up strained relations with Asad. Prime ministerial meetings between Rifa'i and his Syrian counterpart, Abd-al-Ra'uf al-Qasim, led to a series of summit meetings between heads of state, highlighting the attempt to patch up differences between the two quarreling neighbors.[68]

Immediately after the second Saudi-mediated meeting between Rifa'i and Qasim in October 1985, the Gulf press reported that Rifa'i agreed to a Syrian request to deport those opponents of the Damascus regime resident in Jordan.[69] That concession meshes with Syrian statements emphasizing the improvement in bilateral relations with Jordan. Muslim Brothers – on both sides of the frontier – appear to have been pawns once again in the political chess game between Hussein and Asad. Rifa'i's key role in facilitating the move toward reconciliation was underscored when Asad dispatched a personal emissary to Amman that month to attend the funeral of Rifa'i's uncle, former prime minister Abd-al-Mun'im al-Rifa'i. Asad's envoy, Isa Na'ib, minister of state for foreign affairs, was the first high-ranking Syrian official to visit Jordan in five years.[70]

While Rifa'i played troubleshooter in the contest with the

Islamic activists, the royal family was free to take the high road on Islamic issues. Throughout 1985, the crown placed a renewed emphasis on religious topics, foremost among which has been the special Hashemite attachment to Jerusalem. On numerous occasions the king reaffirmed his commitment to regaining the Islamic holy places lost in the 1967 war. At the August 1985 Arab summit in Casablanca, he spoke at great length on the religious aspect of the Palestine issue:

> The talk about Palestine necessarily means talk about the holiest of the holy places. All of us know the acts to which the holy mosque has been exposed. All of us know what this means if it continues. . . .[71]

And when an interviewer asked whether the king would respond favorably to an invitation from Israeli Prime Minister Shimon Peres to follow Sadat's lead and come to Jerusalem to pursue peace talks, he responded (speaking in English):

> Jerusalem has a very special place in my heart . . . as the last Arab and Muslim ruler to have had the responsibility of securing the rights of Muslims and Christians in the Holy City. . . . Jerusalem is also the burial city of my great grandfather, who led the great Arab revolt. So, after a history of well over 1,000 years, I am not about to be the first under any circumstances to legitimize Israeli annexation by going there.[72]

At the same time, Hussein began to speak ominously about the specter of radical Islam spreading throughout the Middle East, bringing down states like Jordan in its wake. In an interview with the Public Broadcasting System in January 1985, the king said that the dangers posed by Iran and "radical Islamic fundamentalism" were not limited to the possible destruction of Iraq, but rather included "greater fragmentation and greater tragedies [throughout the entire region] than what we have seen in Lebanon already."[73] According to his brother Crown Prince Hassan,

one of the major aspects of concern is the possibility
that the present situation [in the Arab-Israeli dispute]
will lead to a primitive war between extreme confession-
al groups that actually threatens the fabric of our societies. . . . the grim possibility facing the Middle Eastern
countries at present is that of sliding into a prolonged,
fierce and all-destroying war.[74]

Hussein Turns on the *Ikhwan*

In November 1985, the king made an abrupt turnaround in
policy toward the Muslim Brotherhood and entered the domestic battle over Islamic politics for the first time. Until
then, his statements and actions had been confined to esca-
lating the Islamic stakes on foreign affairs, such as support
for the shah, an alliance with Iraq, and the reestablishment
of relations with Egypt, while highlighting the traditional
role of Islam in domestic politics. But now, Hussein began
to meet the growing internal Islamic challenge head-on.

As part of his regional political calculus, Hussein agreed
to a Saudi-sponsored mediation to warm up bilateral relations
with Syria, which had ranged from cool to frigid for the past
eight years. One of the stumbling blocks to better relations
that the king offered to remove was the *Ikhwan* activists
agitating against the Asad regime. In his November 2 speech
opening Parliament, the king lashed out at militant mosque
preachers and called on the lawmakers to pass regulations
banning "uncontrolled, exaggerated preaching and the devia-
tion from the method of effective, objective preaching."[75]

One week later, he took the unprecedented step of offering Syria a public apology for underground *Ikhwan* opposition activity against the Syrian government conducted from
Jordanian territory. The extent of Hussein's recantation of
past statements regarding the Jordanian *Ikhwan* is quite
remarkable. The following excerpts from the king's remarks
are from a front-page *Jordan Times* story headlined "King:
Subversive elements plotted and caused Jordanian-Syrian
rift":

But all of a sudden we discovered the truth about the whole affair and we realized what was happening. It emerged that some groups which have had to do with the bloody events in Syria were actually living in Jordan, hiding behind religious groups and pretending to be adhering to religion. This group has been connected with international organizations based in foreign and Arab and Islamic capitals hatching plots against the Arabs. The group's members were in reality outlaws committing crimes and sowing seeds of dissension among people.

I hereby announce that:
I was quite deceived along with a large section of the Jordanian people by this criminal group. I am pained by what had happened because I am not in the habit of denying the truth or condoning deception.

I warn all citizens against the *evil designs of this rotten group* and urge all citizens to prevent them from implementing their evil plans that aim at causing divisions among Arab ranks and sowing seeds of dissension in our midst through concealing themselves behind religious pretenses and through using our religion to achieve their goals.

I am confident that the vigilant Jordanian family is capable of exposing the *evildoers, deceivers and conjurors* and preventing them from achieving their goals.

I warn this group which went astray and which abused our trust that it has no room amongst us any more. We cannot harbor conspirators or deceivers or those who mean to do harm to our nation and we will not allow anybody to sow seeds of dissension between Jordan and any other Arab country. Anyone who causes harm to our brothers is an enemy of ours.[76] (Emphasis added.)

Rifa'i was almost certainly the principal motivator behind the king's extraordinary shift in policy. Hussein's statements were not written in the form of an apology directed to Asad or as a royal proclamation; they were conceived as a policy directive addressed directly to the prime minister. Within days, foreign radio reports noted that Jordanian security forces, acting under orders from Rifa'i (who also serves as defense minister), had rounded up hundreds of *Ikhwan* members active in the Syrian opposition and extradited them to Damascus.[77] Soon thereafter, Rifa'i's cabinet approved a proposed law prohibiting preachers in the mosques from discussing political issues in their sermons and requiring them to submit drafts of sermons to government authorities prior to their delivery.[78] (Parliament approved the measure several weeks later, but only after progovernment sponsors and *Ikhwan* members of parliament agreed to a compromise in which the government dropped its insistence on the obligatory licensing of preachers.)[79]

Just after Hussein's parliamentary state-of-the-kingdom address, Jordan's House of Representatives was the setting for a highly publicized attempt by the Islamic opposition to discredit the government-endorsed Speaker of the House. In a rare display of defiance, nearly one-quarter of the house members abstained in a vote to reappoint Akif al-Fayiz as speaker. (Fayiz had no opposition.)[80] That same day, militant Islamic activist Shubeilat announced he would place his own name in nomination for House Speaker when Fayiz's term expires, thereby ensuring a direct parliamentary confrontation.[81]

Confronting the Activists

Hussein's twin declarations — his call for legislation against militant preachers and his apology for anti-Syrian *Ikhwan* activity — underscore the magnitude of the Islamic problem facing the regime. Just five years ago, the king had used the *Ikhwan* as a pawn in a gamble of military brinkmanship with Asad that nearly resulted in war. Islamic activists were, at worst, a nuisance. Today, in a complete turnabout from long-standing policy, the king is attacking them directly — both politically and militarily. They have become more than a nuisance.[82]

Islamic issues have moved to the center stage of Jordanian politics. In just seven years, the level of religious activism has intensified from beard-growing and Ramadan-fasting to a level of overt opposition to government policies, a level high enough to demand the personal involvement of the king. Inside Parliament, the activists grow bolder each day; outside, tension is increasing in the mosques and universities. Hussein's apology can only highlight the conflict of strategic goals guiding the king and the *Ikhwan* in their respective policies toward Syria in recent years. In short, the time-honored patron-client relationship between the king and the *Ikhwan* is breaking apart.

Whether the situation will deteriorate into an open rift with the king himself, rather than the activists' current opposition to the king's government and its policies, is unclear. If parliamentary life continues to fail to provide a satisfactory outlet for opposition to government policies or if the country's leaders persist in their efforts to sterilize domestic religious activism for the sake of a more congenial inter-Arab atmosphere, Islamic activism could escalate into direct confrontation with the crown. There is no doubt that Jordan's security apparatus is well equipped to handle any organized antiregime demonstrations or overt agitation; a reenactment of Tehran 1979 is simply not in the cards. But the king's much publicized efforts to negotiate a settlement to the Arab-Israeli conflict "before it is too late" leave him open to charges of treason and capitulation from Islamic activists weaned on the confrontation against Israel, Zionism, and the occupation of the Islamic holy places in Jerusalem. And his personal overture to Asad is sure to fuel resentment among Jordanian Muslim Brothers, whose Syrian counterparts have sacrificed much in their opposition to Alawite rule. What is certain is that Islamic activists are no longer quiescent, passive spectators in Jordan's politics.

3

Facing the King's Dilemma

The emergence of an oppositional Islamic activism is not the only challenge facing Hussein's governing coalition, it is merely the most immediate. Other elements of that coalition are undergoing more evolutionary – but equally profound – changes that threaten to chip away at the foundations of the regime. These changes include the weakening of the traditional role of tribes in Jordanian society and the heightened popular demands for the liberalization and democratization of public life.

That such social transformations should occur in a rapidly modernizing society with weak national identity and shallow social cohesion is not surprising. What is surprising is that Jordan has been able to avoid dealing squarely with these issues until now. Modernization has finally caught up with Jordan; Hussein ought to be ready. He has had decades to grapple with what has come to be known as the "King's Dilemma" – a modern monarch's classic choice between success and survival.[1] But the adrenalin of economic boom and bust accelerated these processes of social change in recent years, perhaps throwing off the king's timetable for social change.

Traditional Role of the Tribes

Since the founding of Jordan, the bedouin have constituted one of the king's most loyal and dependable constituencies. They formed the bedrock of the country's army – the Arab Legion (al-Jaysh al-Arabi) – as well as the state's internal security apparatus. From 1970–1971, tribesmen fought fiercely, and often ruthlessly, to expunge the Palestinian military presence from Jordan's East Bank. To this day, despite the kingdom's increasingly heterogeneous ethnic composition, these "original" Jordanians still control many high-level posts in the army and security services.[2]

Tribal loyalty, however, should not be confused with a selfless sense of Jordanian nationalism. Traditionally, bedouin owed fealty to the monarch not in his capacity as head of state but in his role as *shaykh al-shuyukh*, shaykh of shaykhs. As P. J. Vatikiotis noted in his classic study of the military and Jordanian politics,

> Until 1956 . . . it would be inaccurate to assume that the Bedouin in the [Arab] Legion viewed the state as the basic unit of political organization. The relation of the military to the state in this context was sustained by the primacy of the monarch-chief, not of the nation-state.[3]

Bedouin loyalty grew from a desire to defend the honor of family, tribe, and king, not to protect some abstract notion of Jordanian patriotism. The bedouin accepted the king's right to rule, based on his religious claims, which double as tribal claims, and his personal qualifications as a tribal leader.

Second, the pecuniary aspect of bedouin loyalty should not be ignored. In return for military recruitment and political obedience, tribal leaders receive rewards from the king, government ministries, and the military. Remuneration may come in the form of development projects targeted to tribal lands, weapons allotments, or direct cash payments – such as an envelope from the king – to tribal shaykhs.[4] Paul Jureidini and R. D. McLaurin, writing on the role of the tribes in

Jordan, cite Jordanians who contend that "the bedouin is loyal as long as he (or his tribe) is paid—and well paid."*5

Changing Conceptions of Tribes in Society

During the past 15 years, long-held notions about tribes in Jordan have undergone fundamental change. Modernization, the country's peculiar demographic dynamics, and the king's own state-building efforts have combined to weaken the social status of tribal leaders, dilute bedouin presence in the armed forces, alter the traditional role of the tribes in Jordanian society, and force tribesmen to redefine their own personal relationship to the crown.

Tribes, of course, are not disappearing from Jordanian society. The bedouin merely no longer see themselves as they have in the past. The urban crunch, the competition for academic honors, and the desire to attain business success and social status have placed before the younger generation of Jordanians challenges not faced by their elders in the past decades. Jordanians of bedouin stock have not forgotten— and probably will not forget—their heritage. But that sentimentality just does not mean as much anymore.

> Tribalism in Jordan is on the wane. This is not to say that tribal loyalties are a thing of the past, but that tribal linkages can no longer lay exclusive claim on tribe members' allegiance. . . . For a steadily increasing number of [East Bankers] tribal allegiance is either meaningless or peripheral to their lives and feelings. . . .[6]

---

*Much of the discussion on Jordan's tribes is based on a recent work by Paul A. Jureidini and R. D. McLaurin, *Jordan: The Impact of Social Change on the Role of the Tribes*, The Washington Papers #108, Volume XII (Washington, D.C.: The Center for Strategic and International Studies, Georgetown University, with Praeger Publishers, 1984).

As the younger tribesmen adjust to the pace of a modern technical world, the older generation of tribal leaders must deal with a changing culture that increasingly views their traditionalism as an anachronism. When technocrats call for the rationalization of Jordanian economic and development policy, tribal shaykhs rightfully fear the dimunition of their authority. In response, they try to reassert control over tribal members, only to find the level of obedience far below that to which they have grown accustomed. This, in turn, adds to the perception that their own power is shrinking.

> The growing independence of the individual from his tribe raises serious questions about the power of the tribe to control its members. Thus even though the tribal *shaykh* support the king, it is no longer clear that this support extends beyond the *shaykh* and some of the other senior elders of the tribe and it may not be reflected in or convertible to more generalized support of the members of the tribe. In fact, the palace's payments to the tribe via the *shaykh* are distasteful to many younger members who see them as bribes.[7]

Palestinians in the Military

The interplay of modernization and demographics is felt most deeply in the changing complexion of the armed forces. In Jordan, the role of the army in state-building cannot be overemphasized. As Vatikiotis points out, the creation of a Jordanian army actually preceded the formal establishment of the sovereign state of Jordan by more than 20 years.[8] Indeed, some have postulated that it was the army itself that created Jordan.[9] In any case, few argue with the notion that the military has been the most important element in maintaining the survival and stability of the Hashemite monarchy. And, first and foremost, the army was "a tribal army, a force based on and reflecting the social structure of what were once the major bedouin tribes."[10]

In the past 15 years, the composition of the armed forces has changed dramatically. Although loyal tribesmen and relatives of the king still hold most of the senior positions, Palestinians have gained a significant share of the lower-echelon officer posts.* Reflecting the heterogeneity of the country's demographic makeup, the student body at the kingdom's new military college, Mu'tah University, includes children of bedouin tribesmen, Jordan Valley (*Ghor*) agriculturalists, and Palestinian merchants. As McLaurin and Jureidini note, "the officer corps and especially the army as a whole beneath the senior levels have begun to reflect a very different composition."[11]

Palestinians are in greater demand in the military because they are more likely to have the technical and managerial skills necessary for manning a modern army. Describing the Arab Legion of 30 years ago, Vatikiotis noted the great number of "administration and technical personnel who are Palestinians."[12] Today, as military planners place a premium on a well-educated soldiery, the ratio of Palestinians in the armed forces has grown significantly. (It is hardly surprising that the Jordanian government does not keep such statistics and certainly would not publicize them if it did.) Although education levels among bedouin have risen sharply over the past two decades, they still do not match the performance of Palestinians.

Second, the greater proportion of Palestinians in Jordan's military reflects the greater Palestinian presence in the country. Between 1965 and 1970, Jordan's population grew by about half, almost all the increase due to the influx of Palestinian refugees during and after the 1967 war.[13] And more than three-quarters of Amman's population is itself of Palestinian origin.[14] Even more important, in the years after the

---

*"Palestinians" are here defined as those Jordanian nationals either born west of the Jordan River or claiming parentage from that region.

bloody 1970–1971 civil war, large segments of the Palestinian population resigned themselves to Hashemite rule and opted to become Jordanian nationals.[15] Therefore, not only has Jordan's Palestinian population grown, but the pool of loyal Palestinians has expanded enough to permit the government to institute selective conscription to meet the military's need for a high-tech soldiery. As a result, "conscription and promotion patterns . . . [have given] a much greater role to Palestinians and urban Jordanians and a relatively smaller role to tribal bedouin."[16]

The Paradox of Jordanian Nationalism

The integration of nontribesmen into the mainstream of the armed forces can be viewed as a boon to the king's efforts to build a true Jordanian nationalism. Until recently, the concepts of *state* and *nation* were, for the most part, alien in a country founded less on ideology than on desert folkways. In 1946, when Jordan formally gained its independence, the state was merely an extension of the persona of the king, who himself was little more than primus inter pares among the tribal shaykhs. During his rule, Hussein has worked diligently to forge an appreciation of Jordan as a nation-state, trying to create a sense of Jordanian history and nationality. His task has not been easy. Like many other Arab states, Jordan's borders were demarcated on the map-draped conference tables of Europe in the 1920s. But in contrast to all its neighbors, the concept of Jordan itself did not even exist before this century, and there was no metropolitan center around which to construct one. Over the past decade, with the luxury of a static border with Israel and a domestic scene free of an immediate Palestinian threat, Hussein has made considerable headway toward fostering a sense of Jordanian nationalism. At a time when the requirements of a modern army have demanded changes in recruitment policy, the military has served as a valuable crucible for building such a national character.

But the price of creating the institutions of a modern state is the dimunition of one of Hussein's prime bases of support – the bedouin – and the expansion of a national army whose loyalty has never truly been tested. Since 1971, Jordan's military has seen action only as expeditionary forces aiding the Syrians at the tail end of the 1973 war and in assisting the Omanis quell the Dhofar rebellion in the mid-1970s.[17] To date, the army has not been involved in any serious engagement that directly affected the security and stability of the kingdom. Until that day has passed, the once-unquestioned loyalty of the military cannot be taken for granted.

Similarly, state-building has clashed with the traditional bedouin conception of Jordan as a personalized monarchy in which fidelity is owed to the king, not the state. Paradoxically, and hence the king's dilemma, attempts to build a Jordanian nationalism must come at the expense of some of the most important elements of the status quo. Like many observers, McLaurin and Jureidini note that "Jordan is a Hashemite Kingdom in name, but Hussein's Kingdom in the public mind. . . ."[18] In the long run, it is unclear how tribesmen will deal with a concerted palace effort to superimpose a national identity when, in their view, the old order was working so well.

Although no one can state with certainty what role tribes will play in Jordan's political culture in the future, there seems little doubt that the conventional wisdom no longer applies. Surely, the army is not about to revolt openly against the king (occasional, and usually amateurish, coup attempts notwithstanding), senior commanders will not demand a purge of any nonbedouin from the officer ranks, and tribal leaders will not abdicate their current position as still-potent actors in the decision-making process. But there have been clear indications over the past several years that the old order has indeed changed, and a new, as-yet undefined one is emerging.

Traditionalists Grow Restless

In 1977, the *al-Ra'y* newspaper published a story detailing government plans to amend the Military Retirement Law in order to extend the period of minimum pensionable service from 16 to 20 years. State censors responded quickly by suspending *al-Ra'y*'s publication license for three days.[19] Although the news report was not inaccurate, the government's move was prompted by its acute sensitivity to anything that might provoke discontent and resentment in the military.*

Two years later, when Jordan was enjoying its economic boom, inflation was the most serious domestic problem. According to *Middle East Contemporary Survey*, the "very loyal bedouin were outspoken in voicing dissatisfaction" with the government's inability to control rising prices and growing wage-price disparities.[20] In October 1979, tribal leaders and former army officers marched near Amman to demonstrate against the Badran government's economic policies.[21] In July 1983, bedouin dissatisfaction with government policy escalated into a direct confrontation between Badran and the Bani Hassan tribe in Jordan's northern region. Members of the tribe forcibly prevented security agents from implementing a government plan to fence in some tribal land. In the process, dozens of men from the Bani Hassan were arrested and later imprisoned.[22] Such an overt expression of opposition is even more significant given former intelligence chief Badran's reputation as "bête noire" of Jordan's Palestinian population.[23]

As tribal leaders chafed under Jordan's push for mod-

---

*In Jordan, the government operates the radio and television, but private citizens own and operate the print media. The prime minister and his government may be the target of press criticism; the king, royal family, and fundamental policy decisions are off-limits. Editors are expected to employ their own discretion in discussing issues that fall in the gray area. There is little prior censorship; editors and publishers pay for indiscretion with fines, publication suspensions, and imprisonment.

ernization, the emergent middle class had grown more forceful in its demands for the institution of modern administrative and meritocratic methods in the country's planning and policy-making bureaus. A 1976 law limiting tribal practices in government ministries did little to end traditions of nepotism and favoritism. Finally, in January 1985, the clash between the old and the new spilled over into the kingdom's newspapers.

On January 19, Jordan's English-speaking daily, *Jordan Times*, published a column titled "Detribalism: Toward the Rule of One Law."[24] Several days later, the independent-minded *al-Ra'y*, the *Jordan Times'* much larger, Arabic language sister paper, ran another column titled "We Applaud Abolition of Tribalism in Administration," in which the writer, Abdallah al-Khatib, lashed out at the backwardness of tribal thought.

> Any student of the tribal concepts within our departments will realize that the unhealthy phenomena in these departments will certainly prevent any reform or modernization of this apparatus. The good organizational framework, the carefully wrought laws and regulations, the incentives, the changes in the cadres, and the various administrative procedures will be canceled by the head of this department if he is unable to get rid of the tribe and subscribe to the administrative concept. . . .
>
> To favor Zayd at Amr's expense, to bestow privilege on Zayd at Ziyad's expense, to appoint Ahmad instead of Hammudah, to bypass all the regular steps of appointment for the sake of "our brother," to apply the law to the letter to someone who has no backers in order that another backed person might jump over all kinds of laws and logic, to leave others in the *status quo* – to mention only a few examples – will not only hinder the march of our administrative development and abort their goals, but will also ruin the march of the entire country.[25]

Tension between bedouin traditionalists and liberal-minded modernists had risen to the point at which the king was forced to intervene. On January 27, 1985 Hussein sent a public letter to Prime Minister Obeidat in which he boasted of his bedouin heritage, vowed never to condone the "all-out fragmentation and dismemberment of the tribe," condemned Jordan's media for "exceeding the limits of truth, knowledge and responsibility," and charged several writers with shallowness and "cheap sycophancy."[26] In Jordan's controlled media system, Hussein's warning was unambiguous: "We will not allow the freedom enjoyed by our people to be used as a way to cast doubt, destruction and loss by those who benefit from it."[27]

In a display of opposition rare in recent Jordanian history, Information Minister Leila Sharaf resigned almost immediately after the publication of Hussein's letter.[28] Sharaf, the widow of the king's confidant and former Prime Minister Sharif Abd-al-Hamid Sharaf, had been an outspoken advocate of press freedom, liberalization, and the movement to rid government of anachronistic tribal practices. Hussein's letter was viewed as a direct slap at her efforts, and in her letter of resignation, she harshly criticized the government's crackdown on freedom of expression:

> With all my idealism and simplicity, I thought I had the blessing for pushing an information policy based upon enlightening the citizen on all issues that concern him, moving away from daily interference in his right to think and freedom of expression. . . .But after a good initial response, the government has started to show impatience with even the simplest forms of freedoms and all frank communications with the Prime Minister have disappeared, making it impossible for me to continue in my job.[29]

Fifteen years ago, it would have been unheard of for Jordan's media to denigrate tribes and tribal practices so candidly and for a cabinet minister to state her disagreement with government policy so publicly (especially the cabinet's only woman minister). What is significant is that Sharaf is neither a militant nor a rebel; she is a prime example of the

liberalizing wing of Jordan's social and political establishment. Her principled and much-publicized stand against
tribalism and for freedom of expression set an important
precedent for others to follow. Moreover, the entire episode
underscored the king's particularly uncomfortable and un-
enviable position in the debate.

Postponing Democracy

Hussein has also come under increasing pressure from members of the Jordan elite to speed up the pace of democratization. Prior to 1967, Jordan's Parliament functioned as a representative body for both the East and West Banks of the
river. But martial law was declared during the 1967 war and
Parliament was dissolved in November 1974, one month after
an Arab League summit resolution stripped Hussein of formal conservatorship of Palestinians and appointed the PLO
as their "sole, legitimate representative."[30] Under martial law
regulations, Hussein and various prime ministers have ruled
Jordan by executive fiat. Of course, it should not be inferred
that in any period after 1957 Jordan approximated a limited
constitutional monarchy in anything but name. Political parties have been banned for decades and all decision-making
authority has been vested in the king and his close advisers.
But the structures of Parliament and local government constituted an important symbol to the kingdom's growing,
increasingly wealthy, and modernized middle class. To many,
Parliament's closure meant that Jordan was moving back-
ward, not forward.

Although sensitive to these concerns, Hussein moved
slowly to address them. Throughout 1976 and 1977, special
sessions of the cabinet were convened in all the provincial
capitals, part of what Prime Minister Badran termed "an
objective dialogue with the citizens."[31] Hussein called it "direct and simple democracy"; more critical observers labeled
it an attempt "to promote the impression of greater democratization."[32] In April 1978, one month after a delegation

from Jordan's highly politicized professional organizations met with the king to press for greater democratic freedoms, Hussein announced the appointment of 60 prominent citizens to a purely advisory National Consultative Council (NCC). According to Hussein, the NCC would be an institution in which, "the legitimate expression of the opinions, interests and feelings of the citizens" could be aired "in freedom and responsibility."[33] Throughout the next six years, however, the council proved itself ineffectual, satisfying few desires for the establishment of true democratic institutions. As one observer of legislative development in Jordan has stated,

> The NCC is a manifestation of a general political strategy on the part of King Hussein . . . to utilize the country's political institutions to coopt intellectuals and businessmen, to appease the traditional sectors of society and to mobilize support for Royal policies. Hussein's commitment to these groups, however, is not binding upon him.[34]

In the absence of parties, most political expression is channeled through professional organizations and charitable societies, as well as, of course, religious groups. These are the only outlets for debate and loyal opposition open to Jordan's modernizing elite. Issues addressed by groups of doctors, lawyers, engineers, and architects are not limited to professional concerns. In their capacities as reputable community leaders, they are permitted to work within the narrow limits of Jordan's political debate to oppose certain government policies and lobby for political reform.[35] After Sadat's November 1977 journey to Jerusalem, these groups circulated petitions denouncing the Egyptian leader in language far more forceful than what the king himself used.[36] Among those that signed an anti-Sadat statement appearing in the local press were former Justice Minister Shafiq al-Rusheidat, former Interior Minister Najib al-Rusheidat, and Palestine National Council Speaker Abd-al-Hamid al-Sa'ih.[37] Similarly, professional organizations (along with the faculty of Jordan

University) were outspoken in their criticism of the Arab governments' failure to respond forcefully to Israeli military operations in South Lebanon in 1978; they issued a statement, one not permitted to appear in the local press, charging some Arab governments with a desire to "solve the conflict with the enemy through negotiation and co-existence."[38] In March 1979, these groups were joined by labor unions, women's organizations, and the Committee for Saving Jerusalem in planning a one-hour general strike to protest the Camp David accords.[39]

The issues of liberalization and democratization grew in importance as Jordan's economic boom peaked and began its downward slide. A wide spectrum of Jordanians began criticizing the government for failing to address adequately the problems of inflation and widening wage-price disparities. In 1979, the Badran government sought to defuse opposition by instituting administrative reforms at the local level, and 800 political prisoners were released in January 1980.[40] In 1982, as the economic situation began to worsen, Hussein expanded the NCC to include 75 members; but as is so often the case, partial remedies only fueled demands that the crown was sure to refuse—such as the call for the establishment of political parties.

On the whole, the push to democracy remains a predominantly establishment concern, making it an even more potent issue with which to deal. A magazine called *al-Ufuq*—whose editorials championed democratic rights—was founded in 1982 by Muraywid al-Tal, the brother of former Prime Minister and anti-PLO hard-liner Wasfi al-Tal.[41] The Badran cabinet stripped *al-Ufuq* of its publication license after just five months. Another al-Tal brother, Education Minister Said al-Tal, along with Transport Minister Jamal al-Sha'ir and House Speaker Akif al-Fayiz, figured prominently in the establishment of quasi-political groups such as the Arab Constitutional Alignment in this period.[42] In Jordan, they are the elite.

Hussein finally responded to establishment demands by convening Parliament in January 1984. The assembly was charged with amending the constitution to permit direct elections on the East Bank alone, so that deputies could be chosen to fill the vacant seats of those who had died since the last election, nearly two decades earlier. Under the new plan, a reconstituted Parliament would meet to elect the West Bank deputies, thereby maintaining West Bank representation without popular elections. As discussed earlier, East Bank elections to fill eight vacant seats were held in March 1984, and, for the first time, women were allowed to vote. Four empty West Bank seats were filled in a hotly contested parliamentary ballot in November 1985.

In May 1986, Parliament approved a top-to-bottom overhaul of the kingdom's election laws. Parliament itself was expanded from 60 to 142 members, half of whom will eventually be chosen via direct elections on the East Bank. The West Bank delegation, increased from 30 to 60, will continue to be chosen indirectly by the sitting members of Parliament. Eleven seats were set aside for residents of Palestinian refugee camps on the East Bank, enfranchising tens of thousands of refugees for the first time. An Amman magazine hailed the electoral reorganization as a sign of "the entrenchment of the bases of parliamentary life and the enlightened practice of democracy" in Jordan.[43]

A Questionable Commitment to Democracy

Whether these steps were aimed at liberalizing Jordan's political atmosphere or were just another element of Hussein's inter-Arab and Arab-Israeli policies is unclear. Just after Parliament's convocation, al-Nahar observed that "King Hussein has thus been able to bow gracefully to rising pressure at home for a return to democracy."[44] Since then, various commentators have taken note of the marked change in government appointments, highlighted by the Rifa'i cabinet's "virtual absence of ministers linked to the Jordanian security and military . . . a radical departure from past practice."[45] There is little doubt that the current government does emit at least an aura of greater responsiveness to the modernists and technocrats than did its predecessor.

But there may have been ulterior motives for recalling Parliament that run deeper than the mere desire for democratization of Jordan's political life. In late 1983 and early 1984, Hussein was busily preparing the groundwork for reaching an accommodation with the Palestinian national leadership over forging a common approach toward negotiations with Israel. Promoting his personal credentials as an effective representative of the West Bank Palestinians was an important part of this task. In November 1984, he permitted the PNC to convene in Amman, delivered the keynote address at the convention's opening session, and broadcast the proceedings by state television into the West Bank and throughout Israel.

Parliament's restoration can be understood in light of these actions. When Parliament was convened, Hussein withstood virulent criticism from the Syrians who charged him with violating the Rabat resolutions. At the time, maintaining an image of defiance toward Syria contributed to his initiative toward the Palestinians and the PLO. Moreover, Rifa'i's cabinet is filled with representatives of some of the largest and most powerful Palestinian families such as the Husseinis, the Masris, the Kana'ans and the Nusaybahs, who represent all the major West Bank cities.[46] As al-Nahar argued, "this is being seen as a confirmation of the recent Jordanian policy of expanding Palestinian representation in the legislative and executive branches."[47]

There is little evidence, therefore, that recent moves toward democratization herald a new era in the kingdom's political life. The continued maintenance of martial law suggests that not much has changed. In both May and June 1985, Gulf journals continued to report the presentation of petitions to Rifa'i by hundreds of prominent Jordanians "demanding the release of political prisoners, cancellation of martial law, increase in freedom of the press and speech and legalization of political parties, organizations and all public gatherings."[48] And despite the prospect of national elections, there is little to suggest that organized political campaigning will be permitted or that, once elected, the legislators will be empowered with any substantive decision-making authority.

Hussein's commitment to democratic freedoms and representative institutions appears neither strong enough nor sincere enough to withstand the ebb and flow of his overall regional policies. Until that commitment stands independent of regional concerns, modernists will continue their clamor for more political reform. In the meantime, Hussein's seesaw approach to the "King's Dilemma" — at times tilting to the modernists and at times to the traditionalists — has satisfied no one.

4

Jordan after Hussein

Throughout November 1985, thousands of cheering Jordanians filled the streets of Amman, Aqaba, Irbid, Zarqa, and Salt to celebrate the fiftieth birthday of King Hussein, the preeminent survivor of Middle East politics.

As a country, the Hashemite kingdom is ringed by states — Arab and Jewish — with substantially more potent military arsenals. Across the border, some right-wing Israelis proclaim Jordan to be the rightful homeland for Palestinian nationalists, while at home, Islamic activists have begun their telltale murmur against the king's moderate, pro-U.S. policy. Blessed with nothing to export but cement, fertilizer, and people, Jordan's existence rests squarely on the munificence of friendly states. Somehow, though, the kingdom survives.

And the foremost survivor of all is the Jordanian monarch. Hussein has lived through almost every conceivable personal danger and national threat in a region notorious for coups, revolts, and assassinations. Since he took over from his mentally deranged father in 1952, Hussein has survived two wars with Israel (1967 and 1973), two near-wars with Syria (1970 and 1980), one full-fledged civil war (1970–1971), one nationalist uprising (1957), one Nasserite threat serious enough for the king to request the moral support of British paratroopers (1958), and too many coup and quasi-coup attempts for any but a historical statistician to keep count. (According to reports, the most recent effort was in July 1985.)[1] Hussein has also weathered his share of automobile crashes, bomb explosions, gunshot wounds, and – that symbol of hardworking executives – bleeding ulcers. He has lived through the brutal murder of his grandfather at the hands of Palestinian militants (1951), the vicious killing of his cousin, Iraq's Hashemite King Faisal (1958), and the death of his third wife, Alya, in a helicopter crash (1977). His prime ministers have been blown up and shot down. The young king was brutally honest in his 1962 autobiography *Uneasy Lies the Head* when he said that "Arab lands are not like other lands. Life is all too often held cheaply, and death often passes unheeded."[2]

Hussein, however, is not Superman. In spite of his survival record, U.S. policymakers must be prepared for the day when the king's luck runs out. What can Washington expect from a Jordan after Hussein?

Like many Arab leaders, the cagey and clever king has dealt carefully with the issue of succession. Since his own accession to the throne, there have been three different heirs apparent – all of whom are still living and could compete for the crown in a succession battle. They are Hussein's younger brothers, Muhammad and Hassan, and his eldest son, Abdallah. Two other possible contenders are Prince Faisal, Abdallah's younger brother, and Prince Ali, now just a small child but the first of Hussein's sons born of an Arab Muslim mother.

Muhammad: Not a Contender

Although he is Talal's second son, Prince Muhammad (b. 1941) is the most unlikely candidate of the five to vie for the monarchy. From 1952–1962, Muhammad was crown prince, first in line to succeed the king. Since then, however, he has taken himself out of the running by publicly abdicating his claims to the crown. Between 1971 and 1973, Muhammad served as president of the Council of Tribal Shaykhs, resigning that post for reasons of health.[3] Although he often represents the royal family on ceremonial occasions, he is not a serious contender for the succession.

Hassan: The Consummate Moderate

The king's youngest brother, Hassan (b. 1947), has been crown prince for two decades and remains the most likely candidate to succeed Hussein. Hassan is personally responsible for the planning and implementation of Jordan's economic development projects and is a frequent speaker before international conferences on scientific and technological issues. With increasing frequency in recent years, Hassan has spoken out on matters of public policy, but he is careful not to encroach upon Hussein's authority in political affairs. As the *Middle East Contemporary Survey* stated several years ago, "the mutual respect, trust and loyalty between the two brothers appears as strong as it has always been."[4]

Hassan is by no means, however, Hussein's alter ego. Whereas the king was trained as a soldier and pilot, the crown prince is the palace intellectual, a graduate of Christ Church College, Oxford, with a degree in oriental studies (Arabic and Hebrew).[5] The crown prince has no formal military background and holds the rank of "Honorary General of the Armed Forces."[6] He is not known for particularly close personal relationships with either army or tribal leaders.[7]

From what can be gleaned from published interviews and Hassan's own journal articles, he and his elder brother also part company on more substantive issues. Hassan was just four years old when Hussein witnessed his grandfather's murder and was still an Oxford undergraduate when Jordan lost half its territory in the 1967 war. Having reached political maturity in a period of relative tranquility on the kingdom's western border, Hassan has neither his grand-

father's determination to win over the Israelis through negotiations nor his brother's burden of responsibility for the loss
of the West Bank and Jerusalem.

Hassan's own political crucible was the 1970–1971 civil
war, during which he saw his personal patrimony threatened
by Palestinian extremists. As one military historian noted,
Hassan stood at his brother's side in 1970 as "the Hashemites
were to face the most serious challenge of their troubled
history."[8] Today, that experience is manifested in Hassan's
aversion to all things extremist, both movements and per-
sonalities – whether they be nationalist, leftist, or Islamic.
He has an almost obsessive attachment to the idea of moderation. His political worldview is summed up in the subtitle of
a 1984 book he authored on regional peacemaking – *Search
for Peace: The Politics of the Middle Ground in the Arab East.*[9]

Because he does not view the Israeli military threat as
the primary danger to the maintenance of the Hashemite
regime, Hassan has been more conciliatory than the king on
the issue of the Jewish state. In his 1962 autobiography, for
example, Hussein called the 1947 approval of the UN partition plan for Palestine a "moment of disaster for relations
between the West and the Arabs."[10] In contrast, in *Search
for Peace*, Hassan praised the partition plan as a wise move
that recognized the "immutable facts of human geography."[11]
And the crown prince has been far more explicit than other
Arab leaders in construing acceptance of UN Security Council Resolution 242 as "full recognition" of Israel. In a letter
to *Foreign Policy*, he stated that, with that acceptance,

> Jordan has already accorded full recognition to the sov-
> ereignty, territorial integrity and political independence
> of the state of Israel and its right to live in peace within
> secure and recognized boundaries, free from threats or
> acts of force.[12]

In a 1982 article in *Foreign Affairs*, Hassan outlined the
framework he envisaged for an Israeli-Jordanian peace agree-

ment. Far from some maximalist demands, Hassan was quite forthcoming in listing subjects "proper for discussion," which included "juridical status" such as sovereignty.[13] And in 1984, Hassan offered the option of a borough system for Jerusalem, a much more conciliatory proposal than the requirement of total Arab sovereignty.[14]

When Hassan does denounce the Jewish state, it is often for driving legitimate Arab nationalists into the Israeli Communist Party, thereby "ironically producing the radicals [Israel] claims to fear."[15] He is especially critical of the Soviet Union and the danger of Communist encroachment in the Middle East, lamenting the decades-old failure to resolve the Arab-Israeli conflict as a "tactical victory for the Soviets."[16]

Hassan's main preoccupation is the battle against radicals and ideologues, principally those of the Palestinian and Islamic ilk. Only by taking a forceful stand against all forms of extremism, he argues, can Jordan and its neighbors (Arab and Jewish) avoid a "primitive war between extremist ideological groups that . . . threatens to destroy the social fabric of our societies."[17] He condemns Muslim fundamentalism as a form of "liberation politics" that only seeks solutions through "violence of the autocracy"; he openly disdains "those Palestinians who find our Hashemite tradition, our form of government, and our abiding faith in God distasteful, those blinded by ideology who see us as reactionaries or lackeys or worse."[18] Democratic institutions can have no inherent benefit if they are not "aimed above all at promoting tranquility and future stability."[19]

More than any other Jordanian, Hassan has a personal stake in the kingdom's "future stability." For that reason, he has counseled against making dramatic, public gestures toward settlement with Israel that could provoke backlash at home. Israel and Jerusalem simply are not at the top of Hassan's political agenda. He seems more than satisfied with Jordan's 19-year de facto peace with Israel and is known to be even more hesitant than his brother to invite a surge of Palestinian and Islamic radicalism by seeking to formalize that arrangement in a peace treaty.[20]

Modernization is Hassan's panacea; economic development and social progress are his solutions to extremism. When
asked recently about his vision for the future of Jordan, he
spoke of "Singaporising" the economy – a program of improving management techniques, bolstering export-led industries,
and funding advanced technologies that take advantage of
Jordan's comparative regional advantage of a highly educated labor pool.[21] And his image of the Middle East after
a comprehensive peace settlement is one of a region transformed into an "advanced workshop and a maintenance center of modern technology."[22] That is a far cry from Hussein's
more prophetic vision of the benefits of peacemaking: "I feel
a tremendous responsibility to accomplish something for my
people, something beyond mere economic progress. I want
to help bring about a durable peace, so that my people can
have something I never had – confidence in the future."[23]

Although Jordan's quiescent and largely co-opted Palestinian majority is not currently a major threat to the stability and tranquility Hassan needs to become king, he does
fear what the increasingly militant Palestinians of the West
Bank would do if transported eastward. As the traditional
West Bank elite ages, it is being replaced by a more activist
younger generation, one that grows more polarized each day
among factions of radical nationalists and Islamic activists.
It is this demographic threat – more subtle yet more dangerous than a military danger – that might spur Hassan to
seek a strategic understanding with a sympathetic Israeli
leadership.

On several occasions, Hassan has aired his fears about
the potentially disastrous ramifications of a deluge of Palestinians flooding across the Jordan River. When Amman imposed strict controls over movement across the river bridges,
Hassan explained them as aimed "only at restricting the
demographic move" of West Bankers.

Just to sit back and say Jordan can be the repository
[for West Bank Palestinians] is just impossible. We cannot be a stable repository. Our per capita income has

gone up from less than $400 after the 1967 war to $2,000, which in relative terms is good. But we can't maintain the standard of living or improve on it if suddenly a deluge of people descends on our head.[24]

When some hawkish Israelis proclaim Jordan to be the rightful Palestinian state and urge the relocation of West Bankers eastward, Hassan shudders. He envisages a reenactment of the 1970 Palestinian state-within-a-state scenario and a direct threat to his own rule. This danger could compel Hassan to seek a mutual understanding with a sympathetic Israeli leadership on the control and supervision of the troublesome residents of the occupied territories. Conciliatory statements regarding peace with Israel do not, therefore, foreshadow a new era in bilateral relations. When Hassan warns all who will listen to heed the lessons of Iran and Lebanon, it is the shah and Bashir Gemayel that he recalls. And the memory of Sadat's assassination at the hands of Egyptian Islamic activists is not easily forgotten. Hassan will have even less to do with formal peace negotiations than Hussein. But he is sure to work with the Israelis – at least as closely as his brother does now – to serve their mutual interests in terms of taming an unruly West Bank population.

Abdallah and Faisal: Potential Challengers

If Jordan does face a succession crisis in the near future, Hassan's principal rival for the crown will most likely be his nephew Abdallah, Hussein's eldest son. From the time of his birth in 1962, Abdallah was officially Jordan's crown prince, but that title was stripped from him three years later and conferred upon Hassan when the latter reached age 18. In 1978, King Hussein issued a declaration restating the line of succession and confirming Hassan as heir apparent. At that time, Abdallah was even passed over for second-in-line in favor of his younger half-brother, Prince Ali. Most observers believe that Abdallah has been sidestepped in the royal pecking order to assuage public consternation about his mother, Princess Muna (Toni Avril Gardiner), who was born neither an Arab nor a Muslim.

Today, Abdallah is an officer in the Jordanian army and — like his father — an ex-Sandhurst cadet. Little is known of his policy views. Unlike his uncle Hassan, Abdallah does not yet contribute publicly to the policy debate. But he clearly has kingly ambitions. At a U.S. State Department dinner in May 1985 in his father's honor, the young prince admitted that his current stint in the army is the "best way" to get acquainted with the Jordanian people.[25] Moreover, he dismissed the prescribed line of succession and implicitly criticized Hassan, saying that "picking a leader is not something done automatically because of a given position."[26] Although stripped of his rights as heir, Abdallah has certainly not fallen out of royal favor. He maintains high visibility in the Jordanian press, is often included in meetings with foreign visitors, and regularly represents his father at state functions. As an ex-crown prince, Abdallah will surely be an important factor when the throne becomes vacant.

Faisal (b. 1963) is Abdallah's younger brother, the second son of Hussein and Princess Muna. After graduating from Brown University in June 1985, Faisal enrolled in the virtually obligatory military course in Britain. Like his brother, Faisal does not make public statements on state policy, so little is known of his views on critical national issues. But along with Abdallah, Faisal has a vested interest in the transfer of the kingship to Hussein's offspring, an interest that may make itself more apparent in the event of a succession crisis.*

---

*Observers who enjoy reading much into snippets of biographical information will be interested in the self-evaluation Faisal supplied for his high school's 1981 yearbook. According to the *Washington Star*, Faisal ranked "ZIONISTS" — in "big fat capital letters" — at the top of a list of personal "revulsions," a list that also included "political elections." *Washington Star*, June 11, 1981.

Ali: Future Claimant

Currently second-in-line to the throne, Prince Ali (b. 1975) is Hussein's eldest son by an Arab Muslim — and Palestinian — wife, the popular Queen Alya who died in a helicopter crash. If there has been no succession by the time he reaches age 18, pressure will build on the king to decide whether the kingship will pass laterally to Hassan or, as is tradition, to his then-adult son, Ali. The king has already bestowed the crown princeship on three people; there is no reason to believe he would not change it again. Ali's parentage, representing the fusion of Jordan's tribal and Palestinian ethnic strains, gives his claim to the throne a special attraction.

A murky succession situation grew even murkier in 1979 when Hassan's wife gave birth to their first son, Rashid. In Jordan's patrimonial royal tradition, the kingship is to revert to the sons of Hussein after Hassan's term in office. In 1977, Hassan had no male children, so Hussein's proclamation appointing Ali as Hassan's heir apparent was not problematic. Rashid's presence, however, casts doubt on the likelihood of a tranquil transfer of power from the House of Hassan back to the House of Hussein. The claimants to the throne and the various palace political blocs may use this issue to bring about a full-fledged succession battle immediately upon the death of Hussein.

Filling a Royal Vacuum

A still larger issue haunts any analysis of Jordan's future after Hussein. Will there be a succession at all? A great majority of Jordanians have known no other ruler than Hussein. For decades, his personal approval has been required for every government policy, every significant political appointment, every large armed forces acquisition and maneuver, and every sizable construction project. In the course of a 33-year reign, Hussein has come not only to symbolize Jordan, but to be synonymous with it. As Zaid al-Rifa'i commented, "It is difficult to imagine the Hashemite Kingdom without [Hussein]."[27]

Such a sentiment can certainly not encourage men like Hassan, who has spent much of his adulthood doing exactly that — imagining the kingdom without Hussein. But Hassan and other members of the royal family are not the only ones to ponder the fate of the monarchy. At the critical moment of succession, a weak system like Jordan's is susceptible to more than just the violence of coups, revolutions, and invasions. Parliamentary leaders and local politicians once held power in Jordan. A succession crisis would offer a prime opportunity for those groups to reclaim the free agency they lost in 1957, when Hussein declared himself ready both to reign and rule.[28]

An even more critical variable in all succession scenarios is the role of the military. Men like General Sharif Zaid bin Shakir, commander in chief of the armed forces, General Tariq 'Ala-al-Din, director of general intelligence, and Abd-al-Hadi al-Majali, director-general of public security, are closely tied with the royal family and the kingdom's political elite and have always been powerful players in Jordan's politics. They will surely be pivotal in the succession process, intent on maintaining and securing the military's preeminent position in policy-making. Because no member of the royal family can inherit Hussein's great personal stature within the armed forces and intelligence community, these men are likely to fill the vacuum and try to exert far more political power than the considerable amount they now wield.

Bin Shakir's role will be critical. A distant relative of the king, his early career was marked by participation in an anti-Hussein plot during the 1957–1958 government crisis. But as Hussein has done so often in the past with defeated rebels, he "reformed" Bin Shakir and patronized his rise through the leadership ranks of the armed forces.[29] In August 1970, Bin Shakir was appointed assistant chief of army operations, and, according to an army historian, he "drew up the strategy which finally resulted in the elimination and expulsion of the fedayeen from Jordan.[30] Since he became commander in chief in January 1976 – in a term spanning eight different cabinet rotations – Bin Shakir has grown to be one of a handful of the most powerful men in the kingdom. He will surely wield substantial influence in the post-Hussein era.[31]

Hassan's situation is particularly vulnerable. Even after serving as crown prince for 20 years, members of the royal family have still not reconciled themselves fully to his accession to the throne. In that time, he has alienated Palestinian sentimentalists by his less-than-zealous pursuit of the Palestinian cause, and he has favored modernizing technocrats at the expense of traditional tribal elites. Not only may he face competition within the royal family, but after two decades as crown prince, he may also not have a much firmer base of support among the general public today than he did in 1965. In short, there is no assurance that the Hashemite kingdom as it is known today – a kingdom sculptured by Hussein – can itself survive the king.

5

Domestic Constraints on Peacemaking

As a weak state surrounded by the strong, Jordan's room to maneuver has always been limited by external forces. On the global level, Jordan's reliance on U.S. military and economic assistance has left it open to charges of treason and of pandering to Israel's patron. Under pressure, the king has often responded by assuming rejectionist positions in public and by purchasing Soviet bloc weapons in a hollow roar of defiance. On the regional level, military dangers and economic blackmail have never permitted the kingdom to act independently of the four powers of the Arab world—Egypt, Syria, Iraq, and Saudi Arabia. Instead, Hussein has had to accept humiliation, such as the 1974 Rabat resolution and the recent *Ikhwan* apology to Syria, as the price for survival in a hostile environment. And on the level of Jordanian-Palestinian relations, the kingdom has served—as former Prime Minister Abd-al-Hamid al-Sharaf said—as "shock absorber" for the Palestinian problem, suffering through a Palestinian-inspired civil war and yet offering more than any other Arab state to the Palestinians in return. The king's reward has been political embarrassment, personal frustration, and, of course, civil war. Despite the futility of his efforts, it is to his credit that Hussein still makes at least periodic protestations of independence on vital issues of foreign affairs.

Tacit Accommodation with Israel

By simultaneously maintaining de facto peace with Israel and a public stance of defiance against Israel, Hussein has benefited handsomely while skirting much Arab opprobrium. From the United States, Jordan has received more than $2.5 billion in military and economic aid since the Jewish state was established; more than half of that assistance has been in the form of grants.[1] From the conservative Gulf shaykh-doms, Jordan received even more help, first as an allowance to a struggling fellow monarch and, more recently, as recompense for the kingdom's sacrifice as a confrontation state.

But in many ways, Jordan's prime benefactor in the undeclared state of peace with Israel has been Israel itself. In exchange for maintaining a moderate stance in Arab politics, clamping down on terrorist activity, and keeping West Bank officials and institutions on the government budget, Israeli-Jordanian relations have blossomed over the past 19 years. In a 1985 newspaper analysis, Israeli editor Moshe Zak highlighted seven areas of bilateral agreement and cooperation:[2]

• Water: distribution of resources of the Jordan and Yarmouk rivers.
• Commerce: import of goods over the Jordan River bridges. According to Israeli government statistics, Jordan imported $98.4 million worth of goods from the West Bank and Gaza in 1984.[3] (Jordanian exports to the West Bank are small and, to the Gaza Strip, virtually nonexistent.)
• Travel: tourism policies that accommodate not only West Bankers and Jordanians traveling across the Jordan River, but also groups of Westerners (primarily Americans) visiting holy sites in both countries.* In 1973, the "Open

---

*Jordan's press reported in 1985 that for the first time since the 1967 war, Roman Catholic worshippers have been permitted to visit a holy site on the Jordan River – from the Israeli side – to recreate the Biblical baptism ceremony. Greek Orthodox worship-

Bridges" policy was maintained even during the Yom Kippur war.[4] In 1974, Jordan formalized a policy it had maintained since the 1967 war, allowing foreign visitors to cross over to the West Bank as "pilgrims."[5] According to Israeli government statistics, more than 111,000 tourists entered Israel via the Jordan bridges in 1984. Of that number, many were U.S. citizens participating in religious tour groups. But more than 13,000 of those travelers were themselves Jordanian residents. In 1984, nearly two years after the completion of the Sinai withdrawal, Jordanians visiting Israel outnumbered Egyptians by almost three-to-one.[6] In total, more than a million persons travel across the bridges each year.

• Agriculture: land-use development projects on both sides of the Jordan valley. For example, Zak noted that an irrigation program for the West Bank village of Deir al-Ghusun was funded equally by Jordan, Israel, and a private U.S. aid group, the Catholic Development Fund.[7] Eliyahu Kanovsky, in a 1976 work, referred to several instances of bilateral agricultural cooperation, including the shipment from Israel to Jordan of vegetable seedlings, agricultural education pamphlets, and high milk-yielding sheep.[8] Israeli media reported in 1984 that the two countries were cooperating to exterminate the breeding grounds of malaria-carrying mosquitoes. Most recently, Jerusalem radio reported in December 1985 that with the help of U.S. mediation, Jordan and Israel had worked together to remove a small island interrupting the flow of the Yarmouk River.[9] Israeli Agriculture Minister Arye Nehamkin confirmed the poorly guarded secret of cross-border cooperation in December 1984:

> Before 1967, the Jordan Rift was barren and nothing was growing. Today their side seems to be greener than ours. This is thanks to professional service advisers trained in Israel and the use of the latest agricultural technologies, which we have sold them.[10]

---

pers have been able to visit their baptismal site on the Israeli side since 1981.

• Education: Israeli approval in 1970 of the importation of Jordanian textbooks for West Bank schools, with the sole proviso that all antisemitic and anti-Israeli material be censored.

• Frontiers: two border demarcations (1970 and 1975), both in Jordan's favor. In 1970, Israel returned to Jordan the al-Safi area, southeast of the Dead Sea; in 1975, Israel agreed to move a desert frontier line when it learned that the demarcation was incorrect.[11]

• Security: practical arrangements for preventing terrorist activity along the border.

Over the years, Hussein has met, with diminishing success at secrecy, various Israeli leaders to discuss issues of mutual concern.[12] Most important, the memory of 1970 remains—when Israel, acting at U.S. behest, safeguarded Hashemite rule against a Syrian invasion. And how many other Arab leaders receive birthday greetings from Shimon Peres?[13]

Domestically, Hussein pays little price for this coexistence and cooperation with Israel. Government censors restrict distribution of material referring to the king's accommodation with the Zionists; just days after Hussein's October 1985 UN address calling for prompt and direct negotiations under international auspices—lauded in the United States as a pathbreaking declaration—Jordan's press highlighted a statement by the information minister categorically rejecting direct talks with Israel. Jordanian efforts to woo West Bankers through payoffs and subsidies are portrayed as an effort to fulfill national obligations to the Palestinian people.[14] And few complain about the financial and commercial benefits of West Bank trade and trans-Jordan River tourism.

In addition to the direct by-products of the quiet bilateral arrangement, Jordan reaps untold dividends in terms of the security of its own Western border. Jordan and Israel have a shared interest in monitoring, controlling, and preventing Palestinian nationalist activity in the occupied territories. Although Jordanian government officials and editorial writers may lash out against the harshness of occupation, the king cannot but be pleased with the role Israeli intelligence and security forces play in clamping down on those Palestinians whose politics are about as anti-royalist as they are anti-Zionist.

Avoiding the Risks of Peace

Hussein's legendary reticence to enter direct negotiations with Israel is largely a function of his unwillingness to gamble on improving the status quo when the benefits of simply continuing it are manifest. By his entrance into direct talks – whose outcome no serious observer suggests can lead to a settlement satisfying the maximalist Arab demands – the king risks losing the carefully worked out bilateral relationship. As Zak argued, "Jordan could build this relationship with Israel as long as it was not obliged to sign a formal treaty, which necessitates a territorial arrangement."

When Egypt's Sadat and Israel's Menachem Begin made peace, their job was comparatively simple. Each made concessions, but there was little compromise. In exchange for the entire Sinai peninsula (Taba notwithstanding), Egypt offered all the accoutrements of normal diplomatic relations – embassies, airline rights, tourism, etc. Psychologically, the task was daunting; but once that barrier was surmounted, the outline of a peace arrangement came quickly into focus.

Negotiations between Jordan and Israel would not be so neat. Peacemaking will undoubtedly demand both concessions and compromise. Hussein has certainly attained the maturity to offer Sadat's psychological concession to Israel; if the task were that simple, Jordan's flag would have flown over a Tel Aviv embassy years ago. But a Jordanian-Israeli peace demands painful compromises, political and territorial. Much of the recent diplomatic maneuvering in the Middle East has centered on the means for Hussein to soften the blow of making those compromises, on ways to spread the responsibility for honest brokering, on methods for limiting the loss of pride. The search for "appropriate auspices" – be they in the form of an international conference, a forum, an "accompaniment," a context, or an umbrella—is just such an effort.

Lack of a Domestic Constituency for Peace

Building a foundation for direct talks and peace with Israel is at least as important a task inside Jordan itself as it is within the Arab world as a whole. Lost in the diplomatic shuffle is the extent to which domestic considerations, like external constraints, limit Hussein's foreign policy options. Most observers either overlook or underestimate the role that internal factors play in Jordan's external political calculus. To be sure, domestic opinion has not prevented the king from pursuing some unpopular initiatives, such as his early support for Iraq in the Gulf war and, to a lesser extent, his restoration of diplomatic relations with ostracized Egypt. Although significant in their own right, neither of these moves entailed the sort of diplomatic effort required to do what the United States has wanted Hussein to do for years— enter direct negotiations and sign a peace treaty with Israel. On that issue, the most volatile in Jordanian politics, domestic opposition imposes powerful constraints. And the king is further away today from building a domestic consensus for direct negotiations with Israel than he is in his quest for Arab backing. Indeed, even if Hussein were able to garner Arab support (or, as is more likely, merely Arab acquiescence) for bilateral talks, widespread domestic opposition would probably dissuade him from taking such a giant and potentially suicidal leap toward peace.

Religious opposition to formal peacemaking with Israel would be fierce. Islamic activists care much more about Jerusalem and the Islamic holy places than they do about Bethlehem, Nablus, and Ramallah. Unless Hussein can guarantee the return of the *Haram al-Sharif*—the Temple Mount —to Jordanian sovereignty or control, he is sure to incur their wrath. Negotiators who prefer to leave Jerusalem unsettled until all other problems are resolved fail to realize the enormity of the issue. The return of the holy places to direct Muslim control, without the facade of Jordanian flags guarded by Israeli troops, is the sine qua non of the Islamic activists' agenda; without it, there can be no peace treaty. As author and former UN diplomat Conor Cruise O'Brien recently argued,

> King Hussein, or any successor of Hussein, would be running very serious risks if he concluded *any* treaty with Israel, even one that gave him back all Jordan's lost territory. But if he were to sign a treaty that left Israel in possession of all Jerusalem, he would probably be committing suicide for himself and his dynasty — which he is unlikely to do.[15]

An accommodation on Jerusalem will not by itself either ensure a satisfactory peace or assuage religious antagonism to it. Most Islamic activists have still not begun to come to grips with the notion of a Jewish state on what they perceive to be Muslim land. Most pious Muslims simply do not accept the idea of Israel, and no measure of concession and accommodation can sell them on peace with Israel. It is for that reason that *Ikhwan* parliamentarian Laith Shubeilat criticized the peace process in a recent *Washington Post* interview as a "surrendering process," saying that "all Muslims are not [supportive of it], and we are not afraid of saying it, and we shall never support it."[16]

Over the past decade, Islamic activism has already grown into a nationwide political movement. It has moved away from its traditional client-patron relationship with the crown into an adversarial stance against the king's government and policies. The recent royal and prime ministerial crackdown is sure to aggravate an already tense situation; rapprochement with Syria's Alawite regime places Hussein in league with the Muslim Brotherhood's most despised enemy. As the *Washington Post* noted, "there has been ample evidence, according to government officials and western diplomats, that the religious trend sweeping society was beginning to transform itself into a more organized, politicized and militant form."[17] Facing the Israelis across the negotiating table could be the spark that ignites direct confrontation between the Islamic movement and the king.

Although the religious activists will be the shock troops of opposition to a Jordanian peace initiative, there is little reason to believe that Hussein has forged a consensus for such a move within other elements of his governing coalition. Any formal peace treaty and territorial arrangement over the occupied territories is sure to anger several key East Bank constituencies. Peace will surely have its sweeteners, such as the billions of U.S. dollars given to Israel and Egypt that softened the jolt of peace. But those sweeteners may not be sufficient to overcome the losses to be incurred by

- tribal leaders, whose already diminishing political authority will be tested by Palestinian leaders in the scramble for power that will follow in the treaty's wake;
- military commanders, whose reliance upon the loyalty of the armed forces may prove unfounded when the new, modern army is needed to patrol the West Bank and control dissident Palestinian nationalists;
- many farmers, businessmen, and entrepreneurs, whose government development and commercial assistance funds will be parceled out more frugally to permit at least a modicum of investment in the West Bank;
- liberalizing modernists, whose democratic and libertarian aspirations will be put on hold at least until the kingdom emerges from the post-treaty transition period and Jordan's internal security situation has quieted down;
- educated youth, whose bleak employment prospects will be made worse by the influx of thousands of jobless college graduates from West Bank universities;
- and perhaps most of all, Crown Prince Hassan, whose tentative hold on royal succession is based on the development and nurturing of East Bank constituencies.[18]

Hussein cannot count on vocal support for a Jordanian peace initiative from within his governing coalition. Indeed, not only will most elements of that system be wary of direct talks, but many will likely oppose dealing with the Israelis face-to-face. Even with full political backing, confronting the Islamic activists would be difficult; stamping out the religious opposition without the support of the crown's natural constituencies would be herculean; and dealing with the activists while simultaneously trying to convert those key groups to a policy that runs counter to their own interests would be next to impossible.

In short, Hussein has much to do on the domestic front before entering direct talks becomes a viable policy option. In the meantime, Jordan can continue to enjoy the fruits of its undeclared peace with Israel.

6

Challenges and Prospects

For decades, gauging the stability of the Hashemite regime has been a notoriously risky exercise. Many observers have speculated on Jordan's impending collapse, with each war, each coup attempt, and each parliamentary provocation heralding the abdication of the king and the accession to power of some popularly based regime — Nasserite, Ba'thist, Palestinian, or nationalist.* Today's generation of analysts focuses on the threats of General Ariel Sharon and Rabbi Meir Kahane to flood the East Bank with West Bank Palestinians to substantiate gloomy assessments of the kingdom's future stability. Although they may be right this time,

---

*Epitaphs for the Hashemite dynasty, for example, were prepared after the swift and shocking loss of the country's most advanced, educated, and productive region in June 1967 and after the permissive accommodation to fedayeen demands in the spring and summer of 1970. October 1973 offered several intriguing arguments to support claims of the Hashemites' expectant demise, because it was a war Jordan could not but lose; participation would incur the wrath of the Israelis while lack of it would incur the wrath of fellow Arabs. In the end, Hussein opted for the better part of valor by dispatching a small force of great symbolic value to fight alongside the Syrians — on Syrian territory.

the track record of those betting against the resilience of
Hussein and his Hashemite kinsmen is not heartening. It is
with this caveat that an examination of the kingdom's future
prospects should proceed.

That warning, however, should not obscure the fact that
the current situation and previous crisis periods are fundamentally different. Unlike past experiences, many of the
potential threats of today have arisen from within those elements of society that have helped buttress the regime's precarious existence for so long. Basic notions about economics,
religion, society, and politics are changing, and with that
change comes a weakening of the Jordanian governing system. This paper has dealt with these issues exclusively – at
the expense of even broaching the topic of external influence
on Jordan's internal politics – in order to underscore the grav-
ity of the emergence of destabilizing forces within the kingdom's core political constituencies. These issues have also
been examined individually. But once they are viewed as elements of a larger Jordanian political culture, their impact on
regime stability assumes more portentous proportions.

The kingdom's decade of prosperity has come to an abrupt
and painful end. But statistics alone do not describe accurately the effect boom-and-bust has had – and will continue to
have – on Jordan's domestic situation. Economic opportunity
has long been one of the fundamental elements holding Jordan together. Although it was the only Arab state to offer
citizenship en masse to its Palestinian refugees, the kingdom's real contribution to their welfare has been to render
militancy a nonoption and to offer in its stead a high quality
educational system and a liberal economic climate. The result
was that Jordan gave birth to a generation of stunningly successful businessmen, entrepreneurs, technicians, and skilled
laborers – many working inside the kingdom and many more
in Gulf states and the West. Through their productivity, Jordan enjoyed per capita incomes far higher than other non-
oil exporting Arab countries.[1] Both Jordanian communities –
Palestinian and non-Palestinian – were satisfied, and com-
munal affiliation lost much of its former importance.

When the oil revolution rolled through Jordan, the entire process was accelerated. Thousands more sought employment in Gulf states and sent home billions of dollars in remittances. The government invested heavily in upgrading its educational facilities to cement the kingdom's hold on a comparative regional advantage in skilled labor. Living standards rose at a fever pitch, highlighted by a wave of consumer imports. Millions of dollars were made in real estate speculation, though much of the kingdom's best agricultural land was lost when hundreds of villas were constructed outside Amman. The nationwide examination for university admissions (*tawjihi*) quickly became a litmus test for social mobility; failure to secure a grade high enough to gain entrance to engineering, medical, or architectural schools was a disgrace to one's family. In the meantime, tens of thousands of foreign workers were imported to do the menial work many Jordanians now refused to do themselves. Through foreign policy pragmatism and economic opportunism, most Jordanians were the beneficiaries of an unprecedented era of prosperity. That era, of course, was not without its attendant drawbacks, including inflation, poor distribution of wealth and resources, and a debilitating reliance on imports. Yet most realized that the boom years were about as good as it was going to get in Jordan.

The kingdom's problems, however, were not limited to the normal economic side effects of prosperity. The boom had long-term deleterious effects on Jordanian society. Newfound wealth was an important factor in the acceleration of social forces that began to provoke deep cleavages in the Hashemite governing coalition.

It was in this period that observers first documented an increased popular affiliation with Islam. Many Jordanians began frequenting mosques and donning traditional garb to protest against (and protect themselves from) the accoutrements of prosperity, such as liquor, cosmetics, European fashion, bawdy movies, and mixed-sex socializing. For many, the price to pay for the benefits of economic bounty was far too high.

This period also witnessed the growth of a long-festering conflict between the traditionalists and the modernists. Time-honored tribal practices were simply anachronisms in an economy booming with scores of infant private enterprises and expanding bureaucracies. Technocrats eager for Jordan to make use of its oil-based windfall were exasperated by the groping pace of the *inshallah* – "God willing" – mentality. Conversely, bedouin fearful for their social status refused to countenance any infringement of the prerogatives of custom and tradition by the technocrats.

None of these tensions were new, but they were all aggravated and sharpened by the oil bonanza. Not surprisingly, as long as Jordan's economic pie continued to grow, Hussein and the elite of the governing coalition were able to manage the kingdom's worsening tensions. Employment – either in well-paying jobs abroad or in positions of increasing authority in the rapidly expanding public and private sectors at home – helped defuse much of the nascent anger of these groups.

In 1986, that safety valve no longer exists, and the crisis has passed into a far more dangerous stage. At the kingdom's community colleges and universities, thousands of young men and women are pursuing degrees in engineering and the natural sciences, but barely a trickle can expect to find work after graduation. In anger and frustration, many are turning toward the message of some modern Muslim thinkers that they should weed out the "Western" from the "modern" and turn against the inherent corruption and duplicity of the West. Although fascinated with the advances of Western technology – from space travel to VCRs – they abhor the perceived cultural effect Western ideologies are wreaking on Muslim society.[2]

Meanwhile, the cessation of the flow of easy money from the Gulf has hurt all other segments of Jordanian society. Many Palestinians can no longer count on a life of comfort and relative wealth derived from the paycheck of a relative or two working in the Gulf. Many bedouin can no longer expect to translate their land holdings into ready capital, because the burgeoning land speculation market of recent years has fallen. And many younger tribesmen have realized that though their families still exert considerable power in the kindgom's political life, their own future may very well lie elsewhere.

It is important to note that the current crisis is not just a problem of gloomy economic forecasts, nor even of substantially decreasing standards of living. Jordanians are not about to become an impoverished people. Indeed, compared to most developing countries, Jordan's economic situation is still relatively good. Few other Arabs and scarcely any Africans prefer their own country's quality of life to that of the kingdom's.[3]

Choosing Sides

The troubles facing Hussein's realm are far more profound. If the promise of education and employment has indeed disappeared as a social lubricant, Jordan must deal forthrightly with volatile and conflicting popular demands. Prosperity has proven ephemeral, and there is no ready palliative on which a new sort of social compact can be based. Hard choices must be made, between the traditionalists and the modernists and between the Islamic activists and those elites that control the current Damascus-leaning government. For the first time since the 1970–1971 civil war, there are going to be clear winners and clear losers in Jordanian domestic politics. But because all of the actors in the current contest have played important roles in bolstering the regime throughout its troubled history, there will be only one sure loser—the Hashemites.

The regime's difficulties do not end there. As the decision to hold parliamentary by-elections in 1984 showed, bold steps taken to address one set of popular demands may have unforeseen—and negative—consequences. At that time, Hussein tried to court the modernizing wing of Jordan's political elite by holding out the prospect of democratization and the rejuvenation of parliamentary life. The effort backfired with the election of a bloc of Islamic activists who have since used Parliament as a forum for vituperative assaults on government policy.* In contrast to the Egyptian example, in which the government of President Husni Mubarak has tried to use the expansion of democratic liberties as a tool to divide, co-opt, and undermine the strength of the Islamic movement, the reverse is happening in Jordan. Until a scant few years ago the kingdom had never known a confrontationist Islamic movement. But in 1986, at least partly because of their parliamentary success, Islamic activists are a far more potent political force in Jordan than they were just two years earlier.

The lesson of March 1984 is that making the difficult choices is only half the task facing the regime. Finding an appropriate policy with which to implement those choices may be even more daunting. And because the thread of prosperity no longer exists, there is no clear policy path that can again knit the neat web of constituencies that held the governing coalition together for the past decade and a half.

Hussein will continue to face more policy dilemmas. Tilting at times toward the modernists and at times toward the traditionalists, for example, will become an increasingly dangerous and risky course. It is a policy that pleases no one, yet invites greater demands from everyone. Moreover, it may even exacerbate the regime's problems elsewhere, as the government's current plans to hold national elections to double the size of Parliament may bear out. If the Islamic activists receive a significant electoral boost, the king will have to deal with both an emboldened opposition and a frustrated technocracy. The prospect of a modernists' loss at the polls – with a subsequent undercutting of their claim to some share of political authority – assumes even greater significance if one

---

*Observers who dismiss the Islamic activists' March 1984 success as a result of quirks in the electoral system seem to forget who created the system.

accepts the proposition that a realignment of Jordan's economy will still have to be focused around the one commodity
of which the kingdom maintains a comparative advantage
in the Arab world, its skilled labor pool.

Ironically, the immediate health of the system might
improve if one of the main actors would unilaterally withdraw
from the coalition and turn against it. The current system
was forged in the wake of the civil war, when the weight of
the regime was thrown against the Palestinian militants, and
the other powerful elements in society—including bedouin
leaders, religious traditionalists, and the military—lined up
behind the king. Today, there is no comparable antagonist.
Significantly, there has been no murmur within Jordan's
Palestinian population to take on its old role.

A Coalition against Islamic Activism

A new antagonist may be emerging with the spread of the
Islamic activist movement. Most of the old-time elites—tribal
leaders, technocrats, businessmen, and army and intelligence
chiefs—share an antipathy for the activists' platform, because the activists do not just attack the apportionment of
power within the system; they, implicitly at least, attack the
system itself. If the Islamic movement were to grow in
strength and size—and there is no indication that its already
rapid growth is slowing—those elites could find common
ground in undermining it. Cracking down on the *Ikhwan*
through both government rhetoric and strong-arm tactics,
a policy implemented in November 1985, may be the first
sign of the regime's attempt to sidestep troublesome issues
of domestic politics by focusing on the Islamic threat.

The dangers of this policy are twofold. First, of course,
it only postpones the day when important decisions have to
be made about competing demands among the kingdom's
elites. In the meantime, domestic tensions are sure to increase. Second, by confronting the Islamic activists, Hussein
pits the regime squarely against the most influential social

movement in Jordan today. This policy will certainly drive the activists into a more oppositional stance than they already occupy. So far, they have attacked the prime minister but have not criticized the king personally, even after his scathing denunciation of the *Ikhwan* in early November. They are hesitant to confront the king directly because they are too weak to withstand the repercussions. By cracking down on the insurgent *Ikhwan* now, the regime may indeed be saving itself from a future bloodletting. But the venom of the king's remarks may create a backlash against him by strengthening and emboldening the activists, thereby reinforcing their position as the principal opposition. As has been the case in the past decade, the king's response to the growth of Islamic activism may continue to fuel its expansion. Promoting Islamic activism as the mortal enemy of the regime requires having the wherewithal – military, political, and emotional – to destroy the activists if the confrontation should widen.

The current situation inside Jordan, of course, is far from the stage at which implementing a policy of repression and retribution is even on the agenda. Islamic activists are certainly not antiregime rebels, as they are in Syria. But Hussein should take care that the confrontation with the *Ikhwan* does not deteriorate, for there is no assurance that the regime could withstand the internal tensions that "playing by Hama rules" would be sure to provoke.*

Disturbing Questions

There are too many unanswered questions about Jordanian politics to gamble with predictions about the long-term prospects of the Hashemite regime. But in and of itself, the ex-

---

*"Playing by Hama rules" refers to the Syrian regime's ruthless suppression of a Muslim Brotherhood rebellion in the city of Hama in February 1982. Tens of thousands of local residents were killed by government security forces.

istence of so many fundamental questions says much about the underlying stability of the kingdom. Moreover, many of these questions concern challenges to Jordan's stability that are new and potentially more menacing than the challenges faced by the regime in the past. Among the most important of these are the following:

• With the end of an era of prosperity, can Hussein succeed in restructuring the governing coalition without alienating powerful elements of the status quo?

• Without, inter alia, strengthening the Islamic activist movement, can the regime respond to pleas for greater democratization and liberalization of public life?

• After going untested for nearly a decade, a period in which the demographic composition of the military has undergone a significant overhaul, is the loyalty of the armed forces still beyond question?

• Is Crown Prince Hassan strong enough to claim and maintain the kingship after Hussein?

In the end, the answers to all of these questions may prove to be yes. But to assume so in the meantime is to ignore the very real domestic challenges facing the Hashemite regime.

Conclusion:
U.S. Policy, Jordan, and
the Peace Process

U.S. policymakers may be surprised to learn that King Hussein is weighted down with domestic constraints to his peacemaking efforts that are almost as burdensome as his foreign ones. Promoting the peace process has been at the center of U.S. Middle East policy for more than a decade, and promoting Hussein's role in that process has long been the basis of Washington's bilateral relationship with Amman. All significant U.S. peacemaking efforts, most notably the Camp David accords and the 1982 Reagan plan, envision a pivotal role for Jordan. Indeed, because of Jordan's refusal to join these initiatives, Camp David's framework for West Bank autonomy had no chance of implementation and Reagan's initiative never got off the ground. With both eyes focused on the peace process, Washington has left itself nearly oblivious to the domestic affairs of the East Bank.

Jordan's Special Role

Even when human rights issues assumed a prominent role in U.S. foreign policy making, Jordan remained virtually exempt from examination and criticism. And this is surely not because examiners and critics lacked ammunition. After

104

all, Jordan is a monarchy, constitutional in name but near absolute in fact. Today, the Hashemites rule a population whose origin is overwhelmingly from west of the Jordan River — 70 percent, perhaps. For more than 19 years, the country has been under martial law; political parties were banned nearly three decades ago. Internal dissent is discouraged by one of the Middle East's most loyal and effective security and intelligence forces, and international human rights advocates have cited Jordan with numerous violations of civil, legal, and human rights.[1] Parliament was dissolved in 1974, and for several years thereafter, no democratic institutions existed at all. Since then, Jordan experimented with the purely advisory NCC until Parliament was reconvened in 1984. To date, though, little decision-making authority has devolved to Parliament from where it has resided for nearly as long as anyone in Jordan can remember — in the hands of the king.

Yet, there is wide-ranging, bipartisan U.S. support for King Hussein's Hashemite rule, nary a word of human rights charges leveled at his regime from the usual congressional activists, and a virtual taboo against discussion of the more tawdry aspects of the kingdom's domestic political life.[2]* Reaffirming long-standing U.S. foreign policy, Ronald Reagan, in a toast to a visiting Hussein at a state dinner in November 1981, said "No one should doubt that the preservation of Jordan's security, integrity and its unique and enduring character are a matter of highest importance."[3] And one day later he stated that "the security and well-being of the Hashemite Kingdom of Jordan is a matter of historic and enduring concern for the United States."[4]

---

*Among those members of the Senate Foreign Relations Committee that voted in favor of the June 1985 emergency aid package to Jordan were ranking Democrat Claiborne Pell (R.I.), Alan Cranston (Calif.), Christopher Dodd (Conn.), and John Kerry (Mass.) — all of whom have taken leading roles as human rights watchdogs in the past.

Over the years, U.S. presidents have backed up their strong words with some equally strong deeds. Throughout the early 1960s, Jordan was the largest per capita recipient of U.S. economic and development aid in the world.[5] In 1970, President Richard Nixon and his national security adviser, Henry A. Kissinger, acted forcefully to defend the Hashemites against insurrection and invasion. Throughout the next decade, successive administrations lobbied hard to upgrade weapon transfers and economic support to the kingdom. Most recently, in October 1985, President Reagan wagered some of his personal political capital when he honored a pledge to Hussein to submit to Congress a multibillion dollar arms sale request, even though large majorities of both houses were opposed. Despite criticism from some quarters that Washington has failed "to deliver" on promises of military sales, the U.S. commitment to Hussein has, in fact, stood firm for more than three decades.*

Bases of U.S. Commitment

U.S. support is largely a function of only two factors: geography and personality. If Hashemites ruled the east bank of the Tigris, Euphrates, or some other biblical river (as they did in pre-Ba'thist Iraq), official Washington would not be nearly as interested in their welfare. But because the Hashemites govern the East Bank of the *Jordan* River, placing them in the center of the Arab-Israeli conflict, the kingdom is assured of a central role in U.S. regional political planning.

Second, few leaders of small, poor, powerless, and – in the final analysis – strategically inconsequential Third World states can rival Hussein's masterful ability to sell his nation's political wares to both the U.S. public and the policy-making

---

*Unlike the case of the more affluent Gulf shaykhdoms, who regularly receive U.S. weapons, U.S. support for Jordan is not based on an economic interest.

elite. For decades, Jordan has enjoyed a remarkably benign image in the United States. Much of that image was founded upon U.S. admiration for a king who had cornered the market on moderation in the Middle East. It also incorporated a romantic vision of bedouin society, a respectful image of religious traditionalism, and a somewhat paternalistic view of Jordan's economic prospects. Moreover, the "Plucky Little King's" ability to elude assassination and stymie coup attempts has earned him high marks in a region in which stability and survivability is at a premium.[6]

Hussein has made more than 20 trips to the United States, and each time he has reinforced the perception of the Hashemite monarchy as standing on the brink of declared peace with Israel. In October 1985, Hussein stated in a UN address that he was prepared to negotiate "promptly and directly" with Israel within the framework of Security Council resolution 242 and under international auspices; within hours, the White House hailed Hussein's statement as a courageous move toward peace and formally submitted an arms sale notification to Congress. At the time, the proposed sale was justified as a symbol of U.S. resolve to assist Hussein on the road to peace.* Speaking before the National Press Club in Washington in 1969, 16 years earlier, Hussein laid on the table a strikingly similar offer "as a basis for a just and lasting peace." Soon thereafter, the U.S. government agreed to supply Jordan with millions of dollars in arms, including a squadron of F-104 jets.[7] At that time, the *New York Times* characterized the deal as "primarily a symbolic gesture of American political support for King Hussein, intended to bolster his support among the army officer corps, which has been pressing for new weapons."[8] The pattern has endured.

This is not to suggest that U.S. military and economic largesse has been frittered away over the years. On the con-

---

*Faced with the probability of a precedent-setting congressional disapproval, the White House tabled the arms sale request in February 1986.

trary, Hussein has—by and large—proven himself to be a fairly steady friend and ally to the West. On the Arab-Israeli issue, his tacit accommodation with Israel on such issues as border security, commerce, and tourism has surely been welcome. On strategic issues, Hussein has stood solidly in the anti-Communist camp since his condemnation of the immorality of neutrality in the heyday of the Cold War.[9] As the trend in the Third World moved toward nonalignment, the king did tone down his anti-Communist rhetoric, and at times he has appealed to the Soviet Union for arms when U.S. congressmen attached too many strings to proposed weapons deals. But both Washington and Amman understand that only the United States and its own regional allies such as Israel guard the stability of the Hashemite regime. With that in mind, Hussein has never truly wavered from his very real personal and political affinity for the West. He has had little choice. Therefore, both Jordan and the United States, it seems, would be eminently pleased to maintain the current marriage of convenience indefinitely. Each believes its national interests well served by the relationship.

Peace Process v. Domestic Challenges

In the meantime, though, the United States finds itself dangerously ill prepared to deal with domestic challenges building inside the kingdom. The foreign policy debate remains riveted to Hussein's role in Middle East peacemaking, avoiding troublesome questions surrounding the solidity of the regime's domestic base. In June 1985, for example, Secretary of State Shultz testified before Congress in favor of boosting economic assistance to Jordan. Some of the statistics he cited, including Jordan's projected 30 percent rate of structural unemployment by 1990, were astounding, yet they caused few ripples in the foreign policy debate. And by November 1985, the king had come full circle in his dealings with Jordan's Islamic activists, calling these once-staunch friends of the crown "rotten" and "criminal." Yet few people talk about the rise of Islamic activism in the kindgom.[10] Virtually no one discusses the sort of Jordan that will emerge with the passing of Hussein himself.

In exchange for a bold leap toward formal peace with Israel, the United States can offer Hussein more arms and more aid, the second of which Jordan's ailing economy sorely needs. Indeed, the king's 1985 peace offensive was waged at least partly to lay the groundwork for increases in economic aid needed to ease Jordan's economic woes. And as the Egyptian case shows, the United States remains a loyal patron even when the spirit of peace is not wholeheartedly maintained.

But the prospect of a financial bonanza is simply not enough for Hussein. There are still too many dangers involved to risk the benefits of the current de facto peace by entering public peace talks. Hussein can only lose by meeting Israeli leaders publicly without first securing assurances on certain issues – the holy places in Jerusalem, for example. Making compromises in private discussion prior to an orchestrated public confirmation of a peace agreement will be difficult enough; no Jordanian ruler could endure the popular outrage at what will be perceived to be public bargaining over the pan-Arab and pan-Muslim patrimony. And a failed public peace negotiation is far worse than no negotiation at all.

In the meantime, Hussein still retains the Arab option he has exercised so often in the past. In exchange for conciliation with Syria and obeisance to the collective Arab will, Saudi Arabia will ensure that enough aid reaches Jordan to keep the monarchy afloat. Economic recession may still worsen; periodic infusions of petrodollars will certainly not alleviate the pain of unemployment, commodity shortages, and overcrowding. But, as the king sees it, the kingdom will endure.

Continued endurance, however, will demand more than a stiff dose of Gulf aid; it will require the Hashemite regime to address squarely the fundamental issues chipping away at its long-term domestic stability. Jordan will have to come to grips with an economy that produces little of value but

Jordanians themselves, realizing that the export market for skilled labor has slumped to the point where the high living of the 1970s and early 1980s is a relic of the past. Jordan will have to redefine the relationship between state and Islam, having opted to break up the decades-old patron-client relationship with the Muslim Brotherhood in order to curry favor in Damascus and Riyadh. Jordan will have to determine the proper role of tribes and tribal customs in society, having seesawed between contrary commitments to tradition and modernization. Jordan will also have to respond to impatient liberals' demands for democratization, having postponed for years the reestablishment of popular participation in government decision making. And finally, Jordan will have to stabilize the future of the monarchical system, having survived until now only because the system has not been put to the test of succession.

If Hussein wishes to construct a new and lasting governing coalition, he has only two broad options. Authority can be refocused around either a group of modernists (technocrats, businessmen, and loyal Palestinians) or a group of traditionalists (tribal chiefs, landowners, and non-*Ikhwan* religious leaders). Fundamental differences separate the two groups and mutual interests bind the constituents of each coalition together. Siding with the traditionalists is a low-risk, low-return choice; they have no alternative but to be aligned with the regime, yet they do not represent the innovative, progressive, and forward-looking forces in society that Jordan needs to cultivate if it is to promote its own economic health. Opting for the modernists is a high-risk, high-return option; they have the know-how and entrepreneurial vigor to address Jordan's serious structural problems, but there is no fundamental tie that binds them to the Hashemites. The choice is not simple.

These are the issues that dominate domestic Jordanian politics. Unless they are addressed, the kingdom will become as weak and vulnerable internally as it is externally.

Viewing Jordan solely through the prism of the peace process ignores the magnitude of the kingdom's domestic difficulties. In the end, the peace process is itself the victim of this one-dimensional policy, because it exacerbates Jordan's march toward weakness and vulnerability. And as the Lebanon experience has proved, weak and vulnerable states do not make valuable partners in the pursuit of peace.

Today, the United States can best support the security and well-being of the Hashemite Kingdom of Jordan – as it has pledged to do – by taking stock of the benefits of the undeclared peace both Jordan and Israel reap and by helping Hussein face the difficult domestic choices that *may* free Jordan's diplomatic options in the future.

Notes

Chapter 1

1. Amman Television Service, cited in Foreign Broadcast Information Service – Middle East and North Africa (FBIS), January 23, 1985.

2. *an-Nahar Arab Report and Memo* (Beirut), January 28,
1985, p. 8.

3. *New York Times*, April 2, 1983, citing a *Jordan Times* economic analyst.

4. In 1981, grants from Arab states totaled $1.179 billion,
while workers' remittances from abroad were $1.032 billion, which
together accounted for 49 percent of the GNP of $4.496 billion. See
International Monetary Fund (IMF), *Balance of Payment Statistics*, vol. 36, Yearbook, Part I (Washington, D.C.: IMF, 1985),
333–337 and IMF, *International Financial Statistics* (Washington,
D.C.: IMF, May 1986), 290–293. Unless otherwise noted, Jordanian economic data are drawn from these and earlier editions of
IMF publications.

5. Foreign grants and loans accounted for about 60 percent
of government revenues in the early 1950s; direct revenue contributed only about 40 percent. See Eliyahu Kanovsky, *The Economic
Development of Jordan*, International Bank for Reconstruction
and Development (Baltimore, Md.: The Johns Hopkins University
Press, 1957), 385.

6. See relevant data in various editions of the Colin Legum,

ed., *Middle East Contemporary Survey (MECS)* (New York, N.Y.: The Shiloach Center for Middle Eastern and African Studies, Tel Aviv University, with Holmes and Meier Publishers, Inc.). Also, see Eliyahu Kanovsky, "Jordan's Decade of Prosperity: Will it Persist?" *MECS* 7, p. 371, and *an-Nahar Arab News and Memo*, August 27, 1984, p. 11.

7. In the first quarter of 1973, gold and foreign exchange reserves stood at $296 million (JD 97.2 million); by the fourth quarter of 1981, gold and foreign exchange reserves had grown to $2.03 billion (JD 666.8 million). See Central Bank of Jordan (CBJ), *Quarterly Statistical Series, 1964–1983*, Special Issue (Amman: CBJ, 1984); Gross fixed capital formation rose from $143.7 million (JD 47.2 million) in 1973 to $1.71 billion (JD 565.8 million) in 1981, an increase of 1188 percent. See *International Financial Statistics*, 1984, p. 369.

8. Milton Viorst, "Jordan: A Moderate Role," *Atlantic Monthly* 247 (March 1981), 5. The reference to "no unemployment" in Jordan in the early 1980s is also made by Clinton Bailey, *Jordan's Palestinian Challenge: 1948–1983, A Political History* (Boulder, Colo.: Westview Press, 1984), 136, citing Jean-Pierre Peroncel-Hugoz, "Prosperity under the Shadow of Growing Fundamentalism, Part II," *Le Monde* (via *Ha'aretz*, June 26, 1981) and Henry Carr, "New Prosperity is Creating Frenzy of Business Activity," *International Herald Tribune* (special supplement on Jordan), December 1979.

9. Taken from IMF statistics.

10. Department of Statistics (DOS), *External Trade Statistics* (Amman: DOS, 1984), 5.

11. In 1978, exports to Iraq were valued at $8.8 million (JD 3.4 million); by 1982, they were valued at $173 million (JD 66.6 million), an increase of 1965 percent. See, *External Trade Statistics* and Rami Khouri, "Jordan: Time to Take Stock of Economic Realities," *Middle East Economic Digest (MEED)*, August 10, 1985, p. 9.

12. Estimates for Jordan's exported labor range up to 400,000, but 350,000 is the usually accepted figure. These statistics do not include the number of dependents for these workers.

13. GDP (1981) was $3.531 billion; gross worker's remittances were $1.032 billion, or 29.1 percent. Taken from IMF statistics.

14. Net remittances in 1979 were $15.5 million; in 1981, $887.7 million. The World Bank, *World Tables*, 3rd ed., vol. I, Economic

Data (Baltimore, Md.: The Johns Hopkins University Press, 1983), 301.

15. Ibid. In 1970, remittances accounted for 17.4 percent of export earnings; in 1981, 46.2 percent.

16.

Revenue source	1973	1981	(millions $U.S.)
Direct Arab aid	71.8	1179.0	
Workers' remittances	37.6	1032.0	
Exports (goods)	57.6	734.9	
TOTAL	167.0	2945.9	
GDP	665.5	3531.2	

17. The total value of imports in 1973 was $329.6 million (JD 108.2 million); in 1981, imports were valued at $3.173 billion (JD 1.047 billion) — an increase of 964 percent. *External Trade Statistics*, 3; See *Quarterly Statistical Series*, table 20, "Geographical Distribution of Foreign Trade."

18. Ibid., table 34, "Cost of Living Index."

19. Ibid.

20. In 1975, the population of the East Bank was 1,810,500; in 1981, the population was 2,307,000 — an increase of 27 percent. DOS, *Statistical Yearbook 1984*, no. 35 (Amman: DOS, 1985). In 1975, Jordan produced 50,600 tons of wheat; in 1981, Jordan produced 50,000 tons of wheat.

21. In 1972, Jordan imported 44,228 tons of wheat; in 1981, it imported 348,099 tons of wheat. DOS, *Agricultural Statistical Yearbook and Sample Survey* (Amman: DOS, 1981), 77.

22. In 1981, Jordan imported $3.17 billion worth of goods. *External Trade Statistics*, 1984, p. 3.

23. Ibid. In 1981, Jordan's trade deficit was $2.438 billion.

24. See estimated population figures in *Statistical Yearbook, 1984*, p. 1, based upon the final results of the Housing and Population Census of November 1979. Almost all of the population increase is natural; a small percentage is the product of emigration from the West Bank.

25. Ibid.

26. According to the 1979 census, 1,038,221 out of a total East Bank population of 2,011,051 were under 15 years of age — 51.6 percent. See *Statistical Yearbook, 1984*, p. 5.

27. Ibid., 1. According to the government's 1984 estimates, 1,427,300 people live in the Amman governorate, 55 percent of the country's total population. The second largest concentration of

people is in the Irbid governorate, in which 28 percent of the country's population live.

28. In just three years (1975–1977), inflation in Amman jumped 51 percent, with food prices alone advancing more than 75 percent. Severe food shortages, hoarding, and price gouging were commonplace. See International Labor Organization (ILO), *Yearbook of Labor Statistics*, vol. 43 (Geneva: ILO, 1983) and *MECS* 3, p. 630; 4, p. 573; 5, p. 574.

29. J. S. Birks and C. A. Sinclair, "Hashemite Kingdom of Jordan," *International Migration Project*, no. 4 (Durham, England: University of Durham, 1978, p. 22).

30. *MECS* 3, p. 629.

31. In 1975, there were only 0.4 doctors per 1,000 persons in Jordan; by 1980, the ratio had risen to 1.0/1000. See National Planning Council (NPC), *Five Year Plan for Social and Economics Development 1981–1985* (Amman: NPC, 1981), 12.

32. There were 22,731 telephones in service in Jordan in 1973; by 1981, there were 73,298 – a threefold increase. *Statistical Yearbook, 1984*, p. 152.

33. According to the minister of labor and social development, Jordan's illiteracy rate is just 28.25 percent, and there is virtually no gap between illiteracy rates for males and females. Based upon figures from a 1982 manpower survey, 57 percent of Jordan's employed population, at least 15 years old, said they had some preparatory school training. Also, 78 percent of those 15–30 years old and employed stated they had some preparatory school education. These figures, however, do not reflect an accurate nationwide census and can only be suggestive of the actual literacy conditions in the kingdom. See *Jordan Times*, March 11, 1986; NPC, *Five Year Plan*, 15 and DOS, *Manpower Survey* (Amman: DOS, 1984), 71, 77.

34. See NPC, *Five Year Plan*.

35. Comparison of selected indicators, in $U.S. billion:

Indicator	1973	1981	% increase
GDP (market prices)	.820	3.531	431
Private consumption	.672	3.195	475
Public consumption	.255	.866	239

See IMF statistics.

36. *MECS* 1, p. 475.

37. Ibid., 2, p. 579.

38. Ibid., 4, p. 575.

39. According to Jordan's state budget, 1981 expenditures on fuel subsidies alone were JD 58 million, more than $177 million. See FBIS, January 3, 1983.

40. *MECS* 3, p. 630; *MECS* 4, p. 573.

41. Ibid., 4, p. 574; 5, p. 639.

42. In 1976, army salaries were increased 6–20 percent. Between mid-1980 and early 1981, military salaries were raised twice more. See Ibid., 1, p. 485; 4, p. 575, and 5, p. 639.

43. Ibid., 1, p. 475.

44. Ibid., 4, p. 575; Ibid., 5, p. 639.

45. George P. Shultz, *Jordan and the Peace Process*, statement before the Senate Foreign Relations Committee, June 19, 1985. Reprinted in the *Department of State Bulletin*, August 1985.

46. On July 17, 1985, Kuwait's National Assembly voted to cancel the shaykhdom's $340 million aid package to "confrontation states" – Jordan, Syria, and the PLO. At the time, the assembly's speaker harshly criticized the Jordan-PLO February agreement on joint action as a "capitulationist move," but many observers cite Kuwait's economic difficulties, not political differences, as the rationale for the aid cut off. In 1984, Kuwait had slashed its aid from $561 million to $340 million at least partly "because of declining revenues in the oil market." It is unlikely that Kuwait implemented the complete cutoff of aid, but there has been no confirmed information on the current level of Kuwaiti aid to Jordan. See UPI story in the *Washington Post*, July 18, 1985; FBIS, July 5, 1985; FBIS, July 25, 1985; *Arab News*, March 5, 1986.

47. *Monthly Statistical Bulletin* (Amman: CBJ, April 1985), table 38.

48. FBIS, November 8, 1983.

49. Ibid., January 24, 1985.

50. *MEED*, January 11, 1986, p. 15.

51. Government statistics indicating steady increases in remittances reflect a picture far rosier than the evidence leads one to believe. According to the Central Bank, remittance income in 1984 was up 18 percent over the previous year, reaching $1.27 billion, See, *MEED*, August 31, 1985, p. 15.

52. Joint Publication Research Service, Near East and North Africa Report (JPRS), no. 83060, March 14, 1983.

53. JPRS, no. 84009, November 29, 1983.

54. Private interview with Planning Ministry official, Amman, July 1985.

55. *MEED*, August 24, 1985, p. 14.

56. *Washington Post*, February 3, 1986. According to the article by Jonathan Randal, remittance income in 1985 was $1.1 billion. Even this figure appears high.

57. *MEED*, April 5, 1986, p. 18.

58. *External Trade Statistics*, 3.

59. Ibid., 4–5.

60. Ibid.

61. *MEED*, April 5, 1986, p. 18.

62. Ibid.; see Khouri, "Time to Take Stock," 9.

63. *External Trade Statistics.*

64. Ibid.

65. After the first complete year of operation (1984), the Arab Potash Company lost $37.3 million and the Jordan Fertilizer Industry Company (JFIC) lost $34.1 million. In 1985, JFIC lost another $120 million with projections of losses of $178 million between 1986–1990. As a result, the minister of trade and commerce approved a plan for the purchase of JFIC by the Jordan Phosphate Mines Company in early 1986. *MEED*, August 10, 1985, p. 31; March 15, 1985, p. 23; April 5, 1986, p. 18.

66. JPRS, no. 82577, January 3, 1983.

67. JPRS, no. 84009, March 14, 1983.

68. *an-Nahar Arab Report and Memo*, December 5, 1983, p. 5.

69. *MEED*, May 24, 1985, p. 16.

70. JPRS, Near East and South Asia, no. 83592, June 2, 1983.

71. FBIS, January 3, 1983; JPRS, no. 84009, March 14, 1983.

72. Private interview with Planning Ministry official, Amman, July 1985.

73. *MEED*, December 14, 1985, p. 14. The energy-saving plan entails reducing fuel subsidies and increasing the price of electricity and petroleum-based products. Jordanians currently use 50 percent more energy per capita than the average for the developing world.

74. Projected subsidy outlays for 1984 were as follows: food, $10.4 million (JD 4 million); agricultural products, $18.2 million (JD 7 million); energy, $26 million (JD 10 million), for a total of $54.6 million (JD 21 million). See Budget Department, *Budget Law for the Fiscal Year 1985*, table no. 3. (Amman: Budget Department, 1984).

75. *MEED*, December 14, 1985, p. 20.

76. According to the 1986 budget, the government will only subsidize bread ($27.5 million/JD 11 million) and fuel ($12.5 million/ JD 5 million). See report on the proposed 1986 budget in the *Jordan Times*, December 5-6, 1985.

77. *MEED*, April 12, 1986, p. 17.

78. *Jordan Times*, December 5-6, 1985.

79. See *an-Nahar Arab Report and Memo,* September 26, 1983, p. 4; *MEED*, April 19, 1985 and May 24, 1985, p. 24.

80. *MEED*, April 19, 1985, p. 14.

81. The government's plan includes banning imports of luxury goods similar to, or in competition with, locally produced goods, reducing customs duties on imported capital goods needed to build up local industry, and exempting export goods from income tax. See *MEED* (August 24, 1985), 14.

82. All restrictions have been lifted from the participation of non-Jordanian Arabs in real estate and stock and bond trading, and their investment funds have been protected against nationalization, confiscation, and freezing. *MEED* (February 1, 1986), 22.

83. *Jordan Times*, March 3, 1986.

84. Ibid., March 9, 1986.

85. In 1984, Jordan cut its massive trade deficit by $332 million, 6 percent. See Khouri, "Time to Take Stock," 9.

86. Ibid.

87. In 1984, Jordan exported goods worth $756.7 million (JD 290.6 million); its fuel bill was about $600 million, or 80 percent of the exports. See Khouri, "Time to Take Stock," and *External Trade Statistics*, 3.

88. *Washington Post*, February 3, 1986.

89. *Jordan Times*, March 29, 1986.

90. Quantities of wheat imported and wheat produced domestically: (1,000s of tons)

Year	Imported	Domestic
1977	139.0	62.5
1978	173.3	53.3
1979	201.2	16.5
1980	162.9	133.5
1981	348.1	50.6
1982	209.2	52.3
1983	318.7	-na-
1984	450.5	49.7

From *Statistical Yearbook, 1984*, p. 104.

91. FBIS, April 1, 1985.

92. At the end of 1984, Jordan's external public debt was $2.49 billion (JD 957 million), of which $1.67 billion (JD 641 million) was government debt and $822 million (JD 316 million) was government-guaranteed debt. Of the government debt, Jordan's largest creditors are the United States (23 percent) and Saudi Arabia (20 percent). See *Monthly Statistical Bulletin*, table no. 41.

93. In 1984, domestic revenues ($1.14 billion/JD 437 million) funded only 58 percent of the government's total expenditure ($1.95 billion/JD 746 million). In that year, direct tax revenues (including income tax) amounted to only $166 million (JD 64.1 million), or 8.6 percent of government expenditure. See *Monthly Statistical Bulletin*, tables 36 and 37.

94. From 1982 to 1983, gross capital formation fell 17.6 percent, from $1.7 billion (JD 619 million) to $1.4 billion (JD 510 million). See *Statistical Survey*, table 174, p. 221.

95. For an account of how Jordan narrowly averted default on a $197 million foreign military sales (FMS) loan in FY 1982, see *Arab-Asian Affairs*, no. 120 (September 1983). In recent years, Jordan has raised more than $400 million on the European loan market. In the summer of 1985, Jordan sought a $200 million Euroloan and then increased the amount to $215 million during syndication. According to *MEED*, "The economy's continued deterioration helped to persuade the government to increase the loan. A widening trade gap — from 1984's $2,000 million — is forecast, and the problem is compounded by the continuing slide in official Arab aid and falling remittances from nationals working abroad." See *MEED*, June 29, 1985, p. 12.

96. Khouri, "Time to Take Stock."

97. Regarding the drop in activity at the Amman Financial Market (stock exchange), see statements by Hamdi al-Tabba', chairman of the Federation of Jordanian Chambers of Commerce, FBIS, June 13, 1985. Regarding Jordan's ailing banking system, see *MEED*, May 24, 1985, pp. 24–25.

98. *Wall Street Journal*, January 2, 1986.

99. In 1980, CBJ held $1.14 billion (JD 341 million) in foreign exchange reserves; by the beginning of 1985, those reserves had fallen to $526 million (JD 202 million), a dollar drop of 54 percent. *Monthly Statistical Bulletin*, table no. 4.

100. Shultz, *Jordan and the Peace Process*.

101. Most observers agree on the figure of 125,000 foreign

workers inside Jordan. See, for example, Dieter Weiss, "Development Planning in a Turbulent International Environment — Some Reflections on the Jordanian Case," paper presented at the Study Day on the Economic Development of Jordan, Centre d'Etudes et de Recherches sur le Monde Arabe Contemporain (CERMAC), Université Catholique de Louvain, May 23, 1985, p. 20.

102. JPRS, no. 84117.

103. Ibid., interview with Dr. Mansour Utoum, director of the Labor Ministry's Employment Office.

104. *Jordan Times*, December 5–6, 1985.

105. According to the minister of labor and social development, employers will be subject to fines of about $250 (JD 100) per month for every undocumented foreign worker. Work permits for non-Jordanians were increased in late February 1986 to $216 (JD 75) from $86 (JD 30) for non-Arabs and $72 (JD 25) from $29 (JD 10) for Arabs. *Jordan Times*, January 21, 1986; *MEED*, February 22, 1986, p. 19.

106. *Jordan Times*, May 13, 1986.

107. Ibid., October 27, 1985.

108. Ibid., January 21, 1986.

109. Ibid., November 10, 1985.

110. For a figure of 67,000, see Kanovsky, *MECS*, vol. 7, p. 394. According to some reports, the number of Jordanians studying in foreign universities may be as high as 80,000. See *Middle East International*, February 22, 1985, p. 16. For government statistics, see *Statistical Yearbook*, table 62, p. 82.

111. "Jordan's Search for Jobs," *The Middle East*, March 1986, p. 21.

112. JPRS, no. 84117.

113. Ibid.

114. JPRS, no. 84129, interview with Ali Khreis, director of the Civil Service Commission.

115. FBIS, November 8, 1983.

116. Ibid., January 23, 1985.

117. *Jordan Times*, October 20, 1985.

118. Ibid.

119. On the establishment of the free trade zone, see FBIS, August 22, 1985; on the resumption of air travel between Amman and Damascus, see FBIS, January 2, 1986. All of the recent high-level Jordanian-Syrian meetings have given economic and trade matters high priority.

120. If Jordan received $500 million in aid, it would rank as the third largest recipient of U.S. economic assistance after Israel and Egypt. In 1985, the top five recipients of Economic Support Funds (ESF) were Israel ($1.2 billion), Egypt ($815 million), El Salvador ($285 million), Pakistan ($200 million), and Turkey ($175 million). See International Security and Development Cooperation Act of 1985.

Chapter 2

1. Amnesty International Report, "Jordan: Short Term Detention Without Charge of Political Prisoners," January 1986.

2. FBIS, October 3, 1985.

3. In addition to the controlled and monitored PLO in Jordan, many other small groups of Palestinians, pan-Arabs, Jordanian nationalists, Ba'thists, and Greater Syrians exist within the kingdom. These groups, however, seem to expend more time and effort on internal and internecine quarrels than they do on promoting their political agendas. In any case, they pose no challenge to Jordan's intelligence and internal security agencies. (Personal interviews in Irbid and Amman, summer 1985.)

4. *Jordan's Palestine Challenge*, 137. See also, Aaron D. Miller, "Jordan and the Arab-Israeli Conflict: The Hashemite Predicament," *Orbis* (Winter 1986), 805.

5. For example, in his 1983 survey book on Jordan, Gubser devotes a total of four paragraphs to Islamic issues; in their otherwise insightful study of social change and tribes, Jureidini and McLaurin relegate provocative remarks about the growth of "fundamentalism" to a footnote; Ibrahim's contribution to a 1980 volume on contemporary Islam in Greater Syria offers no evidence to support the claim that "militant Islamic movements are unlikely to succeed in competition with already existing and ever-growing secular nationalism and secular political parties." See Peter Gubser, *Jordan: Crossroads of Middle Eastern Events* (Boulder, Colo.: Westview Press, 1983), 39–40, 111–112; Paul A. Jureidini and R. D. McLaurin, *Jordan: The Impact of Social Change on the Role of the Tribes*, The Washington Papers, no. 108 (Washington, D.C.: Center for Strategic and International Studies with Praeger Publishers, 1984), 89; Ibrahim Ibrahim, "Islamic Revival in Egypt and Greater Syria," in *Islam in the Contemporary World*, Cyriac K.

Pullapilly, ed. (Notre Dame, Ind.: Cross Roads Books, 1980), 169.

6. See, for example, Edward Mortimer, *Faith and Power: The Politics of Islam* (New York: Vintage Books, 1982), 258.

7. "Facts about Jordan," *Arab World File (Fiches du Monde Arabe)*, Nicosia, Cyprus, I-J1; Ibrahim, "Islamic Revival," 167.

8. Hussein visited Iran in March, July, and November 1978.

9. *MECS* 3, p. 631.

10. FBIS, March 2, 1978; September 26, 1978.

11. *MECS* 3, p. 632.

12. *New York Times*, September 14, 1978.

13. Jureidini and McLaurin, *The Impact of Social Change*, 89.

14. *MECS* 3, pp. 633–634; 4, p. 577; also, *New York Times*, September 14, 1978 and November 13, 1978; *Le Monde*, June 21–22, 1981.

15. *MECS* 3, p. 633.

16. Ibid.

17. Ibid., also *Middle East Intelligence Survey* 6, no. 22, Middle East Information Media (Tel Aviv: Israel Press, February 16–28, 1979), 173–174.

18. For terminology on state and popular Islam, see James A. Bill, "Resurgent Islam in the Persian Gulf," *Foreign Affairs* (Fall 1984), 108–109.

19. FBIS, April 4, 1979.

20. Ibid., October 7, 1980.

21. Ibid., November 7, 1980.

22. *The Guardian* (Manchester, England), October 10, 1980.

23. "Khomeyni's Iran was popular not only with the Muslim Brethren but with wider sections of the population – whether for reasons of religious sentiment or for political reasons stemming from support in the PLO, and among the Palestinians generally, for the Iranian revolution." *MECS*, vol. 5, p. 641.

24. See, for example, Gubser, *Crossroads of Middle Eastern Events*, 111.

25. In Syria, the Muslim Brotherhood is the largest, best organized, and most effective opposition group to Asad's regime. Although the Brotherhood may agitate against Muslim rulers in various countries such as Egypt and Jordan, *Ikhwan* antipathy toward Asad is particularly virulent because of his adherence to the Alawite heresy of Shi'ite Islam. Alawites, also known as Nusayris, constitute about 10 percent of Syria's population and are concentrated in the country's northwest region. For centuries, they

have filled the role of Syria's underclass. The Alawite religion deifies Ali, the prophet's son-in-law, and incorporates many Christian characteristics. Although Alawites claim to be good Muslims, most Muslims – especially Syria's Sunni majority – consider them heretics. Most of the men in positions of power around Asad are Alawites.

26. *MECS* 3, p. 631–632.

27. Ibid.

28. *Le Monde*, February 26, 1979.

29. Government ministers were allegedly involved in "staging sex orgies with young girls (including high school pupils) at villas rented for the purpose in exclusive parts of Amman" and with "extending their protection to a chain of brothels established over the past two years in the capital to cater for visiting dignitaries from other Arab countries." See *Foreign Report*, November 21, 1979 and *India Today*, December 16–31, 1979. The less explicit *Le Monde*, which named Arar as one of the accused, referred to the affair simply as a "morals scandal." *Le Monde*, December 21, 1979.

30. *Quarterly Economic Review of Syria, Jordan* (London: Economist Intelligence Unit, Ltd., second quarter, 1980).

31. The other minister was Adnan Abu Awdah. *Le Monde*, December 21, 1979.

32. *Middle East Intelligence Survey* 8, no. 16, November 16–30, 1980, p. 123.

33. FBIS, December 2, 1980.

34. Ibid., December 8, 1980.

35. *New York Times*, December 7–10, 1980.

36. *Middle East Intelligence Survey* 8, no. 16, pp. 112–123; for an official version of the government's response, see *MECS* 5, pp. 650–651.

37. *Middle East Intelligence Survey* 8, no. 16, pp. 122–123.

38. *Le Monde*, February 26, 1980.

39. *The Sunday Times* (London), December 8, 1980.

40. Private interview with Khalifa, Amman, August 1985.

41. *MECS* 5, p. 641.

42. Information concerning *Ikhwan* activity on the campuses of Jordan's universities is taken from private interviews held during the summer of 1985.

43. Nazih Ayubi, "Political Revival of Islam: The Case of Egypt," *International Journal of Middle Eastern Studies* 12 (December 1980): 487.

44. *The Sunday Times* (London), November 30, 1980.

45. Adeed Dawisha, "Much Smoke, Little Fire," *Middle East International*, no. 144, February 27, 1981.

46. *Le Monde*, February 26, 1980.

47. Ibid., June 21–22, 1981; *MECS* 5, p. 641.

48. *Le Monde*, February 26, 1980.

49. *Quarterly Economic Review of Syria, Jordan* (London: Economist Intelligence Unit, Ltd., first quarter, 1980).

50. *Le Monde*, February 26, 1980.

51. FBIS, October 7, 1980.

52. *MECS* 6, p. 675.

53. Ibid.

54. Robert Fraser, ed., *Keesing's Contemporary Archives* (London: Longmas Group Ltd.) January 28, 1982.

55. FBIS, March 14, 1984.

56. Ibid., April 5, 1985.

57. *New York Times*, March 14, 1984.

58. Ibid.

59. Ibid.

60. Ibid.

61. Ibid.

62. In April 1985, for example, Rifa'i's government easily survived a vote of confidence, 48-6. FBIS, April 30, 1985.

63. *MEED*, February 15, 1986, p. 22.

64. *Middle East International*, April 19, 1985, p. 11.

65. FBIS, July 3, 1985.

66. Ibid., December 18, 1985.

67. The 76-article election law is indeed a detailed piece of legislation. For example, article 50 contains the proper procedure for local vote-counting committee chairmen to follow in the event that ballot box keys are lost. See *Jordan Times*, March 29, 1986.

68. Jordan's and Syria's prime ministers met under Saudi auspices in September and October 1985; in November Rifa'i traveled to Damascus to see Asad, and in early December, Qasim traveled to Amman to talk with Hussein. Hussein and Asad met in Damascus at the end of December. The two heads of state exchanged visits to Amman and Damascus in a flurry of diplomatic activity in May 1986.

69. See FBIS, October 22, 1985; November 13, 1985; November 18, 1985.

70. Isa Na'ib, minister of state for foreign affairs, has since

taken a prominent role in the recent surge of bilateral diplomacy. *Jordan Times*, October 21, 1985.

71. FBIS, August 8, 1985.

72. Ibid., February 26, 1985.

73. Ibid., January 29, 1985.

74. Ibid., January 18, 1985.

75. Ibid., November 4, 1985.

76. *Jordan Times*, November 11, 1985.

77. These reports were first made by the Voice of Hope Radio from Marj 'Ayun, Lebanon (FBIS, November 13, 1985), then repeated by Radio Monte Carlo (FBIS, November 18, 1985).

78. See *Jordan Times*, November 17, 1985 and *al-Fajr Palestinian Weekly*, November 29, 1985.

79. *Jordan Times*, December 21, 1985.

80. Thirteen of the 55 attending representatives abstained in the ballot. See *Jordan Times*, November 3, 1985.

81. Ibid.

82. There are many points of parallel between the current situation in Jordan and the situation obtaining in Egypt in the early 1970s; the role of Islamic activists in domestic politics is one of the most instructive. Anwar Sadat used the Egyptian *Ikhwan* in his contest with the Left much the same way that Hussein used their Jordanian counterparts against Asad. Both cases have had at least one similar result – the strengthening and emboldenment of the Islamic activists on the domestic front. Jordan is just beginning to feel the sort of boomerang effects that – of a greater magnitude – toppled Sadat.

Chapter 3

1. Samuel P. Huntington, *Political Order in Changing Societies* (New Haven: Yale University Press, 1968), 177.

2. For example, the commander in chief of the armed forces is Sharif Zaid bin Shakir, a cousin of the king, and the director of public security is a leading member of a powerful tribe from Karak that has long wielded political power in Jordan, the Majalis.

3. P. J. Vatikiotis, *Politics and the Military in Jordan: A Study of the Arab Legion, 1921–1957* (New York: Frederick A. Praeger, 1967), 20.

4. Jureidini and McLaurin, *The Role of the Tribes*, 39.

5. Ibid., 88.

6. Ibid., 40.

7. Ibid., 52.

8. Vatikiotis, *Politics and the Military*, 5.

9. Ibid. Vatikiotis cites a 1948 Israeli Defense Ministry handbook on Jordan. See Agra (pseudonym), *The Armies of the Arab States in the Context of Their Environment* (in Hebrew), Tel Aviv, 1948.

10. Jureidini and McLaurin, *The Impact of Social Change*, 22.

11. Ibid.

12. Vatikiotis, *Politics and the Military*, 29.

13. According to government population figures, in 1965, the East Bank population was 493,400; in 1970, the East Bank population was 723,900 — an increase of 47.9 percent. See *Statistical Yearbook, 1984*, p. 2.

14. Clinton Bailey, "If There's to be a State for the Palestinians, It Must be the Already-Palestinian Jordan," *Los Angeles Times*, December 29, 1985.

15. See Bailey, *Jordan's Palestine Challenge*, and Miller, "The Hashemite Predicament."

16. Jureidini and McLaurin, *The Impact of Social Change*, 62.

17. In 1973, Hussein preferred not to open a Jordanian theater against the Israelis, opting instead to dispatch the 40th Armoured Brigade and the Third Armoured Division to assist the Syrians. See, for example, Richard A. Gabriel and Alan Scott MacDougall, "Jordan," in Gabriel, ed., *Fighting Armies: Antagonists in the Middle East, A Combat Assessment* (London: Greenwood Press, 1983), 33. Gabriel and MacDougall are incorrect, however, when they state that "Jordan has not been involved in any combat operations since the 1973 war." In 1975, a Special Forces Battalion was sent to — and saw action in — Oman when called upon to assist in quelling the Dhofar rebellion. See Anthony H. Cordesman, *Jordanian Arms and the Middle East Balance* (Washington, D.C.: Middle East Institute, 1983), 183. Also, Brigadier S. A. el-Edroos, The *Hashemite Arab Army, 1908–1979* (Amman: The Publishing Company, 1980), 643.

18. Jureidini and McLaurin, *The Impact of Social Change*, 56.

19. *MECS* 1, p. 477.

20. Ibid., 4, p. 572.

21. Ibid.

22. Ibid., 7, p. 628.

23. Many observers confer upon former Prime Minister Mudar Badran such less-than-affectionate titles. For "bête noire," see *Middle East International* (May 17, 1985), 11.

24. FBIS, January 30, 1985.

25. Ibid., January 29, 1985. (Appeared in Jordan on January 24, 1985.)

26. Ibid., January 28, 1985. (Appeared in Jordan on January 27, 1985.)

27. Ibid.

28. Ibid., January 30, 1985. For more on Sharaf, see Bernard Avishai, "Jordan: Looking for an Opening," *The New York Review of Books*, September 27, 1984.

29. Cited in *Middle East International*, February 8, 1985, p. 11.

30. In November 1974, both houses of Parliament authorized amendments to the Jordanian constitution permitting the king to dissolve the assembly and to delay calling elections for a 12-month period. Prior to the by-elections of 1984, called to fill eight vacant seats, parliamentary elections were last held in Jordan in April 1967. See Anne Sinai and Allen Pollack, *The Hashemite Kingdom of Jordan and the West Bank: A Handbook* (New York: American Academic Association for Peace in the Middle East, 1977), 71.

31. *MECS* 1, p. 475.

32. Ibid.

33. Ibid., 2, p. 583.

34. Nabeel A. Khoury, "The National Consultative Council of Jordan: A Study in Legislative Development," *International Journal of Middle East Studies* 13, no. 4 (November 1981): 428.

35. According to *MECS*, the head of the Jordanian Bar Association is Ibrahim Bakr, a member of the PNC and formerly the spokesmen for the PLO's Central Committee; the leader of the Doctor's Union, Hasan Khurays, is a known PLO sympathizer. *MECS* 2, p. 581.

36. Ibid.

37. Ibid.

38. Ibid., 582.

39. Ibid., 3, p. 632.

40. Ibid., 4, p. 576.

41. Ibid., 6, p. 674.

42. Ibid.

43. *Akhbar al-Usbu'*, April 3, 1986, p. 8 cited in FBIS, April 17, 1986.

44. *an-Nahar Arab Report and Memo*, January 16, 1984, p. 4.

45. *an-Nahar Arab Report and Memo*, April 15, 1985, p. 6.

46. Soon after the breakdown of Jordan-PLO coordination in February 1986, there were changes made in the Rifa'i cabinet, most notably a shuffle of several Palestinian ministers.

47. Ibid. Eleven of the 23 new ministers in the Rifa'i cabinet were of Palestinian origin, a slight increase over the proportion (7 out of 16) in the previous government.

48. See reports from Dubai and Kuwait in FBIS, May 20, 1985 and July 5, 1985, respectively.

Chapter 4

1. An East Jerusalem Arabic weekly and Israeli Radio both cited rumors from the East Bank concerning an attempted officer coup. See FBIS, July 19, 1985.

2. Hussein bin Talal, *Uneasy Lies the Head* (New York: Bernard Geis Associates, 1962), 24.

3. *The International Who's Who of the Arab World 1984* (London: The International Who's Who of the Arab World, Ltd., 1983), 369.

4. *MECS* 2, p. 577.

5. *Who's Who of the Arab World*, 226.

6. *Jordan Times*, March 20–21, 1986.

7. Moreover, his ill-temper is legendary; according to reports, the mayor of Amman suffered a heart attack after Hassan took him to task for neglecting to repair a faulty retainer wall before it collapsed and killed several passersby. Taken from private interviews in Amman, August 1985.

8. el-Edroos, *The Hashemite Arab Army*, 451. This mammoth work was written under the patronage of Crown Prince Hassan.

9. Hassan bin Talal, *Search for Peace* (New York: St. Martin's Press, 1984).

10. Hussein, *Uneasy Lies the Head*, 122.

11. Hassan, *Search for Peace*, 131.

12. See letters of correspondence, *Foreign Policy*, no. 60 (Fall 1985), 186.

13. Hassan bin Talal, "Jordan's Quest for Peace," *Foreign Affairs* (Spring 1982), 812.

14. Avishai, "Looking for an Opening," 48.

15. *The Times of London*, September 3, 1982; also, *Jordan Times*, March 22, 1979.

16. *Baltimore Evening Sun*, September 12, 1982. And, for example: "The Russians have been able to exploit the Arab-Israeli conflict to insinuate themselves into a position of power and influence." Hassan, *Search for Peace*, 119.

17. FBIS, January 18, 1985.

18. *Jordan Times*, November 21–22, 1985. In recent months, Hassan has received increased press coverage in Jordan for statements concerning the need for moderation in religion; *Foreign Affairs* (Spring 1982), 806.

19. *Foreign Policy*, no. 60 (Fall 1985), 186.

20. Writing in the *New Republic*, David Pryce-Jones puts Hassan at the top of the list of those in Jordan "who advocate the abandoning of the West Bank on the grounds that the Israelis and the Palestinians deserve one another and should best be left to batter themselves to bits." "The Timid King," *New Republic*, Year End Issue, 1982.

21. *Jordan Times*, November 21–22, 1985.

22. Hassan bin Talal, "Return to Geneva," *Foreign Policy*, no. 57 (Winter 1984–85), 13.

23. Judith Miller, "King Hussein's Delicate Balance," *New York Times Magazine*, April 22, 1984.

24. *Washington Post*, May 19, 1983.

25. Ibid., May 30, 1985.

26. Ibid.

27. Miller, "The Hashemite Predicament."

28. When Hussein's father, Talal, was declared mentally incompetent to rule in 1952, a regency council ran Jordan for several months until Hussein reached the age of majority. From his formal investiture on the throne until the government crisis of 1957, parliamentary leaders held a significant share of political power in the kingdom and Hussein lacked the free rein he now maintains.

29. See references to Bin Shakir's rebellious past in Uriel Dann, "Regime and Opposition in Jordan," *Society and Political Structure in the Arab World*, Menachem Milson, ed. (New York: Humanities Press, 1973), 171, 176.

30. el-Edroos, *The Hashemite Arab Army*, 474.

31. Bin Shakir is reputed to be especially close to Abdallah, an alliance that might have great impact on the choice of the next Jordanian monarch.

Chapter 5

1. *US Overseas Loans and Grants, Statistical Annex I to the Annual Development Coordination Committee Report to Congress, 1984: Obligations and Loan Authorizations, July 1, 1945–September 30, 1983* (Washington, D.C.: AID, Office of Planning and Budgeting), 19.

2. Moshe Zak, "Peace Without an Embassy," *Ma'ariv*, November 1, 1985, cited in FBIS, November 5, 1985.

3. For occupied territory trade statistics, see *Statistical Abstract of Israel* (Tel Aviv: Department of Statistics, 1985), table 27/11, p. 713. Also, see comparable data in Fawzi A. Gharaibeh, *The Economies of the West Bank and Gaza Strip* (Boulder, Colo.: Westview Press, 1985).

4. Eliyahu Kanovsky, *The Economy of Jordan: Implications of Peace in the Middle East* (Tel Aviv: University Publishing Projects, 1976), 143.

5. Ibid., 138.

6. In 1984, 13,056 Jordanian residents visited Israel (including 43 who arrived by air), as compared with 4,563 Egyptians. For tourism statistics, see *Statistical Abstract of Israel*, 1985, tables 4/5 and 4/8, pp. 141, 145.

7. See Pinhas 'Inbari's analysis, "Turning Off the Royal Faucets," *al-Hamishmar* (Israel), in FBIS, November 27, 1985.

8. Kanovsky, *The Economy of Jordan*, 139–140. He cites Israeli press reports that Israel shipped to Jordan some "high-quality sheep" that yielded about 200 liters of milk annually, in contrast to the 30–40 liter yields of East Bank sheep.

9. FBIS, December 3, 1985.

10. *Jerusalem Post*, December 21, 1984.

11. See also, Moshe Zak, "Israeli-Jordanian Negotiations," The *Washington Quarterly* 8, no. 1 (Winter 1985) for background information on these and several other interesting examples of bilateral cooperation.

12. Zak's article "Israeli-Jordanian Negotiations" chronicles in detail these encounters from 1963 to 1977. In 1986, Shimon Peres removed much of the secrecy from his relationship with Hussein when he openly discussed their quiet diplomacy. In May 1986, for example, an interviewer questioned him about the "dialogue" created when he "met with Hussein." In response, Peres noted elliptically, "Let us say that everything you said is correct. I did not say it is correct." FBIS, May 14, 1986.

13. FBIS, November 14, 1985.

14. In December 1985, a group of West Bank notables defied hard-line PLO sentiment and assumed control of the Nablus city council from the Israeli occupation authorities. Said Zafir al-Masri, the new mayor, "We are taking over the municipality to provide services to the people in accordance with the Jordanian municipal law." FBIS, December 11, 1985.

15. Conor Cruise O'Brien, "Political Reality in the Middle East," *Atlantic Monthly*, October 1985, p. 45.

16. *Washington Post*, December 27, 1985.

17. Ibid.

18. Those East Bank constituencies signaled their displeasure with Hussein's flirtation with the potentially destabilizing "peace process" in 1983 by channeling remittance income to Switzerland. Cited by Kanovsky in *MECS*, vol. 7, p. 397.

Chapter 6

1. In 1983, Jordan's per capita GNP was $1,640. In contrast, the People's Democratic Republic of Yemen's was $520; The Yemen Arab Republic's, $550; Egypt's, $700; Morocco's, $760; and Tunisia's, $1,290. Syria's rate was marginally higher ($1,760), while Algeria—a major exporter of oil and natural gas—registered a per capita GNP of just $2,320. See The World Bank, *World Development Report 1985* (New York: Oxford University Press, 1985), 174–175.

2. Many observers have documented the link between joblessness (especially among the technically trained) and Islamic activism throughout the Middle East. In his 1980 analysis of Islamic politics in Egypt, Nazih Ayubi describes a sense of popular frustration that hauntingly resembles Jordan today. Among the symp-

toms of that frustration is the "expansion of university education proceeding at a time when economic opportunities are declining, resulting in delayed employment, poor salaries and working conditions and the increased likelihood of permanent mass unemployment for the educated."

Sa'ad Eddin Ibrahim notes the following relationship between economic crisis and Islamic activism: "In the absence of a credible, secular national vision . . . to enhance the present and future socioeconomic prospects of the middle and lower classes to galvanize the imagination of the educated youth and give them some sense of being essential parts of a grand design, Islamic militancy becomes the alternative." Also on Egypt, Hamid Ansari adds that "even the unemployed militants had the benefit of technical education." Lucien Vandenbroucke cites the "strong link between Islamic revival and frustrated expectations of higher standards of living." He ascribes one of the root causes of "fundamentalism" to the frustration of "blocked social mobility," the product of too many university graduates and too few jobs. These citations are representative of a general observation in the literature on Islamic activism in the region.

See Nazih Ayubi, "Political Revival of Islam: The Case of Egypt," *International Journal of Middle East Studies* 12 (December 1980); Sa'ad Eddin Ibrahim, "Anatomy of Egypt's Militant Groups," *International Journal of Middle East Studies* 12 (December 1980); Hamid Ansari, "The Islamic Militants in Egyptian Politics," *International Journal of Middle East Studies* 16 (March 1984); Lucien Vandenbroucke, "Why Allah's Zealots? A Study of the Causes of Islamic Fundamentalism in Egypt and Saudi Arabia," *Middle East Review* (Fall 1983).

3. No sub-Saharan country (other than South Africa) has a per capita GNP that approaches Jordan's $1,640; the highest is the Congo's $1,230. Moreover, Singapore (7.8 percent) was the single country in the world claiming a higher average annual growth rate than Jordan (6.9 percent) for the period from 1965–1983. See The World Bank, *World Development Report 1985*.

Conclusion

1. According to Amnesty International, 35 people were arrested for political reasons and detained without charge in Jordan in the final four months of 1985 alone. Six of those persons were

reportedly tortured during detention. Amnesty International, "Jordan: Short Term Detention."

2. See the generally laudatory assessment of Jordan's human rights situation in the U.S. State Department's *Country Reports on Human Rights Practices for 1984* (Washington, D.C.: Department of State, February 1985), 1284–1293. For example, the report states that "generally, however, martial law has not much affected the civil rights of Jordanians."

3. *Washington Post*, November 3, 1981.

4. Ibid., November 4, 1981.

5. Jordan ranked first among all countries in terms of U.S. aid per capita, $226, between 1956 and 1965. See Michael C. Hudson, *Arab Politics: The Search for Legitimacy* (New Haven: Yale University Press, 1977), 214.

6. Some simply abbreviate "Plucky Little King" to "PLK." In State Department cables, Hussein was referred to as the "BYK" – "Brave Young King." See John Newhouse, "Profiles: Monarch," *New Yorker*, September 19, 1983, p. 68.

7. For an account of this episode, see Daniel Dishon, editor, *Middle East Record, 1969–1970*, vol. 5 (Jerusalem: Israel Universities Press, 1977), 15, 475–479.

8. *New York Times*, April 25, 1969, cited in ibid.

9. Although Jordan never joined the Baghdad Pact, Hussein was very much an anti-Communist. "In the great struggle between communism and freedom, there can be no neutrality," he declared before the United Nations in September 1960.

10. *Jordan Times*, November 11, 1985.

Index

"O, so you've got a copy of 'Lady Chatterly's Lover'!" exclaimed Bob and Pearl, and they proceeded to make themselves perfectly at home in a strange house. Their hostess has about given up thoughts of a bridge game.

From a cartoon pasted into *Lady Chatterley's Lover* (Florence: Privately Printer, 1928), formerly the property of Jewell F. and Patricia G. Stevens, now in Special Collections, Morris Library, Southern Illinois University, Carbondale.

A Descriptive Bibliography of *Lady Chatterley's Lover,*

With Essays Toward a Publishing History of the Novel

Jay A. Gertzman

Bibliographies and Indexes in World Literature, Number 23

Greenwood Press
New York • Westport, Connecticut • London

FOR MY SISTER ADELE

Library of Congress Cataloging-in-Publication Data

Gertzman, Jay A.
  A descriptive bibliography of Lady Chatterley's lover : with
essays toward a publishing history of the novel / Jay A. Gertzman.
      p. cm. — (Bibliographies and indexes in world literature,
  ISSN 0742-6801 ; no. 23)
    ISBN 0-313-26125-3 (lib. bdg. : alk. paper)
    1. Lawrence, D. H. (David Herbert), 1885-1930. Lady Chatterley's
lover—Bibliography. 2. Lawrence, D. H. (David Herbert),
1885-1930. Lady Chatterley's lover—Criticism, Textual.
3. Lawrence, D. H. (David Herbert), 1885-1930—Publishers.
I. Title. II. Series.
Z8490.5.G47   1989
[PR6023.A93]
823'.912—dc20   89-17181

British Library Cataloguing in Publication Data is available.

Library of Congress Catalog Card Number: 89-17181
ISBN: 0-313-26125-3
ISSN: 0742-6801

First published in 1989

Greenwood Press, Inc.
88 Post Road West, Westport, Connecticut 06881

Printed in the United States of America

The paper used in this book complies with the
Permanent Paper Standard issued by the National
Information Standards Organization (Z39.48-1984).

10 9 8 7 6 5 4 3 2 1

Contents

Preface; Acknowledgements

Proscribed, barbered, pirated, sold and rented as under-the-counter pornography, and accorded best-seller status during the decensorship years of 1959-60, *Lady Chatterley's Lover* affords a case study of a piece of "high literature" deeply penetrating the public consciousness. The objective evidence for this is the set of bibliographical descriptions that form the bulk of this book. In order to clarify the circumstances of the work's publication, marketing, and distribution (in private, piratic, expurgated, trade and mass-market, hard- and soft-bound editions), I have prefixed to the descriptions themselves introductory essays, hoping they both elucidate the novel's publishing history, and indicate the social settings conditioning its production and reception.

In Sections 2 and 3, and Appendix 1, I document the extensive early involvement of Samuel Roth, a New York publisher whose business combined literary classics and "borderline pornography." The essay for Section 2 provides a survey of book-smugglers' distribution methods and of those of the retailers who sold or rented under the counter. I also attempt to account for the variety of piracies and their audiences. The rationale for the expurgated editions, and the methods by which they were prepared, are given in Section 3. More extensive study along these lines (undertaken with respect, not disapprobation, for the instincts and expertise of Samuel Roth, Laurence Pollinger, and Martin Secker) would be fruitful. It could result in specifying those contemporary sexual taboos and notions of sex roles which made Lawrence's own definition of sexual vitality radical, difficult to comprehend, and easy to sensationalize and parody. In order to document the variety of audiences for the novel, and how the book was made available at various "points of sale," I describe, in Section 5, the "Chatterley Sweepstakes," and survey continental editions (Section 4), and both book club editions and mass-market trade paperbacks (Sections 5 and 6). I hope that the level of detail used in describing cloth

bindings, dust jackets, and paperback wrappers (including illustrations, blurbs, lettering and logos) in the bibliographical entries provide evidence of the attractions of these editions for the audiences they were designed to reach. Appendix 1 (which contains the second-longest introductory essay) delineates the strategies for publishing and marketing the sequels and parodies of the novel. These indicate as well as any publications of *Lady Chatterley's Lover* do the cultural contexts which allowed the work to be absorbed willy-nilly into the ethos of British and American society for more than half a century.

Much of this information is tentative; the most oft-used word in many of the introductory sections is "probably." The facts, as far as I have been able to determine them, are in the bibliographical descriptions themselves. It is the public results, not the private intentions, of Lawrence's publishing his last novel that the latter document. However, Lawrence's statement to Edward Dahlberg, only months after the publication of the Orioli edition, is greatly intriguing:

> As for writing pariah literature, a man has to write what is in him and what he can write and better by far have genuine pariah literature than sentimentalities on a 'higher' level. (CL 1138)

This is a strong answer to a question he asked Ottoline Morrell (and himself) a month earlier, as notoriety over *Lady Chatterley's Lover* and *Pansies* built: "Really, why does one write? Or why does one write the things I write! I suppose it's destiny, but on the whole, an unkind one" (CL 1124). I hope that, taken together, the bibliographical entries and introductory essays make the following question worth exploring: are Lawrence's own choices regarding the characters, their actions, and the diction of *Lady Chatterley's Lover* (the third version especially) *themselves* partly a result of his expectations concerning the way pirates, expurgators, merchandisers, smuthounds, and booksellers would not only treat his text but also determine the physical units (the volumes) in which that text was contained?

I refer to the scatology, the sexually-active heroine increasingly contented with the strength of her adulterous commitment to her working-class lover, the crippled aristocratic husband, the hero's violent sexual aggressiveness, and the explicitness of the sex "bouts". The appearance of *Lady Chatterley* as an underground sex-book steered the text in directions about which the author expressed revulsion, but which this perceptive social critic and "Priest of Love" should have in substance (and with clenched teeth) foreseen. If, as Squires (15-20, 174-88) so carefully shows, the novel became more polemical with each re-writing, and if, as he and others state, the work insists on the reader's considering personal regeneration through active subversion of "modern" conventions involving sexuality, class status, and the "cash nexus," then Lawrence would want for it as irresistible a reputation as possible. Of course he hated indignant moralists, compromising publishers, and unscrupulous pirates. "The

beastly marketable chunk of a published volume is a bone
which every dog presumes to pick with me," he wrote in his
introduction to the first bibliography of his works in 1925.
"The voice inside is mine forever" (McDonald 10). Lawrence
needed money and approached *Lady Chatterley's Lover* in a very
businesslike manner. The way in which the words were packaged
was largely beyond his control, even by late 1928. However,
with the appearance of the Orioli edition, he put the process
into operation. The resultant "marketable chunks" provide
effective media for reaching the imaginations of an indeterminate general audience. Perhaps the author could tell
himself, as he did an editor under attack for publishing "The
Escaped Cock," that "you won't lose in the long run. Deadness
is what loses in the long run. Anything that makes 'em
wriggle becomes at last indispensable" (CL 1057).

The bibliographic descriptions are intended to accommodate details of publishing and distribution. My system of
notation for individual entries is as follows:

_____

Always Present:
-First character: arabic number   = *edition*
-Second   "   "   "   = *impression*
Frequently Present:
-subsequent (3rd when used) character: lower case letter =
    issue
-subsequent (sometimes 3rd, sometimes 4th) character: sub-
    scripted number following arabic number or l.c. letter =
    state

_____

An asterisk preceding the first character indicates that
I have not located a copy of the item listed. I have supplied
information regarding dating for many asterisked entries:
this information (enclosed in quotation marks) was found on
the copyright-page printing history of either the entry
itself or a later impression of the same edition, unless
another source (duly noted) was available.

Notations are not strictly chronological (see the
statement on subeditions below). I have indicated, when
ascertainable, the date of printing in the individual
descriptions. Appendix 6 lists the editions chronologically
by either certain or assumed publication date.

The separate listing given to each impression, issue,
and state of an edition is based (tentatively of course) on
the internal and external evidence that I have been able to
accumulate. In the case of perfect-bound paperbacks this is
especially problematical. Individual impressions of these
editions are given separate designations based usually on
statements of printing history often located on the volume's
copyright page. I have not been able to use offset slur,
register measurement, or type batter to detect hidden
printings.

Beginning with Section 3, I have made use of the concept
of "subedition": a discrete set of impressions deriving from

a single set of plates; either the plates themselves or a photolithographed copy of them may have been sent to another publisher by arrangement, or used to issue a "series" (thin-paper, "pocket," commemorative, "cheap"), or to create a reissue with new front matter or editorial apparatus. I treat impressions of individual subeditions as entities by keeping them together; strict chronology or a sequence of impressions by individual publishers is sacrificed to this end.

In the method of arranging entries, and in the bibliographical descriptions for each entry, I have endeavored to follow the suggestions of Fredson Bowers's *Principles of Bibliographical Description*, and those of G. Thomas Tanselle, as contained in the essays by him listed in my Works Cited section. The format of each entry includes (1) quasi-facsimile title transcription, (2) collation, (3) listing of contents, (4) details of typography (measurement of text block and tentative identification of typeface), (5) paper (thickness of individual sheets and total bulk; watermarks), and (6) description of binding materials, colors, lettering and illustration. The notes which conclude the descriptions include price and number of copies printed, if known. These notes are designed to supplement rather than repeat what is stated in the introductory essays, and cross-references are provided when necessary. At times, I do repeat facts given in the essays, when the reader's convenience seems to dictate it.

Apropos of the latter, especially for booksellers I have briefly characterized many editions with subheadings which make their descriptions easily identifiable to the eye as one skims the pages (see also Appendix III). Also for convenience of booksellers and collectors, in the collations I have used inches to indicate length and width of the leaf. Elsewhere, the metric system is employed.

In the collations, when indicating signings of gatherings I use '$' when any leaf other than the first in each gathering is signed. I do not use this symbol to indicate that the first leaf is signed, since that is evident from the lack of square brackets surrounding the signature number. Thus 1-23^8 means the first leaf in each gathering is signed with a consecutive arabic numeral; [1-23]^8 would indicate that the gatherings are not signed and the sequence is inferred. When the 23-letter alphabet is used, the same principle applies.

In item 1.7 below, the underdotting in the title-page transcription indicates a gothic typeface.

For identification of typefaces I have found *Rookledge's International Typefinder* helpful (abbreviated as R). Classification of the faces follows the DIN standard as recommended by Tanselle, "The Identification of Type Faces." For binding colors, the NBS Centroid Color Charts (abbreviated as C) were consulted. For cloth textures, I have

relied on Tanselle's "Bibliographical Description of
Patterns" (abbreviated as T).

The references to the Roberts and McDonald bibliographies designate the places in those two works where descriptions of the relevant volume may be found. In my Copies
Examined line I have used *The National Union Catalogue*
symbols for American libraries, and those of *The British
Union-Catalogue of Periodicals* for British. The collections
of Gerald Pollinger and W. Forster are indicated without
symbolic abbreviation. The word "personal" indicates my own
copy.

The following abbreviations for published works cited
are used:

CL   Moore, Harry T., ed. *The Collected Letters
                of D. H. Lawrence.* 2 vols. New York:
                Viking, 1962. All references are to
                volume 2.

FLC   *The First Lady Chatterley*

JTLJ   *John Thomas and Lady Jane*

LCL   *Lady Chatterley's Lover*

McDonald   McDonald, Edward D. *A Bibliography of the
                Writings of D. H. Lawrence.* Phila-
                delphia: The Centaur Book Shop, 1925.

MM   Moore, Harry T., and Dale B. Montague,
                eds. *Frieda Lawrence and Her Circle.*
                London: Macmillan, 1981.

PW   *Publishers' Weekly*

Roberts   Roberts, Warren. *A Bibliography of D. H.
                Lawrence.* 2nd edition. Cambridge:
                Cambridge University Press, 1982.

In the essays, I have been forced to use an alternate
form to superscript to indicate endnotes, due to the inability of my Toshiba printer consistently to maintain proper
line spacing with this feature. As suggested in the 1985
edition of *The MLA Style Manual*, note numbers are placed
between slashes, as follows: /1/

Acknowledgements

I wish to thank Gerald Pollinger and the Estate of
Frieda Lawrence Ravagli for permission to quote from the
preliminary pages of each entry described in this bibliography.

An earlier version of the essay for Section 2 appeared in
The D. H. Lawrence Review, and I thank the editor, Dennis

Jackson, for permission to reproduce portions of that paper herein.

For acknowledgements of permissions to reproduce illustrations, see the pages on which they appear. I have made
every effort to locate any person or company whose material
may be reproduced herein.

I owe a special debt of gratitude to the following for
their time and their very valuable contributions of informa-
tion and advice: Mr. Louis Bondy, London; Prof. Arthur Efron,
SUNY Buffalo; Mr. and Mrs. W. Forster, Stamford Hill, London;
M. Maurice Girodias, Paris; Mr. Anton Gud, Long Island, N.Y.;
Mr. Seymour Hacker, New York City; Prof. Leo Hamalian, City
College of New York; Mr. Alan J. Kaufman, New York City; Mr.
Patrick Kearney, Santa Rosa, Cal.; Mrs. A. Roth, New York
City; Prof. Karen Burke LeFevre, Rensselaer Polytechnic
Institute; Mr. Gershon Legman, La Clé des Champs, France; Mr.
Arnold Levy, Secaucus, N.J.; Mr. Gerald Pollinger, Esq.,
London; Prof. Warren Roberts, Austin, Texas; Mr. Anthony
Rota, London; Mr. C. J. Scheiner, Brooklyn, N.Y.; Mr. Albert
Sperisen, San Francisco; Prof. Michael Squires, Virginia
Polytechnic Institute and State University; Prof. G. T.
Tanselle, Columbia University; Mr. Allan Wilson, Secaucus,
N. J.; and the staffs of the British Library, the Bodleian
Library, the Nottingham County Library, and the university
libraries of Nottingham (UK), Tulsa, Texas (Humanities
Research Center), California at San Diego (Special Collec-
tions, Central Library), Harvard, Syracuse (Arents), New York
University (Fales), and Southern Illinois (Morris Library).
The staff of the Mansfield University Library was extremely
helpful in handling a large number of diverse requests over a
long period of time. For inaccuracies, I alone am responsible.

So many booksellers and book scouts have helped me that
it is impossible to thank them individually. I would like to
name three from whom I acquired many volumes: Lucile Coleman,
North Miami, Florida; Peter Howard, Berkeley, California; and
Ivan Stormgart, Boston, Mass.

I must especially thank several people who opened their
homes, offices, and libraries to me. Without the freely-given
and amazingly extensive information on erotic bookselling and
bibliography that Cliff Scheiner volunteered, I could not
have written the first three sections of this book. On two
occasions in 1985 and 1988, Bob and Eileen Forster gave me
free access to their superlative Lawrence collections and
provided delightful company and conversation as well. Gerald
Pollinger did the same on my visit to his offices in May
1988. On four occasions from 1985 to 1988 Mrs. Adelaide Kugel
(Samuel Roth's daughter) kindly showed me her father's books
in her Manhattan apartment and truly went out of her way to
give me valuable information about him. Arnold Levy's full
archives and fine memory provided many important details, and
he was generous with his time in person and by letter. I
cherish Gershon Legman's correspondence not only because of

the information but also (and chiefly) because these letters
are part of the output of a major American writer.

SECTION 1

The First Edition and Its Authorized Impressions

INTRODUCTORY ESSAY

"[It] . . . will not only revolt decent minded people on account of its theme, but also because of the filthy words . . . . " ("Lewd Book Banned," qtd. in Nehls 3: 264–65); "evil outpouring. . . . diseased mind. He is obsessed with sex" ("Famous Novelist's Shameful Book," qtd. in Nehls 3: 262-63). *Lady Chatterley's Lover* provoked outrage because it challenged readers' tolerances in matters central to their social roles and responsibilities, and to their notions of how to conduct themselves in their most intimate moments. In this respect, Lawrence's challenge went far beyond the use of four-letter "obscenities," as Richard Aldington (308) implies in his fulmination against "the morbid degeneracy of British sex hatred." Although few readers in such cases are honest enough with themselves and/or their peers to openly say so, most adults, whether liberal or conservative, find themselves unable to cope with material which deeply ("shockingly") questions basic assumptions governing self-image and conduct. It is easier to allow authorities such as presidential commissions and school boards (in Lawrence's case the publishers George Doran/1/ and Horatio Bottomley, Home Secretary Joynson-Hicks or Senator Smoot of Utah) to articulate their secret confusion as well as to serve as butts for uneasy snickering. "O lecteur hypocrite, mon semblable, mon frère."

In *Lady Chatterley's* case, Lawrence's characters were disturbing to almost any intelligent reader more or less adjusted to British or American society in the third decade of the twentieth century. There are writers (Michaelis, Clifford) who trivialize human relationships, or excite corrupt but "conventionally pure" feelings. The novel presents the educated classes as secretly insecure and morally as well as sexually paralyzed; the targets here are not fox-hunting bullies or snobs but "bright young people" (Hilda, Tommy Dukes, Duncan Forbes) with liberal ideas on

respectability, birth control, and pre-marital sex. The lower classes are venal and self-destructively ignorant. Most men, as Connie and Mrs. Bolton find, are emotional cripples needing to be smothered with platitudes. Modern marriage, based on sharing with one's spouse commercial success, is sterile; adultery is not a sin unless a visceral, but sacred, bond between the partners exists. As for the love between Mellors and Connie, the latter's submission to her lover's inarticulate libido is absolute, mysterious, and to many feminists the product of a sexual reactionary's imagination. Christianity is also treated contemptuously; Lawrence implied it has lost the necessary "togetherness with the universe," and its pervasive influence is simply another indication that "our old show will come flop." One must add to this the challenge to family values that Connie represents as a wife who chooses sexual gratification over caring for her husband, and the challenge to taboo involved in using scatology in intimate and poetic contexts.

Great works of erotic literature go beyond titillation and excite opposition essentially because of such icon-oclastic challenges. In Lawrence's case the obvious popular focus was his challenge to prurience. Comstockery and British respectability had long provided him with notoriety. His deliberate decision to write about a woman's adultery, to use taboo words, and to issue "my lady" privately and under his own name insured him a choleric struggle with the "censor-morons." Following the example of Norman Douglas, he had *Lady Chatterley's Lover* "privately printed" in Florence in July 1928. His nominal publisher was Pino Orioli, who several months later was to issue Douglas' *Nerinda* (Woolf 100). Erotic works so published sometimes went unprosecuted since they reached only affluent readers not (presumably) as likely as more "common" folk to be debauched (Craig 170-71). Obviously the Orioli *Lady Chatterley* was not so tolerated, and in any case privately printed books were suspect. A 1930 New York court, in convicting a bookseller of distributing Schnitz-ler's *Hands Around*, stated that the designation "privately printed" on its title page carried *a priori* the stigma of indecency (Bogart 370). For Henry Seidel Canby, writing from the towers of Yale in 1924, private printing was "one of the worst methods of issuing a book. It is a sign usually of weakness in the book, distrust distrust of the reader, or fear of the hand of authority" (108).

Canby's three reasons are as important as his tone. They categorize a certain type of work, often privately published, "peddled around waterfronts, in the neighborhood of waxworks and houses of ill fame, by itinerant book-sellers and junk dealers, or . . . pulled from under a counter, with a wink" (Mehring 56). The statement is that of a European poet, recalling his early twentieth-century boyhood, specifically the subversive works in his father's library. These included books on witchcraft, demonology, political radicalism, white slavery, anti-clericism and anti-semitism, and erotic libertinism. This "veritable

black market of unsavory printed matter" (57) included
works of De Sade, Sacher-Masoch, Baudelaire, Huysmans,
Diderot (*The Nun*), Prévost (*Manon Lescaut*). All were kept
in an obscure corner (called "the poison cupboard"), some
under lock and key. The writers were considered "distinguished madmen," their influence on one's friends, not to
mention wife and children, feared, and their books themselves secreted in tabooed corners.

There was little alternative to private publication
open for Lawrence since there was little hope that Secker
or Knopf would take the MS (Nehls 3: 168, 178; CL 1041,
1042); eventually both demurred in favor of an expurgated
edition. See Section 3, pp. 59-61./2/ A small indication of
his problems with the Florence edition is his choice of
title. The announcements Orioli sent out carry the subtitle
John Thomas and Lady Jane (British slang for the male and
female genitalia), which Lawrence decided upon as full
title after Juliette Huxley indignantly suggested it. In a
letter to Martin Secker, 5 March 1928, he noted the change.
However, a letter of 13 March indicates that he had agreed
to reduce it to a subtitle, most probably to please London
and New York publishers. As Squires (14) points out, Aldous
Huxley told him of extensive damage likely to distribution
and sales. On 2 April he responded to Huxley as follows:
"I'll have to leave out *John Thomas*, shall I? What a pity!
But it's too late to leave it from the leaflets. . . ."(CL
1042, 1043, 1046, 1052-53). Now, Lawrence knew on 2 April
that Secker would not publish the novel anyway--as he had
expected. In view of this, his reason for dropping "the
title I want" as subtitle for the Florence edition is
unclear. The decision may have been made before 2 April,
and Knopf, still at that point in the running, would have
balked in any event. Apart from these considerations, and
despite the use of the four-letter words in the text, to
use *John Thomas and Lady Jane* as title or subtitle would
have made confiscation by authorities easier, and caused
serious-minded potential readers to sense hard-core smut by
a "distinguished madman," to be relegated as a tabooed
novelty to a locked cupboard. Lawrence never made such
choices easy for his readers. The final two problems Canby
notes are relevant to this "phallic title" incident, which
indicates just the surface of the hazardous iceberg that an
author who had his work privately printed had to negotiate
in 1928.

The full story of Lawrence's financial management of
the Orioli and Titus editions will be set forth in Michael
Squires' introduction to his forthcoming (1989) Cambridge
edition of *Lady Chatterley's Lover*. Briefly, Orioli
commissioned the same printer, Franceschini, to prepare
both the Lawrence and the Douglas volumes, which are
similar in size, paper-covered boards, statement of
limitation, paper, and unlettered white paper jacket. For
Lady Chatterley, Orioli printed announcements and order
forms (Squires 12) and, with Lawrence's aid, distributed
the work in July 1928 through the writer's friends, who hid
copies and delivered them to booksellers as he instructed

(Squires 189-91). Although annoyed by some British retailers' refusal to distribute after their copies had
arrived (Nehls, III, 325; Moore, *Priest* 563), Lawrence
seemed satisfied that *Lady Chatterley* had found her way
into the hands of most British subscribers. Only 200 copies
remained by September 1928 (Squires 191). At U.S. ports,
customs officials very early began confiscation (CL
1072). According to Squires, Lawrence's private account-
book, in which he recorded costs and profits for the novel,
indicates that "although [he] originally intended five
hundred copies for America, . . . most copies were sold in
England" (223)./3/ Squires also quotes a letter of 27
August, 1928 to Orioli: "it is *useless* to mail copies to
America" (190).

By September, reports of piracies forced Orioli to
purchase the remaining 200 copies and raise the price to 4
guineas ($21)./4/ By early 1929, London booksellers were
asking £6 (Squires 191, 196). Two months later, Lawrence
decided to "launch" his paper-bound "second edition" of 200
copies (see 1.1.c in the bibliographical descriptions
below) against the "dirty orange pirate" (1.6), as he
termed it in "A Propos of *Lady Chatterley's Lover*." Most
copies were sold at 21 shillings to booksellers, rather
than to private individuals, for whom the price was 30
shillings (*Letters* 113). In London, Charles Lahr agreed to
take 112 copies, having been offered a one-third discount
(Squires 193-94; 223). But the "second edition" was badly
outnumbered. By April 1929, with customs officials and
Scotland Yard inspectors seizing copies of the Orioli
issues (CL 1119, 1121), Lawrence knew of three piracies
being sold in both Europe and America (CL 1139): see "A
Propos," and 1.6, 1.7, 1.10 below. He needed an inexpensive
Paris volume with a large printing--a "popular" edition
which would reach the pirates' clientele, and beyond: "so
that anybody can get it" (CL 1139). In 1933, his wife
stated, in her introduction to another Paris edition, that
he wanted "to reach the people he voiced and from whom he
came" (see pp. 100-02 below and entry 25.1).

In a letter to Lawrence on 12 Dec. 1928, Huxley
suggested that Orioli find a Paris publisher who could
photolithograph the Florence edition; the book could sell
at "some reasonable rate between the original 2 guineas and
the 5000 [sic] frcs asked by the pirates" (Smith 304).
Rejecting the idea of using Orioli (see endnote 4 and CL
1106), Lawrence first queried Sylvia Beach, but she
refused, not wishing, after *Ulysses*, to become known as a
publisher of erotica. "What could anybody offer after
Ulysses?" she asked (Beach 93). At some point, Lawrence
called Jack Kahane, soon to found the Obelisk Press, but
then without sufficient capital to oblige. (Obelisk was to
publish many works banned in England and America). "The
book was then the number-one scandal book and it would have
been well worth starting a new imprint just to publish that
one title on the continent" (Girodias 87). The rationale
for this assumption is well stated by Gershon Legman: "In
the 1920s and '30s, erotica publishing in English and

French became inextricably combined with a 'front' or cover of avantgarde literature" (*Private Case* 46). Lawrence also contacted the Pegasus Press, run by Holroyd Reese (see Section 4, pp. 101-04) and Nancy Cunard (Squires 194, CL 1107, 1112, 1122). They might have obliged (in early 1929 Reese proposed a press run of 1000 to start at 100 francs a copy) save for the activities of Scotland Yard in ferreting out copies of the Orioli edition (Squires 195). Frank Groves of Libraire du Palais (Squires 195-96) gave a brief spark of hope (see 1.10 below). Eventually, Beach suggested Edward Titus, husband of cosmetics magnate Helena Rubinstein (Ford 140); since 1926 Titus had been publishing such authors as Lewisohn, Cocteau, Rimbeau, Aleister Crowley, and Kiki under his Black Manikin imprint. He agreed to issue *Lady Chatterley* on condition his volume contain new material regarding the piracies; Lawrence obliged by writing "My Skirmish With Jolly Roger."

The Paris Popular Edition appeared without Titus's imprint; the publisher hoped that in future he could use it and that Lawrence would give him other work (he hoped *Pansies* [Ford 141-42]) to embellish his list. By late April the plates had been made. The price of 60 francs, reported by Squires (196), was far below the 300 or 400 the pirated editions fetched (for prices of specific piracies see 1.6, 1.7, 1.10 and p. 12 below). Titus hired salesmen to secure orders outside France (Ford 141). Through March 1930, there were three printings, totalling between 9,000 and 11,000 copies. In mid-September, sales were still good. As of 1 December, 1930, the author's share of earnings from the edition amounted to 89,151 francs (MM 22; see Ford 143).Titus sent to Lawrence 10,000 francs on 27 Feb. 1930. Mrs. Lawrence received 5,000 francs on 15 September, 10,000 five weeks later, and 20,000 on 1 Dec. 1930 (MM 19, 21, 22). This was followed by two payments of 10,000 francs each in April and August 1931 (MM 30, 34).

The Paris Popular Edition was probably smuggled along with other piracies into England and the U.S., where bookleggers could sell it along with the first edition, European authorized printings (Section 4), and the "privately printed" piracies (Section 2) at a healthy profit. Lawrence was as helpless to stop the bookleggers and pirates or to share in the rewards as Joyce and Frank Harris had been, especially since the piracies had a large foothold by the time his Paris edition appeared.

ENDNOTES

1. ". . . nauseating crudities and vulgarities . . . . He is a voice crying not in the wilderness, Repent Ye! but in the red-light district of a humanity he would debase to the level of his own puerility and degeneracy." (Gross 185-86)

2. It is interesting to note that both Secker and Knopf rejected Radclyffe Hall's *The Well of Loneliness* in 1928. Secker demurred at once, stating that the book would not

make money. At first, Blanche Knopf convinced her husband to offer Hall a contract. The Knopfs backed out after Jonathan Cape was ordered not to publish, stating that they had concluded that only the pruriently curious would buy the novel (Dickson 142-49, 167-69).

3. The notebook held at the Northwestern University library is entitled "Memoranda / D. H. Lawrence." Squires' *Creation of Lady Chatterley's Lover* provides excerpts in Appendix E.

4. It appears that only about one-half of these 200 copies were sold in Lawrence's or Orioli's lifetimes. In 1948, an enterprising American bookseller acquired approximately 100 copies of *Chatterley* at Orioli's Florence warehouse, arranging the purchase from a gentleman with whom Orioli had gone to Portugal as war threatened Europe, and where he died in 1942. These were copies of the first, hardbound, edition (1.1.a below), with the Lawrence signature and with the phoenix on the upper cover. (I received this information in correspondence with the American bookseller in July 1988).

   Why these copies went unsold is unknown, but Lawrence wrote to Secker as follows on 3 Dec. 1928: "Orioli though worries me a bit--I don't hear from him--he doesn't send out *Lady C.* when she's ordered--I'm afraid he's really ill" (*Letters* 111). Within the week, Orioli did write to Lawrence (CL 1103), but the latter had lost enough confidence in him to reject Huxley's idea of sending him to Paris to arrange the "Popular Edition." As for the unsold copies of 1.1.a, it is possible that the increased price (rather than Orioli's illness) may simply have slowed sales, as Lawrence conjectured would happen on 3 September (CL 1091). The early appearance of piracies may have been another factor. As of September 28, 1929, the novelist knew ("this is strictly private") of 50 unsold copies (CL 1202).

   As C. J. Scheiner (see p.14) has cogently suggested, publishers very often retain some copies of books they feel will escalate in value at some indeterminate period after publication. To withhold one-tenth of an edition even of so notorious a publication as a future investment may seem excessive. However, even if this is the basic reason for the unsold copies (undertaken by Orioli in part as a reaction to Lawrence's shrewd financial arrangements with him [see Squires 221-23]), we need not assume that it was an act of animosity on his part toward the novelist. The passages in Orioli's memoirs (232-34) which suggest that attitude may in fact, as Aldington (*Pinorman* 106, 212) asserts, have been written under Norman Douglas' influence.

BIBLIOGRAPHICAL DESCRIPTIONS

[The Orioli Edition]

1.1.a LADY CHATTERLEY'S LOVER | BY | D. H. LAWRENCE |
       PRIVATELY PRINTED | 1928

(8 15/16 x 6 3/8"): π^2 1-23^8, 186 leaves; pp. [4], 1-365,
[366] [2].

CONTENTS: p.[1]: blank, p.[2]: This edition is limited | to
    One Thousand copies. | No.____ | signed.........p.[3]:
    t.p. p.[4]: Florence - Printed by the Tipografia Giuntina,
    directed by L. Franceschini. pp.1-365: text. p.[366]:
    blank. pp.[2]: blank.

TYPOGRAPHY: Text: 35ll.(p.109), 156 x 104mm; 10ll.=44mm.;
    face 3 (2x)mm. Typeface: Transitional (DIN 1.24, Modern
    Baroque). Old Style No 2 (cf. R69), for title page and
    text. Statement of limitation in Jenson Old Style (R34).

PAPER: smooth white laid unwatermarked. Chainlines 25mm.
    apart. Thickness .1mm. Total bulk 20.1mm.

BINDING: paper-covered boards, light grayish reddish brown
    (C45). Lawrence phoenix stamped in black, middle of upper
    cover. White paper label on spine, printed in black,
    lettering enclosed within border of one rule: LADY |
    CHATTERLEY'S | LOVER | D. H. | LAWRENCE |. Endpapers same
    as rest of book. Top edge trimmed; others untrimmed. Blank
    dj, 500 x 230mm. Thickness .05mm. Yellowish white (C92).

PRICE, NUMBER OF COPIES PRINTED: see Roberts, p.101.The bill
    from the printer included the following items: "1000
    copies, handmade paper," "1000 coverpapers -- handmade
    moretto," "1200 labels," "paper for wrappers"(jacket),
    "1500 leaflets" (order forms) (Squires 222).

NOTES: Roberts A42a; McDonald, *Supplement*, #38. At one time
    the Orioli edition was kept in the British Museum
    Private Case (Rose, *Register* I, #2457 and #2512). The
    British Library "de-suppressed" the book "some time after
    1964" (Legman, *Private* 50). The Bodleian copy's accession
    stamp bears the date 15 November 1929, and indicates that
    the copy was donated to the library, not purchased by
    Oxford University. It is kept in the Phi Collection.
        For further details see the following: MSS: Tedlock
    (24-27); DHL's attempts to expurgate: Sagar (223);
    printing: Roberts (109); strategies of retailing: Squires
    (11-14, 188-97, App. E), Hamalian, *D. H. Lawrence*
    (180-83); difficulties with authorities: Squires (195),
    Moore, *Letters* (1120); reviews: Draper (278-84), Nehls
    (III, 261-65).
        Lawrence to Martin Secker, 14 Aug. 1928: "I agree about
    the label on the back of *Lady C.*--I don't like it"

(*Letters* 110). As he often stated, he was pleased with all other aspects of the volume's physical appearance.

The copy at PU is unnumbered; instead is written "out of series" in script. The library purchased the copy from a British bookseller in 1958.

COPIES EXAMINED: PU; NsyU(Arents); OkTU; TxU; NNU(Fales); MH-H(2 copies); PPRF; personal; LO/N-1; OX/U-1; Forster Coll.

1.1.b   as 1.1.a save:

PAPER: very light blue (C180).

NOTE: two copies only; See Roberts A42a, variant (2).

COPY EXAMINED: TxU

1.1.c   as 1.1.a save:

Leaves measure 8 1/2 x 6 3/8".

CONTENTS: p.[2]: Second edition | limited to 200 copies.

PAPER: white wove unwatermarked. Thickness .08mm. Total bulk 17.5mm.

BINDING: Ribbed paper wrappers, light grayish reddish brown (C45); thickness: .13mm. Paper spine label as 1.1.a. Top edge partly trimmed; others untrimmed. No binder's leaves or endpapers.

NOTES: Roberts A42b. Printer's bill lists "200 copies on common paper," "200 cover-papers--handmade moretto," "600 leaflets" (order forms). The printer set up half the text, ran both the hand-made paper and the common-paper copies, and then printed the rest of the copies of both "editions" (Squires 13).

The Manuscript collection (s. v. "Lawrence, D. H. Misc.") at TxU contains a photostat of a false title page for a copy of LCL sent to Egmont Arens of The Vanguard Press (see pp.12-14 below). This page measures 8 1/4 x 5 7/8" and, in a typeface very similar to that used in 1.1.a, reads as follows: JOY GO WITH YOU | BY | NORMAN KRANZLER | THE | PONTE PRESS |. The page is inscribed, in what TxU identifies as Lawrence's hand, thusly: to Egmont Arens | This book, with | best of luck | from N. K. | 1 Sept 1928 |. It is impossible to ascertain whether this page is either a discrete entity or part of a preliminary gathering; if the latter is the case, the copy or copies in which it appears would constitute another state of the Orioli edition. It may, however, have been pasted over the original title page. In any case, it provides an imprint as well as a false title and author to deflect a custom officer's suspicions, and the volume in which it appeared may well have had a false dust jacket (see p.15 below). As for "Kranzler" (German for sick person), perhaps Lawrence is referring to Norman Douglas, although it was the former who was seriously ill in 1928.

Because the size of the false t.p. more nearly resembles 1.1.c than 1.1.a, I assume it was used to camouflage the latter, "common paper," issue.

COPIES EXAMINED: NNU(Fales: rebound, upper and lower covers preserved); TxU; DLC(spine repaired); Forster Coll.

[The "Paris Popular Edition"]

1.2   THE AUTHOR'S UNABRIDGED POPULAR EDITION | [rule] | LADY CHATTERLEY'S LOVER | Including | MY SKIRMISH WITH JOLLY ROGER | Written Especially and Exclusively as an | Introduction to this Popular Edition | BY | D. H. LAWRENCE | PRIVATELY PRINTED | 1929

(7 1/2 x 5 1/2"): π^6 1-23^8, 190 leaves; pp. [4], I-VIII, 1-365, [366], [2].

CONTENTS: p.[1]:t.p. p.[2]: blank. p.[3]: *Tous droits de reproduction, et | traduction et d'adaptation réservés | pour tous pays y compris la Russe.* | Copyright by D. H. LAWRENCE. p.[4]: blank. pp.I-VIII: MY SKIRMISH | WITH | JOLLY ROGER |. pp.I-365: text. p.[366]: blank. pp.[2]: blank.

TYPOGRAPHY: Text: 35ll. (p. 169), 137 x 91mm.; 10ll. = 38mm.; face 2(1.2x)mm. Typeface: title page set in Hollandse Mediaeval (R3), save for author's name, in Garamond (Stempel), R92.

PAPER: smooth white wove unwatermarked. Thickness .07mm. (p.57). Total bulk 15.8mm.

BINDING: ribbed paper wrappers, moderate yellowish brown (C77), printed in black. Upper cover: upper right: 60 Frs | [rule] |. At center: Lawrence phoenix. Lower cover, in lower right: LECRAM PRESS - PARIS |. White paper labelon spine printed in black. In border of one rule: LADY | CHATTERLEY'S | LOVER | D. H. | LAWRENCE |. No endpapers. Top edge trimmed, others untrimmed.

NOTE: Roberts A42c; McDonald, *Supplement* #42. Roberts (102) reports that first printing consisted of 3,000 copies.

COPIES EXAMINED: TxU; personal; LO/1 (rebound, wrappers preserved); NO/U-1 (rebound); Forster Coll.

1.3.a   as 1.2 save:

(7 9/16 x 5 1/2"): π^8 1-23^8, 192 leaves; pp.[8], I-VIII, 1-365, [366], [2].

CONTENTS: pp.[4]: blank. p.[5]: t.p. p.[6]: blank. p.[7]: tous droits. . . LAWRENCE. p.[8]: blank.

PAPER: Thickness .07mm. Total bulk 14.0mm.

BINDING: as 1.2 except top and bottom edges lightly trimmed;
    fore-edge untrimmed.

NOTES: "By mid-August Titus had sold all three thousand
    copies and was printing again" (Squires 197). Ford (143)
    reports second printing was also 3000 copies.

COPY EXAMINED: OkTU (rebound; upper and lower covers
    preserved)

1.3.b   as 1.3.a except:

PAPER: Thickness .08mm. Total bulk 16.1mm.

BINDING: deep red (C13) morocco-grain limp leatherette.
    Spine divided by 5 raised bands. Stamped in gold: LADY |
    CHATTERLEY'S | LOVER |. Reddish gray (C22) endpapers,four
    binder's leaves. Edges trimmed.

NOTE: this may have been printed on cheaper paper and
    rebound either privately or by the bookseller. It may be a
    booklegged piracy. "Wannemaker" (the New York store which
    carried erotica in the thirties?) is written in pencil on
    the first leaf.

COPY EXAMINED: personal

1.4. as 1.2 save:

T. p. as 1.2 save l. 11: 1930 |.

BINDING: as 1.3.a.

NOTES: ". . . as early as 3 February Lawrence had authorized
    a third printing of three thousand copies" (Squires 197).
    Ford (143) states the 3rd printing to have been 5000
    copies.
        Titus sent Mrs. Lawrence a statement of account on 1
    Dec. 1930 (MM 22) which indicates that net profit on
    copies sold fluctuated as time passed. The net worth of
    the first 2,266 copies was 34 francs each; the next 2,600
    copies netted 36 francs each; a subsequent 1,145 copies
    brought 40 francs each.
        On 1 Dec. Titus stated, "I am ordering 5,000 more
    copies to be printed" (MM 23). One assumes this refers to
    a fourth (fifth?) impression. I have not been able to
    distinguish any such printings from 1.4.

COPIES EXAMINED: NNU(Fales); TxU; OkTU; NO/P-1; OX/U-1;
    LO/N-1 (lacks spine label)

SECTION 2
Piracies, 1928–50;
The "Third Edition"

INTRODUCTORY ESSAY

The audience for *Lady Chatterley* during the first thirty years of its existence included the politicians, clergy, and journalists who forced the novel underground. Self-appointed moralists too angered by Lawrence's challenge to their values and personal identity to read more than half a page forged a reputation for Lawrence's last novel which insured it a place not only in thinking people's libraries but in the public mind. Its importance must be measured not only by its poetic evocations of springtime and unspoiled visceral passion but also by the outraged censorship--and prurient curiosity--it stimulated. A consequence of such responses was its adaptation by pirates for diverse readers with dubious ability to understand it, but with great power to keep the book a vital presence in mid-twentieth-century society. Sheerly as regards size of audience, a poet-prophet of Lawrence's powers could ask no more than that as many such readers as possible, shocked, idly curious, or admiring, be delivered into his hands.

The bibliographical descriptions below indicate the extent to which book pirates served the novel's audience; they specify many of the physical forms in which "my lady's" message (shocking, compelling, and profound) was communicated; and, they suggest the extent to which bookleggers were responsible for Lawrence's success at disseminating what he passionately put forth "as a healthy, honest book, necessary for us today." He hated the pirates, but as he worked out his own distribution tactics for the novel during the first year of its appearance, it must have become increasingly clear that it would be through such publishers that his novel would reach many readers.

The present list is incomplete. First, I cannot account for the illustrated edition Lawrence mentions in a letter of 20 July 1929 (CL 1166) as "about to appear in Philadelphia" (it could not be 3.1). The more piracies one examines (some seen only in private libraries of dedicated collectors), the more one realizes that other examples are somewhere extant. A publisher need not have acquired the first edition as copytext; I found unauthorized issues of the Swedish Jan Förlag, the French Obelisk Press, and the Paris Popular volumes. Even the Faro (Samuel Roth) and the Grosset and Dunlap expurgated reprints were pirated. The variety and number of unauthorized printings suggest that *Lady Chatterley* may be the most-pirated twentieth-century novel in English.

The prices varied widely. Huxley (Smith 304) reports that the first piracy, probably the "dirty orange" (1.6), sold for an incredible 5000 francs. This would have been almost $200; did Huxley mean to write "500"? As reported in "A Propos" (90), the "funereal" tome (1.7-1.9) went for between ten and fifty dollars, while the "close replica" (1.10) fetched between 300 and 500 francs. Other prices reported for unspecified piracies varied widely: £2 (CL 1105), $10 (CL 1104), 30 shillings (CL 1103), 300 francs, with a 100 franc discount to booksellers (CL 1122).

However inevitable the pirates, Lawrence never resigned himself to their machinations, and expected a loyal front against those who would steal his livelihood. He suspected various booksellers (Sylvia Beach in Paris, Francis Steloff in New York) of marketing authorized and pirated editions side by side, and of publishing piracies (Squires 193). He even accused a reputable publishing house that had attempted to get his authorization for an unexpurgated American edition: "Those Vanguard Press people must have gone behind my back and cheated me. . ." (CL 1104). Vanguard's efforts are important to the *Lady Chatterley* publishing history because they reveal how circumscribed were the possibilities of legally distributing interdicted literature at the time. They also reveal the pressures to which a prospective publisher could subject the author of such a work.

Vanguard had communicated with Lawrence in July-August of 1928, before any piracies had appeared, for an American privately printed, unexpurgated edition of *Chatterley*. Emphasizing that the novel's power would not survive expurgation, but making no commitment that the book would carry the Vanguard imprint, Jacob Baker, Vanguard's Managing Editor, requested Lawrence to send surreptitiously three copies of the Orioli edition to be photolithographed. The price was to be $10 a copy; royalties were to be 10%. the author was requested not to send any more copies of his Orioli edition to the U.S., because of the danger of piracy, and to turn over to Vanguard all outstanding American orders received to date. Copies were to be sent to

Baker, Rex Stout, and Egmont Arens (see 1.1.c, NOTES). The offer was made dependent on Lawrence's providing Vanguard (which had recently taken over the Macy-Masius list) with at least one future work, although, as Baker mentions, this would mean Lawrence's abrogation of his agreement with Knopf./1/ Vanguard, established in 1926 with the aid of a grant from the American Fund For Public Service, published titles (some considered radical) aiming to improve the working classes, and was instrumental in fighting the 1929 Clean Books Bill. It had a reputation for clear, attractive book design (Tebbel, III: 181,401). The Macy-Masius list included *Americana Esoterica*, Louys' *Songs of Bilitis*, D. H. Clark's *Female*, and *Immortalia*, a collection of bawdy songs, limericks, and parodies. The first-mentioned work carried this imprint: "Privately published by Macy-Masius." Vanguard's anti-censorship activities were serious: it defended booksellers arrested for selling its books, and lobbied for a revision of the New York State statutes to shift prosecution from individual dealers (always the easiest targets for John Sumner's Society for the Suppression of Vice) to the publishers (PW 9 Mar 1929: 1217; 22 Feb. 1930: 983; 14 July 1934: 138). In 1938, it published, under its own imprint, Sheila Cousins' *To Beg I Am Ashamed*, after the London publisher (Routledge) had withdrawn this autobiographical novel by a London prostitute.

In view of this, how interesting it would have been had the first authorized American edition of *Lady Chatterley's Lover* carried the Vanguard imprint in 1929! Sumner would certainly have brought suit, and one imagines a liberal such as Judge Woolsey liberating *Lady Chatterley* a few years before the *Ulysses* decision, thus radically altering the book's printing history (and destroying that element of its fascination which depended on its clandestine reputation). In 1932, Henry Hazlitt, editor of *The Nation*, quoted Morris Ernst concerning the consistent failure of the Society for the Suppression of Vice to gain convictions when "a book was published with an established publisher's imprint" (289). *Chatterley* would have been a celebrated case. Consider the Smoot-Cutting Debates on the floor of the Senate in March 1930, where Smoot of Utah, advocating that Customs officials are capable of deciding at a glance whether or not an imported book should be destroyed, referred to works "so disgusting, so dirty and vile that the reading of one page was enough for me." *Chatterley*, for him, was a prime exemplar (*Cong. Rec.* 18 March 1930: 5491; see Paul 55–62).

Even if Vanguard published without its imprint, Lawrence would have received a share of the profits, although having to take on faith that the share was a just one. He was at first enthusiastic (CL 1081–82), but, as Squires (191) reports, about a month after Baker's letter, Lawrence had decided on advice of his New York agent not to pursue the matter. Perhaps, he felt as he did when considering a Pegasus Press [Holroyd Reese; see pp.5, 102–03] Paris edition: "*How am I to keep a check on him?*" (Zytaruk 376). The stipulation requiring Lawrence to send

to Vanguard a future work, while fair to the latter, would have enforced disloyalty to Knopf, and, considered strictly from a business point of view, this may have hurt Lawrence in the long run with London and New York publishers. In December 1928, considering the rising tide of piracies, Lawrence was second-guessing his decision: "since now I get *nothing*, & they [pirates] do as they like" (Zytaruk 366). Did Vanguard ultimately respond with a pirated edition, as Lawrence suspected? There is no evidence of this, although 1.7 below does advertise its American origin: "American Eagle [on both title pages], with six stars round its head and lightning splashing from its paw, all surrounded by a laurel wreath . . . " ("A Propos" 90).

In any event, Vanguard may not have prevented American pirated editions, for they appeared very early. The Orioli volumes were at first very scarce in the U.S., since customs officials were alerted for them soon after publication; Paris, where the Popular Edition originated, was very far away. Therefore, copies (some of them imported) were made available to America by experienced international "bookleggers." However, C. J. Scheiner, one of the foremost contemporary dealers in, and students of, erotica, believes that more would have been printed domestically, since that was easier and precluded involvement with customs./2/ He points out that after 1928, it was also cheaper: a constricted market for *éditions de luxe* (erotic or otherwise) meant that for typesetting, printing, binding and storing, artisans had to reduce prices or not work at all. There were many job printers, several on the lower east side of New York, who would oblige, either during the day or at night. It behooved the publisher to pick up printed sheets quickly, so that smuthounds might not get wind of the edition and track it down. Frank Harris' 1925 letters are full of bitterness toward a New York publisher (most probably Esar Levine) for allowing unbound sheets to remain with the printer until they, and Levine, fell into the hands of the law (Tobin and Gertz 326-30). As stated below (pp. 27-28) Sam Roth experienced a reversal with his expurgated piracy of *Chatterley* because he lacked the cash to pick up his copies from the binder. The latter had the text reset, fabricated an imprint, and issued the work himself.

It is worth reviewing the U.S. bookleggers' methods of importation and domestic distribution of censored erotica, with an eye to considering McDonald's opinion (40-41) that no individual pirates got rich by "doing" *Lady Chatterley*. Perhaps, but the variety of approaches to distribution suggest that the publishers and smugglers, if not the printers, were well rewarded for their diligence. Scheiner believes that "organized crime did all the wholesale importing," and this hypothesis implies a lucrative business with a loyal clientele.

IMPORTATION

1. Bookleggers would ship to the U.S. through southern ports (Hamalian, "Samuel Roth" 902). The banned books may have been carefully hidden under innocuous ones to which

customs would pay little heed. Possibly, this is the "Texas dodge" Lawrence suggested Orioli try in September 1928 (CL 1091). The previous May, he had confided to his staunch distributing ally Koteliansky, "I may try to slip 200 copies into America in crates" (Zytaruk 342). See the third method listed below.

2. Bookleggers would use false dust jackets, and unlettered cloth (see 1.9 Var.[3], 8.1, 25.2 Var.[2]) or paper-covered boards. Lawrence himself had Orioli use the former with twenty copies of the first edition sent to England (CL 1091); he sent at least one copy to Vanguard with a false title page (see above, 1.1.c NOTES). Beach suggested American purchasers of *Ulysses* use false dust jackets (Fitch 119); Scheiner finds this practice "very common." His colleague, Arnold Levy,/3/ reports that false labels would be printed on paperbacks. Brome (194) describes this method as effective in shipping Harris' *My Life and Loves* to France.

3. Bookleggers would secrete unbound signatures in packing cases, or individually wrap them, for domestic and/or foreign shipment. Noel Fitch (134) reports copies of *Ulysses* being shipped from England to America in this way. Nos. 1.7 and 1.8 below are very strangely gathered; it is doubtful that this was the reason, but worth mentioning.

4. Bookleggers would contract "agents," perhaps simply bookloving tourists, to attempt to get copies past customs. Beach and Frank Harris did so (Brome 194-95; Fitch 119-21). For Beach, a man in Canada smuggled copies across the border. Beach also had an offer from the publisher Mitchell Kennerly, who knew a ship captain willing to smuggle thirty copies a month from France.

DOMESTIC DISTRIBUTION

In America, booklegged copies of *Lady Chatterley*, the majority of which were domestically produced, but which included copies of European pirated editions, the Paris Popular edition, and the Orioli, reached bookstores by truck. "The driver, always a different one, asked how many copies of *Ulysses*, or *Lady Chatterley's Lover*, were needed. The bookseller could have ten or more at $5, to be sold for $10" (Beach 180). "There are more bookleggers than bootleggers in America. . . . Shipments [reach] Los Angeles, Frisco, New Orleans, Atlanta, Boston. . . ." (Roth, *Frank Harris* 243-44). Talese (81-85) describes a small army of "secondary distributors," travelling the back roads of America with under the counter copies of magazines and books, depositing them with booksellers whose reputation as dealers in sexually explicit materials was locally well-established. These distributors operated from coast to coast. Frieda Lawrence met an "elegant young man from Hollywood" (Jake Zeitlin?) who "had sold enough Lady C's to keep [Edward Titus, publisher of the Paris Popular Edition] for a year" (MM 32).

Scheiner informs me that booklegging tactics prior to the late twenties differed from those employed during the 1930s. Perhaps the 1930s were characterized by more efficient modes of transportation and more resourceful personnel; organized crime infiltrated booklegging as it did

other illicit American transport activities in the late 1920s. After 1940, according to Scheiner, returning servicemen brought back enough cheap copies to flood the market by mid-decade.

Where might one find copies of *Lady Chatterley*? The novel could be sold openly in Paris. Brentano's, Galignani's (Caffrey 51, Ford 85) and Shakespeare and Company were favorites with tourists. In London, where, 1930, "everyone was reading Lady C" (MM 4), Charles Lahr and Edward Goldston (CL 1117, 1127), would have stocked the Orioli and the Paris editions, and possibly the piracies as well. Near Chancery Lane was "William Jackson" (Books) Ltd (Frederick C. Joiner and Alan Steele), who acted as agents for Orioli and who had extensive U.S. and Paris connections (Mumby and Norrie, 5th ed., 370-71)./4/ Important booksellers in America who were enemies of the "censor-morons" included Frances Steloff (Gotham Book Mart), the Holliday Book Shop (CL 1104) and Harry Marks (all of New York; see Ford 28, 85), Horace Townsend, (Philadelphia; see *New York Times* 25 Jan. 1930: 1), Williams (Boston), Ben Abramson (Argus, Chicago and New York), Covici McGee and Kroch and Brentano's (Chicago), Harry Schwartz and C. N. Caspar (Milwaukee), and, on the west coast, Jake Zeitlin and Stanley Rose. Both Scheiner and Legman, among others, praise The Gotham Book Mart and the Argus Bookshop as sources of interdicted literature. (See also Tebbel, III: 408, 642-43; Covington 48-50; Rogers 144-56.) Girodias (202) describes Steloff as "our single American trade client" for the Obelisk Press *Tropic of Cancer*; "streams of tiny orders . . . sometimes for six copies at a crack!" were received from her. Steloff also dealt with "William Jackson."/5/ It should be noted that U.S. scholars could legally petition for exemption of their indivivdual copies from the Customs ban (Paul 126). See Section 6, endnote 2.

The most likely practice for a "jolly roger" was to print about 1000 copies of "my lady" at a time and to offer large percentages of the printing to such respected establishments for sale to their sophisticated clients. In a letter to me (4 Aug. 1985), Gershon Legman states that in the thirties sexually-explicit books "would be sold in large batches to the main outlets for erotica." Such stores had another advantage than steady sales: if necessary, their owners could enlist the aid of influential clients or friends, who might wish to continue to purchase materials there and/or avoid being mentioned as clients. Thus, in case of police action, they might speak for the bookseller to local authorities./6/ This may cause smut-sniffers to steer clear. In any event, due to the threat the latter posed (or because the bookseller's financial health was not dependent on selling pirated editions), established, eclectic shops tended to trust only proven customers willing to pay the going prices for the books; only a small number of such collectors were needed (Hoffmann 292). However, the large audience for erotic literature meant a large market, and anyone for whom prurience fired a little

persistence could, rather easily, "ask around" to find
someone somewhere in town "in the know." That someone might
well be a book or cigar store owner who, having gained the
trust of a dealer with the stature of an Abramson or
Steloff, had invested in copies of one or more notorious
interdicted items. In Britain, the source might be the
proprietor of a "rubber shop." Such an establishment sold
condoms, trusses, medicines with allegedly aphrodisiac
powers, books exploiting curiosity about military discipline and esoteric diseases, and borderline erotica./7/

One supposes that, in the outlets noted above, in the
more modest and specialized antecedents of today's "adult"
bookstores, in general bookstores with special shelves or
sections for esoteric materials, or in drug or cigar
stores, interdicted erotica was kept out of sight of casual
browsers, who might have included Sumner-inspired smuthounds. The cigar store, serving an all-male clientele with
some of whom the owner could easily become familiar, was an
especially promising source of under-the-counter classics.
The following is a hypothetical example of how the process
might work at one of the more modest book, drug, or cigar
stores on the east coast of the U. S. (assuming Lawrence's
novel was in stock)./8/ Our *Lady Chatterley*-hunter would,
upon entering, encounter display racks of gossip, pin-up,
art, and nudist magazines, collections of bawdy jokes,
books about celebrities, and "racy" romantic or mystery
novels. Making his (most likely not her) way with the
proprietor beyond the shelves of *Broadway Brevities*,
Smokehouse Monthly, and Sam Roth's *Beau* or *Two Worlds*, he
might find himself in a small back room, where very quickly
he would be told the price of what the owner had on hand (a
price which might vary based on the owner's assessment of
the customer's financial status); he would pay in cash, and
would be asked to leave by the back door. On further
visits, our now-trusted customer could purchase photographs
of couples coupling in various positions, or scatological
and pornographic illustrated stories ("Tijuana Bibles"), or
32 or 64 page "readers." If he preferred full-length books,
there were (for example) privately printed tales of exotic
metamorphoses of men into sofas purchased by madams for
Parisian whorehouses, or variations on the secret lives of
Victorian and Gilded Age coxcombs, or the memoirs of
Casanova (black boards, linen spine, red endpapers, top
edge gilt, edges untrimmed--imitative of the fine collections in many a baronet's library). Erotica could be
consumed conspicuously, even if shelved with respectable
discretion (as in the example above, pp.2-3). The variety
of erotica's large appeal afforded ample room for bodice-
ripping hackwork, but also for some very good writing
indeed (Balzac, Schnitzler, Hunecker, Cleland, Rocester).
Such were the fish (some ephemeral, some immortal) with
which the unexpurgated *Chatterley* swam, during the years
when the printed word was considered influential enough to
corrupt./9/

Was most of the legally interdicted material purchased
in these back rooms (and under the counter), or by mail

order? Here British and American experience in the between-the-wars period differs. In Britain purchasing and selling interdicted books incurred less risk from police or self-appointed crusading moralists than in the U.S. This would explain why, as *Publishers Weekly* reported on 20 July 1935, specialists in compiling mailing lists of interested parties were flourishing in America. The most resourceful underground publishers--Jack Brussel, Samuel Roth, Ben Rebhuhn ("Obscene Book" 32) or Esar Levine ("Publisher Is Held" 17)--may have, in their brochures, discreetly found ways to suggest that they handled such "privately printed" material, while ostensively advertising borderline or acceptable erotica, which was published under imprints such as Faro or Panurge. Even without covert suggestion, such publishers could have received queries about the legally forbidden. Tony Gud, who was on the scene, thinks this was likely./10/

In fact, some of Roth's circulars and dust jacket advertisements list some works which were "privately printed" as well as many which bear imprints. His 1936 conviction for distributing obscene materials using the U.S. mails was based in part on the mail order sale of the notorious *Ananga-Ranga*./11/ Clearly, he was able to engage in interstate distribution of banned books using the U.S. mails (this was the charge on which he was convicted). *Chatterley* may have been among these in the early and mid-thirties (although I have seen no brochures advertising it), as it obviously was in 1929. In early 1930, Roth's parole (he had been convicted in 1928 of dealing in obscene materials) was revoked because he had continued to deal in banned books, including *Lady Chatterley* (see pp.26-27 below). Testimony from John Sumner and his agents (U.S. v. Samuel Roth 92-94) indicated that clients had written to his Golden Hind Press for copies, not of advertised books, but of *Fanny Hill* and *Chatterley*. Roth responded by requesting payment in advance, after which he arranged delivery of the books. He was doing the same after his prison experience in 1930. The back flap of the dust jacket of Gudaitis' *A Young Man About To Commit Suicide* (Faro 1931) contains a coupon for a reader to fill in, so that the publisher can send him/her notices of "Faro's Limited Editions." These may have been "privately printed" banned books; in the case of *Chatterley*, not Roth's expurgated edition (7.1-7.4), which could be legally mailed, but a complete edition, possibly one of the piracies Roth is suspected of issuing (1.6, 1.11, 1.12, 2.1).

Mail order sale of erotica may have been almost as important in America as direct dealing with retailers. C. J. Scheiner demurs. He thinks under-the-counter bookstore sales were quicker and less risky, and that therefore most banned books (as opposed to those which might reasonably, albeit not infallibly, be considered harmless by authoriti-es) changed hands through direct contact between client and bookseller. One could much more easily judge the earnest-ness of a man dealt with face-to-face than that of a

faceless mail order client. If Samuel Roth was not exactly
unique, there were not many with his industry and daring.
The publisher usually preferred to remain the shadowy
figure behind the middle-man. Gershon Legman cautions
(letter to the author, 4 Aug. 1985) that to distribute
through the mails or by common carrier (i.e., Railway
Express) was a federal crime. It is most likely, therefore,
that the largest number of copies were sold by storeowners
(or through the independent agents who travelled throughout
the country with boxes of material). But both methods were
important.

In purchasing the unexpurgated *Lady Chatterley*, either
through the mails or in person, one could not be sure which
edition he (she?) would get, but could be sure it would be
expensive. Therefore, physicians (including especially
dentists), lawyers, and professors were prime customers,
and these doctors and counselors could use their professional responsibilites as justification, as could stage or
screen stars./12/ Those with tighter pursestrings could
borrow their fill of banned books. Schwartz's Casanova
Bookshop had a lending library of erotic literature,
discretely offered to trustworthy customers (Schwartz,
Fifty Years 51). Sumner cited various urban outlets,
including drug stores, for loaning prohibited works (N. Y.
Society 1931: 13; 1934: 13; see PW 11 March 1933: 941 and
10 June 1933: 1887; *N.Y. Times* 27 Feb. 1933: 17, 1 Mar.
1933: 15). In just a month or so of loaning out *Lady
Chatterley* at 5 or 10 dollars, one could make more than the
40 or 50 that outright sale would generate. Therefore,
almost any dealer who sold banned books would be glad to
rent them, whether he could afford to do so only to trusted
customers or not. There was at least one "Society" dedicated to such rentals, The Esoterica Biblion on 44th Street
in Manhattan.

People who imagined their personal or professional
reputations endangered by visiting a store personally could
order various titles not only by mail order but by telephone, having first ascertained an under-the-counter
numerical listing and calling in the number of the book
desired; a messenger delivered (C.O.D.) for the stipulated
price (Rice 1). Such customers were probably steady,
well-trusted ones.

The most notorious case of prosecution for selling
Lady Chatterley involved the Dunster House Bookshop in
Cambridge, Massachusetts. In 1929 the New England Watch And
Ward Society entrapped the proprietor into selling a copy
of the novel. The latter testified that he had paid $5 and
sold for $15. He had acquired five copies to meet requests
from Harvard faculty (See PW 28 Dec. 1929: 2923). Because
there is evidence (see 4.1) that some booksellers may have
published their own editions of *Lady Chatterley*, it should
be noted that Dunster House had been a private press
publisher since 1919 (Ransom 172, 257), and did have the
resources to put out its own version. This is quite
unlikely, but had it done so, the owner would have been

loath to distribute it in Boston, plagued by Watch and
Ward. Although the latter was losing credibility, and
Dunster House enjoyed high repute, the case resulted in not
only the fining but the incarceration of the bookseller for
distributing obscene material (Bogart 374-76; see Commonwealth v. DeLacey, 271 Mass 327, N.E. 455 [1930]). *John
Bull's* oft-quoted characterization of *Chatterley* as a
"sewer of French pornography" (20 Oct. 1928: 11) reflected
a widespread desire to suppress the work. The large number
of piracies is directly related to the tenor of hostility.

Shortly after the Boston arrest, the district attorney
of Philadelphia, citing Dunster House as a precedent,
raided local bookshops. From a Rittenhouse Square establishment, he seized copies of *Lady Chatterley* along with
other books and prints, and immediately stigmatized the
material as "pure filth," "vile and rotten" (see *New York
Times* 25 Jan. 1930: 1). Publishers, the source of the
merchandise, were difficult to find and prosecute; the
bookseller and his hapless clerks made easy scapegoats.

And yet there was one enterprising and resourceful
publisher whom the authorities hunted down with a vengeance. The most notorious name associated with early
printings of *Lady Chatterley* was not that of a bookseller
but of the enigmatic New York poet, social critic, and
entrepreneur Samuel Roth, who by 1930 had earned the enmity
of men and women of letters as well as guardians of morals.
Sylvia Beach organized an international protest against him
in 1926, after his piracy of several chapters of *Ulysses*
(in expurgated form) in *Two Worlds Monthly*. From the late
twenties through the fifties, he served several jail terms
for publishing works considered pornographic. Hamalian
("Samuel Roth"), and Talese (111-31) have described his
career. His piracies included "editions expurgated and
unexpurgated" of *Lady Chatterley's Lover* (Cacici 246;
Hamalian, "Samuel Roth" 912); see below, pp.21-22, 26-27.
Some internal evidence regarding printing-house style is
given in the entries below for 1.6, 1.7, 1.11, 1.12, and
2.1. Lawrence's description of 1.6, the "dirty orange
pirate" (89), includes a mention of his signature "forged
by the little boy of the piratical family." C. J. Scheiner
reports book-trade gossip which acknowledges that Lawrence
might be correct. As for the illustrated edition mentioned
above (p.12), Lawrence's reference to its being published
in Philadelphia suggests a possible Roth involvement. He
was getting material published there at the time (*The Diary
of a Smut-Hound*, published under the imprint of "William
Hodgson" and written by Roth under the pseudonym of "Hugh
Wakem"). But no evidence can be produced of his involvement, and no illustrated edition which can be placed in the
late twenties has been located.

About the expurgated productions much more is known.
Secker's 1932 "authorized" abridged edition of *Lady
Chatterley*--whose plates parented over sixty impressions by
four different publishers--was clearly based on the 1930

"Samuel Roth" edition (7.1-7.4)./13/ Reproductions of two
pages (pp.26 and 93) of the latter, preserved in the
Nottingham University Library, contain holograph revisions
(by Laurence Pollinger and Martin Secker) appearing, along
with most of the rest of Roth's text, in the published
Secker version. Gerald Pollinger owns the original sheets
("this melancholy relic" [Pollinger 237]) bound in Secker's
moderate brown cloth and inscribed to Pollinger from
Secker. The Secker edition left untouched some parts of the
text which Roth had excised, but in other places made
deeper cuts. See the essay for Section 3, pp.66-69, and
Appendix V. The overwhelming similarity was quickly
recognized by reviewer Henry Hazlitt, who cogently analyzed
the effect of the expurgations (289-92); he also alluded to
the original perpetrator (Roth by this time was already
feuding with *The Nation*):

> And recently one particularly unscrupulous publisher
> brought the book out openly, bowdlerized to get by the
> censors, but with no acknowledgement either of the
> theft or of the bowdlerization. It was sold in many of
> the so-called respectable bookstores, whose owners,
> presumably, would have indignantly refused to handle a
> book in which the organs of the human body, and the
> act by which children are conceived, were described in
> good plain English, but who thought it quite all right
> to act as receivers of stolen goods. (291)

Of one dubious distinction Hazlitt cannot rob his enemy: it
was in the Roth-devised expurgations that *Lady Chatterley's
Lover* was most widely made available in England and America
from 1930 to 1959. The "sex-bouts" were replaced by asterisks (Roth sometimes added transitional phrases), euphemisms were used for four-letter words, and phrases referring
to various parts of the body from the neck to the knees
were either excised or recast (Roth must have studied
literary editors from Bowdler and Plumptre to Francis
Palgrave and Henry Morley). See Section 3 and Appendix V.
The blurbs, of course, turn one's attention elsewhere:

> . . . a thoroughly revised and beautiful edition that
> brings out . . . the sweet decadence which is eating
> away our society to the bone. . . . an exposition of
> the [modern] world in a state of decay (flyer preserv-
> ed at ICarbS).

> Luckily the few changes made, [sic] do not impede at
> all the deep, torrential stream of the narrative (dust
> jacket; see 7.2 below).

> The most daring and most famous of all modern novels .
> . . . Lawrence sees the rottenness of our life, but
> loved it nevertheless (blurb on back of dust jacket of
> Gudaitis' *Young Man About To Commit Suicide* [Faro,
> 1932])

Roth's claims for the narrative integrity of his
version may have originated in the agent Curtis Brown's

telling him, when the former queried Brown about authoriz-
ing "The Samuel Roth Edition," that Lawrence's own expurgations worsened the novel. Adelaide Roth remembers her
father telling her of this conversation./14/ The blurbs
speak to a post-depression mood of world-weariness and
decadence fashionable in the late twenties after a decade
of obsession with sexual experimenting (Allen, *Only
Yesterday* 164-65). This was part of the zeitgeist which
Lawrence understood and deplored, and for which he had an
imaginative solution. Roth knew how to exploit this mood,
and, after Beach's International Protest against him, he
shared its cynicism (see also the essay for Appendix 1,
pp.238-40). Whether or not he understood how this advertising adulterated Lawrence's message as overtly stated in
several (unexcised) passages is immaterial.

If Roth was the first to exploit openly the novel's
sexual explicitness, he was also the first to discover how
openly and legally to publish a version for the general
reader. One way to explain his marketing strategies is to
say that he isolated and focussed on those aspects of the
book--the narrative, the tabooed sexual desires, the strong
silent hero, the curious and vulnerable heroine--which
homogenize it with popular romance. The blurbs addressed
the first two items and the dust jacket illustration and
frontispiece the final two. See especially 7.3 and 7.4
below. Thus he was the first to attempt to mass-market *Lady
Chatterley's Lover* (but without the technical resources to
succeed; for print runs see below). In 1960 Richard
Hoggart, in his introduction to the newly-decensored
Penguin edition, felt the need to refute the criticism (see
pp. 64-65, 130-32 and endnote 1 of Section 7) that *Lady
Chatterley* was basically a pulp romance. The William Faro
edition, due to Roth's bold advertising, initiated the
process which encouraged this impression. The style and
content of his blurbs seem almost quaint in comparison with
those of the Authorized Editions (Section 3) or the U.S.
and British post-censorship paperbacks of the past quarter-
century (Sections 5 and 6). But the theory and purpose is
the same.

"The Samuel Roth Edition" was undertaken (soon after
his release from prison in September 1930; see below, p.26)
for the shrewdest and most ambitious of commercial motives. Assuming correctly that a revision "for the general
reader" could "become one of the sensations of the publishing season," he proceeded without either authorization or
advertisement. His justification, given in his bizarre
anti-semitic tract *Jews Must Live* (189-219), was that a
larger publisher might get wind of the project and an-
ticipate his edition:

. . . without as much as a newspaper announcement of
my intention, [I] threw the book on the market where
it became a favorite overnight. My best hopes for it
were realized. For not only did the book sell rapidly;
it was granted on all sides that I had accomplished my

intention without real injury to the book either as a
sustained story or as a work of art. (193)

Roth's song is partial, but his rationale for the
abridgement must be admired. First, he wished to keep John
Sumner from harassing him. Second, his postal-order
operation required extensive use of the U.S. mails (using,
presumably, lists compiled during his ventures with the
periodicals *Two Worlds Monthly* and *Casanova Jr's Tales*).
These lists were especially important since some advertising possibilities (including the *New York Times*) were
closed to him after the protest against his *Ulysses*
serialization (Hamalian, "Samuel Roth" 896). They also
potentially provided an expanded audience of readers,
especially women, who might be embarrassed to purchase even
borderline or literary erotica in a book, cigar, or drug
store. Third, he wanted to place his books in retail
outlets as well (not only the barbered *Chatterley* but the
more problematical titles in his Faro list [see below]). In
case of legal troubles, penalties were less serious than
the federal offense incurred by operating through the
mails.   Perhaps Roth had his eye on the Gotham Book Mart,
where, the proprietor stated, Lawrence was always the
best-selling author (Rogers 144, 200). It may be that Ms.
Steloff, and other booksellers as well, were too wary of
Roth's notoriety since his Joyce piracies to carry any
production which might be traced to him. On the other hand,
if Roth was involved as deeply as is thought in producing
unexpurgated piracies, she (and others) may have needed
these productions to satisfy requests of some very good
customers. There was another incentive for doing business
with Roth. While other, unexpurgated, editions of *Lady
Chatterley* would be sold under the counter, Roth alone in
1930 (until the Knopf 1932 Authorized Edition) sported a
version which could be shelved, with other Lawrence titles,
for display ("Lawrence Book Revision" 7), as Hazlitt
ruefully acknowledges. Thus it could easily reach those
tolerating only a "revised edition" in their homes. Roth's
net spread wide.

Even without accepting Roth's own words on the matter,
one must assume that his well-conceived distribution
strategies were lucrative. Offering an expurgated *Lady
Chatterley* to a variety of outlets created for him a larger
audience than the other pirates enjoyed. None of this
company (with the possible exception of Roth's parasitic
imitator Nesor, discussed below) identify themselves with
imprints, as the proprietor of William Faro was still
pointing out a generation later, in a resolute self-defense
before the Kefauver Commission investigating in 1955 the
effects of pornography on juvenile delinquency (United
States. *Hearings*. 201-04). Roth's piratical competitors of
the 1930s must have relied exclusively on "bookleggers,"
back-room lending libraries, or furtive telephone sales.
The Faro *Lady Chatterley*, due to Roth's industry, would
have needed to trust the wholesaling strategies of smugglers and retailing practices of booksellers to a much
smaller extent.

One senses beneath the moral indignation of Hazlitt's review grudging acknowledgement of well-rewarded cunning. Frieda Lawrence also alludes to Roth's success, and to some extent parrots his advertisements, in her dust-jacket blurb to the Knopf version: "the only authorized edition . . . after all the expurgated pirated editions . . . even in its revised form it has all the beauty of the original edition, and [suggests] to the greatest possible extent, the original's strength and vigor" (see 17.9 below). It may well have been Roth's industry and success that forced Secker and Knopf to put forth the text they did in 1932.

Roth defends his edition and its reception in an acerbic introduction to his dramatization of the novel ("By Way Of Explanation" 8-11). His revision was done purely for "business": recent prison sentences for publishing interdicted erotica had left him in financial straits. "A man in charge of the biggest retail business in the western world" read and approved of his galleys (and acknowledged their inoffensive character), but shunned the book itself (i.e., he displayed it but instructed salesmen to discourage purchasers) because of Roth's reputation as a pirate./15/ Roth reproduces the text of a letter to the *New York World* (dated 26 Oct. 1930), a reply to the *World* article which appeared the day before. Attempting to refute the article's assertions, Roth declares that he will pay Frieda Lawrence royalties "as soon as she authorizes our edition," that 2,000 copies have been sold at $3 each, that "I was never arrested for being found in possession of a copy of *Lady Chatterley's Lover*," that his revised version is not bowdlerized, and that "at least three smaller publishers" had recently considered issuing an expurgated *Lady Chatterley* but did not know how to improve the work's readability. The accuracy of these statements vary. Roth surely knew more about William Faro's profits and prices than the reporter, whose negative attitude toward Roth was evident throughout the piece. The latter had made and was making extensive efforts to get Mrs. Lawrence's authorization-- after publication. She wrote to Edward Titus on 15 July 1931 that she had met and did not wish to deal with Roth, "an awful man" (MM 33), although he offered her £1,000 (MM 34). A jury acquitted Roth on 10 Sept. 1931 of selling unexpurgated editions of *Chatterley*./16/ As for the state of his Faro text, it would have been bad business to admit the bowdlerization (for which see Section 3, pp. 66-69).

In a letter to the bookseller Harry Schwartz (who said the Faro impressions "sold by the thousands"), Roth says that he spoke to Frieda Lawrence and held her royalties in escrow, against the time when she requested them. He writes that she had almost authorized his edition, but that "at the last minute" Knopf offered a larger sum./17/ The state of Lawrence's will at the time (she might not have been able to give anyone authorization), as well as whatever other publishers may have said about Roth, may also have been factors. "I do not think it honest," he concluded, "to

accuse me of any unfairness to Lawrence, or to his wife" (Schwartz, *Book-Collecting Racket* 24-25).

I can identify four impressions of the Roth abridgement (Legman estimates that these were printed in runs of between 3,000 and 5,000 copies; Adelaide Roth states 2,000-3,000), at three (for the first two impressions), two, and one dollar respectively. In 1931 and 1932 William Faro issued a dramatization by Roth's own hand and two anonymous sequels, both also Faro imprints: *Lady Chatterley's Husbands* and *Lady Chatterley's Friends.*/18/ These works detail Connie's peripatetic exploits in various glamorous European wateringholes. Making only oblique references to bedroom gymnastics, they use Lawrence's plot as a convenient paradigm for a tease. See the essay for Appendix 1, pp. 237-43.

As C. J. Scheiner states, Roth virtually invented the business of selling borderline erotica by mail order. The categories mentioned below (see Appendix IV for a fuller list) replicate those under which contemporary erotic booksellers shelved their front-room stock as described above. William Faro offered gossip or scandal books such as the quite notorious *The Strange Career of Herbert Hoover* and the less successful *Intimate Journal of Rudolph Valentino*; columnist Mark Hellinger's *Moon Over Broadway* was a steady seller. There was titillating romance (*Woman's Doctor*, a novel about abortion, and *Loose Shoulder Straps*) and racy memoirs (*Memoirs and Mistresses*; *Colors and Odors of Love*). Roth himself expurgated a 1927 collection of "racy" stories for men's smokers, *Anecdota Americana* (see Legman, *Horn Book* 485-86). In addition one could order "remainders" such as *Sacred Prostitution and Marriage by Capture* (reprinted by Roth as a "Big Dollar Book") and *Padlocks and Girdles of Chastity*. Another staple were erotic (but suitably barbered) classics: Mendes' *Lila And Colette* and Mirbeau's *Celestine: The Diary of a Chambermaid* (which, with *Chatterley*, comprised the "Modern Amatory Classics"). *Venus In Furs* was offered with the dramatization of Lawrence's novel as part of a series of "Ardent Classics." The Sacher-Masoch title may raise eyebrows, but *The Nation* in 1933 ("Purity" 194) noted it as one of the "more esoteric classics [which] are quite openly displayed in drug-store windows." Finally, there were (purportedly) shocking but true tales: *The Man Who Killed Kitchener* and *The Private Life of Frank Harris*. The magnitude of this enterprize strongly indicates that for a few deep-depression years it was successful, and a larger source of revenue than an underground edition of a banned and booklegged work, done in a small printing as stated above. In a time of financial rough seas and broken weather, it is remarkable that it remained afloat at all; without the expurgated *Lady Chatterley* as a flagship, it may have fairly drowned its ambitious captain. William Faro Inc. ceased publishing in 1932, perhaps because of general financial problems (see the Nesor episode below), but also because of the Knopf authorized expurgated *Chatterley* (for which see Section 3, p. 61). This would have drained off

sales of Roth's edition.

The authorities were always quick to line Roth up in their sights. Six sources suggest that his colleagues thought he had been arrested for either publishing or selling *Chatterley* (Pringle 463; Hamalian, "Lady Chatterley Spectacle" 11; *New York Times* 1031; "Lawrence Book Revision Fought" 7; Wood 31; Ryan 47). The facts, however, are difficult to specify. On occasion, Sumner and his agents tried but failed to attain a conviction, for all they could come up with were the expurgated *Chatterley* and other innocuous Faro titles. Roth himself places one Sumner-inspired raid in May 1931, and states the books to have included the expurgated *Lady Chatterley* (*Jews* 194; see also *New York Times* 8 May 1931: 4). The attorney's brief for this trial states the books to have been *Eastern Shame Girl* and *Celestine* (Adelaide Roth, letter of 7 Dec. 1988). The charge, selling obscene material, was dismissed. As stated above, he won a case involving similar charges in October of the same year. Nor was Roth ever sentenced for *publishing* the Lawrence novel.

Roth's FBI files show that he was arrested in 1928, and jailed in 1930, for selling obscene materials. These included the "grossly obscene" *Lady Chatterley's Lover*. The words are those of the Post Office Chief Inspector, testifying at Roth's Fall 1929 trial (18 [parenthesized here and in the next four paragraphs are page numbers in the stenographer's minutes of United States v. Samuel Roth, C-53-79]). Roth was on parole at the time as a result of the 1928 arrest; that parole was revoked. After four months at Welfare Island, he was immediately remanded to Moyamensing Prison in Philadelphia, where he served two months for selling to a Philadelphia bookseller a copy of *Ulysses*. Presiding Judge John C. Knox, in revoking parole, stated that "The Golden Hind Press was undoubtedly engaged in the sale of *Lady Chatterley's Lover*, an obviously obscene book. This is amply shown by the correspondence introduced into evidence" (transcript of Judge's decision, U.S. v. Roth, p.2). The details relevant to *Lady Chatterley* (the unexpurgated version, of course) are as follows:

1. On October 5, 1929, carrying a search warrant, Sumner and some associates seized approximately 3000 books at the storage loft of Roth's Golden Hind Press, 160 Fifth Ave. At this address Sumner found *Lady Chatterley* (17-18, 27, 32, 78); Roth's own piracy, A. Roth states (possibly entry 1.11 below). He also discovered, together with other titles, part of a print run of Roth's piracy of Sylvia Beach's *Ulysses* (U.S. v. Roth 25-28; *New York Times* 5 Oct. 1929: 22; PW 2 Nov. 1929: 2176; Ryan 43-47; Adelaide Roth, letters to the author, 16 Aug., 7 Sept. and 7 Dec. 1988). On Oct. 4, police arrested Roth and one of his salesman at 122 Fifth Ave, where The Golden Hind Press had its offices. Here the authorities impounded copies of Lawrence's *Sun*, *Oscar Wilde Three Times Tried*, Clement Wood's *Flesh*, Huneker's *Painted Veils*, Huysmans' *Down There*, Schnitzler's

Hands Around, Yama, In A Moorish Harem, and *Amatory Experiences of a Surgeon* (13-15, 17, 23, 25-30; A. Roth, letter of 7 Dec. 1988).

2. A Post Office inspector had "entered into correspondence with the Book Auction [run by Roth and his wife] and The Golden Hind Press" for a three-month period beginning in November 1928. The inspector "did secure [apparently by mail] . . . a book *Lady Chatterley's Lover* . . . . " (17).

3. On Oct. 4 Roth's brother Max was arrested in the Woolworth Building, where (using an alias) he was attempting to sell to two men various interdicted volumes, including *In A Moorish Harem* and *Lady Chatterley's Lover*. One of the men, a lawyer (to whom Max Roth sold a copy of *Chatterley*) turned out to be a special investigator for John Sumner and the other individual was a New York police officer (*New York Times* 5 Oct. 1929: 22; U.S. v. Roth 24).

4. Finally, Sumner himself produced an order blank and a bill of sale for another copy of the novel, on which had been written "please deliver to bearer." Sumner, who confiscated many letters and memoranda on Oct. 5, had apparently helped himself to the item after spying it on a desk at 160 Fifth Ave. (92-93). It indicated that Roth had sold this copy after requesting (and receiving) the money in advance, writing to his correspondent (probably a Sumner agent) that "we cannot keep such an account with safety, either to you or to us, so please send us your check or money order for $18."

This information is in part at variance with that of William Ryan, a student of, and close friend of, Roth during the publisher's later years, who wrote me (15 May 1988) that "by Roth's own testimony in his unpublished autobiography, he served two concurrent six-month terms, 1929 through 1930, the first in New York for selling *Lady Chatterley's Lover*." Possibly, Samuel Roth, writing a quarter-century after the events he is recalling, exaggerates the role of the Lawrence novel in Judge Knox's revocation of his parole (the decision was handed down 27 January, 1930).

On Sept. 11, 1931, Mrs. Roth was acquitted of selling copies of the unexpurgated *Chatterley* by mail order. However, her defense was that she was ill at the time, and that her husband had conducted the business (*New York Times* 10 Sept. 1931: 22; 11 Sept. 1931: 14). This tends to confirm, not contradict, Roth's own culpability.

Roth's real *Chatterley* nemesis was not Sumner or the authorities but business associates who pirated his abridgement and issued it under the Nesor imprint (see 8.1-8.3) in the early thirties. The most plausible account places this pirating in 1932. After a series of complex legal maneuvers, creditors—according to Roth (*Jews* 207-19) —exploited his lack of ready funds by attaching his Faro

assets (unbound sheets kept at a bindery pending payment by Roth) and selling several Faro titles. These works were reset and issued in a bewildering variety of bindings, possibly because one of the creditors owned the bindery. In a letter to Prof. Hamalian,/19/ Gershon Legman states that the execrable *Jews Must Live* was "issued about 1934 as a revenge against Nesor (Rosen? [unidentified]) who had got hold of some of his copyrights, or at least so he explained it." Roth himself told Hamalian ("Samuel Roth" 903) that Nesor evolved into Crown publishers. Roth does not mention a Rosen, but Arnold Levy has suggested that the creditors may have used the name of someone with little connection to the enterprise, as Roth himself had used in "William Faro" the slightly altered name of a cellmate of his at New York's Federal House of Detention in 1929 (Roth *Jews* 190-91). Rosen may have been one of the partners who comprised Nesor. Gershon Legman has written to me (letter of 6 Sept. 1988) that the name "Nesor" implies the surname of a binder, Gene Rose, who had previously worked on Roth's editions (issued without imprint) of interdicted, highly-prosecutable, pornography.

Whatever the case, the episode is another indication that Roth's abridgement was lucrative. Nesor's text is identical to the Faro, but it has obscured the nature of the abridgment by omitting many of the asterisks that Roth used to indicate excisions.

Roth's vengeance, an attack on his own people, was a despairingly self-destructive one. The Nesor episode must have been as traumatic for him as the international *Ulysses* protest, seven years before. His nemesis, in stealing his titles and thus his audience, did more than take bread from his mouth. In treating him as he had Joyce and Lawrence, Nesor threatened his very identity. Also, they were perhaps the key factor in forcing William Faro out of business, although the depression economy and the Knopf "Authorized Edition" of *Chatterley* helped. One other powerful con-tributing factor was the notoriety over the Hoover exposé. In late 1931 the New York Supreme Court issued an injunc-tion against further sales of the book, which its publisher stated had gone through 10 impressions (Hamalian "Samuel Roth" 904). Roth continued to publish borderline erotica until 1936, when (see endnote 11) he was convicted of distributing obscene materials.

The Royal imprint on 9.1 below strongly suggests Crown (Emmanuel Wartels, founder). This edition (reset with text identical to Nesor) may have appeared in 1936 or 1937, the early days of Crown, when the fledgling distributor-pub-lishers needed a title which would sell, and when, not coincidentally, Roth was in prison. The kind of *Lady Chatterley* market that Roth had discovered was anything but ephemeral. See Section 3 for its exploitation by British and American hardcover and paperback reprint publishers.

In encouraging the prurient to try *Lady Chatterley*,

Roth was hardly alone; nor do his books illustrate the only
appeals of this kind. The more sumptuous of the underground
editions defiantly exploit the contemporary reader's obsession with sex by portraying it as a nightmarish force.
Entry 3.1 below, for example, attractively printed in
California for an unknown publisher by Lawton Kennedy,
offers vignettes of a priapic demon forcing naked victims
into a transparent vial to create for him a baby--an
attempt to titillate and to produce *épater le bourgeois*
erotica for the gentleman's library./20/ The style suggests
Wallace Smith; see his illustrations for Ben Hecht's
Fantazius Mallare (Chicago: Colvici-McGee, 1922). That such
a connection between sex and evil adorns Lawrence's novel
about the holiness of the body is ironic. His letter to
Willard Johnson disapproving of the Hecht text and Smith
drawings appeared in expurgated form as a review in the
University of California's *Laughing Horse* (CL 725-27).
Fantasius Mallare's bitter, furtive attitude toward
sexuality and the body revolted Lawrence, as did Clifford's
statement in Chapter 6 from which the illustrator of item
3.1 (Smith?/21/) might have taken his cue: "all the love-
business might as well go. I suppose it would if we could
breed babies in bottles." Lawrence would not have been
amused by the display of a copy in a recent N.Y. Public
Library exhibition on censorship.

Wallace Smith had a varied career as adventurer (with
Pancho Villa in Mexico), author of *Bessie Cotter* (novel
about a Chicago prostitute which was banned in England in
1935 and published by Kahane in Paris), illustrator (Boden-
heim's *Blackguard*, Hecht's *The Florentine Dagger*, and his
own stories), and screen-writer from 1929 until his death
in Hollywood in 1937 (Hansen 289-301, Craig 94-95, PW 6
Feb. 1937: 746). Smith's eclectic talents, cosmopolitanism,
and experience with erotic literature and illustration
would have made him a attractive choice for either Kennedy
or the publisher of this California edition. And Smith
might have seen the job as a way of "getting his own back"
on Lawrence, who characterized his *Mallare* drawings as "so
completely without irony, so crass, so strained and so
would-be" (CL 725).

The "Silver Phoenix" edition (4.1) is unillustrated,
but its binding, red and black title page, running heads,
decorated initials and typography make it a sumptuous item
for an "in-the-know" gentleman's erotica collection.
Lawrence himself noted the skillfully printed (and very
expensive) "close replica" he found in Paris (1.10): the
"real thing" was possibly titillating simply to possess--
especially if the author's (forged) signature completed the
illusion.

The descriptions below indicate that piracies existed
in a large variety of formats for different but overlapping
kinds of markets. There were the early, awkwardly photolithographed facsimiles of the Orioli (some with black
boards and red endpapers) which circulated widely, and the
attractively printed volumes (1.7, 2.1.a, 3.1, 4.1) for

those who were pleased to regard themselves as discriminating connoisseurs whose aristocratic good taste might itself justify their owning the volume. Some of these works, if published by affluent booksellers for their best customers in the medical and legal professions, may have seen shorter and less frequent press runs than the others, have been loaned out less, and have cost even more to purchase. The latter would have been especially true if they were the only copies a seller had on hand at the moment. There were also the Roth abridgements for those mail order customers far from a big city, and/or too respectable to allow "dirty words" a place in their libraries. Another format was the cheaply printed pocket or bedside throwaways (resembling the European authorized editions, and competing with them in bookstalls throughout Europe, Asia, and the Orient) for tourists or servicemen (11.1, 12.1-14.2). For the latter, during World War Two or the Korean Conflict, the novel could offer a kind of rite of passage, or a *vade mecum*: "Lady, you ain't been in the army at-all without you've read *Lady Chatterley's Lover*" (Sara 47). Bookleggers and pirates were not alone, but certainly important, in cultivating and satisfying this variety of curiosities. It is impossible to ascertain exactly how wide their collective net spread; however, it was noted at the 1960 Old Bailey decensorship trial that every one of the three-dozen witnesses "had at one time or another read an underground copy" (Bedford 138).

One notorious early edition has been shown by Craig Munro (222-35) not to be a piracy, although Frieda Lawrence believed it to be. However, Lawrence wanted this printed in London to coincide with the exhibition of his paintings at the Warren Gallery in 1929. The Bloomsbury bookseller Charles Lahr and the owner of the Mandrake Press (P. R. Stephensen; publisher of *The Paintings of D. H. Lawrence*), were involved. In fact, the book was not printed until about a month after the author's death (Davidson's bust, which its frontispiece reproduces, was done on March 2, 1930). Booksellers have referred to this volume as the "third edition" because of the (false) printer's statement (verso of the title page). This, and the date, Munro shows to have been an attempt to conceal from vigilant London authorities the identity of Stephensen and Lahr.

Not surprisingly, Pino Orioli refers scathingly to this edition:

> While British Censorship was making all this fuss about a few copies of *Gian Gastone* (in the Lungarno Series) printed in Florence, a large edition of *Lady Chatterley* was being printed in London on English paper. I have examined this edition. The text is identical with the Florentine edition and it has the Florentine imprint, but the price is lower; and no wonder, considering the bad production of the book. The Home Office people seem to have been unaware of the existence of this edition, which was printed

and circulated under their noses.(238)

His bitterness is occasioned partly by the fact that, ironically, the piracy flourished while his Lungarno edition of *Gian Gastone* (second in the series, after Lawrence's translation of *The Story of Dr. Manette*) led to his prosecution in Florence. The complaint originated with British authorities. They felt that this English translation contained obscenities, and that the work would be imported into England and become available in Soho and Charing Cross bookstores. The Italian courts cooperated, and police had impounded Orioli's stock of the title. The appearance and notoriety of his own edition of *Lady Chatterley's Lover* had motivated this British action; its real purpose was to prevent British authors from privately publishing "indecent" works on the continent (Aldington, *Pinorman* 113-15; Orioli 236-37).

A letter from Frieda Lawrence to Edward Titus (MM 28-29) suggests that only in January 1931 did she learn of the "third edition." She reports Orioli's anger, suggests that the publishers offered her some part of the profits, and swears to Titus that she will try to "stop them," a course of action which Titus felt quixotic: "it is best to let things alone." In later letters, she attempts to refute rumors, and Titus' suspicions, that she had indeed taken money from Lahr (MM 34-35).

A set of sheets from the "second edition" (1.1.c), with pencilled marginalia by Stephensen, was offered for sale by Sotheby's in London on 10-11 July 1986. It is this set (bound in the cloth used by Lahr and Stephensen) to which Munro refers (234-35, note 12) as printer's copy.

ENDNOTES

1. I have seen these letters in a manuscript file, entitled "Orioli--Misc.," at the Humanities Research Center, University of Texas.

2. in a questionnaire returned to the author, 1 March 1986 and an interview, 5 June 1987. As I stated in the Acknowledgements section, p. xii, Mr. Scheiner's expertise was essential to me in writing this essay.

3. in a questionnaire returned to the author, undated but March 1986.

4. Norrie tells of Steele receiving "forty [mail]bags" of LCL in 1929 from Orioli, which if the date is correct, most probably was the paperbound "second edition" (1.1.c) since only 200 copies of the hardbound issue remained by September 1928 (see Section 1, endnote 4), and since Steele had refused to sell his copies of the latter in July of that year. Late in that month he wrote to Orioli, cancelling "William Jackson's" order, fearing the novel's iconoclasm

was too extreme to make it a safe item to stock (Squires
189). Squires states that Lawrence's friend Enid Hilton
picked up these copies from Steele's shop and secreted them
until a more willing seller could be found.

5. Dr. Karen Burke LeFevre, who is researching a study of
The Gotham Book Mart, so stated in a letter to me, 11 July
1987.

6. John Sumner raided the Gotham Book Mart in 1931 and
1936. He was unsuccessful in his prosecutions. His boorish-
ness, and the importance of Ms. Steloff's shop as a
resource for the popularization of contemporary literature,
were pointed out by *Publishers Weekly*. See PW 1 Feb. 1936:
604-05; 21 Dec. 1935: 2229; 14 Nov. 1931: 2234. See also
Rogers 144-46; Tebbel III: 642-43. Compare this deferen-
tial attitude to the statements made in newspapers and
journals about Samuel Roth (and colleagues such as Esar
Levine) throughout the period: see PW 14 Jan. 1933: 124;
Pringle 463; "Lawrence Book Revision" 7.

7. I am grateful to Patrick Kearney (letter of 15 Aug.
1988) for information on these establishments. Alec Craig
mentions them, without explanation, in *Above All Liberties*
(London: Allen and Unwin, 1938): 116.

8. C. J. Scheiner is my main source for the information in
this section, which I obtained in a personal interview with
him on 5 June, 1987. Some of this information was corroborated by Richard (now deceased) and Adelaide Roth
(Samuel Roth's son and daughter) in a personal interview on
3 July 1987, by Allan Wilson in a questionnaire returned 27
July 1987, and by Tony Gud, who published with Roth in the
1930s, in a questionnaire returned to me on 7 July 1987. I
am indebted to Ms. Kugel, Mr. Gud, Mr. Wilson and Mr. Roth
as well as to Mr. Scheiner, and, for information regarding
English practices, to the London booksellers Louis Bondy,
Anthony Rota, and W. Forster.

9. This state of affairs continued, of course, until the
book was de-censored, and might even have had some effect
on the decision. See Craig (161) regarding the confiscation
of a group of books including *Chatterley* in 1953, and
Moore's plea in his anthology of Lawrence's writings on
Sex, Literature, and Censorship for liberation of the novel
from its status as an expurgated "pharmacy paperback" (20,
26).

10. In a letter accompanying a questionnaire returned to
the author, 7 July 1987.

11. Roth was convicted of distributing obscene materials in
1936, the books in question being indiscriminately characterized by the assistant U. S. attorney as the "filthiest"
he had seen (*N. Y. Times*, 4 Sept. 1936: 2, col. 4). Some of
the evidence, as Roth's FBI files show, consisted of
brochures advertising his own version of Ellis's *Kanga

Creek, Hanley's *Passion Before Death*, Rhys Davies' *Bed Of Feathers*, Norman Davey's *Penultimate Adventure*, the *Ananga-Ranga*, Twain's *1601*, and Lewishon's *The Case Of Mr. Crump*. The first four bore an imprint (Black Hawk); the last three did not, and had been officially proscribed. *The Ananga-Ranga* was "privately printed" (although the copyright page identifies The Golden Hind Press, a generic title for Roth's operations rather than a specific imprint). The Lewishon title carries a false imprint, "John Henderson." Roth served three years.

12. A. Roth told me (interview of 3 July 1987) that Samuel Roth's mailing list included not only many physicians and dentists (easy to find in telephone books and other sources), but the membership of the Harvard and Yale clubs. Her biography of her father, when published, will discuss her father's publishing business in detail.

13. Adelaide Roth possesses a copy of an unexpurgated piracy (1.11) in which offending passages on approximately 50 pages are circled in pencil. The passages range from single four-letter words to entire sexually-explicit paragraphs. The book is from her father's (Samuel Roth's) library.

14. So stated in the interview with the author of 3 July 1987.

15. The man may have been Arthur Brentano himself, or possibly Joseph A. Margolies, whom Tebbel (III: 149) identifies as an expert book retailer, the buyer for Brentano's in the late twenties and sales manager for Covici-Friede in 1929. Margolies, like Roth born in eastern Europe and educated in the U.S., was president of the American Booksellers Association in 1944 (PW 27 Jan. 1945: 449). Whomever it was may simply have wanted to make his customers aware of the fact that the version they were purchasing was barbered.

16. See *New York Times* 4 Sept. 1936: 7, col.4. See also United States. *Hearings* 203.
    Roth's failure to obtain Frieda Lawrence's permission did not stop him on at least one occasion from representing himself as having secured copyright for *Lady Chatterley's Lover*. In 1957, when the French film of the novel was being distributed in this country, a New York theatrical producer attempted to stop the film from being shown, on the grounds that, as the *New York Times* stated (3 May 1957), "he had bought the screen rights in 1936 from a Samuel Roth, who, he said, had purchased the rights to the D. H. Lawrence novel from the English author's estate."

17. The Library of Congress Copyright Office contains no records for the Faro *Lady Chatterley*, although Roth did file for copyright on most Faro titles (but not for other reprints of erotic classics).

18. Roth registered the first of these in the copyright office in Washington with his own name as author. For the second title there is no copyright application. Both books, however, were most probably ghost-written. Scheiner, in a note to me of 16 July, 1986, recollects that *Lady Chatterley's Husbands* was done by Anthony Gudaitis, whose *Young Man About To Commit Suicide* was a Faro imprint. See pp. 240-41. He stated that *Lady Chatterley's Friends* was the work of Clement Wood, who published various works with Roth. For internal evidence regarding *Friends*, see A3.1 in Appendix I.

19. This letter is dated "First Day Of Spring 1976"; I am grateful to Prof. Hamalian for showing it to me.

20. I am indebted to Mr. Albert Sperisen of San Francisco (letter postmarked 19 July 1986) for the identification of Kennedy as printer (not publisher) of this edition.

21. The style of Smith's signed drawings in the following books (which he wrote as well as illustrated) suggest in the treatment of small human figures, gnarled hands, and shadows the line drawings in 3.1: *The Little Tigress*, *On The Trail In Yellowstone*, and *Are You Decent?* All were published by Putnam's, in 1923, 1924, and 1927 respectively. The same stylistic qualities are evident in Hecht's *The Florentine Dagger* (NY: Boni and Liveright, 1923). The similarities between 3.1 and *Fantasius Mallare* involve the sinuous, *art nouveau* line with strong vertical rhythms (like those of Clara Tice and Harry Clarke), the initials decorated with naked bound human figures, and the monstrous hands sinisterly forcing human beings into contorted positions.
   In 1924 Covici published Hecht's *The Kingdom of Evil: A Continuation of the Journal of Fantasius Mallare*, with twelve illustrations by Anthony Angarola. The drawings are similar in theme and setting to Smith's, but they differ from those in 3.1 in that Angarola uses white space as alternatively background and foreground.

BIBLIOGRAPHICAL DESCRIPTIONS (PHOTOLITHOGRAPHED PIRACIES [see also 1.3.b above])

[A Piracy of the Paris Popular Edition]

1.5   T.p. as 1.2, but with last two lines excised.

(6 7/8 x 4 15/16): unsigned, 192 leaves; pp.[4], I-VIII, 1-365,[366].

CONTENTS: as 1.2 above, save pp.[2] not present.

TYPOGRAPHY: Text: 35ll.(p.123), 135 x 90mm. 10ll.=39mm.

PAPER: smooth white wove unwatermarked. Thickness .05mm. Total bulk 11.7mm.

BINDING *(but possibly rebound)*: green morocco-grain cloth. Gold-stamped on spine: [thick-thin rule] | LADY | CHATTERLEY'S | LOVER | [rule] | D. H. | LAWRENCE | 1935 | [thin-thick rule]. Blind-stamped border, upper and lower covers. Plain white endpapers. All edges trimmed.

NOTE: For a reset piracy of 1.2, see 10.1 below.

COPY EXAMINED: Forster Coll.

[The "dirty orange pirate"]

1.6   LADY CHATTERLEY'S LOVER | D. H. LAWRENCE | PRIVATELY PRINTED | 1928 [1.1 in an open face display type. Cf. R 392, Castellar]

(9 1/16 x 6"): [1]^2 [2-92]^4, 186 leaves; pp.[4] 1-365, [366], [2].

CONTENTS: p.[1]: t.p. p.[2]:blank. p.[3]: blank. p[4]: This edition is limited to | Five Hundred copies | No. . . . By [forged signature]. pp.1-365: text. p.[366]: blank. pp.[2]: blank.

TYPOGRAPHY: Text: 35ll. (p.175), 157 x 104mm., 10ll.=44mm. Face: 2.5(2x)mm.

PAPER: smooth white laid, chainlines approx. 20mm. apart. Watermark: LOUVAIN BOOK [device: closed book, upper cover showing, on which is "R" in border; scrollwork running along spine and fore-edge] |. Thickness .1mm. Total bulk 20.1mm.

BINDING VARIANTS: (1): calico (T302) cloth, medium orange (C53). Stamped in black on upper cover: Lady Chatterley's

Lover | D. H. Lawrence |. Very light bluish green (cf.
C162) paper spine label printed in yellowish brown. In
border of one rule: LADY | CHATTERLEY'S | LOVER | [decora-
tion: antique vase or cup] | D. H. | LAWRENCE |. Top and
bottom edges trimmed; fore-edge partly trimmed. Endpapers
same as rest of book. (2): Morocco-grain (T402) cloth,
very dark green (cf. C147). All edges partly trimmed. Endpapers white, smooth, bear same watermark as rest of
book.

NOTE: *A Propos* (89): "dirty orange pirate." Lawrence said
this appeared "in London, from New York, towards the end
of 1928."
    Concerning the forged signature in some copies, see
Essay for Section 2, p.20.
    Probably it was this piracy that Huxley had in mind
when he wrote Lawrence, 12 Dec. 1928, of "the spurious
edition, for which [Paris booksellers] ask 5000 francs"
(Smith 304). The price is incredible; could it have been
500? See p.12 above.

COPIES EXAMINED: Var. (1): Forster Coll.; NO/P-1; CU-S;
personal; Var. (2): PU (spine label chipped away).

["Funereal"]

1.7 Lady Chatterley's Lover | [vignette: American eagle,
· · · · · · · · · · · · · · · · · · · · ·

wings spread, laurel wreath and arrows at its feet, 8
stars (around head, left wing, and tail), surrounded by
wreath in strong reddish brown (cf. C40) open 10 mm. at
top; tied ribbons at bottom] | D. H. LAWRENCE | 1928

(9 5/8 x 6 1/4"): [1]^4 [2]^8 [3]^4 [4]^{12} [5-23]^8 [24]^4 [25]^2,
186 leaves; pp.[6], 1-365, [366].

CONTENTS: p.[1]:blank. p.[2]: LADY CHATTERLEY'S LOVER | D. H.
LAWRENCE | [eagle vignette] | PRIVATELY PRINTED | 1928 |
[preliminary title page; ll. 1,2 in open display type,
except A in CHATTERLEY] |. p.[3]: This edition is limited
to | Five Hundred copies.| No....... | By........ p.[4]:
blank. p.[5]: t.p. p.[6]:blank. pp.1-365: text.
p.366: blank.

RUNNING HEADS: appear over thin, thick rules. Versos: LADY
CHATTERLEY'S LOVER Rectos: D. H. LAWRENCE

TYPOGRAPHY: Text: 35ll.(p.143): 156(172) x104mm. 10ll.=43mm.
Face: 3(2x)mm. Typeface: preliminary title page: l.1,
cf. R392, Castellar. See 1.6 and 7.4.$_2$ below. Limitation
statement: Bembo(?), R35. Running headlines in Castellar.

PAPER: smooth white wove unwatermarked. Thickness .11mm.
Total bulk 21.8mm.

BINDING VARIANTS: (1): morocco-grain cloth (T402b), black.
Upper cover: blind-stamped border and (in upper center)
scallop-outlined ornamental decoration (27 x 22mm).
Gold-stamped on spine: [2 rules] I LADY I CHATTERLEY'S I
LOVER I [short rule] I D. H. I LAWRENCE I [2 rules] I
[profile of eagle's head, 6mm. high] I. Lower cover undecorated. Edges lightly trimmed. White wove endpapers.
(2): as (1) save: patterned paper endpapers: diagonal
strips 5-10mm. apart: vivid yellow, grayish reddish brown,
dark reddish brown, grayish olive green.

NOTE: In *A Propos* (89-90), this is described as "funereal,"
"gloomy," "sinisterly high-brow," "like Captain Kidd with
his face blackened, reading a sermon to those about to
walk the plank." Lawrence states it was selling in the
US [in 1929] for between 10 and 50 dollars. He mentions
"two title pages"; See CONTENTS above, p.[2].
    The underdotting in this t.p. transcription indicates a
gothic typeface. The blank space under the first line is
not symbolic; it is required by the word-processing
program employed.
    The monotype cutting of the Bembo typeface occurred in
1929 (Jaspert 20).

COPIES EXAMINED: Var.(1): TxU (copies 1 & 3). Var.(2): TxU
(cop. 2)

1.8   as 1.7 save:

(9 1/2 x 6 1/4"): [1]^4 [2]^2 [3-6]^4 [7-25]^8 [26]^4 [27]^2, 186
leaves; pp.[6], 1-365, [366].

PAPER: Thickness .1mm. Total bulk 22.4mm.

BINDING: as 1.7 above, var. (2).

COPY EXAMINED: personal

1.9   as 1.7 save:

LADY CHATTERLEY'S LOVER I BY I D. H. LAWRENCE I PRIVATELY
PRINTED

(9 5/16 X 6 5/16"): [1-46]^4, 184 leaves; pp.[2], 1-365,
[366].

CONTENTS: p.[1]: t.p. p.[2]: This edition is limited to 300
copies I Each one numbered I From one to three hundred I
NO ...... I By .... pp.1-365: text. p.[366]: blank.

TYPOGRAPHY: Typeface: ll. 1 and 3 of t.p. in Broadway (R484);
limitation st. in Commercial Script (R307: a flowing
script); running heads in Castellar (R392).

PAPER: Thickness .1mm. Total bulk 20.2mm.

BINDING VARIANTS: (1): as in 1.7, var. (1). (2): calico-grain
cloth (T302), dark grayish reddish brown (C47). Decoration

and stamping as 1.7. Edges lightly trimmed. White wove
endpapers. (3): Linen-grain (T304) cloth, deep red (C13).
Gold stamped, upper cover: inner and outer border of two
rules each. In each corner of inner border is a floral
decoration (three branches of three-petaled flowers, seen
edge-on, on background of small dots). No lettering. Spine
and lower cover blank. Top and fore-edge trimmed; bottom
edge lightly trimmed. Plain smooth white endpapers.

NOTE: In the OkTU copy [Var.(1)], a wedge-shaped portion of
    p.89 did not register, due to the leaf being creased
    during imposition so that not p.89 (sig. 9_4v) but its
    verso received part of the impression meant for p.89. When
    the sheet was perfected, the leaf was arranged correctly
    so that p.90 has the correct text on it, but this is
    printed over the wedge-shaped section of text meant for
    p.89. Therefore, despite the printer's discovery of the
    error, the pirate-printers and/or publishers decided to
    sell this copy.
        The Broadway typeface was cut in America in 1929
    (Jaspert 256).

COPIES EXAMINED: Var.(1):OkTU. Var.(2):personal. Var.(3):
    CU-S

    ["close replica"]

1.10   LADY CHATTERLEY'S LOVER I BY I D. H. LAWRENCE I
       PRIVATELY PRINTED I 1928

(9 x 6 5/16"): π^2 1-23^8 186 leaves; pp. [1-4], 1-365,
[366], [2].

CONTENTS: p.[1]:half-title. p.[2]: This edition is limited I
    to 1500 copies.I This is number _____ I. p.[3]: t.p.
    p.[4]: blank. pp.1-365: text. p.[366]: blank.
    pp.[2]: blank.

TYPOGRAPHY: 35ll.(p.145): 156 (172) x 105mm. 10ll.=44mm.
    Face:3(2x)mm. Typeface: t.p. in Bruce Old Style(?) (R173,
    Modern ["Didone"]). DIN 1.34 (Modern Neo-Classical). Spine
    label: ITC Century(?) (R175).

PAPER: smooth white wove unwatermarked. Thickness .12mm.
    Total bulk 24.8mm.

BINDING: Var.(1): paper covered boards, deep yellowish pink
    (C30). Cream paper label on spine: in border of one
    rule: LADY I CHATTERLEY'S I LOVER I D. H. I LAWRENCE I.
    Top edge trimmed, others lightly trimmed. Head and tail
    bands in red and yellow. Plain white endpapers. Dj: plain
    linen-grain cloth (T 304); light grayish yellowish brown
    (C 79). Var. (2): as (1) except that paper-covered boards
    are moderate brown (C58) and the volume is quarter-bound
    in calico (T302) cloth, grayish reddish brown (C46). Top

edge lightly trimmed; others untrimmed.

NOTE: Roberts App.I.B.I & p.110. *A Propos*: "close replica."
   Copies in the Brit. Lib. (copy 1), at Ill. St., Arizona,
   and Harvard have the words "Imprimée [sic] en Allemagne"
   rubber-stamped near the bottom of the title page. It seems
   likely that in *A Propos* Lawrence has confused this volume
   with another, reset, piracy (2.1.a below?); possibly, he
   meant by "printed not photographed" that the text was
   well-printed rather than presenting a faint, partly
   smeared register and uneven margin. At any rate he seems
   to have created a ghost: "European pirated edition of
   fifteen hundred, produced by a Paris firm of booksellers,
   and stamped *Imprimé en Allemagne* . . . . printed, not
   photographed . . . a very close replica of the original,
   but lacking the signature and it gives itself away also by
   the green-and-yellow silk edge of the backbinding [head-
   band?]. This edition is sold to the trade at one hundred
   francs, and offered to the public at three hundred, four
   hundred, five hundred francs. Very unscrupulous booksellers are said to have forged the signature. . . ."(90).
      The Harvard (Houghton Lib.) copy has the numeral "5" in
   the limitation statement changed by hand to "8".
      I would like to make a feeble conjecture regarding the
   involvement of Frank A. Groves in this edition. On 8 March
   1929 Lawrence wrote to Huxley that Groves ("of the
   Libraire du Palais Royal--Groves and Michaux") would
   publish the authorized Paris edition of LCL (CL 1137).
   Squires states (195-96) that "in mid-March [Lawrence]
   learned that Groves had apparently launched a pirated
   edition of the novel printed in Germany."

COPIES EXAMINED: Var.(1): TxU(dj); OkTU; OX/U-1; LO/N-1 (2
   copies; one stamped); MH-H. Var. (2): DLC.

   [Black Moire Cloth: Samuel Roth, publisher?]

1.11   LADY CHATTERLEY'S | LOVER | BY | D. H. LAWRENCE |
       Florence | PRIVATELY PRINTED | 1928 [ll. 1,2,6 in red]

(9 5/8 x 6 1/4"): [1]^2 [2-23]^8 [24-25]^4, 186 leaves; pp.[4],
   1-365, [366], [2].

CONTENTS: pp.[1-2]: blank. p.[3]: t.p. p.[4]: blank.
   pp.1-365: text. p.[366]: blank. pp.[2]: blank.

TYPOGRAPHY: Text: 35ll.(p.200), 156 x 103mm. 10ll.=44mm.
   Face: 2.5 (2x)mm. Typeface: title page in Granjon (R66);
   spine label in Old Style No. 2 (R69).

PAPER: smooth white laid; chainlines approx. 25mm. apart.
   Watermarked: WARREN'S | OLDE STYLE [l.1 arranged in
   semi-circle] |. Thickness .1mm. Total bulk 20.04mm.

BINDING VARIANTS: (1): moire fine rib (T 102bd), black. Cream

spine label, bordered in red (vertical rules intersected
by horizontal rules 6mm. from top and bottom edges of
label): LADY | CHATTERLEY'S | LOVER | BY | D. H. LAWRENCE
|. Deep reddish orange (C 36) endpapers. Edges lightly
trimmed. (2): as (1) except dotted-line cloth (T 108);
moire pattern present.

NOTE: T.p. very similar to 2.1 below. The linotype version of
Granjon dates from 1928 (Jaspert 108).

COPIES EXAMINED: Var.(1): personal (copy 1). Var.(2): OkTU;
ICarbS

1.12.a as 1.11 save:

$[1]^2$ $[2-24]^8$; leaf size, no. leaves, pag. as 1.11

PAPER: unwatermarked, otherwise as 1.11.

BINDING VARIANTS: Var. (1): as 1.11, var. (1), but endpapers
strong purplish red (C255). Fore and bottom edges
untrimmed; top edge lightly trimmed. Headband in red.
Var. (2): as 1.11 var. (2).

NOTE: The copy at ICarbS is in the dust jacket used with some
modifications in advertising copy for at least three
impressions (see 7.1, 7.3, 7.4 below) of the Roth expurgated edition. Apparently, a bookseller or owner placed
it there. The dj is described s.v. 7.1 below, but it
should be noted here that the jacket forced (it does not
really fit) onto the present volume differs from that of
7.1 in that the coupon on the front flap and the advertisement on the back cover are not present here. These are
the only places on the dj where the publisher is identified, which he could not afford to be for 1.12. The
front-flap statement of abridgement (part of the blurb)
could (if indeed the publisher issued it with 1.12) serve
to deceive smuthounds.

COPIES EXAMINED: Var.(1): personal (copy 2); TxU. Var. (2):
ICarbS

1.12.b as 1.11 save:

Leaf size, collation as in 1.12.a.

PAPER: unwatermarked. Thickness .06mm. Total bulk 13.6mm.

BINDING: as 1.12.a except: cream paper spine label: [rule] |
D. H. Lawrence [swash w] | Lady [swash y] | Chatterley's
[swash y] | Lover | Privately Printed [swash y] |
[rule]. Endpapers strong red (C12). Top edge trimmed.
Fore edge lightly trimmed. Bottom edge untrimmed. Head
band in red.

NOTE: the swash letters on the label are similar to those on
some copies of *Lady Chatterley's Husbands*, John Hamill's
Strange Career of Mr. Hoover under Two Flags, *The Intimate*

Journal of Rudolph Valentino, Clement Wood's *Warren Gamaliel Harding: An American Comedy*, Wood's *Herbert Clark Hoover: An American Tragedy*, and the third impression of Roth's abridgement of *Chatterley* (see 7.3 below). All were published in 1931-32 by Samuel Roth under his Faro imprint, but were probably prepared by a New York job printer who may have served many other publishers. It is possible that Roth's brother Max did the presswork.

COPIES EXAMINED: PPRF; OkTU

RESET PIRACIES [see also 25.10, 25.12, 26.1 and 27.5 s.v. Continental Editions; 18.1 s.v. Authorized Abridged Editions]

  [published by Samuel Roth?]

2.1.a LADY CHATTERLEY'S I LOVER I BY I D. H. LAWRENCE I *Florence* I PRIVATELY PRINTED I 1928 [ll. 1,2,6 in red]

(8 7/8 x 6 1/4"): [1]^2 [2-23]^8, 186 leaves; pp.[4], 1-365, [366], [2].

CONTENTS: p.[1]: blank. p.[2]: This edition is limited I to One Thousand copies. I No.......... p.[3]: t.p. p.[4]: blank. pp.1-365: text. p.[366]: blank. pp.[2]: blank.

TYPOGRAPHY: text: 35ll. (p.215), 150 x 102mm; 10ll. = 43mm. Face: 2.4 (1.4x)mm. Typeface: Transitional (DIN 1.24, Modern Baroque). Century Expanded (R114).

PAPER: smooth white wove. Watermark: Utopian [in script] above device of two sets of scales enclosed by long-necked bottle. Thickness 1.3mm. Total bulk 25.7mm.

BINDING: strong purplish red (C255) paper covered boards. Paper carries pattern of chain and wire lines. Paper label [moderate gray (C265)] on spine. [Enclosed in rectangular border of broken red lines:] *D. H. LAWRENCE* [swash D, H, L] I [floral decoration in red] I *Lady* [swash L] I *Chatterley's* [swash C] I *Lover* [swash L] I [floral decoration in red] I PRIVATELY I PRINTED I. Lines 3-5 in non-flowing decorative script]. Top and bottom edges trimmed; fore edge untrimmed. Moderate gray (C. 265) endpapers with laid paper pattern to match boards. Top edge stained gray. Head and tail bands in red and white.

NOTES: reset in a slightly different typeface than the first edition (with inverted commas for quotations as per English and American practice), and with some of the typographical errors corrected, but with type set so that each page carries the same number of lines as does the

Florence (Orioli) printing. T.p. very similar in typeface and arrangement to 1.11, 1.12. The spine label script is identical to that used on the labels of several books published by Roth, as described s.v. 1.12.b above.
See Roberts Ap. IB.III.

COPIES EXAMINED: personal; PU; ICarbS; TxU; DLC (rebound); MH (rebacked)

2.1.b as 2.1.a save:

t.p.: ll. 1,2,6 printed in black.

Leaves measure 8 13/16 x 6 1/4".

PAPER: Unwatermarked. Thickness .09mm. Total bulk 19.2mm.

BINDING: very light greenish blue (C171) paper-covered boards, with chain (approx. 40mm apart) and wire line pattern; endpapers to match boards. Black head and tail bands. All edges trimmed.

NOTE: p.[2] blank (no limitation statement).

COPIES EXAMINED: personal; OkTU; NcU; ICarbS; MH (rebacked)

[demon vignettes]

3.1 *Lady Chatterley's* | *Lover* | *By* D. H. Lawrence | [vignette of naked demon with streaming hair from ears to below shoulders, ending in beaked serpents' or birds' heads. He carries a long handled spoon in his right, and a crucible in his left, hand.] | *Privately Printed* | Florence, Italy | 1928

(9 1/2 x 6 3/8"): [1-19]^8 [20]^4, 156 leaves; pp.[4], [1-2], 3-307, [308].

CONTENTS: pp.[4]:blank. p.[1]:t.p. p.[2]:blank. pp.3-307: text. p.[308]:blank.

TYPOGRAPHY: Text: 41ll.(p.163), 160 x 103mm. 10ll.=38mm. Face: 3(2x)mm. Typeface: Transitional (DIN 1.24, Modern Baroque). Century Old Style (R62).

PAPER: Yellowish-white (C92) ribbed "laid," chainlines approximately 25mm apart. Watermark: *Linweave* [script L] *Text* [script T] [device: script L and T interwoven] (America) |. Thickness .13mm. Total bulk 21.5mm.

BINDING VARIANTS: (1): calico-grain cloth (T302), pale reddish purple (C244), cream paper label on spine: [thick rule, 2mm] | [thick rule, 1mm.]| *Lady* | *Chatterley's* | *Lover* | [diamond] | D. H. LAWRENCE | [thin rule] | [thick rule, 1mm] | [thick rule, 2mm.] |. Top and fore edges

partly trimmed, bottom edge trimmed. Endpapers: grayish
white (C153), with pale blue (C185) hair-vein pattern.
Cf. T1104. Head and tail band in red. (2): as (1) save
spine label: light greenish yellow (C101); endpapers
white laid paper.

DECORATIONS [see also title page transcription]:
  a. Line drawings, chapter headpieces:
    CH. II: demon, penis erect, holds transparent vial under
    left arm, pointing to man whose right arm is raised in
    protest. Naked male and female figures cower at demon's
    feet in postures of enervation or despair.
    CH. VI: demon lifts naked male and female by the hair
    towards the top of the vial; one man pulls on the woman's
    left ankle. Nude figures lie at demon's feet.
    CH. X: demon forces with index finger of right hand the
    male into the neck of the vial as female tries to push the
    male away. Male figures stand or lean against demon's
    ankles.
    CH. XIV: vacant-eyed demon, half-reclining on left elbow,
    mixes with his wand the vial half-full of liquid in which
    are swirled two or more human figures; the earth beneath
    him burns with islands of flame.
    CH. XVIII: vial, half-full of bubbling liquid, rests
    against penis and thighs of demon. Against his left flank
    are four naked females, three of whom fondle babies. Four
    men sit, stand, or walk at his right. At the end of his
    wand the demon holds for inspection a human child, curled
    in foetal position.
  b. Chapter titles within thin rules, over which is a
    decorated border of undulating fig leaves, white on black
    background.
  c. 7-line initial, first word on novel. Letter "O" formed of
    two naked figures, each body arched in semicircle, arms of
    each bound to ankles of the other.

NOTES: Remarkable are this volume's good press work and
    design, and its sinister pictorial narrative.
        Displayed (#254) at the NY Public Library 1984 censor-
    ship exhibit; t.p. reproduced in *Censorship*. NY: Oxford
    U. Press, 1984: 117.
        Albert Sperisen identifies the printer as Lawton
    Kennedy of San Francisco (fl. 1933-1960); the publisher
    remains unknown. Mr. Sperisen was a partner of Kennedy in
    the Black Vine Press, circa 1935-37. If the illustrator
    was Wallace Smith (or if it was a conscious imitator),
    Lawrence's dislike of his illustrations for Hecht's *Fan-
    tasius Mallare* would have been known in California (where
    Smith was active from 1929 to 1937) from the Lawrence
    review in *Laughing Horse*. See p. 29 above.
        There are unbound copies at TxU and OkTU; these may
    have been distributed by bookleggers who shipped them in
    this way to avoid detection.

COPIES EXAMINED: Var.(1): TxU; OkTU. Var.(2): CU-S.

[silver phoenix on spine]

4.1 DAVID H. LAWRENCE | [rule] | LADY CHATTERLEY'S | LOVER |
     [dot] Printed complete | from the original manuscript |
     [Lawrence phoenix] | [ll.2,5 and last two words in l.4
     in red]

(9 7/16 x 6 3/8"): [1]⁴ [2-27]⁸ [28]⁴, 216 leaves; pp. [4],
[I-IV], V-VII, [VIII], [1-2], 3-417, [418], [2].

CONTENTS: pp.[4]:blank. p.[I]: half-title. p.[II]:blank.
     p.[III]: t.p. p.[IV]: blank. pp.V-[VIII]: untitled and
     unattributed introd., purportedly by DHL, on probable
     response to novel's themes and diction. p.[1]: section
     title. p.[2]: blank. pp.3-[418]: text.

RUNNING HEADS: versos: [thick, thin rule] | LADY [dot]
     CHATTERLEY | [thin, thick rule] |. rectos: [thick, thin
     rule] | D [dot] H [dot] LAWRENCE | [thin, thick rule] |.

TYPOGRAPHY: Text: 32ll. (p.153): 164 x 101mm. 10ll.=46mm.
     Face: 3(2x)mm. Typeface: Garamond Stempel(?), R92. Tran-
     sitional. DIN 1.24, Modern Baroque. Three-line decorated
     initial (white on black background) begins each chapter.

PAPER: rough white wove unwatermarked. Thickness .12mm. Total
     bulk 31mm.

BINDING: calico-grain cloth (T302), very deep red (C14). On
     spine, silver-stamped: D. H. LAWRENCE | [rule] | LADY |
     CHATTERLEY'S | LOVER | [Lawrence phoenix] |. White rough
     unwatermarked endpapers. Top edge stained v. deep
     red. Top edge trimmed, others partly trimmed. Red head
     and tail bands.

NOTE: In a letter to me (4 Aug. 1985), Gershon Legman states
     that this was published by Chicago bookseller Ben Abramson
     "about 1930." Pages V-[VIII] contain the text of "Dirty
     Words," purportedly by Lawrence but unattributed here.
     Roberts (App. II.II) states that this essay first appeared
     in the U.S. in 1931.

COPIES EXAMINED: TxU; personal

     [p.149: "Grammer" for "Grammar"]

5.1 LADY CHATTERLEY'S | LOVER | BY | D. H. LAWRENCE |
     FLORENCE | PRIVATELY PRINTED | 1928 [ll. 1,2,6 in red]

(8 3/16 x 5 1/2"): [1]² [2-11]¹⁶, 162 leaves; pp.[4], 1-315,
[316], [4].

CONTENTS: pp.[1-2]:blank. p.[3]:t.p. p.[4]:blank. pp.1-315:
    text. p.[316]:blank. p.[4]: blank.

TYPOGRAPHY: Text: 38ll.(p.168): 162 x 102mm.; 10ll.=41mm.
    Face 2.5(1.5x). Typeface: old face; DIN 1.13, modern
    Renaissance. R4, Pastonchi(?). T.p., chapter titles, and
    spine label in Futura(?): R 254. Sans Serif (DIN 1.52,
    Modern Linear).

PAPER: Smooth white laid. Impressed with chainlines ap-
    prox. 30mm. apart. Watermark same as 2.1.a above. Thick-
    ness .1mm. Total bulk 18.1mm.

BINDING: Var. (1): calico-grain cloth (T302), strong red
    (C12). Cream paper label on spine: [decoration made of
    short horizontal and vertical rules intersecting at 90°
    angles] l Lady l Chatterley's l Lover l [v-shaped decorat-
    ion] l D. H. Lawrence l [decoration as in l.1] l [ll.2-4
    in red]. Top edge trimmed. Fore and bottom edges lightly
    trimmed. Plain white endpapers.Var. (2): as (1) save
    moderate blue (C182) cloth. Var. (3): as (1) save moderate
    green (C145) cloth.

NOTE: There are transcription and spelling errors in the
    text, two of which occur on p. 149: "haughty" for mighty;
    "Grammer" [sic] for "Grammar."
        The futura typefaces originated circa 1927-30 (Jaspert
    277).

COPIES EXAMINED: Var.(1) and (2): personal. Var.(3): TxU

        ["Chatterly"]

6.1   LADY CHATTERLY'S [sic] l LOVER l BY l D. H. LAWRENCE l
       PRIVATELY PRINTED l 1928

(9 x 5 7/8"): [1]^2 [2-11]^{16}, 162 leaves; pp.[4], 1-314, [6].

CONTENTS: pp.[1-2]:blank. p.[3]:t.p. p.[4]:blank. pp.1-314:
    text. p.[6]:blank.

TYPOGRAPHY: text: 40ll. (p.172): 174 x 102mm; 10ll.=43mm.
    Face: 3(1.5x)mm. Typeface: Transitional (DIN 1.24, modern
    baroque). Gloucester Old Style (R126). T.p., ll.1-2 in
    Parsons(R. 239).

PAPER: smooth white wove unwatermarked. Thickness .1mm. Total
    bulk 19.3mm.

BINDING VARIANTS: (1): embossed paper boards, very dark red
    (C17), with black veined marbleized pattern. Fine morocco-
    grain cloth (T402b) quarter-binding, deep red (C13).
    Plain white endpapers. All edges trimmed. Black-stamped on

spine: [two rules] | LADY | CHATTERLY'S [sic] | [short
rule] | LOVER | [two rules] |. (2): as (1) except paper
label on spine: [2 rules] | LADY | CHATTERLY'S [sic] |
LOVER | [short rule] | D. H. LAWRENCE | [2 rules] |.
ll. 2-4 in Plantin (R39)? Top edge stained red. (3): as
(1) but black cloth boards, calico grain (T.302). Gold
stamping on spine, as (1). (4): as (1) except paper-
covered boards of dark green, cf. C146? (same marbleized
pattern) and paper label as (2). (5): as (1) but calico-
grain (T302) cloth with marbleized pattern (moderate
yellow green[C136]; dark greenish yellow[C103]). Quarter
bound in calico-grain cloth, deep green(C142).

NOTE: Italicized words in Orioli ed. reproduced in bold.
Probably produced from letterpress, or relief plates.

COPIES EXAMINED: Var.(1) and (5): personal. Var.(2): TxU,
personal. Var.(3): OkTU. Var.(4): CU-S

["The Samuel Roth Edition"]

7.1   BY D. H. LAWRENCE | [double rule] | LADY | CHATTERLEY'S
| LOVER | [double rule] 1930 [double rule] | WILLIAM
FARO, Inc. [ll. 2, 6 and initial letters in ll. 3-5 in
red]

(9 3/8 x 6 1/8"): [1]^2 [2-21]^8, 162 leaves; pp.[4], 1-313,
[314], [6].

CONTENTS: p.[1]: t.p. p.[2]: Revised, 1930 | by | William
Faro, Inc. p.[3]: blank. p.[4]: *Modern Amatory Classics* |
NUMBER ONE |. pp.1-313: text. p.[314]:blank. pp.[6]:blank.

TYPOGRAPHY: 37ll. (p.165), 160 x 101mm., 10ll.=42mm.
Face: 3(2x)mm. Typeface: De Vinne (R177); Modern (DIN
1.34, Modern Neoclassical). T.p.: ll. 3-5(title) in
Broadway (R484). Spine label in a similar sans serif
display face.

PAPER: Smooth white wove unwatermarked. Thickness .14mm. Total bulk 24.1mm.

BINDING: Linen-grain (T 304) cloth, Black (C267). Endpapers
(1.3mm) medium red (C15). Cream paper label (82 x 33mm.):
LADY | CHAT- | TERLEY'S | LOVER | LAWRENCE |. Top edge
trimmed, others partly trimmed.
Dj: front cover: drawing of woman whose head, in
profile, leans on man's shoulder. Occupies lower two-
thirds of cover. Moderate red, signed: A. 30 K. | Skillin
|. LADY | CHATTERLEY'S | LOVER | D. | H. | LAWRENCE | [ll.
1-3 on upper third of cover]. Mod. red, in the face used
for spine label. Background in light orange yellow
(C70). Behind figures are diagonal strips of moderate
olive green(C125), running from left to right at 20°
angles to the vertical. On spine, in fat-face display

type, mod. red: LADY | CHAT- | TERLEY'S | LOVER | LAWRENCE
|. Back cover, in red: Ad for *Celestine* (compares novel's
"picture of the decadence of French society" to LCL's
description of "the decadence of English society") and LCL
("in a thoroughly revised and beautiful edition that
brings out, even more cogently than before, the sweet
decadence which is eating away our society to the bone").
Front flap, in red: price ($3) and blurb, below which is
coupon for brochure announcing "Faro's limited editions."
Rear flap blank.
    For another state of this dj, see 1.12.a, NOTE.

NOTE: See Roberts Ap. IB.IVa.

COPIES EXAMINED: ICarbS (2 copies, one in dj)

7.2   As 7.1 save:

[1-20]^8, 160 leaves; pp.[4], 1-313, [314], [2].

CONTENTS: p.[1]: blank. p.[2]: *Modern Amatory Classics* |
    NUMBER ONE |. p.[3]: t.p. p.[4]: Revised, 1930 | by |
    William Faro,Inc. pp. [1-313]: text. p.[314]: blank.
    pp.[2]: blank.

PAPER: Thickness .12mm. Total bulk 22.1mm.

BINDING: as 7.1 except: fore-edge untrimmed, bottom partly
    trimmed.

COPIES EXAMINED: PManM; TxU; MH (rebound); personal; NO/P-1

7.3   as 7.1 save:

LADY | CHATTERLEY'S | LOVER | BY | D. H. LAWRENCE | THE
SAMUEL ROTH EDITION AS ORI- | GINALLY PUBLISHED BY WILLIAM |
FARO, Inc. NEW YORK CITY, 1931 [ll. 1-3,6-8 in red]

(8 1/2 x 5 9/16): ftpc. tipped in, + [1]^2 [2-11]^{16}, 162
leaves.

TYPOGRAPHY: Text: 37ll.: 158 x 101mm. 10ll.=46ll.
    Face: 2.5(1.5x)mm. Typeface: t.p. in sans serif (cf. R248,
    4-line Block Gothic).

PAPER: Thickness .1mm. Total Bulk 17.8mm.

BINDING: Var. (1): Paper spine label: in border of 2 rules,
    horizontal rules intersecting vertical 4mm. from top and
    bottom of label: *Lady* | *Chatterley's* | *Lover* | [vine leaf]
    | LAWRENCE |. ll. 1-3 in non-continuous script. Label
    measures 53 x 29 mm. Smooth white endpapers. Top edge
    trimmed, others untrimmed. Var. (2): as (1) save cloth is
    rib (T102), deep blue (C179).
    Dj: Drawing on front in deep brown. Lettering in bluish
    black (C193). Background in light grayish yellowish
    brown. Strips are deep yellow brown. Back cover: ad for

Hamill's *Strange Career of Mr. Hoover*. Lettering on spine and back cover in deep yellow brown. Front flap: blurb ("This is the famous Samuel Roth edition . . . even better than the original. . . ."). Above blurb: $2.00. Rear flap blank.

FTPC.: Line and wash drawing on clay paper surrounded by border of one rule, 174 x 129 mm. Caption: LADY CHATTERLEY I. Reproduced in half-tone of dark grayish yellowish brown (C81). Delicately featured woman, hands clasped in front, faces viewer. At her back is a murky sky and a spacious rural landscape of hills, hedgerow, coal mine, and cottages. Monogram: A.-[19]30-K. SKILLIN I.

NOTES: See Roberts App.IB.IVb. The frontispiece represents a corroboration of the illustrator Mahlon Blaine's characterization of the Roth expurgations as "The Louisa May Alcott Edition" (see essay for Section 3 below [p. 66]). The back of the dust jacket of Anthony Gudaitus' *Young Man About To Commit Suicide* (NY: Faro, 1932) contains a blurb for the publisher's *Lady Chatterley's Lover* which states "now in its seventh large printing." Since the price is $2.00, I assume the book to be the 1931 version, which from the copies seen I can only identify as the third impression.

COPIES EXAMINED: Var. (1): personal(dj); OkTU (dj); TxU. Var. (2): Forster Coll.

7.4.$_1$ LADY I CHATTERLEY'S I LOVER I BY I D. H. LAWRENCE I [floral ornament] I The Samuel Roth Edition as Originally I Published by William Faro, Inc.; I New York City, 1932

(8 15/16 x 5 15/16"): Ftpc., tipped in, + [1-20]^8, 160 leaves; pp.[6], 1-313, [314].

CONTENTS: pp.[1-2]: blank. p.[3]: half-title. p.[4]: blank. p.[5]: Revised, 1930 I William Faro, Inc. pp. 1-313: text. p.[314]: blank.

TYPOGRAPHY: Text: 38ll.(p.83), 163 x 41mm. 10ll.=46mm. Face: 3(2x)mm. Typography: t. p. in Caslon Old Face #2 (R59). Spine label in Sans Serif. Ftpc. caption in a modern face (Bodoni Book [Linotype], R154?)

PAPER: smooth white wove unwatermarked. Thickness 1.3mm. Total bulk 25.4mm.

BINDING: Var. (1): ribbed cloth (T102), medium olive green (C125). Cream paper label on spine: [type ornaments] I [rule] I LADY I CHATTERLEY'S I LOVER I [type ornament] I LAWRENCE I [rule] I [type ornaments] I. All edges trimmed. Smooth white endpapers. Var. (2): as (1) except ribbed cloth, moderate olive brown (C95).
    Dj, state 1: front: strips in gold, background in pale orange yellow (C73). Drawing, lettering, front flap, spine as 7.3. Back: THE BIG DOLLAR BOOKS I Which Sold for From

$2 to $20 in Other Editions (list of 25, including the 2
parodies. Begins Roth's *Private Life Of Frank Harris*, ends
Wood's *Herbert Clark Hoover; An American Tragedy*.)

FTPC: as in 7.3, but in medium-gray tones.

NOTES: Roberts (see Ap.IB.IVc) records frontispieces in the
    1930 and 1931 impressions, but I have seen them only in
    7.3 and 7.4.
        By 1929, reprint publishers had made one dollar a
    prevalent price, and many bookstores had "dollar
    counters." (Tebbel, III: 210-11).
        There may be a "Samuel Roth Edition" with the Big
    Dollar imprint. Some Faro titles (for example Wake's
    Sacred Prostitution And Marriage By Capture [New York |
    THE BIG DOLLAR BOOK COMPANY | 1932]) were so issued.
    Others carry a copyright statement attributed to this
    company. Ms. Adelaide Roth has informed me (letter of 19
    Jan. 1988) that there is no such LCL imprint in her
    father's library; nor is one listed in the OCLC data base.

COPIES EXAMINED: Var.(1): personal, ICarbS. Var.(2): OkTU
    (dj, state 1)

7.4.$_2$ As 7.4.$_1$ save:

t.p.: ll. 1-3 in slightly opened display type.

TYPOGRAPHY: as 7.4.$_1$ except typeface: ftpc. caption in
    Hollandse Mediaeval(R3)?, spine label in Bodini Book
    (Linotype), R(154)?

BINDING VARIANTS: (1): linen-grain (T304) cloth, light gray
    (C264); edges, endp. as 7.4.$_1$. Spine label as 7.4.$_1$ but
    typeface different (see typography) and ornament between
    title and author shaped differently. (2): as (1) but
    net-grain cloth (T118), deep purplish blue (C197). (3):
    as (1) but calico cloth (T302), vivid green (C139). (4):
    as (1) but rib (T102) cloth, light bluish gray (C190); no
    ornament after title (1.5) on spine label.
        Dj: state 2: as 7.4.$_1$ above but on front, background in
    medium greenish blue (C173). Front flap, at top:
    Originally published | *at $3* | .

COPIES EXAMINED: Var.(1): OkTU; personal; TxU (copy 1). Var.
    (2): personal. Var.(3): LO/N-1, personal (dj, st.2); TxU
    (Copy 2; dj, st.2); Var.(4): personal

    [Nesor imprint]

8.1   LADY | CHATTERLEY'S | LOVER | BY | D. H. LAWRENCE |
       [device: sun with rays(?)] | Published by | NESOR
       PUBLISHING CO.

(9 x 6"): [1-20]^8, 160 leaves; pp.[4], 1-316.

CONTENTS: p.[1]: half-title. p.[2]: blank. p.[3]: t.p.
    p.[4]: blank. pp.1-316: text.

TYPOGRAPHY: Text: 37ll. (p.127), 162 x 111mm. 10ll.=42mm.
    Face: 3(1.5x)mm. Typeface: Century Schoolbook (R119).
    Transitional (DIN 1.24 Modern Baroque). Apparently printed
    by a relief process.

PAPER: smooth white wove unwatermarked. Thickness .12mm.
    Total bulk 21.4mm.

BINDING: Var.(1): calico (T 302) cloth, deep blue (cf. C183).
    No lettering, label, or design on binding. All edges
    trimmed. Plain white endpapers. Var.(2): calico cloth,
    light olive brown (C94). On spine is white paper label:
    in border of two rules, horizontal rules intersecting
    vertical 4mm. from top and bottom of label: Lady |
    Chatterley's | Lover | [vine leaf] | LAWRENCE | (ll. 1-3
    in non-flowing decorative script as in label for 2.1.a and
    7.3. Var.(3): as Var. (1) but paper spine label, as
    Var.(2) save no border.

NOTE: See Roberts App. IB.Va and b. C. J. Scheiner stated to
    me (17 Aug. 1988) that Jack Brussel experimented with a
    process ofphotographically etching metal; the plates could
    be used to run off 1000 copies of an exclusive-appearing
    "limited edition" at a time. It is possible that the
    Nesor firm knew of this process either through Brussel or
    because of the use of a common printer.

COPIES EXAMINED: var.(1)-(3): personal.

8.2   As 8.1 except:

TYPOGRAPHY: as 8.1, but seems printed by lithographic
    process.

BINDING: as 8.1 save very light yellowish green cloth (134).
    Gold-stamped on spine: [rule] | LADY | CHAT- | TERLEY'S |
    LOVER | LAWRENCE | [thin-thick rule] |.

COPY EXAMINED: DLC

8.3   As 8.1 except:

(8 15/16 x 5 5/8"): [1-10]^{16}, 160 leaves; pp.[4], 1-316.

TYPOGRAPHY: Text: 37ll. (p.127), 161 x 112mm. 10ll.=41mm.
    Face, typeface: as 8.2 (lithographically printed).

BINDING VARIANTS: (1): as 8.2 but mod. yellowish green cloth
    (C136). (2): as 8.2 but brilliant blue calico cloth
    (C177), stamped in red (so reported in Roberts Ap.
    IB.V.b.): [rule] | Lady | Chatterley's | Lover | [star] |
    D. H. LAWRENCE | [rule] |. (3): As 8.2 above, save spine
    stamping in red (no rules), as reported by Roberts, Ap.

IB.V.a. (4): as 8.2 but very deep red (C14) cloth, linen
grain. Gold stamping on spine. (5): as 8.2 but brilliant
blue (C177) calico cloth, stamped in gold. (6): as 8.2 but
very dark green (C147) calico cloth. (7): deep yellow
brown (C78) calico(?) cloth, paper label on spine as in
7.4.$_1$ above. (8): as 8.2 save cloth is black. (9): as 8.2
but calico cloth, deep blue (C 183). White paper label on
spine, as 8.1 Var.(2). (10): as 8.2 but light bluish gray
cloth (C191). (11): as 8.2 but calico-grain cloth,
brilliant blue (C177).
     DJ: state 1: Drawing and lettering on front cover as in
7.2 above, but in deep brown. Background in light grayish
yellowish brown. No strips (rays) of color. Back cover and
both flaps blank. State 2: as (1) but rays present, in
moderate greenish blue.

NOTE: The Roth paper labels on binding variants (7) and (9)
     make for interesting evidence of the relation between
     7.1-7.4 and 8.1-8.3. The use by Nesor of dj modelled on,
     and paper labels used by, Roth lend weight to the explana-
     tion for the Nesor edition postulated in the essay
     accompanying this Section (Nesor may have originally
     overprinted the labels for Roth). Also, note that the copy
     seen of Var.(7) is in the dj used for 7.4.$_1$ above.

COPIES EXAMINED: Var.(1): personal(dj, st. 1). Var.(2):
     TxU(c. 3). Var.(3): TxU(c. 1). Var.(4): TxU(c. 2).
     Var.(5): personal, TxU(c. 4). Var.(6): TxU(c. 5). Var.(7):
     TxU(c. 6; in dj as 7.4.$_1$), OX/U-1. Var.(8): personal.
     Var.(9): OkTU(dj, st. 2). Var.(10): personal(dj, st. 1)
     Var.(11): OX/U-1.

     [The Royal Imprint]

9.1   LADY | CHATTERLEY'S | LOVER | BY | D. H. LAWRENCE |
      [floral decoration] | PUBLISHED BY | ROYAL PUBLISHERS

(8 x 5 1/8"): [1-10]^{16}, 160 leaves, pp.[4], 1-316.

CONTENTS: [1]: half-title. p.[2]:blank. p.[3]:t.p. p.[4]:
     blank. pp.1-316:text.

TYPOGRAPHY: Text: 36ll. (p.127): 157 x 104 mm. 10ll.=42mm.
     Typeface: Transitional; DIN 1.24, Modern Baroque. Cf.R125,
     Comenius.

PAPER: smooth white wove unwatermarked. Thickness 08mm. Total
     bulk 16.1mm.

BINDING: paper-covered boards, embossed with marbled design.
     Strong reddish brown(C 40). Stamped in black on spine,
     running left to right: LADY CHATTERLEY'S LOVER -- LAWRENCE
     | [stamped vertically]: ROYAL |. All edges trimmed. Plain
     white end papers.

Dj: The Skillin illus., as in Roth and Nesor DJ, but reproduced on back as well as front cover. Lettering reproduced on back as well as front, and, as is the drawing, in red. Lettering on spine as in Nesor and Roth, but imprint present, which reads ROYAL |. Flaps blank.

NOTE: The imprint may corroborate Roth's statement (Hamalian "Samuel Roth" 902) that the perpetrators of the Nesor piracy were the founders of the Crown Publishing Company, operated from 1936, the year Roth was sentenced to prison for distributing pornography. It is possible, however, that Roth himself may have issued 9.1 upon his release from prison, as a countermove.

COPIES EXAMINED: OkTU(dj); personal

[Reset piracy of the Paris Popular Edition]

10.1   T.p. as 1.4 above.

(7 1/2 x 5 1/2"): [1]^8 2-17^8, 136 leaves; pp.[6],I-VI,1-260.

CONTENTS: pp.[1-2]:blank. p.[3]:t.p. p.[4]:blank. p.[5]: Tous droits de translation . . . . Copyright by D. H. LAWRENCE. p.[6]:   blank. pp.I-VI: "My Skirmish With Jolly Roger" pp.1-260: text.

TYPOGRAPHY: Text: 46ll.(p.133), 157(168) x 110mm. 10ll.=33mm. Face 2.5(1x)mm.

PAPER: smooth white wove unwatermarked. Thickness .1mm. Total bulk 13.7mm.

BINDING: calico-grain (T.302) cloth, strong purplish blue (C196). Blind-stamped border, upper cover. Stamped in dark blue on spine: D. H. LAWRENCE | LADY | CHATTER- | LEY'S | LOVER |. Edges trimmed, top edge stained blue. Plain white endpapers.

NOTE: this is reset from the Paris Popular Edition. The British Library catalogue states it was done in the Netherlands, c.1943. This library's copy has a ball-point inscription dated 1949 on p.[5]. There is an advertisement for *De tweede Lady Chatterley*, in Dutch, pasted to the free front endpaper.

COPY EXAMINED: LO/N-1

[a piracy of the Grosset And Dunlap expurgated edition]

11.1   *LADY* | *CHATTERLEY'S* | *LOVER* | *By* | D. H. LAWRENCE | GROSSET & DUNLAP | PUBLISHERS NEW YORK | *By arrangement*

with Alfred A. Knopf

(8 x 5 7/16"): [1]^8 [2-20]^8, 160 leaves; pp.[1-4], 7-322.

CONTENTS: p.[1]: LADY | CHATTERLEY'S | LOVER | This book is *complete* and *unabridged*! From first page to last it is exactly as | the author wrote it and as originally | published. p.[2]: blank. p.[3]: t.p. p.[4]: blank. pp.7-322: text. p.322, after last line of text: THE END | Kawsar Press |.

RUNNING HEADS: rectos and versos: LADY CHATTERLEY'S LOVER

TYPOGRAPHY: text: 38ll.(p.51): 171(183) x 100mm. 10ll.=43mm. Face 3(2x)mm. Typeface: Times New Roman(Monotype); R53.

PAPER: Thickness .06mm. Total bulk 13.2mm.

BINDING: stiff paper wrappers, medium orange (C53); calico texture. Printed in black: upper cover: LADY | CHATTERLEY'S | LOVER | *By* | GROSSET & DUNLAP | PUBLISHERS NEW YORK | *By arrangement with Alfred A. knopf* [sic] |. Spine (bottom to top): LADY CHATTERLEY'S LOVER | *By* D. H. LAWRENCE. lower cover: *Price in U.S.A. Tow* [sic] *Dollars* | *Price in Europe and Continent* | *Ten Chillings* [sic] |.

NOTE: This work is neither complete nor unabridged! In fact, Grosset and Dunlap reprinted the Knopf "authorized" abridged edition (which used Secker plates) from 1934 through the early forties. See Section 3, and entries 17.10-17.11, 17.30-17.31 below. The text, as stated above, is based On Roth's.

COPY EXAMINED: CU-S

[A set of (related) piracies of the Jan Förlag Swedish Edition]

12.1   [in square border with edges rounded and top and bottom rules 3mm thick]: *Lady* | *Chatterley's* | *Lover* [all 3 ll. in non-continuous script]

(8 1/4 x 5 5/16"): [1]^8 2-3^8 [4-5]^8 6^8 [7]^8 8^8 [9-12]^8 13^8 [14-15]^8 16-19^8, 152 leaves; pp.[4], 7-303, [304], [2].

CONTENTS: p.[1]: t.p. p.[2]: blank. p.[3]: Unexpurgated | authorized | Edition |. p.[4]: blank. pp.7-303: text. p.[304]: THE END | Oprae [sic] Press |. pp.[305-06]: blank.

RUNNING HEADS, rectos and versos: LADY CHATTERLEY'S LOVER

TYPOGRAPHY: text: 39ll.(p.115): 176(190) x 115mm. 10ll.=44mm.
Face 3(2x)mm. Typeface: cf. R69, Old Style No.2 and R67,
Imprint (transitional); DIN 1.24, Modern Baroque.

PAPER: smooth white wove unwatermarked. Thickness .07mm.
Total bulk 12.0mm.

BINDING: stiff paper wrappers, light bluish green (C163).
Printing in dark blue. Upper cover: [in noncontinuous
script, in square border with edges rounded, as on
t.p.]: *Lady | Chatterley's | Lover |*. [below square
border]: *By |* D. H. LAWRENCE | THE ONLY ORIGINAL EDITION |
PUBLISHED IN SWEDEN |. On spine, bottom to top: 20 $
LADY CHATTERLEY'S LOVER by D.H. LAWRENCE |. Lower
cover: Price 20 Kr. or 20 Shillings. | OPERA PRESS |.
No endpapers. Edges trimmed.

NOTES: The title page, p.3, and upper cover imitate the Jan
Förlag editions, published in Sweden from 1942 to 1956
(see #27.1-30.4 below). Numerous spelling errors, syntax
errors, and transposed and upside-down letters in the
present set of volumes indicate that the typesetters did
not know English. These piracies were possibly circulated
in India, north Africa and the middle east during World
War II, and in the far east after the war. C. J. Scheiner
says piracies of this kind were circulated in Korea and
China for purchase by American soldiers during the early
1950s. The present edition, and the related editions
described below, seem printed by letterpress, not photolithography (perhaps because the latter technology was not
available). There seem to be three separate resettings of
type (12.1; 13.1; 14.1-14.2) in the copies I have seen (in
12.1 two separate typefaces are used [for example pp.124-
25]). With the exception just noted, the same typeface is
used for each volume seen; however, on many pages spelling, punctuation, and spacing between paragraphs vary in
the first three volumes listed (each page retains the same
number of lines and begins and ends with the same word).
Some misspellings are common from version to version;
surely a common copy-text (and probably a common store of
type) was used.

COPY EXAMINED: CU-S

13.1   Lady | Chatterley's | Lover | *By | D,*[sic] *H,*[sic]
        Lawrence [ll.4,5 in non-flowing calligraphic script]

(8 5/16 x 5 1/2): [1-19]^8, 152 leaves; pp.[1-6], 7-303,
[304].

CONTENTS: p.[1]:blank. p.[2]:blank. p.[3]:t.p. [p.4]:blank.
p.[5]: Unexpurgated | autborized [sic] edition | Edition
|. pp.7-303:text. p.[304]: THE END | Lotus Press |.

RUNNING HEADS: as 12.1

TYPOGRAPHY: text: 39ll.(p.115): 178(186) x 113mm. 10ll.=44mm.
Face 3(2x)mm. Typeface: cf. R67, Imprint (transitional);

DIN 1.24, Modern Baroque.

PAPER: smooth white wove unwatermarked. Thickness .06mm. Total bulk 10.3mm.

BINDING: stiff paper wrappers, yellowish white (C92).
Printing in dark blue. Upper cover: [in noncontinuous
script, in square border with edges rounded]: *Lady |
Chatterley's | Lover* |. [below square border]: By |
D. H. LAWRENCE | THE ONLY ORIGINAL EDITION | PUBLISHED IN
SWEDEN |. Line 4 in open-faced, shadowed display type. On
spine, bottom to top: LADY CHATTERLEY'S LOVER by D. H.
LAWRENCE |. Lower cover: Price 20 kr. or 15 Shillings.
No endpapers. Edges trimmed.

NOTE: sig. [7] is incorrectly folded in copy seem; pp. 101-04
precede pp. 97-100; pp.109-12 precede pp.105-108. Also,
p.[201] signed 202.

COPY EXAMINED: personal

14.1   [no title page]

(8 5/16 x 5 1/2"): [1]^6 2-19^8, 150 leaves; pp. 7-303, [304],
[2].

CONTENTS: pp.7-303: text. p.[304]: THE END | Lotus Press |.
pp.[2]: blank.

RUNNING HEADS: as 12.1

PAPER: smooth white wove unwatermarked. Thickness .07mm. Total bulk 11.8mm.

BINDING: as 13.1 except: (1) wrappers moderate greenish blue
(C173); (2) no identification of press on lower cover,
but the latter is partly chipped away in the copy seen.

COPY EXAMINED: CU-S(lower cover partly chipped away)

14.2 Lady | Chatterley's | Lover | By | *D. H. Lawrence* (1.5
in non-continuous script)

as 14.1 save:

(8 3/8 x 5 13/16): [1]^8 2-19^8, 152 leaves; pp. [1-4], 7-303,
[304], [2].

CONTENTS: p.[1]: t.p. p.[2]: blank. p.[3]: [swelled rule, as
in Jan Förlag editions] | *Unexpurgated | authorized |
Edition* | [swelled rule] |. p.[4]: blank. pp. 7-303: text.
p. [304]: THE END | Lotus Press |. pp.[2]: blank.

PAPER: Thickness .06mm. Total bulk 12.1mm.

BINDING: as 13.1 save paper wrappers are medium orange (C53).

NOTE: On t.p. of copy seen is rubber-stamped, in Arabic, a
     bookseller's identification: "Mr. Sulaiman Hajab. News
     papers and Magazines. Suez" [Egypt].
     I am assuming, because of the regularity of the text and
     collation of this and 14.1, that they are parts of a
     single impression.

COPY EXAMINED: CU-S

          [Drug-store "secondary" paperback, 1949]

15.1   LADY [two rules] ǀ CHATTERLEY'S ǀ LOVER ǀ *By* ǀ
        D. H. Lawrence ǀ A Travellers Pocket Library ǀ Best
        Seller ǀ [pub. device; triangular design] ǀ WARD-HILL
        BOOKS ǀ [2 rules] New York [2 rules] ǀ. [2 vertical
        rules run from below R (1.3) to above A (1.6) and
        continue from just below 1.7 to above W in 1.9)].

(6 1/2 x 4 1/4"): [1-5]^{16}, 80 leaves, pp.[1-2],3-160.

CONTENTS: p.[1]:t.p. p.[2]: LADY CHATTERLEY'S LOVER ǀ
     Copyright, 1949. ǀ All Rights Reserved. ǀ All names used
     in this story ǀ are fictitious. Any resemblance ǀ to any
     person, living or dead, is ǀ purely coincidental. ǀ
     PRINTED IN CANADA. pp.3-160: text.

TYPOGRAPHY: 42ll.(p.135): 132 x 82mm. 10ll.=31mm.
     Typeface: Times Roman (R.52): Old Style. DIN 1.13, Modern
     Ren.

PAPER: smooth white wove unwatermarked. Thickness .06mm. To-
     tal bulk 5.8mm.

BINDING VARIANTS: (1): stapled. Paper wrappers, laminated.
     Upper cover: yellow, with male (in brown) and female nude
     (in red and white); an abstract design imitative of the
     cover of the first and second impressions of the
     Penguin/NAL authorized expurgated edition (18.1 below).
     Above drawing: [in triangle, blue on white background:]
     102 ǀ A CURIOUS AND UNUSUAL LOVE AFFAIR ǀ LADY
     CHATTERLEY'S ǀ LOVER D. H. LAWRENCE. Below drawing, on
     purple background: HERE, AT LAST, IS THE STORY THAT WAS
     TALKED OF IN WHISPERS! On spine: 102 [blue on white
     triangle] ǀ top to bottom: [in red on yellow background:]
     LADY CHATTERLEY'S LOVER [in white on purple background:] ǀ
     102 in triangle, as above]. Blurb on lower cover, in blue
     on white background, between rules. spine. Inside of both
     covers red with white stripes and logo. (2): as (1)
     except: upper cover: drawing is of man in business suit,
     standing between pair of woman's hands, wrists together,
     palms upward. Predominant colors white, deep blue, strong
     yellow green, dark purplish red, vivid reddish orange.
     Spine: blue background replaces purple. Inside lower
     cover: advert for *10 Lessons in Sex Technique*. Inside of
     upper cover is blue, with white stripes and logo.

NOTE: On p. [2]: "Copyright 1949." This edition contains the
    expurgations and bowdlerizations of the "authorized
    abridged edition," but reproduces only about one half of
    the "authorized" text. Perhaps declaration of copyright is
    made in the same spirit. At foot of t.p. for var. (2): -1-
    [pagination] l. Another state?
        The 160-page format is typical of erotic paperbacks
    which "secondary distributors" (see Section 5, p. 133)
    sold to adult bookstores through the 1960s (United
    States III: 94-95).
        Hancer (370) lists three other Ward-Hill titles:
    Gropper, *Passion is a Gentle Whip* (#100, 1949), Sacher-
    Masoch, *Venus In Furs* (#103, 1949), and Sinclair, *Pagan In
    Silk* (#104). He reproduces the upper cover of #103; it is
    similar in illustration and design to the *Chatterley*.

COPIES EXAMINED: Var.(1): personal. Var.(2): personal.

    [The "Third Edition"]

16.1 LADY CHATTERLEY'S | LOVER | BY | D. H. LAWRENCE |
      PRIVATELY PRINTED | 1929

(8 1/2 x 5 1/2"): tipped in front. + [1]^8 2-23^8, 184 leaves;
pp.[4], I-364.

CONTENTS: p.[1]: half-title. p.[2]: Third edition | limited
    to 500 copies. | No........ p.[3]: t.p. p.[4]: Florence -
    Printed by the Tipografia Guintina, directed by
    L. Franceschini. pp.I-364:text.

TYPOGRAPHY: Text: 35ll.(p.165), 147 x 102mm.; 10ll.=46mm.
    Face 3(2x)mm. Typeface: text in Garamond (Berthold)?,
    R 94. Transitional (DIN 1.24, Modern Baroque).
    T. p. in Jenson Old Style. Old Face (DIN 1.13, Modern
    Renaissance).

PAPER: smooth white wove unwatermarked. Thickness .07mm.
    Total bulk 15.1mm.

BINDING VARIANTS: (1): linen cloth (T 304) over flexible
    boards, brownish orange. Lawrence phoenix stamped in
    black on upper left of upper cover. Smooth white
    endpapers; all edges trimmed. (2): as (1) except Phoenix
    in upper right of upper cover. (3) as (1) except Phoenix
    in lower right of upper cover.

FRONT.: half-tone black-and-white reproduction of Jo Davidson
    bust of Lawrence; black border. Measures 104 x 71
    mm. Tipped onto t.p.; bust faces limitation statement.

NOTE: No longer, since Munro's (222-35) researches, con-
    sidered a piracy: see Essay above, p.30-31. The Cambridge

University Exhibition Catalogue (23) says this edition "may even incorporate [Lawrence's] own last corrections."

COPIES EXAMINED: Var. (1): personal; OkTU; TxU; Forster Coll. Var.(2): LO/N-1; NO/U-1. Var.(3): Forster Coll.

SECTION 3

The Authorized Abridged Edition, 1932–68

INTRODUCTORY ESSAY

An expurgated edition of *Lady Chatterley's Lover*, "authorized" by Laurence Pollinger, Frieda Lawrence's literary executor, and in fact prepared by him and Martin Secker (Pollinger 237), was published by Secker in February and by Knopf in September 1932. That the work was bowdlerized as well as expurgated, and that it obscured the motivations of the characters as well as the author's intentions, was clearly stated in early reviews./1/ However, it was this version which was most readily available to readers in America--and to a lesser extent in England, where the proximity of continental editions of course made them easier to come by. During the many years when reading *Chatterley* was a rite of passage for young people, and for all sorts a way of getting "in the know," it was the "authorized" edition which one had to look out for: either to read or to beware of purchasing. The following list makes clear that it was in any case a very steady seller. There were eight separate editions (copies printed from one setting of type); I have identified 65 separate impressions. This version remained in print in America for at least a year after the 1959 decensorship decision. In England, remarkably, it was published in paperback as late as 1968.

However "authorized," it was based upon a piracy. See the essay for Section Two for Samuel Roth's expurgated version (in print 1930-32), his success in distributing it in bookstores and through the mails (pp.22-24), and Secker and Pollinger's adaptation of his text as a basis for the "authorized" edition (p.21). Secker and Knopf use no copyright notice; they felt the work was really in the public domain, since Lawrence never could secure copyright for the Orioli edition./2/ This did not stop Roth from using a copyright line in his edition (7.1-7.4), although no record of its registration exists in the copyright office of the Library of Congress.

Not all of these editions were in fact "authorized" by the Lawrence estate; for one example, see 18.1; the term most accurately refers to the expurgated text prepared for the Secker edition of 1932, which was so authorized. All of the volumes listed below contain this text (the original version of which--Roth's--was *not* authorized).

Because this version was prepared for a large number of general readers, and because of the various formats (hard cover, pocket editions, paperbacks, "dollar books," and uniform editions of complete works), its history contains interesting evidence of publishing strategies and printing practices. There are certainly many formats and methods of appeal represented. Testimonials from Frieda Lawrence and other authorities were as important in early thirties hardcover issues as in 1959 paperbacks. So were blurbs, used to draw a reader's eyes away from the words "authorized" or "abridged" and towards allusions to sexual explicitness, adultery, and the notorious author's honesty, courage, and prophetic vision. The dust jacket and paper wrapper illustrations present an iconography at which Lawrence may have choked, but which various popular artists make quite arresting: lush grass (22.1) and early spring flowers (20.3; 20.6), a humble cottage deep in the forest (19.1), a man and a married woman engaged in what a different generation than the present one could call "making love" (17.22; 21.1). Whether in crown octavo, thin-paper, pocket, or paperback format, and whether printed in runs of 2,000 or 700,000, the "authorized" editions were for a mass-market as opposed to a specialized academic trade, and as physical objects they show what this meant during the thirty-year period when a great writer's reputation was being forged in the public mind.

Martin Secker printed eight impressions between 1932 and 1934; Secker and Warburg no longer have records for the work,/3/ but Roberts ascertained that the first printing was 3400 copies. In early 1935, Secker was deeply in debt (Mumby and Norrie, 5th ed., 349), and Heinemann acquired his Lawrence list (the Authorized Edition being 19th of the 22 titles listed in a pamphlet announcing the transfer). From then until 1956, the house's subedition consisted of 21 impressions from the Secker plates, in "thin-paper," "pocket," and finally the "Phoenix" Edition. There was a cloth-bound pocket edition published in 1953 by Chatto and Windus by agreement with Heinemann (see 19.1 below), but the British paperback of the Authorized Edition did not appear until 1958, published by Ace Books (see 22.1), again by agreement with Heinemann. There were two Ace editions between 1958 and 1961; I have found 15 impressions.

Ace Books was sold to Four Square in 1961. The imprint name, as Victor Weybright, then of New American Library (NAL) (294-95) states, was that used on the pipe tobacco manufactured by Godfrey Phillips Ltd. Phillips "knew less than nothing of the book business . . . . After a series of inadequate mergers and losses . . . the Godfrey Phillips interests were acquired [in 1966; T. L.

Bonn, in Crider 192, states 1961] by NAL so the business [was] a wholly owned subsidiary, under a managing director who has made a series of contracts to publish Playboy trivia and Girodias pornography." Weybright writes in disdain of the decisions of his former NAL partner Kurt Enoch, and goes on to say (295-96) that the New English Library (NEL) was content to republish NAL titles, including Signet Classics (see Mumby and Norrie, 5th ed., 514-15). He also asserts that Enoch secured for NEL contracts with contemporary American writers such as Irving Wallace and Harold Robbins. The Signet Classics titles NEL reprinted did not include the unexpurgated *Lady Chatterley*, which obviously the Lawrence estate would not have allowed. Items 23.8 and 24.1 indicate that Four Square published the abridged edition two years after the first British (Penguin and Heinemann) unexpurgated editions appeared and that, six years later, the same Secker/Heinemann abridgement was issued under the NEL imprint. The 1962 volume was impressed from plates of the second Ace Books subedition. NEL's 1968 volume is apparently a new edition. The first line on p. [4] of the latter, indicating that the work is *the* "authorised" edition, was removed.

In the United States, Knopf (see 17.9) first published the authorized version (the firm did clearly state, not only on the dust jacket, as did Secker, but on the title page, that it was "abridged"). I have found only one impression, in 1932. If indeed this was the case, and if Roberts' information about the press run (2000) is correct,/4/ why? Secker's text went through eight in three years. If, as I have suggested in the essay for Section 2, Samuel Roth's success motivated the authorized edition, one would expect aggressive publishing strategies. Knopf was an established and highly respected concern, with a unique reputation among American trade publishers for producing fine books at reasonable prices (its *Chatterley* had the same attractive decorated cloth binding as had the other items in its important Lawrence list). Frieda Lawrence's dust-jacket blurb, as stated earlier, is a direct challenge to Roth's advertising copy. Although the Faro imprint was out of business by 1933, the Roth version might have been available by mail order (with many other Faro titles) as a "Big Dollar Book"; the back covers of the dust jackets of many Faro titles so designate them. The Nesor text (see 8.1-8.3 and the essay for Section 2) was flourishing, and perhaps the young and energetic publishers distributed very effectively, above and below counters. Knopf, with the advertising and the many outlets available to him, could have trounced them if he had chosen to, and perhaps did; the evidence is inconclusive. Possibly the unfavorable reviews of the Authorized Edition discouraged this very scrupulous publisher. Perhaps he felt that to compete at all with Roth (or Nesor) was beneath him, or bad for the reputation of his house.

In any event, in 1934 Knopf sold the rights to the Authorized Edition to Grosset and Dunlap, where it became one of 109 titles in the Novels Of Distinction series./5/

Along with reprints of such writers as Hemingway, Wilder, Huxley, Forester, and Morley, it carried the popular price of $1.00. Another Grosset and Dunlap subedition, in the Madison Square Books series, appeared in the early forties. Again there were two impressions, which appeared with a large variety of other reprints, including romances, mysteries, and westerns. They were distributed to established bookstores, drug stores, railway newsstands, and "5 and 10s," as well as by mail order. In the thirties, cheap reprints would have had press runs of from 10,000 to 50,000 copies per impression (Tebbel III: 203, 494). This was a step toward the audience mass-produced paperbacks were to reach after World War II: a close enough step to inspire hand-wringing about books being sold by the same methods tooth paste, cough medicine, and soda were. What injury to public taste, queried conservative bookmen, might result from publishers standardizing and packaging their product for bargain-hunting truck drivers or shopgirls looking for a few hours' pleasure (Butler 15-25)? Be that as it may, such people comprised a significant segment of the Authorized *Chatterley's* audience.

The American paperback appeared twelve years earlier than the British. From 1941 to 1948, Penguin Books were distributed from the New York office headed by Kurt Enoch, who was aided from 1945 on by Victor Weybright. Because of differences regarding distribution and cover format with London director Allen Lane, and because of the competition between the two branches which these differences caused, the American branch broke with Lane in 1948 to form the New American Library (NAL), which distributed in drugstores and newsstands as well as bookstores. NAL fiction titles were termed "Signets" (Schreuders 37-46, 88; Schick 138-44).

The list on p.[2] of 20.1 includes two titles Allen Lane especially disliked: Cain's *Mildred Pierce* and Caldwell's *God's Little Acre*. Upon the latter's release, Lane suggested facetiously that Weybright change the imprint's name to "Porno Books." He also disliked the decision to publish Faulkner and J. T. Farrell (Weybright 182). In fact, NAL had, with its predecessors Avon, Pocket, and Popular Library, discovered an audience similar to that which frequented the front rooms of the "adult" bookstores of the thirties, the tastes of which Samuel Roth ("William Faro, Inc.") was the first to exploit by mail order (see Section 2)--initially with the (unauthorized) antecedent of the Authorized Edition (for its edition of the latter NAL contracted with Knopf). Of course, Weybright and Enoch appealed with a much larger and more varied range of titles than could Roth, and with a cheaper product distributed with enormously improved resources to drug stores, subway and airport newsstands, "5 and 10s," cigar and stationery stores (Davis 16-17, 46-48; Bonn 15-17, Schick 103-07). Their first impression of *Chatterley* comprised 280,370 copies at 25 cents each;/6/ the run of the first "Samuel Roth Edition" (see 7.1-7.2 above) was probably 3,000 copies at $3 each. However, comparison of the Faro and NAL blurbs, titles in print, and cover illustrations (see 7.1-7.3;

20.1-20.10 and 21.1-21.4) suggest that NAL captured in
their outlets the mass readership Roth was gesturing toward
with his mail order operation. "Good reading for the millions": both imprints were built upon the stout prop of the
best writers, classic and modern. Both reprinted some
sexually-explicit writers, in abridgement when prudent. NAL
wedded "commerce and conscience" (Davis 113), although in
1959 the Grove Press disagreed. And this was Roth's claim,
although James Joyce (in 1928), the Lawrence estate (in
1930), and Senator Estes Kefauver (in 1954; see U.S.
Senate. *Hearings*) disagreed.

That the American Authorized version appeared in paper
so much earlier than the British indicates that *Lady
Chatterley* was more widely known in abridgement here than
in Britain, where complete continental editions (see
Section 4) were easier to come by in any case. Perhaps this
was the reason for the 12-year lag, although the disdain of
William Heinemann Ltd (which arranged the first paperback
with Ace Books) and Alan Lane (Penguin) for either the
commercialization of erotica or the abridgement strategy
(see essay for Section 6, pp.181-83) may have been the
determining factors.

The latter was a sore point with traditional publishers, and with legal authorities and critics. The 1953 NAL
impression (the first Signet Giant *Chatterley*; see 20.7)
carried a more noticeable labeling of the work as "authorized" (but not "abridged") on the cover, title page, and
p.[1] (Crider 188). This was a response to a Federal Trade
Commission complaint (1950) about Signet's placement of its
notices of abridgement (in 35 titles). In 1951, NAL was
directed to place the notice on the title page and front
cover (Schick 145). Note, however, that the words "abridged" or "expurgated" do not appear in this or subsequent
printings of the "authorized" NAL versions until 1959 (see
21.4), although it previously had been used, on p.[1]. With
20.7, "Authorized" replaces "abridged." The absence of an
explicit abridgement notice was used by Grove to counter-
sue NAL after the former published a complete edition in
1959. Grove felt NAL had deliberately obscured the distinction between its abridgement and the complete work.

In 1959, PW reported (20 July: 37) that the NAL
Chatterley was a slow but steady seller until the French
film (1955; distributed in US in 1956) of the novel became
the subject of an early-1959 censorship controversy
(Bosmajian, ed. 164-65). Then 450,000 were printed to meet
demands of drugstore outlets. Sutherland (*Off. Lit.* 16)
reports that in July 1959 650,000 copies were sold (NAL
records indicate that the month would have been August; see
Madison 554). In an open letter to the trade (PW 31 Aug.
1959) to counter a similar report by Grove, NAL stated
"under the still effective agreement [with the Lawrence
estate], we had sold 1,500,000 copies in eleven printings
before Grove came out with its unexpurgated hardcover
edition. We expect to continue with this Signet edition
which is preferred by many distributors and readers." A PW

article on 10 Aug. (pp.42-43) reproduces covers of both the abridged and unexpurgated NAL editions: they are very similar./7/

There is an interesting contrast between the number of copies of the authorized edition sold through 11 printings and the number of copies of NAL's bestseller—*God's Little Acre*—purchased from 1946 and 1957: over six million (Schick 142). However, sales of the Lawrence title show it to be a very important property for NAL (Schick 142), and of enormous influence in popularizing the novel. Consider that NAL's first printing alone was probably larger than the total press run of the separate subeditions put out by Heinemann, Secker, Grosset and Dunlap, and Knopf. It was also paid the dubious compliment of imitation by another, even more abridged, unauthorized paperback (see 15.1, var.[1]).

The above illustrates different British and American lineages for the Authorized edition. Another aspect of this version's history also shows variation from one country to the other: blurbs and illustrations used to stereotype the work for popular consumption. A Heinemann dust jacket shows a man and a woman embracing deep in the woods (17.22). Vanguard's recreates one of Connie's early visits to the gamekeeper's hut. The Ace paperback's cover reproduces a swatch of lush grass; the New English Library's a single red rose. These are remarkably restrained covers for these firms. The former's *Women In Love*, *The Plumed Serpent*, and *The Virgin And The Gipsy* tease viewers with nubile young women. Heinemann's jacket advertising discusses the faithfulness of the abridgement to the author's purpose, and Lawrence's criticism of modern industrialism. Vanguard stresses the latter, and, as does Secker, suggests that the author's last novel, with its "phallic tenderness," may be his best. This scrupulous avoidance of sexually-oriented packaging does not mean that prurience was not a British motive for publishing and reading novels. Sutherland (*Off. Lit.* 20) describes Ace as a "downscale" firm which confessed that "people are willing to plow through a lot of intellectual stuff for two or three lines of what-not. We get a great many appreciative letters—mostly from prisons." Ace, NEL, and Four Square distributed in cigar stores, pharmacies, rail and air terminals, as well as bookstores, and marketed with this audience in mind (Sutherland *Off. Lit.* 29). For it, some combination of prurience with romantic fantasy would be a motive for buying literature. However, British publishers did not exploit it in the case of *Lady Chatterley*. Perhaps, because *Chatterley* was a banned, and in their cases barbered, book, they did not choose to force the issue.

One would expect from Allen Lane's contempt for American paperback illustration that New York advertisers would most aggressively exploit popular fantasies to "package" *Chatterley*. The American cover art "hypes" the novel as mildly erotic romance (see also Section 5, pp.131-32 and Section 7, pp.212-13), and would suit quite well the

Roth parodies of 1931 and 1932, or a Hollywood film. This kind of "packaging" encourages a view which Richard Hoggart's Introduction to the 1960 Penguin edition vigorously denies (possibly at the suggestion of Lane): that what Lawrence (himself!) had in fact produced was a

> straightfoward novelette, which fabricates a wish-fulfillment love affair between a very commonplace novelettish hero [strong, silent, disillusioned] and an equally commonplace titled novelettish heroine . . . . enthrall[ed] in a purely Eleanor-Glyn-like spell . . . . It is the pure tone of pulp. (Brophy, Levey, and Osbourne 133-34)/8/

American packaging represents a much "harder sell" than the British, but the appeal is no more daringly "indecent" a focus on prurience than is the latter. Grosset and Dunlap commissioned "Skrenda" for one of a suite of portraits of graceful, heavy-lidded, dreamy women in evening dress (17.30); another example of his work appears on the dust jacket of a novel the title of which might serve as the caption for any of these illustrations: *Playgirls In Love*. Skrenda's soft-edged delineation of aristocratic affluence and conventional romantic yearning is as far from Lawrence's intentions as the very different, prurient, association of sex and demonic torture which is the theme of the illustrations for a piracy of the same period (3.1). Of the NAL paperback covers, one would expect just what one finds: a man and a woman lying among flowers, teasing each other with them. There are two exceptions. The sixth impression shows the (possibly naked) couple embracing; the woman's wedding ring (combined with the blurb, "The Great Novel That Shocked The World") may have suggested adultery too closely. The seventh impression's cover art returns, with slight variation, to that of impressions three through five. A second noteworthy variation in cover art appears on the first and second impressions, a near-naked couple superimposed on the playing-card suits of spade and diamond. The design is signed by one of the most successful paperback illustrators, Robert Jonas, who stated that "for books in which the poetic predominated I used poetic, associative images" (Schreuders 44). Similar designs may be found on covers for Caldwell's *Trouble In July*, McCullers' *The Heart Is A Lonely Hunter*, and Cain's *Serenade*. The *Chatterley* design perhaps suggests a "shuffling" of partners.

It is difficult to account for the change from this imaginative cover to the later ones, all of which suggest the pulp magazines or movie posters. But this must be just the reason: NAL's representational illustrations hint at an alluringly romantic narrative, as its blurbs do at a risqué one (see also the essay for Section 7, pp.212-13). Only underground editions of erotica, such as entry 3.1, could include wantonly explicit illustration. See the discussion of this edition on pp.28-29 above. A mainstream pre-sixties paperback romance could no more approach sexuality in this way than it could through scatological language. One may

describe a typical example of the genre by adapting the witty epitome of "sex-pulp" (see Section 5, pp.134) writer Jack Woodford and saying that it is a "sex novel with its panties discreetly in place."/9/ It had to be obliquely suggestive, even sentimental, as the Authorized Edition of *Chatterley* was. To be fair, NAL's biographical information is accurate and interesting (although Lawrence did not approve the Authorized Edition in 1928 as stated). Grosset and Dunlap's front-flap blurb (17.30) stresses the theme of adultery. Knopf's quotation of Frieda Lawrence has been discussed above (p.24).

To understand just what were the tolerances of respectable society were for *Lady Chatterley*, let us try to classify the kinds of deletions and bowdlerizations Samuel Roth devised, and Laurence Pollinger and Martin Secker revised in 1930 and 1932 respectively. Here is *The New Yorker's* assessment of Roth's version:

> . . . an edition . . . with all the censorable passages deleted and a good deal of the rest re-written, apparently by someone around the office. It takes a pretty good book to stand being hashed up like that, but the firm of William Faro, Incorporated, had faith in the ability of D. H. Lawrence and was game to make the attempt. ("Books, Books, Books" 76)

Mahlon Blaine, one of Roth's illustrators, once off-handedly referred to the Faro *Chatterley* as the "Louisa May Alcott edition."/10/ The demure Lady Chatterley portrayed in the Roth frontispiece (see 7.3, 7.4) seems a reflection of Blaine's epithet, which, however facetious, is accurate both as regards the strictness of the edition's accommodation of Mrs. Grundy and, as we shall note later, its lack of sensitivity for feminine self-assertion. As far as the latter is concerned, Blaine's epithet would be even more apt for the Authorized Edition.

Excisions go beyond 4-letter scatological and erotic obscenities to words for bodily parts and functions ("womb," "phallus," "orgasm"), references to nakedness and sexual intercourse, and passages describing copulation and Mellors'--but especially Connie's--thinking about the psychological effects of sexual fulfillment. Bowdleriza-tions involve the kinds of substitutions summarized below (see Appendix V for a systematic collation of Chapter 10):

ORIOLI ED.	ROTH/SECKER ED.
fuck, jazz	love
sleep with	love (Roth: also "have")
womb	heart

bed	house ("She's been in my house afore. . . .")
cunt	love ("bit o' love")
loins	limbs
penis	passion [Roth; Secker adds "liver"]
feel	touch
shit	things
intercourse	affair
change of life	dangerous age
began to urinate in	made a privy of

Roth is careful to let the reader know that a "love-bout" is about to commence. He does so by asterisks but also by judicious use of the text, even at the risk of retaining very occasionally a word such as "naked." Secker more strictly excludes this, but finds "crisis" necessary near the end of Chapter Three, where it may raise the smut-sniffer's hackles more than Roth's substitution ("joy") but where it accomplishes ably Roth's own goal of keeping the narrative flowing, while of course arousing prurient interest. In the Faro and Secker texts this is always kept alive while being frustrated. The Faro provides its first row of dots where Connie and Michaelis first have intercourse. Actually, Lawrence's language is discreet enough to preclude expurgation at the point the asterisks appear, but the shrewd Roth provides the titillation gratis. The situation is one some readers (just those who would enjoy the other Faro titles and the romantic films Lawrence sneers at in his Chapter 11) were accustomed to from years of reading "borderline" erotica; they probably not only enjoyed but would have felt cheated without it. A different sort of bonus exists, by the way, for readers of the Authorized Edition: it has one more chapter than the Orioli or Faro, Secker and Pollinger having split Chapter Ten into Ten and Eleven at the point where the second (omitted) love-making episode commences.

Roth is as strict with Lawrence's text as ever a post office censor was with him; the ubiquitous substitution of "love" for "fuck" is only the most obvious example. However, Secker and Pollinger, apart from the necessary removal of allusions to John Thomas and Lady Jane for British readers, are generally more censorious than Roth, even using a different substitution for "fuck" ("*make* the little flame brilliant") late in the final chapter: to avoid the impression of a "code" which the reader can replace with the original? In Chapter 10, both editions will not allow the gamekeeper to be seen caressing "the

curve of [Connie's] crouching loins" or "her flank," or, a
bit later, with "his wet body touching hers." In the
Authorized Edition, Mellors and Connie are not even seen
(after sex) walking through the woods together, although
the dialogue at this point is innocuous. Roth allows all
but Mellors' putting his hand under Connie's dress,
including her marvelling about her lover's "touch upon her
living body" and her "new nakedness." Secker's edition
simply uses the excision of these paragraphs to break the
tenth chapter into two here. Late in the same chapter ("11"
in Secker) both Roth and the authorized edition excise
Mellors' yearning for "the sleep with the woman in his
arms," and a paragraph later, in the same context, change
"sleep" to rest, lest the notion of male and female
sleeping together be entertained. In Chapter 16/"17"
(although in both editions Mellors does watch "the full
curve of her hips" as Connie goes upstairs), Roth, but not
Secker, allows Lawrence to tell us that her lover's passion
has "torn" her slip. Earlier, Roth does not find it
necessary to delete her confession of running naked in the
rain (although her musing on Mellors' compliment regarding
her "arse" is censored). Secker removed about 40 lines
here, apparently to avoid any image of the woman's naked
body.

There is another possible motive (although a sub-
conscious one) than businesslike prudence for some of the
excisions/11/; again the Authorized Edition seems slightly
more culpable than Roth's in this connection. Connie's
struggle to understand her sexual needs and the magnitude
of her desire for Mellors is essential to the novel's power
and originality. Lawrence writes from Connie's point of
view: "To her it meant nothing except that she gave herself
to him [Michaelis]." For the last five words Roth substitutes "a man must have his way." In Lawrence's novel,
Connie's growing independence of convention, and her
ambivalent impulses for dominance and submission, are
dramatically revealed. From her affair with Michaelis
onward, the expurgations obscure this. "Men were very kind
to the *person* she was," Lawrence writes, "but rather cruel
to the female, despising her or ignoring her altogether";
ironically, this is true of the three (male) expurgators.
In fact, they have made his very next line unintelligible
in their ardor to excise the words "womb," "loins," and
"breasts."

Secker's cuts in Chapters 10 and "17," described
above, are examples. Another is the passage late in Chapter
10/"11" where Connie thinks with rapture of being pregnant
by Mellors. The Roth and Secker texts are identical here,
at pains to exclude not the fact of pregnancy but precise
words for the sexual organs. As a by-product of the
expurgation, however, a female perspective is nearly lost,
because Connie's emotions regarding pregnancy ("if I had
him inside me as a child") so often are expurgated. A
particularly disturbing example (anti-feminist in a very
different way than Lawrence could be accused of being)
involves Connie's exultation in sensing "a child in me" and

"a new life" in her "womb." In context, the latter could
have been bowdlerized as "heart," as elsewhere. As it is,
by deleting the two sentences, Roth reveals inadvertent
squeamishness about, indifference for, or contempt of this
intimate revelation of Lawrence's heroine's sensibility,
and her irresistible passion for Mellors. Connie's aggressive, independent side is effectively toned down also, as
her momentary desire to treat the gamekeeper as "temple
servant" to her "Bacchante" is obscured. Another instance
is the Authorized Edition's Chapter 17, where Clifford's
annoyance at his wife's "running out stark naked in the
rain, and playing Bacchante" is cut. A longer Secker/Pol-
linger excision in the same chapter occurs when Connie,
just before leaving for Venice, recognizes her deepening
commitment to Mellors. The 250-word passage (which Roth
retains in part) describes the woman's acceptance without
guilt of her "sensual self," despite the "reckless devil"
she had "to be strong to bear" the night before. The
diction here is very similar to the notorious description
of the previous night's love-making, which at the 1960
British trial of the Penguin edition (see Section 6 below,
pp.179-81) was used by the prosecution as an example of
deviant sexuality. Roth removes any reference to the fact
that this passion was aroused by any night-time or
"phallic" activity, and purges the following three paragraphs, but--if indeed expurgation can admit degrees of
badness--Roth allows a bit more of Connie's psychic
development to come through at this point, and elsewhere,
than does the Authorized Edition./12/

    Roth, of course, initiated the shrewd emasculations
(and defeminizations) in the first place. Lawrence's own
abridgements are preserved at the Humanities Research
Center, University of Texas, in a typescript the author
sent to Knopf in 1928./13/ (For a collation, see Michael
Squires' forthcoming Cambridge University Press edition of
the novel.) The author bowdlerized, as did Roth, but the
former's euphemisms are limited to what he knew Secker and
Knopf would see as hopelessly scatological and obscene
references:

ORIOLI ED.	KNOPF TYPESCRIPT
over-fuck	over indulge myself in sex
penis	loins, bowels of compassion, jouster, little Lancelot, sex
gone into	known
open her thighs	yield

fuck	be Sir Pestle and Lady Mortar, enjoy, coition, sex pleasure, cuddlin'
cunt-awareness	blood
arse	behind, tail
shits and pisses	comes an' goes

Lawrence excises much less than Roth or Secker, which explains why he uses more bowdlerizations for "penis" than does the Authorized Edition. Some of its heavily expurgated sentences Lawrence himself did not revise at all. And he would never had eliminated whole passages, specifically the following, which Roth and Secker cut: Connie's first intercourse with Michaelis (Chapter 3); Dukes' monologue about his flaccid penis and vocabulary in Chapter 4; the first three love-bouts, and Connie's growing adulation after the third (Chapter 10); her rainy romp with Mellors and his approval of her "two secret openings" in Chapter 15; the "night of sensual passion" in the next chapter; and Sir Malcolm's boisterous luncheon conversation with Mellors in Chapter 17.

During the period February–April 1928, when he still believed Secker and/or Knopf could prepare an edition of the novel for the general public, Lawrence's letters stressed that he would not tolerate excision of whole "sections." He sent one carbon copy of the typescript to each publisher, asking that they continue the expurgations in the manner he had suggested by his holograph revisions, blue-pencilling any "substantial revisions" and sending them to him for approval (CL 1041). At the same time he was willing to cut "more and more" in the hope of producing a "feasible" edition to complement the "immaculate" Orioli (CL 1042). Apparently Secker "lifted shocked hands of indignation" (CL 1055) before Knopf did; by early April Lawrence requested Pollinger not to send the carbon type-script to Chatto. By mid-April he was acknowledging that despite Knopf's willingness, the project would fail (CL 1056). See the essay for Section 1, endnote 2.

It does not appear that Secker and Pollinger even consulted the revised typescript in 1932. Perhaps they no longer had access to it, for Lawrence asked that it be sent to the Huxleys when he decided not to try another London publisher (CL 1053). It is a strictly academic point, for the British publisher had in hand the version of an expurgator who through bitter experience had been brought to appreciate, as Lawrence admitted he did not, "what was supposed to be proper and what not" (CL 1041).

ENDNOTES

1. See for example, Henry Hazlitt, *The Nation* 7 Sept. 1932: 214-15; V. S. Pritchett, *Fortnightly Review* 1 April 1932: 536-37; *Times Literary Supplement* 25 February 1932: 130. These are reprinted in Draper 285-92.

2. So stated in a letter in the Arents archive at Syracuse University (see Chapter 5, endnote 1): William Koshland of Knopf to Frieda Ravagli, 10 June 1954.

3. I was so informed in a letter of 17 January 1986.

4. William A. Koshland, Chairman of the corporation, kindly informed me on 16 January 1986 that a thorough search for records of this title proved that publication records for it no longer exist.

5. The publisher informed me in a letter of 14 January 1986 that records for books of this period are unavailable.

6. A copy of the contract and information regarding printings were found in the NAL file on deposit at the Fales Library, New York University. See Notes to 20.1 below. I wish to thank the publishers for allowing me to see this material.
    The contract with Knopf grants Penguin (American Branch) exclusive Canadian rights and non-exclusive rights elsewhere. The agreement was to be for three years, to be extended automatically.

7. A letter to me from NAL on 11 June, 1985 (see Note to 21.4) gives the number of copies of the abridged edition sold in 1959: 812,390.

8. For other observations equating *Lady Chatterley's Lover* with pulp romance, see Section 2, pp.21-22; Section 7, endnote 1; and the essay for Appendix 1, pp.239-40.

9. Contemporary pornographic novelist Richard E. Geis: "Jack [Woodford] used to say a sex novel was a romance novel with its panties down" (Geis 2).

10. Adelaide Roth recalled this during an interview with the author, 3 July 1987.

11. I am indebted to Ms. Theresa Higgins, a student assistant who helped prepare the collations in Appendix V, for discovering the following rationale for revision.

12. I have found one writer who feels that the expurgations were "truly the best and fairest attitude toward the book," because the Authorized Edition provided for readers "all of Lawrence's social comment and trenchant criticism of the times, all of his social philosophy, indeed all of his intriguing contrast of the naturalness of love versus

sanctimonious artificiality . . . . Only the gutter words
and the [indecent] expressions . . . were omitted" (Whitman
67). This is a radically different assessment of the matter
than that of Graham Hough, made four years before the
British de-censorship. Since Lawrence could not cleanse his
four-letter words of prurient connotations, their excision
was not crucial. The total candor used in describing
intercourse was also more strident than necessary. The
novel's merit lay in the lovers' discovery of their mutual
need. The loss of "specific sexual detail" in the abridgement was regrettable, but it "suffers less by the omissions
than has often been alleged"(162).

13. *John Thomas And Lady Jane*, ts., Humanities Research
Center, University of Texas at Austin. Listed by Vasey
(219) as E182f. I would like to thank the Center for
sending me a microfilm of this typescript, and Gerald
Pollinger and the Lawrence Estate for permission to see it.

BIBLIOGRAPHICAL DESCRIPTIONS

> *[First plating (letterpress) of the Secker "parent edition"]*

17.1 LADY CHATTERLEY'S | LOVER | BY D. H. LAWRENCE | LONDON | MARTIN SECKER | NUMBER FIVE JOHN STREET ADELPHI

(7 7/16 X 4 7/8"): A–U^8 X^4, 164 leaves; pp.[1-8], 9-327, [328].

CONTENTS: [1-4]:blank. p.[5]:half-title. p.[6]:blank. p.[7]: t.p. p.[8]: AUTHORIZED BRITISH EDITION | *First Published February 1932* | LONDON: MARTIN SECKER LTD., 1932. pp.9-327: text. p.[328]: [rule] | PRINTED IN GREAT BRITAIN BY | THE DUNEDIN PRESS, LIMITED, EDINBURGH |.

TYPOGRAPHY: text: 38ll. (p.161): 147(156) x 93mm. 10ll.=38mm. Face 3(2x)mm. Typeface: Scotch 2(linotype)?, R.186. Modern ("Didone"). DIN 1.34, Modern Neo-classical.

RUNNING HEADS: rectos and versos: LADY CHATTERLEY'S LOVER

PAPER: ribbed white laid unwatermarked. Impressed with chain-lines approx. 25mm. apart. Thickness .14mm. Total Bulk 24.8mm.

BINDING: calico-grain cloth (T.302), moderate brown (C. 58). Blind stamped double border, upper and lower cover. Gold-stamped on spine: | [thin rule] | [thick rule] | LADY | CHATTERLEY'S | LOVER | [dot] | D. H. | LAWRENCE | SECKER | [thick rule] | [thin rule] |. Fore and top edges trim-med. Bottom edges partly trimmed. Plain white endpapers.
    Dj: yellowish white (C.92) paper, lettered in red. Front cover, at top: [rule] | LADY CHATTERLEY'S | LOVER | BY D. H. LAWRENCE | [rule] | [at bottom]: [rule] | AUTHORIZED BRITISH EDITION | [rule] |. On spine: [rule] | Lady | Chatterley's | Lover | [square within border] | LAWRENCE | AUTHORIZED | BRITISH | EDITION | [rule] | SECKER | [rule] |. Back cover: In double border: LATEST | FICTION | [rule] | [list of 6 titles, beginning Lothar's *Clairvoyant*, ending Gunther's *Bright Nemesis*]. Front flap: Mr. Lawrence's latest | --and in the opinion of | many critics, his greatest-- | novel, now available for the | first time to the general public | in an authorized abridged | edition. In lower right: 7s. 6d. | net |.

NOTE: Roberts (A42d) reports that 3440 copies were printed. In January 1986, Secker and Warburg informed me that its records regarding the Secker printings of this edition have been lost.

COPIES EXAMINED: TxU (dj); ICarbS; OkTU (2 copies); personal; NO/P-1; NO/U-1; Forster Coll.

17.2   "reprinted February 1932"; as 17.1 save:

TP: added after author's name: *SECOND PRINTING* |.

(7 3/8 x 4 7/8"): coll. as 17.1

CONTENTS: p.[8] (added as l.3): *Reprinted February 1932*

PAPER: total bulk: 24.1mm.

BINDING: color of cloth: light blue (C181). Double border,
    upper and lower covers, stamped in black. Spine lettering
    stamped in black.
        DJ: As 17.1 save front cover: added as l.6: *Second
    Printing* |. Wrap-around band, red, lettering in black: on
    front and back: D. H. LAWRENCE'S | GREATEST NOVEL |. On
    spine: 7s. 6.d.

COPY EXAMINED: ICarbS, personal (dj)

*17.3   "reprinted May 1932"

17.4   "reprinted October 1932"; as 17.1 save:

TP: added after author's name: *FOURTH PRINTING*

(7 3/8 x 4 7/8"): [A]^6 B-U^8 X^4, 162 leaves; pp.[4], 9-327,
[328].

CONTENTS: p.[1]: half-title. p.[2]:blank. p.[3]:t.p. p.[4]:
    AUTHORISED BRITISH EDITION | *First Published February 1932*
    | *Reprinted February 1932* | *Reprinted May 1932* | *Reprinted
    October 1932* | LONDON: MARTIN SECKER LTD.,1932. pp.9-327:
    text.

PAPER: rough white laid unwatermarked. Chainlines approx.
    25mm apart. Thickness .11mm. Total bulk 18.5mm.

BINDING: as 17.2. Endpapers white, impressed with chain-lines
    the width of which is the same as it is in the leaves.
    DJ as 17.1, but *Fourth Printing* added, middle of front
    cover. Back cover bears ad for Secker Pocket Ed. of DHL's
    poems and tales. Front flap: 4 blurbs for LCL from London
    periodicals. Price (7s 6d) in lower right.

NOTE: This volume may not be part of the "Pocket Edition,"
    which may refer to the smaller (6 15/16 x 4 1/2") format,
    in red cloth with "Pocket Edition" on the dj. However, the
    terms "pocket" and "thin-paper" may be used interchange-
    ably: the Pocket Edition of *The Lost Girl* has a list of
    titles in the "thin-paper" edition on p.[2]. See NOTES to
    17.13 below.

COPIES EXAMINED: Forster Coll.; OkTU(dj)

*17.5 "June 1933" -- subedition: first 3/6 impression.

17.6   second 3/6 impression: "July 1933"; as 17.1 save:

(7 1/8 x 4 7/8"): [A]^6 χ^1 B-U^8 X^4, 163 leaves; pp.[6],9-327, [328].

CONTENTS: pp.[1-2]: blank. p.[3]: half-title. p.[4]:blank. p.[5]:t.p. p.[6]: AUTHORIZED [sic] BRITISH EDITION | *First published February 1932* | *Reprinted February 1932* | *Reprinted May 1932* | *Reprinted October 1932* | *Three-and-Six Edition* | *First published June 1933* | *Reprinted July 1933* | LONDON: MARTIN SECKER LTD., 1933 |. pp.9-327:text.

TYPOGRAPHY: 38ll.(p.161): 145(155) x 42mm. 10ll.=37mm. Face 3(2x)mm.

PAPER: smooth white wove unwatermarked. Thickness .13mm. Total bulk 21.5mm.

BINDING: linen grain (T304) cloth, strong reddish orange (C35). Black stamped, upper cover: LADY | CHATTERLEY'S | LOVER |. Black-stamped on spine: LADY | CHATTERLEY'S | LOVER | D. H. LAWRENCE | SECKER |. Lettering in Sans Serif. Plain white endpapers. (Dust jacket not seen).

NOTE: A disjunct leaf bearing pp.15-16 is pasted in after A6.

COPY EXAMINED: LO/N-1

*17.7   "January 1934" (*English Catalogue* lists as "Pocket Edition," Feb. 1934; size "7 x 5 1/2").

*17.8   "March 1934" (NOTE: In 1935, Secker sold its Lawrence list to Heinemann). See Powell ([9]), and 17.11 below.

[The only(?) plating of the Knopf subedition]

17.9   [in double border, inner one decorated, in orange]: D. H. LAWRENCE | [swelled rule, in orange, 34mm long] | LADY CHATTERLEY'S | LOVER | AUTHORIZED ABRIDGED EDITION | [pub.'s logo,in orange: running borzoi in oval] | MCMXXXII | NEW YORK: ALFRED [dot] A [dot] KNOPF

(7 1/2 x 5 1/8"): [A]^8 B-T^8 U^4 [X]^8, 164 leaves; pp.[1-8], 9-327, [328]. Sig.[X]5 signed X (relic of Secker plates)

CONTENTS: p.[1]:blank. p.[2]: list of 11 Lawrence titles (beginning *St. Mawr*, ending *David*) and Luhan's *Lorenzo In Taos*: The best portrait we are ever likely to get | that [sic] strange genius, D. H. Lawrence |. p.[3]: section title p.[4]: blank. p.[5]:t.p. p.[6]: FIRST AMERICAN EDITION | ["rights reserved" statement: 2 ll.] | MANUFACTURED IN UNITED STATES OF AMERICA p.[7]: section title. p.[8]: blank. pp.9-327:text. p.[328]:blank.

TYPOGRAPHY: Text: 38ll.(p.145), 145(155) x 92mm. 10ll.=
37mm. Face: 2.5(1.5)mm.

RUNNING HEADS: as 17.1

PAPER: smooth white wove unwatermarked. Thickness .12mm.
Total bulk 17.6mm.

BINDING: Calico grain cloth(T 302), medium orange (C 53).
Upper cover, black-stamped: LADY CHATTERLEY'S | LOVER | [2
rules] Spine: in black: LADY | CHATTERLEY'S | LOVER |
[short double rule] | D. H. LAWRENCE | ALFRED [dot] A
[dot] KNOPF |. As Roberts (A42e) states, "spine is
decorated with black and green horizontal rules; title and
author's name appear on green panel background. There is a
vertical green and black decorated rule in the center of
the middle portion of the spine." Lower cover (lower
right), on green panel: BORZOI | [logo as on tp] | BOOKS
|. Top edge trimmed and stained deep orange; others partly
trimmed. Smooth white endpapers.
Dj: Front cover: [in white on strip of black]: D [dot] H
[dot] LAWRENCE | Authorized Abridged Edition [in black on
white background] | [in white on purple background]: LADY
| CHATTERLEY'S | LOVER | [in black on white background:
6-line statement from Frieda Lawrence, acknowledging the
present "*only authorized edition. . . after all the
expurgated pirated editions. . . even in its revised form
it has all the beauty of the original edition, and . . .
suggests to the greatest possible extent, the original's
strength and vigor.*"] Spine: [set horizontally in white on
black background: D [dot] LAWRENCE | [set vertically, in
white on purple background]: LADY CHATTERLEY'S | LOVER |
[set horizontally, white on black ground]: borzoi logo |
ALFRED [dot] A [dot] | KNOPF |. Back cover: photo of
DHL. Front flap: price ($2.50) and list of 10 Lawrence
titles. Lower flap: blurb for *Lawrence in Taos*.

NOTES: as Roberts states (A42e: "first authorized expurgated
edition, American impression"), 2000 copies printed at
$2.50, Sept. 1, 1932. The binding conforms to that of
other Knopf editions of Lawrence. Knopf, more than any
other American trade publisher of the period, was sensitive to the techniques of fine printing and usually
provided full colophons with details regarding book
design. There is no colophon here, for the typography is
of course Secker's.
Mrs. Lawrence's reference to "all the expurgated
editions" alludes most probably to the Roth expurgations
(N.Y.: Faro, 1930, 1931, 1932; #7.1-7.4 above); see essay
for Section 2, p.24. Roth himself states (Schwartz 24-25)
that he almost came to terms with Mrs. Lawrence but that
Knopf advised against it. Snyder (13; #103) notes that
this is abridged but calls it "our first complete modern
love story. All other editions published in America were
pirated."

COPIES EXAMINED: TxU(dj); personal(dj); OkTU; Forster Coll.

[First plating, Grosset and Dunlap "Novels of Distinction" subedition, 1934"]

17.10   (in border of strong pink [C. 218], decorated with
        artificial leaves in white [each side measures 8 mm,
        top and bottom measure 22mm.]): LADY | CHATTERLEY'S |
        LOVER | *by* | D. H. LAWRENCE | *author of* | AARON'S ROD,
        THE LOST GIRL | WOMEN IN LOVE, Etc. | [floral dec. in
        pink] | [rule] | GROSSET & DUNLAP | *Publishers* | *by
        arrangement with* | ALFRED A. KNOPF

(7 3/4 x 5 3/8"): [1]^4 [2-21]^8, 164 leaves; pp.[6], 9-327,
[328], [2].

CONTENTS: p.[1]: half-title. p.[2]:blank. p.[3]:t.p.
    p.[4]: FIRST AMERICAN EDITION | *All rights reserved--no
    part of this book may be reprinted in* | *any form without
    permission in writing from the publishers* | MANUFACTURED
    IN THE UNITED STATES OF AMERICA |. p.[5]:   section title
    p.[6]: blank. pp.9-327: text. p.[328]: blank pp.[2]:

TYPOGRAPHY: Text: same as Knopf subedition, 17.9 above.

RUNNING HEADS: as 17.1

PAPER: smooth white wove unwatermarked. Thickness .12mm.
    Total bulk 21.3mm.

BINDING: black calico-grain (T. 302) cloth; blind-stamped
    pub's device [bird in nest over G D] lower right corner of
    upper cover. Silver-stamped on spine: LADY | CHATTERLEY'S
    | LOVER | GROSSET | & DUNLAP |. Lettering on black back-
    ground, which interrupts at top and bottom of decorated
    spine a network of squares comprising a checkerboard
    pattern in silver and green on black background. Top edge
    trimmed, stained green; fore and bottom edges partly
    trimmed. Plain white endpapers.

NOTES: See Roberts, p. 111. Binding and t.p. design uniform
    with other DHL works in G & D's Novels of Distinction
    series, which was introduced in its 1934 catalogue: "The
    physical appearance of these books will inspire every
    booklover with their worthiness of a place in their [sic]
    libraries." There are 109 fiction titles -- at the popular
    reprint price of $1.00 each -- including three of the
    Lawrence titles and works by Huxley, Forester, Hemingway,
    Morely, and Wilder.
        First leaf of Knopf ed., containing on verso list of
    DHL works published by Knopf's Borzoi imprint, not
    appropriate here. Thus the inconsistent preliminary
    pagination, as in the Madison Square subedition below.
        Tebbel (III: 203,494) suggests that press runs for
    cheap reprints might have been between 10,000 and 50,000
    copies. See essay above, p.59.
        In-text signatures are "fossils" of the Secker/Knopf

plates; they are not used to collate gatherings in the present edition.

COPY EXAMINED: personal

17.11   as 17.10 save:

T.P. as 17.10 but border in black.

(8 1/16 x 5 3/8): [1-19]^8 [20]^4 [21]^8, 164 leaves; pag. as 17.10.

PAPER: Thickness 1.3mm. Total bulk 22.0mm.

BINDING: no blind-stamped pub. device; otherwise as 1.10.

COPIES EXAMINED: CU-S; ICarbS

[subedition: first Heinemann plating, "January 1934." Heinemann Australian Edition?]

17.12   LADY CHATTERLEY'S | LOVER | BY D. H. LAWRENCE | LONDON | WILLIAM HEINEMANN LTD

(6 7/8 x 4 3/8"): π^2 A-K^{16}, 162 leaves; pp.[4], 9-327, [328]. $5 signed [sig. no.]* |; sig. D5 signed D*. |.

CONTENTS: p.[1]: half-title. p.[2]: THE NOVELS OF D. H. LAWRENCE | THIN-PAPER EDITION | [20 titles, starting *White Peacock*, ending *Love Among The Haystacks*. LCL 19th.] p.[3]:t.p. p.[4]: AUTHORIZED [sic] ABRIDGED EDITION | *First published February* 1932 | *Reprinted February, May, October* 1932 | *June, July* 1933; *January* 1934 |. pp.9-327:text. p.[328]: PRINTED IN GREAT BRITAIN BY | NEILL AND CO., LTD., | EDINBURGH.

TYPOGRAPHY: text: 38ll.(p.145), 146(156) x 93mm. 10ll.=38mm. Face3(2x)mm.

RUNNING HEADS: as 17.1 above

PAPER: smooth white wove unwatermarked. Thickness .08mm. Total bulk 13.28mm.

BINDING: Linen-grain cloth (T.304), strong red (C12). Stamped in gold on spine: [thin-thick rule] | *D. H.* | *LAWRENCE* | [dot] | LADY | CHATTERLEY'S | LOVER | *Heinemann* | [thick-thin rule]. Plain white endpapers, all edges trimmed.
    Dj: Front cover and spine blue with white lettering and triple borders, outer two in white and inner one in black. Front cover, inside borders: POCKET [dot] EDITION [dot] THE [dot] WORKS [dot] OF | D [dot] H [dot] LAWRENCE | LADY CHATTERLEY'S | LOVER [last two lines in black on orange band in upper third of cover, which is superimposed on the blue background and borders and runs from fore-edge

of front cover to lower edge of spine. At bottom, outlined
in orange: Lawrence phoenix.] At bottom: LONDON: WILLIAM
[dot] HEINEMANN [dot] LTD. On spine: star [in orange] |
[following four lines in black on orange background]: LADY
| CHATTERLEY'S | LOVER | 19 | star [in orange] | star [in
orange] | star [in orange] | [Lawrence phoenix [in orange]
| POCKET | EDITION | 3s.6d. | NET | Heinemann |. Back
cover (white with black printing) contains, in triple
border in orange, author's name in blue display type, and
biographical note, which continues on back flap. Back flap
states that Lawrence's work is here "issued in what he
called this 'brave red' pocket edition." Front flap has
list of the Pocket Edition, 22 titles starting *White
Peacock*, ending *Fantasia of the Unconscious*.

NOTE: As Heinemann acquired the Secker Lawrence list in 1935
    [see 17.13], this volume seems an anomaly; it may be an
    Australian edition. This would explain the use of the word
    "abridged" on p.[4], which is replaced by "British" on
    other impressions of this edition. My copy bears the
    ticket of an Adelaide bookseller.
        In this and later Heinemann impressions the word
    "L'Amour" (p.13, l.3) contains a capital "A"; earlier
    impressions had used (as did the Orioli ed.) a lower-case
    letter.

COPY EXAMINED: personal

[First Heinemann plating for the home market, 1935(?)]

17.13 LADY CHATTERLEY'S | LOVER | BY D. H. LAWRENCE | LONDON
       | WILLIAM HEINEMANN LTD

(7 1/4 x 4 7/8"): [A]^8 B-T^8 U^{10}, 162 leaves; pp.[4], 9-327,
[328]. Sig. U2 signed U*

CONTENTS: p.[1]: half-title. p.[2]: THE NOVELS OF D. H.
    LAWRENCE | THIN-PAPER EDITION | [21 titles, starting *White
    Peacock*, ending *A Modern Lover*. LCL 19th.] | [short rule]
    | *Essays* | [2 titles]. p.[3]:t.p. p.[4]: AUTHORIZED [sic]
    BRITISH EDITION | [short rule] | *First published February
    1932* | *Reprinted February, May, October 1932* | *June, July
    1933* | *January, March 1934* | *July 1935* | PRINTED IN GREAT
    BRITAIN | AT THE WINDMILL PRESS, KINGSWOOD, SURREY |.
    pp.9-327:text. p.[328]:blank.

TYPOGRAPHY: text: 38ll.(p.149), 147(153) x 92mm. 10ll.=38mm.
    Face3(2x)mm.

RUNNING HEADS: as 17.1 above

PAPER: smooth white wove unwatermarked. Thickness .13mm.
    Total bulk 24.6mm.

BINDING: Linen-grain cloth (T.304), strong red (C12). Stamped

in black on upper cover, first letter each line almost
flush with joint: LADY I CHATTERLEY'S I LOVER I. Blackstamped on spine: LADY I CHATTERLEY'S I LOVER I
[rectangle, 8x2mm.] I D. H. I LAWRENCE I HEINEMANN I.
Blackstamped, lower right of lower cover: Heinemann
windmill. All edges trimmed. Plain white endpapers.

NOTES: Heinemann commemorated its 1935 acquisition of
    Secker's DHL list with a pamphlet containing an "Apprecia-
    tion" by Richard Aldington and a list of 22 titles, the
    present one being 19th. The pamphlet, blue with an orange
    phoenix and white lettering, was supposed to suggest the
    dj design for the "Pocket Edition," the price of which was
    3s 6d per volume. It appears that the "thin-paper" and
    "pocket" "editions" may have been different formats, but
    of the same price. No. 17.12 could pass for crown octavo
    [7½ x 5"]; it is a slightly larger, and a thicker, volume
    than 17.12 or 17.14, which could be, in contrast, a
    "pocket" format. But the list in 17.12 [p.2] is headed
    "Thin-Paper Edition." The terms "thin-paper" and "pocket"
    are not clearly distinguished in Heinemann catalogues or
    series statements. When the Phoenix Edition was introduc-
    ed, in 1956, that format was made distinct from the Pocket
    Edition. See other impressions listed below, and especial-
    ly 17.32.

COPY EXAMINED: personal

17.14   "November, 1936"; as 17.13 save:

(6 7/8 x 4 5/16"): collation, no. of leaves, pagination as
17.13 above.

CONTENTS: as 17.13, except: p.[2]: 27 titles listed, beginn-
    ing with *White Peacock*, ending with *A Modern Lover*.
    p.[4]: added after l. 7: I *November 1936* I.

TYPOGRAPHY: text: 38ll.(p.149), 147(159) x 91mm. 10ll.=37mm.
    Face 2(1.5)mm.

PAPER: smooth white wove unwatermarked. Thickness .07mm.
    Total bulk 12.9mm.

BINDING: calico-grain cloth (T.302), deep red (C13). Gold-
    stamped on spine: [thin rule] I [thick rule] I *D. H.* I
    LAWRENCE I [dot] I LADY I CHATTERLEY'S I LOVER I *Heinemann*
    I [thick rule] I [thin rule]. All edges trimmed. White
    endpapers.

COPIES EXAMINED: NO/P-1; Forster Coll.

*17.15   "October, 1937"

17.16   "June, 1938"; as 17.13 save:

Leaf size: 6 11/16 x 4½".

CONTENTS: p.[2]: list contains 30 titles, ending with

Reflections. List headed THE NOVELS OF D. H. LAWRENCE I.
p.[4]: last two lines read *October 1937* I *June 1938* I.

TYPOGRAPHY: 138ll.(p.149), 147(157) x 93mm. 10ll.=37mm. Face
2(1.5)mm.

PAPER: thickness .07mm. Total bulk 13.3mm.

BINDING: as 17.14 above.

COPIES EXAMINED: NO/P-1; NO/U-1

*17.17   "July, 1938"

*17.18   "July, 1939"

*17.19   "March, 1940"

*17.20   "September, 1940"

*17.21   "November, 1940"

*17.22   "June, 1941"

17.23   LADY CHATTERLEY'S I LOVER I BY D. H. LAWRENCE I
         [pub. device: windmill over rule; W and H on either
         side] I WILLIAM HEINEMANN LTD I LONDON :: TORONTO

(7 1/4 x 4 3/4"): [A]^8 B-T^8 U^{10}, 162 leaves; pp.[4],
9-327,[328]. Sig. U^2 signed U*

CONTENTS: p.[1]:half-title. p.[2]: list of 30 Lawrence
   titles, beginning *White Peacock*, ending *Reflections.*
   p.[3]:t.p. p.[4]: AUTHORIZED BRITISH EDITION I [short
   rule] I First Published February 1932 I Reprinted
   February, May, October 1932 I June, July, 1933; January,
   March 1934 I July 1935; November 1936; October 1937 I
   June, July 1938; July 1939 I March, September, November
   1940 I June 1941, June 1942 I PRINTED IN GREAT BRITAIN AT
   THE WINDMILL PRESS, KINGSWOOD, SURREY I. pp.9-327: Text.
   p.[328]: blank.

TYPOGRAPHY: 38ll.(p.149): 147(157) x 92mm. 10ll.=38mm. Face
   2(1x)mm.

RUNNING HEADS: as 17.1

PAPER: rough white wove unwatermarked. Thickness .1mm.
   Total bulk 19.9mm.

BINDING: coarse linen (T.304c) cloth, deep reddish orange
   (C.36). Stamping in black: upper cover: LADY I
   CHATTERLEY'S I LOVER I. Spine: LADY I CHATTERLEY'S I LOVER
   I [rectangle, 8x2 mm] I D. H.I LAWRENCE I HEINEMANN
   I. Lower cover, lower right: pub. device [windmill]. Let-
   tering in Sans Serif. All edges trimmed.
      DJ: front cover: watercolor, reproduced in half-tone.
   Man and woman lying under tree, kissing. Strong light

filters through foliage in center of picture, illuminating grass and path but not lovers; woman (brown hair, neck bare) wears brown; man with reddish-brown hair dressed in long black cloak. Predominant colors: vivid purplish blue, brilliant greenish yellow, pale yellow, brown, black. Lettering in reddish orange: LADY | CHATTERLEY'S | LOVER | D [dot] H [dot] LAWRENCE |. Spine and back cover white with blue lettering. Spine: Lady | Chat-| terley's | Lover | [star, in red] | D. H. | LAWRENCE | 6/- | net | Heinemann |. Back cover: biographical note, continued on back flap, ending: "No headstone was over his grave, save a phoenix (which was his own design) done in stone by a peasant who loved him." The pamphlet with Aldington's "Appreciation," first published 1932, is still offered gratis. Front flap blank.

COPY EXAMINED: OkTU(dj)

17.24   as 17.23 save:

coll: [A]^8 B^8 C-I^{16} K^{18}, L^{16}, 162 leaves; pp. [4], 9-327, [328]. K2 signed K*

CONTENTS: p.[4], 1.9: June 1941; June 1942; September 1947 |.

PAPER: smooth white wove unwatermarked. Thickness .07mm. Total bulk 12.1mm.

BINDING: spine of dj lettered in dark blue: Lady | Chatterley's | Lover | *by* | D. H. | LAWRENCE | [logo: windmill] | Heinemann |. Front flap blank save price, in lower right: 7s6d | NET |.

COPY EXAMINED: Pollinger coll.

*17.25   "January 1948"

17.26   "March 1949"; as 17.24 save:

Coll: [A]^{16} B-I^{16} K^{18}. $5[-C] signed [sig]* |. K2 signed K |. C4 signed C*

CONTENTS: p.[4]: . . . *June 1942; September 1947* | *January 1948; March 1949*

PAPER: smooth white wove unwatermarked. Thickness .08mm. Total bulk 14.4mm.

BINDING: dj: lettering on upper cover reads: LADY | CHATTERLEY'S | LOVER | *by* | D. H. LAWRENCE |. Back flap, under blurb, is notice for *Tales* and *Plumed Serpent*.

COPY EXAMINED: Forster Coll.(dj); Pollinger Coll.(dj)

17.27   "1950"

[in triple border, the middle one decorated with type

ornaments]: D. H. LAWRENCE | [French rule] | LADY |
CHATTERLEY'S | LOVER | [Heinemann windmill] | WILLIAM
HEINEMANN LTD | MELBOURNE :: LONDON :: TORONTO [11.3-5 in
open-face display type]

(6 13/16 x 4 1/4"): coll., no. of leaves, pagination as
17.23. $5[-K] signed [sig.]*; K2 signed K; K6 signed K*

CONTENTS: as 17.23 except p.[4]: . . . | 1942, 1947, 1948,
   1949, 1950.

TYPOGRAPHY: 38ll.(p.101), 147(158) x 93mm. 10ll.=43mm. Face
   2(1x)mm.

RUNNING HEADS: as 17.1

PAPER: smooth white wove unwatermarked. Thickness .08mm.
   Total bulk 15.8mm

BINDING: deep reddish orange? (C36) cloth, linen grain
   (T304). Goldstamped on spine: [thin-thick rule] | *D. H.* |
   LAWRENCE | [dot] | LADY | CHATTERLEY'S | LOVER | *Heinemann*
   | [thick-thin rule]. Plain white endpapers, all edges
   trimmed.
      Dj: Front cover and spine as 17.12, save no price on
   spine. Front flap: "The author's intellectual purpose in
   writing this book can be clearly discerned from this
   version, in spite of the cuts it has sustained. 7/6 net."
   Also advert for Aldington's *Portrait of a Genius But* . . .
   Back flap: list of 13 titles in Pocket Edition, "other
   titles in active preparation."

NOTE: This is the first impression of the Heinemann "Authorized Edition" to be listed in the *English Catalogue*.

COPIES EXAMINED: NO/P-1; Forster Coll.(dj); personal

*17.28   "1951"

17.29   "1952"; as 17.23 save:

LADY | CHATTERLEY'S | LOVER | BY D. H. LAWRENCE | [Heinemann
windmill, over rule; W on left, H on right of windmill] |
WILLIAM HEINEMANN LTD | MELBOURNE :: LONDON : : TORONTO

sig. I5 signed I*; sig.K2 signed K*; sig. K6 signed K**

CONTENTS: as 17.23 except p.[4]: . . . 1950 | 1951, 1952

RUNNING HEADS: as 17.1

PAPER: smooth white wove unwatermarked. Thickness .1mm. Total
   bulk 17.36mm.

BINDING: Linen grain (T304) cloth, strong red (C.12). Black
   stamped on upper cover: LADY | CHATTERLEY'S | LOVER |. On
   spine: LADY | CHATTERLEY'S | LOVER | [rectangle, 8x2 mm] |
   D. H. | LAWRENCE | HEINEMANN [all but last line on spine

in sans serif; all lettering on upper cover in sans
serif] l. Plain white endpapers; edges trimmed.

COPY EXAMINED: NO/P-1

[*subedition: Grosset & Dunlap "Madison Square Books"*]

17.30.$_1$ LADY l CHATTERLEY'S l LOVER l *by* l D. H. LAWRENCE l
GROSSET & DUNLAP l PUBLISHERS NEW YORK l *By
arrangement with Alfred A. Knopf*

(8 x 5 1/4"): [1]-[8]^{16}, [9]^4, [10-11]^{16}, 164 leaves, pp.[6],
9-327, [328],[2].

CONTENTS: same as Grosset and Dunlap Novels of Distinction
subedition, 17.10 above.

TYPOGRAPHY: as 17.9 above.

RUNNING HEADS: as 17.1 above.

PAPER: rough white wove unwatermarked. Thickness .13mm
(sig[2]1); .1mm(sig[9]3). Bulking 2.1mm(sig.[2]);
.38mm(sig[9]). Total bulk 22.0mm.

BINDING: Black cloth, fine bead grain (T. 202b). Stamped in
light greenish blue (C. 172). Upper cover: LADY l
CHATTERLEY'S l LOVER l D. H. LAWRENCE l. On spine: LADY l
CHATTERLEY'S l LOVER l D. H. LAWRENCE l GROSSET & DUNLAP
[on background of light greenish blue squares] l. Edges
unstained, trimmed. Smooth white endpapers.
   DJ: front cover: line and wash drawing of seated woman,
with shrubs, leaves, iron-wrought fence and stone column
in background. Woman wears stylish ball gown; eyes are
shaded and introspective, and lips are parted. Signed
SKRENDA29. Colors: black, white, very pale yellow. In
white on red background, in ornamented display type: *LADY
CHATTERLEY'S l LOVER l D. H. LAWRENCE* l. Spine: Drawing
continues. Author and title (?) in white on red background. At foot of spine is publisher's name. Back cover
bears list of "Madison Square Books," 24 titles, including
Max Brand's *Iron Trail*, O'Hara's *Appointment in Samara*,
Rinehart's *Circular Staircase*, Norman Lindsay's *Cautious
Amorist*. Back flap: blurb for *Farewell To Arms*. Front
flap: blurb for LCL: "The theme . . . concerns the right
of a married woman to have a child by another than her
husband. . . ."

NOTES: See Roberts, p.111.
   Sigs. from the Secker/Knopf eds. exist, randomly
scattered throughout the leaves, and not used for collation in this subedition. The 4-leaf sig. [9] is printed on
a slightly thinner paper than is the rest of the book.
   For a similarly posed, fashionable, yearning woman by
Skrenda see the dj for May Christie's *Playgirls in Love*

(Grosset and Dunlap, copyright 1932).
    In a letter dated Jan. 14, 1986, Grosset and Dunlap
informed me that records for out of print books published
before 1960 are not available.

COPIES EXAMINED: ViSaRC; personal(dj, spine of dj rubbed)

17.30.$_2$ as 17.30.$_1$ save:

Leaves measure 7 3/8 x 5

PAPER: smooth white wove unwatermarked. Thickness .1mm. Total
    bulk 19.1mm.

BINDING: as 17.30.$_1$ [top edge unstained]

COPY EXAMINED: personal

17.31   T.P. as 17.30

(7 3/4 x 5"): $[1-7]^{16}$ $[8]^{12}$ $[9-10]^{16}$ $[11]^8$, 164 leaves;
pp.[6], 9-327, [328], [2].

CONTENTS: as 17.10

TYPOGRAPHY: as 17.9

RUNNING HEADS: as 17.1

PAPER: smooth white wove unwatermarked. Thickness .11mm.
    Total bulk 19.6mm.

BINDING: lettering and decoration in very pale blue (C.184);
    otherwise as 17.30.
    DJ: lower cover carries list of 30 titles, starting with
Faith Baldwin's *District Nurse*, ending with Margaret
Wilson's *The Able McLaughlins*. (Only one title from
17.30.$_1$ included: *The Circular Staircase*. Lower flap: ad
for Ruth McKenney's *My Sister Eileen*.

COPY EXAMINED: OkTU(dj)

        [subedition: Heinemann Phoenix Ed. 1956]

17.32   D. H. LAWRENCE | [short French rule] | *Lady
        Chatterley's* | *Lover* | [Lawrence phoenix] |
        WILLIAM HEINEMANN LTD | MELBOURNE :: LONDON :: TORONTO

(7 3/4 x 5"): $[A]^{16}$, $B-I^{16}_*$, K^{18}_*, 162 leaves; [4], 9-327,
[328]. Sig. I5 signed I*; K2 signed K*; K6 signed K*|*

CONTENTS: p.[1]:half-title. p.[2]: THE PHOENIX EDITION OF
    D. H. LAWRENCE [list of 28 titles in 20 vols]. p.[3]:t.p.
    p.[4]: AUTHORISED BRITISH EDITION | [short rule] | FIRST
    PUBLISHED 1932 | REPRINTED 1932 (three times), 1933

(twice) | 1934 (twice), 1935, 1936, 1937, 1938 (twice), 1939, | 1940 (three times), 1941, 1942, 1947, 1948, | 1949, 1950, 1951, 1952, 1953 | REPRINTED IN THE PHOENIX EDITION 1956 | PRINTED IN GREAT BRITAIN | AT THE WINDMILL PRESS | KINGSWOOD, SURREY |. pp.9-327: text. p.[328]: blank.

TYPOGRAPHY: 38ll.(p.326), 152(158) x 93mm. 10ll.=39mm. Face 3(2x)mm.

RUNNING HEADS: as 17.1

PAPER: smooth white wove unwatermarked. Thickness .06mm. Total bulk 11.8mm.

BINDING: linen-grain (T304) cloth, strong blue (C. 178). Silver-stamped on spine: [thick rule] | D. H. | LAWRENCE | *Lady* | *Chatterley's* | *Lover* | [thick rule] |. Head and tail bands in red, with red place marker. Plain white endpapers. All edges trimmed.
    DJ: background in vivid yellowish green (C129). Front cover: D. H. [swash letters] | LAWRENCE | THE PHOENIX EDITION | LADY | CHATTERLEY'S | LOVER | WILLIAM HEINEMANN LTD. [ll. 1,2 in white; ll.3 and 7 in black; ll. 4-6 in red, in cartouche with white background]. Spine: green background; white rule divides it from upper cover: PHOENIX | EDITION | OF D. H.| LAWRENCE | [rule] | Lady Chatter- | ley's | Lover | [rule] |. [ll. 1-4 in black, rest in white]. Back cover: list of volumes in Phoenix edition. Flap of front cover: Lawrence phoenix and two paragraphs on Lawrence: "an example to an industrial age suffering from 'sex in the head'. . . . " Flap of back cover: "Though larger in format and more lavishly produced than the old 'pocket' edition, The Phoenix Edition is being offered at a similarly low price."

NOTE: *Eng. Cat.* lists publication date as May 22, 1956; price 10s 6d. Mumby and Norrie (487) state that a Lawrence revival in the 1050s led to the Phoenix Edition.

COPY EXAMINED: TxU(dj)

17.33 as 17.32 save:

Leaves measure 7 3/16 x 4 3/4".

TYPOGRAPHY: 38ll.(p.303): 148(157) x 91mm. 10ll.=39mm. Face 2(1.5x)mm.

PAPER: smooth white wove unwatermarked. Thickness .08mm. Total bulk 15.6mm.

BINDING: strong red (C.12) cloth. Silver-stamped on spine: D. H. | LAWRENCE | *Lady* | *Chatterley's* | *Lover* | [Lawrence phoenix] | HEINEMANN |. All edges trimmed.
    DJ: background color moderate green(C.145). Upper cover: l.3, added after author's name, is a Lawrence phoenix in red and black. On spine: same as above for

first 8 lines. Added, in black, starting l. 9: | 10 |
[rule, in white as above] | [logo: windmill over rule] |
HEINEMANN

COPIES EXAMINED: OBgU (rebound); NO/P-1(dj); Forster Coll.;
   OX/U-1

17.34   as 17.33 save:

coll.: $5 signed [sig.]*; K6 signed K$^{*'*}$

CONTENTS: p.[4]: 1.9" 1958 |.

NOTE: Still in print, 1961 (at 12/6).

COPY EXAMINED: Pollinger Coll.

["Authorized" Indian Edition, 1943?]

18.1   Lady Chatterley's Lover | BY | D. H. LAWRENCE |
        CENTRAL BOOK DEPOT | ALLAHABAD

(7 1/8 x 4 15/16"): π^2 [1]^8 2-22^8 23^4, 182 leaves; pp.[4],
[1], 2-360.

CONTENTS: p.[1]:half-title. p.[2]:blank. p.[3]:t.p. p.[4]:
   AUTHORISED INDIAN EDITION 1943 | PRINTED BY J. K. SHARMA
   AT THE ALLAHABAD LAW JOURNAL | PRESS, ALLAHABAD AND
   PUBLISHED BY THE CENTRAL BOOK DEPOT | ALLAHABAD. pp.[1] –
   360:text.

TYPOGRAPHY: Text: 34ll.(p.225): 135(148) x 93mm. 10ll.=39mm.
   Face 3(2x)mm. Typeface: Bembo(?). Old Style (Mod.
   Ren., DIN 1.13). Printed from type, or perhaps letterpress
   plates.

RUNNING HEADS, rectos and versos: LADY CHATTERLEY'S LOVER |.

PAPER: smooth white wove unwatermarked. Thickness .06mm.
   Total bulk 13.1mm.

BINDING: calico grain (T302) cloth, light grayish green
   (C154). Stamped in black. Upper cover: LADY | CHATTERLEY'S
   | LOVER | D. H. LAWRENCE |. On spine: LADY | CHATTERLEY'S
   | LOVER. | D. H. LAWRENCE | CENTRAL | BOOK DEPOT |. Plain
   white endpapers. All edges trimmed.

NOTE: text follows Secker abridgement. In a letter dated 3
   Jan. 1986, Mr. Gerald Pollinger of Laurence Pollinger Ltd.
   kindly informed me that the Lawrence estate has no record
   of this edition being authorized. Perhaps the publisher
   got the permission of a Dominion government official.
      In 1959, a Bombay bookseller was convicted of selling a
   copy of the unexpurgated LCL. The work was still banned in
   India as of 1968; the expurgated edition was available

(either the present volume or the Heinemann, or perhaps
both; see Shah 104-05).

COPY EXAMINED: TxU

[Vanguard Library Edition, 1953]

19.1   LADY CHATTERLEY'S | LOVER | [opened swelled rule] |
        D. H. Lawrence | [pub. device: Trojan warrior with
        spear and shield, in oval border] | THE VANGUARD
        LIBRARY | LONDON

(6 7/8 x 4 6/16"): [1]^{16} 2-8^{16}, 128 leaves; pp.[4], [1-4],
5-245, [246], [6]. $1(-[1]) signed L.C.L -- [sig. no.]

CONTENTS: pp.[1-2]: pastedown. pp.[3-4]:blank. p.[1]: half-
    title: THE VANGUARD LIBRARY | NO. 22 | LADY CHATTERLEY'S
    LOVER. p.[2]: list of 22 titles, starting with Maughan's
    The Razor's Edge, ending with LCL. p.[3]:t.p. p.[4]:
    PUBLISHED BY | CHATTO & WINDUS | IN ASSOCIATION WITH |
    WILLIAM HEINEMANN LTD | 99 GREAT RUSSELL ST. W.C.1 | First
    issued in | *The Vanguard Library* | 1953 | PRINTED IN GREAT
    BRITAIN BY | HAZELL WATSON & VINEY LIMITED | AYLESBURY AND
    LONDON | ALL RIGHTS RESERVED |. pp.5-245: text. pp.[246],
    [1-2]: list and description of first 21 titles in Vanguard
    Library. pp.[3-4]: blank. pp.[5-6]: pastedown.

TYPOGRAPHY: Text: 46ll.(p.29), 146(154) x 88mm. 10ll.=89mm.
    Face 2.5(1x)mm. Typeface: Lutetia(?), old style. DIN
    1.13, modern Ren.

RUNNING HEADS: rectos and versos: LADY CHATTERLEY'S LOVER

PAPER: rough white wove unwatermarked. Thickness .1mm. Total
    bulk 13.3mm. (excluding pastedowns).

BINDING: embossed calico grain cloth, deep orange yellow (cf.
    C.72). On spine, stamped in gold on red on rectangle of
    deep reddish brown: [2 rules] | [triangle] | [rule] | LADY
    | CHATT- | ERLEY'S | LOVER | [dot] | LAWRENCE | [rule] |
    [triangle] | [2 rules] |. At tail of spine, gold-stamped:
    Trojan warrior. All edges trimmed. Top edge stained purple.
    Dj: front cover: D. H. | LAWRENCE | *Lady Chatterley's Lover*
    | [line drawing in purple in white oval: man kneeling, using
    hammer and saw; woman standing in right foreground, lost
    profile. The figures are staring at each other. Hut and
    trees in background] | 3/6 | NET | THE VANGUARD LIBRARY |.
    Lines 1,2 in white on deep purple (C.220) background; rest
    of lettering in deep purple on strong orange (C.50) back-
    ground. On spine: [in white on deep purple background:] D.
    H. | LAWRENCE | [in deep purple on white background:] | LADY
    | CHATTER- | LEY'S | LOVER | [on yellow background with
    white stripes:] [3 rules, in purple, on yellow background
    with white stripes] | [logo: warrior, in purple on white
    background] | [3 rules in purple on yellow background with

white stripes] | [in purple on white background:] No. 22 |
VL [swash] |. Lines 1,2 (author's name) set top to bottom;
rest set vertically. Back cover: on white background, in
purple, is three-paragraph blurb: "His prophetic and
unconventional mind penetrated beneath our era's crust of
industrialism to the dark welter below; for those who
chose at first to ignore his themes, events such as the
spread of psychoanalysis and the rise of Fascism have
offered fresh warnings. . . . New phallic tenderness . . .
held up to an age suffering from 'sex in the head'. . . .
Now it is acknowledged as a great book--the quintessence
of Lawrence." Front flap: note on jacket (designed by
Edward Bawden, vignette by Biro). Back flap: first 22
titles in Vanguard Library. Begins Maughan's *Razor's Edge*;
ends LCL.

NOTES: I believe this to be the 1953 "printing" listed verso
    t.p. in the Heinemann Phoenix Ed. (17.32 above). The
    description of the novel in Vanguard's #31 (Clostermann's
    The Big Show) refers to Lawrence's "dying testament," and
    to his description of "a new phallic tenderness."

COPIES EXAMINED: Forster Coll; personal; Pollinger Coll.(all
    in dj)

*19.2

19.3   as 19.1 save:

CONTENTS: p.[2]: list of 30 titles, ending Menen, *The
    Backward Bride*. p.[4]: ll.9-10: *Reprinted* 1955 | *Reprinted*
    1956 |. pp.[246], [1-2]: list and description of first 30
    titles in Vanguard Library.

BINDING: dj: front cover: D. H. | LAWRENCE | [rule] | *Lady
    Chatterley's* | *Lover* | [drawing of man in brown coat with
    knapsack over shoulder, embracing woman with light blue
    blouse and dark blue coat; background of trees and leaves.
    Signed Biro. Predominant colors brown, blue, greenish
    blue] | THE VANGUARD LIBRARY 3/6 | NET |. [ll. 1-3 in
    yellow, 1.4 in white, 1.5 in red on strip of yellow]. On
    spine: Lady | Chatterley's | Lover | D. H. | Lawrence |.
    No. 21 | [logo] |. Back cover: Blurb, as 19.1. Flaps:
    jacket designer's credit (Biro), list of Vanguard titles.

NOTE: listed in *Ref. Guide To Current Lit.* for 1957.

COPY EXAMINED: Forster Coll.

    *[First printing Penguin (first American branch) edition,
    1946]*

20.1   D. H. LAWRENCE | *LADY* | *CHATTERLEY'S* | *LOVER* |

[pub. device: walking Penguin] | PENGUIN BOOKS, INC. | NEW YORK

(7 1/8 x 4 1/8"): no sig.[perfect bound], 132 leaves; pp.[4], 1-260.

CONTENTS: p.[1]: *About This Book* (". . . . The present version is the abridged version approved by Lawrence himself and originally published by Alfred A. Knopf, Inc., in 1928 [sic]"). p.[2]: List of Penguin and Pelican books, beginning *Lovely Lady,* ending Hansen's *America's Role in the World Economy.* p.[3]: t.p. p.[4]: Published by Penguin Books, Inc., and | Reprinted by Arrangement with Alfred A. Knopf, Inc. | FIRST PENGUIN BOOKS EDITION, SEPTEMBER, 1946 | *All rights reserved* . . . | Penguin Books, Inc., 245 Fifth Ave, New York . . . | Penguin Books Limited, Harmondsworth, Middlesex, England | PRINTED IN THE UNITED STATES OF AMERICA |. pp. 1-260: text.

TYPOGRAPHY: text: 44ll.(p.3), 157 x 89mm. 10ll. = 35mm. Face3(1.5x)mm. Typeface: Times Roman (R.52), old style. DIN 1.13, modern Ren.

PAPER: smooth white wove unwatermarked. Thickness .06mm. Total bulk 8.9mm.

BINDING: paper wrappers, laminated. Upper cover: pink, yellow, black. Drawing of near-naked woman and naked man, framed by intertwined playing card symbols (spade and diamond respectively). In black, in yellow strip at top: 610 [walking penguin logo] |. Above drawing, on pink background: LADY CHATTERLEY'S | LOVER |. Below drawing, in black, on right half of cover: D[dot]H[dot]LAWRENCE |. Below drawing and name of author is blank strip 5/16" wide, followed by black strip, 3/4" from bottom of cover, on which is printed in white: PENGUIN BOOKS |. At spine edge, above author's name: jonas|. Spine: on yellow background: 610 |. Set top to bottom, on white background: LADY CHATTERLEY'S LOVER D. H. LAWRENCE |. Lower cover: photo of Lawrence, and three paragraphs on his life and writings ("He sought his apocalypse chiefly in sex and that was the reason for the obloquy dealt him by Mrs. Grundy.") Strips in yellow (at top), and in yellow and black (at bottom), run from front cover to spine and lower cover. Penguin logo on bottom strip of lower cover. Plain smooth white endpapers, thickness .1mm. Edges stained pink.

NOTES: Harry T. Moore: "*Lady Chatterley's Lover*, a book dealing with love as a serious, major, and sacred theme, was taboo over here and in his native England . . . . Meanwhile, a mutilated edition that sold chiefly as a drugstore paperback had parodied what he really wrote . . . ." (Moore,"LCL as Romance" 262). Moore is probably referring to the NAL edition. However, see the more mutilated edition published by Ward Hill Books (15.1 above), one binding variant of which carried on the upper

wrapper a male and female nude modelled after the illustration on the wrapper of 20.1.
     Weybright (183) praises Times Roman's beauty and
utility: ". . . it saved some 15 percent on paper in the
manufacture of a book with normal margins."
     The cover design is signed [Robert] "Jonas," who
stated that "for books in which the poetic predominated I
used poetic, associative images" (Schreuders 44).
     The first impression comprised 280,370 copies (25¢).
In the NAL archive at Fales Library, N.Y.U., the number of
total copies of each impression is listed on an undated
typed sheet headed "Expurgated Edition of *Lady Chatterley's Lover.*"
     The contract with Knopf grants Penguin (American
branch) exclusive Canadian rights and non-exclusive rights
elsewhere. The agreement, on file with NAL archival
materials at Fales Library, NYU, was for three years, to
be extended automatically.

COPY EXAMINED: personal; KyU

20.2 "December, 1946." copies: 101,418. As 20.1 save:

CONTENTS: as 4.1 save p.[4]:. . . | SECOND PENGUIN BOOKS
    EDITION, DECEMBER, 1946.

PAPER: smooth white wove unwatermarked. Thickness .06mm.
    Total bulk 9.2mm.

BINDING: as 20.1 but red replaces pink on upper cover.
    Wrappers unlaminated. Endp. as 20.1

COPIES EXAMINED: INS, personal

20.3 "March 1948." copies: 303,035. As 20.1 save:

CONTENTS: as 20.1 except p.[2]: list of other recommended
    Penguins: begins *Lovely Lady*, ends with Smith's *Strange
    Fruit*. Included 4 titles by Caldwell, 2 by Faulkner,
    Lewisohn's *The Tyranny of Sex*, Frank's *Desire Me*, Joyce's
    Portrait.

PAPER: Smooth white wove unwatermarked. Thickness .05mm.
    Total bulk 7.9mm.

BINDING: paper wrappers. Upper cover: white lettering. [First
    two lines in purple strip at top:] 610 | THE GREAT NOVEL
    THAT SHOCKED THE WORLD | LADY CHATTERLEY'S | LOVER |
    D[dot]H[dot]LAWRENCE | [drawing of smiling woman (heart-
    shaped, girlish face), her head and top of left shoulder
    visible, lying amid small flowers. A man's hand holds red
    flower just over her head] | [blank purple strip, 5/16"] |
    [in olive green strip, 3/4":] A SIGNET BOOK |. Predominant
    colors dark green, red, yellowish pink, brown. Spine and
    lower wrapper as 20.1, but purple and green strips replace
    yellow and black, and logo on lower cover replaced by:
    Published by the New American Library |. No endpapers.
    Edges stained pink.

COPY EXAMINED: TxU

*20.4   "May 1948."   copies: 101,835

20.5   "January 1949." copies: 49,540.

D. H. LAWRENCE | *LADY* | *CHATTERLEY'S* | *LOVER* | [logo, in oval
border: N [dot] A [dot] L | Si[sic]GNET | BOOKS] | A SIGNET
BOOK | Published by THE NEW AMERICAN LIBRARY

CONTENTS: as 20.3 except p.[4]: . . . THIRD PRINTING,
    FEBRUARY, 1948 | FOURTH PRINTING, MAY, 1948 | FIFTH
    PRINTING, JANUARY, 1949|. At bottom, in rectangular
    border: *SIGNET BOOKS are published by* | *The New American
    Library of World Literature, Inc.,* | *245 Fifth Avenue, New
    York 16, New York* |. Below border: PRINTED IN THE UNITED
    STATES OF AMERICA

TYPOGRAPHY: as 20.1

PAPER: smooth white wove unwatermarked. Thickness .04mm.
    Total bulk 7.5mm.

BINDING: as 20.3

COPY EXAMINED: personal

20.6   "January 1950." copies: 49,540. As 20.1 save:

T.P. as 20.5

CONTENTS: as 20.1 save p.[2]: 18 Signet titles, beginning
    with Cain's *Mildred Pierce*, ending with *Walden*. p.[4]: . .
    . THIRD PRINTING, FEBRUARY, 1948 | FOURTH PRINTING, MAY,
    1948 | FIFTH PRINTING, JANUARY, 1949 | SIXTH PRINTING,
    JANUARY, 1950 | At bottom, in rectangular border: *SIGNET
    BOOKS are published by* | *The New American Library of World
    Literature, Inc.,* | *245 Fifth Avenue, New York 16, New
    York* |. Below border: PRINTED IN THE UNITED STATES OF
    AMERICA

PAPER: Smooth white wove unwatermarked. Thickness .05mm.
    Total bulk 8.8mm.

BINDING: upper cover: [on 3/4" orange strip at top:] 610 |
    [3-line logo as on t.p.] THE GREAT NOVEL THAT SHOCKED THE
    WORLD | [in white:] LADY CHATTERLEY'S | LOVER | [in
    yellow:] D. H. LAWRENCE | [illus. of woman and man embrac-
    ing; her right hand, wedding ring(?) visible, rests on his
    bare shoulder. Only the heads and the man's shoulder are
    shown (his profile is lost), leaving one to guess that the
    couple are naked. Background of flowers and leaves.
    Predominant colors pale orange yellow, green, light brown]
    | [in 1/16" strip of blue at bottom:] SIGNET BOOKS |.
    Lower wrapper and spine as 20.1, but printing in spine on
    orange background, strips at top and bottom in yellow and
    blue. Lower cover, on orange strip at top: . . . Good

Reading for the Millions |. No endpapers. Edges stained
pink.

NOTE: this is the only impression with this cover art. See
essay above, p.65.

COPIES EXAMINED: Nott. County Lib., personal

20.7   "November 1953." copies: 237,150. Subedition: Signet
        Giant (S1086). As 20.1 save:

T.p. reset after l.4: A Complete Reprint of the | Authorized
American Edition | [logo, in oval border: N[dot]A[dot]L |
SIGNET | BOOKS] | A SIGNET BOOK | Published by THE NEW
AMERICAN LIBRARY

CONTENTS: as 20.6 except p.[1]: Destined To Love: 4-paragraph
        blurb. ". . . . Then a chance meeting with Mellors. .
        . reawakens the emotions she had so long repressed, and
        the passion that flames between these two hungering
        spirits drastically alters their destinies." At bot-
        tom: THIS BOOK IS A COMPLETE REPRINT OF THE AUTHOR- | IZED
        AMERICAN EDITION APPROVED BY LAWRENCE HIM- | SELF AND
        ORIGINALLY PUBLISHED BY ALFRED A. KNOPF IN | 1928. [sic]
        p.[2]: list of 5 titles, starting with Sons and Lovers and
        ending with Appointment In Samarra. p.[4]: as 4.6 save . .
        . SIXTH PRINTING, JANUARY, 1950 | SEVENTH PRINTING,
        NOVEMBER, 1953 |.

PAPER: thickness .08mm. total bulk 11.3mm.

BINDING: Front cover illus., signed [James] "Avanti," a
        version of the one for 20.3-20.5 but more of woman's body
        shows: a less youthful female with parted lips and half-
        closed eyes. Her breasts are covered. Her right hand is
        not visible; therefore, no wedding ring is included. From
        her picnic basket protrudes a paperback book, painted in
        the same strong reddish brown as is the rose. In gold
        strip at top: S1086 | [logo: SIGNET GIANT arranged on
        black border encircling price (35¢)] | One of the World's
        Most Famous Modern Novels | A Complete Reprint of the
        Authorized American Edition | [on red background:] Lady
        Chatterley's | Lover | [in white, superimposed on illus:]
        D. H. LAWRENCE |. At bottom, printed in pink, in black
        strip: A SIGNET GIANT |. Predominant colors pink, green,
        yellowish green, reddish brown. Spine in black on gold
        background: S1086 | [set top to bottom:] LADY CHATTERLEY'S
        LOVER | D. H. Lawrence | [left to right, in pink, on strip
        of black: Signet Giant logo]. Lower wrapper: three brief
        statements on Lawrence by Arnold Bennett, Richard Al-
        dington, Anthony West. Strips at top and bottom in gold
        and black, printing at bottom in pink. Signet Giant logo
        at top. No endpapers. Edges stained yellow.

NOTES: In 1954, Barney Rosset recognized that this edition
        "had gone through about seven printings - which shows the
        potential of the book . . . ."(Rosset to a friend in
        Paris, requesting two copies of the unexpurgated text be

sent to him to force a test case, March 31, 1954; in
Arents coll., Syracuse U.)
       To accommodate a price rise (to 35¢), the "Signet
Giant" series was introduced in 1950. This is the first
impression of LCL to be so designated. For the Federal
Trade Commission complaint (1950) about Signet's placement
of their notices of abridgement (in 35 titles), see the
essay above, p. 63.

COPIES EXAMINED: Forster Coll., ICarbS, personal

*20.8 "July 1957." copies: 155,145. New cover ordered.

*20.9 "August 1957." copies: 12,075.

*20.10 "January 1958." copies: 32,045.

       [2nd (reset) NAL edition (1958-59)]

21.1   "December 1958." copies printed: 51,415

D. H. LAWRENCE | *Lady* | *Chatterley's* | *Lover* | A Complete
Reprint of the | Authorized American Edition | [pub. device,
in oval border, as on tp of 18.5 above] | A SIGNET BOOK |
Published by THE NEW AMERICAN LIBRARY

(7 1/8 x 4 1/4"): unsigned (perfect bound), 128 leaves;
pp. [1-4], 5-253, [254], [2].

CONTENTS: p.[1]:blurb, as in 20.7 above. Under rule:
    ". . . approved by Lawrence himself and originally
    published by Alfred A. Knopf." p.[2]: list of 4 titles,
    starting with *Sons and Lovers* and ending with *Winesburg
    Ohio*. p.[3]:t.p. p.[4]: as 20.7 save publishing history:
    . . . | ELEVENTH PRINTING, DECEMBER 1958 |. pp. 5-253:
    text. p.[254],[1]: list of titles. p.[2]: HOW TO BUILD A
    LOW COST LIBRARY

TYPOGRAPHY: 44ll.(p.137), 155 x 90mm. 10ll.=34mm. Face
    3(2x)mm. Typeface: as 20.1.

PAPER: smooth white wove unwatermarked. Thickness .08mm.
    Total bulk 11.5mm.

BINDING: paper wrappers, white and deep pink (C3), lettering
    in deep red (C13) and black. Upper cover [in outer borders
    of gold, red, and white, with lettering in black except as
    noted]: D1428 | [next 4 ll. in box at upper left]: SIGNET
    | 50c | DOUBLE | VOLUME | D. H. LAWRENCE | [in pink]: The
    great novel that shocked the world | Lady Chatterley's |
    Lover | [in red]: A Complete Reprint of the | Authorized
    American Edition | [drawing of seated, embracing couple
    against background of deep pink sky with white clouds] |
    [in lower right, in red]: A SIGNET BOOK |. Spine, on gold
    background: D | 1428 | [top to bottom:] LADY CHATTERLEY'S

LOVER   D. H. Lawrence | [logo: Signet Double Vol., as on u.c.]. Lower cover: photo of author, quotes from Bennett, Aldington, West, against cloud and sky motif as on upper cover. Edges stained red.

COPIES EXAMINED: TxU, personal

21.2   "August 1959."   copies: 715,000. As 21.1 save:

CONTENTS: as 21.1 except for p.[2]: four titles given, beginning *Sons and Lovers*, ending *Studs Lonigan*. p.[4]: as 21.1 save: FIRST PRINTING SEPTEMBER 1946 | TWELFTH PRINTING AUGUST 1959 |. p.[254], [1]: list of 10 titles, starting with *Huckleberry Finn*, ending with *Scarlet Letter*.

BINDING: [in red:] D1428 | [logo]: [in red:] 1428 | [in white:] SIGNET BOOKS [in oval encircling price (50¢)] |. [In large (x-height 28mm) display type (strong vertical stress, hairline serifs) in brilliant yellow:] Lady | Chatterley's | Lover [last word in title extends into drawing, in blue outline on black, of fully dressed man (shirt, slacks, shoes) and woman embracing, lying on the earth]. | [below figures, in reddish-pink:] The great novel that shocked the world | [in white:] D. H. LAWRENCE | [in pink:] A COMPLETE REPRINT OF THE AUTHORIZED AMERICAN EDITION | [in white:] A SIGNET BOOK |. On spine, on white background: D | 1428 | [set top to bottom:] [in bluish green:] Lady Chatterley's Lover [in black:] D. H. LAWRENCE |. Lower cover: portrait, blurbs by Bennet, Aldington, West.

NOTE: This impression has a new cover, very similar to the unexpurgated NAL ed. of the same month [see 37.1 below]

COPIES EXAMINED: personal, TxU

*21.3   August 1959. copies: 36,000.

*21.4   September 1959. copies: 11,800.
        [NB: I have not located a copy of this impression; however, the NAL archive at the Fales Library, NYU, contains proof copy of the first leaf, with its state-ment "To The Reader," and the second (the t.p. and its verso). Transcription is given here.]

TP: as 21.1

CONTENTS: [p.1]: "This is the only expurgated edition authorized by the Lawrence estate. . . . The book has remained in print [since 1946], selling well over two million copies. It was the *only* edition . . . admissible through US customs and in general circulation in the United States until quite recently." p.[2]: list of titles. p.[3]:t.p. p.[4]: *Published as a SIGNET BOOK* | *By arrangement with Alfred A. Knopf, Inc.* | FIRST PRINTING SEPTEMBER 1946 | FOURTEENTH PRINTING SEPTEMBER 1959

NOTE: A letter to me from Alan J. Kaufman of NAL in June, 1985 kindly gives the number of copies of the abridged version sold in 1959: 812,390. Madison (554) reports that the public accusations between Grove and NAL in the summer of 1959 resulted in 650,000 copies being sold. See Section 5.

On 25 May 1988, Gerald Pollinger stated that the Lawrence Estate approved of NAL ceasing to publish its expurgated edition.

[First Ace Books Edition, April 1958]

22.1   LADY CHATTERLEY'S | LOVER | D. H. LAWRENCE | THE HARBOROUGH PUBLISHING CO. LTD. | 35 GREAT RUSSELL STREET, LONDON W.C.1

(7 x 4 1/2"): [1]^8 2-20^8, 160 leaves; pp.[1-4], 5-315, [316],[4]. $1(-20) signed LC-[sig. no.]. Sig. 20$_1$ signed CL-20.

CONTENTS: p.[1]: half-title. p.[2]: THE WORKS OF D. H. LAWRENCE [27 titles] |. p.[3]:t.p. p.[4]: AUTHORISED BRITISH EDITION | First published 1932 | Reprinted 1932(three times), | 1933(twice), 1934(twice), | 1935, 1936, 1937, 1938(twice), | 1939, 1940(three times), 1941, | 1942, 1947, 1948, 1949, 1950, | 1951, 1952, 1953, 1956. | First Ace Books Edition, April 1958 | Printed in England by Hunt, Barnard & Co., Ltd., | at the Sign of the Dolphin, Aylesbury, Bucks.|. pp.5-315: text. p.[316]: ad for Danielson's *Love in the South Seas*, pp.[4]: Ace booklist: 50 titles, under headings of General Fiction, General Nonfiction, and War Titles, beginning *A House Is Not A Home*, ending *Johnny Purple*. Fiction includes works by James Baldwin, Steinbeck, Lessing, Renault, Moravia, Mailer.

TYPOGRAPHY: Text: 38ll.(p.97), 147(159) x 86mm. 10ll.=38mm. Face 2.5(2x)mm. Typeface: Times Roman (DIN 1.13, modern Ren.)

RUNNING HEADS, rectos and versos: LADY CHATTERLEY'S LOVER

PAPER: rough white wove unwatermarked. Thickness .1mm. Total bulk 17.9mm.

BINDING: paper wrappers; upper cover bears lettering on background photograph of lush, unmowed grass: The first authorised British | paper-back [sic] edition | *Lady* | *Chatterley's* | *Lover* | *A Novel* | *D. H. Lawrence* (ll. 1-2 in white, sans serif; ll. 3-5 in white, non-continuous script; ll. 6-7 in yellow, same script). In upper left, black in yellow circle: 3/6 |. Upper right, black on yellow clover-leaf design: ACE BOOKS |. Below leaf, in yellow: H190. On spine, in yellow and white on black background: set horizontally: [Ace logo] | H190 | [set

vertically]: *Lady Chatterley's Lover* [title in script as on upper cover] D. H. LAWRENCE | [in yellow circle]: 3/6 |. Lower cover: photograph portrait of author. All edges trimmed.

NOTE: Sutherland (*Off. Lit.* 20): "In 1958, a downmarket British publisher, Ace, brought out the abridged *Chatterley* (it went through four editions in twelve months)." See essay for Section 3, p.60.
     The Ace, Four Square, and New English Library volumes were published with the approval of the Lawrence Estate (Gerald Pollinger, interview with the author, 25 May 1988).

COPIES EXAMINED: Forster Coll.; Pollinger Coll., personal

22.2   "April 1958"; as 22.1 save:

CONTENTS: as 22.1 except p.[4]: . . . First Ace Books edition,   April 1958 | Reprinted April 1958 |

PAPER: rough white wove unwatermarked. Thickness .1mm. Total bulk 16.6mm.

COPY EXAMINED: NO/P-1

*22.3   "July 1958"

*22.4   "August 1958"

*22.5   "January 1959"

*22.6   "May 1959"

*22.7   "September 1959"

*22.8   "January 1960"

*23.1   *Second Ace Books edition, "Reset June, 1960"*

*23.2   "Reprinted July 1960"

*23.3   "Reprinted August 1960"

*23.4   "Reprinted September 1960"

*23.5   "Reprinted September 1960"

23.6   "Reprinted October 1960"

LADY CHATTERLEY'S | LOVER | D. H. LAWRENCE | THE HARBOROUGH PUBLISHING CO. LTD. | 44 BEDFORD ROW, LONDON W.C.1

(7 x 4 5/8"): [A]^{16} B-G^{16} [H]^{16}, 128 **leaves**; **pp.**[1-4], 5-256.

CONTENTS: p.[1]:half-title. p.[2]: THE WORKS OF D. H.

LAWRENCE [26 titles; *Aaron's Rod* no longer present].
p.[3]: t.p. p.[4]: AUTHORISED BRITISH EDITION | Bound
Edition first published in England by | William Heinemann
Limited, London, W.C.1 | [next 7 lines reproduce printing
history as in Heinemann Phoenix subedition, 17.32 above]
First Ace Books edition April 1958 | Reprinted April 1958
| Reprinted July 1958 | Reprinted August 1958 | Reprinted
January 1959 | Reprinted May 1959 | Reprinted September
1959 | Reprinted January 1960 | Reset June 1960 | Re-
printed July 1960 | Reprinted August 1960 | Reprinted
September 1960 | Reprinted September 1960 | Reprinted
October 1960 | (Printer's statement: Love & Malcolmson).
pp. 5-256: text.

TYPOGRAPHY: Text: 46ll.(p.33), 144 (153) x 88mm. 10ll.=32mm.
Face: 2.5(1.5x)mm. Typeface: Times Roman (DIN 1.13, Modern
Renaissance).

RUNNING HEADS: rectos and versos: LADY CHATTERLEY'S LOVER

PAPER: rough white wove unwatermarked. Thickness .1mm. Bulking 13.8mm.

BINDING: as 22.1 above.

NOTE: ". . . an expurgated edition published in Britain . . .
sold nearly a quarter of a million copies in nine months
last year [1960]" (Bedford 146).

COPY EXAMINED: personal

*23.7   "Reprinted March, 1961"

*23.8   *First Four Square (paperback) subedition, 1962*

NOTE: Ace Books was sold to Four Square in 1961. The Signet
Classics titles NEL reprinted did not include the
unexpurgated LCL, which obviously the Lawrence estate
and Penguin would not have allowed. Item 24.1 (and
Whitaker's *Cumulative Book List*; see 24.1, NOTES)
indicate that Four Square published the abridged
edition two years after the first British (Penguin and
Heinemann) unexpurgated editions appeared and that, six
years later, the same Secker/Knopf abridgement was
issued under the NEL imprint -- both from the text of
the second Ace Books edition (23.1). The first line on
p. [4], indicating that the work is *the* "authorised"
edition, was removed.

New English Library Edition, 1968(?)

24.1   LADY | CHATTERLEY'S | LOVER | *D. H. LAWRENCE* | [each
letter boxed by thin rules] NEL: | THE NEW ENGLISH
LIBRARY

(7 x 4 1/2): [A]^{16} B-G^{16} [H]^{16}, 128 leaves; pp.[1-4], 5-256.

CONTENTS: p.[1]: half-title. p.[2]: blank p.[3]:t.p. p.[4]:
as 21.6 above through line 24 save 1.1 not present.
Beginning 1.25: Reprinted March 1961 | First Four Square
edition, 1962 | [asterisk] | Republished by the New
English Library Limited | February 1968 | [conditions of
sale: 5 lines regarding rebinding of the work being
prohibited] | *NEL Books are published by the New English
Library Limited from Barnard's Inn | Holborn, London, EC 1
Made and Printed in Great Britain by Ivor Nicholson and
Watson | Ltd, Redhill, Surrey* |. pp.5-256: text.

TYPOGRAPHY: 46ll. (p.97), 143(151) x 86mm. 10ll.=34mm. Face:
3(2x)mm.

PAPER: smooth white wove unwatermarked. Thickness .07mm.
Total bulk 11.3mm.

BINDING: paper wrappers. Upper cover: background in brilliant
green (C.140). Photograph of one red rose, with leaves,
long stem, and thorns. In black, at top: [each of first
three letters boxed:] NEL 2114 FOUR SQUARE 5/- | [rule] |
D H | Lawrence | [in lower right, in white:] *Lady |
Chatterley's | Lover* |. On spine: pub's logo, 2114 |.
Running top to bottom: LADY CHATTERLEY'S LOVER D. H.
LAWRENCE [author's name in white] |. Set vertically: 2114
|. Lower cover, at top: PUBLISHED BY THE NEW ENGLISH
LIBRARY LIMITED [logo] | [rule] | photo of Lawrence, below
blurb: ". . . . The subject of a notorious court case for
obscenity, it is bold, erotic, and outspoken. No reader
has ever been quite the same after reading this book."
Below photo is price list for nine countries (Australia,
Belgium, France, Germany, Italy, Netherlands, New Zealand,
Switzerland, UK [5/-]).

NOTES: Apparently a new edition (face size larger, although
text block smaller, than   23.6). In *Whitaker's Cumulative
Book List*, 1968-69, as "new edition," published February
1968.
  Perhaps this expurgated edition was published as late as
1968 because some people would not want in their homes or
libraries a complete version. However, there is no
indication in the book or on the covers that it is in fact
expurgated. Perhaps the lack of a lubricous cover was a
sign that it was (see essay above, p.64). It is noteworthy
that this edition was published in more countries than the
(unexpurgated) Penguin edition.
  Mumby and Norrie (514): NEL absorbed Four Square.

COPIES EXAMINED: LO/N-1(rebound, paper wrappers preserved);
NO/P-1; Forster Coll.; Pollinger Coll.

SECTION 4

Continental Editions in English, 1933–60

INTRODUCTORY ESSAY

The first unexpurgated continental edition of *Lady Chatterley's Lover*, "not to be introduced into the British Empire or the U. S. A.," appeared in European bookstalls in 1933, under the imprint of The Odyssey Press of Hamburg, Paris, and Bologna. In her "Open Letter" prefixed to the text, Frieda Lawrence states that she authorized an expurgated edition (Secker 1932) to make the novel, "or as much of it as England would allow," widely available in that country. Odyssey's "well-printed" edition, with the "little typographical mistakes" corrected, and issued at an affordable price for everyone, served, she hoped, to further introduce the work to general readers. Lawrence "wanted to reach the people he voiced and from whom he came."

The Paris Popular Edition (1.2–1.4; see pp.4–5 above), arranged by the author himself, had been printed in three impressions of 3,000 copies each in 1929–30. Edward Titus closed his Black Manikin Press in 1932 (Ford 158). By 1933, rights to the unexpurgated continental edition were held by The Albatross Press, which on 25 January of that year signed a contract with Frieda Lawrence, agreeing to publish no later than March 31, 1933./1/ Odyssey, therefore, was an alternate imprint of The Albatross, a fact corroborated by the general appearance of the books themselves (with the exception of the paper wrappers: Albatross are color-coded, and carry the logo and double borders on upper and lower covers; Odyssey covers were simply printed and of neutral colors). Both imprints have paper jackets. They bear very similar colophons, which the publishers felt were "innovative" for inexpensive paperbacks ("Tauchnitz" 1645); those of both imprints name the printer (Brandstetter) and the paper-mill (Bautzen). Both books have attractive monotype faces and page layout by the distinguished typographer Hans Mardersteig. They are also equal in size, fitting for the coat pockets of the early 1930s ("Tauchnitz" 1645). Identical prices in reichmarks,

lire, French and (later) Swiss francs are listed on the lower
covers. Finally, verso the upper covers are blurbs in
English, German and French, to attract Europeans not familiar
with English as well as tourists of various nationalities.
Even the imprint names have similar connotations of peregrin-
ation, serendipity (fortunate homecomings to all manner
mariners), and spirituality (the albatross was supposed to
carry souls to safe havens). Also, both names carry similar
spellings in English, French, and German (PW 14 Dec. 1946:
3217).

Both imprints carry a copyright notice naming [Max]
Christian Wegner, one of the managers of Albatross. The other
two were British publisher John Holroyd Reece (of whom more
below), and Kurt Enoch, already experienced in the German
book trade and responsible for conceiving the format and
design of the volumes (Schick 32-33). These men effected a
successful, innovative business, exploiting an audience of
English-speaking tourists and natives of countries throughout
Europe for modern literature, including adventure, mystery,
love stories, biography, historical and psychological novels,
and humor and satire (by 1939, when the war forced a halt to
operations, there were 13 Lawrence titles). They realized
that travellers' tastes and social class had changed from
those of the previous, more aristocratic and less iconoclastic generation (Dickson 152). An enthusiastic *Publishers'
Weekly* reported in 1932 ("Tauchnitz" 1643-45) that with
headquarters in various capitals, Paris-based Albatross had
been able, through the good offices of Curtis Brown, Ltd., to
make contacts with many writers and their agents. The firm
solved difficult promotion and distribution problems by
exploiting the railway line from Verona (where the books were
printed) to Leipzig and Hamburg (where they were sent to a
score of depots convenient for reaching booksellers in
various countries). The emphasis on contemporary writers and
the attractive "modern" format provided strong competition
for Tauchnitz, the leading publisher of continental reprints
since the mid-nineteenth century. In 1935 the two companies
merged (Schick 32-33; Davis 23-25). Also in that year Penguin
began operations in England, using format and design similar
to Albatross (Morpurgo 181).

The Odyssey imprint seems to have been used to publish
works which had encountered objections on the basis of erotic
content or scatological language: the best example other than
Chatterley is Joyce's *Ulysses*. The firm had an extensive
list and probably did not want its customers to feel they
ought to think of Albatrosses as "bedside throwaways" or the
kinds of books "one reads with one hand." Not that the
Lawrence and Joyce titles fit this description save in
notoriety, but they were banned books which would have to be
discarded after being read, or sneaked through customs. This
reputation is in fact the reason given, in a memo from
Albatross' editorial office in 1947, for its decision not to
sue Jan Förlag for flooding the market with the latter's
edition of *Chatterley* (27.4, 28.1-29.1) at that time being
distributed in Switzerland and France. The memo is preserved
in a Humanities Research Center file ("Lawrence, D. H.

Misc.") and reads in part: "Neither does it cast a very good reflection on us to be the publisher of this book even if it sells like hotcakes." I take this to mean that a court case would associate Albatross with a current attempt to dis- tribute a proscribed book, and probably with past practice of doing so under the camouflage of the Odyssey imprint.

Odyssey published seven impressions of *Chatterley* (25.1- 25.7) between 1932 and 1935. The 1936 eighth impression was issued in Paris with the Obelisk imprint. The owner was Jack Kahane, to whom Lawrence had offered a cheap edition of *Chatterley* in 1929, after Beach refused and before Titus was approached (see 1.2, the "Paris Popular Edition). Kahane, then beginning his publishing career (Joyce's *Haveth Childers Everywhere*), refused, Lawrence thought through timidity, but Kahane asserts because his finances were unsteady and the project might have to be abandoned. He states that this incident led to his·founding of the Obelisk Press, as a "natural sanctuary" for authors with censorship problems (Kahane 223-26). As I mentioned in the essay for Section 1 (p.4 above), Gershon Legman (Introduction 46) throws some acerbic light on this, stating that erotica publishers in the 1920s and 30s wished to identify their products with avant- garde literature "in Paris and Florence." Obelisk was, he says, such an "imitation avant-garde firm," which published "mostly semi-erotic trash," but also Henry Miller. However, if Kahane had not published what he did (including non-trashy fiction by Norah James, James Hanley, Peter Neagoe, or Radclyffe Hall), he would not have developed the audience he did. Also, as Kahane's son, Maurice Girodias, states (230), his father, unlike Titus, the Crosbys, Cunard, and Lowenfels, was an experienced businessman with some capital to spare. By 1934, he was in a position to publish *Tropic Of Cancer*, however cautiously: the "one man in the whole world" who would do so, according to Miller's agent (Ford 363).

Why and under what circumstances did Kahane publish the eighth impression of *Chatterley*? The most likely explanation (at least the simplest) is that as it had recently been and perhaps still was "the number one scandal book" (Girodias 87; see p.3 above), he wanted it for his list and purchased the rights from Albatross in 1936, the copyright remaining with the latter (clearly, as indicated by the file of interoffice memos referred to above, the firm still had the copyright in the mid-1940s). In a letter to me (15 Oct. 1988), Maurice Girodias recalls his father speaking of a visit to Holroyd Reese "presumably at the time that deal [regarding the Obelisk printing] was made."

Verso the title pages of the fifth (1934) and seventh (1935) impressions of the Odyssey Press *Chatterleys* (25.5 and 25.7), and of the eighth impression (25.8), one reads that the copyright is held by "Les Éditions Du Pégasus, Paris." It is quite possible that this "Pegasus" represents the same publishers as does "Odyssey." As mentioned in Section 1, Holroyd Reese (with Nancy Cunard) owned a Pegasus Press in Paris in the late 1920s. Lawrence approached him regarding an authorized Paris edition of *Lady Chatterley's Lover* before he

went to Titus (CL 1107, 1112; see p.5 above). Ford states
that Radclyffe Hall's *Well of Loneliness* was published under
this imprint until "Reese closed the Pegasus in the early
thirties" (359). Lovat Dickson confirms this (151-54). Reese,
he says, published Hall's novel under his Pegasus Press
imprint. ". . . Already the Pegasus edition was displayed in
every English bookshop in Paris" (170). This was in 1928,
when the Albatross enterprise was still in the planning
stage, and before the Odyssey Press was founded. Kahane
eagerly added *The Well Of Loneliness* to the Obelisk list in
1933 (Ford 359, 414). I assume he did the same with the
Lawrence title in 1936.

This helps explain the "Éditions Du Pégasus" in the
Chatterley copyright statements, but not why this statement
attributed copyright to Odyssey in the early (1933) impressions, and to Pegasus thereafter. Whatever liaison existed
between Kahane and Reese is unclear. If there was one, it
might help explain why Kahane got *Chatterley* from Odyssey. It
may also be why the title was published under the Pegasus
imprint in 1938 (25.11)--especially if Reese and Kahane were
sharing profits. Girodias mentions Reese only as a "flagrant
adventurer" (241). He also says that, Albatross being "shaky"
in the late 1930s, Kahane conceived an idea for another continental reprint series, modelled after Tauchnitz, Albatross,
and Penguin. However, the "international situation" prevented
it from developing. Could this plan, formed with a member of
Hachette who would have provided "distribution and financing"
(241), have included Reece?

Even if there was a connection between Reece and Kahane,
it does not fully explain why Odyssey sold the work to Kahane
in 1936. The seven impressions in three years indicate a
steady seller; was Kahane able to pay very well for it? In
contrast, Odyssey published *Ulysses* from 1932-39 (Slocum and
Cahoon 30), issuing three impressions from 1932 to 1935
(before the British Bodley Head edition), and one in 1939.
One can imagine that after 1935, the title would have been
less attractive to Paris publishers (including Odyssey)./2/
Chatterley was a different story. Perhaps Kurt Enoch had
something to do with the agreement; he acted as Kahane's
distributor for *Cancer*, using his experience with clandestine
methods to good effect (Girodias 202).

Kahane only published one impression (25.8), possibly
because of piratical competition. The Pegasus imprint (1938)
of this edition (25.11) may be an example. It states that the
copyright is held by "The Pegasus Press, Paris." Verso the
title page we find that it is the "ninth impression," which
is consistent with the Odyssey and Obelisk statements (the
colophon in some copies reads "eighth impression"). The new
edition (26.1) which carries the Pegasus imprint contains no
copyright information. Both volumes may be piracies, as 25.9
obviously is. One should note, for whatever it may be worth,
that Frieda Lawrence's introduction is not present (see 25.8,
NOTES). I have found no information identifying the Pegasus
Press of the late 1930s, but it is unlikely that Reese would

compete with Kahane at that point. It is possible they were partners in this venture.

I do not know how large any individual impressions of any of the Paris editions were.

The Swedish Jan Förlag editions also have a rather interesting publishing history, which involves Frieda Lawrence and The Albatross Press. The file of Albatross' interoffice memos mentioned above was written in a spirit of dismay and controversy. In 1946, that house printed 20,000 copies for post-war travellers, but was dismayed to find that the Swedish publisher had invaded the French and Swiss markets (in 1946 the latter printed one impression of its second edition, with two binding variants [26.1], and one impression [two issues] of a third edition [27.1]). Albatross threatened to sue under the Swiss copyright law if restitution was not made. It is clear from the memos that the Jan Förlag printings (which began in 1942 [25.1] and continued to 1956 [28.2]) were sanctioned by Mrs. Lawrence and Lawrence Pollinger (all carry the notice "Unexpurgated authorized Edition"). Albatross felt this was unfair; Lawrence Pollinger countered that the 1933 contract allowed Frieda to assign rights as she wished. In any event, Albatross decided not to publish a post-war *Chatterley*, for the reasons discussed above. It should be added that they also faced competition for the Scherz Phoenix paperback of *The First Lady Chatterley*, published in Berne (see 54.1-54.4 below).

The Jan Förlag edition attracted at least two piracies: 27.5, 12.1-14.2.

The statement of responsibility in Japan's Keimeisha volumes (25.12; a subedition from plates made from the Odyssey Press version) suggests, falsely, that this publisher had permission of the Lawrence Estate./3/ The book was probably issued in the early 1950s. In 1950, a Japanese-language unexpurgated edition of *Chatterley* resulted in heated public debate, and in 1952 and 1953 trials ended with the publisher being fined (Moore, Introduction 29). Another noteworthy Keimeisha publication, probably dating from the same period, was Miller's *Sexus*. The large presence of the American military in Japan and Korea in the early 1950s may well have motivated these editions, which would have been sold in stores such as Tuttle's in Tokyo. This shop operated concessions in Army Post Exchanges in four Japanese cities (PW 12 Jan, 1952: 155). See #25.12.$_1$ below.

In view of the competition, it is interesting that Heinemann, which aggressively increased its continental activities after the war, published its Netherlands edition in 1956. It is possible that Barney Rosset's 1954 plans to challenge censorship laws with an unexpurgated American edition (see Caffrey 49-63) was a factor in its appearance (see the Introductory Note to Section 8 below). There were two impressions in four years. Some serendipity was involved. Because the plates were handy for the first clothbound de-censorship British edition, Heinemann was able to put the

latter on sale less that a month after the Old Bailey decision.

ENDNOTES

1. This information can be found in a MS file headed "Lawrence, D. H., Misc." at the Humanities Research Center at the University of Texas at Austin. The file contains inter-office memos of the Albatross Press dating from 1946 to 1948 regarding the Jan Förlag editions of *Lady Chatterley's Lover*.

2. The Olympia Press catalogue for 1958, and the *Cumulative Book Index*, 1957-58, list a printing of *Lady Chatterley's Lover* (12,000fr., $3.50). Maurice Girodias, Olympia's owner, was the son of Jack Kahane of Obelisk, so it is possible that plates of that impression, if they survived the war, were available. *Lady Chatterley* is not listed in the Olympia catalogue for 1956, nor in that for 1962. I have found no copies, and believe that, like several other advertised Olympia titles, it was in fact never published. It is not in Kearney's handlist of Olympia publications. I have found no pirated edition published and/or distributed by an American "secondary [paperback] distributor" in the early 1960s. Had Olympia issued an edition, it is quite likely that within a few years Collectors Publications, which pirated many Girodias titles, would have offered a *Lady Chatterley* also. See the essay for Chapter 5, pp.136.

3. In an interview with me on 25 May 1988, Gerald Pollinger stated that the Keimeisha copyright statement is not accurate.

BIBLIOGRAPHICAL DESCRIPTIONS

[First plating of the Odyssey Press parent edition]

25.1   LADY CHATTERLEY'S | LOVER | *by* | D. H. LAWRENCE | THE
       ODYSSEY PRESS | HAMBURG [dot] PARIS [dot] BOLOGNA

(7 1/8 x 4 3/8"): π^4 I-22^8 23^6, 186 leaves; pp.[8], I-359,
[360], [4]. $1(-\pi)$ signed 56, [sig. no]. $2 signed 56,
[sig. no.], with * superscripted to sig. no.

CONTENTS: pp.[1-2]:blank.p.[3]: half-title. p.[4]:blank.
   p.[5]:t.p. p.[6]:COPYRIGHT 1933 | BY THE ODYSSEY PRESS,
   CHRISTIAN WEGNER, HAMBURG | IMPRIMÉ EN ALLEMAGNE |. pp.[7-
   8]: open letter from Frieda Lawrence. pp.I-[360]:text.
   p.[1]:blank. p.[2]: THIS EDITION IS COMPOSED IN |
   BASKERVILLE TYPE CUT BY THE | MONOTYPE CORPORATION. THE |
   PAPER IS MADE BY THE PAPIER- | FABRIK BAUTZEN. THE
   PRINTING AND | THE BINDING ARE THE WORK OF | OSCAR
   BRANDSTETTER [dot] ABTEILUNG | JAKOB HEGNER [dot] LEIPZIG
   |. p.[3]: advert for Joyce's *Ulysses*. p.[4]:blank.

TYPOGRAPHY: text: 36ll.(p.195): 147 (153.5) x 84mm.
   10ll.=50mm.   Face: 3(1.5)mm. Typeface: Monotype Baskerville (see colophon). Transitional (DIN 1.24, modern
   baroque).

PAPER: smooth white wove unwatermarked. Thickness .08mm.
   Total Bulk 16.0mm.

BINDING: ribbed paper wrappers, medium blue (C182), printing
   in black. Thickness .34mm. Upper cover: LADY CHATTERLEY'S
   | LOVER | BY | D.H.LAWRENCE |. On spine: LADY | CHATTER- |
   LEY'S | LOVER | BY | D. H. | LAWRENCE | THE | ODYSSEY |
   PRESS |. Lower cover: RM 2.80 - FRS 18 - Lire 14 | NOT TO
   BE INTRODUCED INTO THE BRITISH EMPIRE OR THE U.S.A. Verso
   upper cover is brief statement in English, German, and
   French about the present inexpensive, "unexpurgated and
   carefully revised" edition "within the reach of every
   purse" conforming to the author's wishes (as Mrs. Lawrence
   states on p.[7]). No endpapers. All edges trimmed.

NOTE: See Roberts A42f.

COPIES EXAMINED: personal, NO/U-1; Forster Coll., OX/U-1

25.2   as 25.1 save:

CONTENTS: p.[6]:as 25.1 save ll. 1-2: *Second Impression* |
   [star] |. p.[2]: ll.5-9: FABRIK BAUTZEN, THE PRINTING AND
   | THE BINDING OF THIS SECOND IM- | PRESSION ARE THE WORK
   OF | OSCAR BRANDSTETTER [dot] ABTEILUNG | JAKOB HEGNER
   [dot] LEIPSIG

BINDING: Var. (1): paper wrappers are moderate blue (C182).

Var. (2): rebound, poss. by publisher or bookseller: half-bound linen-grain (T304) cloth; moderate yellow green (C120); paper-covered boards with marbling design (T1108; Gloster[?]), predominant colors green, orange, yellow. All edges trimmed. Plain white endpapers. No lettering on binding.

NOTE: for other bindings with no identifying lettering, see 1.9 Var. (3), 8.1 Var. (1).

COPIES EXAMINED: Var. (1): OkTU; Var. (2): personal

25.3   as 25.1 save:

CONTENTS: p.[6]:as 25.1 save ll. 1-2: *Third Impression* | [star] |. p.[2]: ll.5-9: FABRIK BAUTZEN, THE PRINTING AND | THE BINDING OF THIS THIRD IM- | PRESSION ARE THE WORK OF | OSCAR BRANDSTETTER [dot] ABTEILUNG | JAKOB HEGNER [dot] LEIPSIG

PAPER: Thickness .07mm. Total Bulk 16.2mm.

BINDING: paper wrappers are light blue (C.181). Prices listed on lower wrapper as in 25.1 save SFR 3.50 added after RM 280.
    Dj: light yellow (C.86), printed in black. Front cover (first four lines as upper cover of wrappers): [thick rule] | *NEW CHEAP EDITION* | [thin rule] | of D. H. Lawrence's great novel | unexpurgated and authorised with | a foreword by Frieda Lawrence. | [thin rule] | RM 2.80 [wavy dash] SFR 3.50 [wavy dash] FRS 18 [wavy dash] LIRE 14 | [thick rule] |. Spine: wording identical to that on spine of wrapper. Back cover and both flaps blank.

NOTE: The "New Cheap Edition" statement refers, I assume, to the Odyssey Press edition rather than to this third impression of same, since the price is the same as for the first impression. Odyssey did publish a "thin-paper" *one-volume Ulysses*. However, it was advertized as "cloth-bound," and also as more expensive than the two-volume paperbound issue. See Slocum and Calhoun (30).

COPIES EXAMINED: personal, CU-S

*25.4

25.5   as 25.1 save:

LADY CHATTERLEY'S | LOVER | *By* | D. H. LAWRENCE | THE ODYSSEY PRESS | PARIS

Leaves measure 7 1/8 x 4 1/4.

CONTENTS: p.[6]: . . . Fifth Impression | [star] | COPYRIGHT 1934 | BY LES ÉDITIONS DU PÉGASE, PARIS |. p.[2]: THIS EDITION IS COMPOSED IN | BASKERVILLE TYPE CUT BY THE | MONOTYPE CORPORATION, THE | PAPER IS MADE BY MONTGOLFIER | BROTHERS, ANNONAY, THE PRINT- | ING AND THE BINDING OF

THIS | FIFTH IMPRESSION ARE THE | WORK OF THE PROTAT
BROTHERS, MACON

PAPER: thickness .08mm. Total bulk 16.1mm.

BINDING: paper wrappers, dark blue (C183). Unribbed paper
(thickness .36mm). Verso of both upper and lower cover is
blank. At bottom of lower cover: FRS 18 [short rule] SFR
3,50 [short rule] LIRA 14 | NOT TO BE INTRODUCED INTO THE
BRITISH EMPIRE OR THE U.S.A.
    Dj: as 25.3 save for back cover which carries price and
statement of restricted distribution (as on lower wrapper).

COPY EXAMINED: NO/U-1 (d.j.: flap of upper wrapper lacking)

*25.6

25.7   as 25.1 save:

CONTENTS: p.[6]: *Seventh Impression* | [star] | COPYRIGHT
    1935 | BY LES ÉDITIONS DU PÉGASE, PARIS |. p.[2]: THIS
    EDITION IS COMPOSED IN | BASKERVILLE TYPE CUT BY THE |
    MONOTYPE CORPORATION, THE | PAPER IS MADE BY MONTGOLFIER |
    BROTHERS, ANNONAY, THE PRINT- | ING AND THE BINDING OF
    THIS | SEVENTH IMPRESSION ARE THE | WORK OF THE PROTAT
    BROTHERS, MACON |. pp.[3-4]: blank.

PAPER: thickness .08mm. Total bulk 15.8mm.

BINDING: paper wrappers, yellowish white (C92). Lettered in
    blue (paper wrappers not ribbed in this impression). No
    blurbs verso upper cover. Press not named at bottom of
    spine. No listing of prices on lower wrapper.

COPIES EXAMINED: TxU, personal

[subedition: Obelisk Press, 1936]

25.8   [within abstract unlinked ribbon-like designs in deep
    red, at both sides of ll. 1, 4, 6-8]: LADY | CHATTERLEY'S
    LOVER | *by* | D. H. LAWRENCE | [vertical ribbon-like
    design in deep red] | THE | OBELISK PRESS | *PARIS*

(7 7/8 x 5 1/8"): t.p., tipped in, + π^2 I-22^8 23^6, 185
leaves; pp.[6], I-359, [360], [4]. $1(-$\pi$,2,7) signed 56,
[sig. no.] |. $2(-$\pi$) signed 56, [sig. no.] with * super-
scripted to sig. no. |.

CONTENTS: pp.[1-2]: blank. p.[3]: half-title. p.[4]:blank.
    p.[5]: t.p.(tipped in) p.[6]: *Eighth Impression* | [star] |
    COPYRIGHT 1936 | By LES ÉDITIONS DU PÉGASE, PARIS
    |.pp.I-[360]: text. p.[1]: blank. p.[2]: THIS EDITION IS
    COMPOSED IN | BASKERVILLE TYPE CUT BY THE | MONOTYPE
    CORPORATION, THE | PAPER IS MADE BY MOULIN-VIEUX, |

PONTCHARA-SUR-BREDA, THE | PRINTING AND BINDING OF THIS |
EIGHTH IMPRESSION ARE THE | WORK OF PROTAT BROTHERS, MACON
|. pp.[3-4]: blank.

TYPOGRAPHY: text: as 25.1.

PAPER: rough white wove unwatermarked. Thickness .1mm.
    Total bulk 18.4mm.

BINDING: paper self-wrappers, medium orange yellow
    (C.71). Upper cover: lettering (same as t.p.) in black,
    with abstract ribbon-like design in dark blue. On spine,
    lettering in black, pub. device in dark blue: LADY |
    CHATTERLEY'S | LOVER | BY | D. H. LAWRENCE | [pub. device:
    obelisk with book at base; name of press on the obelisk] |
    THE | OBELISK PRESS | PARIS |. Lower cover and lower flap
    blank. Top edge trimmed; others untrimmed. No endpapers.

NOTE: Neither this nor the Pegasus Press impressions include
    the Introduction by Frieda Lawrence. This may be a clue to
    unauthorized issues, but the Introduction may simply have
    been excised because the last paragraph refers to other
    editions (of the first two versions) of *Lady Chatterley*
    being issued "over the same [Odyssey Press] imprint at
    some future date." This was not about to happen; 25.7 is
    the final Odyssey impression of any of the three versions.

COPIES EXAMINED: personal

25.9   as 25.8 save:

coll.: π^4 I-22^8 23^6, 186 leaves; pp.[8], I-359, [360], [4].
$1(-$\pi$,1,2,7) signed 56, [sig. no.] |. $2(-$\pi$) signed 56,
[sig. no.] with * superscripted to sig. no. |.

CONTENTS: pp.[1-4]: blank. p.[5]: half-title. p.[6]: blank.
    p.[7]:t.p. p.[8]: *Eighth Impression* | [star] | COPYRIGHT
    1936 | By LES ÉDITIONS DU PÉGASE, PARIS |.

BINDING: paper self-wrappers. Flap of upper cover:
    UNEXPURGATED | AUTHORISED | COPYRIGHT | EDITION | OF |
    D. H. LAWRENCE'S | CLASSICAL NOVEL | PRICE: 50 francs.
    Lower flap blank.

COPIES EXAMINED: TxU, OkTU, ICarbS, CU-S

        *[A photolithographic piracy of the Obelisk or Pegasus
        Press impression of the Odyssey Press parent edition]*

25.10   [within abstract unlinked ribbon-like design, at both
        sides of ll. 1,4,6]: LADY | CHATTERLEY'S | LOVER | *by* |
        D. H. LAWRENCE | VOL. I [VOL. II]. [line 6 in sans
        serif]

    (6 11/16 x 4 1/8"): vol. I: no sigs, 84 leaves; pp. [2],

1-166.
vol. II: no sigs., 99 leaves; pp.[2], 167-360, [2].

CONTENTS: vol. I: p.[1]:t.p. p.[2]: blank. pp.1-166:text.
    vol. II: p.[1]:t.p. p.[2]:blank. pp.167-360:text. p.[1]:
    blank. p.[2]: THIS EDITION IS COMPOSED IN | BASKERVILLE
    TYPE CUT BY THE | MONOTYPE CORPORATION, THE | PAPER IS
    MADE BY MOULIN-VIEUX, | PONTCHARA-SUR-BREDA, THE |
    PRINTING AND BINDING OF THIS | EIGHTH IMPRESSION ARE THE |
    WORK OF PROTAT BROTHERS, MACON

TYPOGRAPHY: vol. I: 36ll.(p.55): 129 x 77mm. 10ll.=35mm.
    Face: 2(1x)mm. vol. II: 36ll.(p.273): 131(136) x 77mm.
    10ll.=32mm. Typeface: as 25.1.

PAPER: ribbed white wove unwatermarked. vol. I: thickness
    .06mm. Total bulk 6.8mm. vol. II: thickness .07mm. Total
    bulk 7.7mm.

BINDING: paper wrappers, deep pink (C.3).Printed in black on
    upper cover: LADY | CHATTERLEY'S | LOVER | [French rule] |
    BY | D. H. LAWRENCE | VOL. I [VOL. II] | [all but last
    line in sans serif, both vols] |. On spine, top to bot-
    tom: LADY CHATTERLEY'S LOVER. All edges trimmed.

NOTES: The title pages as well as the contents are photolith-
    ographed. The former are identical to those used for the
    Obelisk and Pegasus Press volumes, with the following
    exceptions: 1) the ribbon-like decorations are of course
    in black, not in red. 2) the imprint is removed; thus the
    lines THE | OBELISK [PEGASUS?] PRESS | PARIS are not
    present, although the decorations surrounding them are. 3)
    The vol. numbers are of course added, in a different
    typeface.
        I could not collate the gatherings without harming
    the structure of the book, but they are irregular, some
    consisting of four, others of 10 or more leaves. The book
    is side-stitched and the wrappers glued to the first and
    last leaves; no endpapers. The volumes are smearily
    lithographed, with many lines lightly or inconsistently
    impressed and others quite thick and black. The page
    numbers are crudely drawn on the lithographic plates, with
    p. 360 so drawn although this page was unnumbered in the
    Obelisk impression. The colophon is identical to that of
    the latter, and to one state of the Pegasus Press im-
    pression.
        I have seen two states of the latter, in one of which
    (TxU) the colophon is the same as that of the Obelisk
    volume; therefore the pirate-publishers of the present
    volume could have used it as well as the Obelisk. Another
    copy of the Pegasus impression (at LO/N-1), representing
    probably a latter state, has a colophon reading NINTH
    IMPRESSION, which is correct. See 25.10 below.

COPY EXAMINED: Prof. A. Efron, SUNY Buffalo

[subedition: Pegasus Press, 1938]

25.11.$_1$ as 25.8 save:

T.p. 1.7: PEGASUS PRESS replaces OBELISK PRESS |.

sheet size: 7 1/2 x 5." $1(-π,2,7) signed.

CONTENTS: p.[8]: *Ninth Impression* | [star] | COPYRIGHT 1938 |
    BY, THE PEGASUS PRESS, PARIS |. (colophon, p.[2], as in
    Obelisk Press subedition).

PAPER: Thickness .09mm. Total bulk 17.8mm.

BINDING: Upper cover: same as Obelisk Press impression but
    PEGASUS replaces OBELISK. On spine: LADY | CHATTERLEY'S |
    LOVER | BY | D. H. LAWRENCE | THE | PEGASUS PRESS | PARIS
    |. Flaps as 25.8 but I have not seen copy with bottom of
    front flap intact. See state 2 of this impression, below.
    All edges partly trimmed.

COPIES EXAMINED: NNC (rebound), TxU (flaps not present),
    personal (front flap clipped).

25.11.$_2$ as 25.11.$_1$ save:

Leaves measure 7 3/4 x 5 1/8"

CONTENTS: p.[2]: colophon, 1.7, revised to read NINTH
    IMPRESSION

PAPER: smooth white wove unwatermarked. Thickness .08mm.
    Total bulk 17.6mm.

BINDING: Front flap reads: 75 francs |.

COPY EXAMINED: personal

25.11.$_3$ as 25.11.$_2$ save:

CONTENTS: p.[8]: 1.4: no comma (2 blank spaces) after BY |.

COPY EXAMINED: British Lib.

[subedition (unauthorized): Keimeisha of Tokyo]

25.12.$_1$ LADY CHATTERLEY'S | LOVER | *by* | D. H. LAWRENCE |
    KEIMEISHA | TOKYO

(6 13/16 x 4 1/4"): t.p., tipped in, + [1-23]^8 [24]^2, 186
leaves; pp.[2], I-359, [360], [2], (1)-(8). $1,2 signed as
in 25.1, but not used in collation.

CONTENTS: recto tipped in leaf: t.p. verso: Title | LADY
    CHATTERLEY'S LOVER | Author | D. H. Lawrence | Publisher |
    Pearn Pollinger & Higham Ltd. | through Mr. Lewis Bush,
    c/o The British Literary Centere[sic], Ltd. p.[1-2]: Open
    letter from Frieda L. pp.I-[360]: text. p.[1]:Annotation
    p.[2]: blank. pp.(1)-(8): glossary of English words and
    equivalent in Japanese for each chapter of the novel.

TYPOGRAPHY: Text: 36ll.(p.177), 146(151) x 83mm. 10ll.=
    43mm. Face 2(1x)mm.

PAPER: smooth white wove unwatermarked. Thickness .07mm.
    Total bulk 14.7mm. (not including tipped-in t.p. leaf,
    which is on sized paper identical to endpapers, and which
    measures .06mm).

BINDING: white paper wrappers, printed in red. Upper
    cover: LADY CHATTERLEY'S | LOVER | by | D. H. LAWRENCE |
    KEIMEISHA | TOKYO |. On spine: LADY | CHATTER- | LEY'S |
    LOVER | BY | D. H. | LAWRENCE |. Paper cover measures
    .32mm in width). Smooth white (sized) endpapers. All edges
    trimmed.

NOTES: As stated on p. 104 above, this edition is not author-
    ized by the Lawrence Estate. Lewis Bush was a resident of
    Tokyo, and a literary journalist who wrote for English-
    language audiences about the far east.
      Regarding the statement on the verso of the tipped-in
    leaf, it should be noted that as of 1952, United States
    (and presumably British) publishers and agents could neg-
    otiate directly with the Japanese. Prior to that date, all
    contracts had to be approved by the Supreme Commander of
    the Allied Powers (see PW 13 Sept. 1952: 1006).

COPIES EXAMINED: TxU(copy 1), OkTU

25.12.$_2$ as 25.12.$_1$ save:

Last sig. is [23]; it contains eight leaves.

CONTENTS: Only 4 pages of Annotations at end, covering
    ch. I-IX only.

COPY EXAMINED: TxU (copy 2)

25.12.$_3$ as 25.12.$_2$ save:

CONTENTS: No statement of responsibility verso t.p. Pasted-in
    ticket (58 x 45mm) carries this statement.

BINDING: Dj: light gray (C264) with Japanese characters in
    red on upper cover. Lower cover: publisher's device(?):
    elephant. In lower right: ¥395.|

COPY EXAMINED: TxU, copy 3.

25.12.$_4$ as 25.12.$_2$ save:

CONTENTS: verso t.p., added after 1.6: This book is published
in Japan by arrangement with | Mrs. Frieda Lawrence, c/o
Pearn Pollinger & Higham Ltd. | through Mr. Lewis Bush,,
c/o The British Literary Centere[sic], Ltd.

COPY EXAMINED: NO/P-1

NOTE: On 25 May, 1988, Gerald Pollinger informed me that the
Keimeisha copyright statement is not accurate.

*[Another, undated, Pegasus Press(?) edition; possible
piracy]*

26.1   T.p. as 25.11 save for an additional line added at
bottom, in a different typeface: A COMPLETE AND
UNEXPURGATED EDITION |.

(9 x 6"): unsigned; pp. [4], 7-275, [276].

CONTENTS: p.[1]: half-title. p.[2]: Privately Issued |.
p.[3]: t.p. p.[4]:blank. pp.7-275: text. p.[276]: blank.

TYPOGRAPHY: text: 4711.(p.103): 177(189) x 117mm. 10ll.=38mm.
Face 3(2x)mm. Typeface: Old Face (DIN 1.13, Modern
Renaissance). Cf. Hollandse Medieval (R3) or Leamington
(R42).

RUNNING HEADS: versos: D. H. LAWRENCE |. rectos: LADY
CHATTERLEY'S LOVER |.

PAPER: smooth white wove unwatermarked. Thickness .1mm.
Total bulk 15.0mm.

BINDING (but probably rebound): linen grain (T304) cloth,
medium blue (C182). Gold-stamped on spine: [two rules] |
[two rules] | LADY | CHATTERLEY'S | LOVER | [short rule] |
LAWRENCE | [two rules] | [two rules] | [two rules] |.
Endpapers light gray (C264); free endpapers measure .3mm.
All edges trimmed, sprinkled with red. Head and tailbands
in yellow and green.

DECORATIONS: Decorated Gothic initials, bordered, begin each
chapter. Tailpieces end each chapter (abstract design).

NOTES: The book is tightly rebound, with probably the first
and last leaves excised; I cannot with any confidence
collate the gatherings, although it may be bound in 12s.
It is possible that this is a piracy using the Pegasus
imprint. C. J. Scheiner has told me that he has seen
Chatterley titles printed in Paris, allegedly by under-
world figures active in the late 30s. The Pegasus imprint
would place the book c. 1938.
The printing style uses single inverted commas for
quotations. Italicized words in the Orioli edition are
printed in boldface.

The typeface features a sloping e-bar, angled stress,
and oblique serifs, with little contrast between thick and
thin strokes. It is similar to that used for the limitation statement in the Orioli edition. The book is printed
from letterpress on good quality paper, and these
elements, together with the typeface and decorations,
provide an ersatz-sumptuous air fitting a gentleman's
erotica collection.

This particular edition is not in any library I have
visited. I found a copy in a used bookstore in Philadelphia.

COPY EXAMINED: personal

[First Jan Förlag Swedish edition, 1942]

27.1   *Lady* | *Chatterley's* | *Lover* | [swelled rule] | BY D.
H. LAWRENCE | *Jan Förlag - Stockholm* [ll. 1-3 in
non-continuous script]

(7 13/16 x 5 1/8"): [1]^8 2-24^8, 192 leaves; pp.[8], 9-379,
[380], [4]. $(-[1]) signed [sig. no.] *Lady Chatterley's
Lover* [on direction line] |.

CONTENTS: pp.[1-2]: blank. p.[3]:half-title. p.[4]:blank.
p.[5]: t.p. p.[6]: *Copyright 1942* | *by Jan Förlag* |
Stockholm | *Printed by* | *Victor Pettersons Bokindustri,
Stockholm* | *1942.* p.[7]: [swelled rule] | *Unexpurgated* |
authorized | *Edition* | [swelled rule]. p.[8]:blank.
pp.9-[380]: text. p.[1]: blank. p.[2]: THIS EDITION IS
COMPOSED | IN OLD STYLE TYPE CUT BY | THE LINOTYPE
CORPORATION. | THE PAPER IS MADE BY THE | FINBRUKEN PAPER
MILL. | THE PRINTING OF THIS | IMPRESSION IS THE WORK OF |
VICTOR PETTERSONS | BOKINDUSRTI, | STHLM, SWEDEN,
1942.| pp.[3-4]:blank.

TYPOGRAPHY: Text: 36ll.(p.177), 147(156) x 86mm. 10ll.=41mm.
Face: 3(2x)mm.
Typeface: see colophon. DIN 1.24, modern baroque.

PAPER: smooth white wove unwatermarked. Thickness .07mm.
Total bulk 16.5mm.

BINDING: paper self wrappers (chain-lines approximately
25mm. apart); deep reddish orange (C36). Upper cover:
[ll.1-3 in square border with edges rounded and top and
bottom lines thick (3 mm.):] *Lady* | *Chatterley's* | *Lover* |
BY D. H. LAWRENCE | *Jan-Förlag - Stockholm* [ll. 1-3 in
non-continuous script]. Spine: *Lady* | *Chatterley's* | *Lover*
| [swelled rule] | D. H. | LAWRENCE | *Jan-Förlag* |. Lower
cover: *Kr 12:-* |. In lower right: printer's logo:V and P
worked together in oval. Flap of upper wrapper: *In
Preparation:* D. H. LAWRENCE | The Rainbow | *Kr. 12:-* |.
Lower flap blank. Top edge trimmed, others lightly
trimmed.

NOTE: Jan Förlag also published English language editions of Lawrence's *The Rainbow* (1942) and Lewisohn's *The Case Of Mr. Crump* (1943).

COPIES EXAMINED: personal, Forster Coll., LO/N-1

27.2   as 27.1 save:

CONTENTS: p.[6]: *Copyright 1942 | by Jan-Förlag | Stockholm | Second edition |*. p.[2]: last line of colophon reads STHILM, SWEDEN, 1943.

BINDING: paper self-wrappers bear no chain-lines. Flap of upper wrapper: D. H. LAWRENCE | The Rainbow | *Kr.* 12:-

COPIES EXAMINED: personal, Forster Coll.

27.3   as 27.1 save:

size of sheets: 7 1/2 x 5"

CONTENTS: p.[6]: *Copyright 1945 | by Jan Förlag | Stockholm | Third edition |*. p.[2]: last line of colophon reads STHLM, SWEDEN, 1945.

PAPER: Thickness .08mm. Total bulk 17.6mm.

BINDING: Var.(1): light grayish brown (C60) paper-covered boards, reinforced with strips of white linen at corners of fore-edges. Quarter-bound in linen-grain (T304) cloth, vivid deep red(C17). All edges trimmed, top edge stained purplish white. Endpapers yellowish white (C92). Head and tail bands in red. Gold-stamped on spine: [double rule] | Lady | Chatterley's | Lover | [rule] | D. H. | LAWRENCE | *Jan Förlag* | [rule] | [double rule] |. Var.(2): as (1) save endpapers ribbed, impressed with chainlines.

COPIES EXAMINED: Var.(1): personal, MH. Var.(2): TxU

[subedition: "Branner English Library," 1945]

27.4   as 27.1 save:

Lady | Chatterley's | Lover | [French rule] | BY D. H. LAWRENCE | JAN-FORLAG [asterisk] STOCKHOLM | och | POVL BRANNER'S FORLAG | KOBENHAVN

collation: as 27.1 save [1]^8 ($\pm$[1]3) [t.p. leaf a cancel].

CONTENTS: as 27.1 save: p.[6]: COPYRIGHT 1945 | by | JAN-FORLAG [asterisk] STOCKHOLM |. p.[2]: 1.10 reads STHLM, SWEDEN, 1945.

PAPER: Thickness .08mm. Total bulk 16.6mm.

BINDING: black paper wrappers. Upper cover: *D. H. Lawrence*
    | *Lady* | *Chatterley's* | *Lover* | [decoration in red and
    green: rose with leaves] | BRANNER | ENGLISH [union jack]
    LIBRARY [ll. 1,6,7 in green, ll. 2-4 in white. Dec. in-
    scribed "s.v. otto.s." Initials in ll.1-4 swash] |. On
    spine, pink on black background: *D. H. Lawrence* | *Lady* |
    Chatterley's | *Lover* | [2 rules] | BRANNER | ENGLISH
    [union jack] LIBRARY | [typography as on upper cover].
    Lower cover white, plain. No endpapers. Top edge rough
    trimmed. Fore and lower edges roughtrimmed.

NOTE: see also 28.1 Var.(1) below.

COPY EXAMINED: personal

   *[A photolithographic piracy of the Jan Förlag "second
    edition"]*

27.5   *LADY CHATTERLEY'S* | *LOVER by* | D. H. LAWRENCE |
        UNEXPURGATED EDITION | [three asterisks] | THE ROCKMAY
        PRESS | MCMLVI

(6 13/16 x 4"): unsigned; pp.[1-8], 9-379, [380], [4].

CONTENTS: pp.[1-4]:blank. p.[5]:half-title. p.[6]:blank.
    p.[7]: title page. p.[8]:blank. pp.9-[380]:text. pp.[4]:
    blank.

TYPOGRAPHY: Text: 36ll.(p.33), 128 x 75mm. 10ll.=39mm. Face
    2(1x)mm.
    Typeface: Linotype Olde Style

PAPER: smooth white wove unwatermarked. Thickness .05mm.
    Total bulk 10.1mm.

BINDING: linen grain cloth, deep brown (C.56). Lawrence
    phoenix stamped in orange on upper cover. On spine,
    running bottom to top: [vine leaf] *LADY CHATTERLEY'S LOVER*
    [vine leaf] |. Blindstamped at tail of spine:
    publisher's logo (I and U-shaped ornament [Greek phi?]
    worked together in oval).
        Dj: Light yellowish green (C.119) lettered in blue on
    front cover: [in double border: *LADY CHATTERLEY'S* | *LOVER*
    by | D. H. LAWRENCE | [star] | UNEXPURGATED EDITION | THE
    ROCKMAY PRESS |. On spine, top to bottom: *D. H. LAWRENCE* |
    [star] | *LADY CHATTERLEY'S LOVER* |. On back cover: pub-
    lisher's logo, as described above. Flaps of d.j. blank.

NOTE: the Greek phi is pronounced "fie"; the word "Phi" is
    used to designate the erotica collection of the Bodleian
    Library, Oxford.

COPY EXAMINED: Forster Coll.

[Second Jan Förlag edition; 1946]

28.1   *Lady | Chatterley's | Lover* | [rule] | BY D. H.
           LAWRENCE | *Jan Forlag - Stockholm* [ll. 1-3 in
           script]

(7 3/4 x 5 1/16"): [1]⁸ 2-24⁸, 192 leaves; pp.[8], 9-380,
[381-82], [2]. $(-[1]) signed [sig. no.] *Lady Chatterley's
Lover* [on direction line] |.

CONTENTS: pp.[1-2]: blank. p.[3]: half-title. p.[4]: blank.
    p.[5]: t.p. p.[6]: *Copyright 1942 | by Jan Förlag |
    Stockholm | Second edition* | p. [7]: [rule] | *Unexpurgated
    | authorized | edition* | [rule] | p.[8]: blank.
    pp.9-[381]: text. pp.[382]: THIS EDITION IS COMPOSED | IN
    OLDE STYLE TYPE CUT BY | THE LINOTYPE CORPORATION. | THE
    PAPER IS MADE BY THE | FINBRUKEN PAPER MILL. | THE
    PRINTING OF THIS | IMPRESSION IS THE WORK OF | VICTOR
    PETERSONS BOKINDUSTRI,| STHLM, SWEDEN, 1946. |.
    pp.[1-2]:blank.

TYPOGRAPHY: Text: 36ll.(p.177), 148(155) x 86mm. 10ll.=
    41mm. Face 3(2x)mm.
    Typeface: see colophon (DIN 1.24, Modern Baroque).

PAPER: smooth white wove unwatermarked. Thickness .08mm.
    Total bulk   16.2mm.

BINDING: Var. (1): same as 27.4 above. Var. (2): paper
    wrappers, yellowish-white (C.92), lettered in blue.
    Upper cover: [ll. 1-3 in square border with edges rounded
    and top and bottom lines thick (3 mm.)]: *Lady |
    Chatterley's | Lover* | BY D. H. LAWRENCE | *Jan Förlag -
    Stockholm* |. On spine: LADY | CHATTERLEY'S | LOVER |
    [swelled rule] | D. H. | LAWRENCE | Jan Förlag |. Lower
    cover: *Kr. 12:--* | *Bound Kr. 15:- -*| [pub. device in lower
    right corner] |. Top edge rough-trimmed. Fore- and bottom
    edges partly trimmed. No endpapers. Var. (3): as 27.3
    above.

NOTE: On p.[6], "second edition" may refer to the resetting
    of type for this 1946 edition, although the term is used
    differently in 27.2, to denote a second *impression* (1942)
    of the first edition.

COPY EXAMINED: Var.(1):TxU   Var.(2): Forster Coll. Var.(3):
    LO/N-1

[Third Jan Förlag edition, 1946 and 1950]

29.1.a   *Lady | Chatterley's | Lover* | [rule] | BY D. H.

LAWRENCE | *Jan Förlag - Stockholm* [ll. 1-3 in non-flowing script]

(7 1/4 x 5 1/8"): 1⁸, 2-24⁸, 192 leaves; pp.[1-8],9-380, [381-82], [2]. $(-[1]) signed [sig. no.] *Lady Chatterley's Lover* (on direction line).

CONTENTS: pp.[1-2]:blank. p.[3]: half-title. p.[4]: blank. p.[5]: t.p. p.[6]: *Copyright* | JAN FÖRLAG | *Stockholm* | *Vepe* | [rule] | Victor Petersons Bokindustriaktiebolag | Stockholm 1946 |. p.[7]: [rule] | *Unexpurgated* | *author-ized* | *edition* | [rule] |. p.[8]: blank. pp.9-[381]: text. p.[382]: blank. p.[2]: blank.

TYPOGRAPHY: Text: ll.36, p.177. 149(155) x 86mm. 10ll.=40mm. Face 3(1.5)mm.

PAPER: smooth white wove unwatermarked. Thickness .08mm. Total bulk: 16.8mm.

BINDING: same as 28.1 Var.(2)

NOTE: This edition contains the same number of pages of text as the second edition (28.1), but it is reset. On p.14, l. 11: "Abvious." Corrected in later impressions.

COPIES EXAMINED: personal, PU.

29.1.b   as 29.1.a save:

CONTENTS: p.[6]: *Copyright 1942* | *by Jan-Förlag* | *Stockholm* | *Second edition* | [same as 25.2]. p.[382]: last line of colophon reads STHILM, SWEDEN, 1946.

BINDING: grayish olive (C.110) paper-covered boards, reinforced with strips of white linen at corners of fore-edges. Quarter-bound in linen-grain (T304) cloth, deep red (C13). All edges trimmed, top edge sprinkled with grey. Endpapers white. Head and tail bands in red. Gold-stamped on spine:[double rule] | Lady | Chatterley's | Lover | [rule] | D. H. | LAWRENCE | *Jan Förlag* | [rule] | [double rule]

COPY EXAMINED: personal

29.2   as 29.1.a save:

leaves measure 7 3/4 x 5 1/8".

CONTENTS: p.[6]: last line reads Stockholm 1950 |.

TYPOGRAPHY: Text: 36ll., p.177: 148(155) x 87mm. 10ll.=41mm. Face: 2(1.5)mm.

PAPER: smooth white wove unwatermarked. Thickness .08mm. Total bulk 16.7mm.

BINDING: Var. (1): as 28.1 Var.(2). Var. (2): Light yellow brown

(C76) paper-covered boards flecked with green. Linen strips
at foreedges of boards, as in 29.1.b. Quarter-bound in deep
red (C16) linen grain cloth, stamped as in 29.1.b. Yellowish white (C92) endpapers. All edges trimmed. Red head
and tail bands. Top edge stained reddish-brown.

COPIES EXAMINED: personal [Var. (1) and (2)], TxU [Var. (1)
and (2)].

[Fourth Jan Förlag edition, 1953]

30.1   LADY | CHATTERLEY'S | LOVER | BY D. H. LAWRENCE | *Jan
         Förlag [dot] Stockholm* [ll. 1-3 in opened display type]

(7 1/2 x 5"): [1]^8 2-19^8 20^4, 156 leaves; pp.[8],9-309,[310],
[2].

CONTENTS: p.[1]: blank. p.[2]: blank. p.[3]: half-title, in
open-faced display type. p.[4]: blank. p.[5]:t.p. p.[6]:
Copyright | JAN FÖRLAG | *Stockholm* | Continental Edition |
[short rule] | This edition must not be sold in the |
British Empire or the U.S.A. | Victor Peterson Bokindustri
Aktiebolag | Stockholm 1953 |. p.[7]: *Unexpurgated* |
authorized | *edition* |. p.[8]: blank. pp.9-[310]: text.
pp.[2]: blank.

TYPOGRAPHY: Text: 44ll. (p.225): 149(154) x 89mm. 10ll.=40mm.
Face 2(1.5x)mm.
Typeface: R153, Bauer Bodoni. DIN 1.34, modern neo-classic.

PAPER: smooth white wove unwatermarked. Thickness .07mm. Total
bulk 12.9mm.

BINDING: stiff paper wrappers (.24mm thick), pale
yellow (C.89), calico grain pattern. Lettering in dark
blue, as in 28.1 Var.(2) save lower wrapper is blank
except for printer's device (V, P worked together in circle).
Top and bottom edges trimmed, fore-edge untrimmed.

COPY EXAMINED: personal; MH

30.2   as 30.1 save:

LADY | CHATTERLEY'S | LOVER | BY | D.H. LAWRENCE |
Jan Förlag - Stockholm [ll. 1-3 in open display type]

PAPER: thickness .06mm.

BINDING: stiff paper wrappers (.24mm thick), pale
yellow (C.89), calico grain pattern. Lettering in dark blue.
Upper cover: Lady | Chatterley's | Lover | *by* | *D. H.
Lawrence* | [decoration: 5 stylized leaf designs] | JAN-FÖRLAG
[dot] STOCKHOLM |. Lower cover blank. On spine, top to
bottom: *JAN-FÖRLAG* [dot] STOCKHOLM |. Lower cover contains
printer's device in lower right.

120   *Lady Chatterley's Lover*

COPY EXAMINED: CU-S

[*third impression of fourth Jan Förlag ed., 1956*]

30.3   as 30.1 save:

(7 3/16 x 4 3/4"): [1]^8 2-18^8 19^{12}, 156 leaves; pp.[8],
9-309, [310], [2].

CONTENTS: p.[6], last line, ends STOCKHOLM 1956 |.

PAPER: Thickness .07mm. Total bulk 11.8mm.

BINDING: as 30.2 save wrappers pinkish white (C9). On spine,
    running top to bottom: [leaf decoration] Lady Chatterley's
    Lover *by D. H. Lawrence* [leaf decoration] |. Lower cover
    blank.

COPY EXAMINED: British Lib. (rebound, wrappers preserved)

30.4   as 30.3 save:

coll: [1]^8 2-18^8 19^4 20^8

PAPER: thickness: .07mm. Total bulk: 13.4mm.

BINDING: as 30.2.

COPY EXAMINED: Forster Coll.

[*Heinemann Netherlands edition, 1956*]

31.1   LADY CHATTERLEY'S | LOVER | *by* | D. H. LAWRENCE | *Complete*
         unexpurgated | *edition* | WILLIAM HEINEMANN/NEDERLAND |
         THE HAGUE

(8 x 5 1/2"): [1]^6, [2-16]^8 [17]^6, [18]^8 140 leaves;
pp.[1-4],5-279, [280].

CONTENTS: p.[1]:half-title. p.[2]:blank. p.[3]:t.p. p.[4]: This
    edition must not be introduced | into the British Empire
    or the U.S.A. | *Copyright 1956 William Heinemann/Nederland*
    | Manufactured in the Netherlands |. pp.5-279:text.
    p. [280]: blank.

TYPOGRAPHY: Text: 41ll.(p.159): 155 x 100mm, 10ll.=36mm.
    Face:2(1.5)mm.
    Typeface(incl. t.p.): Garamond (Monotype)? (R91). Transit-
    ional (DIN 1.24, Modern Baroque).

PAPER: smooth white wove unwatermarked. Thickness .12mm. Total

Bulk: 18.3mm.

BINDING: calico grain cloth (T. 124b), white, with spine
lettering in gold within gold-stamped border with a star at
each corner, on background of deep reddish purple (C.238):
[rule] | LADY | CHATTERLEY'S | LOVER | [star] | LAWRENCE |
[rule] |. At tail of spine, gold-stamped: HEINEMANN |
[rule] | NEDERLAND |. White head and tail bands. Plain
white endpapers,.5mm thick. All edges trimmed.
   DJ: pale yellowish pink (C31), with strip at bottom (5mm
high) in deep purplish red. Front cover: *Lady | Chatterley's
| Lover* | COMPLETE | UNEXPURGATED EDITION | D. H. LAWRENCE
[11.1-3 in white, nonflowing script; 11.4-5 in deep purplish
red, sans serif type; 1.6 in pale yellowish pink on deep
purplish red background] |. On spine: *Lady Chatterley's Lover*
[top to bottom, nonflowing script in deep purplish red on
white background] | D. H. | LAWRENCE | [rule] | HEINEMANN
| NEDERLAND | [11.3-6 run left-right] |. Back cover: photo
of author. Front flap: Lawrence ". . . holds up [Connie and
Mellors] as an example to an industrial age suffering from
'sex in the head'. . . . LADY CHATTERLEY'S LOVER has long
been acknowledged to be a novel of great power and
beauty" [this material repeated from Phoenix expurgated
edition, see 15.32 above]. At bottom right: 15sh. Back
flap: 5 Lawrence titles.

NOTES: Heinemann published an unexpurgated Phoenix edition for
the home market in 1961: 46.1 below.
   The Cambridge U. exhibition catalogue (24) states that
the Dutch typesetters produced "a new crop of typos."

COPIES EXAMINED: TxU(dj); personal; OkTU; personal; NO/P-1

31.2.$_1$ as 31.1 save:

(7 3/4 x 5 1/4"): [1]^6, [2-17]^8 [18]^6, 140 leaves; pp.[1-4],
5-279, [280].

COPY EXAMINED: personal (no dj)

31.2.$_2$ as 31.2.$_1$ save:

Leaves measure 7 3/4 x 5 1/8"

PAPER: smooth white wove unwatermarked. Thickness .1mm. Total
Bulk 14.1mm.

BINDING: on spine: [rule] | LADY | CHATTERLEY'S | LOVER |
[star] | LAWRENCE | [rule]
Dj: as 31.1 save lower flap is blank.

COPIES EXAMINED: personal(dj), FMFIU

[Heinemann post-censorship impression for home market, 1960]

31.3.$_1$ as 31.1 save:

T.p.: Imprint change, beginning l.7: [pub. device: W. H.,
windmill in center] | HEINEMANN | LONDON MELBOURNE TORONTO

(8 x 5 3/8): [1-16]^8 [17]^4 [18]^8

CONTENTS: p.[4]: William Heinemann Ltd | LONDON MELBOURNE TORONTO
    | CAPE TOWN | AUCKLAND | THE HAGUE | © 1960 D. H. Lawrence
    Estate | Printed in Holland |.

PAPER: thickness .11mm. total bulk 16.8mm.

BINDING: linen-grain cloth (T304), vivid red (C11). Sil-
    ver-stamped on spine: [rule] | LADY | CHATTERLEY'S | LOVER
    | [star] | LAWRENCE | [rule] | HEINEMANN |.
    DJ: moderate green (C145) and red. Front cover: [on green
    background]: Lady | Chatterley's | Lover | [Lawrence
    phoenix in red and black] | [in white strip, black
    lettering]: COMPLETE AND UNEXPURGATED | [on red back-
    ground]: D. H. LAWRENCE | [11.1,2,3,6 in white] |. On
    spine: top to bottom: D. H. LAWRENCE | Lady Chatterley's
    Lover |. set vertically: COMPLETE | UN-| EXPURGATED |
    EDITION | HEINEMANN |. Back cover in green, with list of
    Phoenix Edition (23 titles in 21 vols) and adverts for
    Phoenix and Moore's *D. H. Lawrence Miscellany*. Front flap:
    2 paragraphs on DHL. At lower right: 16s | NET |. Back
    flap: 5 titles of studies and collections of Lawrence.

NOTES: Full-page advert in *Bookseller*, Nov. 12, 1960, p.2065,
    placed just after the British decensorship decision,
    stated the volume would be "out early December." This
    edition was still in print in 1970, for it was listed in
    British Books In Print, although the Heinemann Phoenix
    (unexpurgated) Ed. (see below, 46.1) was published in
    1963. The Phoenix edition cost 30 shillings, while 31.3 was
    priced at 16s.

COPIES EXAMINED: Notts. County Lib.(2 copies, dj), TxU(dj),
    personal(dj), Pollinger Coll. (dj)

31.3.$_2$ as 31.3.$_1$ save:

PAPER: Thickness   .08mm. Total bulk 14.9mm.

BINDING: dj: ticket pasted over price on front flap, reading:
    80p | NET |.

COPIES EXAMINED: NO/U-1; CU-S(dj)

SECTION 5

Post-Censorship U.S. Editions, 1959–88

INTRODUCTORY ESSAY

"First unexpurgated legally-sanctioned American edition": even a label for the Grove Press' 1959 *Lady Chatterley* requires a fistful of words. The events attending the
publication of this watershed edition called for millions of
words, not a few of them from the Postmaster General, the
publishers of Grove, New American Library, and Pocket Books,
the executors of the Lawrence estate, and some of the most
eminent lawyers, literary critics, and advertising strateg-
ists of the day. Perspectives on these events have been
accurately recorded by Charles Rembar, Warren Roberts, Alec
Craig, John Sutherland, and Raymond Caffrey. However,
important details still await clarification. These involve
the volume's publishing history as affected by the following:
the Press' efforts to prepare and advertise a scholarly
edition, Rembar's successful defense of the book against the
Post Office's charges of obscenity, and the attendant
pressures of the "Chatterley Sweepstakes" in July and August
1959. In the light of these circumstances, the state of
Grove's text of the novel is also noteworthy (see Notes to
32.1).

Lady Chatterley's decensorship meant that it did not
have to be sold furtively to the pruriently curious who,
however clearly some of them may have understood its author's
message, had forged its reputation as a "d.b." Barney Rosset
of Grove started Lawrence's novel on its way to respectability, and to the shrine of acknowledged classics. The
implications of this are profound. Therefore, Rosset's
promotion and distribution tactics for both his hardcover and
paperbound editions are especially interesting to compare to
those of contemporary and later American publishers. None
could afford completely to forget that a once notorious and
banned book glows, however faintly, with the aura of a
glamorous, shady past. The fire is almost, but not quite,
extinguished even when the novel becomes a trade paperback
classic instead of a mass-market star attraction.

Judge F. Van Pelt Bryan's favorable decision, on July 21, 1959, included this:

> . . . the format and composition of the volume, the advertising and promotional material and the whole approach to publication, treat the book as a serious work of literature. The book is distributed through leading bookstores throughout the country. There has been no attempt by the publisher to appeal to prurience or the prurient minded.

In 1954 Bennet Cerf had written to Rosset that with any such project the publisher would be "placing more than a little of his bet on getting some sensational publicity from the sale of a dirty book." (Caffrey 54). Knowing that he must show more was at stake, Rosset took great pains to produce a scholarly edition: witness the Introduction by Mark Schorer, his Bibliographical Note at the end of the volume, the letter from Archibald MacLeish, the dust jacket testimonials from Jacques Barzun, Edmund Wilson, and Harvey Breit, and the elaborately informative blurb on the jacket flaps. Rosset's efforts, including his attaining of affidavits from a dozen authorities, are described in detail by Caffrey (52-56). The conservative typographic design and undecorated binding and dust jacket also convey a dead-serious intent. With modifications, they set a standard Grove used in the next decade to publish many works which, prior to the Grove editions, were associated with red endpapers, black boards, lack of copyright statements or publisher's names, Mexico City or Paris imprints, cryptic logos, authorial pseudonyms, erotic and/or satanic illustrations, "Old Face" type, false limitation statements, smeary photolithography, and high prices. While Grove's volume is not designed very differently from one of Lawrence's novels published a generation earlier by Martin Secker or Thomas Seltzer, Rosset's purpose was more ambitious, in a scholarly and a business sense, than that of a Thomas Seltzer, Jack Kahane, Pino Orioli, Ben Abramson, Martin Secker, Alfred Knopf, Samuel Roth, or Victor Weybright. At least in retrospect, the stakes were higher. What must Roth (see Sections 2 and 3) have thought, sitting in a federal penitentiary in July 1959 (whence he had been sent for outraging Estes Kefauver and presumably the country by publishing pornography which included Beardsley's *Under The Hill*), and contemplating Rosset's potential clientele and status, made possible by the Supreme Court analysis of his own case in 1957?

Grove used two types of publicity: that preparing the trade and the public for *Chatterley* as a literary masterpiece, and that aimed at minimizing the damage of the "Chatterley Sweepstakes," which followed Judge Bryan's decision as several paperback firms turned the claim that the novel was in the public domain to their own advantage. Promotion was handled by the firm of Sussman and Sugar, which had represented the most prestigious American presses: Harvard University, Random House, Simon and Schuster (Rembar 70; Caffrey 66). Its efforts are preserved in the Arents

archive at Syracuse University./1/ It prepared informative, decorous advertisements in leading newspapers, most of which were accepted (Rembar 71-72). One partial exception, at which the *Times* and the *New Yorker* balked (PW 13 July 1959), was a newspaper advertisement reading simply "The Post Office ban forbids us to tell you where you can buy a copy of *Lady Chatterley's Lover*." In smaller type Lawrence, Schorer, MacLeish, and Grove are identified. An eight-page Digest of Public Opinion quoted newspaper editorials throughout the country criticizing the Postmaster General's refusal to allow the book to be mailed. Order forms sent to booksellers were accompanied by a letter from Rosset explaining the moral superiority of an "honest" complete edition and stating that the legal advice he sought assured him that attempts to suppress his edition would fail. In late May, Rosset narrated a radio program (advertised in the *N. Y. Times*) which presented a brief history of literary censorship and simulated the voices of Lawrence, Mellors, Connie, and Judge Woolsey. The program ended with an announcement that *Chatterley* could be purchased "at all good book stores." The extent to which such efforts could win favor in 1959 is described by an Assistant District Attorney in New York at the time:

> In substance, did the publisher (or distributor or dealer) print an evocative cover, advertise prior banning, display the item massed with other borderline items, and urge in various ways erotic, deviant, or scatological appeal? If so, let him not justify by claiming historical importance, or literary artistry, that, quite obviously, was not even remotely the basis of his sales appeal. (Kuh 78)

The shrewd advantage Rosset had gained by his agreement with The Readers' Subscription book club (see Notes for 32.1 below) provided an additional forum for his intentions. This was a specialized club, in its tenth year of operation, which offered avant garde works to a largely academic clientele needing to stay abreast of current trends (Craig 157); its alternate selection to the Grove *Chatterley* was an edition of Freud's letters. In the recent past it had offered *Flowers of Evil*, *Finnegan's Wake*, and Arendt's *The Human Condition*. Book clubs were very important for extensive distribution at the time, and the specialist variety was just gaining prominence (Tebbel IV, 363-64). The club newsletter for April quoted the MacLeish letter as incentive. In early August, a large advertisement placed in the N. Y. *Times* soliciting new members also quoted MacLeish, mentioned the court decision proudly, and offered to anyone by coupon a copy of the Bryan "historic" decision.

The Sweepstakes strategy required more combativeness. After the trial, competing unexpurgated paperbacks appeared from companies of varied reputations. Pocket Books was one of the most prestigious. Its early entry (with a formidable first printing of 100,000 copies) shows that the potential of *Lady Chatterley* in 1959 was significant enough to exercise even a well-off firm. Its edition (36.1) was published only eight days after the court decision. This was rapidly

followed by the editions of the New American Library (37.1; published July 31) and Pyramid Books (38.1), out by early August). The "Tabloid Publishing Company" issued a newspaper-format piracy (35.1) reset word for word from the Grove text. It was being sold in New York and Connecticut in early August (in the latter state police soon confiscated copies because of the ease with which juveniles could purchase them from newsstands). There was also New American Library's reissue of the expurgated edition (21.1-21.4). Of course, a $6.00 hardcover could not compete with 35 or 50 cent paperbacks printed in runs of over a million copies. New York bookseller Arnold Levy/2/ describes

> the upright rack of paperbacks on sale at my corner candy store in Brooklyn--all filled with *different editions* of LCL! And, as a topper, there was a N. Y. Times size newspaper-like edition for sale too. It was a sight for sore eyes!

As Mr. Levy puts it, as far as *Lady Chatterley* was concerned, "anything went."

Rosset could hardly have been surprised at the appearances of the competing paperbacks, but he did not condone the events with inaction. Grove sued the NAL on July 23, charging that firm's use of the word "authorized" (but not "abridged") to describe its expurgated edition was misrepresentation. At this point, Rosset countered with Grove's own paperback version, printing on the cover "This is . . . the only unexpurgated edition ever published in America." NAL countersued, claiming this was false, as did the distributor for the Pocket Books edition, later in August. See 33.1, 36.1, and 37.1, Caffrey 76-77, and Sutherland, *Off. Lit.* 15-17. Grove skirmished with truck banners, window stickers, and posters color-keyed to the dust jacket. Page-length announcements to the trade and the public explained Grove's motives for, and problems attending, publication. Letters to dealers solicited loyalty to Grove's edition over the "hitch-hiking" paperback publishers./3/

The Lawrence estate, which authorized the Knopf-NAL version, would not take royalties from Rosset (Sutherland *Offensive Lit.* 13-14), unless he provided it with 10% of hardcover and 50% of paperback sales plus all rights to subsequent printings (Arents archive, typescript of letter from Laurence Pollinger headed "EXTRACT".). Laurence Pollinger's opposition to Rosset is carefully chronicled by Caffrey (58-63, 75-76). For a possible reason for it, beyond an agent's refusal to be pushed into giving up control of a valuable property, see the Introductory Note to Section 8 below. The Estate still considers the NAL printings to constitute the only authorized unexpurgated American version (Pollinger 239; letters, Gerald Pollinger to the author, 12 Aug. 1985, 3 Jan. 1986). Throughout the summer of 1959, however, Rosset kept his idealistic motives paramount, for they were, in fact, his best advantage at the time.

In his three-page (late July) letter to booksellers he reiterated that he alone had borne court costs, had volunteered to pay costs of anyone involved in legal action for selling the work, had accepted additional expenses of shipping by Railway Express, had "mobilized the support of the American public for this important fight," had advertised responsibly, and had made the book a legitimate bestseller. He solicited loyalty to his cloth edition, and to the soon-to-appear Grove paperback, which he labeled (somewhat disingenuously, with the NAL and Pocket volumes about to come out), as the "*first and only* complete, uncensored, uncut version" (see 33.1) in the U.S., and the only one with scholarly introduction and preface. A draft (Arents: Rosset to William Callahan of Dell Publishing, 6 Aug. 1959) of another open letter, to wholesalers to whom Dell distributed the Grove paperback, stated that the latter alone guaranteed to purchasers that they would be getting the uncut novel which Grove had now become famous for defending. As an example of the loyalty Grove hoped to receive, a statement from the prestigious Gotham Book Mart promising Ms. Steloff's exclusive patronage was quoted. This draft contains an interesting redlined passage, to the effect that Dell and Grove would have priced the paperback at 75 cents but for the competition; the alternate price of 50 cents at least will limit the number of teenagers whose purchases may well precipitate local prosecutions of booksellers; Grove alone plans to defend its edition against these. Grove alone would have been satisfied with a hardcover at a price only adults could afford, thus not providing enemies of free expression with an "into-whose-hands" issue. In any event, Rosset promised that his paperback would have a prurient-free cover design and a promotion campaign aimed at delineating Grove's idealistic motives.

Sussman and Sugar deserved the "special presentation edition" (32.5.b below) which Rosset prepared for them after the Bryan decision; they sharply focussed, as was so necessary, on Grove's responsible public service, while making clear the firm's tough-minded perseverance in defense of its investment. Apropos of the latter was a realistic concession to human curiosity: an advertisement on which the type was set irregularly to suggest a rhythmically-swaying hammock. This was low-key, witty, and erotically suggestive, but, as Rembar might argue, normally so, given the community (especially the popular media) standards of the time. The undulating type stated that "the warm pleasant days of summer are perfect for reading 'Lady Chatterley's Lover'." In a hammock, or perhaps on a sofa, or a bed? With one hand? Or with a friend: "there are tales of couples reading Lawrence on couches: putting him aside to lie on them" (Tindall vi).

Although the Grove Press could hardly have created a new audience for *Lady Chatterley*, its book design, its publicity campaign, and its distribution practices surely did more than extend the novel's availability to the randy, the scholarly, and the vast majority of us who fall between these extremes. It made it possible for readers not to have to frequent the back rooms described in Section 2, the cheap paperback or

"dollar-book" counters of the various outlets (see Section 3) which sold unacknowledged bowdlerizations, or any bookstores a tourist might visit in Europe (Section 4). Fooling customs officials became a thing of the past, as did brown paper mail-order wrappers. The shred of daring associated with owning a Paris or Swedish edition needed no longer be resorted to as an aphrodisiac. It was necessary for Barney Rosset to redirect the course of the novel's reputation. The strategy and its implications are clear in Charles Rembar's excellent account (see especially 94-99; 118-26) of his argument before Judge Bryan regarding the average person in the community, and its standards. He took full advantage of the new legal guidelines the Roth Case had set up for ruling on pornography. Community standards should not be set, the counselor averred (97), by outraged moralists or by the pruriently curious, but by intelligent readers. These proper readers may be sexually aroused, but not in a prurient way. Rather, given the amount of sexual explicitness considered normal in TV and film in 1959, such readers would encounter and recognize a level of "erotic realism" (Kronhausen 25-29; 249-60) which did not involve moral discomfort. Rembar acknowledged that prurient curiosity would be the motive for most of the interest stimulated by *Chatterley*, and that most citizens would not support its publication, regardless of their desire to read it. However, "an 'average' notion of what is objectionable [should not] control the freedom to write and be read" (125). Rembar, a brilliant lawyer, pushes back the boundaries of literary taboo in order to remove *Chatterley* from the category. This process, as sociologists have observed, is a dynamic one in modern culture, especially when sexual explicitness is concerned (Polsky 192-97; McGrath 194-96).

What this suggests is that one can theoretically winnow down (not actually limit) the "readership" of the book to a small group of those enlightened enough to purchase it for careful reading. It is this group for which it is supposedly designed; this indeed is the group Sussman and Sugar's promotion efforts focus upon (the less sophisticated mass may be left to hear of the Grove edition willy-nilly, and of course they will). The cognoscenti were, in fact, the group Lawrence had in mind with his Florence edition, although, as Mrs. Lawrence's introduction to the Odyssey Press first printing (25.1) points out, he also wanted to reach the common people "from whom he came." This, as well as a counter to the pirates, was why Lawrence published his own Paris Popular Edition (1.2-1.4; see p.4 above).

Once the Grove strategy in its purest form takes precedence, the book becomes codified as a classic, the "erotic realism" no longer a cause for concern. Many people forget its reputation for prurience and the motives for reading it change. Publishers and prospective readers still know this reputation of course, as this essay and the accompanying descriptions will show. However, most of today's readership pick up the book with less diverse (or "insalubrious," as strict moralists used to say) motives than formerly. I do not mean the book has lost its reputation for

sexual explicitness, nor that readership is reduced; quite the opposite is true, given printing and distribution practice from 1959 to date. I mean that those among us whose fascination with the vagaries of sexual expression requires outlet in materials with unblushing erotic and scatological explicitness no longer make *Chatterley* a high priority *for this purpose*. (Nor would they ever have done, but for the moral outrage which selectively struck Lawrence so strong a blow in 1928). However, was not some of *Chatterley's* vitality lost by its de-censorship? The strictly prurient-minded, and the outraged puritans (however "grey in every fibre," as Lawrence described Home Secretary Joynson-Hicks in "Pornography and Obscenity") must be counted as part of the *Chatterley* reading community. Lawrence may have hated them, and what they did to him, but, in hindsight, their opinions helped publicize his book, and gave it a better chance of having an effect--if not on them (and even this is problematical), then on those directed to it by their fears.

At the present time, hostility toward *Chatterley* might come from Christian fundamentalists who deplore the "religion" of "secular humanism," and from women who find the kind of sexuality Lawrence advocates "pornographic" in the sense of inhibiting feminine civil rights and self-awareness. These groups can hardly be excluded from the 1980s reading community for the novel. Are they necessarily impervious to Lawrence's language and theme? Do not those who approach a book with guilty curiosity or moral indignation help create a reputation which makes it ultimately more accessible, even if its effect may be to their minds different from that which most critics now think Lawrence "intended"? Do not they influence how it is read, and who reads it, as much as literary reviewers do? Is not their theoretical exclusion as proper readers a sign, ironically, of the novel's decline in vital public interest?

These are not questions by which advertisers or lawyers should be guided. Nor are Rosset, Rembar, or Sussman and Sugar responsible for *Lady Chatterley* no longer being the indispensable "pariah literature" (Lawrence's phrase; see p.viii above) it was in 1959 and before. TV, film, and the general commercialization of the youth culture were then well on the way to replacing books with music and film as the artforms most absorbing to the public imagination. However, it is significant to see the redefinition of the novel's audience being concurrently worked out by its pioneering liberators. For one indication of *Lady Chatterley's* current status as a classic, see pp.249-50 and A13.1 below, the comic strip version (1986). Herein, the once-notorious "phallic novel" is treated as an Establishment icon which the iconoclastic cartoonist labors to reduce to absurdity.

It is also interesting to analyze the methods which Grove's competitors at the time, and both Grove and those rivals during the past generation, used to sell the book. With the exception of the tabloid piracy, with its pulp-inspired lubricity ("smothering passions"; "recent movie starring French sexpot"), they have appealed to the most

"legitimate" reasons for reading *Chatterley*, without exclud-
ing from these sex and romance. The differences between these
tactics and those of the packagers of the Authorized Edition
(see Essay for Section 3, pp.62-66) are ones of degree, and
depend on evolving standards of public taste and morality.
Back-cover and first-page paperback blurbs during the summer
of 1959 carefully suggested reading for learning about the
opposition of social hypocrisy to natural instinct, and
pointed to Lawrence's acute psychological analysis, his
insights on sexuality and the health-giving effects of its
free expression. These did not preclude the publishers'
categorizing the novel as erotic romance, although that the
love-affair was adulterous was not emphasized. The NAL cover
had small line drawings of a fully-clothed man (shirt,
slacks, and even shoes in place) and a woman lying amid
flowers, embracing. Pyramid followed with a very similar
drawing of a couple walking hand-in-hand. In both cases,
clothing (the males' especially) is that of 1959: the Pyramid
gentleman is in a business suit. The strategy may have been
to have the contemporary purchasers (largely male?) identify
easily with the characters. The Pocket Books lower-cover
blurb reads largely as literary criticism, but does mention
"virile gamekeeper" and "impotent husband." The cover is
unillustrated. However, the decorated oval border, reminiscent of a mirror, on the title page and cover may be a
version of the picture-frame device for paperback bindings,
which, from the 1940's onward, was used--usually enclosing an
illustration--to suggest a passage into a fantasy world (Bonn
102, 115; see his plate 14). In 1959, this title in itself
possessed a fascination which might have made this device
work. Advertising's shrewd appeal to the furtive need for
sexual fantasizing does not disappear with a larger tolerance
for "erotic realism" as healthy and acceptable by community
standards.

Since the 1960s, sexually explicit mass media advertising for clothing, cologne, films, and books demonstrates how
integral stimulating the erotic imagination is to attracting
purchasers. The nature of this appeal is still prurient;
however, it never strays beyond, if it enters at all, the
shadowy borderland apparently exempt today from interdiction.
It is true, however, that the near borders of the "hard core"
itself have responded elastically to this advertising, not
without protest by conservatives who feel that there remains
a consensus regarding what self-indulgent sexual deviance is.
The blurbs and cover designs for paperback impressions of
Chatterley in the late seventies and early eighties, although
such advertisements hardly provoked the concern that those
for men's underwear or women's cologne did, can be discussed
as examples of an explicit return to the prurient appeals
which the 1959-60 first printings of these editions were
obliged to disdain. Before glancing at the 1970s "packaging,"
however, let it be emphasized that none of the post-censorship printings have focussed on a prurient "hard sell," by
any reasonable definition of the epithet "hard" during the
past twenty years. The dust jacket of the Modern Library
edition (34.1-34.4) is more typical in stating the novel's
importance to be related to its status as a modernist work

and to its exploration of the individual's obligations to
social conventions of her or his time. The publisher's own
obligation is clearly that of providing inexpensive literary
classics. The early 1960s blurbs on NAL covers (see 37.15)
convey a similar message. The Bantam 1968 edition (42.1)
speaks of Lawrence's "daring" and his "explicit declaration
of faith." The back cover reproduces his wish regarding
"complete, honest, and clean" sexual awareness. Pocket, Black
Cat, Bantam, and NAL covers remained bright-colored, decorous
posters throughout the sixties.

It is erotic fantasy and romance that substitutes for
what Kuh (see p.125 above) stigmatizes as a basic "erotic,
deviant, or scatological appeal." Book designers sometimes
return to the appeals made by the illustrations of the
authorized abridged editions of the 1930s. The dust jacket of
the Greenwich House subedition (32.15) reproduces a painting
of Connie discovering Mellors bathing, and touts a unique
(and "liberated") love story. The volume reproduces Lawrence's erotic paintings, and would make a suitable gift for
a contemporary sensibility. The Bantam cover art circa 1974-
87 (see 42.9) summarizes in one drawing two other memorable
scenes: a naked woman crowned with wild flowers, and the same
person walking toward a vivid green clearing and a tiny
cottage. The artwork on the upper cover of the first impression (42.1), more subtly suggestive, reproduces wild flowers,
perhaps in seed, perhaps in bloom, standing erect high above
weeds, implying a natural process of decay and sexual
regeneration, and movingly illustrating the "sturdy blue-
bells" over which Clifford drives his wheelchair in Chapter
13. One might see a similar tableau walking in the woods, and
be surprised by a vigorous, irresistible natural growth. This
is a trade paperback in a series of Modern Classics produced
for an audience specified as discriminating and well-educated. Therefore, Bantam contracted "sophisticated" covers
(Crider 59). Another possible stimuli to erotic romance is
the simple black design NAL used for the Lawrence novel and
other reprints of once-controversial love stories (see 37.24,
37.26); black, the traditional color of erotica, connotes the
taboo and the mysterious. The series' *Fanny Hill* contains
this blurb for *Chatterley*: "The famous story of a lovely
woman who flouts convention for the sake of an overwhelming
love."

The 1970s were a "liberated" decade in the U.S.; during
this time Grove and NAL used soft-core erotica as front-cover
illustration. The Black Cat printings of the mid-seventies
(32.11-32.15) displayed on the front cover a softly-lit
photograph of a naked couple gently enjoying each other's
nearness. This was followed in 1982 by the movie tie-in
impression (33.16), in some copies of which sixteen of the
frankest possible stills from the Just Jaecklin film were
bound in. Probably throughout the same period, and continuing
into the early 1980s, NAL's cover art (37.32-37.40) featured
a "trompe d'oeil" cartoon of a candidly nubile brunette. When
the cover is turned upside down the drawing reveals a
silhouette profile of man (on left) and woman -- both appear
to be in passionate convulsions. From this upside-down

perspective the white space surrounded by black suggests a vulva. These two covers are interesting examples of clever and at the same time sensational paperback illustration for trade (not mass-market) books which were widely distributed in college bookstores (see below). The NAL artwork may be an example of "college humor" intended to attract undergraduates, and professors, to this edition as opposed to those of Bantam or Grove. A white background had long been favored by mass-market illustrators working to create subtle erotic suggestions (Peterson 65-67; Coser 219). Its use in trade titles is part of the evidence that the distinction between the latter and mass-market paperbacks had by the seventies become tenuous (Tebbel IV, 350-51; Smith 10). Such covers also show how tolerant an atmosphere for sexual explicitness had developed since the 1940s and 50s, when cover art for NAL's expurgated editions (see 20.1, 20.3, 20.6, 20.7, 21.1) was considered salacious for using pulp romances and Hollywood posters as models. See also the Avon and Berkley paperback covers for *The First Lady Chatterley* (52.1-52.2, 53.1 below, and the essay for Section 7).

By the mid-eighties, there had been retrenchment from the iconoclasm of the seventies. The most recent Bantam and NAL printings feature front-cover reproductions of classic (42.23) and contemporary (37.41) paintings the erotic undertones of which are of the same unimpeachable stature as is the Lawrence novel. Whatever the style or period, replication in packaging, as a backhanded compliment to successful gimmickry, has been a prime characteristic of the paperback bandwagon (Smith 7-8, Bonn 85; see essay for Appendix 1, p.247, and for Section 7, pp.212-13). Such "piggybacking" helps a later edition share the attention and sales generated by an already-marketed competing edition. The Chatterley Sweepstakes was simply an earlier, notorious example.

Blurred boundaries between mass-market and trade publishing should not obscure the fact that, as far as the practicalities of advertising are concerned, the distinction is real. The trade (originally dubbed "egghead" [Davis 208]) paperbacks are geared toward either a more intellectually-oriented or more educated (and therefore presumably more responsible) audience than that which the mass-market book attracts. It may be more accurate to say that one purchases a trade book with the intention to read it with care, as opposed simply to be entertained. Trade titles are to be found at bookstores; they are not distributed to "points of sale" such as railway stations, airports, newsstands and supermarkets, where the limited rack space is used for best-selling books in behalf of which promotional campaigns attempt to take full advantage of a short shelf life (Smith 18, Coser 357). A trade title represents a perennial commodity which brings in a steady if unspectacular income over a long period of time. It is a prestigious item "requiring little additional expenditure for promotion" (Smith 60), as *Chatterley* has been for both NAL and Grove since 1959, and for Bantam since 1968. Sometimes, such mainstays begin as mass-market bestsellers, as did *Chatterley* in 1959-60, at least for Grove: over two million sold. Pocket Books sold

1,750,000; NAL sales totalled 1,250,000 during the first 14 months of publication (see notes for 33.1, 36.1, 37.1)./4/

In 1959, one could purchase the unexpurgated paperbacks at various points of sale, although the choice may have been limited in various sections of the county (but not New York City, see p.126 above). Publishers would not want their distributors to deal in competing editions, and the independent distributors themselves possibly took pains to see that their clients displayed only the edition they provided (see notes to 33.1). Since the early sixties, one would most likely find paperback printings only in the literature sections of bookstores. College bookstores are especially important; the origin of the "serious" (i.e. trade) softcover involved the perception that the mass-market publishers could, with a bit of horizon-broadening, serve the interests of the campuses, which since the war had attracted so many young people (Bonn 51, Davis 210-11). This is important in understanding Lawrence's, and *Lady Chatterley's*, contemporary reputation. College students form a significant cross section of the literate population, and if it is not intellectuals and those to whom they profess who are drawn to Lawrence and his work today, it is general readers with an openness to what academics say about the eternal theme of erotic romance. In addition, students' book budgets are nearly depleted by the required course texts which professors know must themselves include as many paperbacks as possible (Davis 210-11; Bonn 61). Paperbacks are affordable, and can be marks of status in the makeshift shelves of dorms and off-campus apartments: a sign that the owners have graduated (on the advice of peers and teachers) from Robbins, Cartland, and Sheldon to Lawrence, Jong, Nin, and Fowles.

Classic authors also depend for present-day readers on the large chain bookstores. These carry generous selections of Lawrence materials which, although not as prominent as current movie tie-ins and blockbuster hopefuls in their flashy cardboard display racks, and unlikely to benefit from autograph parties for the latest chroniclers of New York Yuppiedom, are cause for optimism nonetheless. They are good evidence that the impression made on many young readers by The Priest Of Love, whether in a required course reading or elsewhere, is too strong for the book business to begin to ignore. For example, Sonenschein et. al. (145), researching mass media erotica for the 1970 Commission On Obscenity and Pornography, found that among thirty-two women interviewed, the four most widely-read erotic novels (the most prominent source of these women's knowledge about sexuality) were *Valley Of The Dolls*, *The Carpetbaggers*, *Lady Chatterley's Lover*, and *Candy*. This was almost a decade after the Chatterley Sweepstakes.

Another source of Lawrence's, and *Lady Chatterley's*, continuing reputation is the book club editions and their audiences. Doubleday, a highly successful reprint publisher, organized many such clubs and 40.1 may have been an entry in its Literary Guild. Such organizations, selling through bookstores, department stores, and magazine advertisement,

reach many kinds of readers. In 1960, one kind of subscriber was the upwardly mobile young college graduate who may or may not have kept up with his/her reading since college, but who would have found cheap hardcover editions a convenient way to maintain the reading habit and build a personal library (Tebbel IV: 109, 361, 364). Recent brochures of the International Collector's Library version (41.1) list its *Chatterley* under the category "Romance and Passion," along with titles such as *The Thorn Birds, Dr. Zhivago, Wuthering Heights, Pride and Prejudice, Peyton Place, Love Story*. The club offers "a library of the most-beloved literature of all time in elegant collectors editions. . . from timeless novels to modern classics. . . " Each work is bound in one of five styles, the *Chatterley* being accorded the "Jade Green Louis XVI." The finely printed and bound tomes which at one time legitimatized the rich (therefore trusted) man's private erotica collection may have become defunct in the post-censorship era, but the status-allure of "the finest traditions of bookmaking art" still exists, as the recent Chatham River Press edition also shows (see 32.23). For more on book clubs, see Section 6, pp.184-85.

It is often remarked, and impossible to deny, that one result of the *Chatterley* decensorship was a spate of prurient-interest paperbacks, which made a lot of money for what are termed "secondary" or "adults only" publishers and distributors. The latter placed their wares in adult bookstores, newsstands, and (depending on books' level of lubricity) at other outlets at which mass-market paperbacks could be purchased. It was the between-the-wars predecessors of the secondary distributors who moved pirated copies of banned books from southern ports to points of sale throughout the country (see essay for Section 2, p.15). As the 1971 United States Commission on Obscenity (III: 88-98) carefully explains, by the late 1960s, there were several dozen such companies, most located in Southern California and New York. Their market had become saturated, especially because the number of retail outlets did not proliferate as greatly as publishers hoped they would when legal concepts of obscenity were liberalized. Secondary publishers never had large-scale financial or technical resources, nor the ability to appeal to the broad general standards of taste. They represented as little a threat to their mainstream counterparts, either in volume of distribution or net profits, as Samuel Roth had to Alfred Knopf, Grosset and Dunlap, or the New American Library. However, the flooded secondary market suggests a temporary bonanza for these distributors and publishers, which can be traced to the greater freedom to publish sexually-oriented material occasioned by three major decensorship trials of the early sixties (*Chatterley, Tropic of Cancer, Fanny Hill*).

This liberalization changed the "Seconaries'" modes of operation. Prior to 1959, Adults Only paperbacks shared many characteristics of the mainstream genre novel: mystery and detective, adventure, romance. The "love bouts" in these "Sex Pulps" were hinted at; the diction was circumspect. The covers featured little more nudity, or "bosoms and bottoms,"

than the mass-market genre paperbacks (United States. Commission III: 91), in which group, as I have suggested above, the Authorized Edition of *Chatterley* could take its place, as could the Avon and Berkley editions of *The First Lady Chatterley*. The 1949 piracy of NAL's Authorized Edition, 15.1, shows how closely a secondary paperback could ape the mass market. From about 1965 onward, new guidelines for the secondary product began to evolve, and the Sex Pulps were transformed into "hard-core" entertainments with little story-line. The subject matter become largely copulation and its techniques, described as graphically as had Miller and Lawrence; the language included all the obscene and scatological diction which was accepted as necessary for these two writers' aesthetic goals (United States. Commission III: 92). The entire process is interestingly documented by Richard E. Geis (2-16, 26-36), himself a successful pornographic novelist from 1960 to 1985.

Adult films and magazines evince the same process of greater license. As for mainstream publishers, the appearance of classic and contemporary erotic literature in paperback beginning in the early sixties is well documented by Sutherland (*Off. Lit.* 28-31). For the expansion, therefore, of the boundaries of erotic explicitness, for whatever mixture of entrepreneurial, aesthetic, self-exploratory, or prurient motives publishers, writers, and readers may have had, the appearance of the "complete Lady C" in America is a pioneering exemplar. Would Lawrence say "one up to it," especially in view of his own intolerance (see "Pornography and Obscenity") for what he considered pruriently titillating?

Blurbs for the Sex Pulps and the post-censorship *Chatterley* paperbacks are sometimes difficult to distinguish from each other; while this may simply mean that such formulae for illicit sexual passion (not, of course, the only cover advertisements for the Lawrence novel) admit of little variety, it is worth noting some examples, since they are obviously effective for both kinds of book: "The shocking story of an incredible love affair" (*Strange Lust* [Intimate Editions]), or "a tempestuous novel of a woman's strange desires" (*Mask Of Lesbos* [Beacon]), are more dramatically stated versions of blurbs on the bindings of 36.1, 37.1, 37.21, 42.1 above. Sometimes the differences between Sex Pulps and mainstream paperback "packaging" must be measured by how often both have been under fire from local district attorneys and senatorial committees for the crime of displaying "erotic, deviant, or scatological appeal."

"Appropriateness" in book advertising is a matter of taste. Whatever the approach, sex and love are used with a novel such as *Chatterley* as a "come-on," which is inevitably misleading in the light of any literary analysis of the book. Misleading and shallow, but not irrelevant. The "packaging," whether dust jacket, overheated blurbs, or pulp or "sophisticated" paperback covers, focusses on a mind-set that teasing publisher and enticed purchaser share; a context, in fact, which conventional middle-class moral imperatives have made inevitable, and which insures that sexuality ("sex in the

head") will be identified with furtive desires still associated with prurient motives (even more so in 1989 than in
1959 or 1978). Lawrence needs such readers. His message is
for them. They apparently still need him, in a way that,
where yearning humanity is concerned, makes the distinction
between hard-edged prurience and intellectual self-discovery
more legally than pragmatically substantive.

A final note on possible unlocated editions published
since Judge Bryan's decision: the 1971 United States Commission On Obscenity And Pornography tells us that "virtually
every book written in English which was originally thought to
be obscene at the time of publication has been reissued by
secondary publishers" (92). I have not found evidence that
this is true of *Lady Chatterley's Lover*. For the possibility
of the Paris-based Olympia Press having done so, see the
essay for Section 4, endnote 2. In the United States, Collectors Publications pirated many Olympia volumes during the
sixties; the firm does not advertise *Chatterley* among them,
nor have I located any copies. Less likely reprinters would
be Pendulum (Atlanta), Brandon House (Los Angeles), Greenleaf
(San Diego), Lancer, Fleur de Lis, or Ophelia (all of New
York). Collectors Publications is the most likely candidate,
and if this firm did not reprint the Lawrence novel it may be
because Olympia did not do so. However, as C. J. Scheiner has
pointed out,/5/ the ubiquitous paperback editions from 1959
onward would make any such venture by a secondary publisher
unprofitable. The closest approach to such a reprinting
occurs in a 1961 English-language Danish publication reissued
by Lyle Stuart (see essay for Appendix 1, p.249) in 1966 and
advertised for sale by Collectors Publications. A 12-page
chapter in this book, Ove Brusendorff and Poul Henningsen's *A
History of Eroticism: The XXth Century*, consists of lengthy
excepts from *Chatterley* joined by brief plot summaries.

ENDNOTES

1. This essay, and the bibliographical descriptions below,
draw heavily upon the Arents Library (Syracuse University)
Grove Press archive, a rich collection of correspondence,
legal briefs, news clippings, advertising copy, and memoranda. I cite these documents when identifying marks make
them easier to find, and prefix such citations as "Arents."
When I do not do this, it is because they have no identifying
characteristics other than those mentioned in the context of
the discussion, and I hope it is clear from the context that
they are to be found in the archive. I wish to thank the
staff of the library for their cooperation.

2. in a letter to the author, postmarked 5 May 1988.

3. See *Publishers Weekly*, 7/13 and 8/17, 1959. The Arents
Archive contains many clippings of advertisements, for
example from the Los Angeles *Times*, July 26, and the Pitts-
burgh *Press*, June 28. Other issues of PW relevant to the
Grove edition and its consequences in 1959: 5/11,p.74;
5/25,p.242; 6/8, p.94; 7/6,p.110; 8/17,p.70; 8/24,p.78;

9/17,p.106; 9/28, p.90; 10/5, p.106; 10/12,p.74; 10/19,p.66; 11/2,p.82.

   The "Chatterley Sweepstakes" was not limited to editions of the novel. There was a parody, *Lady Loverley's Chatter* (A7.1), and even an aerosol perfume, packaged in "shocking pink" and "passionate purple" (not in Centroid color charts) and entitled "Lady Chatterly's [sic] Instant *Sexx* [sic]." See *The Insider's Newsletter* [women's section], Nov. 23, 1959: 8.

4. A *New York Times* list of paperback bestsellers from 1941 to 1956 (reproduced in Davis 289-90) lists *Lady Chatterley's Lover, Tropic of Cancer* (1961), and *Lolita* (1959) as having sold 3 1/2 million copies each. This is an extremely conservative estimate for LCL. In any event, it contrasts to Dr. Spock's *Baby And Child Care* (1946; 18 1/2 million) and *Peyton Place* (1957; 10 million). Hackett and Payne state (40) that through 1965 NAL and Pocket Books had sold, combined, 6,314,580 copes; they place the work fifth on the list of paperback bestsellers.

5. In a letter to the author (undated but May 1988).

BIBLIOGRAPHICAL DESCRIPTIONS (for other POST-CENSORSHIP U.S.
    EDITIONS, see 47.5 and 47.6 below)

*[Grove Press hardbound Edition, 1959: pre-publication
    impressions (numbers 1-4)]*

32.1.$_1$ LADY | CHATTERLEY'S | LOVER | *by D.H. Lawrence* |
        With an Introduction by MARK SCHORER | GROVE PRESS
        INC. [dot] NEW YORK

(8 x 5 3/8"): [1]-[13]^{16}, 208 leaves; pp.[2],[i-iv],v-xxxix,
[lx],[2],1-368,[4].

CONTENTS: pp.[2]:blank. p.[i]:half-title. p.[ii]:blank. p.[iii]:
    title page. p.[iv] *Introduction* by Mark Schorer, | Copyright
    © 1957 by Grove Press, Inc. | *Letter from Archibald MacLeish*,
    | Copyright © 1959 by Grove Press, Inc. | This edition is
    the third manuscript version, | first published by Guiseppe
    Orioli, Florence, 1928.| *Grove Press Books and Evergreen
    Books* | *are published by Barney Rosset at Grove Press,
    Inc.* | *795 Broadway New York 3, N.Y.*| MANUFACTURED IN THE
    UNITED STATES OF AMERICA |. p.v-vii: letter from Archibald
    MacLeish. p.[viii]:blank. pp.ix-xxxix: Introduction by
    Mark Schorer. p.[lx]:blank. p.[1]: fly-title. p.[2]:blank.
    pp.1-365: text. p.[366]:blank. pp.367-68: BIBLIOGRAPHICAL
    NOTE signed M.S. pp.[4]:blank.

TYPOGRAPHY: Text: 34ll.(p.51), 157 x 102 mm; 10ll.=44mm; face
    3(2x)mm.
    Typeface: modern Neoclassical (DIN 1.34). Linotype Caledonia.
    Pagination (3mm) centered 4mm below text.
    Following internal pages unnumbered: viii,xl-xli,[2],366.

PAPER: smooth white wove unwatermarked. Sheet size: 44 x 33
    offset (Arents coll., McKillin and Sons to Grove, 3/19/59).
    Thickness .095mm. Total Bulk 20.8mm.

BINDING: linen grain (T 304) cloth boards, yellowish gray
    (C 93); quarterbinding is of a calico grain(T 302), deep
    blue(C 179). Gold-stamped on spine (top to bottom, save last
    two lines): LADY CHATTERLEY'S LOVER | *D. H. Lawrence* | GROVE
    | PRESS |. No head or tail bands. All edges trimmed. Plain
    white endpapers.
      Dj: State 1: coated paper. Front cover and spine strong
    yellow (C.84), lettered in black (ll.1,2,3,5), white
    (ll.4,6), and blue (7,8): LADY | CHATTERLEY'S | LOVER | *BY*
    | D.H. LAWRENCE | IN ITS ORIGINAL UNEXPURGATED EDITION |
    INTRODUCTION BY MARK SCHORER | PREFACE BY ARCHIBALD MACLEISH
    |. On spine, reading top to bottom: LADY CHATTERLEY'S |
    LOVER D.H. LAWRENCE |[title in black, author in blue] |. Set
    horizontally, in white: GROVE PRESS |. Back cover in white
    with black lettering [comments by Jacques Barzun, Edmund
    Wilson, Harvey Breit, all defending sexual explicitness and
    4-letter words]. At bottom, under rule: GROVE PRESS, INC.,
    795 Broadway, New York 3, N. Y.|. Flaps contain blurb; 1st
    paragraph (front flap) quotes Harry Moore: "The time is

overdue for an American publisher to make a fight for *Lady
Chatterley's Lover* . . ." Front flap, upper right: $6.00
| .

PRICE, NO. OF COPIES PRINTED: As Roberts, p.106, reports,
published May 4, $6.00. A 10-column table in the Arents
archive (see the essay above, endnote 1) lists the printing
history in more detail than that given to Roberts by
Grove's publicity director in 1959. Three printings were
ordered in March (on the 17th, 26th, and 31st) of 15, 5,
and 15 thousand, respectively. A fourth, ordered April 16,
of 10,000 makes a total of 45,000 before publication.
Clearly, sales were brisk despite the use of the U. S. mails
being impossible before Judge Bryan's decision on July 21.
Publishers' Weekly announced the Grove hardback as a
"candidate" for its Best-Seller of the Week list May 11;
its first appearance on the list was in the May 25 issue,
with 40,000 copies sold and a new (5th?) printing under way.
Readers' Subscription, Inc., a small book club with a mainly
college-educated clientele, contracted with Grove (Arents
archive: Letter of Agreement, 19 March 1959) to distribute
15,000 copies (no plates were sent) and sold 10,588 (Arents:
Royalty Statement, 30 June 1961). Members of such book
clubs usually had to wait months after trade publication
(Grannis 216) to receive copies. However, Readers' Subscription's newsletter, *The Griffin*, listed the Lawrence
(at $4.95) as its April selection. The success of the
Grove venture, obviously, required winning the court case
brought against it by the Post Office, and at an early
date (partly to forestall piracy).

TYPOGRAPHICAL NOTE: p.290, l.16 reads: . . . same," same
Hilda. Corrected in post-publication impressions (see below).

NOTES: See Roberts pp.105-06. On May 6, postal inspectors
impounded 24 cartons, containing 164 copies and 20,000
circulars, as obscene, thus nonmailable. (PW 18 Jan. 1960:
101). Grove appealed, precipitating the decensorship trial.
    The jacket presented a problem for booksellers: the
background in olive brown faded, especially in display
windows. For the eighth printing of the jackets (accompanying
the 10th printing of the book) a two-color scheme was
ordered; with the 11th book printing a slightly darker
background color was instituted [no copies seen in two-color
jackets] (undated memo to Algen Lithographers, Arents coll).
    At least two passages appearing in the authorized expurgated
editions survive in the Grove Press version: 1) p.19,
ll..13-14 (Chapter 2): "She was not a 'little pilchard |
sort of fish,' like a boy." The Orioli ed., and the MS.,
read "like a boy, with a boy's flat breast and little
buttocks." 2) p.31, ll. 8-9 (Chapter 3): "There was
something curiously | childlike and defenseless about
him." Orioli, and MSS., read "There was something curiously
childlike and defenseless about his naked body: as children
are naked." Prof. Schorer consulted the MSS, but he did
not collate the Grove galleys line-by-line with the Orioli
Edition. As the text was prepared, and the expurgated text
(one assumes) collated with the unexpurgated, some errors

were probably inevitable. See Caffrey 64–65 for Schorer's copy-texts (he first used the Odyssey Press and Jan Förlag editions, and then corrected some but not all of the copy against the Orioli). There were no doubt additional omissions. When Grove checked its edition against the NAL paperback, it found the latter included single words and whole phrases not in the Grove edition (Arents: interoffice memo, 31 Aug. 1959).

COPIES EXAMINED: TxU(cop.2,4, both dj); personal(dj); OkTU(dj)

32.1.$_2$ as 32.1.$_1$ save:

CONTENTS: p.[iv]: publisher's address not present.

BINDING: d.j.: state 1: as 32.1.$_1$ State 2: back cover, under rule: 64 University Place [replaces 795 Broadway] I.

NOTE: see Roberts p.112 (The error on p.290, noted above, is uncorrected). Grove was moving its offices in April and May of 1959.

COPIES EXAMINED: personal(dj, st.1); TxU(copy 5, dj, st.1; copy 3, dj, st.2); Forster Coll.

*32.2   [ordered 17 March 1959]

*32.3   [ordered 26 March 1959]

*32.4   [ordered 31 March 1959]

[Grove Press hardbound edition, post-publication impressions (5–14)]

32.5.a   as 32.1.$_2$ save:

CONTENTS: p.290, l.16: . . . same," said Hilda I.

BINDING: Var.(1): as 32.1. Var.(2): yellowish gray cloth, no blue quarterbinding. Spine lettering as above, but stamped in black.

TYPOGRAPHICAL NOTE: In response to a reader's query (see Arents: letter, J. Schmidt to E. Smyth, 17 Aug. 1959; Caffrey 65), Schorer ordered the word "unusual" on p.2, l.28 changed to "unused," as DHL had written in the MS. It is possible that the change was effected for the 14th printing, but I have seen no copies with this change. The paperback version does not carry it, but the Modern Library editions do.

NOTES: The correction on p.290 was probably made with the fifth printing. See Arents archive, letter, D. Giles to Grove Press, 5 May 1959; holograph note on letter suggests the Press checked the sentence after letter was received.

The address on the back cover of the dj (see 32.1.$_2$ above) was changed to the University Place address with the 9th printing, in mid-June(Arents: invoice from Algen Press to Grove, 17 June 1959).

Binding Var.(2) is possibly a remainder (secondary) binding; At Christmas 1959, Grove offered booksellers "one free for [each] ten" (Arents archive: undated flyer).

There were 14 printings altogether, the last one (20,000) being ordered on July 22nd. This, and the first post-publication printing of May 16, which it equalled, were the largest orders (See also "Lady Chatterley" 102-04). In June the Grove hardback had risen to fourth, and in July to 2nd on the best-seller list. PW's August 24 issue reported 160,000 copies in print; the novel was then second on the list (it never challenged Uris' *Exodus* for first). Sales slackened during the early fall; by November the title was no longer on the list. The latest approximation of copies sold (Oct. 12) was 160,000. Hackett and Burke (177-78) give a similar figure.

The hardback is not listed in Grove's 1961 catalogue; it was replaced with the paperback version, and, by arrangement with Random House, the Modern Library Edition.

COPIES EXAMINED: NN(Var.1); personal(Var.[2]); TxU(copy 1,6 [both var.(2), both dj st.2])

*32.5.b   probably as 32.5.a save:

CONTENTS: special presentation leaf tipped-in(?) at front headed THE ARRON SUSSMAN EDITION

BINDING: Var(1): Nigerian goatskin, gilt lettering and top edge gilt. Var.(2): quarter-bound calf with gilt lettering

NOTE: After the court decision, Rosset had 15 copies specially bound and presented as the "Aaron Sussman Edition," as a tribute to the advertising strategies of the president of the firm he contracted to publicize the hardback. (See the "repro" of limitation statement in the Arents Archive). In 1934, Sussman helped Random House introduce *Ulysses* to serious readers. See PW 14 April 1934: 1449.

*32.6   [ordered 20 May 1959]

32.7   [ordered 26 May 1959]

32.8   [ordered 3 June 1959]

32.9   [ordered 10 June 1959]

32.10   [ordered 24 June 1959]

32.11   [ordered 1 July 1959]

32.12   [ordered 9 July 1959]

32.13   [ordered 17 July 1959]

*32.14   [ordered 22 July 1959]

[Subedition: Greenwich House, 1983]

32.15   as 32.5.a save:

D. H. LAWRENCE | LADY CHATTERLEY'S LOVER | WITH PAINTINGS BY
D. H. LAWRENCE | AND A FOREWORD BY MORELAND PERKINS | [Rule]
| *Greenwich House Classics Library* | [rule] | Greenwich House
| Distributed by Crown Publishers, Inc. | New York

(8 x 5 1/8"): no sig., 192 leaves; pp.[1-18], 1-365, [366].

CONTENTS: p.[1]:half-title. p.[2]:biographical note. p.[3]:
    t.p. p.[4]: Copyright © 1983 by Greenwich House, | a
    division of Arlington House, Inc., | . . . . This 1983
    edition is published by Greenwich House, a division of
    Arlington House, Inc., | distributed by Crown Publishers,
    Inc. | . . . . h d f e d c b a|. p.[5]-[7]: FOREWORD. p.[8]:
    ABOUT THE PAINTINGS p.[9]: A GALLERY OF PAINTINGS BY |
    D. H. LAWRENCE | [Lawrence phoenix] pp.[10]-[16]: black
    and white reproductions of the paintings published first
    by Mandrake Press in 1929. p.[17]: fly-title. p.[18]:blank.
    pp.1-365:text. p.[366]:blank.

PAPER: smooth white wove unwatermarked. Thickness: .09mm.
    Total bulk: 18.7mm.

BINDING: deep purple(C.219) paper-covered boards. On spine,
    top to bottom, stamped in silver: LADY CHATTERLEY'S LOVER
    | D. .H. LAWRENCE Greenwich House. At bottom right of
    lower cover: ISBN no. Plain white endpapers. All edges
    trimmed. Head and tail band in purple.
    Dj: coated paper, white with black and purple letter-
    ing. Front cover:[in black]: THE COMPLETE ORIGINAL UNEXPURGATE
    EDITION | [in purple]: LADY | CHATTERLEY'S | LOVER | [in
    black]: WITH THE EROTIC PAINTINGS OF D. H. LAWRENCE |
    [reproduction of painting by Peter Fiore: Connie gazes at
    Mellors washing (from ch. 6). Predominant colors red,
    brown, white, blue.] | [in purple:] D.H.LAWRENCE |. Flaps
    contain blurb, ending, ". . . Lawrence -- revolutionary
    poet of desire -- has created one of the most tender,
    poignant, and liberated love stories of all time." On back
    cover: list of Greenwich House Classics Library; 10 titles,
    beginning *Huck Finn*, ending *War And Peace*. Spine, top to
    bottom: LADY CHATTERLEY'S LOVER | D.H. LAWRENCE Greenwich
    House |. Line 1 in purple, 1.2 in black.

NOTE: p.2: "unusual." The reading Schorer wished here ("unused"),
    although appearing in the Modern Library ed., is not used;
    it was requested in 1959 (see notes to 32.1.$_1$). p. 290: .
    . . same," said Hilda. The readings in chapters 2 and 3 in
    the Grove hardback are of course also present here. See
    Notes for 32.1 above. I cannot ascertain whether or not
    Grove authorized this printing, or 32.19-32.23 below.

COPY EXAMINED: personal

*32.16

*32.17

32.18   as 32.15 save:

CONTENTS: p.[4]: last line reads: h g f e d

COPY EXAMINED: personal(dj)

[subedition: Chatham River Press, 1983]

*32.19

*32.20

*32.21

*32.22

32.23   as 32.15 save:

[rule] | CHATHAM RIVER PRESS CLASSICS | [rule] | D. H. LAWRENCE
| [rule] | [French rule] | LADY | CHATTERLEY'S | LOVER | With
Paintings By | D. H. LAWRENCE | AND A FOREWORD BY | MORELAND
PERKINS | CHATHAM RIVER PRESS [dot] NEW YORK

(8 1/2 x 5 1/8"): no sigs, 192 leaves; pp.[i-iv], v-vii,
[viii-xviii], 1-365, [366].

CONTENTS: p.[iv]: Chatham River Press Classics have been
    designed and produced for the | discerning book lover.
    . . . The text is printed on a fine | acid-free paper . .
    . . The pages are gilded | . . . . The cover | design . .
    . | re-creates the finest features of the age-old trad-
    itions of | Europe and American antiquarian book design .
    . . . | . . . This 1983 edition is published by the
    Chatham River Press, | a Division of Arlington House, Inc.
    | Distributed by Crown Publishers. . . .| k j i h g f e |
    Reprint. Originally published: New York, Greenwich |
    House, 1983. . . . p.[ix]: no Lawrence phoenix.

PAPER: smooth white wove, unwatermarked. Thickness: .095mm.
    Total Bulk: 19.0mm

BINDING: quarter-bound black morocco (with diagonal gold
    fillet on upper and lower covers) over nonpareil marbled
    paper boards (grey, black, yellow, red, blue). On upper
    cover, enclosed in decorated border, gold lettering on
    black panel: LADY | CHATTERLEY'S | LOVER |. Oval ticket
    stuck to boards reads GENUINE | BONDED LEATHER | [short
    French rule] | PEEL OFF |. On spine, in green panels bordered

with decorated rules: LADY | CHATTERLEY'S | LOVER | D. H.
LAWRENCE | CHATHAM | RIVER | PRESS |. Six raised bands. On
lower right of lower cover: ISBN no. Marbled endpapers
(nonpareil, to match boards). All edges gilt.

COPY EXAMINED: personal; Pollinger Coll.

[Grove Press paperback edition, 1959-to date]

33.1   LADY | CHATTERLEY'S | LOVER | BY D. H. LAWRENCE | *With
        an Introduction by Mark Schorer* | GROVE PRESS INC. [dot]
        NEW YORK

(6 1/2 x 4 1/4"): unsigned, pp.[1-4],5-384.

CONTENTS: p.[1]: statements about novel by Jacques Barzun and
   Harvey Breit. p.[2]: blank. p.[3]:t.p. p.[4]: *Introduction
   by Mark Schorer,* | Copyright © 1957 by Grove Press, Inc. |
   Letter from Archibald MacLeish, Copyright © 1959 by Grove
   Press Inc. | This edition is the third manuscript version,
   | first published by Guiseppe Orioli, Florence, 1928. |
   MANUFACTURED IN THE UNITED STATES OF AMERICA |. pp.5-6: letter
   to publisher from Archibald MacLeish. pp.7-36: Introduction
   by Schorer. pp.37-375:text. pp.376-77: Bibliographical
   Note. pp.378-84: text of Judge Bryan's decision in Grove
   vs. US Post Office.

TYPOGRAPHY: Text: 39ll.(p.153), 143 x 83mm. 10ll.=35mm.
   Face 3(1.5x)mm. Typeface: Times New Roman (Monotype), R53.
   Old Style. DIN 1.13, modern Renaissance.

PAPER: smooth white wove unwatermarked. Thickness .06mm. Total
   bulk 14.1mm.

BINDING: Var. (1): coated paper wrappers, white. Upper cover: |
   [upper left:] FG5 | America's #1 Bestseller at $6.00 / Now
   50 ¢ | THIS IS THE GROVE PRESS EDITION, | THE ONLY UNEXPURGATE
   VERSION | EVER PUBLISHED IN AMERICA | LADY | CHATTERLEY'S
   | LOVER | *BY* D. H. LAWRENCE | COMPLETE AND UNABRIDGED |
   [ll. 12-15 printed in red circle, set at 45 degree angle:]
   This and only this | is the uncensored | edition making |
   today's headlines! | INTRODUCTION BY MARK SCHORER | PREFACE
   BY ARCHIBALD MACLEISH [ll. 1-2,6-8,10-11, 16-17 in black;
   ll. 3-5 in red; 1.9 in purple; ll. 12-15 in yellow] |. On
   spine, top to bottom: FG5 LADY CHATTERLEY'S LOVER [in
   black] | D. H. LAWRENCE [in purple] |. At tail, horizon-
   tal: GROVE PRESS [in red] |. Lower cover: THIS AND ONLY
   THIS IS THE COMPLETE | REPRINT OF THE FAMOUS | GROVE PRESS
   $6.00 BEST SELLER! | *Only this Famous Grove Press Edition*
   | *Offers You All These Features* | [dot] Complete, unexpurgate
   text pre- | cisely as D. H. Lawrence wrote it! | [dot]
   Preface by Pulitzer Prize winner | and former Librarian of
   Congress | Archibald MacLeish! | [dot] Introduction by
   noted critic and | teacher Mark Schorer! | [dot] Lengthy
   excerpt from the original | Federal Court decision which

de- | clared the Grove Press edition "not | obscene!" [ll.
1-3 and dots in red; rest in black] |. Edges stained light
bluish green (C163).
Var. (2): as (1) save lower cover: NEVER BEFORE IN
PAPERBACK! [in red] |; blurbs from N.Y.*Times* and E. Wilson
(printed in black save first line, in red).

NOTES: p.38, 1.26: "unusual"|. p.54, 1.2: ". . . like a
  boy."|. p.65: 1.9: ". . . defenseless about him."|.
  [See Notes to 30.1-4 and 30.5-14.₁ above.]
    PW, Aug. 22, 1959, p.107: Grove "has printed nearly 1.3
  million copies of the 50¢ paperback." The figure equals the
  number printed by the New American Library.
    Grove chose Dell as printer and distributor, because of
  its preeminence as a paperback distributor since the "blockbuster" *Peyton Place* and *Anatomy of a Murder* (Arents:
  draft of letter, Rosset to Wm. Callahan, 6 Aug. 1959).
    The "this and only this" notice regarding an unexpurgated,
  newly decensored classic was subsequently used by Grove for
  its paperbacks of Miller's *Tropics* and by Putnam for its
  Fanny Hill.
    For lawsuits against Grove over its paperback front cover
  advertising, see notes to 36.1 and 37.1, and p. 126 above.

COPIES EXAMINED: personal(Var. [1] and [2])

     [subedition: first Black Cat printing, 1962]

3.2   as 33.1 save:

LADY | CHATTERLEY'S | LOVER | BY D. H. LAWRENCE | *With an*
Introduction by Mark Schorer | *A Black Cat* [logo: cat's face]
Book | GROVE PRESS, INC. [dot] NEW YORK

Sheets measure 6 3/8 x 4 1/4"

CONTENTS: p.[1]: About | *Lady Chatterley's Lover* | [Three
  paragraphs on the importance of the Grove Press challenge
  to censorship.] p.[4]: 1. 7 reads: First Black Cat Edition
  1962 |. p.384: second half of page contains advert for Moore's
  Intelligent Heart.

PAPER: Thickness .06mm. Total bulk 13.7mm.

BINDING: upper cover: [in red]: An Evergreen Black Cat Book [cat
  logo in black, below which is BA9] 50 ¢ | THIS IS THE COMPLETE
  UNEXPURGATED GROVE | PRESS EDITION WHICH MADE PUBLISHING |
  HISTORY AS A $6.00 BESTSELLER [ll.2-4 in blue] | LADY |
  CHATTERLEY'S | LOVER | D. H. LAWRENCE | INTRODUCTION BY MARK
  SCHORER | PREFACE BY ARCHIBALD MACLEISH [ll. 5-10 in
  black] | [ll. 11-13 in blue circle, printed at 40 degree
  angle]: This and only this | is the ORIGINAL | Grove Press
  Edition|. On spine: running top to bottom: [in black:]
  LADY CHATTERLEY'S LOVER [in blue:] D. H. LAWRENCE |.
  Running left to right: [in red:] BA-9 | [in black: cat

logo] | [in red:] GROVE | PRESS |. Lower cover: logo and
price, as on u.c.; 5-line statement regarding trial in
blue; blurbs by Wilson (in black) and Breit (in red). Edges
stained blackish blue(C 188).

NOTES: The revised wording in the blue circle, u. c., is a result
of the agreement between Grove and NAL. The first printing
was planned to be 100,000 but was changed in January 1962
to 60,000 [Arents archive: memos from Richard Brodney
(Dec. 1961) and Joyce Sudborough (Jan. 8, 1962)]. A chart
in the archive gives the month and year of publication, and
the number of copies, for the second through 7th printings;
this is the source for the figures given below for 33.2-33.8.
    The Black Cat paperback carries the same expurgated
passages (on pp.54 and 65), and the "same, said Hilda" reading
(on p.305).
    The Black Cat second printing of Frank Caprio's *Variations
In Sexual Behavior* contains a 3-page list of titles,
beginning with LCL and *Tropic of Cancer*, and including Wm.
Longgood's *The Poisons in Your Food*, Sybille Bedford's *The
Trial of Dr. Adams*, Mortimer Hunt's *The Natural History of
Love*, Lindner's *Rebel Without A Cause*, Balzac's *Droll Stories*,
Henry Olson's *Sexual Adjustment in Marriage*, and Caprio's
Female Homosexuality.

COPY EXAMINED: TxU

33.3   as 33.2 save:

Sheets measure 6 3/8 x 4 3/16"

CONTENTS: p.[4]: 1.7: Second Black Cat Printing 1963 |.

BINDING: The word EVERGREEN not present on 1.1 of upper and
lower cover.

NOTE: Arents: number of copies: 40,000 (April 1963)

COPIES EXAMINED: personal, NSyU(Arents)

*33.4   (Arents: no. of copies printed: 25,000; Oct. 1964)

33.5   as 33.2 save:

CONTENTS: p.[4]: 11.7-8: First Black Cat Edition 1962 | Fourth
Printing--1966 |.

PAPER: Thickness .06mm. Total bulk 14.22mm.

BINDING: price changed to 75¢.

NOTE: Arents: 15,000 copies (Aug. 1966).

COPY EXAMINED: Notts. County Lib.

33.6 as 33.5 save:

CONTENTS: p.[4],1.8: Fifth Printing |.

PAPER: Thickness .08mm. Total bulk 18.24mm

BINDING: price changed to 95¢. In lower left of lower cover:
    Printed in U.S.A. |. Edges unstained.

NOTE: Arents: no. of copies printed: 15,000 (Dec. 1968).

COPY EXAMINED: MMeT

*33.7   (Arents: no. of copies printed: 16,500; Nov. 1969).

*33.8   (Arents: no. of copies printed: 11,000; May 1971).

*33.9

*33.10

33.11   as 33.2 save:

sheets measure 7 x 4 1/8"

CONTENTS: p.[4]: 11.7-14 read: No part of this book may be
    reproduced, for any | reason, by any means, including any
    method of | photographic reproduction, without the permission
    | of the publisher.| First Black Cat Edition 1962 | Tenth
    Printing | DISTRIBUTED BY RANDOM HOUSE, INC., NEW YORK |
    Manufactured in the United States of America |. p.384: no
    ad for *Intelligent Heart*.

PAPER: Thickness .06mm. Total bulk 14.3mm.

BINDING: white coated paper wrappers. Upper cover: [in blue]:
    B-9 [in black: cat logo] [in blue:] $1.50 | [in purple:]
    Lady Chatterley's Lover | [in green:] by D. H. Lawrence |
    [photograph of man's head, in profile, eye closed, turned
    slightly toward woman (head and neck visible) who stares
    straight ahead. One of man's hands rests just below woman's
    neck. Predominant colors (very muted) strong yellow (C84)
    and dark olive brown (C96). Photo surrounded by double border
    rounded at edges.] [in blue:] Introduction by Mark Schorer
    | [in green:] Preface by Archibald MacLeish |. On spine:
    top to bottom: [in black:] LADY CHATTERLEY'S LOVER [in
    blue:] BY [in green:] D.H. LAWRENCE |. [Set left to right,
    at bottom:] B-9 | [cat logo] | GROVE PRESS [logo in black,
    rest in blue]|. Lower cover: price and logo, and two
    blurbs by Wilson and Breit, headed by: The complete |
    Grove Press Edition | that made | publishing history |.
    [ll. 1,3,4 in purple, 1.2 in green]. At bottom in blue:
    Photo by Martin Keoniges Printed in U.S.A. | [in black:]
    394-17293-0 |. Edges stained bluish-green.

COPY EXAMINED: personal

33.12   as 33.11 save:

CONTENTS: p.[4]: 1.12: Eleventh Printing |. p.384: on direction
    line: *3-74* |.

PAPER: Thickness .1mm.   Total bulk: 21.6mm.

BINDING: edges unstained.

COPY EXAMINED: personal

33.13   as 33.11 save:

CONTENTS: p.[4]: 1.12: Twelfth Printing | Manufactured in the
    United States of America | DISTRIBUTED BY RANDOM HOUSE, INC.,
    NEW YORK | Grove Press, Inc., 53 East 11th St, | New York,
    N.Y. 10003 |. p.384, on direction line: *1-75* |.

BINDING: Price after cat logo on upper and lover covers:
    $1.95 |. Lower cover, directly above number: Grove Press,
    Inc., 53 East 11th Street, New York, New York 10003 [as on
    p.[4]|. Edges unstained.

COPY EXAMINED: personal

33.14   as 33.13 save:

CONTENTS: p.[4]: 1.12: Thirteenth Printing |. 11.15-16: GROVE
    PRESS, INC. 196 WEST HOUSTON STREET, | NEW YORK, N.Y.
    10014 |. p.384, on direction line: 1-76|.

BINDING: address of press changed on lower cover; same as
    that given on p.[4].

COPIES EXAMINED: DLC, personal

33.15   as 33.14 save:

T.p: printing begins 2 3/4" from top of page.

Pagination: [1-4], 5-383, [384].

CONTENTS: p.[4]: 1.4: Copyright © 1957 by Grove Press, Inc.|.
    added as 1. 7: All Rights Reserved |. 11.13-19: Fourteenth
    Printing 1977 | ISBN: 0-394-17293-0 | Grove Press ISBN: 0-
    8021-4107-2 | Manufactured in the United States of America
    | Distributed by Random House, Inc., New York | p.[384]:
    no direction line.

BINDING: in black under address of press: ISBN: 0-394-17293-0
    |.

COPY EXAMINED: personal

[subedition: "Revised Black Cat Edition 1982"]

33.16.1   as 33.15 save:

(7 1/16 x 4 1/8"): [1-4], 5-192, [8], 193-384. [Eight clay-
paper sheets bound in at p.192.]

CONTENTS: p.[4]: 11.13-22: First Black Cat Edition 1962 |
    First Revised Black Cat Edition 1982 | First Printing Revised
    Black Cat Edition 1982 | ISBN: 0-394-62424-6 | Library of
    Congress Catalog Card Number: 82-48044 | Photos, by Georges
    Pierre, from the film *Lady Chatter-* | *ley's Lover.* |
    Manufactured in the United States of America | GROVE
    PRESS, INC., 196 West Houston Street, | New York, N.Y.
    10014 |.

TYPOGRAPHY: text: 3911.(p.153), 140 x 84mm. 1011.=34mm. Face
    3(2x)mm.

PAPER: smooth white wove unwatermarked. Thickness .06mm. Total
    bulk   12.6mm.

BINDING: Coated paper wrappers. Upper cover: two scenes from
    film, one Mellors and Connie in silhouette, the other, in
    flesh-tones, the lovers lying in the bracken, heads and
    Connie's left hand, with wedding(?) ring, visible. [In red:]
    Lady Chatterley's | Lover [in white:] [cat's face logo] |
    B-479 | $3.50 | [in blue:] By | D.H. Lawrence |. On spine,
    on background of light blue: [right to left, in white:] [cat
    logo] | Grove | Press | [top to bottom:] [in red:] Lady
    Chatterley's Lover | [in black:] D.H. Lawrence | [in white,
    right to left:] B-479 |. Lower cover, on background of light
    blue: [in black:] The Complete Grove Press Edition | That
    Made Publishing History |. [blurbs from Wilson and Breit,
    slightly condensed from 31.11-15; 14 lines] | [rule in white]
    | [next four lines in red]: With 16 pages of full-color
    illustrations from | the film directed by Just Jaecklin,
    starring | Sylvia Kristel, Nicholas Clay and | Shane Briant,
    distributed by Cannon Films. | [rule in white] | [in black:]
    With a Preface by Archibald MacLeish |. Credits, publisher's
    address and ISBN in lower left, in white. Logo and price in
    white in upper right.

ILLUSTRATIONS: each sheet contains on recto and verso a
    separate "still," in color, from Just Jaecklin's film of the
    novel, distributed by Cannon Films.
    a. Connie and Clifford's wedding reception
    b. Fox-hunting
    c. Clifford on battlefield
    d. Mellors "taking" Connie on the floor of the hut
    e. Mellors bathing
    f. Connie and Mellors conversing in his cottage
    g. Mellors carrying Clifford
    g. Clifford attempting to operate motorized wheelchair as
       Connie and Mellors attend him
    i. Connie masturbating
    j. Connie and Mellors bedecked with flowers
    k. Mellors "taking" Connie in the woods
    l. Connie holding a chick as Mellors watches
    m. Connie and Mellors embracing
    n. Connie and Mellors in bed
    o. Connie, bare-breasted, undressing

p. Connie and Mellors talking, colliery(?) in background

NOTE: for other movie tie-ins see 44.35-44.40 and 49.1 below.
   The cover photo of the reclining lovers is very similar
   to a "still" from the 1955 Kingsley Pictures film of the novel

COPY EXAMINED: personal

33.16.$_2$ as 33.16.$_1$ save:

pagination as 33.15 (no illustrations)

PAPER: Thickness .06mm. Total bulk 11.3mm.

BINDING: price given as $3.95. On lower cover, four lines in
   red regarding film excised.

COPY EXAMINED: personal

33.16.$_3$ as 33.16.$_2$ save:

CONTENTS: p.[4]: 1.21 reads: Grove Press Inc., 920 Broadway,
   New York, N.Y. 10010 [sans serif typeface]|.

PAPER: Thickness .07mm. Total bulk: 14.7mm.

COPY EXAMINED: personal

33.16.$_4$ as 33.16.$_3$ save:

CONTENTS: p.[4]: 1) ISBN no. changed, 1.16: 0-8021-3068-2. 2)
   1.21 printed in same typeface as rest of page.

BINDING: upper wrapper: cat's face logo, series no., and
   price excised. Spine: series no. (B-479) at bottom excised.
   Lower : 1) series no. excised from cat's face logo at upper
   right. 2) ISBN no. excised at lower left. 3) machine-readable
   strip added in black at lower right, with new ISBN no. added
   below.

COPY EXAMINED: personal

[Modern Library Edition, 1960(?)]

34.1   Lady | Chatterley's | Lover | BY D. H. LAWRENCE | *With*
        an Introduction by | Mark Schorer | [logo:torchbearer]
        | The Modern Library | *New York*

(7 x 4 3/4"): [1]^{16} [2-5]^{32} [6]^{16} [7]^{32} [8]^{16}, 208 leaves;
pp. [i-iv], v-xxxvii, [xxxviii], [1-2], 3-376, [2].

CONTENTS: p.[i]: half-title: THE MODERN LIBRARY | *OF THE WORLD'S*
   BEST BOOKS | [swelled rule] | Lady Chatterley's Lover |
   [swelled rule] | *The publishers will be pleased . . .*

[6-line offer of ML list]. p.[ii]:blank. p.[iii]:t.p.
p.[4]: 1.1: First Printing |. Four lines copyright infor-
mation for Schorer Intro. and MacLeish letter, as in 30.1-
30.14 above, followed by: This edition is the third
manuscript version, first | published by Guiseppe Orioli,
Florence, 1928, and | by arrangement with Grove Press,
Inc. | RANDOM HOUSE is the Publisher of THE MODERN LIBRARY
| BENNETT CERF [dot] Donald Klopfer ! Manufactured in the
United States of America |. pp.v-[vii]: MacLeish letter.
p.[viii]: blank. pp.ix-xxxvii: Schorer Introd. p.[xxxviii]:
blank. p.[1]: section title. p.[2]:blank. pp.3-344: text.
pp.345-46: Bibliographical Note |. pp.[347]-376: transcript
of Judge Bryan's decision. p.[1]: full-page illus. advert
for *American College Dictionary*. p.[2]: blank.

TYPOGRAPHY: text: 36ll. (p.173), 139 x 94mm. 10ll.=37mm.
    Face 2(1x)mm.
    Typeface: Times New Roman (Monotype), R53. Old Style. DIN
    1.13, modern Renaissance.

PAPER: smooth white wove unwatermarked. Thickness .05mm. Total
    bulk 12.6mm.

BINDING: linen-grain (T304) cloth, light gray(C.264). Upper
    cover, in center: gold-stamped outer border with torch-
    bearer at lower right corner. Gold-stamped inner border
    encloses dark green (C.146) panel, in which,in gold: *Lady
    | Chatterley's | Lover* | D. H. | LAWRENCE |. On spine:
    dark green rectangular panel, enclosed by gold rules,
    above which is torchbearer, in gold. In panel: *Lady* !
    Chatterley's | Lover | D. H. LAWRENCE | [1 mm. gold
    triangular decoration] | MODERN | LIBRARY |. Lower cover
    undecorated. Top edge stained greenish gray. All edges
    trimmed. Decorated endpapers (medium gray, white) with
    Rockwell Kent design:"m" "l" and open book, torchbearer
    in panel in center.
        dj:(state 1): white coated paper. Front cover: uneven
    non-continuous border of unequal width (10 -14mm) in gray
    and tan (simulating printed-paper design?), lettered
    (save 1.5) in black: Lady | Chatterley's | Lover | By
    D. H. LAWRENCE | [in tan]: Complete / Unexpurgated |
    Introduction by Mark Schorer | *Preface by* Archibald
    MacLeish | A MODERN LIBRARY BOOK |. Spine: [tan block,
    same design as front cover] | Lady | Chatterley's | Lover
    | [star, in tan] | *D.H.* | *Lawrence* | [gray block] | [tor-
    chbearer, in tan] | MODERN | LIBRARY | [in tan block:] 148
    |. Back cover: Advert and order form for ML books. Front
    flap: price ($1.95), blurb, beginning: This is the
    unexpurgated version | . . . , first published in Amer-|
    ica by The Grove Press. . . . [The novel] is by now so |
    well established . . . | that readers may be inclined to
    overlook its continuing and | growing relevance to our own
    period in | history when questions of individuality | in
    conflict with civilization are perhaps | more urgent than
    ever. It is for this rea-| son among others that this
    unexpurgated | version of Lawrence's novel is welcome at |
    this time. Back of jacket: complete list of ML books,

beginning *The Education of Henry Adams*, ending *Wisdom of Israel*. Titles in italics.

NOTES: published by arrangement with Grove, and supplants the latter's hardbound ed. PW, 17 Aug. 1959, notes the agreement between Rosset and Cerf, and that "Random House is recognizing the position that Grove Press has earned as the only publisher to fight for the unexpurgated edition." Rosset solicited such statements during the "Chatterley Sweepstakes" of summer 1959, and such acknowledgement from Cerf may have helped booksellers decide to give precedence to the Grove hard and paperback editions over the competing paperbacks. It should be noted that in 1954, Cerf refused to endorse Rosset's project (see essay above).

In the first six months of the book's appearance 5480 copies were sold. From 1961 to 1968, at $1.95 a copy, sales reached 26,000 copies. At $2.45, 4,600 copies were sold during the year beginning in mid-1968 (Arents: memo of royalty agreements between Grove and Random House, 30 April-30 Oct. 1960). In April 1966 a book club (Doubleday; see 40.1 below) expressed interest in *Chatterley, and Our Lady Of The Flowers* (Arents: letter from E. Harper of Grove to treasurer of Random House, 29 April 1966).

The correction in the novel's ninth paragraph, first sentence, from "unusual" to "unused" was made for the ML edition (Arents: letter from Grove to Random House, Aug. 1959). This is the only edition to date with this corrected reading. Two expurgated passages remain, as in the Grove text: p.20, l.10: ". . . like a boy."l. p.31, l.24: ". . . defenseless about him."l.

The binding design, by Joseph Blumenthal, was used from the 1940s until 1963. Each title was available in only one color cloth (Neavill 33). See below.

COPIES EXAMINED: personal(dj, st.1), TxU (2 copies,dj, st.1)

34.2   as 34.1 save:

CONTENTS: p.[iv]: no statement of printing history. pp.[2]: list of Modern Library Giants, beginning Anderson and Grimm, *Tales*, ending *The Wisdom of Israel*.

BINDING: linen-grain (T304) cloth, brilliant bluish green (C.159). Upper cover, blind-stamped: torchbearer in hexagonal border with MODERN LIBRARY below border. Spine, silver-stamped [torchbearer] l [rule] l LADY CHATTERLEY'S l LOVER l *D. H. Lawrence* [ll. 3-5 top to bottom] l [rule] l MODERN LIBRARY l. Edges unstained, trimmed.
DJ: ML list, inside jacket, printed in different style: titles in lower case.

NOTE: the style of binding of 34.2, more economical than that of 34.1, was used from fall 1963 to 1966; the list did not appear inside the jacket after 1963. See Neavill 34.

COPY EXAMINED: personal(dj, st.1); MH

34.3   as 34.2 save:

CONTENTS: p.[1]: half-title contains title only. p.[4]:
names of Cerf and Klopfer removed. pp.[2]: as 34.2 but the
typography has been redesigned.

PAPER: Thickness .04mm. Total bulk: 11.6mm.

BINDING: Var.(1): black calico cloth (T302), black. Blind-stamped
u. c. has m and l (in center) and border rounded at upper
right   and lower left; other corners squared. Spine silver-stamped
as above but with differently-designed torchbearer in
border at top. Plain white endpapers. Var.(2): as (1) but
cloth is dark red (C13); endpapers in light orange yellow
(C70), with Kent-designed torchbearer.
   Dj(state 2): back flap mostly blank; offer of free list
at bottom.

NOTE: the binding, designed by Neil Fujita to reflect contemporary graphic design, was used beginning 1968, but
with new endpapers which he designed. The plain endpapers
were used after a 1970 decision not to add new titles to
the ML series, because paperbacks were cutting deeply into
sales (Neavill 37).

COPIES EXAMINED: personal(Var.[1]), ICarbS(Var.[2], dj st.2),
CU-S (Var.[2], dj st.2)

        [subedition: "Second Modern Library Edition," 1983]

34.4   as 34.3 save:

D[dot]H[dot]LAWRENCE | LADY | CHATTERLEY'S | LOVER [ll. 2-4
in white on black background, enclosed in black panel 33 x
78mm with an inner border in white] | WITH A PREFACE BY
ARCHIBALD MACLEISH | AND AN INTRODUCTION BY | MARK SCHORER |
[logo: torchbearer] | MODERN LIBRARY | NEW YORK

Leaves measure 7 1/4 x 4 3/4"

CONTENTS: p.[i]: woodcut (by Stephen Alcorn), 74 x 56mm: woman
in beret, walking stick in gloved hand, in foreground;
background of factory with smokestack, man with sack over
shoulder, walking along railroad. p.[4]: SECOND MODERN
LIBRARY EDITION | May 1983 |. ll.3-19: copyright, rights
reserved statements, edition statement, Cat. In Pub. data,
ISBN no (0-394-60430-X). Last line reads: Manufactured in
the United States of America |. p.[1]: *Author's Note*
(brief biography). p.[2]: blank.

RUNNING HEADS: rectos and versos: *LADY CHATTERLEY'S LOVER* |.

PAPER: Thickness .06mm. Total bulk 14.2mm.

BINDING: morocco-grain paper-covered boards, moderate reddish
brown (C43). Centered on upper cover: torchbearer in black

panel with inner border, 24 x 28mm. Gold-stamped on spine:
Lady I Chatterley's I Lover I D. H. I Lawrence I Modern
Library I. Endpapers in red, light brown and black, with
torchbearer in repeated pattern. Edges unstained, trimmed.
Brown head and tail bands.

   dj: light tan ribbed paper. Upper cover: D[dot]H[dot]LAWRENCE
I LADY I CHATTERLEY'S I LOVER [ll. 2-4 in white, in red
panel with white inner border] I [woodcut, as on p.(i)] I
MODERN LIBRARY I. Spine: [torchbearer] I D.H.LAWRENCE I
LADY I CHATTER- I LEY'S I LOVER [ll. 2-4 in white, in red
panel with white inner border] I MODERN I LIBRARY I. Lower
cover: history and purpose of ML. Front flap: Upper right:
$7.95 I. Below torchbearer in black panel is 24-line blurb
for novel: ". . . a classic of modernist fiction I and
courtroom controversy. . . . the temptation of adultery
and the pursuit of sexual I fulfillment; and the question
of the individual's I responsibility to self and society."
I JACKET DESIGN BY R. D. SCUDELLARI I JACKET WOODCUT BY
STEPHEN ALCORN. Back flap: biographical sketch. Back of
jacket: list of ML books; begins Aristotle, ends *Thirty
Famous One-Act Plays*.

TYPOGRAPHICAL NOTE: Vignettes added above chapter titles.

NOTE: The reissues of some ML titles began in the late '70s,
   after rising prices of reprints prompted a feeling that
   attractive hardbound reprints were once again desirable
   (Neavill 37).

COPY EXAMINED: personal

            ["Tabloid Publishing Company", 1959]

35.1   COMPLETE BOOK I UNEXPURGATED I LADY I CHATTERLEY'S I
        LOVER I [in white on black circle used as background:]
        THIS I IS I THE I UNCENSORED I EDITION I MAKING TODAY'S
        I HEADLINES I BY D. H. LAWRENCE I [in white on black
        square positioned in upper right parallel to ll. 1 and
        2]: 25¢ [ll. 3-5 in red]

sheet size: 22 7/8 x 16": pp.[1], 2-47, [48]. The tabloid format
consists of 24 sheets, 4 columns per page.

CONTENTS: p.[1]: title. p.2, bottom of column 4: Published by
   I Tabloid Publishing Corp. I 33 West 42nd St. I New York,
   NY I. pp.2-[48]: text. p.[48]: blurbs for novel ("smothering
   passions and fulfilled desires, ... recent movie starring
   French sexpot Danielle Darrieux"), photo of Lawrence ("lover
   of life spiced with unbridled passions"), quotes from Barzun,
   Breit, NY *Times*.

TYPOGRAPHY: 9711 (p.30, col. 2), 420 x 60mm. 10ll.=46mm. Face:
   3(2x)mm.

PAPER: thickness .08mm. Total bulk 1.52mm.

NOTE: The text is reset from the Grove Press edition. This
   tabloid was on sale in Connecticut newsstands by early August,
   1959, soon after the decensorship decision; because the
   publication was sold in locations where juveniles congregate,
   it was removed from newsstands in Norwalk and Bridgeport,
   Connecticut by local police (PW 7 Sept. 1959: 33).

COPIES EXAMINED: TxU, NSyU(Arents)

[Pocket Books Edition, 1959]

36.1.1   *D. H. Lawrence* [calligraphic display type] | Lady |
          Chatterley's | Lover | [decoration] | With an Appendix
          containing the decision | of United States District
          Court rendered | by Federal Judge Frederick van Pelt
          Bryan | [arranged in half-oval around line drawing of
          perched bird:] CARDINAL | EDITION | [rule] | POCKET
          BOOKS, INC. [dot] NEW YORK [lines 2-5 enclosed in
          decorated oval border]

(6 5/16 x 4"): no sigs (perfect bound),192 leaves; pp.[6], 1-378.

CONTENTS: p.[1]: continuation of blurb began on lower cover;
   copy begins: has suffered censorship to such a degree . .
   . . p.[2]: blank. P.[3]: t.p. p. [4]: This CARDINAL
   edition includes every word contained in copy No 402 of
   the | signed limited edition . . . | 1928. It is printed
   from brand-new plates . . . | easy-to-read type.[four
   lines] | [rule] | L A D Y C H A T T E R L E Y ' S
   L O V E R | CARDINAL edition published July, 1959 | 1st
   printing ....July, 1959 | This edition reproduces
   exactly the text of the 1928 | Italian edition, . . . | In
   any case where the original text has been ren- | dered
   incomprehensible by [typographical errors], the present
   pub- | lisher has inserted the correct interpretation in
   italics in | brackets after the original word or phrase.
   Near gutter margin: L | Printed in U.S.A. | [rule] |
   [three-line notice of registered trade mark, with logo and
   price at left] |. p.[5]: flytitle. p.[6]: blank. pp.1-354:
   text. pp.[355]-378: text of Bryan decision.

TYPOGRAPHY: 37ll.(p.131), 141 x 87mm.; 10ll. = 37mm.; face
   3(1.5x)mm.
   Typeface: Caledonia. Modern Neoclassical (DIN 1.34).

PAPER: smooth white wove unwatermarked. Thickness: .05mm.
   Total bulk 11.3mm.

BINDING: paper wrappers. Upper cover: background in dark
   purplish red (C259) with 5/8" vertical strip in black adjacent
   to spine. [in white:] A complete and unexpurgated edition
   of | this century's most celebrated love story | [arranged
   in decorated oval border on light greenish-blue (C172)
   background; title in black, author in white, decoration in

purple:] Lady | Chatterley's | Lover | *D. H. Lawrence*
[calligraphic display type] | [decoration] | Including the
complete text of | Federal Judge Frederick vanPelt Bryan's
| precedent-setting opinion on | the censoring of this
modern classic |. In vertical strip: [at 30 degree angle,
in black set within greenish-blue square] 35¢ | CARDINAL |
EDITION | C-363 | THE | COMPLETE | BOOK |. On spine on
black background: [set left to right:] FICTION | C-363 | 3
| [set top to bottom, first 3 words in white, rest in
greenish-blue:] LADY CHATTERLEY'S LOVER [dot] D. H. Lawrence
| [set left to right:] POCKET | BOOKS | INC. |. Lower
cover in greenish blue, with 1/4" strip of black overlapping
from spine, printed in black save first three words, in
purple: *Lady Chatterley's Lover* [display type] . . . tells
of a love affair between | Constance Chatterley and a
virile game- | keeper who worked for her impotent hus- |
band. . . . . a story | symbolizing the blight of modern
civili- | zation and the basic superiority of natural |
impulses to the sophisticated immoralities | of an inbred
society. . . . | It has also been widely attacked as
"obscene" | and *(Continued on the first inside page)* | [22
lines in all]. Edges stained yellow.

NOTES: First in the "Chatterley Sweepstakes": published Wed. 29
July 29, 6 days after the court decision, in an impression
of 1,000,000 copies. The second impression ("printing") was
400,000. Madison (554) states that one million were sold
in six days and that the second printing was 870,000. In late
August, Pocket Books distributor, Bookmobile Inc., sued
Grove for stating on its paperback cover that the latter
book was the only unexpurgated US ed. The suit was denied,
albeit only on a technicality. See PW 10 Aug. 1959: 42; 7
Sept.: 33; 26 Oct.: 29). See notes to 37.1 and p.126 above.
   This edition was Pocket Books' second-best seller in
1959: 1,750,000 copies (PW 18 Jan 1960,p.90). Through
1959, the firm's bestselling novel was Zola's *Nana* with
2,637,000 sold since 1941 (Schick 132). Sales of the
latter were helped by an extremely sensuous cover illustration. The Pocket edition's cover, for reasons attendant
upon the Bryan decision (see essay above), was not illustrated
However, since the 1954 congressional investigations and
criticisms of lurid paperback covers, more sophisticated
"poster" designs had often replaced representational
drawings (Bonn 103, Davis 240) for safe newsstand and
drugstore sales.
   Pocket Books made literacy tests to determine how much type
could fit on a page without producing eyestrain. Times Roman
9/10 pt. gave the best results (Schick 132). But the typeface
here is Caledonia.

COPIES EXAMINED: CU-S, personal(cop. 1)

36.1.$_2$ as 36.1.$_1$ save:

PAPER: thickness: .06mm. Total bulk 14.1mm.

COPIES EXAMINED: personal(cop. 2), ICarbS

*36.2   August 1959?

*36.3   August 1959?

36.4   as 36.1.₁ save:

  CONTENTS: p.[4]: 1.9: 4th printing .... August 1959 |.
     1.16: C [above "Printed in U.S.A.; replaces "L" of 1st
     ptg.] |.

  PAPER: Thickness .06mm. Total bulk 12.6mm.

  BINDING: edges unstained.

  COPY EXAMINED: personal

         *[subedition (unauthorized?); produced in Jerusalem
          from Pocket Books format]*

36.5   as 36.1.₁ save:

  t.p.:   last four lines excised.

  (6 1/4 x 4 1/8"): [1-11]¹², 192 leaves; pp.[6], 1-378.

  CONTENTS: p.[4]: L A D Y   C H A T T E R L E Y 'S
     L O V E R | 1st printing ....August, 1959 | This
     edition reproduces exactly the text of the 1928 | Italian
     edition, . . . | In any case where the original text has
     been ren- | dered incomprehensible by [typographical
     errors], the present pub- | lisher has inserted the correct
     interpretation in italics in | brackets after the original
     word or phrase. | REPRINTED IN ISRAEL | BY STEIMATZKY'S
     AGENCY | PLATES BY OFFSET SH. MONSON, JERUSALEM |.

  TYPOGRAPHY: 140 x 85mm.; 10ll.=36mm.

  PAPER: Thickness .07mm. Total bulk 15.2mm.

  BINDING: crackle-grain cloth, deep blue(C179). Gold-stamped
     on spine: D. H. LAWRENCE | [short rule] | LADY | CHATTERLEY'S
     | LOVER |. Edges trimmed, unstained. Plain white endpapers.

  COPY EXAMINED: personal

36.6   as 36.1.₁ (including Contents) save:

  Leaves measure 6 1/4 x 4"

  PAPER: Thickness .05mm. Total bulk 11.1mm.

  BINDING: coated paper wrappers. Upper cover (black save for
     3/8" vertical strip in gold adjacent to spine): [in blue:]
     A complete and unexpurgated edition of | this century's most
     controversial love story | *L*[swash]ADY | CHATTERLEY'S |

L[swash]OVER | [in red:] D. H. LAWRENCE | [in blue:] Including
the complete text of Federal Judge | Frederick vanPelt Bryan's
precedent-setting | opinion on the censoring of this modern
classic |. In gold strip: 50¢ | [logo: reading kangaroo] |
50142 | The Complete | Book | POCKET | BOOKS | INC. |. Spine,
on gold background: [left to right:] 50142 | [top to bottom:]
LADY CHATTERLEY'S LOVER [dot] D. H. Lawrence | [left to
right:] [kangaroo logo] POCKET | BOOKS | INC. |. Lower cover:
same as 36.1, but set differently on gold background and with
last two lines not present. ll. 19-21: *(back cover is continued
on the inside half title)* | PUBLISHED BY POCKET [logo] BOOKS
INC. PRINTED IN U.S.A. | [rule] |. Edges unstained.

NOTE: According to Schreuters (29) this version of the kangaroo
logo was used from 1964 to 1977.
    A similar cover design was used for Durrell's *The Black
Book* (first Cardinal Giant Pocketbook edition "March
1962." There is no kangaroo logo.

COPY EXAMINED: personal

    *[Signet NAL Unexpurgated Ed., 1959 [for NAL
    "authorized" expurgated ed. see 20.1-21.4]*

37.1   D. H. LAWRENCE | *Lady* | *Chatterley's* | *Lover* | *A Complete
        Authorized Reprint of the* | *Unexpurgated Edition* | N [dot]
        A [dot] L | SiGNET | BOOKS | A SIGNET BOOK | Published
        by THE NEW AMERICAN LIBRARY [ll. 2-4 in calligraphic
        display type; ll. 7-9, enclosed in oval border, a
        publisher's device]

(8 1/8 x 4 1/4"): no sigs., 144 leaves; pp. [1-4], 5-283, [284],
[4].

CONTENTS: pp.[1-2]: To the Reader: p.[3]: t.p. p.[4]: COPYRIGHT
    ©, 1959, BY THE NEW AMERICAN LIBRARY | OF WORLD LITERATURE,
    INC. | *All rights reserved--*| *no part of this book may be
    reprinted in any form* | *without permission in writing* |
    from the publishers | *Published as a SIGNET BOOK* | *by
    arrangement with Alfred A. Knopf, Inc.,* | *Wm. Heinemann
    Ltd. and the Literary* | *Executor of the Author's Estate.*|
    First Printing This Edition, July 1959 | *SIGNET BOOKS are
    published by* | *The New American Library of World Literature,
    Inc.* | *501 Madison Ave, New York 22, New York* | PRINTED IN
    THE UNITED STATES OF AMERICA |. pp.5-283: text. p.[284]:
    How To Build | A Low-Cost Library |. pp.[4]: list of 31 Signet
    titles, beginning with Sourian's *Miri* and ending with
    Shute's *On The Beach*.

TYPOGRAPHY: 45ll. (p.175), 157 x 88mm; 10ll.= 34mm. Face: 3(2x)mm
    Typeface: Modern Ren (DIN 1.13). Times Roman(?)

PAPER: smooth white wove unwatermarked. Thickness .05mm(p.193).
    Total bulk 10.1mm

BINDING: Coated paper wrappers. Upper cover: black background.
Blue 29mm-wide horizontal strip at top, with 3 lines of
text: [in black]: D1736 |. [In white]: NOW UNEXPURGATED |
[in black]: AUTHENTIC AUTHORIZED EDITION [dot] A SIGNET
BOOK | [next three lines in large (x-height 28mm) display
type (strong vertical stress, hairline serifs) in brilliant
yellow:] Lady | Chatterley's | Lover [last word in title
extends into drawing, in blue outline on black, of fully
dressed man (shirt, slacks, shoes) and woman embracing,
lying on the earth]. | [below figures, in reddish-pink:]
The great novel that shocked the world | [in white:] D. H.
LAWRENCE |. On spine, white background: [left to right, in
black:] D | 1736 | [top to bottom:] [in dark blue:] Lady
Chatterley's Lover [in black:] D. H. LAWRENCE |. Lower
cover white, bears photo of Lawrence and blurbs by A. Bennett,
R. Aldington, A. West. All edges stained red. At bottom:
PUBLISHED BY THE NEW AMERICAN LIBRARY | Cover printed in
U.S.A. Edges stained red.

NOTES: Published July 31, 1959. See essay above (p.126) for
Grove's lawsuit against the NAL expurgated edition and NAL's
countersuit upon the appearance of the Grove paperback. Only
NAL could claim permission from the Lawrence estate, Weybright
having acquired the rights from Knopf for the "Authorized
Abridged Edition" in 1946 (Weybright 288-89). "NAL is now
making up for dealers a rack card on which newspaper stories
and editorials about the book and the film [the French version,
censored in US] will be produced" (PW 20 July 199: 37-38). NAL
also countered Grove's "Letter to the Trade" with one of its
own. The two-page note To the Reader which begins the NAL
unexpurgated edition is an attempt to describe the history
of the firm's involvement with the book and its lawful
interests in it.
    There must have been much jockeying for position by dis-
tributors, each probably pressuring his accounts to display
only the edition he provided. Publishers would want the
distributor they chose not to provide customers with more
than a single edition (Arents: letter, D. Young to McFadden
Publishers, 30 Nov. 1961). In any event the NAL unexpurgated
version, distributed by Independent News Inc., was not on
its list of 1959 top-sellers, although the competing
paperback editions of Pocket, Dell (Grove's distributor),
and Berkley (First Lady Chatterley; see 53.1 below) each
attained second place for those firms (PW 18 Jan. 1960: 90).
It is possible that dealers, out of respect for Rosset's
risks, favored the Grove edition. A telegram in the Fales
archive at N.Y.U. (Weybright to Laurence Pollinger, 20
Oct. 1960) places the number of copies sold to that date
at 1,250,000, which was 750,000 less than Grove. NAL ran
an ad in trade journals in September 1959 listing five of
its best-sellers. Chatterley was second on the list (Arents:
clipping headed "September: A Month To Remember").
    NAL did keep its expurgated version in print. See Essay
for Section 3, p.63 and NOTES to 21.4 above.
    When Grove and NAL settled their suits, the former
acknowledged that NAL's contract with, and payment of
royalties to, Lawrence's estate gave its edition "a certain
standing not shared by other publishers in this country." Grove

also recognized NAL's exclusive paperback rights in Canada and other Berne Convention countries (PW 12 Oct. 1959: 23). The Canadian decensorship trial was precipitated by seizure of copies the of the NAL edition. In court in April, 1960, Victor Weybright, director of the press, testified that 173,000 copies had been sold in Canada (PW 25 April 1960: 58).

COPIES EXAMINED: personal, ICarbS

37.2   as 37.1 save:

CONTENTS: p.[2]: changes involving combination of two paragraphs into one, the NAL Authorized Edition no longer being in print. p.[4]: 1.12: *Second Printing This Edition, August 1959* |.

COPY EXAMINED: personal

*37.3   August, 1959 (date given in Fales Library, NYU, archive: memo, 7 Aug. 1959. See Section 3 above, endnote 6).

*37.4   August, 1959. Date and number of copies (50,000) found in Fales: memo, 13 Aug. 1959.

*37.5   Sept., 1959. Fales: memo, 21 Aug. 1959. No. of copies: 50,000.

*37.6   Sept. 1959. Fales: memo, 3 Sept. 1959, states that there were to be changes in cover and front matter, and that there were 125,000 copies printed.

*37.7   Sept. 1959 (Fales: memo of 10 Sept. 1959).

*37.8   Oct. 1959. This was the third Canadian printing; there were 25,000 copies ordered for Canada with statement "third printing, October 1959" on copyright page. Fales: memo of 23 Sept. 1959.

*37.9

*37.10

*37.11   May 1960. There was a rush order for 105,000 copies (Fales: memo of 18 April 1960).

*37.12   May 1960. 15,000 copies for Canada (Fales: memo of 18 April 1960).

*37.13   August 1960 (Fales: Memo of 19 Aug. 1960). In Oct. 1960 Weybright informed Pollinger that sales of the unexpurgated ed. had reached 1,250,000 (telegram, 20 Oct. 1960). There was a rush printing of 50,000 copies, because at this point the Canadian court decision made it legal for Canadian dealers to sell the book.

*37.14   Feb. 1961. Several typos were reset, and the mistake
          regarding Frieda Lawrence's relation to Baron Von
          Ricthoven was corrected (from "sister" to "cousin")
          Fales: memo, 7 Dec., 1960.

37.15   as 37.1 save:

CONTENTS: p.[4]: ll.3-15: *All rights reserved.* I *No part of
    this book may be reprinted without* I *written permission
    where protected by copyright* I *under the Berne Convention.*
    I *Published as a SIGNET BOOK* I *By arrangement with* I *Wm.
    Heinemann Ltd. and the literary* I *Executors of the
    Author's Estate.* I *First Printing This Edition, July, 1959*
    I *Fifteenth Printing This Edition, November, 1961* I SIGNET
    TRADEMARK REG. U.S. PAT. OFF. AND FOREIGN COUNTRIES I
    REGISTERED TRADEMARK--MARCA REGISTRATA I HECHO EN CHICAGO,
    U.S.A. I [final four lines as in 37.1.]. pp.[284]-[3]:
    list of Signet titles, beginning *Sons and Lovers*, ending
    On The Beach. p.[4]: How To Build I A Low-Cost Library I.

PAPER: thickness .08 mm. Total bulk: 11.9mm.

BINDING: coated paper wrappers. Upper cover: [ll.1-3 in 1"
    strip of black, at top:] COMPLETE I UNEXPURGATED I
    AUTHENTIC AUTHORIZED EDITION I [ll. 4-7 on red back-
    ground:] *Lady* I *Chatterley's* I *Lover* I D. H. LAWRENCE I
    [ll.8-13 on yellow rectangle on black background:] "This
    Signet Edition is the only complete I unexpurgated version
    of LADY CHATTERLEY'S I LOVER authorized by the estate of I
    Frieda Lawrence for U.S. publication." I LAURENCE POL-
    LINGER, Literary Executor I to the Estate of the late Mrs.
    Frieda Lawrence I A SIGNET BOOK I [.1,3,14 in blue; 1.2 in
    yellow; ll. 4-6 in white; rest in black]. At right of line
    4, in black: logo [D1736 I SIGNET I 50¢ I BOOKS; ll.2 and
    4 arranged in oval around price]. [left to right:] Spine,
    on black background: [in white:] D I 1736 I [top to
    bottom, in yellow:] Lady Chatterley's Lover I [in white:]
    D. H. LAWRENCE I. Lower cover: [in yellow, on black
    background:] . . . one of the most I beautiful and tender
    love stories I . . . . tenderness and passion were I the
    only weapons [against materialism. Ten-line blurb]. I [in
    white on red background: 8-line statement regarding the
    unexpurgated text.] I [in yellow rectangle as on u.c.:
    statement from L. Pollinger]. Edges stained red.

COPY EXAMINED: personal

NOTE: In Canada, Heinemann held publishing rights to Lawren-
    ce's works, and thus an agreement was needed.

*37.16

*37.17

*37.18

*37.19

37.20   as 37.15 save:

t.p.: added after l.4: WITH AN AFTERWORD BY HARRY T. MOORE |.

pagination: pp.[1-4], 5-299, [300], [4].

PAPER: thickness .06mm.   Total bulk 10.0mm.

CONTENTS: p.[4]: ll.3-4: Afterword © 1962 by | The New
    American Library of World Literature, Inc. |. ll. 12-13:
    executors of the author's estate, | *who have authorized*
    this softcover edition. | *l.15: Twentieth Printing This*
    Edition, May, 1963 |. [284]: blank. pp.285-99: Afterword.
    pp.[300]-[4]: list of titles, beginning Baldwin's *Go Tell*
    It On The Mountain, ending Moravia's *Conjugal Love.*

BINDING: price stated as 60¢.

COPY EXAMINED: personal

NOTE: Harry Moore's "afterword" is dated April 26, 1962. It
    was printed at end of the text so as to avoid resetting
    (Fales: memo of 19 Nov. 1959).

37.21   as 37.20 save:

CONTENTS: p.[4]: *l.15: Twenty-first Printing This Edition,*
    June, 1964 |. pp.[300]-[3]: list of titles, beginning
    O'Connor's *Violent Bear It Away*, ending Moravia's *Conjugal*
    Love. p.[4]: Explanation of Signet's four paperback
    series.

BINDING: upper cover: blurb in yellow background by Aldington
    replaces Pollinger statement: The great novel that shocked
    the world ... | "He can enter the very soul of another man
    or | woman...with a vividness which makes his | experience
    of them our own." | --RICHARD ALDINGTON |. Series state-
    ment above logo reads P2513 |. On spine, at top in yellow
    square: series statement.

COPY EXAMINED: personal

*37.22

*37.23

37.24   as 37.21 save:

CONTENTS: p.[4]: l. 14 (statement of first printing) excised.
    l.14: *Twenty-fourth Printing This Edition* |. l.20: 1301
    Avenue of the Americas, New York, New York 10019 |.
    p.[300]: list begins with Fielding's *Birthday King.*

BINDING: upper cover, on black background: logo in blue:
    price 75¢, series number (at right of logo). | D. H.
    LAWRENCE | [ll.3-5 in red border, which ends 3/4" from
    bottom of cover:] *Lady* | *Chatterley's* | *Lover* | COMPLETE

[dot] UNEXPURGATED | AUTHORIZED EDITION | A SIGNET BOOK |
[1.2 in white, ll.3-7 in yellow; 1.8 in blue].
Spine: left to right: SiGNET [in oval, in blue on black
background] | [in black on white background:] T | 2754 |
[set top to bottom; first three words in red, rest in
black, all on white background:] LADY CHATTERLEY'S LOVER
[dot] D. H. LAWRENCE |. Lower cover: in black border are
three statements (printed in red, black, and blue respectively) as in 37.21, but phrased a bit differently.
Below border: PUBLISHED BY THE NEW AMERICAN LIBRARY |.

COPY EXAMINED: personal

*37.25

37.26   as 37.24 save:

CONTENTS: p.[4]: 1.15: *Twenty-sixth Printing This Edition* |.

NOTE: NAL used a very similar binding format for *Memoirs of
Fanny Hill* (first printing, 1965). Page [2] contains a
blurb for *Chatterley* (see Essay above). Series number
given as Q3674. The other books advertised on this page
are *Tom Jones*, *Forever Amber*, and *Moll Flanders*.

COPY EXAMINED: CU-S

*37.27

*37.28

*37.29

*37.30

*37.31

37.32   as 37.26 save:

t.p.: imprint change, ll.8-12: [pub's device:] S within C | A
SIGNET MODERN CLASSIC from | NEW AMERICAN LIBRARY | [rule] |
TIMES MIRROR |.

CONTENTS: p.[4]: [double rule] | CAREFULLY SELECTED, EDITED,
AND PRINTED, | SIGNET CLASSICS PROVIDE A TREASURY OF THE
WORLD'S | GREAT WRITINGS IN HANDSOMELY DESIGNED VOLUMES |
[double rule] |. [ll.6-18 as ll.1-13 in 37.26, save 1.14,
where SIGNET MODERN CLASSIC replaces SIGNET BOOK.] 1.19:
Thirty-second printing This Edition |. To left of ll.20-22
(ll.15-17 in 37.26): logo (S within C). ll.22-26: SIGNET,
SIGNET CLASSICS, MENTOR AND PLUME BOOKS | *are published
by The New American Library, Inc.,* | *1301 Avenue of the
Americas, New York, New York 10019* | PRINTED IN THE UNITED
STATES OF AMERICA |. pp.[300]-[4]: list of Signet Clas-
sics, beginning *Huckleberry Finn*, ending *Wuthering
Heights*. Both 50¢.

PAPER: Thickness .06mm. Total bulk 10.3mm.

BINDING: white background, black lettering in Sans Serif.
cover: THE COMPLETE UNEXPURGATED VERSION | OF THE WORLD-
FAMOUS NOVEL | D. H. LAWRENCE | [rule] | LADY CHATTERLEY'S
| LOVER |. [Near spine edge, running bottom to top:] A
SIGNET MODERN CLASSIC [dot] CQ486 [logo] |. Lower half of
cover occupied by half-length drawing ("t. upshur") of
nude woman with face half-covered by luxuriant black hair,
nipple of right breast in pink. Spine: [left to right:]
[logo] | SIGNET | CQ | 486 | [top to bottom:] LADY
CHATTERLEY'S LOVER D. H. LAWRENCE 451-CQ486-095|. Lower
Cover: two-paragraph blurb ("tenderness and passion were
the only weapons which would serve man from self-destruct-
ion" . . . . "complete unexpurgated text"), followed by L.
Pollinger statement as in 37.26. Last line reads: THE NEW
AMERICAN LIBRARY PUBLISHES SIGNET, MENTOR, CLASSICS & NAL
BOOKS |. Edges unstained.

NOTE: Times Mirror acquired NAL in 1960 (Crider 191, Davis
281). For discussion of the cover illustration, see
pp.131-32 above. This drawing bears some similarity to the
photo design on the front cover of the 1972 paperback
edition of Marco Vassi's *Contours Of Darkness*, published
by the Olympia Press in 1972.

COPY EXAMINED: personal

37.33 as 37.32 save:

CONTENTS: 1.17: *Thirty-third Printing This Edition* |.
Although the rest of the wording is unchanged from 37.32,
some lines are set differently. 11.10-18 in 37.32 are
condensed into 11.10-16.

PAPER: thickness: 06mm. Total bulk: 9.7mm.

BINDING: paper-covered boards, white. As 37.32 save a black
outer border on upper cover. Added as line 1, upper cover:
L1183 $1.95 |. At foot of spine: logo: NAL in oval,
bisected at top and bottom by short rules. Same logo at
bottom of lower cover, at right of DURABOUND |, which is
surrounded on three sides by rectangle open at left, near
logo.

COPY EXAMINED: personal

37.34 as 37.33 save:

CONTENTS: 1.19: *Thirty-fourth Printing This Edition* |.

BINDING: u.c.: added near spine edge, before logo and after
CQ486: | [dot] | 95¢ |. At top of spine, below logo:
SIGNET | MODERN | CLASSIC |.

COPIES EXAMINED: personal, PinU

37.35   as 37.34 save:

CONTENTS: 1.19: *Thirty-fifth Printing This Edition* I.

BINDING: u.c.: near spine edge: A SIGNET MODERN CLASSIC [dot]
    CY820 I [dot] I $1.25 I. At bottom of spine, top to
    bottom: 451-CY820-125 I.

COPY EXAMINED: OkTU

37.36 as 37.35 save:

CONTENTS: p.[4]: 5 lines removed, as is statement regarding
    printing history. After publisher's address (1.20): 36 37
    38 39 40 41 42 I PRINTED IN THE UNITED STATES OF AMERICA
    I.

PAPER: thickness: .5mm. Total bulk: 10.7mm.

BINDING: upper cover, 1.1: A SIGNET CLASSIC[dot]451-
CW1077[dot]150 [logo] I. Spine: 11.5-6: CW I 1077 I. At
    bottom, top to bottom: 0-451-51077-1 150 I.

COPY EXAMINED: personal

*37.37

37.38   as 37.36 save:

CONTENTS: p.[4]: first numeral in 1.20: 38 I.

BINDING: price indicated as above on spine and u.c. is $2.25.

COPY EXAMINED: PP

*37.39

37.40   as 37.38 save:

CONTENTS: p.[4]: address change, 1.19: *1633 Broadway, New
    York, New York 10019* I. pp.[300]-[4]: list of titles
    begins *Lord Jim*, ends *Marble Faun* (both $1.95).

PAPER: thickness: .05mm. total bulk 8.8mm.

BINDING: u.c.: text and illustration surrounded by brownish-
    gray border. At top: logo [on brownish-gray background, in
    red] 451-CE1787 [dot] $2.75 I SIGNET CLASSIC I. Spine:
    background in brownish-gray. At top: [logo] SIGNET I
    CLASSIC I CE I 1787 I. At bottom: 0-451-51787-3 275 I.

COPIES EXAMINED: personal, Pollinger Coll.

37.41 as 37.40 save:

t.p.: after 1.8 (logo): A SIGNET CLASSIC I rule] I NEW
AMERICAN LIBRARY I [rule] I.

CONTENTS: p.[4]: added as line 1.4: Cover painting by Mark
    English I. 1.20 reads: 41 42 43 44 45 46 47 48 49 I.

pp.[300]-[4]: list begins *Lord Jim* ($2.50), ends *Tobacco Road.*

BINDING: coated paper wrappers. U.c., printed in white: [rule] [in oval cartouche, on black background bordered in white and orange:] *Signet Classic* [rule] | D. H. LAWRENCE | [rule] | *Lady | Chatterley's | Lover* | [at bottom:] 451- CE1787 [dot] $2.75 |. Printing superimposed on painting of nude woman, back to viewer and in shadows, removing garment. Water pitcher, also in shadows, occupies right foreground. On spine, superimposed on part of painting: left to right: logo |. Top to bottom: [in cartouche:] *Signet Classic* |. left to right: CE | 1787 |. top to bottom: *Lady Chatterley's Lover* | D>H> LAWRENCE | 0-451- 51787-3 275|. L.c.: in black on white background: cartouche logo, three blurbs, machine-readable identification strip, ISBN number, as on spine.

NOTE: NAL has kindly informed me (letter, Alan J. Kaufman to the author, 11 June 1985) that there had been 41 printings, totalling 3,040,000 copies, to that time. Mark English, the illustrator, designed the Bantam Shakespeare series.

[Pyramid Books Edition, 1959]

38.1   The | Complete and Unexpurgated | Edition of | Lady | Chatterley's | Lover | D. H. LAWRENCE | [pub. device: pyramid with P, B inscribed on sides; surrounded by wreath, below which is PYRAMID ROYAL on ribbon] | Published by | PYRAMID BOOKS, 444 Madison Avenue, New York 22, N. Y.

(7 1/16 x 4 1/8"): unsigned, perfect bound; pp. [1-8], 9-383, [384].

CONTENTS: p.[1]: summary of Judge Bryan's decision. pp.[2-3]: blurbs from various newspapers regarding the *Chatterley* decensorship case. p.[4]:blank. p.[5]:t.p. p.[6]: Lady Chatterley's Lover | by D. H. Lawrence | Pyramid Books Edition | August 1959 | Copyright 1959 | by Almat Publishing Corporation | All Rights Reserved | *Printed in United States of America* | p.[7]: section title p.[8]: blank. pp.9-355: text. p.[356]: blank. pp.[357]-383: transcript of Bryan decision. p.[384]: Pyramid logo (as on t.p.).

TYPOGRAPHY: text: 40ll.(p.11): 151 (155) x 89mm. 10ll. = 33mm. Face: 3(2x)mm.
Typeface: Times Roman (R52). old style; DIN 1.13, Mod. Renaissance

RUNNING HEADS: rectos and versos: LADY CHATTERLEY'S LOVER |.

PAPER: rough white wove unwatermarked. Thickness .08mm.
   Total bulk 14.7mm.

BINDING: Paper wrappers, black. Upper cover: [in upper
   right:] logo, as on t.p., in white, with series number
   (PR25) price (50¢) below I [on same line as wreath of
   logo, in yellow:] UNEXPURGATED I [in white, last two lines
   parallel to first word of title:] the complete uncut I
   edition of one of I the world's most I controversial
   novels I [in orange:] LADY I CHATTERLEY'S I LOVER I [in
   white:] Including the full text of the I famous decision
   by Federal I Judge Frederick vanPelt Bryan I which lifted
   the Post Office ban I [in yellow:] D.H. LAWRENCE I. On
   spine [title in yellow, rest in white:] left to right:
   PR25 I LADY CHATTERLEY'S LOVER D.H. Lawrence I [left to
   right: PYRAMID ROYAL I. l.c., printed in white and yellow,
   contains blurb: ". . . psychologi- I cally brilliant and
   vigorous novel I . . . "spirit- I ual" . . . "shocking" .
   . . "inspiring" . . . I "erotic" . . . . 'great I personal
   expression of [Lawrence's] attitudes on I sex and our . .
   . a touching love story you'll never forget." (19 lines).
   Edges stained orange.

NOTES: Pyramid started its Royal line, featuring "the very
   best fiction and non-fiction for your reading pleasure,"
   in 1956 (Crider 243). Titles included *The Moonstone, The
   Scarlet Pimpernel, The Compact Bible, Père Goriot*;
   nonfiction subjects ranged from handwriting analysis to
   professional basketball.

COPIES EXAMINED: personal, TxU, NcU

38.2   as 38.1 save:

The I Complete and Unexpurgated I Edition of I LADY
CHATTERLEY'S I LOVER I D. H. Lawrence I [triangle] I PYRAMID
BOOKS I 444 Madison Avenue, New York 22, New York

CONTENTS: p.[1]: blurb: ". . . story of the degrading of
   natural impulses by modern industrial society . . . first
   such story to tell the whole truth -- to dispense with
   euphemism and hypocrisy, to describe completely the most
   basic and uninhibited experiences of the characters."
   pp.[2-3]: nine blurbs from newspapers. p.[6]: LADY
   CHATTERLEY'S LOVER, *by D. H. Lawrence* I Pyramid Books
   Edition: Second Printing *March 1962* I Copyright © 1959 by
   Almat Publishing Corporation I All Rights Reserved I
   Printed in the United States of America

PAPER: smooth white wove unwatermarked. Thickness .07mm.
   Total bulk 15.2mm.

BINDING: Paper wrappers, white. Upper cover: in upper left:
   logo [triangle in red] I PYRAMID BOOKS I PR-40 I 50¢ I.
   [to left of logo:] D. H. Lawrence I [next 3 lines in red]
   Lady I Chatterley's I Lover I [drawing of apparently naked
   man kissing woman's forehead; predominant colors orange,
   dark red, brown] I Unexpurgated I the complete edition I

of the world's most | controversial novel |. On spine: PR-
40 | 50¢ | [set top to bottom, first 3 words in red:] LADY
CHATTERLEY'S LOVER D. H. Lawrence |. At base of spine, set
vertically: PYRAMID BOOKS |. Lower wrapper, in red: About
the 'Lady' . . . [blurb: "words such as 'spiritual'
'shocking' 'inspired' 'erotic' have been wedded to
describe this beautiful and uninhibited book . . . long
banned by the Post Office. . . famous judicial decision .
. . 'touching and unforgettable love story.'] At bottom:
ad for Statler's *Japanese Inn*. Edges stained light orange.

COPY EXAMINED: Pollinger Coll.

[Milestone Edition, 1960]

39.1   Lady Chatterley's Lover | [decoration] | *by* | D. H.
        Lawrence | Milestone Editions | New York

(7 1/8 x 6): [1-10]^{16}, 160 leaves; pp.[1-6], 7-320.

CONTENTS: p.[1]:half-title p.[2]:blank. p.[3]: t.p.
        p.[4]:First printed 1928 | This complete text first
        published in Great Britain 1960 | Reprinted 1960 | © 1960
        The Estate of D. H. Lawrence | Printed in U.S.A. p.[5]:
        fly-title. p[6]: blank. pp.7-319: text. p.320: This book
        was set in Video Baskerville . . . . | The conversion to
        electronic (cathode ray tube) char-| acter creation
        permits the use of the most mod-| ern composing
        techniques while maintaining the | detail of the original
        type cuttings. | This Milestone Edition was set, printed
        and | bound by The Haddon Craftsmen, Inc., Scran-| ton,
        Pennsylvania. | *Typography and design by* | *Millicent La*
        Roque. | [in lower left corner, printed vertically: HB9C.]

TYPOGRAPHY: text: 39ll. (p.139), 178 x 110mm. 10ll.=45mm.
        Face 3(2x)mm. For typeface see CONTENTS above.

PAPER: rough white laid; impressed with chain-lines approx.
        20mm. apart; unwatermarked. Thickness .11mm. Total bulk
        20.2mm.

BINDING: Var.(1): linen-grain cloth(T304), deep green(C142);
        quarter bound in calico-grain cloth(T302), dark
        green(C146). Upper cover: facsimile of Lawrence's signa-
        ture, gold-stamped in lower right. On spine: panel in deep
        yellowish green (C132); gold stamped therein: [thick-thin
        rule] | LADY | CHATTERLEY'S | LOVER | [rule] | D. H. |
        Lawrence | [thin-thick rule]. At tail of spine: *M* |
        [rule] | MILESTONE | EDITIONS. Edges trimmed. Yellowish-
        brown endpapers, thickness -- .12mm. Head and tailbands in
        green. Var.(2): as (1) but faint marbling pattern on
        endpapers; predominant color light orange yellow.

NOTE: The printing history on p.[5] is identical to that in

the Penguin paperback, 2nd printing (see 44.2): perhaps
that, and not an American edition, was used as copytext.
This edition is not authorized by the Lawrence Estate.

COPY EXAMINED: personal

[Doubleday (Book Club?) Edition, 1966(?)]

40.1   *Lady Chatterley's* | *Lover* | [decoration] | D. H.
        LAWRENCE | NELSON DOUBLEDAY, Inc.| *Garden City, New
        York*

(8 1/4 x 5 1/2"): [1-10]^{16}, 160 leaves, pp.[6], [1], 2-313,
[314].

CONTENTS: p.[1]:half-title. p.[2]:blank. p.[3]:t.p. p.[4]:
The text is the third manuscript version, | published in
Florence in 1928 by Orioli | *Distributed in Canada by
permission* | *of Laurence Pollinger Limited* | *Printed in
the United States of America* |. p.[5]: flytitle. p.[6]:
blank. pp.[1]-313: text. p.[314]:blank.

TYPOGRAPHY: 39ll.(p.61), 166(173) x 100mm. 10ll.=43mm. Face
3(2x)mm.
Typeface: Times Roman (R52). old style; DIN 1.13, Mod.
Renaissance

RUNNING HEADS: rectos and versos: LADY CHATTERLEY'S LOVER

PAPER: smooth white wove unwatermarked. Thickness .1mm.
Total bulk 17.8mm.

BINDING: Linen-grain (T303) cloth, moderate yellow green
(C136). Upper cover: gold-stamped rule of small flowers,
vertically placed 35mm. from fore-edge. Spine, running top
to bottom: [in light brown:] D. H. Lawrence [row of
floral dec., gold stamped] | [in black]: Lady Chatterley's
Lover [row of floral decoration, as on u.c. | [in light
brown, horizontally placed at tail of spine]: Nelson |
Doubleday |. Top and bottom edges trimmed, fore-edge
untrimmed. . Endpapers strong reddish orange(C35), but
verso of free front and back endp. white. Head and
tailbands in green.

NOTE: The above might have been acquired from Modern Library
and Grove but the text is not Grove's. The wording verso
t.p., indicating that the book was sold in Canada with the
permission of the Lawrence estate, suggests an agreement
with NAL (see 37.1, Notes).
    The Arents Archive of Grove Press materials at Syracuse
Univ. contains a document indicating an unnamed book
club's interest in *Chatterley* and *Our Lady of the Flowers*.
The writer, treasurer for Random House, feels Grove should
accept because both it and Modern Library will benefit

from the added publicity (and stature?) to be accorded the titles (letter, E. Harper to Grove Press, 29 April 1966). See Essay above, pp.133-34.

COPY EXAMINED: personal

40.2   as 40.1 save:

collation: [1-8]^{12} [9-12]^{16}

PAPER: thickness .08mm. Total bulk 15.22mm

BINDING: morocco-grain brownish pink (C33) paper covered boards, quarter-bound moderate bluish green (C164) paper. Upper cover: vertical rule of small flowers, approx. 55mm from fore-edge. Spine as 40.1 above. Plain white endpapers.Top and bottom edge trimmed, fore-edge lightly trimmed.

NOTE: In my personal copy on p.312, at the gutter edge, 24mm. from bottom of page, appears: J 18 I. The ICarbS copy reads K 23 I.

COPIES EXAMINED: ICarbS, OAU, personal

[International Collector's Library]

41.1   *Lady Chatterley's* I *Lover* I [decoration] I D. H. LAWRENCE I INTERNATIONAL COLLECTORS LIBRARY I *Garden City, New York*

(8 1/8 x 5 1/2"): [1]^{4} [2-3]^{12} [4-11]^{16}, 156 leaves, pp.[6], [1], 2-305, [306].

CONTENTS: p.[1]:half-title. p.[2]:blank. p.[3]:t.p. p.[4]: The text is the third manuscript version, I published in Florence in 1928 by Orioli I *Distributed in Canada by permission* I *of Laurence Pollinger Limited* I *Printed in the United States of America* I. p.[5]: flytitle. p.[6]:blank. pp.[1]-305: text. p.[306]:blank.

TYPOGRAPHY: 40ll.(p.61), 167(173) x 100mm. 10ll.=43mm. Face 3(2x)mm.
    Typeface: Times Roman (R52). old style; DIN 1.13, Mod. Renaissance

RUNNING HEADS: rectos and versos: LADY CHATTERLEY'S LOVER

PAPER: Smooth white laid; impressed with chainlines approx. 20mm apart. Unwatermarked. Thickness .09mm. Total bulk 16.5mm.

BINDING: morocco-grain paper covered boards, deep bluish green(C165). Upper cover: gold-stamped decorated border enclosing blank inner panel. Elaborate outer border of

type ornaments and floral decoration. Spine divided into 6 sections by 5 raised bands, gold-stamped with five decorated panels. In top panel: D. H. | LAWRENCE |. In third panel: LADY | CHATT- | ERLEY'S | LOVER |. In bottom panel: INTERNATIONAL | COLLECTORS | LIBRARY |. Endpapers light yellowish green(C134), flecked with brown (thickness 1.2mm). Headband in light brown. Black placemarker bound in. Top and bottom edges trimmed, fore-edge lightly trimmed.

NOTE: Although reset, this is another version of the Double-day (book club) edition, in a slightly more sumptuous format.

COPY EXAMINED: personal

[Bantam Edition, 1968-date]

42.1   *The Complete and Unexpurgated | 1928 Orioli Edition of | LADY CHATTERLEY'S LOVER | [rule] | D. H. LAWRENCE | Preface by Lawrence Durrell | Edited and with an Introduction by | Ronald Friedland | [pub. logo: rooster, with lettering encircling it: [dot] BANTAM BOOKS [dot] LONDON NEW YORK TORONTO*

(7 1/16 x 4 1/4"): unsigned; pp.[i-vi], vii-xxiv, 1-360.

CONTENTS: p.[1]: 2 paragraphs on Lawrence's life: ". . . The search for a full, intense life, lived in harmony with deep, instinctual energies . . . . subtlety in exposing the forces which deny life . . . LCL is one of his most daring and deliberate creations, and his most explicit declaration of faith." p.[ii]: list of Bantam Modern Classics, 13 titles, starting with *All The King's Men*, ending with Queneau's *Zazie*. p.[iii]:t.p. p.[iv]: LADY CHATTERLEY'S LOVER | *A Bantam Modern Classic* | *published February 1968* | [copyright information, 611.] | [rule] | Bantam Books are published by Bantam Books Inc., a subsidiary of Grosset & Dunlap, Inc. Its trademark . . . . Bantam Books, Inc., 271 Madison Avenue, New York, N.Y. 10016.[6 lines] | [rule] | PRINTED IN THE UNITED STATES OF AMERICA |. p.[v]: Contents p.[vi]:blank. pp.vii-xi: Preface. p.[xii]:blank pp.xiii-xxiv: Introduction |. pp.1-328: text pp.329-360: *A Propos of Lady Chatterley's Lover.*

TYPOGRAPHY: 42ll.(p.73): 152(157) x 88mm. 10ll.=36. Face 3(1.5x)mm.
Typeface: Times Roman (R52). old style; DIN 1.13, Mod. Renaissance

RUNNING HEADS: versos: *D.H.L.* Rectos: *Lady Chatterley's Lover* (pp. viii-xi: rectos and versos: *Preface* |. pp.xiv-xxiv: rectos and versos: *Introduction* |. pp. 331-59: rectos: A Propos of *Lady Chatterley's Lover* |.)

PAPER: smooth white wove unwatermarked. Thickness .08mm.
Total bulk 15.2mm.

BINDING: coated paper wrappers. Upper cover: Predominant
color is light purplish blue (C199). Photograph of meadow,
weeds, and wild flowers. In upper left quadrant of upper
cover, in white: The | Unexpurgated | 1928 Orioli |
Edition | D. H. | Lawrence | [rule] | Lady | Chatterley's
| Lover | [rule] | With a Preface | by Lawrence Durrell |.
[in upper right, near spine, running bottom to top]: NY
4089 [asterisk] 95¢ [asterisk] A BANTAM MODERN CLASSIC
[Bantam logo] |. On spine: 95¢ | [rule] | NY4089 | [Bantam
logo in blue] | A BANTAM | MODERN CLASSIC | [rule] | [set
top to bottom:] D.H. Lawrence [dot] Lady Chatterley's
Lover |. Lower cover: blurbs by author, Durrell, sunburst
design in orange with Bantam logo at center. Series number
and price in strip at fore edge, as on u.c.

NOTE: The Bantam Modern Classics series was begun in 1968,
and LCL was one of the first fifteen titles. The list
included the best 20th-century writers.
    The Lawrence estate does not consider this edition to be
the "authorized" one, but does acknowledge it. Bantam's
rights descend from Grosset and Dunlap, which firm dealt
originally with Knopf (letters, Gerald Pollinger to the
author, 12 Aug 1985, 3 Jan. 1986; interview, 25 May
1988). See essay for Section 3, pp.61-62, and 17.9, 17.10.

COPY EXAMINED: TxU

*42.2 "August 1969" [N.B.: the dates assigned to each
printing for the second through 18th printings are taken
from p.[4] of 42.18]

42.3 "June 1970"; as 40.1 save:

CONTENTS: 11.3-4: *2nd printing | 3rd printing |.*

COPY EXAMINED: personal

*42.4 SUBEDITION: "Bantam edition / February 1971"

*42.5 "January 1972"

*42.6 "June 1972"

*42.7 "November 1972"

*42.8 "August 1973"

42.9 "January 1974"; as 40.1 save:

The Complete | And Unexpurgated | 1928 Orioli Edition | D. H.
| Lawrence | [rule] | Lady | Chatterley's | Lover | Preface
by | Lawrence Durrell | Edited and with | an introduction by
| Ronald Friedland | [logo, around which is printed: [dot]

BANTAM BOOKS [dot] LONDON NEW YORK TORONTO] | A NATIONAL
GENERAL COMPANY

CONTENTS: p.[ii]: Bantam Lawrence titles: *The Fox, Chatterley, Virgin and Gypsy, Women in Love*. p.[iv]: LADY
CHATTERLEY'S LOVER | *A Bantam Modern Classic / published
February 1968 | 2nd printing ... July 1969 | 3rd print-
ing... May 1970 | Bantam edition published September 1971
| 2nd printing | 3rd printing | 4th printing | 5th
printing | 6th printing |*. 11.11-16: copyright informa-
tion. 11.17-23: information regarding address and trade-
mark of publisher. 1.24: PRINTED IN THE UNITED STATES OF
AMERICA |.

TYPOGRAPHY: Author and title on upper cover, title on spine
and on lower cover, printed in ITC Firenze (R435)

BINDING: white coated paper wrappers. Upper cover: water-
color(?) of naked brown-haired woman (visible from waist
up) with back to viewer, walking toward distant cottage
under towering tree. From her hair (bound with bow at nape
of neck) flow various brightly colored daisies, wild-flow-
ers, and ferns. In black: The Unexpurgated | 1928 Orioli
Edition | [rule] | Lady | Chatterley's | Lover | [rule] |
D. H. Lawrence | [rule] | With a Preface by Laurence
Durrell [in upper right, bottom to top]: N7159 [asterisk]
95¢ [asterisk] A BANTAM BOOK [logo] |. Lower cover in
black: Lady | Chatterley's | Lover | [rule] | "This is the
real point of | this book. I want | men and women to be
able | to think sex, | fully, completely, | honestly, and
cleanly." | -D. H. Lawrence |. Spine: [left to right:]
[logo, with rooster in red] | NOVEL | 95¢ |. Running top
to bottom: Lady Chatterley's Lover D.H. Lawrence |. [set
vertically:] 553 | 07159 | 095 |.

NOTE: it is interesting to see this cover (identified in
42.18 below as by Bill Edwards) replacing fairly quickly
the one used for the first impression. The change of
subedition may be the reason, or perhaps the first
illustration was thought too subtle to attract attention.
However, the audience for this "trade" paperback., as for
the Signet NAL for the same time period (see #37.32),
would have included specialty book stores, chains, and,
especially, college stores. The elimination of the series
designation was due to "the line between school and
general titles becoming less clear-cut."(Crider 59).
   Display type used on binding same as that on t.p. of
43.1 below.

COPY EXAMINED: personal

42.10   "April 1975"; as 42.9 save:

CONTENTS: added as 1.11: *7th printing* |.

COPY EXAMINED: personal

42.11.₁   "October 1975"; as 42.10 save:

CONTENTS: p.[4]: added as l.12: *8th printing* |.

COPY EXAMINED: MH

42.11.₂   "October 1975"; as 42.10 save:

t.p.: last line, under logo, excised.

CONTENTS: p.[4]: LADY CHATTERLEY'S LOVER | *A Bantam Modern
   Classic / published February 1968 | 2nd printing...August
   1969 3rd printing...June 1970... | Bantam edition
   published September1971 | 5th printing January...1972 7th
   printing...November 1972 | 6th printing...June 1972 8th
   printing...August 1973 | 9th printing | 10th printing |
   11th printing* |

PAPER: sheets bulk 16.5mm.

BINDING: upper cover, spine edge: price stated as $1.25.
   At top of spine: [logo] | NOVEL | [rule] | $1.25 |. Last
   line at bottom: 125 |.

COPY EXAMINED: OkTU

*42.12   "May 1977"

42.13   "October 1978"; as 42.11.₂ save:

CONTENTS: p.[4]: l.4: *Bantam edition / September 1971 |
   5th printing...January 1972 9th printing...January 1974 |
   6th printing...June 1972 10th printing...April 1975 |
   7th printing...November 1972 11th printing...October 1975
   | 8th printing...August 1973 12th printing...May 1977 |
   13th printing...October 1978* |. l.16, after copyright
   statements: ISBN 0-553-12592-3 | *Published simultaneously
   in the United States and Canada* |. p.360, at bottom: offer
   of Bantam catalogue.

BINDING: u.c.,at edge of spine, running bottom to top:
   12592-3 [asterisk] $2.25 [asterisk] A BANTAM BOOK [logo]
   |. Spine, at top: [logo] | NOVEL | $2.25 |. At bottom: 0-
   553-12592-3 |.

COPY EXAMINED: personal

42.14   "September 1979"; as 42.13 save:

CONTENTS: p.[4]: l.4: *Bantam edition / February 1971 | 5th
   printing...January 1972 10th printing...April 1975 | 6th
   printing...June 1972 11th printing...October 1975 | 7th
   printing...November 1972 12th printing...May 1977 | 8th
   printing...August 1973 13th printing...October 1978 | 9th
   printing...January 1974 14th printing [large dot]
   September 1979* |. l.16: ISBN   0-553-13530-9

BINDING: u.c., near spine: 13530-9 [asterisk] $2.50 [aster-

isk] A BANTAM BOOK [logo] |. New price and ISBN number on
top and bottom of spine respectively.

COPY EXAMINED: personal, Pollinger Coll.

42.15   "July 1980"; as 42.14 save:

CONTENTS: 1.10: *15th printing...July 1980* |. 1.16: ISBN 0-
553-14472-3 | last line: 24 23 22 21 20 19 18 17 16 15 |.

BINDING: u.c., near spine: 14472-3 [asterisk] $2.95 [aster-
isk] A BANTAM BOOK [logo] |. New price and ISBN number on
top and bottom of spine respectively. Lower cover: at
bottom left is machine-readable grid and ISBN no.

COPY EXAMINED: personal

42.16   "April 1981"; as 42.15 save:

CONTENTS: p.[4]: last line, digit as extreme right is 16 |.

COPIES EXAMINED: personal; PP

*42.17   "February 1982"

42.18   SUBEDITION: "Bantam Classic edition / January 1983";
as 42.16 save:

[pub. logo: b enclosed by C] | [within rules, running across
page]: A BANTAM CLASSIC[dot] | Lady Chatterley's | Lover | by
D. H. Lawrence | The Complete and Unexpurgated 1928 Orioli
Edition | Preface by Lawrence Durrell | Edited and with an
Introduction by Ronald Friedland | [logo: a bantam] | BANTAM
BOOKS | TORONTO [dot] NEW YORK [dot] LONDON [dot] SYDNEY

Size of leaves: 6 7/8 x 4 1/4

CONTENTS: p.[1]: 2-paragraph biography of author. p.[2]: List
of Bantam Classics: 35 titles, beginning with *Canterbury
Tales*, ending with *Chatterley*. p.[4]: LADY CHATTERLEY'S
LOVER | *A Bantam Book / February 1968 | 2nd printing
...August 1969   3rd printing...June 1970 | Bantam
edition/February 1971 | 5th printing...January 1972 11th
printing..October 1975 | 6th printing...June 1972 12th
printing...May 1977 | 7th printing.November 1972 | 13th
printing...October 1978 | 8th printing...August 1973 14th
printing. September 1979 | 9th printing...January 1974
15th printing...July 1980 | 10th printing...April 1975
16th printing April 1981 | 17th printing...February 1982 |
Bantam Classic edition/January 1983 | Cover Art by Bill
Edwards* |. 1.20: ISBN 0-553-21097-1 |. 1.30: 0 27 26 25 24
23 22 21 20 19 18 |. p.360: no catalogue offer.

PAPER: Thickness .08mm. Total bulk 16.9mm.

BINDING: Printing in sans serif. Upper cover: 21097-1
[asterisk] $2.25 | [within rules, repeated across both
covers and spine]: A BANTAM CLASSIC[dot] | [at bottom of

drawing]: Lady Chatterley's Lover | by D. H. Lawrence |
The Unexpurgated 1928 Orioli Edition |. Spine, in sans
serif: set left to right: [logo: b within C] | [within
rules:] BANTAM CLASSIC[dot] | [rooster logo | $2.25 | [top
to bottom:] Lady Chatterley's Lover[dot] D.H. Lawrence |
[set right to left:] 0-553- | 21097-1 |. Lower cover:
blurb: "Lyric and sensual . . . . scenes of intimate
beauty . . . . vision of individual regeneration through
sexual love. . . . erotic celebration of life." Blurb by
Durrell, note of preface and introduction, machine-
readable grid, ISBN number.

COPIES EXAMINED: personal, PP

42.19   as 42.18 save:

CONTENTS: p.[2]: list of Bantam Classics: 43 titles, starting
with *Beowulf*, ending with *Chatterley*. p.[4]: last digit
at right, bottom of page: 19 |.

BINDING: upper cover: 21149-8 [asterisk] $2.75 |. On spine:
price changed to $2.75. At tail of spine:last line reads
21149-8 |. Lower cover under grid: ISBN no.: 0-553-21149-8
(different from that given on p.4).

COPY EXAMINED: personal

42.20   as 42.19 save:

Added to last line on t.p.: [dot] AUCKLAND |.

CONTENTS: p.[4]: last digit at right, bottom of page: 20 |.

COPY EXAMINED: personal

*42.21

42.22   as 42.20 save:

CONTENTS: p.[2]: list of 50 titles, beginning *Beowulf*, ending
Sherlock Holmes. p.[4]: *last digit at right, bottom of
page: 22* |.

*BINDING: upper cover, at top: 21262-1 [asterisk] IN U.S.
$2.95 (IN CANADA $3.50) |. Inside u.c., top to bottom: N O
553-21262-1>>295 |. On spine, under rooster logo: IN U. S.
| $2.95 | [rule] | IN CANADA | $3.50 |. At tail of spine,
last line: 21262-1 |.*

COPY EXAMINED: personal

42.23   as 42.22 save:

*CONTENTS: p.[4]: 1.3: 2nd printing...August 1969 10th
printing...April 1975 | 3rd printing...June 1970 11th
printing October 1975 | 4th printing...February 1971
12th printing...May 1977 | 5th printing...January 1972
13th printing...October 1978 | 6th printing...June 1972*

*14th printing...September 1979 | 7th printing...November
1972 15th printing...July 1980 | 8th printing...August
1973 16th printing...April 1981 | 9th printing...January
1974 17th printing...February 1982 | Bantam Classic
Edition / January 1983 | 7 printings through October 1987
| Cover painting, A Letio by F. Zandomeneghi | Galleria
Arte Moderna, Florence. | Courtesy of Scala/Art Resource,
New York. |* Last line reads: 0 32 31 30 29 28 27 26 25 24
23 | .

PAPER: Thickness: .08mm. Total bulk: 15.4mm.

BINDING: Background moderate greenish blue (C173). Upper
    cover: 1.3: Lady Chatterley's Lover | by D. H. Lawrence |
    [painting, bordered at top and bottom with white rule:
    young woman lying in bed, in white shift or nightgown,
    face turned toward wall or panel on which are swirling
    floral patterns. Predominant colors white, dark brown,
    silver, blue] | The Unexpurgated 1928 Orioli Edition | .
    Inside upper cover: number as above; machine-readable
    grid. Lower cover: blurbs as above, but set differently.
    Grid on white background.

COPY EXAMINED: personal

42.24   as 42.23 save:

CONTENTS: p.[4]: last digit at right, bottom of page: 24 | .

BINDING: as 42.22.

NOTE: that p.[4] credits the painting reproduced on the cover
    of 42.22 suggests that copies of 42.24 exist with the
    binding of 42.23, but I have not seen such copies.

COPY EXAMINED: personal

    [Buccaneer Books, 1983]

43.1   D. H. LAWRENCE | Lady | Chatterley's | Lover | [rule]
        | BUCCANEER BOOKS, INC.

(8 1/2 x 5 1/2"): [1-9]^{16}, 144 leaves; pp.[2], [1-4], 5-283,
[284], [2].

CONTENTS: pp.[2]:blank. p.[1]:t.p. p.[2]: THE COMPLETE
    UNEXPURGATED EDITION | OF THE WORLD-FAMOUS NOVEL |
    Copyright © 1983 by Buccaneer Books, Inc. | International
    Standard Book Number: *0-89966-375-3* | For ordering
    information, contact: | BUCCANEER BOOKS, Inc. | Box 168,
    Cutchogue, N.Y. 11935 | pp.[3-4]: blank. pp.5-283: text.
    p.[284]: blank. pp.[2]:blank.

TYPOGRAPHY: text: 45ll. (p.15), 179 x 102mm. 10ll.=39mm. Face
    3(2x)mm.

Typeface: Times Roman (R52). old style; DIN 1.13, Mod.
Renaissance. Title, on t.p., set in ITC Firenze.

PAPER: smooth white wove unwatermarked. Thickness   .07mm.
Total bulk 11.7mm.

BINDING: linen-grain(T304) cloth, yellowish gray(C93).
Gold-stamped on spine, top to bottom: LADY CHATTERLEY'S
LOVER   D. H. LAWRENCE I [vertically set, at tail: [logo:
Ren. galleon] I BUCCANEER All edges trimmed. Plain white
endpapers. Head and tail bands in red.

NOTE: probably issued without d.j., for libraries. The title,
on t.p., is set in ITC Firenze, as in 42.9-42.17 above.

COPY EXAMINED: personal

SECTION 6

Post-Censorship British Editions, 1960–88

INTRODUCTORY ESSAY

The circumstances under which *Lady Chatterley's Lover* was de-censored in England were quite different than those which applied a year earlier in America. Penguin Books, and its founder Allen Lane, were respected institutions, as sound in stature as in capital. Lane did not need to make a lot of money, establish a specialty, or deliver a body-blow to the censors. The avowed reason for the Penguin *Chatterley* (and for several other titles issued at the same time) was to establish, on the thirtieth anniversary of the author's death, a "Lawrence Million": that many copies of his work in Penguin reprints (Morpurgo 314)./1/ A reformed Obscene Publications Act had been passed in 1959; although the Director of Public Prosecutions (D.P.P.) quickly decided to proceed against Penguin, evidence is conflicting (Loth 214, Morpurgo 314–16) regarding whether or not Lane believed it inevitable. Morpurgo points out that the firm's other Lawrence titles were now used in colleges, and that Penguin, which no one would accuse of the mass-market sensationalism that might be thought to motivate Ace or Pan Books, did not initially bother to consult a lawyer. On the other hand, Lane's own testimony at the Old Bailey trial indicates that without the new law's protection, Penguin may not have risked possible prosecution:

> [Although] we had considered [publishing *Chatterley*] in 1950 . . . we wouldn't be in the position we are in today to defend it. This year, the fact that the new Act was now on the Statute Book and that there had been a trial in America decided us that this was a book we should do now. (Rolph 142)

Rosset had published with the intention of forcing a court test of an established, repressive practice. Of course, Judge Bryan's decision and the subsequent availability of the title in the U.S. may have led Penguin to believe that sensible public officials (and tired customs officers/2/) would greet

its own version with tolerance. That the D.P.P. did not do so was contingent on the Penguin format: not an expensive hardback but a three-shilling-and-sixpence (albeit tactfully designed and printed) paperback, which would easily fall into the hands of shop girls and working class boys, some of whom were angry at the Establishment (Sutherland, *Off. Lit.* 22, Craig 172). The paperback appeal was particularly to the young, who bought these books even when only a little less expensive than the hardbacks. To acquire and provide safe housing for the latter was a sign of a sober-minded citizen but the former could be treated as irreverently as any other expendable item with which one blithely rambled about (Mumby and Norrie, 5th ed. 424).

The prosecution stressed the subversive elements: four-letter words gratuitously used, the general immorality (especially for a British female) of exalting sexual pleasure over Christian obligations, and the specific licence Lawrence gives (circumstances notwithstanding) to adultery. Also fully scrutinized was the apparent sodomy in Chapter 16 (in America, Charles Rembar forestalled discussion of this by invoking the Whole Book provision)./3/ Lawrence probed at the most untouchable British taboos. He did so, as Graham Hough (159-62) shows, with pent-up fury at having his message restricted by what he felt were demonic and prurient-minded enemies of compassion and "warm-hearted" communion. The special hostility Horatio Bottomley and others felt in 1928 for *Lady Chatterley's Lover* did not end with its de-censorship. In 1968 Lawrence Durrell remarked "it is strange the effect of this taboo [the four-letter words]. I have seen people turn white with rage at a mention of this book" (ix). Geoffrey Gorer (180) explains that British family life and values require the dutiful wife and mother not to become unfocussed by entertaining the possibility of personal sexual gratification. The liberal attitude prevailed with the jury, but such a struggle for minds and hearts was not easily resolved, despite what the expert witnesses might climb the academic bandwagon to say about Lawrence's respect for marriage and his puritanism. Perhaps Penguin's own sigh of relief is evident in its dedication of post-trial impressions with the Hoggart Introduction (44.11 et. seq.) to the jurors.

None of the Prosecution's arguments would have been nearly as strong as conservatives thought they were if paperback publication (even by Penguin) at 3 shillings 6 pence had not been at issue. Part of Lane's initial unconcern was the lack of objection to Nabokov's *Lolita* (published in hardback), in which intercourse between a sophisticated adult and a teenage girl is explicitly described. The novel had come out in 1959 (there was no scatological diction therein) and the D.P.P. had not moved against it (Craig 114). Nor had he interfered with T. E. Lawrence's *The Mint* when, in 1955, a limited edition was issued with the four-letter words: the trade edition (also in hard covers) replaced them with empty space (Craig 116). The debate in the House of Lords (in December 1960) suggests that the chief focus of concern involved mass-produced softcovers which were popular with

teenagers and the working class generally. The Earl of Craven:

> I made a trip up the M1. . . . the day that *Lady Chatterley's Lover* went on sale to the public and there [in a restaurant], at every serving counter, sat a sniggle of youths. Every one of them had a copy of this book held up to his face. . . . They held the seeds of suggestive lust, which was expressed quite blatantly, by glance and remark, to the girls serving them. . . . We have given a shove to the ball of promiscuity which is, in any case, rolling downhill at an alarming rate. (Rolph 269)

Lord Amwell:

> I would let [only] the libraries, both public and private, have the book in its unexpurgated form. But . . . anyone who wants to read the book should produce his *bona fides* that he is not pornographically minded, and that he has some consideration for the future of literature and the interests of art. (Rolph 273)

For these guardians of culture, the "rough-handed [truck] drivers" Mumby and Norrie (443) describe as double-parking outside bookshops to buy a copy prove that the working classes have not the enlightened self-restraint necessary to uphold moral values. Sutherland (*Off. Lit.* 23-24) points out that the jury's decision was seen as an affirmation of the proletariat's, and young people's, right to read, without having to prove their loyalty to the respectability which binds the middle-aged middle classes. Witness Richard Hoggart's defense of the book was along these lines, as was the lower-wrapper blurb on Penguin's trade edition of Rolph's *The Trial of Lady Chatterley*: "For it was not just a legal tussle, but a conflict of generation and class."/4/ For further evidence Sutherland (24) quotes the Pan Books' blurb for Sillitoe's *Saturday Night and Sunday Morning*: "Thirty years have passed since D. H. Lawrence's proletarian hero - Lady Chatterley's Lover - shook the bookshops. Now, from the Lawrence country, comes a new author . . . " In this connection it is interesting that the British judge appeared to be in favor of continuing the ban (Rolph 237-48), and that several public libraries, including (because of opposition from the City Council) Nottingham's, did not purchase the book (Thompson 114-20).

While in America the book's liberation was contingent on its being marketed on the basis of literary merit not prurient fascination, in England there was a slightly different focus: the jury found the novel not likely to corrupt or deprave those millions ready to spend a nominal sum to read it. That it had been published in a non-prurient format by a firm everyone saw as an exemplary conservator of English tradition was, however, an important element in this decision.

Sutherland (*Off. Lit*.172-74) describes the preeminent position Allen Lane and his Penguins had attained since World War II. Penguins had the status of hardbacks, were welcomed in all kinds of bookstores, and their unillustrated covers were a token of their seriousness. This made it possible for respectable British book buyers to feel easy about being seen purchasing and reading the Penguin *Chatterley*. This firm, as one of its directors, Sir William Emrys Williams, testified, would not publish an expurgated, thus "dirty," "unwholesome" edition (Bedford 145). Frederick Warburg (194-95) opines that Lane was risking little in precipitating the trial. He reasoned that, apart from the fact that the new law allowed the book to be banned without the publisher being subject to criminal proceedings, if Lane and his enterprize were even faintly in danger of conviction, it would cause "a crisis of unforeseeable proportions." Actually, it was only the publishing house, not Lane, which was at risk at the Old Bailey. Unlike Warburg, who, only a few years before, had to appear in the dock at the beginning of his trial for publishing an obscene work, Lane was allowed to sit with his lawyer throughout (Craig 162).

There was no "Chatterley Sweepstakes" in the U.K. No paperback publisher could compete with Penguin, whereas U.S. firms were initially outselling the (unauthorized; see Section 5, pp.125-26) Grove hardback. Lane's reputation, as well as the gentlemanly traditions of British publishing, were also factors. Penguin sold three million copies in the first year, after having initially printed 200,000 (in itself double the usual number and twice as many as needed for the Lawrence Million [Morpurgo 315]). After the trial, Hazel, Watson and Viney printed 800,000 more copies in two press runs. Rubber plates were flown to Holland on 3 November where 250,000 copies were prepared. Western and Cox and Wyman also impressed large runs, which were followed by reprintings by Cox and Wyman and the Utrecht firm. See 44.2-44.10. Pollinger (238) says that 1,986,121 copies were sold during the first six weeks of publication, and 1,240,435 during the first six months of 1961. The windfall profits were serendipitous; when Penguin became a public company in April 1961, its shares sold very well and at high prices (Morpurgo 328-29).

Unlike Grove's or NAL's edition, Penguin's called for no special publicity. Its unillustrated covers were not necessitated by legal considerations of serious intent, but by an inviolable axiom of Allen Lane's "programme," precisely stated by his biographer and colleague: "that no other paperback could ever be mistaken for a Penguin and that no Penguin could ever have thought to have been produced by some other firm" (Morpurgo 218). While the US softcover editions of *Chatterley* started as mass-market books, Penguin's (despite the initially large press runs) had from the first most of the characteristics of trade paperbacks. It was only in the mid-seventies, after Lane's death, that one finds cover illustrations at all, and then dignity is preserved with, in the case of *Lady Chatterley's Lover* and *The First Lady Chatterley*, a suite of photographs combining variously the youthful beauty of the (clothed) human body, the fragil-

ity of flowers, the tenderness of lovers, and the elemental toughness of their background (see 44.22-44.27, 44.39, 45.1). Even the 1982 movie tie-in impression (44.36) is elegantly designed with the pale yellow blank space as prominent as the characters themselves. Mellors brandishes a key to the hut; even here, "phallic" does not mean, as Lane contemptuously put it, "bosoms and bottoms." There is of course highly charged erotic meaning, "sensitively" implied. The same is true of the suite of photographs by Peccinotti (44.22, 56.1, 58.1), with their implication that the owners of the hat and the coat are elsewhere, exploring their bodies and consciousness.

Lane's "points of sale" were those of hardbacks: bookstores, which since World War II, when Penguins won stature as a symbol of British resilience, had made space for them in part as a patriotic gesture. Not needing to attract the eyes of patrons of drug or cigar stores, transportation centers, or food markets, the Penguin covers remain unique, even if this means changing the cover artwork now that American trade paperbacks are using classical paintings on their covers. In 1985, Penguin advertised a "New Look" to take place over an 18-month period, combining Penguin Classics, Penguin English Library, and Penguin American Library into the "brand new series of Penguin Classics-- creating the most comprehensive library of world literature from any paperback publisher. Penguin offers *five times* as many classic literature titles as Bantam . . . ." (Advertisement in PMLA 100 [Nov. 1985]: 1114). Penguin saw the value of the academic market in Britain from the first and in both England and the U.S. takes the strongest possible advantage of it (Morpurgo 248-49, 382). For copyright reasons it does not distribute *Lady Chatterley* (which is not included in the Penguin Classics series) in this country.

Just as the British paperback *Chatterley* has a different history than the American versions, so have the British hardbacks, which have been controlled by Heinemann. Its Phoenix Edition (17.32-17.34, 46.1-46.3), a standard set (none such exists in the US), replaced in the late 1950s the old "thin-paper" or "Pocket" volumes (17.12-17.31) taken over from Secker in 1935. Mumby and Norrie (487) credit a Lawrence revival in the late 1950s for the change. The Phoenix *Chatterley* is no longer available. Heinemann reset the work in 1981 (46.1), in a more austere format which is some 80 pages shorter and is possibly targeted primarily for sale to libraries. Since plans were underway for the Cambridge University Press authoritative edition of Lawrence at that time, and since Heinemann was expected to publish its texts in "their Phoenix edition: a plain text in hardback for the general reader" (Black 55), it is strange that the reset edition appeared when it did. Perhaps the decision had nothing to do with the Cambridge plans. In the mid-1970s, Heinemann made agreements with book clubs and the omnibus edition publisher Peter Hamlyn's Octopus Books to reprint the Phoenix text. The strength of the book clubs (since the 1969 Booksellers' Association decision to allow the clubs simultaneous publication of new fiction), the success of the

Octopus format (see below, and entries 47.1-47.6), and an increasing cost of living in Britain, may have subsequently made the Phoenix Edition difficult to sell. The current Heinemann edition may be targeted for a smaller audience of library borrowers and academics, the market for the Phoenix edition having been taken over, largely, by the omnibus collections. In any event, Heinemann may be presently allowing the book clubs and (especially) Octopus to increase the marketability of its individual hardbacks by their extensive advertising methods.

Omnibus (at times known in the trade as "Pickles"/5/) editions represent another incarnation of Lawrence's work until recently not found in the U.S. At least two firms, imprints of the B. Dalton and Walden chains, do now offer their own four-novel single volume formats (47.5 and 47.6). Peter Curwen tells us that the Heinemann/Octopus editions date from 1976, and were conceived to "breathe new life into a novel which has run out of steam in hardback format." They were sold only to wholesalers through the W. H. Smith outlet [which was given 50% discount], thus "guarantee[ing] sale of an entire print run combined with minimal distribution and selling costs." Under these conditions the price could be kept at the same level as that of a new novel. The idea worked well and earned good press reviews, with half the total number (1,500,000) being sold outside England (36). The innovative Peter Hamlyn, who had declared early in his career that the English would buy in quantity attractive and cheap books, acquired Octopus from Rupert Murdoch in 1976 and by 1979 had made it the largest of all hardback U.K. publishers (Norrie 6th ed.: 113-15).

Both British book club *Chatterleys* were printed from Heinemann plates. The Heron (46.4-46.5) is illustrated; otherwise it and the Guild (46.6) subeditions of the Phoenix edition are bound in a similar grade of imitation leather with gold stamping (see also the US book club editions [40.1, 40.1], discussed in the essay for Section 5). The format imitates the traditional look of a custom-bound 19th-century tome from a gentleman's library. The clients the book clubs discovered in the 1970's form an important group of contemporary readers. Sutherland (*Fiction* 189-94) and Curwen (84-85) describe them. Members of a book club (The Literary Guild and W. H. Smith's Book Club Associates are the largest) would not be likely to include the truck drivers, prurient adolescents, or classless young adventurers whom conservatives stigmatized as wrongly motivated, morally ambivalent readers of the Penguin paperback. They may be new readers, they may well be young, but they are likely to be college-trained, upwardly mobile people, who have settled down in comfortable flats or homes, commute to bureaucratic or professional positions and accept themselves and their aspirations as middle-class. They do not have a great amount of time (or money) to spend choosing reading matter for themselves (and for their children's education), nor to regularly read reviews or browse in bookshops. Being addicted to consumerism, they find that commercial lending libraries do not provide the satisfaction of ownership. Able to choose in the

privacy of their own homes from a list of books (some new, most reprints) advertised as selected by respected bookmen, they can assure themselves of having on their shelves works which reflect modern good taste, not the avant garde. That *Lady Chatterley's Lover* can be included (on both sides of the Atlantic) by organizations which appeal to these motives for buying books indicates the extent to which it has outgrown its reputation for subversive indecency and has become integrated into the canon of twentieth century literary classics. If this audience analysis has any validity, one suspects that most book club readers would not be prepared to identify with Mellors, as did some Penguin witnesses at the Old Bailey, as a proletarian hero.

Book clubs "package" some classic novels (as the Authorized Edition was in the thirties) as erotic romance (see essay for Section 5, pp.133–34). Of course, Lawrence does not exploit what Sutherland (*Fiction* 192–93) describes as the stereotyped characters and diction, formulaic plot, and "soothing" messages of genre fiction, although there are some who attack *Chatterley* as containing these elements (see essay for Section 3, p.65). Regardless of the advertising, readers of Heron or Guild subeditions are as free as any others to see in Lawrence's story a radical challenge to established ways of ignoring sexual desire as a foundation for human relationships. It was this serious appeal to intellectual value that won freedom for the Grove edition in 1959. Paperback blurbs still tend to sell the work that way; from 1960 through the seventies Penguin (44.11, 44.22, 44.36) and Heinemann (see the omnibus subedition 47.4) also suggested that Lawrence's message is especially relevant to the young and disenfranchised in a country wrestling with social injustice. These publishers were merely using appeals to which their own audiences were susceptible. For the same purpose, American versions have managed to hint, with cover art at least, that *Chatterley* satisfies the ubiquitous prurient interests most of us acknowledge in our psyches (see essay for Section 5, pp.129–32, 135–36). A publisher is a businessperson, and is guided by what is effective. S/he uses the available media to run his/her business; this is especially true of the advertising-conscious marketers of book club and omnibus editions. It is the writers who have messages, and the responsibility of keeping these alive is ultimately that of the readers, to whom publishers cannily deliver the work in various formats.

A major event in the history of *Lady Chatterley's Lover* will be its appearance in the Cambridge University Press definitive edition, edited by Professor Michael Squires. There will be both a clothbound and a paperback impression with full editorial apparatus (Black 57). "Granada will issue an edition for the general reader without the scholarly apparatus" (Pollinger 241). Exactly how its appearance will affect future reprintings of the editions now in print in England and America is yet to be made public.

ENDNOTES

1. Other writers accorded this "literary equivalent of a peerage," as Allen Lane's biographer J. E. Morpurgo (267) puts it: Shaw, Wells, Waugh, Georges Simenon, Agatha Christie.

2. The assiduousness with which British customs confiscated copies of the Grove Press edition is open to question. Loth reports "a lot of people brought copies of the unexpurgated American edition into the country without interference by the customs" (211). Bedford (132) confirms Loth's observation. However, Frieda Lawrence's daughter Barbara Barr had a different experience. A newspaper clipping tipped in to a copy of 1.10 at LO/N-1 states that twelve copies belonging to her were confiscated by customs officials, and adds that "in recent weeks travellers from the United States had copies impounded by Customs at London Airport." (I regret that I have been unable to locate the newspaper in which this story appeared).

   The Defense made a strong point of appealing to the jury's fairness to British students who might not have been able to see unexpurgated copies of a key book by a major novelist. Even with tourists' carry-backs unconfiscated, there could hardly be enough to go around. Also, even if U.S. paperbacks were brought in without challenge, reputable booksellers could not sell them. See also the essay for Appendix 1 (p.246) and A7.2 below.

   Please note (see p.18 above) that 20th-century British booksellers were more likely to provide under-the-counter copies than were their American counterparts. A propos of the availability of the unexpurgated *Chatterley* in the U.S. prior to summer 1959, the Tariff Act of 1930 granted scholars the opportunity to petition the Secretary of the Treasury to allow them to import for private study single copies of works which their colleagues acknowledged to possess ". . . established literary or scientific merit." From 1935 on, such petitions for *Chatterley* were successful (Paul 126-27).

3. In addition to the edited transcript of the trial in Rolph (the Penguin paperback, unlike the hardback privately issued by Lane for friends, leaves out the debate in the House of Lords), excellent discussions of the trial are found in Loth (210-21), Sutherland, *Off. Lit.* (10-31), and Craig (163-71).

4. This appeal was not limited to 1960. Both LCL, and the 1986 comic book version (see A13.1 and pp.249-51 in Appendix I), were advertised as follows in the Christmas 1988 catalogue of the mail order distributor Last Gasp Of San Francisco: "You have read the (hilarious) comic version by [cartoonist] Hunt Emerson, now read the original and discover the possible political reasons for the banning of this literary classic."

5. So dubbed after one of its originators, Charles Pick, managing director of the Heinemann group (Pollinger 239).

BIBLIOGRAPHICAL DESCRIPTIONS (for another POST-CENSORSHIP
     BRITISH EDITION, see 31.3 above)

     [Penguin Edition -- special proof copies]

44.1   D. H. LAWRENCE | [French rule] | *Lady Chatterley's
        Lover* | PENGUIN BOOKS

(7 3/4 x 4 7/8"): [1]^{16} 2-10^{16}, 160 leaves; pp.[4], 5-317,
[318], [2]. $1(-[1]) signed L.C.L.-[sig.#]

CONTENTS: p.[1]: half-title: PENGUIN BOOKS | 1484 | LADY
     CHATTERLEY'S LOVER | D. H. LAWRENCE | [penguin logo] |.
     p.[2]: blank. p.[3]:t.p. p.[4]: Made and printed in Great
     Britain | by Hazell Watson and Viney Ltd | Aylesbury and
     Slough |. pp.5-317: text. p.[318]: blank. pp.[2]: blank.

TYPOGRAPHY: Text: 40ll.(p.65), 153(157) x 89mm. 10ll.=38mm.
     Face 3(2x)mm. Typeface: R.91, Garamond 156(Monotype).
     Transitional. DIN 1.24, modern baroque.

PAPER: rough white wove unwatermarked. Thickness .06mm.
     Total bulk   11.5mm.

BINDING: paper wrappers, white. Upper cover: D. H. LAWRENCE |
     [French rule] | *Lady Chatterley's Lover* | PENGUIN BOOKS |
     PROOF ONLY |. Spine and lower cover blank.

NOTE: perfect bound; collation based on signatures.
     Norrie (6th ed.: 182) says that Penguin sent proof copies
     to booksellers, contrary to the firm's usual practice.

COPIES EXAMINED: OkTU, TxU, personal

     *[Penguin: first pre-trial, and two post-trial impres-
     sions]*

44.2   as 44.1 save:

(7 1/8 x 4 3/8"): [1]^{16} 2-10^{16}, 160 leaves; pp.[4], 5-316,
[317-18], [2]. $1(-[1]) signed L.C.L.-[sig.#]

CONTENTS: p.[4]: Penguin Book Ltd, Harmondsworth, Middlesex |
     AUSTRALIA: Penguin Books Pty Ltd, 762 Whitehorse Road, |
     Mitcham, Victoria | [short rule] | First Printed 1928 |
     This complete text first published in | Great Britain 1960
     | Made and printed in Great Britain | by Western Printing
     Services Ltd | Bristol |. pp.5-[317]: text. p.[318]:
     blank.

TYPOGRAPHY: Text: 40ll.(p.65), 153(156) x 88mm. 10ll.=38mm.
     Face 3(2x)mm.

PAPER: rough white wove unwatermarked. Thickness .06mm.
Total bulk 11.1mm.

BINDING: coated paper wrappers, orange and white. Upper
cover: vertical strips of orange at spine (17mm) and fore-
edge (20mm). Lettering on white background. [in orange:]
PENGUIN BOOKS I [rule] I [in black:] LADY I CHATTERLEY'S I
LOVER I [Lawrence phoenix in yellow and black] I D. H. I
LAWRENCE I [rule] I COMPLETE AND 3/6 UNEXPURGATED [price
in orange] I. On orange strip at foreedge, in oval, in
black on white background: penguin logo. Spine: [orange
strip, 17mm.] I [on white background, in black save logo
in orange, set top to bottom:] D. H. Lawrence [penguin
logo] Lady Chatterley's Lover I [set left to right:] 1484
I [rule] I [orange strip, 20mm] I. Lower cover: orange and
white, as on upper cover (logo at foreedge). [in orange:]
PENGUIN BOOKS I [in black:] [rule] I [portrait of Lawrence, with three paragraph biographical sketch] I [rule] I
[in orange:] PENGUIN BOOKS I. Edges trimmed, unstained.
Recto: blurb from *Times* about Lawrence "coming into his
own in 1960." List of seven works by Lawrence published by
Penguin "to mark thirtieth anniversary of [his] death."
Begins *Women In Love*, ends *Letters*. Verso upper wrapper: statements by Lawrence about the "sex relation"; and
(by publisher) denying that the novel is "in any sense of
the word, pornographic." The censorship was caused by
attacks on "the language," which "ignored the tenderness.
. . . It has taken over thirty years for it to be possible
to publish the unmutilated version in the country." Also:
statement by Anthony West; "Cover device by Stephen Russ."
Offer of Penguin list.

NOTES: Printed (by Hazell, Watson, and Viney) in order to
establish the fact of publication. When prosecution became
inevitable, Penguin turned over twelve copies to the
police. Publication date was set for August 25. Penguin so
notified Scotland Yard when the 12 copies were handed over
(Craig 162-63).
    For Lane's dislike of the American branch's garish
covers, see Essay for Section 3 (p.62) above. Some copies
of the pre-trial impr. were mistakenly, and for Penguin
and its printer embarrassingly, put on sale in Nottingham
and other locations in England. They were quickly withdrawn. Penguin did include warnings with its advance
shipments to the effect that the book should not be sold
before the original publication date of 25 August (*Bookseller*, 20 Aug., 1960: 989; PW 5 Sept. 1960: 41). This
printing, warehoused pending the court decision, numbered
200,000. Publication date was Nov. 10. After the decision,
Hazell, Watson, and Viney printed, from new plates, at
first 300,000 and then 500,000 more copies (*Bookseller* 5
Nov. 1960: 1043; 12 Nov. 1960: 2036).
    The Cambridge U. exhibition catalogue (25) states that
the University library received its copy (as per copyright
deposit regulations, one assumes) on 19 October.
    Lane's original intention in publishing the unexpurgated
Chatterley, according to Morpurgo (314), was to make the

200,000 copy run indicate that Penguin had 1,000,000
copies of Lawrence (a "Penguin Million") in print.
  Information regarding printing of the first Penguin
impression was found in the following issues of *The Bookseller* for 1960: 11/5,p.1043; 11/12,pp.2036, 2062, 2064,
2065; 11/19, p.2099, 2123.

COPIES EXAMINED: OkTU; NO/P-1(copy 1)

*44.3   [300,000 copies]

*44.4   [500,000 copies]

    [Post-Trial Impressions]

*44.5   Printed in the Netherlands by N. V. Drukkerij Busch
          in Utrecht. Rubber plates were flown to Holland the
          day the censorship decision was announced. This, *The
          Bookseller* reports, was the first "reprinting."
          Copies numbered 250,000 (*Bookseller* 12 Nov. 1960:
          2036 [this is also the source for #44.6-44.8 below]).

44.6   as 44.2 save:

CONTENTS: p.[4]: 1.9-10: by Western Printing Services Ltd |
    Bristol |.

NOTE: I have found no information on the number of copies
    Western printed.

COPIES EXAMINED: personal, Forster Coll., NO/P-1(copy 2),
    ICarbS

*44.7   There were 100,000 printed by Hunt, Barnard from
          rubber plates supplied by Hazell, Watson and Viney.

*44.8   Immediately after the decision, Cox and Wyman began
          plating and printing 600,000 copies (order raised
          from 300,000).

44.9   as 44.6 save:

(7 1/8 X 4 1/4"): [A]^{16} B-K^{16}, 160 leaves. $1(-[A]) signed T
- L.C.L.- [sig. no.]

CONTENTS: p.[4], 1.8: Reprinted 1960 | Made and printed in
    Great Britain | By Cox and Wyman Ltd | London, Reading,
    and Fakenham

TYPOGRAPHY: Text: 40ll., p.97, 152(157) x 90mm. 10ll.=39mm.
    Face: 3(2x)mm.

PAPER: smooth white wove unwatermarked. Thickness .08mm.
    Total bulk 13.1mm.

COPY EXAMINED: personal

44.10   as 44.8 save:

$1 signed L.C.L.-[sig. #]

CONTENTS: p.[4], l.8: Reprinted 1960 | Made and Printed in
    the Netherlands | by N. V. Drukkerij Busch | Utrecht |.

NOTE: Pollinger (238) states that sales from November to
    December 1960 totalled 1,986,121.

COPIES EXAMINED: OkTU, TxU

44.11   as 44.9 save:

added after l.3: WITH AN INTRODUCTION BY | RICHARD HOGGART |
PENGUIN BOOKS

(7 1/8 x 4 1/4"): [A]^{16} B-E^{16} F^8 G-L^{16}, 168 leaves;
pp.[i-iv], v-xiv, [xv-xvi], [1-4], 5-316, [317-18], [2].
$1 (-[A]) signed T-L.C.L.-[sig.#]

CONTENTS: p.[iv]: l.8: Second edition, with an introduction
    by Richard Hoggart, 1961 | Introduction copyright © by
    Richard Hoggart, 1961 | Made and printed in Great Britain
    | by Cox and Wyman, Ltd., | London, Reading, and Fakenham
    |. pp.v-[xv]: Introd. p.[xvi]: blank. p.[1]: PUBLISHER'S
    DEDICATION [to jurors who adjudged novel not obscene at
    the 1960 trial] |. p.[2]: blank. p.[3]: section title.
    p.[4]:blank. pp.5-[317]: text. p.[318]: blank. p.[31920]:
    Penguin list of Lawrence titles. Begins *Kangaroo*, ends
    Twilight. p.[320]: ad for Moore's *Intelligent Heart*.

TYPOGRAPHY: Text: 40ll.(p.97), 152(157) x 90. 10ll.=37mm.
    Face:3(2x)mm.

PAPER: Thickness 08mm. Total bulk 13.7mm.

BINDING: upper wrapper: author's name followed by: [short
    rule] | *with an introduction by* | RICHARD HOGGART |. Lower
    wrapper: no photo. Three paragraphs on novel: excerpt from
    novel regarding public's hostility to sex as "natural and
    vital," history of the work's banning, plot summary.
    Blurbs from E. M. Forster, TLS. Under rule: *For copyright
    reasons this edition is not | for sale in the U.S.A. or
    Canada |*. Verso l.c.: advert for *Rolph's Trial of Lady
    Chatterley*. Verso u.c.: photo of Lawrence, biographical
    sketch, credit for cover design, offer of Penguin list.

NOTE: unlike previous impressions, this one is perfect-bound.
    Gathering was inferred from signings.
        During first six months of 1961 sales totalled 1,240,435
    (Pollinger 238). Morpurgo (325-26) states that Penguin
    projected modest sales but because of trial publicity
    profits were £112,000.
        Copyright notice probably refers to fact that NAL

editions, both expurgated (20.1-21.4) and unexpurgated (37.1), had been authorized by the Lawrence estate.

COPIES EXAMINED: TxU, OkTU, LO/N-1

44.12   as 44.11 save:

CONTENTS: p.[4]: ll.9-12: Reprinted 1961 | Introduction copyright © by Richard Hoggart, 1961 | [short rule] | Copyright © 1960 D. H. Lawrence Estate |.

BINDING: lower cover: copyright statement: last two words excised.

NOTE: one of my personal copies has a paper sticker reading "6/-" covering price (3/6 in orange) on upper cover. This copy contains clippings for the Melbourne (Australia) *Advertiser* for September 1965, when the ban on the novel was lifted in that country. The sticker reflects the Australian price of the Penguin edition (in this case, the 1961 impression).

COPIES EXAMINED: personal(2 copies)

44.13   as 44.12 save:

No sigs.; perfect bound.

CONTENTS: p.[1]: three-paragraph biographical note added under half-title. p.[4], l.2: Penguin Books Pty Ltd, Ringwood, Victoria, Australia. l.7: Reprinted 1961, 1965 |. ll.12- 14: Made and Printed in great Britain | by C. Nicholls & Company Ltd | Set in Monotype Garamond |.

BINDING: verso both covers blank.

COPY EXAMINED: Pollinger Coll.

44.14   as 44.13 save:

t.p.: Penguin logo above imprint statement

CONTENTS: p.[4]: ll.8-15: Reprinted 1961, 1965, 1966 | Introduction copyright © by Richard Hoggart, 1961 | [short rule] | Copyright © 1960 D. H. Lawrence Estate | Made and printed in Great Britain | by C. Nicholls & Company Ltd | Set in Monotype Garamond |. ll.16-23: This book. . . . subsequent purchaser |.

NOTE: the 8ll. statement at bottom of p.[4], called the "[Gerald] Pollinger line", was devised to clarify a public lending right dispute between public libraries and publishers, who objected to the commercial rebinding of paperbacks in boards for use in libraries. This encouraged multiple lendings and discouraged sales. The practice, which Morpurgo calls "profit-purloining" (264-65), might have led to hardback publishers postponing the granting of paperback rights (see *Bookseller* 5 Nov. 1960: 1843, 12

Nov. 1960: 2024; 11 Dec. 1960: 2412; Pollinger 238-39).
Heinemann alone, Pollinger explains, was granted hardback
rights by the Lawrence Estate.

COPY EXAMINED: personal

44.15   as 44.14 save:

CONTENTS: 1.8: Reprinted 1961, 1965, 1966, 1967 I.

COPY EXAMINED: personal

44.16   as 44.15 save:

t.p.: added after imprint: *in association with William
Heinemann Ltd*

leaves measure 7 1/8 x 4 1/4"

CONTENTS: p.[4]: 1.8: Reprinted 1961, 1965, 1966, 1967, 1969
I. [short rule] I Copyright © the Estate of D. H. Lawrence, 1960 I Introduction copyright © by Richard Hoggart,
1961 I [short rule] I Made and printed in Great Britain I
by C. Nicholls & Company Ltd I Set in Monotype Garamond I
[Pollinger statement] I. p.[1]: MORE ABOUT PENGUINS I.
p.[2]: list of 26 Lawrence titles.

PAPER: thickness .06mm. Total bulk 13.4mm.

BINDING: coated paper wrappers, white. Upper cover: [upper
    right: penguin logo, in oval with orange background] I [in
    blue:] Lady Chatterley's I Lover I [in orange]: D. H.
    Lawrence I [in silver: Lawrence phoenix] I [in orange:]
    With an introduction by Richard Hoggart I. On spine,
    orange background, set top to bottom: [in black:]
    D.H.Lawrence [in white:] Lady Chatterley's Lover [in
    black:] 140014845 [penguin logo] I. Lower cover: [in
    black:] Complete and unexpurgated [in upper right:]
    penguin logo, on orange background I [22 line plot
    summary. ". . . honest, healthy book, necessary for us
    today. The greatest writers of our day, and millions of
    readers, have united in agreement with him."] I Cover
    design by Heather Mansell, incorporating an illustration
    by I Stephen Russ I For copyright reasons . . . U.S.A. I
    [Prices: UK 25p, 5/-; Canada $1.15 (also New Zealand,
    Australia, South Africa)]. [At lower right] 140014845

COPY EXAMINED: Pollinger Coll.

*44.17   "1969"

*44.18   "1970"

44.19   as 44.16 save:

 CONTENTS: p.[4]: 1.8: Reprinted 1961, 1965, 1966, 1967,
    1969(twice), 1970, 1971 I.

BINDING: on spine, above Penguin logo: ISBN 0 14 | 00.1484 5
|. Lower cover: list of prices (40p 8/-, UK; Canada
$1.65). At lower right: FICTION | ISBN 0 14 | 00.1484 5 |.

COPY EXAMINED: personal, Pollinger Coll.

44.20   as 44.19 save:

CONTENTS: p.[4], l.8: Reprinted 1961, 1965, 1966, 1967, 1968,
1969 (twice), 1970, 1971, 1972

COPY EXAMINED: Pollinger Coll.

*44.21   "1973"

44.22   as 44.20 save:

leaves measure: 7 1/8 x 4 1/2"

CONTENTS: p.[iv]: addresses of offices on England, Australia,
Canada, New Zealand. l.11: Reprinted 1961, 1965, 1966,
1967, 1969(twice), 1970, 1971, 1972, 1973 (twice) |.

BINDING: coated paper wrappers, white. Upper wrapper: [pen-
guin, in black, no oval border] | D. H. LAWRENCE [in
greenish yellow; A and W worked together; final stroke of
A and first stroke of W shared] | [in black:] LADY
CHATTERLEY'S LOVER | [photo of tattered and patched coat
on hook, with bouquet of flowers (daisies) in lapel (part
of the suite of photos by Harri Peccinotti used for
Penguin LCL and JTLJ). Colors: light olive brown,
yellowish brown, deep brown, white and yellow]. Lower
wrapper: Lawrence phoenix, photo of DHL, summary of novel,
credits (H. Peccinotti, Notts. Public Library), price (UK
40p; Canada $1.65; Australia $1.35). Spine: D.H.LAWRENCE
[A and W worked together] LADY CHATTERLEY'S LOVER ISBN 0
14 | 00.1484 5 [penguin logo, (no oval border)] |.

NOTE: Flowers on upper cover possibly represent the "roaring"
flowers Notts. miners, incl. DHL's father, wore in their
coats. For similar art work on Penguin impressions of *John
Thomas and Lady Jane*, see 58.1-58.4 below.
    Illustrated covers on Penguins appeared only after Allen
Lane's death (7 July 1970).

COPY EXAMINED: LO/N-1

44.23   as 44.22 save:

CONTENTS: p.[iv]: . . . 1973 (twice), 1974 |.

BINDING: Upper cover: colors in photo are yellowish green,
grayish olive, grayish brown, white and pale yellow (flowers). Lower wrapper: Price 50p, $1.95 Canada.

COPY EXAMINED: OkTU

44.24   as 44.23 save:

CONTENTS: p.[4], 1.11: 1973 (twice), 1974 (twice) I.

BINDING: Upper wrapper: predominant colors in illustration are strong reddish brown, deep brown, light brown, deep red. Lower wrapper: prices: UK 80p; Australia and N. Z. $2.10; Canada $1.95 I.

COPY EXAMINED: Forster Coll.

*44.25   "1975"

44.26   as 44.23 save:

CONTENTS: p.[iv]: Reprinted . . . 1974 [sic], 1975 (twice)

BINDING: Front wrapper: colors in photo as 44.22. Prices on lower wrapper: United Kingdom 75p; New Zealand $2.55; Canada $2.25.

COPY EXAMINED: OkTU

*44.27   "1976"

44.28   as 44.26 save:

CONTENTS: p.[1]: expanded biographical note (4 paragraphs). p.[4]: 11.1-5: addresses include 625 Madison Ave., USA], 41 Steelcase Road West, Markham, Ontario, Canada. Reprinted . . . 1975 (twice), 1976, 1977 I. p.[2]: advert for S&L; list of 7 titles, beginning AR, ending JTLJ.

PAPER: sheets bulk 12.42mm.

BINDING: Front wrapper illus. in colors as in 44.22. Prices on lower cover: United Kingdom 75p I Canada $1.95 I.

COPY EXAMINED: personal

*44.29   "1978"

*44.30   "1978 (twice)"

*44.31   "1979"

*44.32   "1979 (twice)"

*44.33   "1980"

44.34   as 44.28 save:

CONTENTS: p.[iv]: 11.1-5: addresses for England, US, Australia, Canada, N.Z. . . . . Reprinted . . . 1976, 1977, 1978 (twice), 1979 (twice), 1980 (twice) I. 11.18-19: Made and printed in Great Britain I by Hazell, Watson & Viney Ltd. p.[1]: MORE ABOUT PENGUINS I AND PELICANS I. p.[2]: blank.

BINDING: white background lettered in black. D [dot] H |
LAWRENCE | [rule] | Lady Chatterley's | Lover | [illus.,
enclosed in black border; drawing by Yvonne Gilbert of
man, fully dressed, arms around woman, hair unbound, who
stands with her back to him, dressed in a slip, holding a
daisy. The figures seem to be in their twenties. Large
water-pitcher in left fore-ground. A rifle stands on shelf
at right. Predominant colors brown, orange brown, pinkish
white] | [Penguin logo] |. Spine orange with black
lettering set top to bottom: D[dot]H[dot]LAWRENCE Lady
Chatterley's Lover ISBN 0 14 | 00.1484 5 | [penguin logo]
|. Lower cover: blurb, as in 44.35 var.(2). Cover il-
lustration by Yvonne Gilbert | Photograph of D. H.
Lawrence by courtesy of Nottingham Public Libraries |. At
bottom: photo of author. Prices: UK £1.00 | AUST $3.50 |
(recommended) | CAN $2.95 |. In lower right: Fiction |
ISBN 0 14 | 00.1484 5|.

COPY EXAMINED: Pollinger Coll.

44.35   as 44.34 save:

CONTENTS: p.[4]: Reprinted . . . 1979 (twice), 1980 (twice),
1981 |.

BINDING: Var.(1): as 44.34. Var.(2): upper cover: pale yellow
(C89) background. Still photo from film. Mellors (Nicholas
Clay, on right), Connie (Sylvia Kristel), he holding
before her face the key to the cottage she has asked for.
Both dressed warmly against damp weather, posed against
misty background. Lettering in brown. Above photo: [two
fancy rules] D. H. LAWRENCE [two fancy rules] | Lady
Chatterley's | [two fancy rules] Lover [two fancy rules]
|. Below photo: [thick, thin rule] | Now a sensual film
starring | Sylvia Kristel | [thin-thick rule] | Penguin
logo [in oval with orange background, placed to right of
11.5-7] The typeface imitates the logo for the film as
reproduced on lower cover: [two fancy rules] a JUST
JAECKLIN film [two fancy rules] | SYLVIA KRISTEL in | Lady
Chatterley's Lover | [two fancy rules]. Above the rule,
blurb: Compassion, reverence, and desire | are interwoven
in this revolutionary novel. . . . his most complete and
beautiful study of mutual love. | Writing to liberate the
generations who, he felt, had | regarded sex merely as an
embarrassment or a | mechanical act, he said about the
book: '. . . To me [LCL] is beautiful | and tender and
frail as the naked self is.' (Followed by cast of film.)
On spine, on light red background, set bottom to top: D.
H. LAWRENCE Lady Chatterley's Lover ISBN 014 | 00.1484 5
|. Set vertically: Penguin logo. Prices: UK £1.25; Aust.
$3.95; Can. $2.95.

NOTE: for tie-ins with the Jaecklin film, see #31.16 above
and 49.1 below. The story line of this film follows *The
First Lady Chatterley*, film rights to LCL being the
property of a French firm.

COPY EXAMINED: Var.(1): MH (rebound, upper and lower wrappers preserved); Var.(2): Pollinger Coll.

*44.36   "1981 (twice)"

44.37   as 44.35 Var.(2) save:

CONTENTS: p.[iv]: Reprinted . . . 1978 (twice), | 1979 (twice), 1980 (twice), 1981 (twice), 1982 |. . . Made and Printed in Great Britain | by Hazell Watson & Viney | Ltd. Aylesbury, Bucks | Set in Monotype Garamond |.

COPY EXAMINED: NO/U-1(rebound, wrappers preserved)

*44.38   "1982"

*44.39   "1983"

44.40   as 44.37 save:

CONTENTS: p.[iv]: . . . 1982(twice), 1983, 1984. . . . |. 11.19-22: Printed and bound in Great Britain by | Cox and Wyman Ltd., Reading | Set in Monotype Garamond |. p.[1]: MORE ABOUT PENGUINS, PELICANS | AND PUFFINS [17ll., with addresses of branches in US, Canada, Australia, New Zealand, India]. p.[2]: blank.

PAPER: sheets bulk 12.5mm.

BINDING: as 44.34 save: lower cover: UK £1.95 | AUST $3.95 | (recommended) | CAN $4.95 |. In lower right: Fiction | ISBN 0 14 | 00.1484 5|.

COPY EXAMINED: personal

[Second Penguin Edition, 1984]

45.1   D. H. LAWRENCE | [rule] | *Lady Chatterley's Lover* | WITH AN INTRODUCTION BY | RICHARD HOGGART | [logo: penguin in oval] | PENGUIN BOOKS | *in association with William Heinemann Ltd*

(7 1/8 x 4 3/8): no sigs.; pp.[i-iv], v-xv, [xvi], [1-4], 5-314, [6].

CONTENTS: p.[i]: biographical note as 44.28. p.[ii]: blank. p.[iii]: t.p. p.[iv]: first 12 ll. as 44.40. 1.13 reads: 1979 (twice), 1980 (twice), 1981 (twice), 1982 (twice), 1983, 1984 (twice) |. ll.19-23: Made and printed in Great Britain by | Cox & Wyman Ltd. Reading | Filmset in Linotron Bembo by | Rowland Phototypesetting Ltd. | Bury St. Edmonds, Suffolk |. [At bottom:] Pollinger line. pp.v-xv: Introduction. p.[xvi]:blank. p.[1]: PUBLISHER'S DEDICATION. p.[2]: blank p.[3]: section title. p.[4]: blank. pp.5-314: text. p.[1]: MORE ABOUT PENGUINS,

PELICANS | AND PUFFINS p.[2]:blank. pp.[3-5]: ENGLISH AND
| AMERICAN LITERATURE [list of 14 titles, beginning with
Ward's *Helbeck of Bannisdale*, ending with *Barchester
Towers*. p.[6]: blank.

TYPOGRAPHY: 40ll.(p.117): 148 x 89mm. 10ll.=37mm. Face
2(1x)mm. Typeface: see CONTENTS above.

PAPER: smooth white wove unwatermarked. Thickness .06mm.
Total bulk 12.6mm.

BINDING: same as 44.40, save for price list on l.c.: UK £2.50
| AUST. $4.95 | (recommended) | NZ $8.95 | CAN $4.95 |.

COPY EXAMINED: personal

*45.2   "1985"

*45.3   "1986"

*45.4   "1987"

45.5   as 45.1 save:

t.p.: last line excised.

CONTENTS: p.[4]: PENGUIN BOOKS | Published by the Penguin
Group | 27 Wrights Lane, London W8 5TZ, England | [add-
resses for N.Y., Australia, Canada, N.Z.; 4 lines] |
Penguin Books LTD., Registered Offices: Harmondsworth,
Middlesex, England | [pub. history, 7 ll. Line 8: 1985,
1986, 1987, 1988 |. p.[1] list of 9 Penguin offices
throughout the world. p.[2]: blank. pp.[3]-[4]: list of
Penguin mystery and crime novels; 12 titles. p.[5]:
Penguin Books Of Poetry (29 titles). p.[6]: Penguin Poetry
Library, 17 titles.

BINDING: lower cover: photo of Lawrence excised. Penguin logo
below blurb, with list of prices in UK (£3.50), Aust. NZ,
Can. At right is machine-readable strip.

NOTE: On 25 May 1988 Gerald Pollinger kindly informed me that
the total amount of copies of the Penguin *Lady Chatterley's Lover* sold to December 1987 is 4,681,330.

COPY EXAMINED: personal

[Heinemann Phoenix Edition, 1963(?)]

46.1   D. H. LAWRENCE | [French rule] | *Lady Chatterley's
        Lover* | PREFACED BY THE AUTHOR'S | *Apropos of Lady
        Chatterley's Lover* | [Lawrence phoenix] | WILLIAM
        HEINEMANN LTD | MELBOURNE :: LONDON :: TORONTO

(7 1/4 x 4 7/8"): [A]^{16} B-L^{16} M^8, 184 leaves; pp. [8], 9-364, [4].

CONTENTS: p.[1]:half-title. p.[2]: THE PHOENIX EDITION OF
D. H. LAWRENCE (list of 28 titles, beginning *Women In
Love*, ending with 3 vols. of the short stories; asterisk
after LCL indicates its availability in expurgated and
unexpurgated eds)|. p.[3]:t.p. p.[4]: First Printed 1928 |
This complete text | first published in Great Britain 1960
| *Apropos of Lady Chatterley's Lover* | First published
1930 | This edition 1961 | Printed in Great Britain | by
The Windmill Press Ltd | Kingswood, Surrey |. p.[5]:
CONTENTS |. p.[6]:blank. p.[7]: fly-title. p.[8]:
blank. pp.9-43: text, *A Propos*. p.[44]: blank. p.[45]:
fly-title. p.[46]: blank. pp.[47]-364:text,
LCL. pp.[4]:blank.

TYPOGRAPHY: text: 38ll., p.65, 146(156) x 95mm. 10ll.=38mm.
Face: 3(2x)mm.
Typeface: Pilgrim (linotype)?, R183. Modern (DIN 1.34,
Mod. Neoclassic).

RUNNING HEADS, rectos and versos: pp.10-43: APROPOS OF LADY
CHATTERLEY'S LOVER |. pp.[48]-364: LADY CHATTERLEY'S LOVER
|.

PAPER: smooth white wove unwatermarked. Thickness .1mm. Total
bulk 20.46mm.

BINDING: vivid red (C11), calico grain cloth(T 302). On
spine, stamped in silver: D. H. | LAWRENCE | *Lady* |
Chatterley's | *Lover* | [Lawrence phoenix] | HEINEMANN |.
Plain white endpapers. Edges trimmed.
   DJ: Background in strong yellowish green(C131). Upper
cover: [ll.1-2 in white]: *D. H.* [swash D and H] | LAWRENCE
| [phoenix in red and black] | [ll.4-5 in black]: THE
PHOENIX EDITION | *Complete and unabridged* | [ll.6-8 in red
on white background, in cartouche bordered by two sets of
rules in black, with white triangular-shaped designs at
left and right:] LADY | CHATTERLEY'S | LOVER | [in black,
at bottom of cartouche:] *Prefaced by the author's* |
APROPOS OF LADY CHATTERLEY'S LOVER | [in black, below
cartouche]: WILLIAM HEINEMANN LTD. |. On spine: THE |
PHOENIX | EDITION | OF D. H. | LAWRENCE | [rule] | Lady |
Chatter- | ley's | Lover | COMPLETE | AND | UNEXPURGATED |
22 | [rule] | [pub's logo: windmill] | HEINEMANN [ll.6-10,
15 in white; rest in black] |. Lower cover: list of
Phoenix eds. Flap of lower cover: description of Phoenix
eds: ". . . a form which does full justice to their
position as classics of English literature. Though larger
in format and more elaborately produced than the old
'pocket' edition, The Phoenix Edition is being offered at
a similarly low price." Front flap: blurb, similar in
phrasing to that on the Phoenix expurgated edition (see
17.32-17.34).

NOTE: the price was 15s. For the Heinemann expurgated Phoenix
edition, see 17.32-17.34; for the Heinemann unexpurgated

edition published in the Netherlands in 1956 and for the home market in 1960, see 31.1-31.3.

Although the date of publication is stated on p.[4] to be 1961, both *The Cumulative Book Index* and *British Books In Print* (1970) list the publication date as 1963. I am assuming the statement on p.[4] refers to the Heinemann unexpurgated edition (31.1-31.3), although that appeared in Dec. 1960. See 46.2 below. Entry 31.3 was kept in print through at least 1970, probably because it was half the price of the Phoenix Edition.

COPIES EXAMINED: OkTU(dj), NO/P-1(dj), OX/U-1; Forster Coll.(dj); Pollinger Coll.(dj).

46.2   as 46.1 save:

(7 3/8 x 4 1/2"): [1]^{16} [2]^8 [3-12]^{16}, 184 leaves; pp.[1-8], 9-364, [4].

CONTENTS: p.[2]: no asterisk after LCL or explanation of its availability in expurgated and unexpurgated eds. After first 22 vols. is short rule, followed by nine more titles, beginning FLC, ending *Phoenix*. p.[4]: William Heinemann Ltd I 15 Queen St., Mayfair, London W1X 8BE I LONDON MELBOURNE TORONTO I JOHANNESBURG AUCKLAND I *Apropos of Lady Chatterley's Lover* I First published 1930 I This edition 1961 I First published 1928 I This complete text first published in Great Britain 1960 I Reprinted 1974 I 434 4772 4 I Printed in Austria I by Weiner Verlag, Vienna I .

TYPOGRAPHY: Text: 38ll., p.84, 149(155) x 96mm. 10ll.=37mm. Face:3(2.5)mm.

PAPER: smooth white wove unwatermarked. Thickness .1mm. Total bulk   20.5mm.

BINDING: Dj: £ 2.60 net on front flap, booklist on back flap, beginning FLC, ends *Selected Literary Criticism*. Statement regarding Phoenix edition ends with "classics of English Literature."

NOTE: the signing in this edition are relics of the first impression: sig. [3]8-[12]8 signed F, G, *et seq*.

COPIES EXAMINED: OkTU(dj), NSyU, Pollinger Coll.

46.3   as 46.2 save:

coll.: [A]^{16} B-K^{16} L^8 M^{16}, 184 leaves. Sig. I5 signed I*; sig. K5 signed K*; sig. L5 signed L*

CONTENTS: p.[2]: list of titles includes *Twilight* and *Studies*. p.[3]: l.7 of t.p., after Lawrence phoenix, reads: HEINEMANN : LONDON I. p.[4]: l.2: 10 Upper Grosvenor Street, London W1X 9PA I. l.11: Reprinted 1961, 1979 I SBN: 434 40722 4 I Printed in Great Britain by I REDWOOD BURN LIMITED I Trowbridge and Esher I.

BINDING: at base of spine, replacing HEINEMANN: NBS I.
    dj: on spine, "22" excised.

COPY EXAMINED: Pollinger Coll.

[subedition: Heron Books, 1969]

46.4   D. H. LAWRENCE I LADY I CHATTERLEY'S I LOVER I *original*
        illustrations by I *Sandra Archibald* I [pub. logo:
        heron, grass, trees] I *Distributed by* I HERON BOOKS
        [ll. 2-4 in red]

(7 7/8 x 4 3/4"): unsigned; front., 8 plates (possibly tipped
in), + pp.[6], 1-355, [356], [2].

CONTENTS: p.[1]:blank. p.[2]: sunburst design in light gray,
    encircling first two words of: *A Collection distributed by*
    Heron Books I. p.[3]: half-title, in red. p.[4]: front.
    port. of Lawrence, signed D. B.. p.[5]: t.p. p.[6]:
    Published by arrangement with I *William Heinemann Ltd.,*
    London I © *1969, Illustrations, Edito-Service, Geneva* I.
    pp.1-35: text, *A Propos*. p.[36]:blank. p.[37]:fly-title.
    p.[38]:blank. pp.39-[356]:text, LCL. p.[1]: *This book,*
    designed by I *William B. Taylor* I *is a production of* I
    Edito-Service S.A., Geneva I [sunburst design in light
    gray] I *Printed in Switzerland* I. p.[2]:blank.

TYPOGRAPHY: text: 38ll.(p.139): 137(143) x 90mm. 10ll.=35mm.
    Face 3(2x)mm.

RUNNING HEADS, rectos and versos: pp.2-35: APROPOS OF LADY
    CHATTERLEY'S LOVER I. pp.39-[356]: LADY CHATTERLEY'S
    LOVER I.

PAPER: smooth white wove unwatermarked. Thickness: text
    leaves: .09mm. plates: .09mm. Total bulk 17.8mm.

BINDING: imitation(?) morocco leather, very dark green(C147).
    Upper cover: gold-stamped: four borders enclosing blank
    inner panel. Borders decorated with geometrical motifs;
    middle two borders enclosed by rules. Outer and inner
    borders consist of dentelles. Spine divided into five
    panels: first, third and fifth decorated with dentelles
    similar to those on upper cover. Decorated borders at top
    and tail of spine. In 2nd panel: D. H.I LAWRENCE I [short
    rule] I COMPLETE I WORKS I. In 4th panel: LADY I
    CHATTERLEY'S I LOVER I. Lower cover undecorated. Endpapers
    in light and dark green, with repeated heron motifs
    (rosettes in oval border) in checkerboard design. Edges
    trimmed. Head and tailband in black and gold. Gold
    place-marker bound in.

ILLUSTRATIONS:

a) line and wash drawings in light grayish tones, each on
   recto of unnumbered leaf. Each signed S[andra] A[rchi-
   bald].
   –Facing p.56(Ch.3): Connie walking alone through bracken
   ("Aware of growing restlessness"?)
   –Facing p.108(Ch.8): Standing before mirror, left hand
   over face, Connie grieves at her "slacken[ing]" body.
   –Facing p.156(Ch.10): Connie kneels to fondle new-born
   chicks. Mellors (thin, shock of hair over eyes, hatchet-
   faced) looks on.
   –Facing p.186(Ch.10): restless Mellors walking toward
   Wragby, gun on shoulder.
   –Facing p.254(Ch.14): Connie "nestl[ing] up" to Mellors
   in bed.
   –Facing p.268(Ch.15): Connie, naked, coming "belly-for-
   ward" through the rain.
   –Facing p.310(Ch.17): Two women in period swimming
   dresses: Connie and Hilda in Venice?
   –Facing p.344(Ch.19): Mrs. Bolton comforting Clifford
b) frontispiece (uniform for series): Lawrence at about age
   30; line drawing. Signed D.B.

NOTE: On 25 May 1988, Gerald Pollinger stated to me that
   these volumes were distributed by mail order.

COPIES EXAMINED: DLC(rebound), LO/N-1; OX/U-1

46.5   as 46.4 save:

D. H. Lawrence | LADY | CHATTERLEY'S | LOVER | Original
Illustrations by | Sandra Archibald | [logo: ES on petals of
stylized flower; semicircle of s-shaped lines]

Leaves measure 7 13/16 x 4 3/4"

CONTENTS: p.[2]:blank. p.[6]:last line reads: ©
   Illustrations, Editio-Service S. A., Geneva | [in lower
   right: 13 048 17 |. p.[1]:last line reads: *Printed in
   France* |. [no sunburst design]

BINDING: morocco-grain imitation leather, deep brown(C56).
   Upper cover, gold stamped: inner border of six rules
   enclosing blank panel; surrounded by decorated band with
   floral designs. Outer border of four rules. Spine:
   elaborately ruled floral design as on u.c. interrupted by
   panel on which is gold-stamped: D. H. | LAWRENCE | [rule]
   | LADY | CHATTERLEY'S | LOVER |. Lower cover undecorated.
   Edges trimmed. Headband in brown and gold. Yellow place
   marker.

COPY EXAMINED: LO/N-1; Pollinger Coll.

   [subedition, Guild Publishing, 1981]

46.6   as   46.1 save:

Lady Chatterley's | *Lover* | D. H. LAWRENCE | PREFACED BY THE
AUTHOR'S | *Apropos of Lady Chatterley's Lover* | GUILD
PUBLISHING LONDON

(8 1/4 x 5 1/4"): unsigned; pp.[1-8], 9-364, [4].

CONTENTS: p.[1]:half-title. p.[2]:blank. p.[4]: *Apropos of
    Lady Chatterley's Lover* | First published 1930 | *Lady
    Chatterley's Lover* | First published 1928 | This complete
    text first published in Great Britain 1960 | This edition
    published 1981 by | Guild Publishing | by arrangement with
    William Heinemann Ltd | Printed in Great Britain by | St.
    Edmundsbury Press, Bury St Edmunds, Suffolk

TYPOGRAPHY: 38ll.(p.187): 147(153) x 95mm. 10ll.=38mm.

PAPER: smooth white wove unwatermarked. Thickness .1mm.
    Total bulk 18.5mm.

BINDING: imitation morocco leather, deep reddish brown(C41).
    Upper cover, gold-stamped: four borders, outer one
    decorated. Blank inner panel decorated with abstract and
    floral patterns. Spine divided into five sections by
    gold-stamped rules. First, third, fourth, fifth sections
    decorated. In second: LADY | CHATTERLEY'S | LOVER | [rule]
    | D. H. | LAWRENCE |. Lower cover undecorated. Edges
    trimmed. Headband in red and white. Endpapers deep red,
    dec. with repeated abstract design in gold (Verso free
    front endpaper and recto free rear endpaper plain).

COPIES EXAMINED: personal, Forster Coll.

46.7   as 46.6 save:

CONTENTS: added as 1.9: Reprinted 1985

BINDING: endpapers deep red, rectos and versos, but un-
    decorated.
        Dj: coated paper, medium pink C.5). Front cover: in
    rectangular panel (145 x 68mm): [ll.1-3 in border of 4
    rules:] LADY | CHATTERLEY'S | LOVER | [portrait of DHL] |
    D H LAWRENCE [last line in border of 4 rules] |. On spine,
    in rectangular panel: [ll.1-3, and 1.4, in separate
    borders of four rules each:] LADY | CHATTERLEY'S | LOVER |
    D H LAWRENCE |. At base of spine, in double border: pub.
    logo [G and P worked together]. Back cover: portrait of
    DHL. Front flap: "banned thirty years. . . amazing
    intensity of feeling . . . [Constance] finds sensual
    release and fulfillment." Back flap, set top to bottom:
    credit for jacket design (M. Buckingham); at bottom left:
    4214 |.

NOTE: In a letter to the author, dated 23 Sept. 1987, Gerald
    Pollinger stated that a 1985 reprint of the Guild Publish-
    ing volume was issued by W. H. Smith and Book Club
    Associates (which is operated jointly with Doubleday).

COPY EXAMINED: Pollinger Coll.

[Heinemann/Octopus Collected (7 work) Edition, 1976]

47.1   [in white panel on green background, in thin, thick
          borders]: D. H. LAWRENCE | [decorated rule] | SONS AND
          LOVERS | ST. MAWR | THE FOX | THE WHITE PEACOCK | LOVE
          AMONG THE HAYSTACKS | THE VIRGIN AND THE GIPSY | LADY
          CHATTERLEY'S | LOVER | HEINEMANN/OCTOPUS

(9 1/4 X 5 3/4"): [1-30]^{16}, 480 leaves; PP.[1-13],14-960.

CONTENTS: p.[1]:half-title. p.[2]:blank. p.[3]:t.p. p.[4]:
     1.7: *Lady Chatterley's Lover* first published in Great
     Britain in this | complete and unabridged text in 1960 |.
     11.9ff: This edition first published in 1976 by | William
     Heinemann Limited . . . in association with Octopus Books
     Limited . . . | Copyright © The Estate of D. H. Lawrence
     1911, 1913, 1923, 1925, 1930, 1960 | Printed in Great
     Britain by Jarrold & Sons, Ltd. Norwich |. p.[5]:
     CONTENTS. p.[6]: blank. pp.[7-9]: INTRODUCTION. p.[10]:
     blank. p.[11]: section title. p.[12]: blank. pp.[13]-300:
     S&L. pp.[301-02]:blank. p.[303]: section title. p.[304]:
     blank. pp.[305]-400: *St.Mawr* pp.[401-02]:blank. p.[403]:
     section title. p.[404]:blank. pp. [405]-448: *Fox.* pp.[449-
     50]:blank. p.[451]:section title.p.[452]:blank. pp.[453]
     669: *White Peacock.* pp.[670-72]: blank. p.[673]: section
     title. p.[674]: blank. pp.675-[699]: *Love Among Haystacks.*
     pp.[700-02]: blank. p.[703]: section title. p.[704] blank.
     pp.[705]-758: *Virgin And The Gipsy.* pp.[759-60]: blank.
     p.[761]: section title. p.[762]:blank. pp.[763]-960:
     Chatterley.

TYPOGRAPHY: Text: 5111, p.926, 198(204) x 118mm. 1011.=37mm.
     Face 3.5(2x)mm.
     Typeface: Times Roman(R52)? Old Style. DIN 1.13, mod. Ren.

RUNNING HEADS: (rectos and versos) in italics: [title of
     work]

PAPER: smooth white wove unwatermarked. Thickness .08mm.
     Total bulk 39.5mm.

BINDING: very deep red (C14) paper covered boards, fine
     morocco-patterned paper. Gold-stamped on u.c., in gold
     border of thin, thick lines: D. H. | LAWRENCE | [fancy
     rule]. Author and publishers' names goldstamped on
     spine. Endpapers deep bluish green (C165), with author's
     name, repeated across page, in light bluish green. Red
     head and tail bands.
        Dj: deep green (C142), lettering in white, 2 rules in
     gold. Front flap: blurb for novels, £3.95(lower left). LCL
     "probably the most notorious novel ever written. It was
     not available to the public except in pirated and expur-

gated editions until 30 years after his death. . . ."
Lower flap: other titles in the series, aim of which is to
provide "new hardback library of collected works by
outstanding twentieth-century writers . . . .
Thus it is possible to own in one book an authoritative
collection. . . ."

NOTE: The Heinemann/Octopus editions are authorized by the
Lawrence estate. See Essay for Section 6 above, p.183-84.

COPIES EXAMINED: TxU(dj), NO/P-1(dj)

[Shortened (4 work) Heinemann/Octopus Subedition, 1983]

47.2   D. H.| LAWRENCE | [2 rules] | Sons and Lovers | Women
in Love | Love Among the Haystacks | Lady Chatterley's
Lover | Octopus/Heinemann

(9 x 5 3/4"): no sigs; pp.[1-9], 10-858, [6].

CONTENTS: p.[1]:half-title. p.[2]:blank. p.[3]:t.p. p.[4]:
1.4: *Lady Chatterley's Lover* first published in Great
Britain in this | complete and unabridged text in 1960 |.
ll.6ff: This edition first published in 1976 by | William
Heinemann Limited . . . in association with Octopus Books
Limited . . . | Copyright © The Estate of D. H. Lawrence
1911, 1913, 1923, 1925, 1930, 1960 | Printed in the United
States of America | by R. R. Donnelley and Sons Company
|. p.[5]: CONTENTS p.[6]:blank. p.[7]: sec. title. p.[8]:
blank. pp.[9]-299: *Sons and Lovers*. p.[300]:blank.
pp.[301]: section title. p.[302]: blank. pp.[303]-626:*Women In Love*. pp.[627-28]: blank. pp.[629]:section title.
p.[630]:blank. pp.[631]-656:*Love Among the Haystacks*
pp.[657-58]:blank. p.[659]:section title. p.[660]:blank.
pp.[661]-858: *Chatterley*. pp.[6]:blank.

TYPOGRAPHY: 51ll., p.759, 198(205) x 119mm. 10ll.=41mm.
Face 3(2.0x)

RUNNING HEADS: (rectos and versos) in italics: [title of
work]

PAPER: smooth white wove unwatermarked. Thickness .07mm.
Total bulk 33.7mm.

BINDING: fine morocco-grain paper covered boards, very deep
red(C14). Upper cover: in gold-stamped decorated double
border: [floral design] | D.H. | Lawrence | [floral
design] | Sons and Lovers | Women in Love | Love Among the
Haystacks | Lady Chatterley's Lover | [decoration] |. On
spine, gold stamped: [dec] | D.H. | Lawrence | [dec] | [2
rules] | Sons and Lovers | Women in Love | Love Among the
| Haystacks | Lady Chatterley's Lover | [6 rules] |
Octopus/Heinemann |. Lower cover undecorated. All edges
gilt. Marbled endpapers, antique spot (T1206); gray,

black, deep reddish brown, white. Headband in red and white.

NOTE: The plates used in 47.1 for LCL were probably used for 47.2.

COPY EXAMINED: personal; OX/U-1

[shortened (2 work) Chancellor Press subedition, 1983]

47.3   as 47.2 save:

D. H. Lawrence | [thin-thick rule, in medium gray] | Sons and | Lovers | Lady Chatterley's | Lover | CHANCELLOR | [abstract dec.] PRESS [abstract dec.]

(8 11/16 x 5 5/8"): unsigned, pp.[1-13], 14-502, [2].

CONTENTS: pp.[2]:blank. p.[3]: half-title. p.[4]:blank. p.[5]:t.p. p.[6]: *Sons and Lovers* first published in Great Britain in 1913 | *Lady Chatterley's Lover* first published in Great Britain in this | complete and unabridged text in 1960 | This edition first published in Great Britain in 1983 by | Chancellor Press | 59 Grosvenor Street | London, W.1. | ISBN: 0 907486 40 1 | Printed and Bound in Great Britain by Collins, Glasgow. p.[7]:Contents. pp.[8-10]: blank. p.[11]: section title. p.[12]:blank. p.[13]-300: *Sons and Lovers.* pp.[301-02]:blank. p.[303]: section title. p.[304]:blank. pp.[305]-502: *Chatterley.* pp.[2]:blank.

PAPER: smooth white wove unwatermarked. Thickness .06mm. Total bulk 19.5mm.

BINDING: morocco-grain paper-covered boards, dark reddish brown(C44). Upper and lower covers undec. except for single vertical rule stamped in silver approx. 3mm. from hinge. On spine, silver stamped, running top to bottom: D. H. LAWRENCE Sons and Lovers | Lady Chatterley's Lover | CHANCELLOR | [dec.] PRESS [dec.] |. All edges trimmed.

COPY EXAMINED: LO/N-1

[4- work Chancellor Press subedition, 1985]

47.4   as 47.2 save:

t.p., ll.8-9: CHANCELLOR | [dec.] PRESS [dec.] |.

Leaves measure 8 3/4 x 5 1/2"

CONTENTS: p.[4]: l.7 . . This omnibus volume first published
in 1983 | This edition published jointly in 1985 by |
William Heinemann Ltd and Martin Secker & Warburg Ltd. |
. . . and Chancellor Press | an imprint of the | Octopus
Publishing Group p.l.c. | 59 Grosvenor Street | London W1
| ISBN 0 907486 96 7 | Printed in the United Kingdom

PAPER: thickness .06mm. Total bulk 32.3mm.

BINDING: paper covered boards, pale greenish yellow(C104).
upper cover, in gray border: THE BEST OF | [rule] | [ll.
3-4 in very deep red]: *D. H.* | *Lawrence* | SONS AND LOVERS
| WOMEN IN LOVE | LOVE AMONG THE | HAYSTACKS | LADY
CHATTERLEY'S | LOVER | COMPLETE AND UNABRIDGED [author's
name, and titles, in shadowed sans serif] |. On spine:
ll.1-10 as on u. c. At tail: CHANCELLOR | [dec.] PRESS
[dec.] |. Lower cover contains blurb: in LCL, "one of the
most controversial novels ever written, . . . Lawrence
launches a savage attack on the hypocrisies of society and
also celebrates the power and beauty of physical love."
At bottom: REC. U.K. RET. PRICE £9.95. Endpapers pale
orange yellow(C73). Edges trimmed.

COPY EXAMINED: personal

[Amaranth Press 4-work subedition, 1985]

47.5   as 47.2 save:

MASTERS LIBRARY | [rules under lettering on l.1] | D. H. |
LAWRENCE | [double rule under lettering on l.4] | Sons and
Lovers | Women in Love | Love Among the Haystacks | Lady
Chatterley's Lover | Amaranth | P [dot] R [dot] E [dot] S
[dot] S

Leaves measure 9 x 5 5/8".

CONTENTS: p.[4]: l.6ff: This volume first published by
arrangement with Viking Penguin Inc. | and Grove Press,
Inc. in 1983 jointly by | William Heinemann . . .
Octopus Books Ltd. . . . | This edition published 1985 |
Copyright © The Estate of D. H. Lawrence . . . | Amaranth
Press is the exclusive imprint of B. Dalton | Booksellers,
Minneapolis, Minnesota | ISBN 0 8300 0400 9 | Printed in
the United States of America | by R. R. Donnelley and Sons
Company

PAPER: Thickness .06mm. Total bulk 32.1mm.

BINDING: morocco-grain leather, very pale blue (C184),
quarterbound deep blue (C183) leather. Upper cover:
gold-stamped double rule. In center, gold-stamped within
dec. rules: D. H. | LAWRENCE |. Vertical double rule
approx. 15mm from hinge. Spine divided into 4 sections by
three raised bands. Gold decorated borders in all but 2nd

section, in which is inscribed in gold on blue background:
D. H. | LAWRENCE | [dot] | SONS AND LOVERS | [dot] | WOMEN
IN LOVE | [dot] | LOVE | AMONG THE HAYSTACKS | [dot] |
LADY CHATTERLEY'S | LOVER | [dot] [gold border around
lettering] |. At tail: AMARANTH | P [dot] R [dot] E [dot]
S [dot] S |. Lower cover, at bottom, gold-stamped: BONDED
LEATHER. Marbled endp., nonpareil (T1202). All edges gilt.
Head and tailband in blue and gold.

NOTE: A Christmas offer, 1985, by B. Dalton offered a uniform
    14-vol. set of The Masters Library for $149.99. The
    Lawrence vol. was individually priced at $14.98.

COPY EXAMINED: Personal

[Longmeadow Press 4-work subedition, 1985]

47.6 as 47.5 save:

The Works of | D. H. | LAWRENCE | [floral dec.] | SONS AND
LOVERS | WOMEN IN LOVE | LOVE AMONG THE HAYSTACKS | LADY
CHATTERLY'S [sic] LOVER | [floral dec.] | COMPLETE AND
UNABRIDGED | [rule] | *Longmeadow Press* | [rule]

CONTENTS: p.[4]: last 4 ll. read: Copyright © The Estate of
    D. H. Lawrence. . . | ISBN 0 681 31924 0 | Printed in the
    United States of America | by R.R. Donnelley and Sons
    Company |.

BINDING: morocco-grain leather, black. Upper cover, gold-
    stamped: decorated double border, open 17mm at center at
    left and right, with art nouveau floral design at each
    corner. The six petals of the flower at each corner are
    very pale purplish-blue (C202). *The* | *Works* | *of* | D.H.|
    LAWRENCE | [floral dec; petals colored as stated above] |
    COMPLETE | AND | UNABRIDGED |. There is a circular gold
    sticker on u.c.: [floral dec.] | *Classics Library* | *The*
    Works of | *D.H. Lawrence* | *$14.95* | 0-681-31924-0 |
    [floral dec] |. Spine divided into four sections by three
    raised bands. Gold-stamped: [floral dec., petals in
    purplish-blue] | [double rule] | [rule] | [in square
    border:] D.H. LAWRENCE | [rule] | [double rule] | [floral
    dec. as above] | SONS AND LOVERS | [dot] | WOMEN IN LOVE |
    [dot] | LOVE AMONG | THE HAYSTACKS [dot] | LADY
    CHATTERLEY'S | LOVER | [double rule] | [double rule] |
    LONGMEADOW | PRESS |. Lower cover, gold-stamped at lower
    right: BONDED LEATHER |. Endpapers medium blue (C181),
    with gold floral decorations repeated across pastedown and
    free endpapers.

NOTE: this volume is on sale in WaldenBooks chain stores,
    and may be that chain's version of the omnibus Lawrence to
    counter Dalton's (47.5).

COPY EXAMINED: personal

[New (not Phoenix) Heinemann edition, 1981]

48.1   D. H. LAWRENCE ¦ *Lady Chatterley's Lover* ¦ PREFACED BY
THE AUTHOR'S ¦ *Apropos of Lady Chatterley's Lover* ¦
HEINEMANN : LONDON

(8 3/4 x 5 1/8"): [1-18]^8, 144 leaves; pp.[1-6], [1-2],
3-277, [278], [4].

CONTENTS: p.[1]:half-title. p.[2]: The two earlier versions
of *Lady Chatterley's Lover* ¦ are published by Heinemann
under the titles ¦ *The First Lady Chatterley* ¦ *John Thomas
and Lady Jane* ¦. p.[3]: t.p. p.[4]: William Heinemann Ltd
¦ 10 Upper Grosvenor Street, London W1X 9PA ¦ LONDON
MELBOURNE ¦ TORONTO ¦ JOHANNESBURG AUCKLAND ¦ First
published 1928 ¦ This complete text first published in ¦
Great Britain 1960 ¦ Reprinted (reset) 1981 ¦ *Apropos of
Lady Chatterley's Lover* ¦ first published 1930 ¦ SBN 434
40732 1 ¦ Printed in Great Britain by ¦ Billing & Sons Ltd
¦ London, Guildford, Oxford and Worcester ¦. p.[5]:
Contents p.[6]: blank p.[1]: section title, "Apropos"
p.[2]:blank. pp.3-28: text p.[29]: section title, LCL
p.[29]: blank. pp.3-[278]: text, LCL. pp.[4]: blank.

TYPOGRAPHY: 43ll.(p.93), 166 x 106mm. 10ll.=37mm. Face
3(2x)mm.
Typeface: R73, Ehrhardt(?) Transitional. DIN 1.24, modern
baroque.

PAPER: smooth white wove unwatermarked. Thickness .1mm. Total
bulk 14.6mm.

BINDING: Linen grain (T304) cloth, very deep red (C17). Gold-
stamped on spine: *Lady* ¦ *Chatterley's* ¦ *Lover* ¦ D. H. ¦
LAWRENCE ¦ HEINEMANN ¦. Plain white endp. Edges trimmed.

COPY EXAMINED: LO/N-1

NOTE: see essay for Section 6, pp.183-84 above, and Black
157.

48.2   as 48.1 save:

CONTENTS: p.[4], l.8: Reprinted (reset) 1981,1982 ¦.

BINDING: Dj: coated paper, vivid red(C11). Upper cover: DH
LAWRENCE ¦ [vertical rule at spine edge in black and
white] ¦ Lady ¦ Chatterley's ¦ Lover ¦ [vertical rule at
fore-edge; horizontal rule at bottom; both in black and
white] ¦. l.1 in black, ll.3-5 in white. l.2: decorated L
with flower entwined. Lower cover same as upper. On spine:
D. H. LAWRENCE LADY CHATTERLEY'S ¦ LOVER [top to bottom;
name in black, title in white] ¦. At tail, vertically set:
pub. logo, windmill, W, H over HEINEMANN ¦. Front flap: ".
. . an example to an industrial age suffering from 'sex in
the head'. . . . 'It will bring me only abuse and hatred

again'. . . ." Back flap blank save for SBN: 434 40732 1
|.

NOTE: Price in 1985: £7.95.

COPY EXAMINED: personal(dj)

[Magazine format movie tie-in, 1982]

49.1   [cover title] Vol.1 No.8 | COMPLETE BESTSELLERS [set on
        45-degree angle] | LADY | CHATTERLEY'S | LOVER |
        --Now a Major Film Starring-- | SYLVIA KRISTEL and
        NICHOLAS CLAY | D. H. LAWRENCE | THE COMPLETE BEST-
        SELLING BOOK AS ORIGINALLY PUBLISHED [lettering in
        white, brilliant purple, and black] |. Illustrations of
        Connie, in period dress, and Connie and Mellors making
        love. Predominant colors purple, reddish brown, pale
        orange yellow]

sheet size: 10 1/2 x 8 5/16"; pp. 1-96.

CONTENTS: p.1: half-title. p.2: About The Author (2-paragraph
    sketch: ". . . now widely recognized as the foremost
    English writer of his generation." p.3: Contents. . . .
    appeared early in 1982 as a major motion picture starring
    Sylvia Kristel (who won international screen fame as
    "Emmanuelle" . . . . LADY CHATTERLEY'S LOVER is directed
    by Just Jaeckin and released by Columbia Pictures. Under
    rule: Vol. 1 No. 8 © 1982 Viaduct Publications Ltd. "Lady
    Chatterley's Lover" first appeared in 1928. ISBN 0 86326
    002 0. 2nd column: Cover Painting by T. Chantrell Text
    illustrations by Kim Raymond. Printed by Oy Lansa Suomi in
    Finland. Typeset by the Yale Press Ltd. London SE25.
    Origination by Wandlegraphics, Mitcham, Surrey.
    Distributed to the trade by Seymour Press Ltd. . . .
    pp.4-96: text.

TYPOGRAPHY: 68ll. (p.96, col 1): 241(251) x 90mm. 10ll.=38mm.
    Face:2(1.5)mm.
    Typeface: Times Roman(?)

RUNNING HEADS: versos: COMPLETE BESTSELLERS |. rectos: LADY
    CHATTERLY'S [sic] LOVER |.

BINDING: paper covered wrappers. Upper cover described above.
    verso upper wrapper: advert for previous issue (vol.
    1, no. 7: Bates' *Fair Stood the Wind for France*). Lower
    wrapper contains title and blurbs by Seymour-Smith,
    Spilka, Moynahan. Recto lower wrapper: advert for David
    Niven, *The Moon's A Balloon* (vol 1, no. 6).

ILLUSTRATIONS(line drawings, in the manner of pulp mag. or
    adult comic strips; Connie is full-breasted, with full
    lips and long hair):
    p.4: Connie in period overcoat and wide-brimmed hat

p.9: Connie, alone, lying amidst bracken
p.11: Michaelis with head on Connie's lap
p.21: Connie comforting Mellors' daughter as he looks on
p.25: Connie naked before her mirror
p.45: Connie lying on grass; Mellors unbuttoning his shirt
p.81: Connie and Mellors eating

NOTE: this is not a complete list of the illustrations. There
is a crossword puzzle on p.47. No. 27 across: "muddiness."
For other movie tie-ins see #31.16, 44.35 above.
   Pollinger (241) states that the copy-text for this is
the Odyssey Press edition (25.1-25.7).

COPY EXAMINED: NO/P-1

SECTION 7
The First Lady Chatterley, 1944–88

INTRODUCTORY ESSAY

Lawrence considered the possibility of publishing the first version of *Lady Chatterley's Lover* with Secker and with Knopf. As he wrote to Orioli in July 1929, "it has hardly any fucks and shits, and no address to the penis, in fact hardly any of the root of the matter at all . . . . I wish you would just glance through the hot parts, and tell me just how hot they are" (CL 1167). The work was not published, however, until 1944. Its printing history mirrors, but in smaller scope, the events which marked the career of the final version. Benchmarks include attempts to censor, "packaging" for general audiences, expurgation, disputes between publishers, the appearance of the continental edition, and involvement in the 1959 "Chatterley Sweepstakes."

Dial Press published *The First Lady Chatterley* in March, 1944 (50.1). Tebbel (III, 95) and Bosmajian (24-25) describe the consequences. On May 29, John Sumner, who had pursued Samuel Roth (see 7.1 and essay for Section 2) for his 1930 expurgated edition and was still active as Secretary for the New York Society for the Suppression of Vice, filed a complaint. A New York magistrate ruled the book "clearly obscene" and bound over Dial Press for trial. The indictment stated that Lawrence's "central theme," and the book's "dominant effect," is that "it is dangerous to the physical and mental health of a young woman to remain continent"; Connie's major ambition is "the gratification of her sexual desire." Although Sumner had since 1928 made *Chatterley* a prime target, Dial Press professed surprise when he showed up at its offices with a search warrant and seized some 400 copies. The press declared that it had received no complaints and, somewhat disingenuously, that the book had been favorably reviewed./1/ However, in the same month that *The First Lady Chatterley* was issued, Lillian Smith's novel of interracial sexual relations in the South, *Strange Fruit*, encountered the first of several censorship attempts.

For six months Dial could not distribute its Lawrence title in New York state. By that time there had been three printings, the first of which was advertised in Dial's spring list (in PW, 8 April 1944, p.1419) as consisting of 10,000 copies. The work led the publisher's list, although the two which followed, an autobiography by Salvator Dali and James Street's *By Valor Armed*, had print runs of 25,000 and 50,000 respectively. In November, New York State Special Sessions Court judged in Dial's favor, there being reasonable doubt of obscenity. When New York booksellers were allowed to stock Dial's *The First Lady Chatterley*, it sold 1,000 copies in the first two days (Tebbel, III, 95; Bosmajian, 24-25).

Obscene or not, in the 1950s *The First Lady Chatterley* was sold in paperback editions which provide good examples of the sexual suggestiveness attacked at the time by parents, educators, and of course politicians. The front cover of the Avon edition (52.1-52.3) depicts a beautiful woman in a nightgown (resembling film star Joan Crawford) staring directly at the reader; the blurbs, in the fashion of movie posters, advertise "One Woman's Great Love," "white heat," and "the crowning fire of human experience." Avon published magazines as well as paperbacks, and its cover illustrations during the 1940s and earlier 50s were similar to those of the pulp magazines, with yearning, voluptuous women shown touching, flirting with, or otherwise exciting men. The covers for the NAL "authorized" editions are in a similar style (see 20.3, 20.6, 20.7). Avon epitomized for critics such as those on the Gaithings Committee (House of Representatives, 1950) On Current Pornographic Materials the paperback industry's "pornographic" cover drawings and content. In the same year, Avon's *First Lady Chatterley* was one of thirteen titles cited in Fall River, MA as "indecent, obscene or impure, or manifestly tend[ing] to corrupt the morals of youth." The other publishers involved were NAL, Pocket, Bantam, Lion, and Popular Library (Davis 219). Avon shared the hard-edged erotic "come-ons" with its competitors, as it did a list mixing mysteries and thrillers with titles by fine writers (in Avon's case Farrell, Caldwell, Louys, Lawrence, and Algren). In 1952, with *The Amboy Dukes* the Avon bestseller, Lawrence's *The Virgin and The Gypsy* also sold well. Davis (96) suggests that the latter "was published for the value of its title and Lawrence's prurient reputation rather than for its literary merits." Perhaps "in addition to" would be more accurate, for the prestige value of the classic reprint has always motivated paperback publishers, who apparently feel strongly that classics built a readership's trust, and--even more importantly--that the audiences for "softcore" erotica and for fine writing are as overlapping as are aesthetic and erotic impulses (Davis 96-98; Crider 18-23; Schreuders 31-36). See the essays for Sec. 5, pp.129-32 and Sec. 3, pp.62-66.

Avon's second impression of *The First Lady Chatterley* was published in the mid-fifties, and the quotation from Lawrence at the top of the title page regarding the essential rightness of passionate impulse may have been meant as a response to critics of the paperback packaging as well as a

substitute for the preliminary leaf introducing the reader to
the book's content. The cover illustration depicted a blonde
woman, eyes closed and lips parted, towered over by a man
whose the dungaree-clad leg she grasps; his dominating hand
rests firmly on her hair and forehead. The Berkley 1958
edition (53.1) replicates this woman's head, without background; her slightly-altered features, now in close-up, may
have reminded browsers of those of actress Marilyn Monroe.
Berkley's owners were trained at Avon, and published pulp
magazines before moving on to paperbacks. The preliminary
leaf (p.[1]) reproduces a passage from the end of Chapter 4
describing Connie's "rippling thrills" after her first love-
making with Parkin. The diction Lawrence's novels sometimes
share ("peals of bells," "her own short wild cries") with
that of contemporary romantic stories and films which could
not delineate intercourse directly was easily exploitable by
paperback executives who understood the imaginations of a
mass market audience. For the supposed affinity of *Lady
Chatterley's Lover* with pulp romance see the essay for
Section 3, p.65, and the Philip Wylie review of Dial's *First
Lady Chatterley* as discussed in endnote one of this essay.

The packaging of the Penguin edition (56.1-56.9), which
first appeared in 1973, of course contrasts strikingly with
the nineteen-fifties American paperbacks, as did its *Lady
Chatterley's Lover*, to a smaller extent, with the 1959
"Chatterley Sweepstakes" volumes. See essay for Sec. 6,
pp.182-83 and 44.1-44.10 above.

During the Grove Press decensorship case in 1959,
Berkley advertised to the trade that its edition of the first
draft "can be freely displayed, sold, and sent through the
U.S. mails . . . " The copy refers to the censorship case
settled in Dial's favor in 1944; see 50.1 below. For the
"Chatterley Sweepstakes," see pp.124-27, and notes to 36.1
and 37.1 above. This title was definitely a profitable entry:
one of Berkley's best-sellers in 1959 (PW 18 Jan. 1960: 90).
There was a large printing of 31 July 1959, and a 4-page
advertising brochure (see PW 17 Aug. 1959: p.32). The Berkley
text was the nearly-unabridged one Dial used, not the
abridged and expurgated one Avon issued.

The Dial edition treated the text of Lawrence's MS in
the way many wished the Authorized Edition of the third
version had adapted the Orioli text. Four-letter taboo words
were printed with dashes replacing all but the first letter.
For the Australian edition (51.1) the editors performed "a
few minor expurgations . . . in order to conform with local
requirements." They thus reduced the novel by about 15,000
words. The first description of love-making is untouched, but
the other sexually-explicit passages are significantly cut.
These involve Connie and Parkin's fondling each other
(Chapter 11), their nakedness (17), that part of their
dialogue which includes the word "fuck" (12, 24), "balls"
(22), or "shit" (12), discussions of the value of what
[Parkin] has "got atween [his] legs" (15), and Connie's final
rumination on what "the warmth of the man inside her" (24)
means to her. As did Samuel Roth and the Authorized Edition

of the Orioli version, the Australian publisher substitutes "love" for "fuck" (12) and provides a few lines of his own when continuity is damaged by excisions (11,12)./2/

Avon is less puritanical than Peter Huston. Although its edition also substitutes "love" for the f-word (and on p.191 relocates Parkin's "kick in the balls" to "the teeth"), its expurgations are consistently shorter. However, it also makes deep cuts unrelated to perceived obscenities. The reason was that paperback publishers needed to limit costs of printing and paper by restricting the size of their books to a specified number of signatures (Crider 225). The Avon edition, as "specially revised and edited" (so stated in the first but not the second impression), consists of approximately 85,000 words. The excisions create interruptions in dialogue and make underlying themes less clear. They often eliminate interior monologues, and discussions between characters, through which Lawrence contrasts philosophical orientation and, more important, compulsive emotional responses to events. The cuts also eliminate significant details such as Clifford's interest in coal-mine engineering and Duncan and Connie's youthful socialism./3/ The state of the Avon text is camouflaged by such blurbs as "available for the first time to millions of Avon readers" (52.1), and "overwhelming candor and beauty" (52.2). The dust jacket of the third impression, a 12mo cloth-bound subedition produced as part of a series of inexpensive reprints of literary classics, is more aggressive in this regard: "the naked first draught" by an author "who took the smut out of society's taboo words."

Whatever blurb-writers may fantasize, *The First Lady Chatterley* never approached the notoriety of the third version, and thus it engendered fewer legal disputes between publishers. There was one such case. In late January 1947, Heinemann lawyers appeared in Chancery to request, on behalf of A. S. Frere, a court order which would withdraw from sale "all copies of a book named *The First Lady Chatterley*, which was imported into this country from Australia [the Huston edition, 51.1] and sold by the Atlas Publishing and Distributing Company. An interim injunction was granted pending settlement" (*Bookseller* 1 Feb. 1947: 111). I have found no notice of the outcome of this case. According to one (unknown) bookseller's note laid into one of the two copies at OkTU, the result was that "sale of the book in the UK was forbidden." This copy was used as evidence. The other (dated on the flyleaf 17 Jan. 1947, and signed by the Commissioner For Oaths) has underlinings indicating passages similar (not usually identical) to those in the third version. In the margin are references to the page numbers in the Heinemann Authorized Edition (17.12-17.29; 17.32-17.34 above) in which the underlined phrasing appears. It is possible that these copies were used as evidence in the injunction mentioned above. I have found no evidence that Heinemann attempted to· prevent Huston from distributing in Australia on the grounds that the latter was usurping its colonial rights to the novel (i.e., the third version, *Lady Chatterley's Lover*). Heinemann did plan to distribute aggressively in Australasia in 1947

(*Bookseller* 1 Feb. 1947: 3; see also PW 30 Nov. 1945), and had been selling the Authorized Edition of the third version there since 1934 (see 17.12).

There was one Continental Edition of *The First Lady Chatterley*, published by a post-war rival of Albatross, Scherz Phoenix Books, the appearance, list, and distribution of which mirrored Holroyd Reese's firm (see essay for Sec. 4, pp.100-04 above).

In the early 1950s Heinemann entertained the possibility of a one-volume edition of all three versions, but at the time the censorship of the third version caused the plan to be shelved. See the Introductory Note to Section 8 below.

ENDNOTES

1. Philip Wylie's opinion in the *New York Times* Book Review, 9 April 1944, sec.7: 7, was distinctly unfavorable, although he disliked all three versions and pointed out that the first version was "incomparably cleaner" than the third one. He remarked, as others have done (see essay for Sec. 3, p.65) the similarity of the plot to conventional romantic pot-boilers, and noted that the book was "as close as genius should permit itself to get to rubbish."
   For the lower court case, see People v. Dial Press, 182 Misc. 416 (Magis. Ct. 1944).

2. Expurgations in the Peter Huston edition are found in the following chapters and pages:

CHAPTER	PAGE(S)
11	159-62
12	168-71
15	204
17	225-26
22	296
24	321,327

3. I have not made a systematic listing of the Avon excisions but they occur in the following chapters: 3, 5, 8, 11, 12, 15, 17, 21, 22, 23, 24.

[Dial Press, 1944]

50.1   The First Lady Chatterley | BY D. H. LAWRENCE | [pub's
        device: in strap-work frame: winged child riding lion]
        Dial Press: New York

(7 15/16 x 5 5/16"): [1-9]^{16} [10]^{10} [11]^{16}, 170 leaves; pp.
[i-iv], v-xviii, [1-2], 3-320, [2].

CONTENTS: p.[1]: half-title. p.[2]: blank. p.[3]: t.p. p.[4]:
    This book is complete and unabridged in contents, and | is
    manufactured in strict conformity with Government |
    regulations for saving paper. | Designed by William B.
    Meinhardt | Copyright, 1944, by The Dial Press, Inc. |
    Printed in the United States of America by | The Haddon
    Craftsmen, Inc., Scranton, Pa. | pp.v-xiii: FOREWORD BY
    FRIEDA LAWRENCE |. p.[xiv]: blank. pp.xv-xviii: A
    MANUSCRIPT REPORT BY ESTHER FORBES |. p.[1]: fly-title.
    p.[2]: blank. pp.3-320: text. pp.[2]: blank.

TYPOGRAPHY: text: 32ll.(p.42), 147(154) x 98mm. 10ll.=46mm.
    Face 3(2x)mm.
    Typeface: Caledonia(?), R.174. Modern neoclassical, DIN
    1.34. Title page in Normande (R.436; decorative fat and
    thin face).

RUNNING HEADS: versos: *D. H. LAWRENCE* rectos: *THE FIRST LADY
    CHATTERLEY* |.

PAPER: smooth white wove unwatermarked. Thickness .1mm.
    Total bulk 18.1mm.

BINDING:linen-grain(T304) cloth, medium gray(C265). Stamped
    in black on spine: [French rule] | D. H. | LAWRENCE |
    [dec.] | THE | First Lady | Chatterley | [French rule] |
    Dial [flowing script] |. All edges trimmed, top edge
    stained gray. Plain white endpapers.
      Dj: moderate greenish blue(C173), lettered in white and
    black. Upper cover:| [in flowing script, in black]: *An
    original and hitherto Unpublished Novel* | BY | D. H.
    LAWRENCE | The | First Lady | Chatterley | [French rule] |
    [first 4 words only in script; *With a foreword by* | Frieda
    Lawrence | [in double border in white]: "Better than 'Sons
    and Lovers.' This is the *real* | Lawrence in the prime and
    vigor of his talent." [ll. 1,2,3,9, 10 and first 4 words
    of l. 8 in black; ll. 4,5,6 and last 2 words of l. 8 in
    white.] Spine: D. H. | LAWRENCE | THE | First Lady |
    Chatterley | [flowing script]: Dial [ll.1,2 in black;
    others white] |. Flaps and lower cover white. L.c.: ex-
    cerpts from Forbes' MS Report. Flaps contain blurb,
    stating the present version's superiority to the third
    one, which "dwindles to a tract on sex and a fantasy of
    wish-fulfillment." FLC "moves so much faster that the

reader never gains the detachment to go skipping through
for 'hot' passages. . . . Lady Chatterley is not yet a
nymphomaniac . . . . We are better able to recognize
ourselves in [her situation]."

NOTES: Esther Forbes, who states (p.xv) that she had in-
spected the drafts of the first and second versions, was a
novelist, historian, and publicity director for Houghton-
Mifflin (PW 13 May, 1944: 1984-95).
    Roberts (A42g) reports a first printing of 7500 copies.
Dial's notice for this title in its spring 1944 list (PW 8
April, 1944: 1419) states the printing was 10,000 copies.

COPIES EXAMINED: personal, OkTU, CU-S(dj), Forster Coll.

50.2   as 50.1 save:

CONTENTS: p.[4]:ll.4,5: First Printing March 1944 | Second
    Printing April 1944

PAPER: Thickness .07mm. Total bulk 13.7mm.

COPY EXAMINED: NO/P-1, personal

50.3   as 50.1 save:

CONTENTS: p.[4]: ll.4-6: First Printing March 1944 | Second
    Printing April 1944 | Third Printing June 1944

BINDING: DJ: Top right of front flap: $2.75.

COPY EXAMINED: TxU(dj)

*50.4 "January 1945"

*50.5 "November 1945"

50.6   as 50.3 save:

CONTENTS: p.[4]: 7 lines about paper-saving regulations
    removed. First line begins printing history. ll.4-6:
    January 1945 | November 1945 | October 1946

PAPER: Thickness .08mm. Total bulk 15.7mm.

BINDING: medium gray calico grain (T302) cloth. Top edge
    unstained.On front flap of dj: $3.00.

COPIES EXAMINED: TxU(dj); personal; NO/P-1

    *[Australian Edition, 1946(?), reset from Dial Press
    Edition]*

51.1.₁ The First Lady Chatterley | BY D. H. LAWRENCE | Dial

Press: New York | Peter Huston: Sydney [11.3-4]
preceded by printer's logo: flying horse, cloud]

(8 x 5 1/2"): [1-20]^8, [21]^4, 164 leaves; pp.[1-6], 7-327,
[328].

CONTENTS: p.[1]:half-title. p.[2]: blank. p.[3]: Registered
at the G.P.O., Sydney, for | transmission by post as a
book. | *This edition differs slightly from the original
American version,* | *published by Dial Press, Inc., in that
a few minor expurgations* | *have been made in order to
conform with local requirements.* | Copyright 1944, by The
Dial Press, Inc. | Wholly set up and printed by Deaton &
Spenser Pty. Ltd., | Douglass Street, Sydney, and
Published by Peter Huston, | Sydney.|. p.[4]:blank.
p.[5]:t.p. p.[6]: blank. pp.7-15: A FOREWORD BY FRIEDA
LAWRENCE |. p.[16]:blank, pp.17-20: A MANUSCRIPT REPORT BY
ESTHER FORBES |. p.[21]: section title. p.[22]:blank.
pp.23-327:text. p.[328]:blank.

TYPOGRAPHY: Text: 32ll.,p.119, 142 (152) x 97mm. 10ll.=
44mm. Face 2.5(1.5)mm. Typeface as 50.1

RUNNING HEADS: versos: *THE FIRST LADY CHATTERLEY* |. rectos:
D. H. LAWRENCE |.

PAPER: Smooth white wove unwatermarked. Thickness .1mm. Total
bulk 16.8mm.

BINDING: Var.(1): linen grain(T304) cloth, dark green (C146).
Blind-stamped, upper cover: THE | First Lady | Chatterley
|. On spine, gold stamped: The FIRST | LADY | CHATTERLEY
| D. H. LAWRENCE | [pub. device: p,h in rectangle] |.
Plain white endpapers, all edges trimmed.Top edge unstained. Var.(2): yellowish gray(C93) cloth, linen
grain(T304). Lettering stamped in gold on upper cover as
well as spine. Top edge stained gray.
    DJ: same as 50.1 above, save for spine (pub's logo on
spine (flying horse), author's name absence), and flaps
(carry same copy, but set differently. Bottom of front
flap: Price: 12/6).

NOTES: A likely date for appearance of this edition was 1946.
The final Dial impression appeared that year. Injunction
was sought by Heinemann in January 1947 against importation of the Australian edition to England (see essay
above, p.214-15). Furthermore, it would have been difficult to find paper and book-binders in war-time Australia (PW 17 Nov. 1945: 2237).
    In 1946, Sydney was the largest city in Australia and,
with Melbourne, had the largest number of bookstores (see
PW 30 Nov. 1946: 1298-1308).

COPIES EXAMINED: Var.(1): TxU(copies 1-3; c. 3 in dj), OkTU(2
copies, used as exhibit in 1947 trial), personal, Forster
Coll., LO/N-1. Var. (2): NO/P-1(dj), personal(dj)

51.1.$_2$ as 51.1.$_1$ save:

CONTENTS: p.[3]:t.p. p.[4]: as p.[3], 46.1.$_1$, but for final 2
   lines, in sans serif, which read: Printed by P. H.
   Henricks & Co., Pty. Ltd., | Dick Street, Balmain.

BINDING: as 51.1.$_1$, Var.(2)

COPY EXAMINED: TxU (copy 4)

[*Avon Edition, 1950*]

52.1.a   [decorated rule] | *The First* | *Lady Chatterley* | *by*
            D. H. LAWRENCE | *(Author of "Love Among the*
            Haystacks") | [line drawing of Shakespeare's head,
            unfinished: left ear not present] | AVON
            PUBLISHING CORP. | 119 W. 57th St. New York 19,
            N.Y. | [rule] | *Published by arrangement with The*
            Dial Press, Inc. | [decorated rule]

(6 1/2 x 4 1/4"): unsigned; pp.[1-2], 3-220, [4].

CONTENTS: p.[1]: t.p. p.[2]: THE FIRST LADY CHATTERLEY |
   COPYRIGHT, 1944, BY THE DIAL PRESS, INC. | [dot] | *AVON*
   REPRINT EDITION | COPYRIGHT, 1950, BY AVON PUBLISHING CO.,
   INC. | PRINTED IN U.S.A. pp.3-220: text. p.[1]: list of 15
   titles, starting with Maugham's *Liza of Lambeth*; ending
   with Bromfield's *Man Who Had Everything*. p.[2]: advert for
   "Modern Short Story Monthly": 27 titles, beginning Buck's
   Great Stories of China; ending O'Hara's *All The Girls He*
   Wanted. p.[3]: advert for 4 O'Hara titles. p.[4]: advert
   for Algren's *Never Come Morning* and *Neon Wilderness*,
   Dortort's *Burial of the Fruit*, Shulman's *Amboy Dukes*.

TYPOGRAPHY: 40ll. (p.155):141 x 89mm. 10ll.=35mm. Face
   2(1.5x)mm. Typeface: R52, Times Roman(?) Old Style. DIN
   1.13, Mod. Ren.

PAPER: Smooth white wove unwatermarked. Thickness .06mm.
   total bulk 9.6mm.

BINDING: upper wrapper: predominant color black. Avon logo in
   concentric circle, outer circle lettered POCKET SIZE BOOKS
   238. Below: ANC | [in yellow, at right of logo]: "THIS
   BOOK REVEAL(S) A DEEPER UNDERSTANDING OF | THE
   RELATIONSHIP BETWEEN A MAN AND A WOMAN | THAN ANYTHING WE
   HAVE EVER READ." -- Jacob H. Lowrey | [in orange:] *The*
   First | Lady Chatterley | *by* D. H. LAWRENCE | [woman,
   possibly in bed wearing low-cut nightgown, blond hair and
   blue eyes, staring directly at viewer. Three flowers
   (daisies?) in background] | SPECIALLY REVISED AND EDITED
   FOR AVON BOOKS |. On spine,top to bottom: [in red:] D. H.
   LAWRENCE [in yellow on red background]: *THE* FIRST LADY
   CHATTERLEY [in red on yellow background:] AVON [in white
   cirle:] 238 |. Lower wrapper: 3-para. blurb, beginning:
   "Sexual fulfillment was to D. H. Lawrence the crowning

fire of human experience. . . . " Headed "The Story of One
Women's Great Love. Inside upper wrapper: blurb, ending ".
. . as it came originally, in white heat, from the
inspired pen of the master psychologist and poet laureate
of human passions . . . ." Inside lower wrapper: list,
beginning *The Saint Goes West*, ending Clarke's *Tawny*.
Edges stained red.

NOTES: "Avon Publishing Company Inc.," according to Crider
(22), was one of a set of names for companies which later
became "Avon Publications, Inc." (see 52.2). This and
other "predecessor companies" flourished from 1949-51. The
address, 119 W. 57th, was an early one for Avon. This
is the location listed in the firm's *The Virgin And The
Gypsy*, which bears an early Shakespeare Head logo (dated
by Schreuders [34] as 1944) and an advertisement for *The
1946 Avon Annual*. The logo on the front cover was first
used in 1949; the Shakespeare head on the tp appeared from
1947 to 1952 (Schreuders 34-36).
   This edition is stated to be "available soon" in list of
Lawrence titles in Avon's *Women In Love*, which carries
copyright dates of 1948 and 1950. In 1950 Avon greatly
expanded its line with 12 new titles per month (Schreuters
34). It also experimented with selling paperbacks,
including some prestigious titles, in vending machines
(Crider 19).
   The abridgement notice at the bottom of the upper
wrapper may be a result of the Federal Trade Commission's
complaint about the lack of clear abridgement notices on
paperbacks (see Essay for Ch. 3, p.63). It does not appear
in the second impression.
   The woman on the upper cover bears some resemblance to
the film actress Joan Crawford.

COPY EXAMINED: personal

52.1.b   as 52.1.a save:

CONTENTS:p.[2]: last line reads PRINTED IN CANADA pp.[1-3]:
blank. p.[4]: Canadian address of the distributor,
American News Company, given.

BINDING: as 50.1.a except that the series no. (238) not
present on upper wrapper, in logo, or at tail of spine.
Lower wrapper: list begins with Gruber's *French Key
Mystery*, ends with *First Lady Chatterley*. Canadian address
of American News Company given.

COPY EXAMINED: personal

52.2   as 52.1 save:

"Nothing that comes from the deep, pas- | *sional soul is bad,
or can be bad."* | --D. H. LAWRENCE | The First | Lady
Chatterley | *D. H. Lawrence* | AVON PUBLICATIONS, INC. | 575
Madison Ave. | New York 22, N. Y.

CONTENTS: p.[2]: Copyright, 1944, by The Dial Press, Inc.

Published by | arrangement with The Dial Press, Inc.
Printed in U.S.A. pp.3-213: text. pp.214-20: A NOTE BY
FRIEDA LAWRENCE. p.[1]: note on five DHL titles ". . . the
same overwhelming candor. . . . " pp.2-3: advert and
blurbs for *Virgin and the Gypsy*, *Love Among the Haystacks*,
A Modern Lover, *Women In Love*, *Aaron's Rod*, and two short
stories in anthologies. p.[4]: advert and blurb for 3
Aldous Huxley titles.

TYPOGRAPHY: text: 139 x 88mm.

PAPER: smooth white wove unwatermarked. Thickness .06m. Total
bulk 8.8mm.

BINDING: coated paper wrappers. Upper cover: predominant
background color gold. Upper left: [in black rectangle]:
AVON | [in red rectangle: 35¢] | [in black rectangle]:
T-114. [1st line even with AVON]: "A power astonishingly
rich . . . | darkly physical and overwhelming"! | --LONDON
TIMES | [rule in red] | [in black on white background]: D.
H. LAWRENCE | [rule in black] | [next 2 lines in white on
red background]: THE FIRST | LADY CHATTERLEY | [rule in
black] | [in black border is drawing of blond woman in
low-cut gown, eyes closed and lips parted, her head
resting on left leg of dungaree-clad man whose hand
touches her hair (only leg of man and head and shoulders
of woman visible)] |. In lower left foreground is a leaf
or flower] | [at bottom left]: AN AVON | RED AND GOLD |
EDITION |. On spine, top to bottom: [rule in black] | [in
white on red background]: D. H. LAWRENCE | [rule in black]
| THE FIRST LADY CHATTERLEY | [rule] | [logo on red
background] | [in white on black background]: 35¢ | T-114
|. Lower cover: in upper right, white on red circle: 35¢
|. In black on gold background: D. H. LAWRENCE | Writes of
the Soul | and Body of Woman -- | In one of the Famous |
Novels of Our Time | [rule] | [in center of page, black on
red background]: *Avon Red and Gold Library* |. Below this
are blurbs by Jacob Lowrey and Elizabeth Bowen.

NOTES: According to Hancer (69-70), Avon's T series dates
from the mid-fifties. T109, *Various Temptations*, is
copyright 1955. Entry 52.2 (T-114) is advertised in Avon's
edition of *The Rainbow* (both are "Red and Gold" Avons),
and in *Love Among the Haystacks*. Both give the price at
35¢.
    The address is that of Avon Publications Inc., rather
than that of the earlier organization, Avon Publishing
Corp. (see 52.1 above).
    There is no abridgement notice in this impression, which
is helpful in dating its appearance before 1958, when the
Federal Trade Commission requested that Avon make clear
statements regarding excisions (Crider 23).

COPIES EXAMINED: personal, CU-S

[Shakespeare House subedition, 1951?]

52.3   [rule] | The First | Lady Chatterley | BY D. H.
        LAWRENCE | "I see thee in the hemisphere advanced |
        and made a constellation there!" | *From Ben Jonson's
        "Mr. William Shakespeare"* | Shakespeare House | 575
        Madison Avenue New York 22 | [rule]

Coll: [1-7]^{16}

CONTENTS: p.[1]:t.p. p.[2]: THE FIRST LADY CHATTERLEY |
    Copyright, 1944, | by the Dial Press, Inc. | Copyright,
    1951, | by Shakespeare House, Inc. | PRINTED IN U.S.A.
    pp.3-213: text. pp.214-20: A Note by Frieda Lawrence
    p.[1]:blank. pp.[2-4]: list of Shakespeare House (15
    titles, beginning with *Rubaiyat*; ending with *Butterfield
    Eight*), including FLC: ". . . profound understanding of
    the intimate relations of men and women. . . "

TYPOGRAPHY: 40ll., p.93. 141 x 89mm., 10ll.=35mm. Face:
    2(1.2x)mm.

PAPER: smooth white wove unwatermarked. Thickness .08mm.
    Total bulk: 10.8.

BINDING: embossed linen-grain paper covered boards, grayish
    blue (C186), stamped on lower right of u.c. with
    Shakespeare-bust medallion in gold, three stars around
    head, on background in deep blue. Quarter-bound in black
    morocco-grain cloth; gold fillet on outer edges of cloth;
    pattern of star-bursts in gold on quarterbinding, upper
    and lower covers. Spine stamped in 7 panels with stars,
    except on 2nd and 7th panel, lettered in gold on back-
    ground of strong blue. In 2nd panel: THE | FIRST | LADY |
    CHATTERLEY | [dot] | D. H. LAWRENCE |. In bottom panel:
    SHAKESPEARE | HOUSE |. Top edge gilt, all edges trim-
    med. Purple place-ribbon bound in. Endpapers embossed with
    calico design matching boards.
        DJ: dark greenish blue (C174) with three bands of white,
    each intersected with black rule. UC: [in white]: The
    First | Lady Chatterley | [in black]: D. H. LAWRENCE |. On
    spine: [rules continued from upper cover] [set top to
    bottom on dark greenish blue background:] THE FIRST | LADY
    CHATTERLEY | D. H. LAWRENCE [first 4 words in white] |.
    [Set vertically, in center of third band in white:]
    Shakespeare | House |. Lower cover blank except for rules
    in white and black, continued from upper cover. Front
    flap: HERE IS THE NAKED, | first draught of | one of the
    most storm-provoking novels | of modern times -- *Lady
    Chatterley's | Lover* |. Blurb describes Lawrence as one
    "who took the smut out of society's taboo words"; FLC "one
    of the crowning achievements." After the "shock of
    Lawrence's honesty," reader will understand novel's
    "overwhelming candor, warmth, and beauty."

NOTES: The blurbs suggest more strongly than the paperback
    impressions that this edition is unexpurgated, which it is

not. The headnote on pp.[2-4] extols the series' design
as bringing "luxury of fine books . . . to home libraries," and its contents as "selected to insure reading
enjoyment for the entire family." A similar line of low-
cost reprints of literary classics was Pocket Books'
"Collectors Editions," published from 1950-52 (Crider
226).

COPIES EXAMINED: personal, TxU, Forster Coll.(all dj), NO/P-1

[Berkley unexpurgated ed., 1958]

53.1   The | First | Lady | Chatterley | D. H. Lawrence |
        With a note by | Frieda Lawrence | [pub. logo:
        fleur-de-lis] | BERKLEY PUBLISHING CORP. | 145 West
        57th Street [dot] New York 19, N. Y.

(6 3/8 x 4 1/8"): unsigned; pp.[1-4], 5-239, [240].

CONTENTS: p.[1]: blurb headed THE CONSUMMATION | OF LOVE |.
    Quotes passage from the end of Ch. IV (". . . she heard
    and did not hear her own short wild cries as the rolling
    of the magnificent thrills grew more and more tremendous.
    . . ."). Concludes with quote from F. R. Leavis. p.[2]:
    blank. p.[3]: t.p. p.[4]: COPYRIGHT © 1944, BY THE DIAL
    PRESS, INC. | *Published by arrangement with* | *The Dial*
    Press, Inc. | BERKLEY EDITION, SEPTEMBER, 1958 | PRINTED
    IN THE UNITED STATES OF AMERICA|. pp.5-232: text. pp.232-
    39: A NOTE BY FRIEDA LAWRENCE p.[240]: advertisement for
    three Lawrence titles: *Captain's Doll*, *Woman Who Rode*
    Away, *Virgin And The Gypsy*. Price 35¢ each.

TYPOGRAPHY: text: 42ll.(p.33), 140 x 88mm. 10ll.=33mm.
    Face 2.5(1.5x)mm. Typeface: Times Roman. Old Style. DIN
    1.13, Mod. Ren.

PAPER: smooth white wove unwatermarked. Thickness .07mm.
    Total bulk 9.0mm.

BINDING: coated paper wrappers, yellow. Upper cover: logo in
    upper left: BERKLEY | [fleur-de-lis] | BOOKS | BG – 150 |
    50¢ |. At right of logo: D. H. LAWRENCE | [next two lines
    printed in yellow on red background]: The original version
    of | LADY CHATTERLEY'S LOVER | *The First* | *Lady Chatterley*
    | COMPLETE AND UNABRIDGED |. [Lower half of cover contains
    drawing of woman's face, her blonde hair in disarray, eyes
    closed, lips parted.] On spine, set top to bottom: [in
    red:] THE FIRST LADY CHATTERLEY [in black]: LAWRENCE |
    [set left to right:] [logo] | BG-150 |. Lower wrapper:
    blurb, including quote from London *Times* used on front
    wrapper of 52.1, headed *SONG OF THE FLESH*, lettered in red
    and black. States FLC "was the original [version] and was
    the favorite of his wife, Frieda Lawrence. This edition is
    the only unexpurgated printing of the book to appear in
    paperback form. Edges stained yellow.

NOTES: The text is that of 52.1.
    The illustration imitates part of the one depicted on
the wrapper of 52.2. The use of detail from the wrapper of
an earlier impression is common in Avon and other paperback titles; another example is *Aaron's Rod*. The woman on
the cover of 53.1 resembles film actress Marilyn Monroe.
    Berkley was founded in 1954 by two executives from Avon
(Schreuders 34); from a false start with pulp magazines,
the firm began with groups of 17 titles, each group
containing 8 novels and a mix of Westerns, mysteries,
humor, and anthologies. Berkley Giants date from 1955
(Schreuters 101).

COPY EXAMINED: personal

*53.2   [published 31 July, 1959, as reported in PW 18 Jan.
        1960: 90]

[Scherz Phoenix Continental Edition, 1946]

54.1   D. H. LAWRENCE I THE FIRST I LADY CHATTERLEY I
            [logo: flying bird, above PHOENIX arranged in
            semi-cirle] I THE SCHERZ PHOENIX BOOKS I ALFRED
            SCHERZ PUBLISHERS I BERNE / SWITZERLAND

(7 1/8 x 4 1/2"): [1]^8 2-19^8 20^4, 156 leaves; pp.[1-4],
5-310, [311-12]. $(-sig[1]) signed [sig. #] The First Lady
Chatterley I.

CONTENTS: p.[1]: half-title. p.[2]:blank. p.[3]: t.p. p.[4]:
    First Edition I Printed in Switzerland 1946 (Effingerhof
    S. A. Brugg)I. pp.5-13: Foreword by Frieda Lawrence.
    p.[14]: blank. pp.15-18: MS Report pp.19-[311]: text.
    p.[312]: list of Scherz Phoenix Books (begins Aldridge's
    Sea Eagle, ends Deeping's *Seven Men came back* [sic]), con-
    tinued on inside of lower wrapper (begins Deeping's *The
    Secret Sanctuary*, ends Wells' *Apropos of Dolores*).

TYPOGRAPHY: Text: 34ll., p.97, 140(147) x 85mm; 10ll.=40mm.
    Face 3(2x)mm.
    Typeface: R.6, Kennerley(?). old style; DIN 1.13, mod.
    Ren.

PAPER: smooth white wove unwatermarked. Thickness .07mm.
    Total bulk 14.3mm.

BINDING: paper wrappers, yellow. Upper cover: [in black
    banner, at top:] SCHERZ PHOENIX BOOKS I 53* I Extra volume
    I [ll. 4-6 on white background bordered by rules shaping
    an open book]: D. H. Lawrence I *The First* I *Lady
    Chatterley* I [pub. logo, as on t.p. but in black] I [in
    black banner]: ALFRED SCHERZ PUBLISHERS BERNE I. On
    spine, running bottom to top, in white, on white and
    yellow striped background: D. H. LAWRENCE / THE FIRST
    LADY CHATTERLEY I. At top (vertical, on white background):

53*| Extra Volume |. Lower wrapper: pub. logo. Inside
lower wrapper: list (see CONTENTS above). Inside upper
wrapper: 2-paragraph blurb; excerpts from Forbes' "MS
Report." Under rule: PHOENIX PUBLISHING Co. | PARIS |
BERNE/LONDON |. Edges trimmed. No endpapers.

COPIES EXAMINED: Forster Coll., NO/U-1 (rebound)

54.2   as 54.1 save:

D. H. LAWRENCE | THE FIRST | LADY CHATTERLEY | [logo: flying
bird, above PHOENIX arranged in semi-cirle] | PHOENIX
PUBLISHING CO. LTD. | SCHERZ & HALLWAG | BERNE PARIS LONDON

(7 1/4 x 4 1/2"): [1]^8 2-18^8 19^{12}, 156 leaves. $(-sig[1])
signed [sig. #] The First Lady Chatterley |. Sig. 19$_3$
signed: 20* The First Lady Chatterley |.

CONTENTS: p.[4]: Printed in France | Imprimerie Chaix Paris
    p.[312]: list of Scherz Phoenix Books (begins Aldridge's
    Sea Eagle, ends Golding's *Glory of Elsie Silver*), con-
    tinued on inside of lower wrapper (begins Goudge's *Bird in
    the Tree*, ends Wilde's *House of Pomegranates*).

PAPER: smooth white wove unwatermarked. Thickness .06mm.
    Total bulk 11.8mm.

BINDING: paper wrappers, yellow. Upper cover, in black banner
    at top: PHOENIX BOOKS |. last line, in black: NOT TO BE
    INTRODUCED INTO THE BRITISH EMPIRE OR THE USA | [Above
    this, in black banner]: PHOENIX PUBL. CO LTD. PARIS |.
    Inside lower wrapper: list (see CONTENTS above). Inside
    upper wrapper, under rule: PHOENIX PUBLISHING CO. LTD. |
    SCHERZ & hALLVAG | BERNE PARIS LONDON |.

COPIES EXAMINED: MH, TxU, OkTU, NO/P-1, LO/N-1, Forster Coll.

54.3   as 54.2 save:

t.p., 11.6,7: SCHERZ & HALLWAG | BERNE (SWITZERLAND) / PARIS

(7 1/4 x 4 1/4"): [1]^{16} [2-9]^{16} [10]^8 [11]^4, 156 leaves.

CONTENTS: p.[4]: Second Edition 1947 | Printed in Switzerland
    by Effingerhof Brugg |. p.[312]: list begins Aldridge, *Sea
    Eagle*; ends Gibbs, *The Interpreter*. (List inside front
    wrapper begins Golding, *Glory of Elsie Silver,* ends
    Winwar, *Life of the Heart*.

PAPER: Rough white wove unwatermarked. Thickness .1mm. Total
    bulk 16.5mm.

BINDING: upper cover: black banner at bottom reads PHOENIX
    PUBL. CO LTD. BERNE |.

NOTE: this impression is signed as 52.1, but the folding of
    sheets does not correspond to the signatures.

COPY EXAMINED: personal

54.4   as 54.3 save:

t.p.: 11.5-7: PHOENIX PUBLISHING CO. | PARIS | BERNE/LONDON

[1]^{16} 2-10^{16}, 160 leaves; pp.[1-8], 5-310, [311-12], [2].

CONTENTS: pp.[4]: blank. p.[5]: half-title. p.[6]: blank.
    p.[7]: t.p. p.[8]: blank. pp.5-[311]: text. p.[312]:
    blank. p.[1]: Printed in France | Imprimerie Chaix, Paris
    | Dépot légal No 26 | 3e trimestre 1949 |. p.[2]: blank.

BINDING: as 54.1 save wrappers are deep pink (C3). List on
    lower wrapper begins Bromfield, *Early Autumn*, ends Wilde,
    House of Pomegrantes.

COPY EXAMINED: Forster Coll.

        [First British Edition, 1972]

55.1   D. H. LAWRENCE | *The First* | *Lady Chatterley* | *(The*
        first version of 'Lady Chatterley's Lover') | WITH A
        FOREWORD BY | FRIEDA LAWRENCE | [pub. device: windmill,
        W,H] | HEINEMANN : LONDON

(7 1/2 x 5 1/4): [A]^{16}, B-H^{16}, 128 leaves; pp.[4],[i-v],
vi-xv, [xvi]; [1], 2-232,[4].

CONTENTS: p.[1]:blank; laid down to upper cover. pp.[2-4]:
    blank. p.[i]: half-title. p.[ii]: THE PHOENIX EDITION OF
    D. H. LAWRENCE (22 titles, followed, after short rule, by
    9 other volumes including the present one) |. p.[iii]:
    t.p. p.[iv]: address of pub.; First published by The Dial
    Press, Inc., U.S.A., 1944 | First published in Great
    Britain 1972 | 434 407364 [printer's statement (Cox and
    Wyman)] |. pp.[v]-vii: PUBLISHER'S NOTE |. p.[viii]:
    blank. pp.[ix]-xv: foreword. p.[xvi]:blank. pp.[1]-232:
    text. pp.[1-3]: blank. p.[4]:blank; laid down to lower
    cover.

TYPOGRAPHY: Text: 37ll.(p.109), 168.5 (177) x 106mm;
    10ll.=44mm.
    Typeface: Baskerville 169 (monotype); R78. Transitional.
    DIN 1.24, Mod. Baroque.

RUNNING HEADS, rectos and versos: THE FIRST LADY CHATTERLEY

PAPER: white wove smooth unwatermarked. Thickness .09mm.
    Total bulk 13.4mm.

BINDING: Calico-grain cloth (T.302), strong blue(C178).
    Gold-stamped on spine, top to bottom: The First | Lady
    Chatterley | D. H. LAWRENCE |. At tail: pub. device:
    windmill,WH |.

Dj: white laminated paper. upper cover: [1.1 in black,
11.2-4 in grayish blue]: D. H. Lawrence | The First Lady |
Chatterley | the first version of Lady Chatterley's Lover
| [line and wash portrait head of DHL by Larry Learmonth].
Spine: [in black: D. H. Lawrence |. [in blue:] The First
Lady Chatterley |. Pub. device at bottom. Lower cover:
Heinemann Lawrence list. Front flap: summary of novel.
Rear flap: blurb for JTLJ.

NOTE: There are no chapter headings, and all words are fully
    spelled out, in this edition. As Roland Grant points out
    in the Publisher's Note,there was no indication of Chapter
    divisions in Lawrence's MS.
        The price was £2.50.
        The Heinemann JTLJ and FLC are companion volumes; see
    note to 57.2 below.

COPIES EXAMINED: TxU(dj), OkTU(dj), MMeT(rebound), NO/P-1(dj)

    [Penguin edition, 1973]

56.1   D. H. LAWRENCE | *The First* | *Lady Chatterley* | *The*
          first version of | *Lady Chatterley's Lover* | With a
          Foreword by | *Frieda Lawrence* | [logo: penguin in
          oval] | PENGUIN BOOKS

(7 1/8 x 4 3/8"):perfect bound; pp.[1-4], 5-253, [254], [2].

CONTENTS: p.[1]: biographical note. p.[2]:blank. p.[3]:
    t.p. p.[4]: [11.1-5: publisher's addresses] [short rule]
    First published in the U.S.A. 1944 | First published in
    Great Britain by Heinemann 1972 | Published in Penguin
    Books 1973 | [short rule] | Made and printed in Great
    Britain | by Richard Clay (The Chaucer Press), Ltd, |
    Bungay, Suffolk | Set in Monotype Garamond | [11.16-24:
    Pollinger line]. pp.5-[7]: PUBLISHER'S NOTE |. p.[8]:
    blank. pp.9-[16]: FOREWORD BY FRIEDA LAWRENCE |.
    pp.17-253: text. p.[254]: blank. p.[255]: offer of Penguin
    newsletter. p.[256]: Lawrence Penguin list.

TYPOGRAPHY: Text: 3911., p.87, 147 x 90mm. 1011.=37mm. Face
    3(1.5)mm.
    Typeface: see CONTENTS, p.[4]. DIN 1.24, mod. baroque

PAPER: smooth white wove unwatermarked. Thickness .06mm.
    Total bulk 10.6mm.

BINDING: coated paper wrappers, white. Upper cover: logo[pen-
    guin] | [in brownish-orange:] D.H. LAWRENCE [A and W
    worked together] | [in black]: THE FIRST LADY CHATTERLEY |
    [photo: one of Peccinotti's suite of photographs for the 3
    Penguin *Chatterleys*: woman in white, walking through dark
    wood. Sun- or moon-light illuminates dress, hat, and one
    tree trunk, all set upon background of deep shadows. See

44.22 and 58.1 Predominant colors white and black] |.
Spine: [top to bottom]: D. H. LAWRENCE [A and W worked
together] THE FIRST LADY CHATTERLEY ISBN O 14 | 003741 4
[Penguin logo, set vertically] |. Lower cover: [Lawrence
phoenix | blurb ". . . not really revolutionary polemic
or manifesto at all, but a beautiful, rather pastoral
tale. . . . " | "For copyright reasons this edition is not
for sale in the USA." | photo of DHL; prices: UK 35p..
Aust., N. Z.: $1.20. Canada $1.50 |. Edges trimmed.

COPIES EXAMINED: OkTU, NO/P-1, NO/U-1

*56.2 "Reprinted 1974"

*56.3 "1975"

56.4   "1977"; as 56.1 save:

CONTENTS: p.[4]: 1.10: Reprinted 1974, 1975, 1977 | [short
rule] | Made and printed by | Hazell Watson & Viney Ltd, |
Aylesbury, Bucks |.

PAPER: thickness .05mm. Total bulk 8.6mm.

BINDING: Lower wrapper: No copyright statement. List of
prices: UK 80p; Canada $2.50; Australia $2.25(rec.). ISBN
0 14 00.3731 4

COPY EXAMINED: personal

*56.5 "1979"

*56.6 "1981"

*56.7 "1982"

56.8 "1983"; as 56.1 save:

CONTENTS: p.[4]: 1.10: Reprinted 1974, 1975, 1977, 1979,
1981, 1982, 1983 | [short rule] | All rights reserved |
[short rule] | Made and printed in Great Britain by |
Hazell Watson & Viney Limited, | Member of the BPCC Group,
. . . .

PAPER: Thickness .06mm. total bulk 8.9mm.

BINDING: upper cover, in black on white background: D [dot] H
| LAWRENCE | [rule] | The First | Lady Chatterley |
[drawing (oils?) by Yvonne Gilbert: woman, smiling, eyes
downcast, in period costume, walking through woods.
Predominant colors white, brown, light orange] | [penguin
logo in circle on orange background]. Spine, on orange
background, top to bottom: D [dot] H [dot] LAWRENCE The
First Lady Chatterley ISBN 0 14 | 00.3731 4 |. Set
vertically: logo. Lower wrapper: same wording as above,
but arranged differently. Prices: UK £1.95; Aust. and
Canada $3.95.

NOTE: For other Penguin cover illustrations by Gilbert, see
   44.34 above and 58.6 below.

COPY EXAMINED: Personal

*56.9   as 56.8 save:

CONTENTS: p.[4]: Reprinted . . . 1983, 1986 I.

SECTION 8
John Thomas and Lady Jane, 1972–88

INTRODUCTORY NOTE

As Roland Grant of William Heinemann Ltd. explained in his introductions to the Heinemann and Penguin editions of *The First Lady Chatterley* and *John Thomas and Lady Jane*, Willard Hougland (Frieda Lawrence Ravagli's representative) of the Laboratory of Anthropology at Santa Fe, New Mexico transcribed the first and second versions of *Lady Chatterley's Lover* from MSS provided by Mrs. Ravagli. She had Angelo Ravagli bring them from Italy to New Mexico in the late 1930s (see Squires 200). It was in New Mexico that Esther Forbes learned of the existence of the MSS and, after reading typescripts sent her by Mr. Houghton, prepared her "Manuscript Report" for *Dial* in 1944 (see 50.1). In 1951, Mr. Grant saw the second version in typescript (it had been kept in Laurence Pollinger's library), and was encouraged (Pollinger 240) to bring out a one-volume edition of all three works. However, it proved impossible because of the certainty of censorship of the third version in the early fifties (Mondatori of Italy published such a one-volume edition, in Italian, in 1954).

The planned Heinemann edition of all three versions may explain Laurence Pollinger's objection to Barney Rosset's desire to publish the first U.S. unexpurgated authorized edition of *Lady Chatterley's Lover* in 1954. In that year he wrote to Rosset that "someday the unexpurgated version should be published but this is not the time" (Arents archive: letter, Barney Rosset to C. Montague Weekley: 11 Sept. 1959: 4). Caffrey, after a review of the circumstances of the Grove Press publication, states that Pollinger's hostility to Rosset's plans was "mysterious" (63, 75). However, Caffrey quotes Frieda Lawrence regarding Pollinger's loyalty to A. S. Frere and Heinemann (62). This indeed seems to explain it, especially if the three-version edition was still a viable possibility. Frere had written to Mark Shorer in 1954 about this edition being a project sometime in the future (Caffrey

58). It seems to have been Rosset's own opinion (Caffrey 61) that A. S. Frere favored his project in 1954.

BIBLIOGRAPHICAL DESCRIPTIONS

[First Printing in English: Heinemann, 1972]

57.1   D. H. LAWRENCE | *John Thomas* | and | *Lady Jane* | (*the
second version of 'Lady Chatterley's Lover'*) | [pub.
logo: windmill, W, H] | HEINEMANN : LONDON

(8 1/2 5 3/8"): [A]^{16} B-M^{16}, 192 leaves; pp. [i-v], vi-vii,
[viii], [1], 2-372, [4]. Final leaf (M16) laid down to lower
cover.

CONTENTS: p.[i]: half-title. p.[ii]: THE PHOENIX EDITION OF
D. H. LAWRENCE (as 55.1 above) |. p.[iii]: t.p. p.[iv]:
William Heinemann Ltd | 15 Queen St, Mayfair, London W1X
8BE | LONDON MELBOURNE TORONTO | JOHANNESBURG AUKLAND | ©
Italian translation by Carlo Izzo, | Arnaldo Mondadori
1954 | © First publication in English, | The Frieda
Lawrence Estate 1972 | 434 40737 2 | Printed in Great
Britain by | Cox & Wyman Ltd., London, Fakenham and
Reading |. pp.[v]-vii: PUBLISHER'S NOTE |. p.[viii]:
blank. pp.[1]-372: text. pp.[4]: blank.

TYPOGRAPHY: Text: 37ll.(p.185): 167(173) x 106mm.
10ll.=46mm. Face 3(1.5)mm.
Typeface: Baskerville 169(Monotype): see 55.1

RUNNING HEADS: pp.vi-vii: PUBLISHER'S NOTE |. pp.2-372: JOHN
THOMAS AND LADY JANE

PAPER: smooth white wove unwatermarked. Thickness .1mm. Total
bulk 19.6mm.

BINDING: linen-grain (T304) cloth, light reddish brown
(C42). Gold-stamped on spine, top to bottom: *John Thomas* |
and | *Lady Jane* | D. H. LAWRENCE |. Set vertically: pub's
logo.
   Dj: coated paper, white; uniform in design with
55.1. Upper cover: [in black]: D. H. LAWRENCE | [next 2
ll.in dark reddish brown]: John Thomas | and Lady Jane |
the second version of Lady Chatterley's Lover | [Learmonth
portrait in dark grayish red] |. On spine, top to bottom:
[in black:] D. H. Lawrence | [in light gray:] John Thomas
| and Lady Jane |. Set vertically: pub's logo. Front
flap: price (£4), 3 paragraphs on novel, ISBN no. Back
flap: 2 paragraphs on FLC, identification of illustrator
(Learmonth). Lower cover: list of Lawrence novels,
beginning *The White Peacock*, ending *Lady Chatterley's
Lover* " '(final and unexpurgated version).'"

NOTE: see Roberts A42k, who states first printing was 2500
copies.

COPIES EXAMINED: TxU(dj), personal(dj), OkTU, Forster
Coll.(dj), NO/P-1(dj)

[Viking subedition, with revised Introduction]

57.2   D. H. LAWRENCE | *John Thomas* | and | *Lady Jane* | (The
        second version of *Lady Chatterley's Lover*) | [pub's
        logo: Viking ship] | *The Viking Press* | *New York*

(8 3/8 x 5 1/2"): [1-12]^{16}, 192 leaves; pp. [i-v], vi-ix,
[x], [2], [1], 2-372.

CONTENTS: p.[i]: half-title p.[ii]: Viking list of 25 DHL
    titles. p.[iii]: t.p. p.[iv]: © Italian translation by
    Carlo Izzo, Arnaldo Mondadori 1954 | First publication in
    English Copyright © 1972 by | The Estate of Frieda
    Lawrence Ravagli | All rights reserved | Published in 1972
    by The Viking Press, Inc. | 625 Madison Avenue, New York,
    NY 10022 | Published simultaneously in Canada by | The
    Macmillan Company of Canada Limited | ISBN 607-40812-3 |
    Library of Congress card number: 70-185281 | Printed in
    U.S.A. pp.[v]-ix: Editor's Introduction (R. Grant,
    Heinemann). p.[x]: Note that this edition was printed from
    Heinemann sheets, with some typographical changes and
    slightly different MS readings. Publication date for both
    editions: Aug. 29, 1972. p.[1]: section title p.[2]:
    blank. pp.[1]-372: text.

TYPOGRAPHY: as 57.1 above.

RUNNING HEADS: pp.[v]-ix: EDITOR'S INTRODUCTION |. pp.2-372:
    JOHN THOMAS AND LADY JANE |.

PAPER: smooth white wove unwatermarked. Thickness .1mm.
    Total bulk 21.5mm.

BINDING: Calico (T302) cloth, deep reddish orange(C38). On
    spine, top to bottom: [in black]: D. H. Lawrence VIKING |
    [in gold]: *John Thomas and Lady Jane* |. Top edge stained
    strong red.
        DJ, white. Front cover: [in yellow]: *D. H. Lawrence* |
    [in pink]: *John Thomas* | *and Lady Jane* | [in white]: The
    hitherto unpublished | second version of | Lady
    Chatterley's Lover |. Lettering on black square-shaped
    background bordered with yellow. On spine, top to bottom:
    [in gray:] *D. H. Lawrence* [in reddish pink:] *John Thomas* |
    and Lady Jane |. Set vertically, in reddish pink: [logo] |
    [in black:] VIKING |. Back cover: excerpt from Intro-
    duction in black square with yellow border, Standard Book
    Number. Flaps: this draft "by far the longest and most
    serious of the three," contains 20,000 words "deleted from
    the ultimate text . . . has all the explicit sexual pas-
    sages. The different ending poses for readers the question
    'Are you a Parkin man or a Mellors man?'" Front flap, at
    bottom: Jacket design by Mel Williamson. Back flap, at
    bottom: address of press.

NOTE: In the Introduction (vi-vii), Grant says that he wished

to bring out all three versions in one volume in the early
1950s, but could not because of the censorship of the
third version. Pollinger (240) locates plan at the time of
the British de-censorship trial. See pp.230-31 above.

Works In Progress (NY: Literary Guild, 1972) reprints
(pp.15-27) an excerpt from the Viking impression. *Works* is
subtitled *Selections From The Best Books To Be Published
In The Coming Months*, and carries, at the bottom of p.15,
the following: "Copyright © 1972 by the Estate of Frieda
Lawrence Ravagli."

COPIES EXAMINED: MMeT(rebound), OkTU(dj), CU-S(dj)

*57.3   Viking Compass paperback subedition, 1974

57.4   as 57.2 save:

sheet size: 7 3/4 x 5"

CONTENTS: p.[ii]: list of Lawrence works, with asterisks
    indicating those available in Compass editions. Begins
    Sons and Lovers, ends with Viking Critical edition of that
    novel. p.[iv]: 1.5: Viking Compass Edition issued in 1974
    by the Viking Press Inc. 1.13: Second printing June 1974

TYPOGRAPHY: 37ll.(p.185): 158 (165) x 101mm. 10ll.=42mm.

PAPER: thickness .08mm. Total bulk 14.6mm.

BINDING: paper wappers, same design as dj for 55.2. At lower
    left of upper cover, in reddish pink: [logo: viking ship]
    A Viking Compass Book |. [at right, in black:] $2.75 |. On
    spine, top to bottom: [in black:] C342 *D. H. Lawrence* [in
    reddish-pink:] *John Thomas and Lady Jane* [in black]:
    VIKING/COMPASS |. Lower cover has quote from Intro-
    duction, and rephrased copy from front flap of 55.2.

COPY EXAMINED: personal, MH (rebound, front and rear wrapper
    preserved)

        [Penguin Edition, 1973]

58.1   D. H. LAWRENCE | *John Thomas and* | *Lady Jane* | *The
        Second Version of* | *Lady Chatterley's Lover* |
        [pub. device: standing Penguin in oval] | PENGUIN
        BOOKS

(7 1/8 x 4 1/4"): [1]^{12} 2-7^{12} 8-9^{10} 10-16^{12} 188 leaves; pp.
[1-4], 5-376. $1 (-[1]) signed J.T.-[sig. no.]

CONTENTS: p.[1]: biographical note. p.[2]:blank. p.[3]:t.p.
    p.[4]: [ll.1-3: addresses of British, Australian, Canadian
    offices of Penguin] | [rule] | First published in Italian
    by Mondadori | First published in English by Heinemann

1972 | Published in Penguin Books 1973 | [short rule]
| Italian translation copyright © Carlo Izzo, Arnoldo
Mondatori, 1954 | Copyright © The Frieda Lawrence Estate,
1972 | [short rule] | Made and printed in Great Britain by
| Hazell Watson and Viney Ltd, | Aylesbury, Bucks | Set in
linotype Granjon | [Pollinger line] |. pp.5-7: PUBLISHER'S
NOTE |. p.[8]: blank. pp.9-376: text.

TYPOGRAPHY: Text: 39ll. (p.121), 152 (155) x 87mm.
    10ll.=38mm. Face 3(1.5x)mm.
    Typeface: see CONTENTS, p.[4].

PAPER: smooth white wove unwatermarked. Thickness .06mm.
    Total bulk 15.1mm.

BINDING: white coated paper wrappers. Upper cover: [penguin
    logo] | [in orange brown]: D. H. LAWRENCE [A and W worked
    together; decending stroke of A shared with ascending
    stroke of W] | [in black:] JOHN THOMAS AND LADY JANE |
    [dark interior of barn or hut, through opening in door of
    which one sees foliage and a bright light. Heavy coat on
    wall peg, hay-strewn steps, door at left half-open. Wo-
    man's wide-brimmed white hat, with decoration on brim,
    rests on top step near door. Predominant colors green,
    greenish brown] |. On spine, running top to bottom: D. H.
    LAWRENCE [A and W worked together] [dot] JOHN THOMAS AND
    LADY JANE | ISBN 0 14 | 00-3732 2 | [set vertically:
    penguin logo] |. Lower cover: photo of author, credits for
    photos, prices: UK 45p; Australia $1.55; Canada $1.95.
    Above photo: "For copyright reasons this edition is not
    for sale in the U.S.A."

NOTE: The photo illustration on the upper wrapper is one of
    the suite of Peccinotti photos for the Penguin Lawrence
    titles (see 44.22, 56.1).
    The book is perfect bound. I based collation on signing
    of the signatures.

COPIES EXAMINED: OkTU, personal, Forster Coll., NO/P-1

*58.2 "Reprinted 1974"

*58.3   "1977" (first US Penguin ed.)

58.4   as 58.1 save:

CONTENTS: p.[4]: [5 ll. of pub. addresses (England, NY [625
    Madison Ave], Australia, Canada, N.Z.)] | [short rule] |
    First published in Italian by Arnoldo Mondadore Editore
    1954 | First published in English in Great Britain by
    William Heinemann Ltd 1972 | Published in Penguin Books in
    Great Britain 1973 | Reprinted 1974, 1977, 1980 | First
    published in English in the United States of America by
    the Viking Press 1972 | Viking Compass Edition published
    1974 | Reprinted 1974 | Published in Penguin Books in the
    United States of America 1977 | [short rule] | Italian
    translation copyright 1954 by Carlo Izzo, Arnoldo
    Mondadori | First publication in English copyright © The

Estate of Frieda Lawrence Ravagli, 1972 | All rights
reserved | [short rule] | Typeset, printed and bound in
Great Britain | by Hazell Watson & Viney Ltd., | [rest as
58.1]

BINDING: upper cover: predominant colors brown and green.
Lower cover: information regarding "not for sale in U.S.A.
removed; prices raised (UK £1.50).

COPY EXAMINED: personal

*58.5   "1981"

58.6   as 58.4 save:

CONTENTS: Line 10: Reprinted 1974, 1977, 1980, 1981, 1982 |.

TYPOGRAPHY: Text: 39ll. (p.121), 150 (155) x 87mm.
10ll.=38mm.

PAPER: thickness .06mm. Total bulk 12.4mm.

BINDING: Var.(1): coated paper wrappers, white. Upper cover,
printed in black: D [dot] H | LAWRENCE | [rule] | John
Thomas | and Lady Jane | [drawing (predominant colors
white, brown, blue) of young woman and kneeling man. Woman
(heart-shaped face, wearing period dress and shawl,
wedding ring visible on left hand and holding shoe in
right) staring at chick which man (in vest and shirt-
sleeves) holds in his cupped hands] | [penguin logo in
orange oval]. Spine: on yellow background, running top to
bottom: D [dot] H [dot] LAWRENCE John Thomas and Lady Jane
ISBN 0 14 | 00.3732 2 |. Set vertically: [logo]. Lower
wrapper: Lawrence phoenix over blurb, ending ". . . in
many ways quite different from the first and last . . . .
It justifies Lawrence's belief that his novel was, among
other things, about tenderness." Photo of Lawrence, list
of prices: UK £2.25; Aust. $5.95; Can and USA $4.95.
Var.(2): as (1) save: lower wrapper: pasted-in ticket over
prices: UK changed to £2.50.

NOTE: The cover illustration is one of Yvonne Gilbert's
illustrations for Penguin Lawrence works; see 56.8, 44.34
and 45.1 above. The figures are the same Connie and
Mellors; the scene depicted is in Ch. 7 of JTLJ.

COPIES EXAMINED: Var(1) and (2): personal

*58.7   as 58.6 save:

CONTENTS: Line 10: Reprinted 1974, 1977, 1980, 1981, 1982,
1986 |.

Title page (1.6)

Preliminary title page (1.7)

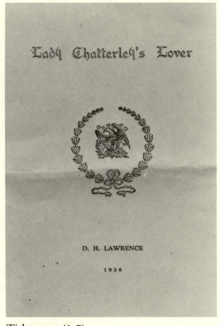

Title page (1.7)

Title page (1.9)

Title page (1.10)

LADY CHATTERLEY'S
LOVER

BY

D. H. LAWRENCE

Florence
PRIVATELY PRINTED
1928

Title page (1.11)

LADY CHATTERLEY'S
LOVER

BY

D. H. LAWRENCE

Florence
PRIVATELY PRINTED
1928

Title page (2.1.a)

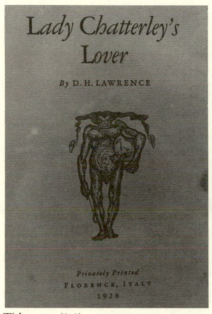

Title page (3.1)

Chapter headpiece (3.1)

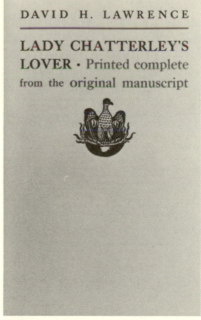

Title page (4.1)

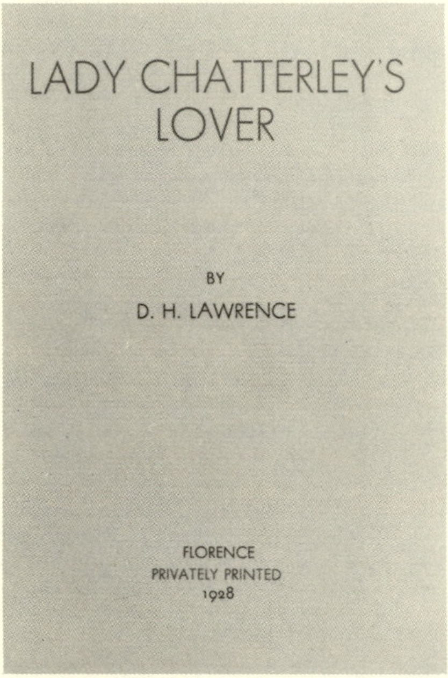

LADY CHATTERLEY'S
LOVER

BY

D. H. LAWRENCE

FLORENCE
PRIVATELY PRINTED
1928

Title page (5.1)

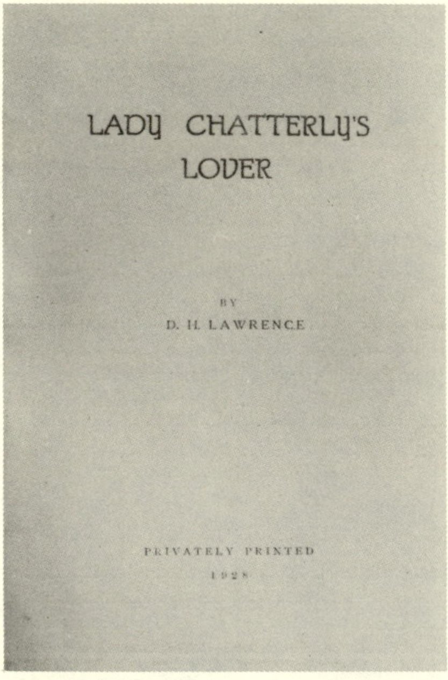

LADY CHATTERLY'S
LOVER

BY

D. H. LAWRENCE

PRIVATELY PRINTED
1928

Title page (6.1)

BY D. H. LAWRENCE

LADY
CHATTERLEY'S
LOVER

1930
WILLIAM FARO, Inc.

Title page (7.1)

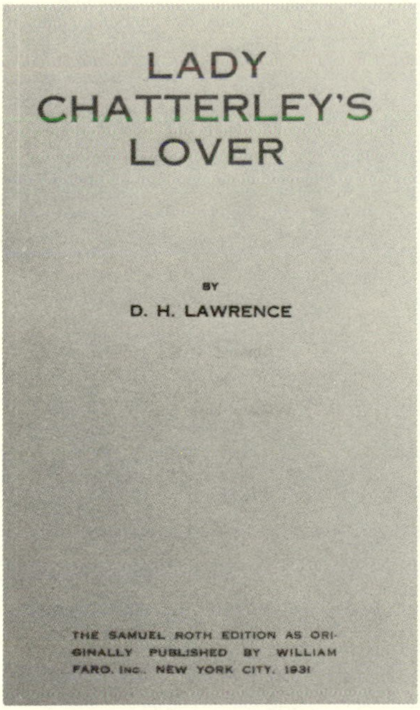

LADY
CHATTERLEY'S
LOVER

BY
D. H. LAWRENCE

THE SAMUEL ROTH EDITION AS ORI-
GINALLY PUBLISHED BY WILLIAM
FARO, Inc., NEW YORK CITY, 1931

Title page (7.2)

LADY CHATTERLEY

Frontispiece (7.4)

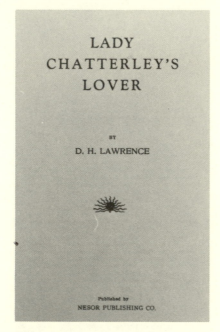

LADY
CHATTERLEY'S
LOVER

BY
D. H. LAWRENCE

Published by
NESOR PUBLISHING CO.

Title page (8.1)

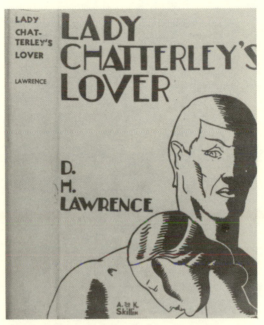

Dust jacket, state 1 (8.1)

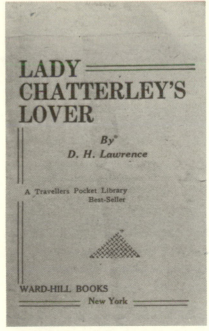

Title page (15.1)

Upper cover (15.1)

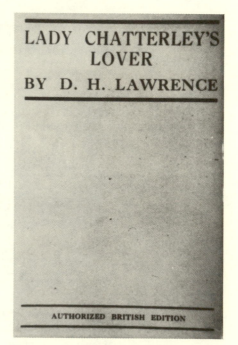

Title page (17.1)

Upper cover of dust jacket (17.1)

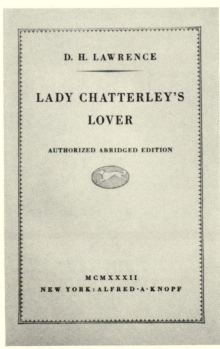

Title page (17.9). By permission of
Alfred A. Knopf, Inc.

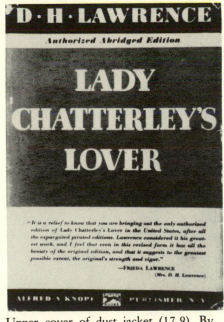

Upper cover of dust jacket (17.9). By
permission of Alfred A. Knopf, Inc.

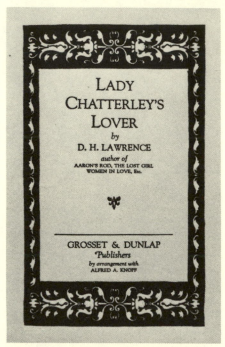

Title page (17.10). By permission of
Grosset and Dunlap, Inc.

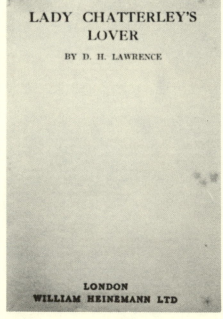

Title page (17.13). By permission of
William Heinemann, Ltd.

LADY
CHATTERLEY'S
LOVER

by

D. H. LAWRENCE

GROSSET & DUNLAP
PUBLISHERS   NEW YORK
By arrangement with Alfred A. Knopf

Title page (17.30.1). By permission of
Grosset and Dunlap, Inc.

Upper cover dust jacket. Illustration by
Skrenda. By permission of Grosset and
Dunlap, Inc.

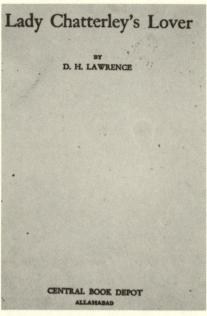

Title page (18.1). By permission of
Laurence Pollinger, Ltd.

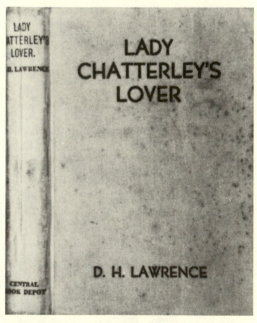

Binding (upper cover and spine) (18.1). By permission of Laurence Pollinger, Ltd.

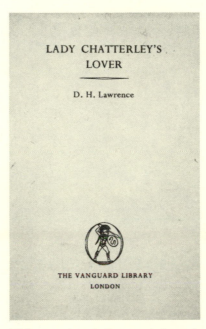

Title page (19.1). By permission of
Chatto and Windus

Title page (25.1)

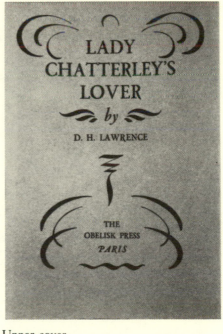

Upper cover

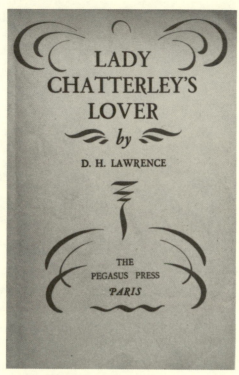

Title page (25.11.1)

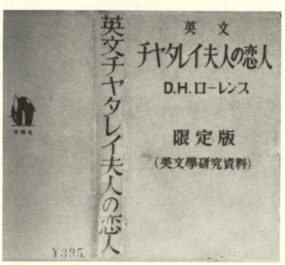 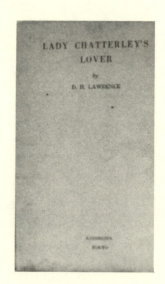

Dust wrapper and upper cover (25.12.3)

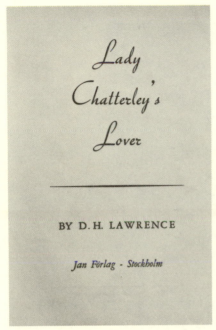

Title page (27.3)

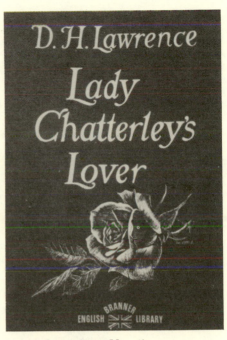

Upper Cover (28.1 Var. 1)

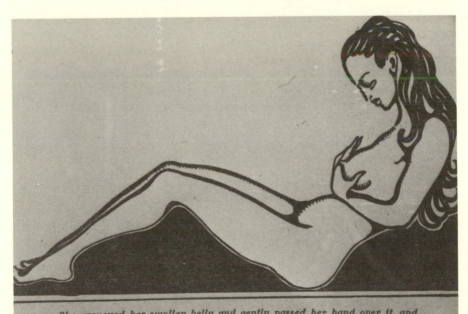

She surveyed her swollen belly and gently passed her hand over it, and
her hard heavy breasts with their protruding nipples — page 13

Frontispiece (A2.1)

APPENDIX I
Dramatizations, Parodies, and Sequels, 1931–86

INTRODUCTORY ESSAY

As Warren Roberts' listing of the parodies of *Lady Chatterley's Lover* in his *Bibliography* made clear, the publishing history of the novel is incomplete without considering the imitations, many of which appeared at peaks of the novel's popularity: the first blush of its infamy in the early thirties, the post-World War return with boot-leg copies of veterans to England and America, and the post-censorship "sweepstakes." The adapters of Lawrence's novel altered its themes, characterization, settings and plot in order to appeal to their audiences. This was done under the supervision of such successful popularizers of erotica as the publishers Samuel Roth, Marcel Rodd, and Lyle Stuart, who utilized the considerable talents of several professional Grub-streeters. There is some objective evidence of their success. To understand the vital hold *Lady Chatterley's Lover* had upon the popular imagination, their efforts are as important as are the expurgations, the pirated texts, the paperback and dust jacket "packaging," and the book club advertisements./1/

As is the case with so much of the early history of the novel, we must consider Samuel Roth (see the Essays for Section 2 and 3), whose dramatization (A1.1) was published under his Faro imprint, as was his expurgated "Samuel Roth edition." The latter (7.1-7.4) ran through at least four impressions in three years; the play, adapted from the publisher's own expurgated version of the novel, seems to have been much less successful. Roth ingenuously admits that, "being pretty nearly all my own work [as opposed to Lawrence's or a ghost-writer's?], [it] is probably very dull."/2/ He recommends his expurgated "version" of *Chatterley* as improving on the original for "a certain purely reading excitement." It is this book that his Introduction, entitled "By Way of Explanation," vigorously defends (see Section Two, p.24). In fact, it is possible that Roth's major reason for publishing the drama, which he duely copyrighted in his

own name, was to convince Frieda Lawrence of his efficacy as a popularizer of *Chatterley.* He might therefore secure her authorization for the novel itself and his expurgated edition of it. She met him in the spring of 1931. "But he was an awful man--he did a play of Lady C so terrible that I can't take his money . . . ." (MM 33). He also wished to return the fire of his many critics (see Section 2, pp.20-25); he expresses snarling contempt for these, as well as for politicians, publishers, and booksellers, not to mention Lawrence himself ("impotent," "self-indulgent"). By 1931 Sylvia Beach's International Protest against him had made him a pariah to whom space in many bookshops, newspaper advertisements, and reviewer's columns were closed. While a Frances Steloff, a Ben Abramson, a Mitchell Kennerly, a Ludwig Lewishon were considered "literati," he found himself stigmatized as a pornographer, a pirate, a "dirty books" man. It must have been hard to bear, and his cynicism surfaces in the play itself. Of course, "By Way Of Explanation" could have with more effect been used as a Foreword to 1931 and/or 1932 impressions of the expurgated *Chatterley*, but this may have meant interrupting print runs of a steady-selling item.

The dramatization (copyright filed April 1931) perhaps was superseded by the two Faro sequels (A2.1, A3.1); the *Husbands* was scheduled for publication in September. Blurbs for the latter, but not the play, appear on the back cover of dust jackets as one of Faro's Famous Dozen, and, in 1932, as one of The Big Dollar Books (see 7.4 above). Sequels might well have ·been considered more attractive and more easily advertised to Roth's extensive mail-order clientele. As *fresh* stories, they offered more variety than an adaptation of an adaptation. That the latter was easily available from the same publisher and contained much of the text of Lawrence's own "version" was a further obstacle to the play's success. Perhaps because Roth sensed its limited appeal, he included it as one of a series of five titles in "The Ardent Classics," providing for it an association with erotica by Catulle Mendes and Sacher-Masoch (the latter's *Venus In Furs* was also a Big Dollar imprint). Since he had based it on his expurgation, he hoped not to receive visits from John S. Sumner or his under-cover agents, and could defiantly give charges of piracy the lie--one can't pirate one's own work.

Despairing self-indulgence and misanthropic cynicism pervade Roth's dramatization. His Mellors, after rescuing Clifford from an out of control wheel-chair, will not accept a reward because, he tells his employer, he acted merely to protect the chicks in its path. Roth puts May, Michaelis, and Hammond in the wrong simply for feckless hedonism, not because their attitudes towards sex and marriage make love into a kind of business agreement and preclude "warm-hearted" unselfish relationships. That would suggest that for sensitive readers a remedy may be possible. Bertha Coutts is unsympathetic because she is a promiscuous "slut," not because of clitoral orgasm, references to which Roth had excised from his edition of Lawrence's novel. As for Clifford, Roth does not make the reader see, as Lawrence does, that Connie's husband uses his disability to bind her to him

with "mind-forged manacles" of pity and wifely obligation.
For Lawrence he is sinisterly repressive as well as pathetic.
For Roth, Lord Chatterley is pitiable and magnanimous, a
helpless victim of his adulterous wife. It is Connie who is
single-minded and imperious. Roth shows her need for sex to
be real, but is silent on what Lawrence teaches: that its
foundation is her craving to realize the tenderness inherent
in her nature as a living creature created for "togetherness."

Thus the Connie of the Faro sequels does not need
Mellors once her sexual infatuation with him wanes. She is at
liberty to become obligation-free and too bewitching for any
one man to possess. In both of these novels, she encounters
with panache and gaiety the variety of sensual experiences
she thinks she needs for self-awareness, in spite of a
resentful Mellors. Her rustic second husband increasingly
finds himself out of his depth in her sophisticated ambience.
Following their publisher's implications, apparently without
a great deal of specific instruction (see below), the writers
of both sequels tell the story of Connie's self-gratifying
worldliness. In so doing, they inevitably come to share the
cynicism in which Roth's dramatization is grounded, for which
he set the tone with such blurbs as "The sweet decadence that
is eating our society to the bone" (see 7.1 above), "[charac-
ters] as delightful as ever to follow--and abuse" (A2.2
below), and "Lawrence sees the rottenness of our life, but
loved it nevertheless" (blurb for the Faro *Chatterley* on the
dust jacket of a novel by "Anthony Gudaitis" [Anton Gud],
author of the first sequel).

On the surface, the sequels appear to be light-hearted
and high-spirited. Their tone is very different from that of
the drama, although the implications of its narrative thread
are developed. Roth gave Mr. Gud no more specific instructions about plot than to "make it dramatic with sensual
overtones."/3/ Although Roth's understanding of popular
entertainment accounts for the high-spirited sensuality, it
does not explain the tenor of his play. His personal concerns
about professional status and self-image may. Perhaps he
aspired to have his work produced as avant-garde drama; four
years earlier, one of his projected enterprises was a
subscription theater./4/ In fact, Adelaide Roth informs me
(letter to the author, 7 Sept. 1988) that three options were
taken on his dramatization. Whatever the case, the Connie of
the sequels is Roth's creation as well as that of his ghost-
writers.

This Connie was an inevitable popular interpretation. In
a shrewd comment in his Introduction ("By Way Of Explanation"
7), Roth opines that *Lady Chatterley's Lover* may become,
thanks to official and self-appointed censors, "the Fanny
Hill of our generation." If so, why blame a publisher in need
of capital for a few business ventures with a novel to which
blue-noses had denied copyright? It was their prudishness,
exemplified by Senator Smoot, whose debates with Sen. Cutting
(March 1930; see Section 2, p.13) were front-page copy across

the country, that had reinforced for the U.S. Lawrence's image as a pornographer. Roth's edition, and, by implication, the drama and sequels into the bargain, respected standards of propriety, and would allow readers to be respectably entertained by "this quaint [pun?] story" while not exacerbating the harm the smut-sniffers had already done. The comparison with *Fanny Hill* is especially interesting because for 200 years its heroine, that sexy and irrepressible bourgeois prostitute, had given people much pleasure; therefore, they were willing to make some effort to acquire copies. A strategy of Roth's sequels was to make Connie's adventures and sensibility a bit like those of the Fanny of Volume II of Cleland's much-prosecuted and perennially-lucrative novel (save that Connie's "revels" are not made explicit). In the second sequel, a self-possessed Connie, confident that the socially-tabooed pleasures she has experienced have been fulfilling, admits her "slavery to love. But it's natural . . . . call it a free whore . . . a non-commercial whore. That's the best of all. That's what the greatest women in all history have been"(p.195). Writing in 1966, Tristram Coffin praises Fanny as "the sweet prostitute (we are with her all the way)," and quotes Dr. Albert Ellis: ". . . Cleland's erotic classic convincingly shows that heterosexual copulation can be glorious, rip-roaring fun."(125-26).

One of Roth's favorite epithets for *Lady Chatterley's Lover* is "sweet." Roth and his ghost-writers well understood Lawrence's bitter criticism of between-the-wars venality and that survives somewhat in the Faro "versions"; however, the mythic bond upon which Connie and Mellors' commitment to each other is founded, and which allows them radically to reject their friends, spouses, and society, does not. It is *Chatterley's* (often pruriently) entertaining rather than its didactic qualities that appeal to a popular audience. "By way of explanation," who is to say (Roth's apology might imply) that these readers' needs should not be served, or that Lawrence himself would not have tolerated their motives for reading in order to be read? If an expurgated abridgement or dramatization will not fully do the job, perhaps a sequel or two, short on Lawrentian introspection and long on *Fanny*-like gaiety, would. And if a serious moral is appropriate, one is forthcoming (as a respectable disclaimer) from the Roth camp: focussing on sexual needs is decadent and self-destructive.

I do not think it appropriate to cry "Poor Lawrence!" He did risk the reputation of a "distinguished madman" (see Section 1 above, pp.2-3) by publishing privately a sexually-explicit, scatological novel which was bound to be denied proper copyright, and then to be interdicted, pirated, and generally become a fascinating object to possess. Inevitably, Connie and her lover could became characters to fantasize about, and fair game for not only thoughtful reflection, but also parlor jokes, and sequels.

Lady Chatterley's Husbands (A2.1-A2.2) was ghost-written by Anton Gud (Anthony Gudaitis), whose *A Young Man About To Commit Suicide* was a 1932 Faro imprint. There were ill-

ustrated and unillustrated impressions, the priority of which
I cannot determine. Perhaps the second impression appeared
without the illustrations (in the lubricous and decadent
style of Rahnghild), out of deference to postal authorities.
Powell notes *Husbands* as "the first sequel," and charac-
terizes it, and the Roth dramatization, as "merely sensational." So it would appear from Roth's instructions to Mr. Gud,
the dust jacket illustration (a shapely woman coyly inspecting a line-up of men), the frontispiece (a nubile nude
inspecting her breasts), and the blurb (readers will find the
shocking Connie and Mellors "as delightful as ever to follow
--and abuse"). Neither Mellors nor Clifford are very important in the novel; therefore the title seems more an attempt
to put the words "Lady Chatterley" before the prospective
reader than to accurately encapsulate the novel's content
(the same is true of A3.1).

    The book describes Connie's drinking and dancing larks
on the Continent with a reluctant Mellors very much in the
background. Clifford, weakened by unrequited love, dies early
and Connie's child is still-born. Hilda emerges as a "tawny
lioness" who marries a sugar-daddy. Connie, before Mellors
joins her, "wreak[s] havoc on herself with her hands";
together, their lovemaking carries a hint of sadism despite
(or perhaps because of) the author's attempt to transplant
some Lawrentian diction: "'Some day,' she cried . . .'you'll
love me to death.'" She grows restless; thus begin her
European adventures, the first of which is a Parisian orgy.

    The author of *Lady Chatterley's Friends* (A3.1) was
Clement Wood, who set to work without consulting Mr. Gud. One
of the best writers Roth relied on through the 1930's, Wood
had also published with Haldeman-Julius and Macy-Macius. The
Faro imprint (see Appendix II) includes three non-fiction
titles by him. In addition, under the pseudonym of Alain
Dubois/5/, he wrote for Faro *Loose Shoulder Straps*. He was
Roth's friend as well as confederate; the latter dedicated
his *The Private Life of Frank Harris* (1932) to "Clement Wood,
The only man I know in America capable of turning this
trick." (Hamalian ["Samuel Roth" 906] states that Wood was in
fact co-author). Wood soon returned the dedicatory compliment
("To Samuel Roth who always enjoys a good tale" [pun?])./6/
In his Prologue to another book published in 1932, Wood
warmly defended Roth against charges of corrupting morals by
issuing *Chatterley*, adding that his employer was a high-
principled man who "has carried out with me every obligation
he has ever made" (Wood 30-31)./7/ In a letter to me of 7
July 1987, Anton Gud implies the same. That Roth is scrupulous in carrying out professional obligations is surely true;
he could not have stayed in business for over thirty years
otherwise. He may have driven hard bargains; he may have not
been able to pay bills promptly; he did not cheat.

    Perhaps it was as a collegial in-joke that Wood put
himself into *Lady Chatterley's Friends*, a.k.a. Alan Dubois, a
writer who introduces Connie and her friends to the literati
of Paris. The character resembles Wood physically ("a tall

austere chap" [p.70]) and in his interests in medieval
European history. On p.94ff, Dubois treats the friends to a
tour of Paris and regales them with his cavalier and sexually
permissive philosophy of life. Connie begins to fall in love
with him, "with his serious outlook on everything, and his
mad pagan soul, in a body equipped with such keen yet disil-
lusioned eyes" (p.112). Wood did not take his Alain DuBois
persona, or this novel, in dead earnest.

A beautiful, sexually active woman's adventures in
exotic lands (Paris, Cairo, the Egyptian desert) especially
unavailable to American readers during the Depression (save
in movie theaters) is clearly the attraction of the book. She
vows to "not now refuse any sensation that life offered her,"
and becomes an epitome of feminine generosity to her adoring
travel companions: Tommy Dukes, Charlie May, and Clement Wood
(appearing as Alan Dubois). The climax of her Egyptian tour
is dinner in a tent with the manservant Mahmed, who bears the
name and the muscular masculinity of the hero of E. M. Hull's
The Sheik, the novel upon which was based the Rudolph
Valentino film. Mellors, meanwhile, plays the malcontent
puritan; the novel's end finds him still in love with Connie
but leaving Cairo for England, as if he must put half a
continent between himself and a pretty blonde leper: which is
how he behaved at the end of the first sequel. His fall is
paralleled by the ascendancy of Clifford's old friends, whom
Lawrence found to be unworthy "mental lifers" but who
flourish in the sequels because they can live by the enlightened, sybaritic Rules Of The Game.

It may be either a sign of the first sequel's success,
or of its lagging sales, but something must have happened to
cause Roth to commission the very busy Clement Wood for the
second. But what? *Friends'* dust-jacket blurb suggesting that
the purchasers of *Husbands* equalled the number of readers of
the Faro *Chatterley* is not sufficient evidence of either confidence or desperation, although the fact that there were two
impressions is promising. Nor are the binding variants for
Woods' sequel evidence of its popularity. That it is not
advertised as a Big Dollar Book (the Faro enterprise failed
in 1932 [see Section 2, p.25]) may mean that it was not worth
doing so. Once the flagship of the Faro fleet, its *Chatterley*, was faced with the competition of the Knopf edition (see
Section 3, p.61), the lesser craft were inevitably to
flounder.

It is highly unlikely that a single press run for either
sequel exceeded 3000 copies, since that would have been the
size of a Faro *Chatterley* printing. Mr. Gud states that Roth
was only "mildly satisfied" with sales, and "thought they
would have done much better" (questionnaire of 7 July 1988).

A final consideration in assessing the popularity of
both novels: their Connie's radical credo of enlightened
promiscuity, in which she both nurtures her men and is free
to explore her own erotic instincts, is an ideal of the
twenties rather than the thirties. She sees sexual fulfillment as a *sine qua non* of human experience; the sequels treat

the concept as a shocking breakthrough for the Modern Woman. Although it would have been difficult even for Roth to have observed in 1931, adults, Frederick Allen states, had by then sufficiently assimilated the New Morality into mundane experience to assess realistically rather than sensationalize the human relationships it made possible (*Only Yesterday* 138-48, 152-65; *Since Yesterday* 105-10).

The "serious" French sequel of 1934 (A5.1-A5.2) is evidence of Allen's observations. D'Orliac makes Connie pay dearly for choosing illicit sexual gratification. She earns the contempt and mistrust of relatives and friends, who withhold from her not only respect and social status, but also financial support. Too poor to marry Mellors (now a forest-ranger in Touraine), she is reduced to house-keeping for him and her child, and regrets having given up Wragby for "Life and nothing more." She now regards Mellors as a protective lover only in bed, and otherwise as her jailor, for he is a social isolate who refuses companionship even when offered by the nearby affable gentry. The latter's curiosity for new sensations causes a dénouement which frees Connie from Mellors. Her second husband is an introspective, dispassionate French count, who understands rather that loves her. He knows she is no heroine capable of living without participating in the moral and social conventions of her society. He recognizes in her a very conventional person who had an unfortunately "romantic" response to her frustrations at Wragby. He will provide for her habitual needs, and gently discipline her never again to forget The Rules of the Game. D'Orliac has little for Mellors to do, save shoot his wife and thus put himself permanently out of the way. He is happy to go to jail, for this is a secretly-desired end for people such as he, who are imbued with the incivil notion that sexuality is impoverished if it is accommodated to financial, social, and intellectual comforts of modern life.

The French and American sequels have as little to do with Lawrence's hero (and persona) as with his teachings and his language. If Knopf and Secker could not stomach them in 1928 (see Section 1, p.3 and endnote 2) one would not expect a different response from other publishers likewise wishing to profit from the sensibilities of their readership. Both Long and McBride, publishing the year after the D'Orliac novel appeared in France, hoped that English and American readers would purchase a book which the McBride dust jacket touted as "the conflict" awaiting "all lovers who believe that life can be reduced to sensual experience." In 1963, Crown Publishers (for whose involvement in the Roth *Chatterleys* see 8.1-8.3; 9.1, and the essay for Section 2, p.28) filed with the Library of Congress Copyright Office for a reprint. I have found no evidence that the book was published. Perhaps they shelved the plan after a close reading of the text, which must have seemed dated by then.

All that Britain produced during the early thirties was a modest parody, *Sadie Catterley's Cover* (A4.1). The humor revolves around the class-consciousness that Lawrence found

debilitating. Sadie and her husband Marmaduke are very upper-
middle-class; they never use the word "sex" because it would
mean losing face with aristocrats. Even the "fourth-under-
gardener" hides his "common" background. He uses the ver-
nacular only while doing what he loves, which is knitting
upholstery, including a bedspread (cover), which functions as
a clever metonymy for his body: "the ponderous primordial
tenderness with which he lifted the bed-spread disclosed some
palpable portion of herself, and a quick convulsion shook her
. . ."(p.27) By having Sadie imitate the gardener's dialect,
the author discreetly parodies Lawrence's four-letter words:
"FUM, COOM," she says, to which he replies, "Tha's got the
nicest, nicest dialect as is." Her husband tosses her out of
the house when he hears what has happened to her diction! She
returns to the gardener and "exposes the core of her physical
jungle" to him; he wraps her in the "piercingly beautiful"
bed-spread.

In Hollywood, California in 1945, a small novelty item
bound in pinkish red and jet black, entitled *Lady Loverley's
Chatter,* appeared. Its distributor was a publisher whose
audience and tactics for reaching it was reminiscent of
Samuel Roth's. Marcel Rodd was indicted in May 1946 by a
Federal Grand Jury for mailing by Federal Express *Call House
Madam*, which he had been advertising as well as distributing
since 1943, and which had been banned by the Postmaster
General in 1945. In February 1946, Rodd opened a sales and
shipping office in New York City and had been sending copies
of the book from there to San Diego. In November, he appealed
his conviction and fine of $2500, stating that the book had
been edited by T. R. Smith, formerly of Boni and Liveright
and editor of the famed anthology *Poetica Erotica* (See PW 23
Feb. 1946: p. 1248; 29 June 1946: p.3333; 16 Nov. 1946:
p.2814).

Lady Loverley hardly classifies as even borderline
erotica, despite its packaging (see A6.1.a), nor as either a
sequel or parody. It uses only the (Spoonerized) title, but
does show that Lawrence's Connie has entered the imagination
as an archetypal erotic heroine an acquaintance with whom had
become as much a rite of passage as a tour of World War II
duty itself. The story concerns a soldier on three-day leave
who strikes up a conversation with a voluptuous woman of
indeterminate age. They discuss her cerebral, possessive but
sexually unresponsive husband (on safari in Africa), jeal-
ousy, adultery, free love, and double martinis before leaving
the cocktail lounge together for "other activity." Lady
Loverley is Venus herself, her beauty an epitome of Anglo-
Saxon, Spanish, near eastern, and African femininity.
Ageless, enigmatic, and irresistible, she requires romantic
conversation, total attention, tactfully-revealed sexual
excitement, and her freedom. The volume's design busily
creates a Hollywood ethos of erotic glamour. Its text-pages
(reinforcing the impression of the binding, dust jacket and
front matter display type) are decorated with exotic head-
and tailpieces, many of nude young women, suggesting (as
small gift-books of love poetry have done since Edwardian

times) an escape from the frustrations of duty into a
"shangri-la" of pleasure and gentle relaxation.

Lady Chatterley's decensorship in 1959-60 occasioned two
parodies and sequels which were aggressively marketed; a book
which sold six million copies in the US and three and a half
million in England during the first 15 months of publication
was a property to build upon. The American impression of Lady
Loverley's Chatter (A7.1; no relation to the 1945 work) is a
patchwork quilt of stills from silent films with captions
consisting of brief quotations from Lady Chatterley's Lover.
An example: Beneath a photo of a man feeding a piece of corn
to a very large chicken with a derby hat: "I suppose if the
love-business went, something else would take its place. It
would be wonderfully refreshing for everybody." One might
make an interesting study of the popular response to "high
literature" by considering which epithets "Warren Watwood"
chose. They include the one regarding extra-uterine conception which formed the basis for the illustrations of an early
piracy (see Section 2, p.29, and 3.1), and some of the
phrases most easily misinterpreted as romantic clichés. None
of these excerpts are scatological or sexually explicit. One
must bear in mind that four mainstream publishers had
recently issued the complete text, in hard and soft covers.
For Macauley to use the passages which these books had
liberated from authorized expurgation would have given
critics of Judge Bryan's decision the evidence they needed
for a damning assessment of the morality of the American
publishing industry. Now, had the "secondary" publishers and
distributors (see Section 5, p.134) been enterprising enough
to do a parody in 1960 (but only after the Tropic Of Cancer
and Fanny Hill verdicts did they feel comfortable in printing
scatology) they would have issued a parody "never before in
paperback." Macauley (in 1960 an imprint of Citadel Press)
could ill afford to play by these rules, as "Warren Watwood"
(probably a pseudonym) well knew.

In compiler Watwood's Foreword, he assumes that Lady
Chatterley's Lover was "unprotected by copyright laws," and
posits an further rationale for publishing, despite the
failure either to request or be granted permission from the
Lawrence Estate to use many excerpts from the novel: only
prudes would object to a bit of fun with a great work. He
forges a bond not only with the "courageous publisher" Barney
Rosset, reiterating the latter's explanation for not adhering
to the Estate's strictures against his Grove Press edition,
but also with the other American "Chatterley Sweepstakes"
publishers (with the exception of the New American Library).
Permission was sought to use the photographs, however.

One of those Watwood acknowledges as helpful in this
regard is the journalist William Iverson. In his The Pious
Pornographers, Iverson uses the title Lady Loverley's
Chatter, not to allude to the 1960 book but in order to refer
facetiously to Lawrence's Connie, whose "'too female' figure,
coupled with her unexpurgated familiarity with huts and horse
blankets" made her a more interesting person for contemporary

readers than Nabokov's Lolita (78). It is an accurate comment
on the existence of the "Sweepstakes" books (including A7.1,
A7.2, A8.1, A9.1, and A10.1). In that its tone is not harshly
pejorative but irreverently candid, it should have evoked a
wry nod of recognition from many publishers and readers, to
whom Iverson is saying with a grin, "I got your number." And
Samuel Roth would surely understand, although he may mention
Fanny Hill as well.

A four-page flyer (at ICarbS) for A7.1, sent by Book
Sales (address on flyer is 352 Fourth Ave., New York) to
booksellers and offering $1.00 off in addition to the usual
trade discount, is one indication that the book was assid-
uously marketed ("the funniest book of the year") as a
promising "spin-off." Another is the full page ad in PW (4
April 1960: 11) trumpeting a 30,000-copy first printing
already sold out before the publication date, and exhorting
booksellers as follows:

> Order Lady Loverley in quantity NOW . . . don't get
> caught short on this guaranteed block-buster that's
> loaded from cover to cover with side-splitting silent-
> film stills uproariously captioned with direct quotes
> from Lady Chatterley. It's a sure-fire rib-tickler
> that's guaranteed to explode the dollar-impulse market.

Lyle Stuart may have had a hand in the advertising. He was
behind the Citadel Press, which had purchased the Macauley
Company in 1943 and retained the imprint (Tebbel IV: 69,
312). A possible Stuart involvement is interesting because he
was (and is) an important mass-market publisher of political
and social commentary, including erotically explicit books
(see below).

The British impression (A7.2) is some evidence that its
predecessor was successful. Its Foreword suggests it was
published before the Old Bailey trial in November 1960, but
possibly after the Director of Public Prosecutions decided to
proceed against Penguin (see essay for Section 6 above). The
captions differ from those in the American version. The names
are not those of Lawrence's characters; instead "Lorna and
Lawrence Loverley" and "Percy Potts" are used. Also, the
British version changes the text so that Lawrence's own words
are replaced by either paraphrase or new copy. The reference
in the Foreword of 7.1 to the "courageous publisher" is left
out, as is the passage scoffing at the killjoy "purists." Was
the British publisher more sensitive to the Lawrence estate's
position regarding the novel, and to Penguin's interests in
its text? Whatever the case, the description of A7.2 in the
Cambridge U. exhibition catalogue could not be used for A7.1:
"stills from silent films to illustrate a parody of the
Chatterley plot."(25)

The statement on the upper cover regarding importation
may suggest that Lawrence's novel could in fact be imported
without confiscation in 1960 (see Section 6, endnote 2), but
might more likely refer simply to the present parody itself,

suggesting that it, unlike the Grove Press edition of the novel, could be safely purchased.

Lady Chatterley's Daughter (A8.1, A9.1-A9.2) was launched as a mass-market paperback and the wrappers feature all the high-powered puffing required to capture the attention of thousands of browsers at drug-store and transportation-center bookracks. As is often the case with paperback art (Bonn 85; Smith 7-8; see essay for Section 5, p.132), illustration and copy imitate closely a model; therefore, the fact that the American edition's packaging is much like the British is some indication of the latter's success. Its front-cover blurb (transposed to the back cover in its American counterpart) refers to the heroine's "guilty secret" and its effect on her "surging passion." Is she drowning in this wave or resisting it? What kind of "release" did her "pent-up desires" necessitate? One must get "under cover" to find out; the illustrations are teasingly ambiguous.

The reference in the upper-wrapper blurb to "six million readers" can only refer to the total number of copies of Lawrence's *Lady Chatterley's Lover* sold in the United States in 1959-60; had *Lady Chatterley's Daughter* sold nearly this many copies, shock and outrage would have indeed been universal. (See Section 5, pp.132-33 and especially endnote 3, Section 6, p.182, and NOTES for entries 31.1, 34.1, 35.1, 42.2, 42.11). Ace Books states "6,000,000 British readers thrilled to this novel," the word "this" being intentionally ambiguous. If called to account for a gargantuan untruth, the publishers could say that the antecedent of "this" is "Lawrence's famous novel." The phrasing of the Consul blurb implies that the thrilling numbers refer to "the serial." This can only mean *Lady Chatterley's Lover*, which, the publisher suggests, only represented early installments of the complete opus now finalized by Ms. Robins' sequel. It is possible that the word "serial" was inspired by the silent film stills which comprise A7.2. The latter would have been in print when A8.1 appeared. Even if so, both Consul and Ace must have banked on the fact that the decensorship of 1959-60 had created a large pool of eager, naive fans of Lady Chatterley.

The cover illustrations aim at a prurient-minded male readership, as do many mass-market paperback covers for Lawrence titles. That for the British Ace edition of *Women In Love* (1959) is a possible progenitor of the Consul cover of *Daughter*. The exception (up until circa 1970) in this regard is *Lady Chatterley's Lover*, for the reasons attending the judicial decisions which finally liberated the unexpurgated text, as discussed in Sections 5 and 6. It is both ironic and unsurprising that the sexual "come-on" is used with a sequel published so soon after those decisions. It is unsurprising although the text itself contains no prurient appeal or taboo language. And it is doubly ironic, because *Lady Chatterley's Daughter* seems from Robins' romantic clichés regarding perfume, kisses, and dashing young soldiers to be written for a respectable female audience. The blurb on

the back of the British wrapper, a low-key and discreetly
worded statement about "the central problem in a woman's
life," is calculated to appeal to them. The appeal to young
ladies is less in evidence in Ace's edition, which also
modifies the cover pose so that it resembles other contemporary American paperbacks (see Bonn, plate 32b).

Ace specialized in genre: Western, Science Fiction,
modern Gothic (Bonn 74). Ace Star Books, Davis (271) states,
was a "quality line" started in 1959. Its cover display for
Lady Chatterley's Daughter is a genre creation, playing upon
the formulae of erotic romance with, as Bonn puts it, "all
the necessary colors and clichés expected by wholesale and
retail book buyers and by readers."(91) As for the story
itself, it takes place during the war. Connie and Oliver are
living peacefully in Sussex, in a centrally-heated farmhouse.
They have become domesticated: clearly comfortable and
functional members of the British middle class. Robins
thoughtfully delineates Claire Mellors' panic-fear of sexual
intercourse, which stems from the contrast she experiences
between her mother's insistent praise of sensuality and the
strict taboos regarding sexual openness which she has
absorbed from her peers and teachers. Her discovery that she
was born out of wedlock completes the trauma. She reacts with
shame, guilt, and resentment for her mother. After a breakdown, she visits Clifford and finds a kindly gentleman with a
social conscience, who tells her he has learned that one
cannot live on an intellectual plane only. Developing the
confidence to think for and believe in herself, she understands how her mother could have wanted to belong totally to
the man she loved, and is prepared to do the same for a
certain badly injured British officer. The happy couple live
at Wragby, which Clifford has selflessly willed to Claire.
Neither the myths Robins recapitulates nor the characters she
describes are Lawrence's, but, if less challenging, they were
much more accessible for her female readers than were those
of *Lady Chatterley's Lover* for the "rough-handed" young men
(See Section 6, p.181) who snapped up the Penguin edition.
The point was surely not lost upon the British or American
mass-market publishers. In the U.S., the peak of Lawrence's
novel's popularity had passed. Ace Books was faced with an
afterglow which might well be exploited by the novelty of a
well-conceived sequel.

A Canadian sequel of 1963 (the year of the decensorship
trial in that country) and a dramatization in English by a
Greek poet in 1969 may be briefly mentioned. The former
(A10.1) occupies only three pages in a collection of the
author's humorous essays. The latter (A11.1) was probably
self-published. The biographical sketch states that the
author, Stavros Melissinos, is a poet,translator (Wilde,
Lorca, Poe, Brecht), and playwright (*O That Naughty Boccac-
cio!* and *Chastity Belt*). A brochure accompanying the play
describes him as "a new Tennessee Williams" and "the foster
brother of Omar Khaiyam." He has written a drawing-room
problem-drama in which a resolute Clifford is the hero,
facing his humiliation and loneliness stoically, for "the
manhood of a person exists in the soul and nowhere else." As

with the other works discussed in this chapter, whatever their merits, much of the interest lies in the extent of the writer's denial or misunderstanding of Lawrence's terms for love and/or psychic health.

In 1973 Lyle Stuart published *Lady Scatterly's Lovers*. In the Introduction, H. Allen Smith reveals that the work was written in 1935 by Gene Fowler, biographer of John Barrymore, novelist, newspaper reporter, and chronicler of "high life" in between-the-wars New York and Hollywood. Inspired by the gift of a pirated copy of Lawrence's novel, he concocted what is strictly speaking neither a parody nor a sequel, but a burlesque account, in what Smith feels is Rabelaisian style with a nod to Twain's *1601*, of the sexual athleticism of Lord Cecil Scatterly, Lady Ophelia, and their friends at Hornsey Hall in Nuttingham. Their cavortings are given a Victorian setting, and there are many fine names (the Laird of Coch-Loch, the Earl of Buggerly) for Fowler's actor friends to enunciate. Another friend was Smith himself (newspaper columnist, and, according to the blurb on the NAL edition of his *Life in a Putty Knife Factory*, a "rowdy, bawdy, breezy humorist"), who recalls that "in the matter of producing vulgar literature, often with a classic swing to it, Fowler was avant-gardish as all hell."

To have published such a book in the thirties would have been socially, not to mention legally, quixotic. It was a likely title for Lyle Stuart to issue in 1973. Stuart began his writing career by publishing with Samuel Roth (Boar's Head, 1953) the sensational *The Secret Life of Walter Winchell*. His first publishing effort was a scandal magazine, *Exposé*. Tebbel (IV: 310-12) states that his books included titles dealing with eroticism and sexual behavior (see essay for Section 5, p.136), among other subjects of a controversial nature, treated in ways calculated to inflame conventional sensibilities. Responsible for *The Sensuous Woman* and *Naked Came The Stranger*, he stated in 1978 that "we started the sex revolution in publishing." His innovative use of mass-market advertising was and is no doubt strengthened by his connections with popular entertainers and journalists.

The final parody is in a very different spirit than all the others; it is the comic-book version (A13.1). It is also a piracy, in that it contains Lawrence's language, although abridged and mixed with modern colloquialisms. The work must be placed in the context of the "Adult" or "Underground" comic strip to understand its perspective on Lawrence (who is credited on title page, under the cartoonist, as the writer). As DeMott (48-52) and Daniels (165-80) show, it is not unusual for this art-form to make informed use of classic literature and mythology, to be extremely iconoclastic regarding any notions of political, moral, and especially sexual convention, and to insist on complete freedom of the artist (and reader) to express and delight in (if not act out) whatever psychosexual impulses s/he wishes to contemplate. The stories are long on contempt for any entrenched authority and short on hopeful solutions; a rock-solid

pessimism concerning politicians and academics often issues in cartoons which strain toward shocking anyone who would balk at absolute freedom from laws or attitudes perceived as authoritarian. This creates a strong bond between the underground comic artists and their readers, who are enormously amused in direct proportion to the amount of shock and disgust the uninitiated feel. For these reasons underground comics, especially in England, are widening their distribution strategies (and audiences) for an "overground" readership (Estren 7-8). DeMott (48, 52) specifies the audience as middle-class males in their late teens and twenties with limited prospects of affluence or improved social status. One can understand why the Lawrence Estate chose not to prosecute the publishers--the latter would have enjoyed not only gaining publicity but also eliciting censure from "the authorities."

Lady Chatterley's Lover was for thirty years a famous banned book; after 1959 it retained in part an aura of notoriety. Its publishers' advertising, throughout the seventies at least, nursed the attendant curiosity. Cartoonist Hunt Emerson's *Lady Chatterley* reverses the position the novel has held as a subversive analysis of sexuality and social class in an industrial society. Instead, he and his publishers consider it as a canonized classic, which, in Penguin, Heinemann, NAL, Grove, or Modern Library editions, is required reading in academic institutions. As such it is fair game for iconoclastic present-day artists. Lawrence's story is made to seem absurd in the same way romantic love stories such as *Jane Eyre* seemed ridiculous to him. It is in this spirit that Lawrence is given "second-billing" on the title page as writer, and that his burlesque profile (all shaggy hair and banana-like nose) is splattered over the back cover of the book. And yet this comic strip version is not an expression of contempt, nor a total negation of the novel. In fact, the importance of Penguin's edition is noted, and the endorsements of fifteen witnesses from the Old Bailey trial are reproduced. A13.1 is a radical recasting of a literary classic so as to make it palatable to the sensibilities of readers of adult comics (whom the artist and publisher must respect as arbiters of one facet of contemporary aesthetic taste). If academics, lawyers, or publishers are offended by callow youth being so served, so much the worse for their prejudice. This rationale is similar to that of A7.1, except that Knockabout Publications' parody is more ambitious; it asks more of its readers than a few minutes' snickering. To read it through, one must encounter some of the language of a major poet. Emerson's bear-like Mellors and pear-shaped Connie are an insalubrious couple, especially with long-stemmed flowers wrapping themselves around their genitals, but there are moments when Connie, pregnant, fairly purrs with satisfaction, causing Mellors to soften his brutal features. The flowers and shrubs writhe with a ridiculous tumescence, and seem to utter snorts of randy, derisive laughter, perhaps mirroring the readers' attitude toward Lawrence's novel, and existence itself. But Emerson's flowers are vital presences nonetheless and too ugly to be dismissed with a sneer. In this, they are like his caricatures.

Despite all, the story and its ending survive, however transformed or adapted to the capacities of a specific set of readers. One could not say as much for some of the other parodies discussed in this chapter, and would have to say the same for the expurgated editions, the poorly-lithographed and stylishly-reprinted piracies, and the paperback wrappers and dust jackets which, whether prurient or not, presented the novel they contained as exotic romance. The changes "high literature" undergo when it becomes part of popular culture are dynamic and inevitable.

ENDNOTES

1. Since I am dealing here only with book-length publications designed as parodies, sequels, or dramatizations, I do not include short stories such as Anthony Powell's excellent "A Reference For Mellors," which appeared in *Winter's Tales* 12. Ed. A. D. Maclean. London: Macmillan, 1966. 135-45. The story was reprinted therein from *Vogue For Men*.

The following plays, probably unpublished, were registered for copyright in The Library Of Congress:
a. Copito, Benjamin. *Lady Chatterley's Lover A Play in Two Acts*. 14 Aug. 1951.
b. Fizell, Becca (Becca Fizell Dunn). *Mrs. Chatterley's Lover A New Play in Three Acts*. 11 Dec. 1957.
c. Guile, Fred Lawrence. *Lady Chatterley's Lover A Play in Two Acts. Adapted from the novel by D. H. Lawrence. Florence, Italy ed.* 5 July 1960.
d. Dorik, Edward (Ed Udovich and John Hart). *Lady Chatterley's Lover A Play in Two Acts*. 4 Sept. 1963 and 27 Jan. 1964.

In addition, The Copyright Office contains an application card dated Jan. 5, 1960, registering a Popular Library Giant (#PC 500) entitled *Lady Chatterley's Daughter*, edited by Lawrence Lariar (a mystery writer, humorist, and cartoonist). The card states that the volume contains "new material." I have been unable to locate a copy of this work; it is unlikely in any case that it would have at all resembled A9.1. It is not in *Books In Print* for 1960, and probably did not appear until 1964. The *American Book Publishing Record* (4: 2893) lists the title, edited by Lariar: "New York: Popular Library, 1964 (c. 1960). unpaged (chiefly illus) . . . . Cartoons on the antics of the nubile American girl." The Vertical File at TxU (VF #G62) contains a copy of the front cover and spine. The cover illustration shows a shapely young woman in pedal-pushers and V-neck sweater reclining on a sofa happily engrossed in *Lolita*. Her niave mother explains to her bug-eyed father, "The librarian said it's all about a little girl just Susie's age."

The following collection of jocular newspaper columns speculating on the subsequent careers of fictional characters contains a paragraph on Mellors (p.68): Martin Levin, *Whatever Happened To Lady Chatterley's Lover?* (Kansas City: Andrews, McMeel and Parker, 1985). A facetious poem and

illustration about *Chatterley* may be found on pp.42–43 of Maurice Sagoff, *ShrinkLits* (New York: Workman, 1980).

2. There is one passage (p.160), in which Clifford explains the importance of Connie's staying with him to preserve "the whole order of my life," which is lifted nearly word-for-word from Chapter 19 of *Lady Chatterley's Lover* (the passage is unchanged in Roth's expurgation).

3. The words are Mr. Gud's, in a questionnaire returned to me 12 July 1988. He also stated that Clement Wood did not consult him when the latter set to work on Roth's second *Chatterley* sequel.

4. A description of this plan appears in a signed article in Roth's magazine *Beau, A Magazine For Men*. March 27, 1927: 49.

5. A. R. Kugel, in a letter of 27 Aug. 1987, identifies Wood as "Dubois."

6. The dedication occurs in *Warren Gamaliel Harding: An American Comedy*, published by Faro in 1932.

7. The defense was in *Herbert Clark Hoover: An American Tragedy*. This was also a Roth publication, although, in view of the legal troubles and subsequent injunction against the Faro scandal book written by John Hamill on Hoover (Hamalian, "Samuel Roth" 904–05), Wood's rewrite of Hamill was published under the imprint "Michael Swain."

BIBLIOGRAPHICAL DESCRIPTIONS

[Roth dramatization, 1931]

A1.1   [rule] | THE ARDENT CLASSICS NUMBER TWO | [rule] | LADY
        | CHATTERLEY'S | LOVER | A Dramatization of his Version
        | of D. H. LAWRENCE'S Novel | by | SAMUEL ROTH | [rule]
        | 1931 WILLIAM FARO, INC. New York 1931 | [rule]

(7 1/4 x 4 11/16"): [1-12]^8, 96 leaves; pp.[8],[1-4],5-13,
[14], [2], 15-63, [64], [2], 65-121, [122], [2], 123-70, [8].

CONTENTS: pp.[1-4]:blank. p.[5]:half-title.p.[6]:list of THE
    ARDENT CLASSICS, 5 titles: *Venus in Furs*, the present
    volume, Mendes' *Lila and Colette*, Sacher-Masoch's *Venus
    and Adonis*, Cheyney's *Pregnant Woman in a Lean Age*.
    p.[7]:t.p. p.[8]: Copyright 1931 | *by* | SAMUEL ROTH
    |. p.[1]: for PAULINE |. p.[2]:blank. p.[3]:section
    title. p.[4]:blank. pp.5-13: BY WAY OF EXPLANATION
    |. p.[14]: blank. p.[1]: section title for Act One.
    p.[2]:blank. pp.15-63:text. p.[64]: blank. p.[1]: section
    title for Act Two. p.[2]: blank. pp.65-121: text. p.[122]:
    blank. p.[1]: section title for Act Three. p.[2]: blank.
    pp.123-170: text. pp.[8]:blank.

TYPOGRAPHY: text: 21ll.(p.82): 130 x 85mm. 10ll.=65mm. Face
    3(2x)mm.
    Typeface: Old Style No. 2(?), R.69. Transitional. DIN
    1.24, Modern Baroque. Title page in sans serif.

PAPER: smooth white wove unwatermarked. Thickness .11mm. Tot-
    al bulk 12.0mm.

BINDING: black linen-grain (T304) cloth. White paper label on
    spine: The | Ardent | Classics | LADY | CHATT- | ERLEY'S
    | LOVER | by | SAMUEL ROTH | [dot] | FARO |. All edges
    trimmed. White endpapers; thickness .10mm.
    DJ: pale yellowish pink (C31), printed in black. Front
    cover: Lady | Chatterley's | Lover | A PLAY [dot] BY
    SAMUEL ROTH | william faro [dot] inc [ll.1-3 in decorative
    display type: R626,Futura Black(?)] |. Set vertically,
    bottom to top: near spine edge, over vertical double
    rule: NUMBER TWO OF A SERIES OF BOOKS CALLED THE ARDENT
    CLASSICS |. Bottom to top. near outer edge, set vertically
    over vertical double rule: ORIGINAL BOOKS OF UNUSUAL
    MERIT AND REPRINTS OF EXPENSIVE LIMITED EDITIONS |. Title
    and vertical rules in red. On spine: bottom to top: LADY
    CHATTERLEY'S LOVER |. Back cover and flaps blank.

NOTES: Roberts Ap.I.A.III. Binding cloth as in 7.1 and 7.2.
    For Samuel Roth's important activities with *Chatterley*,
    see essays for Sections 2,3 and Appendix 1 above, and
    1.11-1.12, 2.1, 7.1-7.4, A2.1-3.1. Roth filed for copy-
    right for this work under his own name (address given as
    Jersey City, N. J.) on April 24, 1931.

COPIES EXAMINED: TxU(dj), personal

[The first Samuel Roth sequel, 1931]

A2.1   LADY | CHATTERLEY'S | HUSBANDS | AN ANONYMOUS SEQUEL
        TO | THE CELEBRATED NOVEL | LADY | CHATTERLEY'S |
        LOVER | PUBLISHED BY WILLIAM FARO, INC. | IN NEW YORK
        CITY, THE YEAR 1931

(8 1/16 x 5 1/2"): [1-15]^8, 120 leaves; pp. [1-8], 9-233,
[6].

CONTENTS: p.[1]: half-title. p.[2]: frontispiece. p.[3]: t.p.
    p.[4]: COPYRIGHT, 1931, BY WILLIAM FARO, INC., | PRINTED
    IN THE UNITED STATES OF AMERICA | ALL RIGHTS RESERVED |.
    P.[5]: FROM THE ANONYMOUS AUTHOR | TO HIS | ANONYMOUS
    READERS |. p.[6]: blank. p.[7]: section title. p.[8]:
    blank. pp.9-233: text. p.[234]: blank. pp.[6]: blank.

TYPOGRAPHY: Text: 26ll.(p.91): 121 (131) x 90mm. 10ll.=45mm.
    Face 2.5(2x)mm.
    Typeface: ITC Century, R175. Modern Face (Didone). DIN
    1.34, Modern Neo-Classic. Title page in Hadriano, a
    display type with extended apex for the A, similar to
    R395, Hadriano Stonecut (but that is shadowed).

RUNNING HEADS: rectos and versos: LADY CHATTERLEY'S HUSBANDS
    | [thick-thin rule] |.

PAPER: rough white wove unwatermarked. Thickness .14mm. Total
    bulk 20.1mm.

BINDING: Moderate Blue (C182) cloth, linen grain (T304).
    Stamped in yellow, upper cover: LADY | CHATTERLEY'S |
    HUSBANDS | [rule] | [floral dec.] |. In yellow on spine:
    [four rules] | LADY | CHATTERLEY'S | HUSBANDS | [rule] |
    [floral dec.] | [four rules] | FARO | [four rules] |. Top
    edges trimmed, others partly trimmed. Plain white end-
    papers.

ILLUSTRATIONS: line drawings (cartoons, each figure with
    heart-shaped face and flowing hair). Each full page,
    captioned (quotation marks appear in text):
    1) p.[2]: frontispiece. Nude woman, lying prone, left hand
       cupped under breast: "*She surveyed her swollen belly and
       gently passed her hand over it, and her hard heavy
       breasts with their protruding nipples* -- page 13"
    2) p.[28]: man and full-breasted woman, eyes averted:
       "*Hilda and Michaelis walked hand in hand* -- page 30"
    3) p.[46]: man [Clifford] lying in bed, left hand protrud-
       ing from covers: "*'Tell her I died smiling, with her
       name on my lips'* -- page 61"
    4) p.[62]: man in shirt, tie and suit jacket, left hand
       on face of apparently naked woman who stares up at him:

"*Proposing a toast to the bride* -- page 94"; drawing
unrelated to text or caption.
5) p.[86]: man (Mellors) fondling naked woman (Connie):
"*And she accepted all his caresses, nearly swooning with
desire* -- page 112"
6) p.[102]: woman (Sir Malcolm's mistress) opening door
for young man: "*She opened the door and was confronted
by a tall curly-haired youth* -- page 132"
7) p.[120]: four burning candles: "'*Maybe you did not
choose the right kind of candle*' -- page 169"

NOTES: The text was printed with spelling errors, including
"Chatterly." There are frequent dropped letters. On p.121
the first three lines of text are repeated; from p.177
onward the text block is set lower on the page than it had
been previously. A very similar printing style, including
running heads, section titles, and typeface, was used for
Faro's anonymous *The Intimate Journal of Rudolph Valentino*, 1931 (for which see NOTES for 1.12.b; see also 2.1.a
and 7.3). All three entries have the same spine label
typeface as the Valentino book, as does A2.2 below.
   All illustrations (including frontispiece) are integral
with the text, not tipped in. Unsigned and unattributed,
they are in the style of "Rahnghild," four of whose
drawings are used in the 1932 Faro edition of *Venus In
Furs*: not the one issued as one of the Ardent Classics
(see A1.1), but the octavo format which attributes
copyright to The Big Dollar Book Company verso t.p.
   The Library of Congress copyright application card lists
the publication date as 15 Sept. 1931. This title is
listed on dj advertisements as one of the Faro Famous
Dozen (see reproduction of list in Pringle 463), and as a
Big Dollar Book (see 7.4.$_1$).

COPIES EXAMINED: personal, NNC

A2.2   as A2.1 save:

(7 9/16 x 5 1/8"): [1-2]^8 [3-8]^{16} [9]^4 [10]^2 118 leaves,
pp.[1-8], 9-233, [234], [2].

CONTENTS: p.[2]: blank. pp.[2]: blank.

PAPER: ribbed white wove unwatermarked. Chain lines approximately 20mm apart. Thickness .14mm. Total bulk 17.1mm.

BINDING: black linen-grain (T304) cloth. White paper label on
spine: [double rule] | *Lady* [swash L] | *Chatterley's*
[swash C]| *Husbands* [swash H] | [two rules] | *FARO* | [two
rules] | [two rules] |. All edges trimmed.
   Dj: white paper wrappers. Upper cover: drawing in brown
and white of woman in tight sweater looking over her
shoulder at a large lineup of men. [rule in brown] | [rule
in white] LADY | CHATTERLEY'S | HUSBANDS | [rule in white]
| [rule in brown] | WILLIAM FARO, INC. N. Y. |. Printing
on 11.2-4 white on brown background, 1.7 in brown. On
spine: LADY | CHATTERLEY'S | HUSBANDS | [rule in brown] |
[rule in white] | FARO | [rule in white] | [rule in brown]

l [ll.1-3 white on brown background; 1.4 in white on brown
background]. Lower cover: advert for Hamill's *Strange
Career of Mr. Hoover.* Back flap blank. Front flap: $2.00 l
We might l offer the human l weakness to see more of
people we like, as an excuse l for the publication of LADY
l CHATTERLEY'S HUS- l BANDS --if one needed an l excuse
for publishing a beau- l tiful and exciting story. The l
world of admirers of Connie l and her gamekeeper husband
lover, l Mellors, will find their favor- l ites as
delightful as ever to l follow -- and abuse.

NOTES: See Roberts App.I.A.IV, who reports the author to be
Samuel Roth.
     This impression is unillustrated. The typeface on the
spine label is identical to that on 1.12.b, 2.1.a, and
7.3. The binding cloth is that of 7.1 and A1.1.
     The dj illustration is not in the style of the in-text
drawings.

COPIES EXAMINED: ICarbS, Forster Coll(dj)

     [the second Samuel Roth sequel, 1932]

A3.1   LADY l CHATTERLEY'S l FRIENDS l [dot] l *A New Sequal*
         [sic] *to* l LADY CHATTERLEY'S l LOVER *and* l   LADY
         CHATTERLEY'S l HUSBANDS l [dot] l 1932 l WILLIAM FARO,
         Inc. l NEW YORK

(7 15/16 x 5 7/16"): [1-14]^8, 112 leaves; pp.[1-9], 10-216,
[8]

CONTENTS: pp.[1-2]: blank. p.[3]: half-title. p.[4]: blank.
     p.[5]: title page. p.[6]: *Copyright 1932* l *by* l WILLIAM
     FARO, *Inc.* p.[7]: THE BOOK [section title] p.8: blank.
     pp.[9]-216: text. pp.[8]: blank.

TYPOGRAPHY: text: 24ll. (p.123): 119 (127) x 89mm.
     10ll.=49mm. Face 3(2x)mm.
     Typeface: Imprint(?), R67. Transitional. DIN 1.24, Modern
     Baroque.

RUNNING HEADS: rectos and versos: LADY CHATTERLEY'S FRIENDS

PAPER: white rough wove unwatermarked. Thickness .16mm. Total
     bulk 20.0mm.

BINDING: Var.(1): black linen-grain (T304) cloth. White paper
     label on spine: [row of dots] l [2 rules] l LADY l
     CHATTERLEY'S l FRIENDS l [large dot] l FARO l [2 rules] l
     [row of dots] l. Var.(2): as (1) save: dotted-line (T108)
     cloth, dark grayish olive (C111).
     Dj: copy on one of the flaps [only segment of jacket
     seen] reads: It seems as if there is to be l no end to the
     adventures of l poor Constance Chatterley l who is now
     Constance l Chatterley Mellors. And, l of course, no one

wants to | see the end: for LADY CHATTERLEY'S HUS- | BANDS
was read avidly by | all the readers of the D. H. |
Lawrence classic, and we | predict that LADY |
CHATTERLEY'S | FRIENDS will even widen | the circle of
her admirers.|. All edges trimmed. Plain white endpapers.

NOTES: C. J. Scheiner (letter of 16 July 1986) has told me
   this was ghost-written by Clement Wood; Adelaide Roth
   confirms this in a letter of 27 Aug. 1987, quoting a pen
   name (Alain Dubois) Wood used for *Loose Shoulder Straps,*
   published by Faro in 1932. Under his own name, Wood wrote
   three non-fiction titles published under the Faro imprint.
      The binding cloth is the same as that used for 7.1, 7.2
   and A2.2.
      There is no copyright record on file for this work.
   See Roberts App.I.A.VI.

COPIES EXAMINED: Var.(1): personal, TxU (both with one flap
   of dj laid in), CU-S(copy 1). Var.(2): ICarbS, personal,
   CU-S(copy 2)

   [First British Parody, 1933]

A4.1   ROBERT LEICESTER | [French rule] | SADIE |
          CATTERLEY'S | COVER | A LEG-PULL | 1933 | CRANLEY &
          DAY

(7 3/8 x 4 3/4"): [A]^8 B-C^8; 24 leaves: pp. [2], [1-8], 9-43,
[44], [2].

CONTENTS: pp.[2]: blank. p.[1]: half-title. p.[2]: BY THE
   SAME AUTHOR | The Hell of Comeliness - *a leg-pull* |.
   p.[3]: t.p.p.[4]: *First Published in October* 1933 *by
   Cranley & Day Limited* | 15a *Harrington Road, London, S.W.*7
   | MADE AND PRINTED IN GREAT BRITAIN BY | THE KEMP HALL
   PRESS LTD., OXFORD |. p.[5]: My tilt at the Roger de
   Coverley [parody of "My Skirmish with Jolly Roger"] |.
   p.[6]: blank. p.[7]: section title. p.[8]: blank. pp.9-
   43: text. p.[44]:blank. pp.[2]: blank.

TYPOGRAPHY: 25ll.(p.17): 113 (148) x 84mm. 10ll.=44mm. Face
   3(2x)mm. Garamont (Amsterdam), R96. Transitional. DIN
   12.24, Modern Baroque.

RUNNING HEADS: rectos and versos: SADIE CATTERLEY'S COVER

PAPER: ribbed, impressed with chain-lines approximately 25mm.
   apart. Thickness .16mm. Total bulk 4.1mm.

BINDING: linen cloth (T304), light blue (C181). Stamped in
   dark blue on upper cover: SADIE CATTERLEY'S COVER |. On
   spine, stamped in dark blue, top to bottom: SADIE
   CATTERLEY'S COVER |.
      Dj: white paper, with red stripes running at 12 degree

angle to the vertical. Front cover, in red: *A leg-pull* |
SADIE | CATTERLEY'S | COVER | [in black:] Robert Leicester
On spine: top to bottom: SADIE CATTERLEY'S COVER |. Set
vertically: 2/6 |. Back cover and flap blank. Front flap
contains blurb: "Those of you who have read D. H.
Lawrence's famous novel. . . must surely be amused with
the delightful caricature of the heroine, here compromised
by Sir Marmaduke Catterley's fourth-under-gardener and
accepting from him the coveted red bedspread with which to
cover her penultimate nakedness."

NOTE: Roberts Ap.I.A.I. Roberts states that Robert Leicester
is "the pseudonym for William S. Scott."
    This, and A7.2, were most likely the kind of books one
could acquire in Britain at "rubber shops" (see essay for
Section 2 above, p.17).

COPY EXAMINED: Forster Coll., TxU

[French sequel, 1935]

A5.1   [in double border, outer one consisting of floral
          designs and inner one of four rules: *Jehanne D'Orliac*
          | LADY CHATTERLEY'S | SECOND HUSBAND | *Translated*
          from the French by | WARRE BRADLEY WELLS | *London* |
          JOHN LONG, LIMITED | 34, 35, & 36 *Paternoster Row*

(7 3/8 x 5"): [A]^8 B-S^8, 144 leaves; pp. [1-8], 9-288.

CONTENTS: pp.[2]: blank. p.[3]: half-title. p.[4]: blank.
    p.[5]: t.p. p.[6]: *Le deuxieme mari de Lady Chatterley*, by
    Jehanne | D'Orliac, was first published in Paris in 1934.|
    English translation first published in 1935. p.[7]:
    statement attributed to André Malraux regarding Lawrence's
    characters and their self-absorption. "The real dialogue
    is between Lady Chatterley and herself." p.[8]: blank. pp.
    9-288: text. (Under rule. p. 288: JOHN LONG, LTD., LONDON,
    ENGLAND, 1935 | WILLIAM BRENDON AND SON, LTD., PRINTERS,
    PLYMOUTH |.

TYPOGRAPHY: Text: 30ll.(p.225), 146 (157) x 90mm. 10ll.=47mm.
    Face 3 (2x)mm.
    Typeface: R91, Garamond 156 (Monotype). Transitional (DIN
    1.24, Modern Baroque).

RUNNING HEADS: rectos and versos: LADY CHATTERLEY'S SECOND
    HUSBAND

PAPER: rough white wove unwatermarked. Thickness: .13mm.
    Total bulk: 20.5mm.

BINDING: Linen grain (T304) cloth, strong reddish orange
    (C35). White paper label on upper cover: [two borders,
    outer one in strong reddish orange, composed of floral
    designs, inner one of four rules:] LADY CHATTERLEY'S |

SECOND HUSBAND | *A Novel by* | Jehanne D'Orliac [1.3 in
strong reddish orange |. White paper label on spine: [row
of floral designs in strong reddish orange] | [rule] |
LADY | CHATTERLEY'S | SECOND | HUSBAND | [floral design in
strong reddish orange] | Jehanne D'Orliac | *JOHN LONG* |
[rule] | [row of floral designs in strong reddish orange]
|. Plain white endpapers. Top edge unstained, trimmed.
Others lightly trimmed.

NOTE: Powell describes this as the "first serious sequel" and
provides a brief plot summary; the Cambridge U. catalogue
(25) makes a similar statement.

COPIES EXAMINED: Forster Coll.; OX/U-1

A5.2   as A5.1 save:

JEHANNE D'ORLIAC | *Lady Chatterley's* | *Second Husband* |
Translated from the French by | *WARRE BRADLEY WELLS* | *Robert*
M. McBride & Company, New York

CONTENTS: p.[1]:half-title. p.[2]:blank. p.[3]: t.p. p.[4]:
LADY CHATTERLEY'S SECOND HUSBAND | COPYRIGHT, 1935 | BY
JEHANNE D'ORLIAC | PRINTED IN THE UNITED STATES | OF
AMERICA | FIRST EDITION |. p.[5]: statement by Malraux.
p.[6]: blank. p.[7]: section title. p.[288]: no rule or
printer's statement.

TYPOGRAPHY: t.p.: 11.1-3 in Koch Kursive.

BINDING: brownish-orange (C54) cloth. Stamped in silver on
upper cover: LADY | CHATTERLEY'S | SECOND | HUSBAND |.
Stamped in silver on spine: LADY | CHATTER- | LEY'S |
SECOND | HUSBAND | [decoration] | D'ORLIAC | McBRIDE |.
Plain white endpapers. Top edge stained reddish-orange.
All edges trimmed.
Dj: coated paper wrappers. Front cover and spine: predomi-
nant color light brown (C57), lettering in white, with
rules in red on white background. U. c.: [rule] | LADY |
[rule] | CHATTERLEY'S | [rule] | SECOND | [rule] | HUSBAND
[rule] | JEHANNE D'ORLIAC | [rule] |. On spine: [rule] |
LADY CHATTERLEY'S [in brown, outlined in white:] SECOND |
[rule] | HUSBAND | [in white:] D'ORLIAC | [rule] | [rule]
| [rule] | McBRIDE | [rule] |. Back cover: notice of three
titles: Deeping's *The White Gate*, Lloyd's *The House in St.*
Cloud, Armstrong's *Escape!* Front flap: price ($2.00);
blurb: ". . . the whole world knows how Constance Chatterley, an English aristocrat, renounced a title and assured
wealth to carry on her passionate relationship . . . .
Here is presented, with all the drama of intensified life,
the conflict that is bound to emerge between all lovers
who believe that life can be reduced to sensual experience." Back flap: advertisement for *Travel* magazine
and coupon for catalogue.

NOTE: Roberts Ap.I.V.
Regarding d.j. coupon, McBride published a wide range of

titles, and specialized in travel books and in fiction by
minor writers.
    There is a copyright card in the Library of Congress
(dated 14 March 1963) indicating that Crown Publishers
intended to publish a reprint of this novel. I have not
located a copy of this reprint.

COPY EXAMINED: personal(dj)

        [Hollywood, 1945]

A6.1.a   LADY LOVERLY'S | chatter | [line drawing of naked
          woman lying under tree] | *by* | MART REB | WITH
          DESIGNS AND DECORATIONS | BY | FRITZ WILLIS | FOR THE
          ARTHUR YEOMAN PRESS

(5 9/16 x 4"): [A–D]⁸, 32 leaves; pp. [1–64].

CONTENTS: p.[1]: half-title. p.[2]: notice of "limited
    edition" of this volume. p.[3]: t.p. p.[4]: Copyright 1945
    by | Marcel Rodd | [rights reserved statement, 3 ll.] |
    [decoration: horses' head] | The Publications of the
    Arthur Yeoman Press are distributed | by the Marcel Rodd
    Company, Hollywood, California, to | whom all correspon-
    dence should be directed. | *Printed in the United States
    of America.* pp.[5–63]: text. p.[64]: decoration: key.

TYPOGRAPHY: Text: 24ll.(p.6), 104 x 75 mm. 10 ll.= 43 mm.
    Face 3(2x)mm.
    Typeface: Times Roman monotype(?), R52. Modern Ren (DIN
    1.13). Times Roman(?). First two lines on t.p., and blurb
    on front and back flap of d.j., in Koch Kursive.

PAPER: smooth white wove unwatermarked. Thickness .12mm.
    Total bulk 4.2mm.

BINDING: paper covered boards, strong red (C12). Upper cover,
    in center: female mask in black and red, on background of
    a black design with uneven edges. On spine, set bottom to
    top: LADY LOVERLY'S CHATTER |. Set horizontally at top of
    spine: REB |. Lower cover undecorated. Edges trimmed.
    Black endpapers.
      Dj: Front cover: predominant colors black, purple,
    white. Head of woman in white; red lips, earring, and
    pearls emphasized. On lower third of cover: *Lady* |
    LOVERLY'S | *chatter* | *by* | MART REB |. Lines 1 and 3 in
    non-flowing script; line 2 in purple. On spine, white on
    black background, set bottom to top: LADY LOVERLY'S
    CHATTER |. Set horizontally at top of spine: REB |. Back
    cover, in white in black border: drawing in light purple
    of naked woman, back to viewer, with flowers and *putti*.
    On lower third of cover: PUBLICATION OF THE ARTHUR YEOMAN
    PRESS | WHICH IS DISTRIBUTED BY | THE MARCEL RODD COMPANY
    | 1656 NORTH CHEROKEE AVENUE | HOLLYWOOD, CALIFORNIA |.
    Each flap contains a vignette of naked woman in light

purple with initials LL worked into design, and blurb:
Front flap: A soldier on furlough meets a woman. | She is
timeless, ageless, eternal. . . . | Laid claim to and
taken into possession | by all, but retained and
maintained by | none, Lady Loverly is everybody's and |
nobody's . . . . At top right of front flap, in light
purple: *one dollar* |. Back flap: . . . A body and a
spirit, She is | so with a stamp and impress alternatively
| mephistophelean and divine | . . . . In the moments of
his bottomless | solitude and urgent need he warmly and |
gratefully embraces her. After the corner | is turned and
the obstacle surmounted,| or friends surround him, he is
free to shun, | and spurn, and snub her. | The Lady
Smiles.

DECORATIONS: headpieces, tailpieces, decorated initials, some
in purple. Line drawings, most of naked women, inter-
spersed with vignettes of mask, armed heads, female lips,
and cupids.

NOTES: Roberts Ap.I.AII.

COPIES EXAMINED: personal(dj), OkTU (dj), ICarbS(dj)

*A6.1.b   "limited edition", number of copies unstated (see
A6.1.a above, p.[2]):". . . bound with a leather
spine imprinted with gold leaf, and printed on
handmade text paper. . . . signed by both author
and artist, has added illustrations tipped in by
hand. . . Copies, at six dollars each, may be
obtained direct from the artist, in care of The
Marcel Rodd Company. . . ."

[post-censorship captioned movie stills, 1960]

A7.1   *Lady* | *Loverley's* | *Chatter* | EDITED AND COMPILED BY |
Warren Watwood | THE MACAULAY COMPANY [dot] PUBLISHERS
| *New York*

(8 1/2 x 5 1/2"): [1]^8 [2-3]^{16}, 40 leaves; pp. [1-80].

CONTENTS: p.[1]: t.p. p.[2]: "*Dedication*: The title of this
book is dedicated to the Rev. W. A. Spooner. Actually,
this sort of volume does not require a dedication. But it
DOES add something of an air, what?" Acknowledgements:
William Iverson, Universal Pictures, United Artists.
"Copyright © 1960, by Warren Watwood | The Macauley
Company Publishers, Inc." p.[3]: Foreword: "For years,
The Lady was expurgated . . . banned . . . praised . .
.forbidden . . . and promptly smuggled into the U.S. and
U.K. by the thousands of copies. Now, a courageous
publisher has defended her so ably in our courts that she
is finally recognized as the great literature she is. At
last, The Lady is officially free to circulate. . . .
Unprotected by copyright laws, she is also free to receive

the irreverent treatment she gets in this book. There are
purists who regard this funning . . . as sacrilege. A pox
on them! . . . . p.[4]: blank. pp.[5-80]: text.

TYPOGRAPHY: [the volume consists of photographs with brief
captions. There are no more than 5 lines of text per
page].

PAPER: smooth white wove unwatermarked. Thickness .1mm. Total
bulk 5.1mm.

BINDING: paper wrappers, medium olive brown (C95). Upper
cover, printed in black: [in circle of deep red:] $1.00 |
LADY | LOVERLEY'S | CHATTER | THIS IS | THE | ABRIDGED |
CENSORED | EXPURGATED | INCOMPLETE | EDITION | NEVER
BEFORE IN PAPERBACK! |. [ll.5-11 arranged to left of still
from foreign film; ll. 5, 6, 11 in white; l. 7 in black on
background of deep red rectangle; l.8 in black; l. 9 in
deep red on background of black rectangle; l. 10 in red,
save first two letters, in black; ll. 11 in white; l. 12
in black, on background of strip in red. On spine, top to
bottom, printed in black: LADY LOVERLEY'S CHATTER |. Lower
cover, printed in black: *Published by* | THE MACAULEY
COMPANY PUBLISHERS, INC. | New York 10, New York |
Distributed by | BOOK SALES, INC. | 352 Park Avenue South
| New York 10, New York |. No endpapers. Edges trimmed.

ILLUSTRATIONS: The book contains approximately 75 stills from
silent films with captions, each a brief excerpt from *Lady
Chatterley's Lover*.

NOTES: Regarding the Dedication (p.[2]), the title is of
course a Spoonerism. William Iverson wrote several
humorous books on the sexual revolution.
      The full-page ad in PW (4 April 1960:11; see essay
above) states that the 30,000 copy first printing sold out
before publication, and a second printing of 30,000 is
being prepared. Three other books are listed in this
advert: D. W. Cory's *Homosexual In America* ($6), *The
Southern History of the Civil War* ($8.50 the set), and
Aleister Crowley's *Magick--In Theory And Practice* ($10).

COPIES EXAMINED: OkTU, ICarbS, TxU

A7.2   as A7.1 save:

imprint change, after l.5: [pub. logo: WHA, 2 quill pens in
black rectangle] | W. H. ALLEN | LONDON | 1960

(8 1/2 x 5 1/2"): [1-5]^8, 40 leaves; pp. [1-80].

CONTENTS: p.[2]: Copyright © 1960, by Warren Watwood | (list
of acknowledgements) | *Made and printed in Great Britain* |
by Gilmore and Dean Ltd., Glasgow, for the publishers, |
W. H. Allen & Co., Ltd., Essex Street, London, W.C.2 |.
p.[3]: *Foreword*: "Banned, censored, expurgated, the poor
Lady is unsure whether she is free to circulate among us,
but at least we can still enjoy a joke at her expense . .

. . We guarantee sophisticated chuckles for sophisticated people."

BINDING: Predominant background color is C94: light olive brown. Upper cover: 1.1 is in circle of strong red and reads 5/- l. 1.12: CAN BE IMPORTED ANYWHERE! l. On spine, top to bottom: LADY LOVERLEY'S CHATTER l. Lower cover: [logo] l W. H. ALLEN l ESSEX STREET [dot] LONDON [dot] WC2 l *Publishers of good books since the 18th century* l.

NOTES: Roberts Ap.IAVII.
      Although the British version may be another edition, the mise-en-page and illustrations are identical to the American version's, and I assume that the new captions were stripped onto the existing plates.
      W. H. Allen published British and American fiction, and biographies of stage and screen personalities (Mumby, 6th ed. 127).
      The *Cumulative Book Index* for 1960 lists the publication date of A7.2 as Oct. 17, 1960.

COPIES EXAMINED: LO/N-1; personal

[post-censorship British paperback sequel, 1961]

A8.1   *Lady Chatterley's Daughter* l [swelled rule] l PATRICIA ROBINS l WORLD DISTRIBUTORS LONDON

(6 5/8 x 4 1/2"): no sigs (perfect bound); pp. [1-6], 7-256.

CONTENTS: p.[1]: blurb: "This is a story which deals with the central problem in a woman's life -- how does she come to terms with love?" p.[2]: Consul Books logo, list of books by Robins (20 titles). p.[3]: t.p. p.[4]: A CONSUL BOOK l [dot] l Copyright © MCMLXI by Patricia Robins l *This CONSUL edition, complete and unabridged,* l *published in England, 1961, by* l WORLD DISTRIBUTORS (MANCHESTER) LTD. l 36 GREAT RUSSELL STREET, LONDON, W.C.1 l Any similarity or apparent connection between l the characters in this story and actual persons, l whether alive or dead, is purely coincidental l Text set in 9 on 10pt. Caledonian l *Made and printed at The Philips Park Press, Manchester* l. p.[5]: section title. p.[6]: blank. pp.7-256: text.

TYPOGRAPHY: text: 39ll.(p.169), 137 x 83mm. 10ll.=38mm. Face 1.5(2x)mm.
      Typeface: see CONTENTS above, p.[4].

PAPER: smooth white wove unwatermarked. Thickness .1mm. Total bulk 13.0 mm.

BINDING: paper wrappers, predominant colors brown and yellow. Upper wrapper: on brown background: in upper left: logo, printed in black on yellow background (man's head, below which, arranged in semi-circle: CONSUL BOOKS). Next two

lines to right of logo: What was the guilty secret | which
held her on the edge | of a surging passion? | [on yellow
background:] LADY | CHATTERLEY'S | DAUGHTER | *Patricia
Robins* | [on brown background:] [drawing of voluptuous
woman in pink slip, facing toward reader but with averted
eyes, lying on bed or sofa with head resting on left arm,
below which is (illegible) artist's monogram] | [in white
circle:] 3/6 | Six million readers thrilled to | the
serial--now the complete story |. On spine, on white
background: in circle: 264 |. [set top to bottom:] LADY
CHATTERLEY'S DAUGHTER | Patricia Robins |. [Set horizon-
tally]: logo, as on upper wrapper. Lower wrapper, on
yellow background: LADY CHATTERLEY'S | DAUGHTER | *Patricia
Robins* | [blurb, as on p.[1], 8ll.] | [drawing, as on
upper wrapper, in black and yellow] |. Edges trimmed,
unstained.

NOTE: The priority of this volume to A9.1 is based on the
front-cover blurb for the latter (see below).
    See endnote 1 above.

COPY EXAMINED: personal

[American paperback version of A8.1]

A9.1   *LADY | CHATTERLEY'S | DAUGHTER* | [swelled rule] | by |
        PATRICIA ROBINS | ACE BOOKS, INC. | 23 West 47th
        Street, New York 36, N.Y.

(7 1/8 x 4 1/8"): perfect bound; pp.[1-4], 5-222, [2].

CONTENTS: p.[1]: blurb, under swelled rule: Claire Mellors,
    the proud and beautiful daugh- | ter of the celebrated
    Lady Chatterley and her | gamekeeper lover, sought from
    each of her | lovers release from the pent-up desires that
    | brought her to the brink of passion but never | beyond.
    . . . p.[2]: list of books by Robins: 20 titles. p.[3]:
    t.p. p.[4]: Copyright ©, MCMLXI by Patricia Robins | Any
    similarity . . . purely coincidental (4 lines) | An *ACE
    STAR BOOK* | published by arrangement with the author. |
    PRINTED IN U.S.A. pp.5-222: text. pp.[2]: list of Ace
    books, beginning Ginzburg's *Unhurried View of Erotica*,
    ending *The One Hundred Stories*.

TYPOGRAPHY: 42ll. (p.47): 136 (147) x 89mm. 10ll.=33mm. Face
    2(1x)mm.
    Typeface: R79, Baskerville (linotype)?. Transitional. DIN
    1.24, modern baroque.

RUNNING HEADS: rectos and versos: LADY CHATTERLEY'S DAUGHTER

PAPER: smooth white wove unwatermarked. Thickness .06mm.
    Total bulk: 7.6mm.

BINDING: coated paper wrappers. Predominant colors brilliant
   yellowish green (C130), light greenish blue (C172). Upper
   wrapper: logo at upper left, in white: K150 | ACE | STAR |
   50¢ [11.2-3 in border] |. Next two lines to right of logo:
   The Sensational Modern Sequel To | D. H. Lawrence's Famous
   Novel | Lady | Chatterley's | DAUGHTER | by | PATRICIA
   ROBINS | 6,000,000 British | readers thrilled to | this
   novel -- now | published for the | first time in America!
   | [to left of last 6 lines is drawing of red-haired woman,
   lips slightly parted, in slip with low decolletage and one
   shoulder strap loose, sitting on bed, staring at (prospective) reader. Artist's signature ("Johnson"? at bottom.]
   On spine: logo as front cover. Set top to bottom: LADY
   CHATTERLEY'S DAUGHTER PATRICIA | [in white:] ROBINS |.
   Lower wrapper: drawing, as on upper wrapper, in blue;
   blurb (on green background: What was she like, the young
   and much- | desired daughter of the famous Lady Chatterley
   | and her gamekeeper-lover? | Was she as bold and wanton
   as her unin- | hibited parents? | Or did a guilty secret
   hold this haughty | beauty on the brink of a surging
   passion? . . . . Edges trimmed, stained yellow.

NOTES: Ace specializes in genre: Western, Science Fiction,
   modern Gothic (Bonn 74). Ace Star Books, Davis (271)
   states, was a "quality line" started in 1959.

COPIES EXAMINED: OkTU, TxU

A9.2   as A9.1 save:

imprint change, 11.8-9: 1120 Avenue of the Americas | New
York, N. Y. 10036

PAPER: Thickness .08mm. Total bulk: 9.3mm.

BINDING: logo on upper wrapper and spine different: in white
   triangle is a black lower case "a"; within the vertical
   strokes forming the bulb of the letter: ace | star |.
   Below the letter: K-233 | 50¢ |.

COPIES EXAMINED: personal, ICarbS

   [Canadian sequel, 1963]

A10.1   [on two-page spread:] [recto: drawing of young woman
         pushing older man in wheelchair while man with gun,
         and rabbit, watch from bushes. verso: older woman
         pushing older man with gun on which sits the rabbit] |
         [dec. rule] | *Lady Chatterley, Latterly* | WALTER
         O'HEARN | *McClelland and Stewart Limited,
         Toronto/Montreal Illustrations by* ED MCNALLY

(8 1/2 x 5 5/16"): [1-6]^{16}, 96 leaves; pp.[1-8], 9-192.

CONTENTS: p.[1]: half-title. p.[2-3]: title pages. p.[4]:
   contents (continued on p.[5]). Below decorated rule: ©
   WALTER O'HEARN 1963. | ALL RIGHTS RESERVED. | No part of
   this book . . . in a magazine or newspaper. [5 ll.] p.[5]:
   contents concluded. Below decorated rule: DESIGN: FRANK
   NEWFIELD | *The Canadian Publishers* | McClelland and
   Stewart Limited | 25 Hollinger Road, Toronto 16 | PRINTED
   AND BOUND IN CANADA BY McCorquodale and Blades (Printers
   (Ltd). p.[6-7]: Introduction. p.[8]: section title. pp.9-
   192: text.

TYPOGRAPHY: Text: 37ll.(p.10): 158 (171) x 97mm. 10ll.=43mm.
   Face 3(2x)mm.
   Typeface: Times New Roman (Monotype), R53. Old Face. DIN
   1.13, Mod. Ren.

RUNNING HEADS: rectos and versos: *Lady Chatterley, Latterly*

PAPER: Thickness .1mm. Total bulk: 10.9mm.

BINDING: paper covered boards, very light bluish green (C162)
   and deep red (C13). Upper and lower cover decorated with
   reproduction of illustrations in the book. On spine, deep
   red in very light bluish green background, set top to
   bottom: WALTER O'HEARN *Lady Chatterley, Latterly* [in
   flowing display type] [pub's device: warrior in chariot,
   horse] McCLELLAND & STEWART |. All edges trimmed. Plain
   white endpapers.
      Dj: Predominant colors black, green, purple, orange, red
   (on white background). Upper cover: Lady Chatterley, |
   LATTERLY | [illustration, as on recto t.p.] | Walter
   O'Hearn |. [Cap. letters in l.1, all letters in l.2 (which
   represent a mixture of display types), and capitals in
   last line in one of following colors: orange, purple,
   green, black, red. These colors also appear in the
   figures' clothing]. Spine, top to bottom: Walter O'Hearn
   [pub. logo, set vertically] [rule] McCLELLAND AND STEWART
   |. Lower cover as upper cover but reproduces illustration
   from verso of t.p. and omits author's name. Front flap:
   blurb, emphasizing the *Chatterley* sequel. Back flap: photo
   of author, brief biography.

NOTE: only pp.9-12 parody the Lawrence novel, detailing
   Connie and Mellors from 1924, through their both taking
   lovers in the thirties, Mellors' growing conservatism, the
   birth of a son, and the couple's reaction to the Penguin
   unexpurgated edition of the novel: Mellors is outraged,
   Connie considers it "too stimulating."

COPIES EXAMINED: NO/P-1(dj); personal(dj)

   [Greek dramatization, 1969]

A11.1   STAVROS MELISSINOS | THE LADY | AND THE GAMEKEEPER | A

stage play based on the story | LADY CHATTERLEY'S
LOVER | By | D. H. LAWRENCE | ATHENS | 1969

(8 3/16 x 5 1/2"): [1-6]^8, 48 leaves; pp. [1-4], 5-94, [2].

CONTENTS: p.[1]: half-title. p.[2]: All rights reserved.
Copyright, by Stavros Melissinos. All | inquiries about
performance rights should be addressed to Stavros |
Melissinos. 89, Pandrossou street, T.T. 116, Athens,
Greece. Tel. 319247|. p.[3]: t.p. p.4; CAST OF CHARACTERS,
and note of acknowledgement from author "for her help with
the translation." pp.5-94: text. pp.[2]: blank.

TYPOGRAPHY: Text: 34ll.(p.18): 152 x 40mm. 10ll.=40mm. Face
3(2x)mm.

PAPER: smooth white wove unwatermarked. Thickness .06mm.
Total bulk: 4.4mm.

BINDING: paper wrappers, white. Upper cover: STAVROS
MELISSINOS | THE LADY | AND THE GAMEKEEPER | [line and
wash drawing of naked, crouched woman, head resting on her
hands and her right knee] | A stage play based on the
story | LADY CHATTERLEY'S LOVER | By D. H. LAWRENCE |
ATHENS 1969 |. [ll.2-3 in red; ll.1-5 in sans serif] |. On
spine, set top to bottom: [star] STAVROS MELISSANOS: "THE
LADY AND THE GAMEKEEPER" [star] |. Lower cover: drawing of
playwright and 3-paragraph biographical sketch. Below
rule: LIMITED EDITION 24 DRACHMAS (C $1.50) Printed in
Greece |. Edges trimmed, unstained.

NOTES: Roberts App.I.A.VIII.
    A 4-page brochure laid into the British Library copy
describes the author as a "poet-sandalmaker" who supplies
the Beatles with footwear and is mentioned in the 1968-70
version of Frommer's *Europe On Five Dollars A Day*.
Melissinos "has become a legend among the hitchers and
hippies who flock through Athens." Blurb on front cover
quotes NBC and BBC respectively as describing the author
as "a new Tennessee Williams" and "the foster brother of
Omar Khaiyam."
    There are numerous typographical errors in the text,
perhaps because the typesetters did not know English. The
book seems to be printed from letterpress.

COPY EXAMINED: LO/N-1

[Gene Fowler parody, 1973]

A12.1   *Lady Scatterly's | Lovers* | [rule] | [typographical
         dec.] | BY GENE FOWLER | *Edited by H. Allen Smith* |
         LYLE STUART, INC. / SECAUCUS, NEW JERSEY

(8 x 5 3/8"): [1-2]^{16} [3]^8 [4-5]^{16}, 72 leaves; pp.[1-6],
7-141, [142], [2].

CONTENTS: p.[1]:   half-title. p.[2]:blank. p.[3]:t.p. p.[4]:
Will Fowler, Gene Fowler, Jr., and Jane Fowler | Morrison,
administrators for the literary estate of | Gene Fowler |
Copyright © 1973 by | Library of Congress Catalog Card
Number: 72-86170 | All rights reserved | No part of this
book . . . Lyle Stuart, Inc., 120 Enterprise Avenue, |
Secaucus, New Jersey 07094. | Manufactured in the United
States of America |.

TYPOGRAPHY: Text: 27ll.(p.25), 141 (150) x 97mm. 10ll.=53mm.
Face 3(2x)mm.
Typeface: Granjon (R66)?. Transitional. DIN 1.24, Mod.
Baroque.

RUNNING HEADS: versos: *LADY SCATTERLY'S LOVERS* |. rectos:
[titles of individual chapters, in italics.]

PAPER: smooth white wove unwatermarked. Thickness .11mm.
Total bulk 8.4mm.

BINDING: linen-grain (T304) cloth, strong red (C12). blackstamped on spine, set top to bottom: FOWLER LADY
SCATTERLY'S LOVERS LYLE | STUART |.
   D.j: coated paper, black. Front cover: GENE | FOWLER'S |
LADY | SCATTERLY'S | LOVERS | EDITED BY H. ALLEN SMITH |.
(11.1-2 in red, 11. 3-6 in white; 11.3-5 in ornamental
display type). On spine, top to bottom: [in red:] FOWLER
[in white, ornamental display type:] LADY SCATTERLY'S
LOVERS [in red:] LYLE | STUART |. On back cover [in red:]
LYLE STUART, INC. | [in white, save backslash in red:] 120
ENTERPRISE AVENUE / SECAUCUS, N.J. 07094 |. Flaps contain
blurb: summary, Fowler's motive for writing the story:
private recitations by male film star friends, including
Barrymore, Carradine, Flynn, Fields. Price on front flap:
$5.95

NOTES: In the Introduction, Smith states that Fowler wrote
this after acquiring a pirated copy of *Lady Chatterley's
Lover* in 1935.
   I am grateful to Arnold Levy of Secaucus, N. J., who
ascertained that 5000 copies of this book were printed,
with some being remaindered (letter postmarked 27 June
1988). Copies were still available in 1987.

COPIES EXAMINED: personal, OkTU, NNC

     [comic strip version, 1986]

A13.1   [cartoon of flowers, shrubs, bee, continued from
          verso] | LADY CHATTERLEY'S | LOVER! | drawn by | HUNT
          EMERSON | written by | D. H. LAWRENCE | [elliptical
          dot] | additional material by | C.A. and G.R. |
          KNOCKABOUT [logo: in rectangle, first word in black
          with each letter surrounded by white square, black

background; second word on white background:] CRACK |
[dot] EDITIONS [dot]

(11 3/4 x 8 3/8"): perfect bound; pp.[1-4], 5-56.

CONTENTS: p.[1]:t.p. p.[2]: [cartoon floral decoration] | The
Cartoon Strip Lady Chatterley's Lover | © 1986 Knockabout
Publications. Published by Knockabout Publications, | Unit
6a Acklam Workshops, 10 Ackam Road, London W10 5QZ | All
rights reserved. No part of this book may be reproduced,
recorded | or transmitted in any form without prior
permission of the publisher. | ISBN 0 86 166 049 8 |
Printed by Jet Offset | We are grateful to Penguin Books
for their stand in publishing | Lady Chatterly's [sic]
Lover in Great Britain. p.[3]: quotation from Lawrence on
British sexual taboos, burlesque profile of Lawrence,
statements by 15 witnesses at the Old Bailey trial on
1960. p.[4]: text. pp.5-56: text.

TYPOGRAPHY: the book consists of cartoon panels.

PAPER: smooth white wove unwatermarked. Thickness .1mm. Total
bulk 3.0mm.

BINDING: coated paper wrappers, predominant colors green,
orange, yellow. Upper cover: [in yellow:] NOT FOR SALE TO
WIVES AND SERVANTS | [in white:] LADY CHATTERLEY'S | [in
red:] LOVER! | [cartoon of nubile woman wearing a toque
and a slip, with riding crop in left hand, riding on back
of wild-eyed unshaven man dressed in period costume of
gardener; his mustache ends are held by the woman in her
right hand and used as reins; flowers and trees in
background] | [in bottom left, on scroll:] HUNT EMERSON: |
& D. H. LAWRENCE. | [logo in lower right, each letter on
white background as on t.p.: CRACK |. Running 3/4" from
spine edge over spine to 3/4" from fore-edge of lower
cover, beginning and ending with jagged border, is
repeated pattern, on yellow background, of cartoon
profiles of D. H. Lawrence. On spine, set top to bottom:
CRACK [logo] HUNT EMERSON LADY CHATTERLEY'S LOVER
KNOCKABOUT |. Lower cover: three cartoon panels with
captions introducing Constance (Lonely, unsatisfied and |
looking for love.), Clifford (Crippled, impotent, and | in
need of an heir.) and Mellors (Rough, randy and
unsuitable). Below panels is ISBN no., and machine-
readable strip. Three-quarter inch strip at fore-edge is
black. At bottom: [in white:] £4 [dot] 95 | [in blue:]
ADULTS | ONLY |. All edges trimmed.

NOTE: Approximately 60% of the characters' speech and the
captions consist of Lawrence's text of *Lady Chatterley's
Lover*.
   This book is distributed in the United States by Last
Gasp Of San Francisco, at $8.95.
   This work, Gerald Pollinger states, is definitely not
authorized by the Lawrence Estate (interview of 25 May,
1988).

Hunt Emerson began drawing cartoons in Birmingham, UK, in 1973. In 1982, he was voted Humorous Cartoonist of the Year by the Society of Strip Illustrators. An anthology of his work appears in *The Big Book Of Everything* (London: Knockabout, 1983).

COPY EXAMINED: personal

APPENDIX II
Chronological Table of Dates of Publication

NOTE: the question mark in parenthesis [(?)] indicates the most likely date of publication.

1928 1.1.a; 1.1.b; 1.1.c; 1.6(?)

1929 1.2; 1.3a; 1.3.b; 1.7(?); 1.8(?); 1.9(?); 1.10(?); 1.11(?); 1.12.a(?); 1.12.b(?); 2.1.a(?); 2.1.b(?); 16.1

1930 1.4; 3.1(?); 4.1(?); 5.1(?); 6.1(?), 7.1; 7.2

1931 7.3; A1.1; A2.1; A2.2(?)

1932 $7.4._1$; $7.4._2$; 17.1; 17.2; 17.3; 17.4; 17.9; A3.1

1933 17.5; 17.6; 25.1; 25.2; 25.3; 25.4; A4.1

1934 8.1(?); 8.2(?); 8.3(?); 17.7; 17.8; 17.10; 17.11(?); 17.12; 25.5; 25.6

1935 1.5(?); 17.13(?); 25.7; A5.1; A5.2(?)

1936 9.1(?); 17.14; 25.8; 25.9; 25.10(?)

1937 17.15

1938 17.16; 17.17; $25.11._1$; $25.11._2$; $25.11._3$; 26.1(?)

1939 17.18

1940 17.19; 17.20; 17.21; $17.30._1(?)$; $17.30._2(?)$; 17.31

1941 17.22

1942 11.1(?); 17.23

1943 10.1(?); 12.1(?); 13.1(?); 14.1(?); 14.2(?); 18.1(?); 27.2

1944 50.1; 50.2; 50.3

1945 27.3; 27.4; 50.4; 50.5; A6.1.a; A6.1.b

1946   20.1; 20.2; 28.1;
29.1.a; 29.1.b; 50.6;
51.1.$_1$(?); 51.1.$_2$.(?); 54.1

1947 17.24; 54.3

1948 17.25; 20.3; 20.4

1949   15.1; 17.26; 20.5;
54.4

1950   17.27; 20.6; 29.2;
52.1.a; 52.1.b

1951 17.28; 52.3(?)

1952   17.29; 25.12.$_1$(?);
25.12.$_2$(?); 25.12.$_3$(?);
25.12.$_4$(?)

1953 19.1; 20.7; 30.1; 30.2

1954

1955 19.2; 52.2(?)

1956   17.32; 17.33; 19.3;
27.5; 30.3; 30.4; 31.1;
31.2.$_1$; 31.2.$_2$; 54.2

1957 20.8; 20.9

1958   17.34; 20.10; 21.1;
22.1; 22.2; 22.3; 22.4; 53.1

1959   21.2; 21.3; 21.4;
22.5; 22.6; 22.7; 32.1.$_1$;
32.1.$_2$; 32.2; 32.3; 32.4;
32.5.a; 32.5.b; 32.6; 32.7;
32.8; 32.9; 32.10; 32.11;
32.12; 32.13; 32.14; 33.1;
35.1; 36.1.$_1$; 36.1.$_2$; 36.2;
36.3; 36.4; 36.5(?); 37.1;
37.2; 37.3; 37.4; 37.5;
37.6; 37.7; 37.8; 37.9(?);
38.1; 53.2

1960   22.8; 23.1; 23.2;
23.3; 23.4; 23.5; 23.6;
31.3.$_1$; 31.3.$_2$; 34.1;
37.10(?); 37.11; 37.12;
37.13; 39.1; 44.1; 44.2;
44.3; 44.4; 44.5; 44.6;
44.7; 44.8; 44.9; 44.10;
A7.1; A7.2

1961   23.7; 37.14; 37.15;
37.16(?); 37.17(?); 37.18
(?); 44.11; 44.12; A8.1;
A9.1; A9.2(?)

1962   23.8; 33.2; 37.19;
38.2

1963   33.3; 34.2(?); 37.20;
46.1; A10.1

1964 33.4; 36.6; 37.21

1965   37.22(?); 37.23(?);
44.13

1966   33.5; 37.24(?);
40.1(?); 40.2(?); 41.1(?);
44.14

1967 37.25(?); 44.15

1968   24.1; 33.6; 34.3(?);
37.26(?); 42.1

1969   33.7; 37.27(?); 42.2;
44.16; 44.17; 46.4; 46.5(?);
A11.1

1970 37.28(?); 42.3; 44.18

1971   33.8; 37.29(?); 42.4;
44.19

1972   33.9(?);   37.30(?);
42.5; 42.6; 42.7; 44.20;
55.1; 57.1; 57.2

1973   33.10(?);   37.31(?);
42.8; 44.21; 44.22; 56.1;
58.1; A12.1

1974   33.11(?);   33.12(?);
42.9; 44.23; 44.24; 46.2;
56.2; 57.3; 57.4; 58.2

1975   33.13(?);   37.32;
42.10; 42.11.$_1$; 42.11.$_2$;
44.25; 44.26; 56.3

1976   33.14(?);   37.33(?);
44.27; 47.1

1977   33.15(?);   37.34(?);
42.12; 44.28; 56.4; 58.3

1978   37.35(?);   42.13;
44.29; 44.30

1979   37.36(?);   42.14;
44.31; 44.32; 46.3; 56.5

1980   37.37(?);   42.15;
44.33; 44.34; 58.4

1981   37.38(?);   42.16;
44.35; 44.36; 46.6; 48.1;
56.6; 58.5

1982   33.16.1; 33.16.2(?);
37.39(?); 42.17; 44.37;
44.38; 49.1; 48.2; 56.7;
58.6

1983   32.15; 32.16(?);
32.17(?); 32.18(?); 32.19;
32.20(?); 32.21(?); 32.22
(?); 32.23(?); 34.4;
37.40(?); 42.18; 42.19(?);
43.1; 44.39; 47.2; 47.3;
56.8

1984   33.16.$_3$(?); 33.16.$_4$
(?); 42.20(?); 42.21(?);
44.30; 45.1

1985   37.41(?); 42.22(?);
45.2; 46.7; 47.4; 47.5; 47.6

1986 42.23(?); 45.3; 56.9;
A13.1

1987 42.24(?); 45.4

1988 45.5

APPENDIX III

Some Well-Known Editions and their Reference Numbers

NOTE: "Edition" is in quotation marks to indicate that this is the publisher's designation; the bibliographical descriptions themselves make clear the distinction between edition, impression, issue, and state.

Orioli edition (1928): 1.1.a; 1.1.b; 1.1.c

"Paris Popular Edition" (1929-30): 1.2; 1.3.a; 1.3.b; 1.4

"Dirty Orange" piracy (1928?): 1.6

"Funereal" piracy (1929?): 1.7; 1.8; 1.9

"Close Replica" piracy (1929?): 1.10

"Demon Vignette" piracy (1930): 3.1

"The Samuel Roth [expurgated] Edition" (1930-32): 7.1; 7.2; 7.3; $7.4._1$; $7.4._2$

"Third Edition" (1930): 16.1

Secker authorized expurgated edition, first impression (1932): 17.1

Knopf authorized expurgated "edition," first appearance (1932): 17.9

Heinemann authorized expurgated "Phoenix Edition" (1956-61[?]): 17.32; 17.33; 17.34

Penguin (first American branch) authorized expurgated paperback edition, first impression (1946): 20.1

Odyssey Press Paris edition (1933-35): 25.1-25.7

Keimeisha Tokyo "edition" (1952[?]): $25.12._1 - 25.12._4$

Jan Förlag Swedish edition, first impression (1942): 27.1

Heinemann unabridged Netherlands edition (1956): 31.1-$31.2._2$

Heinemann unabridged "edition" for the home market, first impression (1960): $31.3._1$

Grove Press edition, first four impression (1959): $32.1._1$-32.4

Modern Library edition, first impression (1960[?]): 34.1

Signet New American Library paperback edition, first impression (1959): 37.1

Penguin(UK) paperback edition, pre- and post-trial impressions (1960): 44.2-44.8

Heinemann unexpurgated "Phoenix Edition" (1963-79): 46.1-46.3

The First Lady Chatterley, Dial Press edition (1944-46): 50.1-50.6

The First Lady Chatterley, Australian edition (1946): $51.1._1$; $51.1._2$

The First Lady Chatterley, Heinemann edition (1972): 55.1

John Thomas and Lady Jane, Heinemann edition (1972): 57.1

APPENDIX IV
The William Faro Imprint

Samuel Roth published under his William Faro imprint (see essays for Section 2, p.25, and for Appendix I, pp.237-43) from 1930 to 1933. The best-selling titles were the expurgated *Lady Chatterley's Lover* (see pp.22-25) and Mirbeau's *Celestine*. In compiling this extremely tentative list, I have consulted the OCLC and REMARC data bases, the copyright records of the Library of Congress, dust jacket advertisements and blurbs on copies which I have seen, and the articles listed in the Works Cited section by Hamalian ("Nobody Knows My Names. . . ") and Ryan. Also extremely helpful have been interviews with Arnold Levy, A. Roth, and C. J. Scheiner, correspondence with A. Roth and William Ryan (who own the largest collections of Roth materials I know of), and various booksellers' catalogues (especially those of Anacapa Books, Berkeley, CA; C. J. Scheiner, Brooklyn, NY; Ivan Stormgart, Boston, MA).

An asterisk [*] preceding an entry indicates that Roth registered the title for copyright and that a card exists so indicating in the Library of Congress.

If (tentative) identification of an anonymous or pseudonymous author has been attempted, his or her name is placed in square brackets.

A (probable) pseudonym is indicated by quotation marks.

Roth republished many of the books listed here either under different imprints, or under the designation "privately published," both simultaneously with the Faro imprint, and at various times in his career from the late twenties through the mid-sixties. See the Mendes title below. The new editions (or impressions) sometimes have altered titles or subtitles, and possibly altered texts. Shortly before, and after, "William Faro" declared bankruptcy, many titles appeared under the imprint "The Big Dollar Book Company" in late 1932 and 1933.

Anon. [Samuel Roth, ed.] *Anecdota Americana. Five Hundred Stories for the Amusement of the Five Hundred Nations That Comprise America.* (1933)

--- *The Intimate Journal of Rudolph Valentino.* (1931)

*--- [Clement Wood]. *Lady Chatterley's Friends. A New Sequal*
    [sic] *to* Lady Chatterley's Lover *and* Lady Chatterley's
    Husbands. (1931)

*Bell, Ralcy Husted. *Memoirs and Mistresses. Colors and Odors
    of Love.* (1931; another, slightly shorter edition of the
    same year carries the subtitle *Amorous Recollections of a
    Physician.*)

*Cheyney, Ralph. *A Pregnant Woman in a Lean Age.* The Ardent
    Classics, #5 (1931)

*"Dubois, Alan" [C. Wood]. *Loose Shoulder Straps.* (1932)

Dickinson, G. Lowes. *Hands Off China! The Letters of a
    Chinese Official.* (1932)

Dutcher, Mary Lee. *Circulation. An Uncensored Study of a
    Newspaper Office.* (1932)

*"Gudaitis, Anthony" [Tony Gud]. *A Young Man About To Commit
    Suicide.* (1932)

*--- *Lady Chatterley's Husbands. An Anonymous Sequel to the
    Celebrated Novel* Lady Chatterley's Lover. Anonymously
    illustrated, possibly by "Rhanghild." (1931)

*Hamill, John. *The Strange Case of Herbert Hoover Under Two
    Flags.* (1931)

*Hellinger, Mark. *Moon Over Broadway.* (1931)

Lawrence, D. H. *Lady Chatterley's Lover.* Modern Amatory
    Classics No. 1. (1930)

*Lennox, Walter. *Woman's Doctor.* (1933)

Lindgren, Lydia. *My Heart in My Throat. The Story of a
    Strange Captivity.* (1932)

McKay, Donna. *A Gentleman in a Black Skin.* (1932)

Mendes, Catulle. *Lila And Colette.* The Ardent Classics, #3.
    (1931). Roth published this title, together with Mendes'
    The Isles of Love, in another edition in 1949 under his
    Boar's Head imprint. This version contained illustrations
    by Rhanghild and decorations by Valetin de Campion. The
    New York Public Library has a copy of a book "privately
    printed" in 1934 entitled *There Are Twenty Good Ways of
    Doing It; An Account of the Sweet Adventures of Lila and
    Colette, behind the Little Red Lights of Paris.*

*Mirbeau, Octave. *Celestine. Being the Diary of a Chamber-
    maid.* Modern Amatory Classics No. 2. (1930)

"Quilter, Daniel" [Samuel Roth]. *Body. A New Study, in Narrative, of the Anatomy of Society*. Illustrated by A. K. Skillin. (1931)

*Roth, Samuel. *Lady Chatterley's Lover. A Dramatization of His* [i.e., Roth's] *Version of D. H. Lawrence's Novel*. The Ardent Classics, #2. (1931)

*---. *Songs Out of Season*. (1932)

*---. *Stone Walls Do Not. The Chronicle of a Captivity*. (2 vols). (1931)

*---. *The Private Life of Frank Harris*. (1931)

*Sacher-Masoch, Leopold Von. *Venus in Furs*. (1931 and 1932; the former part of The Ardent Classics, #1, 12mo. The latter, 8vo., illustrated by "Rahnghild")

---. *Venus And Adonis*. The Ardent Classics, #4. (1931)

*"Vitray, Laura." *The Great Lindbergh Hullabaloo. An Unorthodox Account*. (1932)

*Wood, Clement. *The Woman Who Was Pope*. (1931)

*---. *The Man Who Killed Kitchener*. (1932)

*---. *Warren Gamaliel Harding. An American Comedy*. (1931)

NOTE: The following titles were advertised on dust jackets of Faro volumes. There is no evidence of their ever being published with the Faro imprint. Some may have been published "privately," or with other imprints (Golden Hind, Coventry House), by Roth. In five cases (see the Bell, Bonneau, Wake, "Wakem" and Wood items below) the latter was the case. Possibly, some were not his productions at all but rather those of colleagues: other New York publishers of borderline erotica who may have issued them either "privately" or under their own imprints, and wished to take advantage of Roth's mail-order distribution strategies. Some publishers of borderline erotica active at the time were Esar Levine [Panurge Press], Ben Rebhuhn [Falstaff Press], and Jake Brussel. It is possible that both Roth and one or more other publishers had editions of the same work on the market simultaneously, but this would have been bad for each publisher's business. It did not happen in the case of *Lady Chatterley's Lover*, save for the Nesor episode, where, under pressures of financial exigency, collegiality totally broke down (see pp. 27-28 above).

As postulated in the essay for Section Two, p.18 (see also endnote 11), Roth may have found ways of advertising, with flyers for or on just jackets of his Faro volumes, uncopyrightable interdicted books which he could not openly name.

Anon. *Oscar Wilde Three Times Tried*.

---. [Bonneau, Alcide]. *Padlocks and Girdles of Chastity*. Roth published this under the imprints The Golden Hind Press, in 1931, and The Big Dollar Books, in 1932.

Bell, Ralcy Husted. *Self-Amusement*. Published by The Golden Hind Press in 1929 and, with the added subtitle *and Its Spectres*, by The Big Dollar Book Company in 1932.

Beaumont, Edouard de. *The Sword and Womankind. Being an Informal History of Indiscreet Revelations*. (Published by the Panurge Press, c. 1929)

Symonds, John A. *Sexual Inversion*.

Wake, G.[sic] S. (Charles Staniland). *Sacred Prostitution and Marriage by Capture*. "Privately Printed," 1929; published, in a new edition, as a Big Dollar Book, 1932.

"Wakem, Hugh" [Samuel Roth]. *The Diary of a Smuthound*. (Imprint reads "Philadelphia: Wm. Hodgson"; copyright date is "1930")

Wood, Clement. *Herbert Clark Hoover: An American Tragedy*. (Imprint reads "New York: Michael Swain, 1932").

APPENDIX V

A Collation of "The Samuel Roth Edition" and the "Authorized Edition" with the Orioli Edition: Ch 10

Samuel Roth's unauthorized expurgated edition (7.1-7.4) formed the basis for Secker's Authorized Edition (17.1-17.8) and the subsequent subeditions and new editions (17.9-24.1) which replicate its text. These volumes are described in Sections 2 and 3; see the introductory essay for Section 3, and especially pp.66-69 for an analysis of the strategies of the expurgators. The following collation of Chapter 10 of the first edition of *Chatterley* with the Roth and the Secker text is meant to give a picture of what happened to Lawrence's text when these publishers attempted to produce a version which would pass British and American censors.

The following abbreviations are used:
(R) = the Roth text
(S) = the Secker text
om = omitted
*om = an omission preceded by a row of asterisks
The page and line numbers to the left of the square bracket refer to the Orioli edition.

The Roth and Secker editions are of course no longer in print, but exist in most university libraries, either in special collections or in the stacks. The Orioli edition is quite commonly found in rare book rooms of university libraries in England and America.

This Appendix was prepared jointly by the author and Ms. Theresa Higgins of Nelson, Pa.

```
135:35   loins] body (R) (S)
136:11   his loins] him (R) (S)
136:22-23   to the curve . . . . her flank,] om (R) (S)
137:3-25   With a queer obedience . . . . her breast.] *om (R)
137:8-25   She lay . . . . her breast.] *om (S)
138:4-6   He lay . . . . peaceful.] om (R)
138:4-5   his . . . close.] om (S)
```

```
138:8   her.] her, (R)
138:8-10   It was . . . . Then he] om (R)
138:8-9   He drew . . . knees and] om (S)
138:10   apparently . . . clothing.] om (S)
138:10   Then] then (S)
139:14   "But . . . wistfully.] om (R)
141:27-28   his penis] it (R) (S)
141:33   gone into] captured (R) (S)
142:7   penis] passion (R) (S)
142:7   loins] limbs (R) (S)
143:13   womb] heart (R) (S)
143:26   womb] om (R) (S)
143:26-28   And . . . breasts.] om (R) (S)
148:6-151:20   One time . . . . annoying."] om (R) (S)
     NB: Secker starts his Chapter 11 at
          "The next day . . ." (151:21)
148:6-11   One time . . . . naked.] *om (R)
148:12-15   as . . . . and again.] caressing her. (R)
148:18   secret] om (R)
148:22-25   She felt . . . quiver.] om (R)
148:29-149:12   And when . . . . warmth.] om (R)
149:13   ter] you (R)
149:13   he asked, in] he finally asked, in (R)
149:20   moment,] moment and kissed her. (R)
149:20-23   kissed . . . lantern.] om (R)
150:29-30   and whipped . . . hand.] om (R)
150:33   She . . . again.] om (R)
152:8   intercourse] an affair (R) (S)
152:25-26   She . . . man.] om (R) (S)
157:7-8   She . . . alive.] om (R) (S)
157:25-159:4   He led her . . . . cover himself.] *om (R) (S)
159:6-7   He stood . . . round.] om (R) (S)
159:10-12   She turned . . . . answer.] om (R) (S)
159:20   ,so] as if (R)
159:20   ,so] ,as if (S)
159:23-25   "Don't . . . . again.] om (R) (S)
160:8   in her womb and bowels] om (R) (S)
160:10   womb and] om (R) (S)
160:12-15   --It feels . . . . lovely.] om (R) (S)
160:16-17   "if I . . . child!"] om (R) (S)
160:19-20   one's bowels] one (R) (S)
160:21-22   in one's . . . womb,] om (R) (S)
160:22-23   she was . . . and as if] om (R)
160:22   very] om (S)
160:33   womb] heart om (R) (S)
161:2-3   Iacchos, the bright phallos] Bacchos, (R) (S)
161:5-6   He was . . . her own.] om (R) (S)
161:9   the mere phallos-bearer,] om (R) (S)
161:18   womb and her bowels] om (R) (S)
162:33-35   Connie . . . . holy.] om (R) (S)
163:33   ,beautiful . . . mystery.] om (R) (S)
170:26-27   It seemed . . . necessity.] om (R) (S)
170:33   sleep.] rest om (R) (S)
173:27   he] Sir Clifford (R) (S)
```

Works Cited

Note: I have not included here numerous short articles in either *Publisher's Weekly* or the *New York Times*. Un- published letters and questionnaires sent to me in response to queries are also not listed. All these materials are fully cited in the text of the essays and in the bibliographical descriptions.

Aldington, Richard. *D. H. Lawrence. Portrait of a Genius But . . .* 1950. NY: Collier, 1967.

---. *Pinorman*. London: Heinemann, 1954.

Allen, F. L. *Only Yesterday*. Vol. 1. London: Penguin, 1938.

---. *Since Yesterday*. 1939. N.Y.: Bantam, 1965.

Beach, Sylvia. *Shakespeare and Company*. New York: Harcourt, Brace, 1959.

Bedford, Sybille. "The Trial of Lady Chatterley." *Esquire.* April 1961: 132-36 *et. seq*.

Black, Michael H. "The Works of D. H. Lawrence: The Cambridge Edition." *D. H. Lawrence: The Man Who Lived*. Ed. R. B. Partlow and Harry T. Moore. Carbondale,Ill.: Southern Illinois U. Press, 1980. 49-57.

Bogart, Max. "A Study of Certain Legally Banned Books in the United States, 1900-1950." Diss. New York U, 1956.

Bonn, Thomas L. *Undercover: An Illustrated History of*

American Mass Market Paperbacks. Harmondsworth, Eng.:
Penguin, 1982.

"Books, Books, Books: William Faro, Incorporated." *The New
Yorker* 9 January 1932: 76-77.

Bosmajian, Haig, ed. *Obscenity and Freedom of Expression*. NY:
Burt Franklin, 1976.

Bowers, Fredson. *Principles of Bibliographical Description*.
1949. N. Y.: Russell and Russell, 1962

Brome, Vincent. *Frank Harris: The Life And Loves Of A
Scoundrel*. New York: Yoseloff, 1960.

Brophy, Brigid, Michael Levey, and Charles Osbourne. *Fifty
Works of English Literature We Could Do Without*. N. Y.:
Stein and Day, 1969.

Butler, Ellis Parker. *Dollarature, Or the Drug Store Book*.
Boston: Houghton-Mifflin, 1930.

Cacici, Dante. A Note On The Author. *Bumarap. The Story of a
Male Virgin*. By Samuel Roth. New York: Arrowhead,
1947. 233-56.

Caffrey, Raymond T. "*Lady Chatterley's Lover*: The Grove Press
Publication of the Unexpurgated Text." *Syracuse
University Library Associates Courier* 20 (Spring 1985):
49-79.

Cambridge University Library. *D. H. Lawrence 1885-1930.
Catalogue of an Exhibition at Cambridge University
Library Sept.-Nov. 1985*. Cambridge: The Library, 1985.

Canby, Henry S. *Definitions* (Second Series). New York:
Harcourt, Brace, 1924.

Commonwealth v. DeLacey, 271 Mass. 327, 171 N. E. 455 (1930).

Cong. Rec. 17 March 1930: 5423-32; 18 March 1930: 5488-5520.

Coser, Lewis, Charles Kadushin, and Walter Powell. *Books: The
Culture And Commerce of Publishing*. NY: Basic Books,
1982.

Covington, D. B. *The Argus Book Shop: A Memoir*. Westport, CT:
Tarrydiddle Press, 1977.

Craig, Alex. *The Banned Books Of England*. 1962. Westport, CT:
Greenwood, 1977.

Crider, Allen B, ed. *Mass Market Publishing in America*.
Boston: G. K. Hall, 1982.

Curwen, Peter. *The U.K. Publishing Industry*. Oxford:
    Pergamon, 1981.

Daniels, Les. *Comix. A History of Comic Books in America*.
    N.Y.: Outerbridge and Dienstfrey, 1971.

Davis, Kenneth C. *Two-Bit Culture. The Paperbacking of
    America*. Boston: Houghton-Mifflin, 1984.

DeMott, Benjamin. "Darkness at the Mall." *Psychology Today*.
    February 1984: 48-52.

Dickson, Lovat. *Radclyffe Hall at the Well of Loneliness*. New
    York: Scribner's, 1975.

Draper, R. P. *D. H. Lawrence: The Critical Heritage*. NY:
    Barnes and Noble, 1970.

Durrell, Lawrence. Preface. *Lady Chatterley's Lover*. By D. H.
    Lawrence. NY: Bantam, 1968. vii-xi.

Estrin, Mark J. *A History of Underground Comics*. Rev. Ed.
    Berkeley, CA: Ronin, 1987.

Fitch, Noel Riley. *Sylvia Beach and the Lost Generation: A
    History of Literary Paris in the Twenties*. New York:
    Norton, 1983.

Ford, Hugh. *Published In Paris*. 1975. New York: Pushcart,
    1981.

Geis, Richard E. *How To Write Porno Novels for Fun and
    Profit*. Port Townsend, WA: Loompanics Unlimited, 1985.

Girodias, Maurice. *The Frog Prince. An Autobiography*. New
    York: Crown, 1980.

Gorer, Geoffrey. Rev. of *The Trial of Lady Chatterley*. By. C.
    H. Rolph. *New Statesman* 3 Feb. 1961: 180-81.

Grannis, Chandler B., ed. *What Happens In Book Publishing*.
    NY: Columbia U. Press, 1957.

Gross, Gerald, ed. *Publishers on Publishing*. NY: Grosset and
    Dunlap, 1961.

Hackett, Alice, and James Burke. *80 Years of Bestsellers,
    1895-1975*. NY: Bowker, 1977.

Hamalian, Leo. *D. H. Lawrence in Italy*. N.Y.: Taplinger,
    1982.

---. "Nobody Knows My Names: Samuel Roth and The Underside of

Modern Letters." *Journal of Modern Literature* 3
    (1974): 889-921.

---. "The Lady Chatterley Spectacle." *Columbia University
    Forum* Winter 1960: 6-13.

Hancer, Kevin. *The Paperback Price Guide No. 2*. 2nd ed. NY:
    Harmony Books, 1982.

Hansen, Harry. *Midwest Portraits*. N.Y.: Harcourt, Brace:
    1923.

Hazlitt, Henry. Review of the Authorized Edition of *Lady
    Chatterley's Lover*. *The Nation* 7 Sept. 1932: 214-15.
    Rpt. in R. P. Draper. *D. H. Lawrence: The Critical
    Heritage*. N. Y.: Barnes and Noble, 1970. 289-92.

Hoffmann, Frank. *Analytical Survey of Anglo-American Trad-
    itional Erotica*. Bowling Green, OH: The Popular Press,
    1973.

Hough, Graham. *The Dark Sun A study of D. H. Lawrence*. 1956.
    NY: Capricorn, 1959.

Hoyt, Olga, and Edwin Hoyt. *Censorship in America*. New York:
    Seabury Press, 1970.

Iverson, William. *The Pious Pornographers*. NY: Morrow, 1963.

Jaspert, W. Pincus, W. Turner Berry, and A. F. Johnson. *The
    Encyclopedia of Type Faces*. Poole, Dorset: Blandford
    Press, 1983.

Kahane, Jack. *Memoirs of a Booklegger*. London: Michael
    Joseph, 1939.

Kearney, Patrick. *The Olympia Press Paris 1953-65: A
    Handlist*. London: Black Spring, 1976.

Kronhausen, Eberhard and Phyllis Kronhausen. *Pornography and
    the Law*. NY: Ballantine, 1959.

Kuh, Richard. *Foolish Figleaves? Pornography in--and out of--
    Court*. NY: MacMillan, 1967.

"Lady Chatterley--A Production Challenge." *Book Production*
    Sept. 1959: 102-04.

"Lawrence Book Revision Fought." *New York World* 25 Oct.
    1930: 7.

Lawrence, D. H. "A Propos of *Lady Chatterley's Lover*."
    London: Mandrake Press, 1930. Reprinted in *Sex,
    Literature, and Censorship*. Ed. Harry T. Moore. New

York: Twayne, 1953. pp.89-122.

———. *John Thomas And Lady Jane*. t.s. Humanities Research Center, University of Texas at Austin.

"Lawrence, D. H. Misc." t.s. file. Humanities Research Center, Univ. of Texas at Austin.

Legman, Gershon. Introduction. *The Private Case*. By Patrick Kearney. London: Landesman, 1981.

Letters From D. H. Lawrence To Martin Secker, 1911-1930. MS: Privately Published, 1970.

Lilly, Joseph. "Books And Bookleggers No. 1." *New York Telegram* 6 March 1930, Sec. 2: 1.

———. "Books And Bookleggers No. 2." *New York Telegram* 7 March 1930, Sec. 2: 1.

———. "Books And Bookleggers No. 3." *New York Telegram* 8 March 1930, Sec. 2: 5.

Loth, David. *The Erotic In Literature*. London: Secker and Warburg, 1961.

Madison, Charles. *Book Publishing In America*. NY: McGraw-Hill, 1966.

McDonald, Edward D. *The Writings of D. H. Lawrence, 1925-30: A Bibliographical Supplement*. Phila: Centaur Book Shop, 1931.

McGrath, Peter. "New Themes and Old Taboos." *Newsweek* 18 March 1985. Rpt. in *Censorship: Opposing Viewpoints*. Ed. David Bender and Bruno Leone. St. Paul, Minn: Greenhaven, 1985.   194-96.

Mehring, Walter. *The Lost Library. An Autobiography of a Culture*. Tr. Richard and Clara Winston. London: Secker and Warburg, 1951.

Moore, Harry.,ed. *Collected Letters of D. H. Lawrence*. 2 vols. New York: Viking, 1962.

———. Introduction. *D. H. Lawrence: Sex, Literature and Censorship*. Ed. Harry Moore. NY: Twayne, 1953.

———. "*Lady Chatterley's Lover* as Romance." *A D. H. Lawrence Miscellany*. Ed. Harry Moore. Carbondale: Southern Illinois University Press, 1959.

———. *The Priest of Love. A Life of D. H. Lawrence*. Rev. Ed. New York: Penguin, 1981.

---, and Dale B. Montague, eds. *Frieda Lawrence and Her Circle. Letters from, to, and about Frieda Lawrence*. London: Macmillan, 1981.

Mumby, Frank and Ian Norrie. *Publishing and Bookselling*. 5th ed. London: Jonathan Cape, 1974.

Morpurgo, J. E. *Allen Lane King Penguin*. London: Hutchinson, 1980.

Munro, Craig. "*Lady Chatterley* in London: The Secret Third Edition." *D. H. Lawrence's Lady*. Ed. Michael Squires and Dennis Jackson. Athens, Ga.: U. of Georgia Press, 1985.

Neavill, Gordon B. "The Modern Library Series: Format and Design, 1917-1977." *Printing History* 1 (1979): 26-37.

Nehls, Edward. *D. H. Lawrence: A Composite Biography*. 3 vols. Madison: U. of Wisconsin Press, 1957-59.

New York Society for the Supression of Vice. *Annual Reports*. New York: The Society, 1931 and 1934.

New York Times Biographical Edition. New York: The Times, 1974.

Norrie, Ian. *Mumby's Publishing and Bookselling in the Twentieth Century*. 6th ed. London: Bell and Hyman, 1982.

"Obscene Book Jails A Publisher." *New York Times* 21 Sept. 1935: 32.

Orioli, Pino. *Adventures of a Bookseller*. London: Chatto and Windus, 1938.

Paul, James N., and Murray L. Schwartz. *Federal Censorship Obscenity in the Mail*. New York: Free Press of Glencoe, 1961.

People v. Dial Press, 182 Misc. 416 (Magis. Ct. 1944).

Perkins, Michael. *The Secret Record. Modern Erotic Literature*. New York: Morrow, 1977.

Peterson, Clarence. *The Bantam Story*. 2nd ed. NY: Bantam, 1975.

Pollinger, Gerald J. "*Lady Chatterley's Lover*: A View From Lawrence's Literary Executor." *D. H. Lawrence's Lady*. Ed. Michael Squires and Dennis Jackson. Athens, Ga.: U. of Georgia Press, 1985.

Polsky, Ned. "On the Sociology of Pornography." *Hustlers,
    Beats, and Others*. NY: Doubleday Anchor Books, 1969.
    183-200.

Powell, Lawrence Clark. *D. H. Lawrence and His Critics. A
    Chronological Excursion in Bio-Bibliography*. Pamphlet,
    rpt. from *The Colophon*, Jan. 1940.

Pringle, Henry F. "Throwing Mud At The White House." *Outlook
    And Independent* 9 Dec. 1931: 463.

"Publisher Is Held For Obscene Ads." *New York Times* 16 July
    1935: 17.

"Purity at the Port." *The Nation* 22 Feb. 1933: 194.

Ransom, Will. *Private Presses and Their Books*. New York:
    Bowker, 1929.

Rembar, Charles. *The End of Obscenity: The Trials of Lady
    Chatterley, Tropic of Cancer, and Fanny Hill*. New York:
    Random House, 1968.

Rice, Diana. "Literary Booklegging." *New York Times* 6 Aug.
    1922, Book Review Section: 1, 24.

Roberts, Warren. *A Bibliography of D. H. Lawrence*. 2nd
    ed. Cambridge: Univ. Press, 1982.

Rogers, W. C. *Wise Men Fish Here: The Story of Frances
    Steloff and The Gotham Book Mart*. New York: Harcourt,
    Brace, World, 1965.

Rolph, C. H., ed. *The Trial of Lady Chatterley. Regina v.
    Penguin Books Ltd*. N.p.: Privately Printed, 1961.

Rookledge's International Typefinder. New York: Beil, 1982.

Rose, Alfred. *Register of Erotic Books*. New York: Jack
    Brussel, 1965.

Roth, Samuel. *The Private Life of Frank Harris*. New York:
    Faro, 1931.

---. By Way Of Explanation. *Lady Chatterley's Lover. A
    Dramatization* . . . The Ardent Classics No. 2. By
    Roth. New York: Faro, 1931. 5-13.

---. *Jews Must Live. An Account of the Persecution of the
    World by Israel* . . . N.Y.: Golden Hind Press, 1934.

Ryan, William. "A Lion In A Den Of Daniels." Unpublished
    essay, 1983.

Sagar, Keith. *The Life of D. H. Lawrence*. New York: Pantheon, 1980.

Sara [pseud.]. "So I'm Not Lady Chatterley So Better I Should Know It Now" [short story]. *Commentary* Jan.1963: 44-51.

Schick, Frank L. *The Paperbound Book in America*. New York: Bowker, 1958.

Schreuders, Piet. *The Book of Paperbacks*. London: Virgin Books, 1982.

Schwartz, Harry. *Fifty Years in My Bookstore*. Milwaukee: n.p., 1977.

---. *This Book-Collecting Racket. A Few Notes On The Abuses of Book Collecting*. Part 1. Milwaukee: Casanova Press, 1934.

Shah, A. B. *The Roots of Obscenity*. Bombay: Lalvani, 1968.

Slocum, John, and Herbert Cahoon. *A Bibliography of James Joyce*. New Haven: Yale U. Press, 1953.

Smith, Grover, ed. *Letters of Aldous Huxley*. N.Y.: Harper and Row, 1969.

Smith, Roger N. *Paperback Parnassus*. Boulder, CO: Westview, 1976.

Snyder, Harold Jay. *A Catalogue of English and American First Editions 1911-1932 of D. H. Lawrence*. NY: n.p., 1932. [bookseller's catalogue]

Sonenschein, David, et. al. A Study of Mass Market Erotica: The Romance or Confession Magazine. *Technical Report of the Commission on Obscenity and Pornography*. Vol ix. Wash., D.C.: GPO, n.d. [1971?] 99-164.

Squires, Michael. *The Creation of "Lady Chatterley's Lover"*. Baltimore: Johns Hopkins University Press, 1983.

Sutherland, James. *Offensive Literature: Decensorship in Britain 1960-1982*. Baltimore: Johns Hopkins, 1983.

---. *Fiction and the Fiction Industry*. London: Athlone, 1978.

Talese, Gay. *Thy Neighbor's Wife*. New York: Dell, 1981.

Tanselle, G. Thomas. "The Bibliographical Description of Patterns." *Studies in Bibliography* 23 (1970): 71-102.

---. "The Bibliographical Concepts of *Issue* and *State*," *Papers of the Bibliographical Society of America* 69

     (1975): 17-66.

--- . "The Identification of Type Faces . . . ." *Papers of the Bibliographical Society of America* 60 (1966): 185-202.

---. "A Sample Bibliographical Description." *Studies in Bibliography* 40 (1987): 1-31.

---. "The Description of Non-Letterpress Material." *Studies in Bibliography* 35 (1982): 1-42.

---. "Book-Jackets, Blurbs, and Bibliographers." *The Library* 5th ser. 26.2 (June 1971): 91-116.

---. "Tolerances in Bibliographical Description." *The Library* 5th ser. 23.1 (March 1968): 1-12.

Tarr, Rodger, and Robert Sokan. *A Bibliography of the D. H. Lawrence Collection at Illinois State University.* Bloomington, Ill.: Scarlet Ibis Press, 1979.

"Tauchnitz Has a Rival." *Publishers' Weekly* 9 April 1932: 1643-45.

Tebbel, John. *A History of Book Publishing in the United States.* 4 vols. New York: Bowker, 1978.

Tedlock, E. W., Jr. *The Frieda Lawrence Collection of D. H. Lawrence Manuscripts.* Albuquerque: U. of New Mexico Press, 1948.

The Dunster House Book Shop Case. A Statement by the Directors of the New England Watch and Ward Society. Boston: n.p., 1930.

Thompson, Anthony H. *Censorship in Public Libraries in the United Kingdom During the Twentieth Century.* Essex, Eng.: Bowker, 1975.

Tindall, William Y. Introduction. *The Later D. H. Lawrence.* 1952. NY: Knopf, 1969.

Tobin, A.I. and Elmer Gertz. *Frank Harris A Study in Black and White.* 1931. N.Y.: Haskell House, 1970.

United States. Commission on Obscenity and Pornography. *Technical Report of the Commission* . . . . Vol. III. Washington: GPO, n.d. [1971?]

United States. Senate. Subcommittee To Investigate Juvenile Delinquency of the Committee on the Judiciary. *Hearings on Juvenile Delinquency (Obscene and Pornographic Materials).* 84th Cong., 1st sess. S. Res. 62. Washington: GPO, 1955. pp. 187-211.

United States v. Samuel Roth. C-53-79. U. S. District Ct.,
    So. District of N. Y. 1929.

Vasey, Lindeth. "A Checklist of the Manuscripts of D. H.
    Lawrence." *D. H. Lawrence: A Calendar of his Works*. By
    Keith Sagar. Austin: U. of Texas Press, 1979.

Warburg, Frederick. *All Authors Are Equal*. London: Hutchinson,
    1973.

Weybright, Frederick. *The Making of a Publisher. A Life in
    the Twentieth Century Book Revolution*. NY: Reynel, 1966.

Whitman, Howard. *The Sex Age*. N. p.: Charter Press, 1962.

Wood, Clement. *Herbert Clark Hoover An American Tragedy*. New
    York: Michael Swain, 1932.

Woolf, Cecil. *A Bibliography of Norman Douglas*. London:
    Hart-Davies, 1954.

Zytaruk, George J., ed. *The Quest for Rananim. D. H. Lawrence's
    Letters to S. S. Koteliansky 1914 to 1930*. Montreal:
    McGill-Queen's UP, 1970.

Index
(To the Introductory Essays)

About the Author

JAY A. GERTZMAN is a professor of English at Mansfield University in Pennsylvania. He is the author of *Fantasy, Fashion and Affection: Editions of Robert Herrick's Poetry for the Common Reader* (1986).

Recent Titles in
Bibliographies and Indexes in World Literature

A Guide to Folktales in the English Language: Based on the Aarne-Thompson
Classification System
D. L. Ashliman

Literature for Children about Asians and Asian Americans: Analysis and
Annotated Bibliography, with Additional Readings for Adults
Esther C. Jenkins and Mary C. Austin

A Bibliographical Guide to Spanish American Literature: Twentieth-Century
Sources
Walter Rela, compiler

Themes and Settings in Fiction: A Bibliography of Bibliographies
Donald K. Hartman and Jerome Drost, compilers

The Pinocchio Catalogue: Being a Descriptive Bibliography and Printing History
of English Language Translations and Other Renditions Appearing in the
United States, 1892-1987
Richard Wunderlich, compiler

Robert Burton and *The Anatomy of Melancholy:* An Annotated
Bibliography of Primary and Secondary Sources
Joey Conn, compiler

Intertextuality, Allusion, and Quotation: An International Bibliography of
Critical Studies
Udo J. Hebel, compiler

Backgrounds to Restoration and Eighteenth-Century English Literature:
An Annotated Bibliographical Guide to Modern Scholarship
Robert D. Spector, compiler

They Wrote For Children Too: An Annotated Bibliography of Children's
Literature by Famous Writers For Adults
Marilyn Fain Apseloff, compiler

Americans in Paris, 1900-1930: A Selected, Annotated Bibliography
William G. Bailey, compiler

Research in Critical Theory Since 1965: A Classified Bibliography
Leonard Orr, compiler

Literature for Young People on War and Peace: An Annotated Bibliography
Harry Eiss, compiler